Søren Kierkegaard's Journals and Papers

SØREN KIERKEGAARD'S JOURNALS AND PAPERS Volume 1, A-E

EDITED AND TRANSLATED BY
Howard V. Hong and Edna H. Hong

ASSISTED BY GREGOR MALANTSCHUK

INDIANA UNIVERSITY PRESS
BLOOMINGTON AND LONDON

Copyright © 1967 by Howard V. Hong
ALL RIGHTS RESERVED
No part of this book may be reproduced or utilized in any form or by any means, electronic or mechanical, including photocopying and recording, or by any information storage and retrieval system, without permission in writing from the publisher. The Association of American University Presses's Resolution on Permissions constitutes the only exception to this prohibition.
Library of Congress catalog card number: 67-13025
Manufactured in the United States of America

Contents

CHRONOLOGY vii
TRANSLATORS' PREFACE xiii
INTRODUCTION xxi

SUBJECT HEADINGS

Abstract, Abstraction 3
Absurd 4
Action 9
The Ancients, the Classical 10
Anselm 11
Anthropology, Philosophy of Man 13
Anxiety (*Angst*), Dread 38
Apostle 43
Aristotle 48
Art, Artists, Artistry, the Artistic 50
Asceticism 66
Augustine 71
Authority 73
Being 79
Bernard of Clairvaux 82
Bible 83
Bourgeois Mentality, Philistinism 89
Call, Calling, Vocation 94
Category 101
Catholicism 102
Cause 103
Certainty 107
Change, Coming into Existence 109
Childhood, Children 113
Christ 123
Christendom 153
Christianity 167
Christmas 232
Chrysostom 235
Church 236
Collision, Conflict, Adversity 246
Communication 252
Conscience 320
Contemporaneity 323
Contradiction 328
Corrective 331
Death 334
Demonic 341
Descartes 342
Despair 343
Dialectic, Dialectical 350
Discontinuity, Continuity 355
Don Juan 356
Don Quixote 357
Doubt 358
Dreams 361
Education, Upbringing 362
Enthusiasm 366
Envy 367
Estheticism, the Esthetic 368
Eternity, the Eternal 382
The Ethical, the Ethical Consciousness 389
Equality 441

v

Exist, Existence, Existential 448
Experience 467

The Extraordinary, the Exception 471

BIBLIOGRAPHY 481

COLLATION OF ENTRIES WITH *Papirer* 489

NOTES 497

Chronology

1813

May 5   Søren Aabye Kierkegaard born at Nytorv 2 (new number, 27), Copenhagen, son of Michael Pedersen Kierkegaard and Anne Sørensdatter Lund Kierkegaard.

June 3   Baptized in Helliggeist Church in Copenhagen.

1821

Enrolled in Borgerdydskolen in Copenhagen.

1828

Apr. 20   Confirmed in Vor Frue Church by Pastor J. P. Mynster (later to become Bishop).

1830

Oct. 30   Registered as student at University of Copenhagen.

Nov. 1   Drafted into Royal Guard, Company 7.

Nov. 4   Discharged as unfit for service.

1831

Apr. 25   Finishes first part of second examination (Latin, Greek, Hebrew, and history, *magna cum laude*; mathematics, *summa cum laude*).

Oct. 27   Completes second part of second examination (philosophy, physics, and mathematics, *summa cum laude*).

1834

Apr. 15   Entry I A 1 of journals and papers.

1837

Between May 8 and May 12. On a visit to the Rørdams in Frederiksberg

meets Regine Olsen for the first time (See II A 67, 68).
Autumn. Begins teaching Latin for a term in Borgerdydskolen.

1838

May 19, about 10:30 A.M., S. K.'s entry concerning "an indescribable joy" (see II A 228).
Aug. 8/9 Father dies, 2:00 A.M.
Aug. 14 Father buried in family plot in Assistents Cemetery.
Sept. 7 Publication of *From the Papers of One Still Living*. Published against his will by S. Kierkegaard. (About H. C. Andersen as a novelist, with special reference to his latest work, *Only a Fiddler*.)

1840

June 2 Presents his request for examination to theological faculty.
July 3 Completes examination for degree (*magna cum laude*).
July 19—Aug. 6 Journey to ancestral home in Jutland.
Sept. 8 Proposes to Regine Olsen.
Sept. 10 Becomes engaged to Regine.
Oct. 18 First number of *The Corsair* published by M. Goldschmidt.
Nov. 17 Enters the Pastoral Seminary.

1841

Jan. 12 Preaches sermon in Holmens Kirke (see III C 1).
July 16 Dissertation for the Master of Arts degree, *The Concept of Irony, with constant reference to Socrates*, accepted.
Aug. 11 Returns Regine Olsen's engagement ring.
Sept. 16 Dissertation printed.
Sept. 29 10 A.M.–2:00 P.M., 4:00 P.M.–7:30 P.M. Defends his dissertation. [Around mid-century Magister degrees came to be regarded and named officially as doctoral degrees such as they are now.]
Oct. 11 Engagement with Regine Olsen broken.
Oct. 25 Leaves Copenhagen for Berlin, where he attends Schelling's lectures.

1842

March 6 Returns to Copenhagen.
Nov. 11 S. K.'s brother Peter Christian Kierkegaard ordained.

Johannes Climacus, or De Omnibus Dubitandum Est begun but not completed or published.

1843

Feb. 20 *Either/Or*, edited by Victor Eremita, published.
May 8 Leaves for short visit to Berlin.
May 16 *Two Edifying Discourses*, by S. Kierkegaard, published.
July Learns of Regine's engagement to Fridrich Schlegel.
Oct. 16 *Repetition*, by Constantine Constantius; *Fear and Trembling*, by Johannes de Silentio; and *Three Edifying Discourses*, by S. Kierkegaard, published.
Dec. 6 *Four Edifying Discourses*, by S. Kierkegaard, published.

1844

Feb. 24 Preaches terminal sermon in Trinitatis Church.
March 5 *Two Edifying Discourses*, by S. Kierkegaard, published.
June 8 *Three Edifying Discourses*, by S. Kierkegaard, published.
June 13 *Philosophical Fragments*, by Johannes Climacus, published.
June 17 *The Concept of Dread*, by Vigilius Haufniensis; and *Prefaces*, by Nicholaus Notabene, published.
Aug. 31 *Four Edifying Discourses*, by S. Kierkegaard, published.
Oct. 16 Moves from Nørregade 230 (now 38) to house at Nytorv 2, Copenhagen.

1845

Apr. 29 *Three Discourses on Imagined Occasions*, by S. Kierkegaard, published.
Apr. 30 *Stages on Life's Way*, edited by Hilarius Bogbinder, published.
May 13–24 Journey to Berlin.
May 29 *Eighteen Edifying Discourses*, by S. Kierkegaard, published.

1846

Jan. 2   First attack on S. K. in *The Corsair*.
Jan. 10   S. K.'s reply by Frater Taciturnus in *The Fatherland*.
Feb. 7   Considers qualifying himself for ordination (VII^1 A 98).
Feb. 27   *The Concluding Unscientific Postscript*, by Johannes Climacus, published.
Mar. 9   "Report" (*Corsair*) begun in first NB Journal (VII^1 A 98).
Mar. 30   *A Literary Review* [*The Present Age* is part of this work.], by S. Kierkegaard, published.
May 2–16   Visit to Berlin.
June 12   Acquires Magister A. P. Adler's books: *Studier og Exempler, Forsøg til en kort systematisk Fremstilling af Christendommen i dens Logik*, and *Theologiske Studier*.
Oct. 2   Goldschmidt resigns as editor of *The Corsair*.
Oct. 7   Goldschmidt travels to Germany and Italy.

1847

Jan. 24   S. K. writes: "God be praised that I was subjected to the attack of the rabble. I have now had time to arrive at the conviction that it was a melancholy thought to want to live in a vicarage, doing penance in an out-of-the-way place, forgotten. I now have made up my mind quite otherwise" (VII^1 A 29).

         Date of Foreword to "Bogen om Adler" ("Authority and Revelation"). Not published; MS in *Papirer*.

         Drafts of lectures on communication (VIII^2 B 79-89). Not published or delivered.

Mar. 13   *Edifying Discourses in Various Spirits*, by S. Kierkegaard, published.
Sept. 29   *Works of Love*, by S. Kierkegaard, published.
Nov. 3   Regine Olsen marries Fridrich Schlegel.
Dec. 24   Sells house on Nytorv.

1848

Jan. 28   Leases apartment at Rosenborggade and Tornebuskgade 152 for April occupancy.

Apr. 19 S. K. notes: "My whole nature is changed. My concealment and reserve are broken—I am free to speak" (VIII^1 A 640).
Apr. 24 "No, no, my reserve still cannot be broken, at least not now" (VIII^1 A 645).
Apr. 26 *Christian Discourses*, by S. Kierkegaard, published.
July 24–27 *The Crisis and the Crisis in a Life of an Actress*, by Inter et Inter, published.
Aug. Notes that his health is poor and is convinced that he will die (IX A 216).

Reflections on direct and indirect communication (IX A 218, 221-24, 233-35).

Sept. 1 Preaches in Vor Frue Church (IX A 266-69, 272).
Nov. *The Point of View for my Work as an Author* "as good as finished" (IX A 293). (Published posthumously in 1859 by S. K.'s brother Peter Christian Kierkegaard).

"Armed Neutrality," by S. Kierkegaard, "written toward the end of 1848 and the beginning of 1849" (X^5 B 105-10) but not published.

1849

May 14 Second edition of *Either/Or* and *The Lilies of the Field and the Birds of the Air*, by S. Kierkegaard, published.
May 19 *Two Minor Ethical-Religious Treatises* by H. H., published.
June 25–26 Councillor Olsen (Regine's father) dies.
July 30 *The Sickness unto Death*, by Anti-Climacus, published.
Nov. 13 *Three Discourses at the Communion on Friday*, by S. Kierkegaard, published.

1850

April 18 Moves to Nørregade 43, Copenhagen.
Sept. 27 *Training in Christianity*, by Anti-Climacus, published.
Dec. 20 *An Edifying Discourse*, by S. Kierkegaard, published.

1851

Jan. 31 "An Open Letter . . . Dr. Rudelbach," by S. Kierkegaard, published.

Aug. 7 *On My Work as an Author* and *Two Discourses at the Communion on Fridays*, by S. Kierkegaard, published.
Sept. 10 *For Self-Examination*, by S. Kierkegaard, published.

1851–52

Judge for Yourself, by S. Kierkegaard, written. Published posthumously, 1876.

1854

Jan. 30 Bishop Mynster dies.
Apr. 15 H. Martensen named Bishop.
Dec. 18 S. K. begins polemic against Bishop Martensen in *The Fatherland*.

1855

Jan.–May Polemic continues.
May 24 *This Must Be Said; So Let It Now Be Said*, by S. Kierkegaard, advertised as published.

First number of *The Moment*.

June 16 *Christ's Judgment on Official Christianity*, by S. Kierkegaard, published.
Sept. 3 *The Unchangeableness of God*, by S. Kierkegaard, published.
Sept. 25 Ninth and last number of *The Moment* published; number 10 published posthumously. S. K. writes his last entry (XI^2 A 439).
Oct. 2 Enters Frederiks Hospital.
Nov. 11 Dies.
Nov. 18 Is buried.

Translators' Preface

In richness, insight, variety, and profundity, Kierkegaard's journals are perhaps unexcelled. Lowrie calls Kierkegaard the "greatest of all journal-writers."[1] Certainly his journals are comparable to Emerson's and to Goethe's *Conversations*. Nevertheless, at the outset he had considerable reluctance to do this kind of thing, in spite of the practice and advice of writers whom he regarded highly. His observations on journal-writing are found among his early papers:

* I have often wondered how it could be that I have had such great reluctance to write down particular observations; but the more I come to know individual great men in whose writings one does not detect in any way the kaleidoscopic hustling together of the same batch of ideas (perhaps Jean Paul by his example has given me premature uneasiness in this respect) and the more I recall that such a refreshing writer as Hoffmann has kept a journal and that Lichtenberg recommends it, the more I am prompted to find out just why this, which is in itself innocent, should be unpleasant, almost repulsive, to me. Obviously the reason was that in each instance I thought of the possibility of publication, which perhaps would have required more extensive development, something with which I did not wish to be bothered, and enervated by such an abstract possibility (a kind of literary hiccoughing and squeamishness), the aroma of fancies and mood evaporated.** I think, instead, that it would be good, through frequent note-writing, to let the thoughts come forth with the umbilical cord of the original mood, and to forget as much as possible all regard for their possible use, which would not happen in any case by referring to my journals; rather, by expectorating myself as in a letter to an intimate friend I gain the possibility of self-knowledge and, in addition, fluency in writ-

---

* *In margin:* Resolution of July 13, 1837, made in our study at six o'clock in the evening.

** *In margin of II A 118:* And therefore the entries I have are either so completely cryptic that I no longer understand them or are entirely occasional, and I can also see why usually many entries are from one and the same day, which suggests a sort of day of reckoning, but this is crazy.

1. Walter Lowrie, *Kierkegaard* (London: Oxford University Press, 1938), p. 150.

ing, the same articulateness in written expression which I have to some extent in speaking, the knowledge of many little traits to which I have given no more than a quick glance, and finally, the advantage, if what Hamann says is true in another sense, that there are ideas which a man gets only once in his life. Such practice backstage is certainly necessary for every person who is not so gifted that his development is in some way public.[2]

The apparent wealth of fancies and ideas which one feels in abstract possibility is just as unpleasant, and it develops an uneasiness similar to that which a cow suffers when it is not milked at the proper time. Therefore one's best method, if external conditions are of no help, is, like the cow, to milk oneself.[3]

Before this "resolution" of July 13, 1837, Kierkegaard had, of course, kept reading and lecture notes, sometimes with comments, and had also been hospitable to his own reflections by formulating them in writing on loose sheets or pieces of paper. After September, 1836, he began the practice of transcribing some of these loose entries into notebooks, but he also continued writing on loose sheets. In July, 1835, he began the first of a series of notebooks marked AA, BB, etc., running to 1846. In 1846 he began a series of notebook journals numbered NB 1 to NB 36, which were continued into the year of his death (November 11, 1855). The latest dated entry among the loose sheets is marked September 25, 1855, one week before Kierkegaard was taken to the hospital. Therefore the *Papirer* of all kinds cover a period of about twenty-four years, somewhat more than half his lifetime.

The journals proper and entries on loose sheets do not have the character of a diary, even though an equivalent has been employed as the title in the superb German (ed. H. Gerdes) and Italian (ed. C. Fabro) editions of selections. Lowrie is quite right in saying that the journals are not diaries. "We speak properly of 'The Diary of the Seducer' and of the diary of the young man in 'Guilty/Not Guilty?' where the element of time was essential, but the entries in S. K.'s journals were timeless, they were the records of his thoughts, things he wanted to remember, some of them thoughts he would use ultimately in his writings, very few of them being essentially related to particular dates, and few of them actually dated, except during the first years."[4] Apart from Emil Boesen, Kierkegaard had no confidant other than his journals; yet the personal notion of a diary is present essentially only by indirection. There are, to be sure, entries of personal revelation, but they are quantitatively

---

2. *Søren Kierkegaards Papirer*, ed. P. A. Heiberg, V. Kuhr, and E. Torsting, 20 vols., I–XI[3] (Copenhagen: Gyldendal, 1909-48), II A 118.
3. Ibid., II A 119. II A 208: *Nulla dies sine linea* (Not a day without a line).
4. Lowrie, *Kierkegaard*, p. 107.

minor and some of them are very cryptic. Kierkegaard as a man is not absent, but, as in the published works, personal experience and relationships are usually transmuted into a universality of issues and reflections which thereby become all the more significant for others. The entries of more obvious biographical interest will be the substance of the final volume in the present edition.

Before Kierkegaard's death, Emil Boesen asked him about his various manuscripts and papers. His reply was: "No, let come what may; it depends upon chance. . . ."[5] To have Kierkegaard's papers at all is in a sense providential, if one considers the lapse of almost a century before the completion of the definitive Danish edition and the various custodians and places and conditions of custody. The papers were stored first with Kierkegaard's brother-in-law, J. C. Lund, in Copenhagen early in 1856. His son, Henrik Lund, began making a catalog that year and had a list of 389 items of various kinds before this work was interrupted. In 1858 the papers were moved to Aalborg, Jutland, to Bishop Peter C. Kierkegaard, a brother. H. P. Barfod, the bishop's secretary, resumed work on the catalog in February, 1865, and completed it the same year—472 detailed headings, with numbers 1 to 382 corresponding to Lund's catalog. At the end of his catalog Barfod appended: "Out of consideration for completeness and circumspection it is to be noted that Bishop Kierkegaard, in his depository and among his papers, has at least individual lesser essays and letters which, inasmuch as I have not had opportunity to go through them, are excluded from this catalog."[6]

In the autumn of 1867 Barfod was given a free hand with the papers in order to prepare them for possible publication.[7] Between 1869 and 1877 there were published four volumes of journals from the years 1833 to 1847. In the process manuscripts were clipped, marked, pasted, and corrected as manuscript copy for the printer, and in the process some things were thrown away. Therefore the definitive edition *(Papirer)* is partially dependent upon the earlier edition *(Efterladte Papirer)*. H. P. Gottsched, a theologian from Göttingen, where Kierkegaard's works were coming to be of some significance, took over after Barfod's death in 1869 and completed the edition of eight volumes in 1881. In 1875 the papers were placed in the library of the University of Copenhagen, and they are now in the Royal Library, Copenhagen.

5. Appendix to *Søren Kierkegaards Efterladte Papirer*, 8 vols., ed. H. P. Barfod and H. Gottsched (Copenhagen: 1869-81), VIII, 594.
6. *Efterladte Papirer*, I, p. viii.
7. Ibid., p. ix.

The most fortunate event in the odyssey of the papers was the undertaking of a comparatively full edition of all the papers (journals, notebooks, loose papers, drafts, notes, etc.) by P. A. Heiberg and Viktor Kuhr, who were later joined by E. Torsting. Beginning in 1909 (an edition of 500 copies first noted in Volume VIII^1, 1917), over a period of forty years the editors published eleven volumes of *Papirer*; some volumes are in parts so that the total is twenty separate volumes numbered I to XI^3. Most of the lecture and reading notes, manuscripts of published works (except drafts and marginal notes and comments in Kierkegaard's own copies), letters, and documents have been omitted from the current edition of *Papirer*. The available letters and selected documents pertaining to Kierkegaard were later published as *Breve og Akstykker Vedrørende Søren Kierkegaard*, I–II, ed. Niels Thulstrup (Copenhagen: Munksgaard, 1953–54). The papers yet unpublished in the Royal Library, consisting of notes on reading and lectures, the Schelling lectures, for example, have been made available for the present edition through the courtesy of Niels Thulstrup, editor of the forthcoming supplementary volumes to the *Papirer*.

The Heiberg-Kuhr-Torsting edition of the *Papirer* is a model of scholarly care and comprehension. In the present volume references to the journals and other papers are according to the arrangement and notation (I A 35, X^6 B 70, etc.) in the definitive Danish edition. The texts have been treated with scrupulousness, even to the point of an appendix giving a physical description of the manuscripts and of the writing and critical notations on the texts of manuscripts. In the body of the volumes careful and extensive documentation of references has been carried through.

Lowrie has complained that the Danish publication of Kierkegaard's *Works* has "an immense volume called an Index—which is of no use whatever because it deals only with *words*, without the least selection or discrimination. Even if it were well done, its value would be diminished by half for the fact that it does not include the Journal."[8] The absence of an index, however, should not obscure to us the high quality and immensity of the achievement of the Danish editors of the *Papirer*. (A Danish index of the *Papirer* will be included in the current reissue of the *Papirer* and the publication of supplementary volumes by Gyldendal in Copenhagen.) The present volume and others to come are intended to make the *Papirer* more accessible to English readers by the way of the

---

8. Søren Kierkegaard, *The Christian Discourses* (London: Oxford University Press, 1939), Preface, p. viii.

arrangement and the extensiveness of the selection. A comprehensive index of this and subsequent volumes will appear in Volumes IV and V.

An initial problem which the editors Heiberg and Kuhr faced and which they discuss in particular in the Preface to *Papirer*, I, was the problem of order or organization. "Much could be said a priori for organizing the materials of the new edition simply in chronological order, but quite apart from the presumably justified break with chronological structure for practical reasons, since the material was already separated into three main categories, the very character of the material entailed the judgment that the chronological order of the first main category ought to be broken by substantive categories within individual volumes. As the manuscripts of the first main category come to us from Kierkegaard's own hand, they fall into three groups almost of their own accord: a group with the character of journal entries (from independent utterances and notations to coherent travel sketches); a group related to development of published works of one sort or another (from short pieces and newspaper articles to large works); and a group related to study and reading (from brief aphoristic entries to whole courses and extensive excerpts). According to these three groups the volumes at hand are divided into three sections which for sake of convenience are simply designated as A, B, and C. . . ."[9] The editors also point out that in Group C and partly in Group A Kierkegaard himself had sought additional clustering according to content: theological, philosophical, and esthetic.[10] Besides these shifts from chronological order in favor of emphasis upon content, there are other breaks in chronological ordering because Kierkegaard had also written marginal notes and other additions after the passage of time, even as much as an entire year.[11] Furthermore, in transcribing entries from loose sheets into notebooks Kierkegaard "grouped them according to subjects."[12] The editors conclude: "What is here preserved by not shattering the coherence given by the arrangement in the original manuscripts we have regarded as more essential than what has been lost in chronological clarity, especially since it has been possible to compensate for this loss in another way."[13]

In commenting on Alexander Dru's fine one-volume selection from the *Papirer*, Walter Lowrie was in agreement with this concern of the Danish editors for some stress on an arrangement reflecting content.

9. *Papirer*, I, p. x.
10. Ibid.
11. Ibid., pp. x-xi.
12. Ibid., p. xi.
13. Ibid.

"That book [Dru, *Kierkegaard's Journals*] is invaluable to anyone who would understand the life of Søren Kierkegaard or the development of his thought. But there is more light yet to shine from the twenty big volumes of the Journals, and perhaps more than one scholar will feel prompted to develop this rich mine further. Not now, however, in a biographical interest (for Dru has adequately provided for that), but rather in a topical way. It is now very difficult to get a comprehensive view of Søren Kierkegaard's reflections upon the subjects which chiefly concerned him, for there is as yet no index to the Journals as a whole. It is therefore all the more important that collections should be made of his more important utterances."[14]

Although the plan of the present English edition of selections primarily according to subject is in harmony with an emphasis by Kierkegaard, the Danish editors, and Lowrie upon contiguity of content, the extent to which it exceeds what has been done in this direction is unabashedly in the interest of the reader. A colossal index to the *Papirer* to facilitate a more coherent approach to the content would perhaps be more helpful to a reader than Lowrie admitted, but the reader's use of such an index would still be awkward and fragmented. It is of palpable value, in our judgment, to consolidate the entries on communication, on ethics, on the esthetic, etc., so that the cumulative thought can become apparent. At the same time, however, the sequential character of the entries is preserved by a maintenance of the chronological relationship within each category, insofar as this time-order can be discerned in the materials and in the *Papirer* as published. For those who wish to pursue the serial order of the entries in the present volume, insofar as this can be done on the basis of the *Papirer*, there is an appended table which collates the entries of this volume with the *Papirer* (see pp. 489 ff.).

The forthcoming Volumes II, III, and IV will be subject-centered, like the present volume. Volume V will be devoted to entries from the *Papirer* that are clearly autobiographical in character or are related to Kierkegaard's contemporaries. The detailed index to Volume I-IV will be in Volume IV, and Volume V will have its own index.

In the *Papirer* the term "journal" refers particularly to notebooks which Kierkegaard labeled as journals, AA–NB 36. In a wider, yet very justifiable sense, all entries within category A of the *Papirer* are journal entries. There is, in addition, a moderate number of entries in

---

14. Søren Kierkegaard, *Attack on Christendom* (Princeton: Princeton University Press, 1944), Preface, p. 5.

categories B and C which qualify intrinsically as journal entries because they are Kierkegaard's reflections on issues and ideas. Quite justifiably, therefore, Haecker and later Gerdes in German editions of *Die Tagebücher*, Dru in an English edition of *Journals*, Ferlov and Gateau in the French edition of *Journal*, and Fabro in the Italian *Il Diario* all include items from sections B and C under a title intended primarily to fit section A. Because the present multivolume edition includes letters and papers not included in the journals proper, in other portions of section A, or in sections B and C, the title *Journals and Papers* has been used for the sake of continuity and accuracy. Students of Kierkegaard who wish to pursue detailed studies of particular published works (*Fragments, Postscript*, etc.) are referred to the Danish edition of *Papirer* for the full range of category B.

Even in a multivolume edition *in extenso*, the Danish editors exercised some selectivity and did not print all the papers.[15] Obviously, in the present edition the task of selection is even greater and essentially different. Having made our own selections, we checked the use made of the *Papirer* by scholars throughout the world, especially those in Scandinavia, Germany, England, and America. Among the works collated with our own selections are studies by E. Hirsch, Niels Thulstrup, Torsten Bohlin, Per Lønning, Gregor Malantschuk, Paul Holmer, Edward Geismar, Reidar Thomte, David Swenson, Walter Lowrie, Howard Johnson, T. H. Croxall, Leo Sjestov, Regis Jolivet, Helge Ukkola, Johannes Sløk, James Collins, Valter Lindstrom, and Per Wagndal. In this way the multiplicity of judgments has served as mutual corroboration and extension of selection. Acknowledgment of indebtedness is therefore made to a host of Kierkegaard scholars who have unwittingly contributed to the preparation of this edition, and particularly to Hayo Gerdes, Peter Rohde, Knud Ferlov, Jean J. Gateau, and Cornelio Fabro for the judgment and knowledge embodied in their multivolume editions of selections from the *Papirer* in current German, Danish, French, and Italian editions of selections. We are also indebted to Gyldendal Forlag of Copenhagen for permission to use the text of the *Papirer* and to absorb the editors' notes.

Acknowledgment is gratefully made to Gertrude Hilleboe, Stephanie Schultz, and Ed Miller for translating the Latin, German, and Greek portions of the text, and to Erik Langkjaer for his interest. Editors Miriam S. Farley and Susan Fernandez have been perseveringly helpful in guiding the manuscript through the press.

15. *Papirer*, I, p. xiv.

Special acknowledgment is accorded to the Rask-Ørsted Fond and the Carlsberg Fond for their assistance, including the share which Gregor Malantschuk of Copenhagen has had in the preparation of this volume. His interpretation of numerous points in various entries and his additions to the notes have been invaluable. The compact, penetrating characterizations (in our translation) of Kierkegaard's central concepts in the notes are the results of his long and intimate study of the *Papirer* and the *Works*.

During the initial period of preparatory work on the entire edition, a part-time leave was made possible by awards from the Board of Education of the American Lutheran Church and the Swenson-Kierkegaard Memorial Committee.

By the time the present volume is published, the manuscript of Volume II should be completed and a beginning made on the subsequent volumes. The preparation of Volume I, including planning and selecting for all volumes, has taken longer than we like to remember. Acceleration of work on Volume II and the others has been made possible by a sabbatical leave granted by St. Olaf College and a generous gift from the Louis and Maud Hill Family Foundation, which permits a year of uninterrupted work in Denmark, close to materials and men. We thank the Hill Foundation and St. Olaf College not only for the provision of practical possibilities but for encouragement in hoeing a long row.

St. Olaf College   H. V. H.
Northfield, Minnesota   E. H. H.

Introduction

Unnoticed beyond the boundaries of Denmark and misunderstood within those boundaries, Søren Kierkegaard died on November 11, 1855.

This was the man who, in the words of A. T. Mollegen, "tried to do singlehanded, in the nineteenth century, what God is doing in the twentieth century with the help of two world wars." This remark is now twenty-three years old, but it can stand. Kierkegaard's endeavor was to shatter bourgeois complacency, dispel the illusion of self-redemption, break open the husk of conceit in which men had encased themselves, in the hope that man, open again, might seek God and be found of him.

When I reported Mollegen's remark to Paul Tillich in 1948, our German friend nodded approvingly and said, "Yes, Kierkegaard and God are everywhere succeeding—except perhaps in Russia and America."

I tell you nothing of Kierkegaard's biography, for much of that ground will be covered in Volume V, which is yet to appear. But while waiting for it, we have as required reading the biographical studies written by Walter Lowrie. Here I remind you only that Kierkegaard was a man of private fortune and no public occupation, a layman of the Church of Denmark, who spent the whole of his brief and stormy life in Copenhagen, dying there at the age of forty-two in the midst of a violent attack on the Established Church—a Church which nonetheless he loved.

In an incredibly short twelve-year period there poured from his pen twenty-one extraordinary books, in addition to which he left behind him journals and papers *(Papirer)* which, in print in the Danish, run to eight thousand pages.

Until recently we have had in translation from these eight thousand pages only Alexander Dru's *Selections from the Journals of Kierkegaard* (London: Oxford University Press, 1959). Admirably chosen and accurately translated—but there are no more than 600 pages of them! Just a few nuggets from a mine unworked until Ronald Gregor Smith panned out more of the gold in his book called *The Last Years* (London: Collins,

1965). But still, people who cannot read Danish, Dutch, German, or Italian have been handicapped until now. Zealous translators were relatively quick to give us the works *(Værker)* of Kierkegaard. The papers *(Papirer)* have been slower in coming.

With entire justice Danish scholars have expostulated, "But how can you Americans and English expect to understand Kierkegaard when, not having the *Papirer,* you don't have 'the key to the scriptures'?" I once thought that this was just a bit of Danish self-importance and self-glorification. I think so no more. Having ploughed through all eight thousand pages, I must concede that the *Papirer* are indispensable for the interpretation of this complex man.

Prolific as he was in his published works, Kierkegaard extended himself even further when he was writing for himself. Let it be confessed, the *Papers* are sometimes a bore: verbose, prolix, repetitious. He reverts so often to the same topics, and so much in the same terms, that the impatient reader is tempted to throw the book down with the cry, "We've had this before!" Yet that would be a hasty rejection. For each journal entry gives us some new twist, some new dimension. This is not useless rumination, an endless going over and over again of the same subjects. The fascination of the *Papers* is to watch how concepts *grow* in the recesses of a great man's mind.

I take immoderate pleasure in the fact that Howard and Edna Hong have elected to employ the methodology I recommended to them years ago. Unlike Dru, whose easy guide was chronology, the Hongs went the more difficult route of arranging the journal entries by topics. Yet here is the beauty of it. Within each topical heading, chronology is preserved (insofar as Kierkegaard allows us to date his jottings). Thus we can trace, in many instances, how a concept underwent development in the course of time. Ideas early advanced by Kierkegaard are sometimes stubbornly maintained to the very end. Others are modified or clarified, achieving in the process a high degree of polish.

The *Papers* are worthy of our attention on at least three levels.

One, they contain the thoughts of a man of commanding importance. Like him or dislike him, he has to be reckoned with. Moreover, in the *Papers* we can be sure that this is S.K. himself speaking—which is not always true in the case of his pseudonymous writings.

Two, they include many germinal ideas which never found their way into his published works.

Three, they illumine the published works because in the *Papers* we see both the trial runs (i.e., Kierkegaard winding up and warming up to get ready for a new book) or else Kierkegaard sitting in judgment on his latest book, as his own most severe critic.

The accessibility of this fresh and invaluable material we owe to the Hongs.

If their translation occasionally sounds a little jerky and reads rough, the more the Hongs are to be praised. They are but reproducing faithfully the sometimes roughspun character of the original text from which they were working. Most of the journal entries were jottings, hurried notations. (It is said that Kierkegaard had a desk in every room in his house, in order that whenever an idea occurred to him, even as he was moving from room to room, he could immediately register it. He subscribed to the maxim of Hamann: "There are certain thoughts a man is capable of thinking only once in his life. Write it down!") The translators have wisely decided not to give high English polish to Danish diamonds uncut and rough-edged. Where Kierkegaard was felicitous and eloquent in his mode of expression, the Hongs are. Where he wasn't, the Hongs aren't.

Curiously, the British and the Americans still hesitate about admitting Kierkegaard to the highest ranks of philosophy and theology.

Take, for example, John Updike. In *The New Yorker* for February 26, 1966, he writes a sympathetic and perceptive review of Gregor Smith's translation of selections from the journals dating from 1853 to 1855. Mr. Updike begins his comment in a low key with the cautionary remark, "It is not certain that the United States needs still more translations of Kierkegaard."

In the April 28, 1966, issue of *The New York Review of Books* Mr. W. W. Bartley III sounded aggrieved that any more selections from Kierkegaard were to be forthcoming. He makes a good point, however. He says that we all ought to learn Danish. Thus we could read the whole Kierkegaardian corpus for ourselves—and so be delivered from "selecttions." I agree. But since there is little likelihood of Denmark's reinvasion of the British Isles (or, possibly, of Rhode Island) in our era, we are dependent on the translators who select for us, and we should be grateful to them.

I thought we had reached a stage of philosophical and theological sophistication in which no defense of Kierkegaard is required. Apparently, not so. By "defense" I do not mean that we must kowtow to Kierkegaard, as if he were always in the right. No, he has blind spots and imbalances. I contend only that here is a mind to be met.

The greatness of Kierkegaard cannot be demonstrated in short compass. It can only be asserted. As a bald assertion, then, the greatness of Kierkegaard is fourfold.

He was great as a *prophet*.

In the heyday of nineteenth-century optimism, Kierkegaard foresaw —with a kind of terrifying clairvoyance—the disaster that was about to befall the human race. That which alarmed him most was his age's decision to make "the experiment of doing without the unconditional," i.e., without God. Given this decision, Kierkegaard was able to plot accurately the trajectory of man's fall: from theism, to humanism, to materialism. The legitimate aspirations of the French Revolution rested, unfortunately, on assumptions bound to defeat those aspirations in the long run. "Liberty, Equality, Fraternity" were concepts dear to Kierkegaard. But since men were determined to be quit not simply of kings but also of God and His Church, then the revolutionary watchword must be translated as follows: When men have liberated themselves from God, their struggle for equality produces only equality in mediocrity, and instead of fraternity we end with convention-ridden collectivism. We don't "level up"; we "level down." The Kierkegaardian forecast is this: Unless rewon for Christianity, the West cannot escape the descending logic which reads: from monarchy, to democracy, to Communism—i.e., the abdication of responsible selfhood and the monstrous standardization and regimentation of life. In short, Kierkegaard has foreseen what secularism would be like when it was fully ripe and has maintained that the real trouble with secularism is that man can never remain merely secular. Inevitably man is religious and will turn religious again. If it is not responsible religion to which he turns, it will be daemonic religion. The new "surrogates for religion," springing up "like toadstools after a rain," will be cults in a thousand variations and, as a still more sinister accompaniment, the religion of Statism. Men who have abolished the Absolute will soon invent a new absolute, and Kierkegaard knew what the most enticing of the new absolutes would be: a State which demands of its citizens uncritical allegiance, unconditional obedience, religious devotion, and self-immolation. No one can deny that Kierkegaard was a good diagnostician. History has borne him out.*

---

* One who would learn this aspect of Kierkegaard's thought must search his *Papers* diligently. But his social analyses are to be found sprinkled everywhere throughout his published books, of which, in this connection, I would especially commend *On Authority and Revelation* and *The Present Age*. Of secondary sources, James Collins' *The Mind of Kierkegaard* is best, along with Peter F. Drucker's article on

Kierkegaard was great as a *philosopher*.

It is fascinating to see how Kierkegaard, the reputed father of existentialism, had already anticipated the kinds of philosophical movements which might derive from him, should certain aspects of his thought be accentuated to the neglect of other aspects.

The turn given to things by, for example, a Sartre would not have taken him by surprise. The Kierkegaard who foresaw so much else foresaw this too. He prepared in advance a devastating critique. If one would like to know what is wrong with existential*ism*, Kierkegaard is the one to consult.

With amazing philosophical precision he explains why atheistic existentialism is the wrong answer to the right question.

That which chiefly employed Kierkegaard's dialectical skill, however, was Hegel. For in Hegel he found the philosophical justification, in imposing form, of a *Reich* which, since it was the incarnation of Absolute Reason, must bend all individuals to its will—and break those who would not. This philosophy, utterly inimical to Christianity and potentially destructive of human beings, encountered in Søren Kierkegaard a foe so formidable that no one who has understood him, even though one might be unable to accept the alternative he proposes, could ever again fall prey to rationalistic arrogance, Hegelian or otherwise. "Using the subtlest weapons of logic and philosophy," says Peter F. Rhode very justly, "Kierkegaard performed the feat of demonstrating the impotence of logic and philosophy to deal with the ultimate problems of existence. This demonstration is his real title to fame. It has not been to the belittlement of logic and philosophy; but it has made it difficult for us to abuse these instruments to obtain fictitious solutions of problems which they are

---

"The Unfashionable Kierkegaard" in *The Sewanee Review* for Autumn 1949. Perhaps I may be forgiven for pointing also to my article "Kierkegaard and Politics" in *The American-Scandinavian Review* for Autumn 1955. It is also reprinted in *A Kierkegaard Critique*, of which Niels Thulstrup and I are co-editors (New York: Harper, 1962). I am dumbfounded that William Hubben, in his book *Four Prophets of Our Destiny* (New York: Macmillan, 1960), can be so wide of the mark as to remark in his chapter on Kierkegaard: "Kierkegaard ignored the scientific and social conditions of his time in his quest for the inner freedom. Though he lived and wrote when Karl Marx's *Communist Manifesto* (1848) was published, neither Marx's scientific socialism nor the French socialism of the 1830's seems to have made any impression upon his thinking." What nonsense! Further, I ask how it was possible for so thorough a scholar and so devoted an admirer of Kierkegaard as the great H. Richard Niebuhr to permit himself the imbecility of saying (in *Christianity and Culture*) that "Kierkegaardian existentialism gives up the cultural problem as irrelevant to Christianity."

powerless to solve." Quite in the spirit of Pascal, Kierkegaard has used reason to teach us reason's limits, to show that there is nothing more irrational than the pretensions of the autonomous human reason, and thus to bring us to "the borders of the marvellous." That is, to prepare us for the reception of divine revelation—a revelation not volatilized, as in the case of theological liberalism, nor made synonymous with an evolutionary process culminating in the State, as in Hegel, but a revelation uniquely focused in the God-Man and in the Church his coming created. Kierkegaard's attack on Hegel is, therefore, equally an apology for the Christian Faith. Kierkegaard was much displeased by a German review of his *Philosophical Fragments*. In the *Postscript* he says: "It seems to have escaped the reviewer's attention altogether that the book was nothing more than old-fashioned orthodoxy—presented with a suitable degree of severity." For many, too severe, too orthodox. But there it stands. Our Danish mentor has given us an impressive philosophy of religion which, though surely open to criticism, does not lack admirers and advocates in every major Christian communion today. One might say of Kierkegaard, as the Roman Catholic Church has said of St. Thomas Aquinas: he is to be disagreed with—only with respect. Professor J. V. Langmead Casserley, telling the engrossing story of *The Christian in Philosophy*, says of Kierkegaard that he "cannot allot him any place in this narrative which falls short of the very highest."*

Kierkegaard is great as a *psychologist*. He foresaw not only the disaster which would overtake the human race but also what would follow in the disaster's wake: perplexity, bewilderment, anxiety, paralyzing despair, and the nihilistic mood which creates the spiritual vacuum that makes our present age impotent and unpredictable. The vacuum cries aloud for the Holy Spirit but remains a standing invitation for all manner

---

* To appreciate the philosophical contribution of Kierkegaard, his entire work must be known; but philosophers who are making their initial approach to Kierkegaard might well begin with the twin volumes, *Philosophical Fragments* and *The Concluding Unscientific Postscript to the Philosophical Fragments*. For help from secondary sources, the two best books in English have already been mentioned: Collins' *The Mind of Kierkegaard* and Casserley's *The Christian in Philosophy*. With these should be compared Reinhold Niebuhr's section on "The Loss of the Self in Idealism" in *The Nature and Destiny of Man* (New York: Scribner, 1941) and Charles W. Lowry's brief but admirable treatment of "Existentialism: or Subjectivity in Rebound" in *Communism and Christ* (New York: Morehouse-Gorham, 1953). The differences between Kierkegaard and much of contemporary existentialism have been decisively shown by Walter Lowrie in "Existence as Understood by Kierkegaard and/or Sartre" in *The Sewanee Review* for July, 1950.

of evil spirits to rush in and possess it. In plain words, Kierkegaard knew what the cultural collapse would do to human beings, what kind of mentality it would engender, and thus what kind of priests it would take, what manner of special skills would be required, for communicating the gospel in the new climate.

Charles Williams, praising Kierkegaard in *The Descent of the Dove* (London: Faber & Faber, 1950), comments on how well he comes off in contrast to the old-line apologetics which undertakes to answer agnosticism without ever first having felt its pinch. When will we learn, asks Kierkegaard in *Either/Or*, that people's difficulty with respect to facing Christianity or life itself, particularly "the next day," is no longer doubt but *despair*?

Kierkegaard is only a man, and a curious, misshapen man at that. Yet to read him is to be ushered into the presence of the God "unto whom all hearts are open, all desires known, and from whom no secrets are hid." How thoroughly this servant of God has understood us! Profoundly he interprets to us the meaning of our experience of doubt and despair, of irresolution and timidity, of guilt-consciousness and remorse, of *acedia* and the frenzy of activity by which we would stifle it, of the anxieties we can name and of the *Angst* which remains unnamed. He knows our talent for excuse-making and our virtuosity, when confronted by the claim of God, in evasion. With terrifying adroitness he outmaneuvers us to show—just as the idea occurs—that every attempted escape is a blind alley.

An empirical psychologist Kierkegaard is not; but using himself and the people he knew as Subject A, he has looked deep into the human heart and mind and has described what goes on there—and what it means.*

Kierkegaard is great as a *theologian*. Having analyzed the social ills and the resulting psychological *malaise* of mankind, Kierkegaard proceeds to expound the Christian gospel in its relevance to the questions tortured out of man by means of his existential predicament. Throughout

---

* Every book of Kierkegaard exhibits him in his role as psychologist, student of man. For persons approaching S. K. for the first time, it would be best, in this connection, to begin by reading *Christian Discourses* and *Purity of Heart*. These mastered, one can proceed to the more systematic presentations in *The Sickness unto Death* and *The Concept of Dread*. One of the books richest in psychological insight is also one of the most neglected ones: *Stages on Life's Way*. I know of no good analysis of it in English.

his authorship Kierkegaard's point of reference was a full, orthodox Athanasian-Nicene Christianity, although for strategic reasons he usually kept it concealed. Master pedagogue that he is, Kierkegaard knows that nothing is so useless as the answer to an unasked question. It is like being presented with the solution to the crossword puzzle for which one lacks the corresponding cue-sheet. What could be duller or more pointless? Dangling theology—the theology which comes as purported reply to a question never posed—cannot be assimilated or appropriated. Not that the answers are derived from the questions. This is an epistemological position Kierkegaard repudiates. It is, rather, that the answers, given by revelation, prompt Kierkegaard to try (by a method he calls "indirect communication") to raise with men the questions which, when asked *de profundis*, prepare the inquirer to hear the Christian answer as *answer*.

From first to last, Kierkegaard is a religious writer, a theologian. But not a systematic theologian. Nor is he, in the traditional sense of the term, an apologetic theologian. If this elusive Danish theologian is to be captured at all in a phrase, it would be impossible to improve on the one Brunner chose: he is a missionary theologian. As such, he has tempered the spiritual rapiers needed today for the very special and difficult task—a task not envisaged by the New Testament but accurately described by Kierkegaard as the task—of "Introducing Christianity into Christendom."

Having made so many claims for Kierkegaard, I feel it necessary to surround myself with a great cloud of witnesses.

The verdict of Reinhold Niebuhr is well known: "Kierkegaard is the profoundest interpreter of the psychology of the religious life, in my opinion, since St. Augustine."

Emil Brunner says: "I am convinced that the missionary theology of a man like Kierkegaard in the nineteenth century has done more than any dogmatic theologian, perhaps more than all of them put together."

Cornelio Fabro is summoned as the next witness. While this Roman Catholic monk was Dean of the Department of Philosophy at the College of the Propaganda Fide, he translated into Italian three large volumes of selections from the *Papirer*. Fabro's *Il Diario* has remained a model of excellence, with respect to choice and arrangement, for all other translators, the Hongs included. Padre Fabro writes: "Disciple of Christ, that was Kierkegaard indubitably. Rising above the arid confines of the Reformation, his work can offer to the Catholic theologian precious resources for the preparation of a phenomenology of theological problems, in particular those related to faith; it could therefore lead to a renewal of traditional theology and offer to modern man a theology integral *cordis et mentis.*"

We find New York, Geneva, and Rome in agreement!

But has Copenhagen anything to do with Canterbury? I, as an Episcopalian, am bound to ask: Is Canterbury alone silent? By no means. It will always be to the credit of Anglicanism that it was the Reverend Canon Walter Lowrie, priest of the Diocese of New Jersey, who was chiefly responsible for the translation of Kierkegaard into English. This is not to forget the hero-size pioneer efforts of David F. Swenson, a Congregationalist and professor of the University of Minnesota. An impeccable translator, Swenson's perfectionism was almost his downfall. His veneration for Kierkegaard was so great that he could hardly bring himself to publish any translation he felt to be unworthy of the master stylist whom Danish children have to read for the same reason that we have to read Shakespeare and Milton—just to see what it is possible to do with the language. And so, the Anglican Lowrie at one point wrote to Minneapolis and, in the words of Martin Luther, commanded Swenson to "sin boldly." At a time when Kierkegaard was still unknown in the English-speaking world, Lowrie persuaded the American-Scandinavian Foundation to publish, in cooperation with the Princeton University Press, Swenson's translation of the *Philosophical Fragments.* Later, when Swenson died, Lowrie finished for him the translation of the *Postscript* which the stricken Swenson had about two-thirds done. It was also Lowrie who talked Charles Williams into convincing the Oxford University Press that the translation of Kierkegaard into English was a paramount duty. Oxford, although skeptical, agreed—on condition that Lowrie foot all the bills!

Casserley, whom I have already quoted, does not exaggerate when he hails the translation and publication of Kierkegaard's writings as "perhaps the most important episode in twentieth-century English publishing."

W. H. Auden has said: "To the Oxford, Princeton, and other presses who have been making Kierkegaard available in English, we and our children owe a debt which we could not repay even if we remembered it."

To Auden's list must now be added the honorable name of the Indiana University Press. Thanks to this house and to the labors of the Hongs we shall now have the opportunity, as never before, to explore the rich interplay of a man's mind and to encounter the texture thereof. Some of his thinking, no doubt, deserves to be rejected. But I do not forget what a wise old Lutheran professor at the University of Copenhagen flung at his students in final challenge: "Where Kierkegaard was wrong, that is between Kierkegaard and God. Where he was right, that is between God and *us*."

Howard A. Johnson

Long Beach, California
August 12, 1966

Søren Kierkegaard's Journals and Papers

A series of five periods indicates omissions or breaks in the Danish text as it stands. A series of three periods is used in the few instances of the translators' omissions.

Brackets are used in the text to enclose certain crucial Danish terms just translated or to enclose references supplied by the translators.

Footnote numbers in the text refer to the editors' footnotes, which appear in serial order at the end of the volume. Kierkegaard's notes and marginal comments appear at the bottom of the particular page, at the end of the entry, or in a few special cases as a bracketed insertion within an entry.

Kierkegaard's consciously developed punctuation (VIII^1 A 33-38) has been retained to a large extent. This is evident in the use of the colon and the dash and a minimal use of question marks. Pedagogical-stylistic characteristics (change of pace, variation of sentence-length, and the architecture of sentences and paragraphs) have also been carried over in the main. They are intended as an invitation to reflection and rereading—ideally, aloud.

ABSTRACT, ABSTRACTION

« 1

The abstract character of the Jews shows itself also in their predilection for money—not for property, etc., of money value—for money is a pure abstraction.

II A 708   *n.d.*, 1838

« 2

Abstract concepts are invisible like a straight line—visible only in their concretions.

II A 496   *n.d.*, 1839

« 3

The same thing has happened in the world of the sciences as in the world of commerce. First one traded in kind, then money was invented; today in the sciences all transactions are in paper money, which nobody cares about except the professors.

IV A 6   *n.d.*, 1842-43

« 4

The abstract can produce a prodigious effect. If I say in a talk: There where the road turns, there by the gate where the hired man stands—pure abstractions: *there, road, turns, gate, hired man.*

The gate can be a hundred thousand gates; the hired man can be millions.

This is the eternal *one* of the imagination. Just like the eternal "once upon a time" of the imagination: then man goes out into the morning of life.

VIII^1 A 622   *n.d.*, 1848

ABSURD

« 5

Faith hopes for this life also, but, note well, by virtue of the absurd, not by virtue of human understanding; otherwise it is only common sense, not faith.

IV A 108   n.d., 1843

« 6

N.B. God can appear to man only in the miracle, i.e., as soon as he sees God he sees a miracle. But on his own it is not possible for him to see the miracle, since the miracle is his own annihilation. [*In margin:* N.B.] The Jews expressed this figuratively by saying that to see God is death. It is more accurate to say that to see God or to see the miracle is by virtue of the absurd, for understanding must step aside.

V A 78   n.d., 1844

« 7

Hugo de St. Victor states a correct thesis (Helfferich, *Mystik*, Vol. I, p. 368): "Faith is really not supported by the things which go beyond reason, by any reason, because reason does not comprehend what faith believes; but nevertheless there is something here by which reason becomes determined or is conditioned to honor the faith which it still does not perfectly succeed in grasping."

This is what I have developed (for example, in *Concluding Postscript*[1])—that not every absurdity is the absurd or the paradox. The activity of reason is to distinguish the paradox negatively—but no more.

In an earlier journal or in loose papers[2] from an earlier time (when I read Aristotle's *Rhetoric*) I was of the opinion that a Christian art of speaking should be introduced in place of dogmatics. It ought to relate itself to πίστις.[3] πίστις in the classical Greek means the conviction (more than δόξα,[4] opinion) which relates itself to probability. But Christianity, which always turns the concepts of the natural man upside down and gets the opposite meaning out of them, relates πίστις to the improbable.

This concept of improbability, the absurd, ought, then, to be developed, for it is nothing but superficiality to think that the absurd is not a concept, that all sorts of absurdities are equally at home in the absurd. No, the concept of the absurd is precisely to grasp the fact that it cannot and must not be grasped. This is a negatively determined concept but is just as dialectical as any positive one. The *absurd*, the *paradox*, is composed in such a way that reason has no power at all to dissolve it in nonsense and prove that it is nonsense; no, it is a symbol, a riddle, a compounded riddle about which reason must say: I cannot solve it, it cannot be understood, but it does not follow thereby that it is nonsense. But, of course, if faith is completely abolished, the whole sphere is dropped, and then reason becomes conceited and perhaps concludes that, *ergo*, the paradox is nonsense. What concern there would be if in another realm the skilled class were extinct and then the unskilled found this thing and that to be nonsense—but in respect to the paradox faith is the skilled. It believes the paradox, and now, to recall the words of Hugo de St. Victor, reason is properly determined to honor faith, specifically by becoming absorbed in the negative qualifications of the paradox.

Generally it is a basic error to think that there are no negative concepts; the highest principles of all thought or the proofs of them are certainly negative. Human reason has boundaries; that is where the negative concepts are to be found. Boundary disputes are negative, constraining. But people have a rattle-brained, conceited notion about human reason, especially in our age, when one never thinks of a thinker, a reasonable man, but thinks of pure reason and the like, which simply does not exist, since no one, be he professor or what he will, is pure reason. Pure reason is something fantastical, and the limitless fantastical belongs at home where there are no negative concepts, and one understands everything like the sorcerer who ended by eating his own stomach.

x^2 A 354   *n.d.*, 1850

« 8 *The Absurd*

The spontaneous believer cannot maintain that for reason and for every third person who is not a believer the content of faith is the absurd, and that in order to become a believer everyone must be alone with the absurd.

The spontaneous believer in his immediacy is not integrated, cannot have a redoubling [*Fordoblelse*] within himself, has no room for it. When he talks to another, he well-meaningly, enthusiastically, presents the absurd in the most superlative of superlatives—and hopes this way to convince the other *directly*.

What is lacking is the tension of the dialectical. To understand that for reason it is the absurd, to talk about it in this way quite calmly to a third party, granting that it is the absurd, maintaining the stress that the other must regard it as the absurd—and then still believe it. At the same time it naturally follows that for the believer it is not the absurd.

But the spontaneous believer cannot take himself out of direct continuity with others; he cannot maintain that what for him is the surest thing of all, eternal salvation, is and must be for others the absurd.

From this arises the unholy confusion in speaking about faith. The [immediate] believer is not dialectically consolidated as "the single individual," cannot endure this double vision—that the content of faith, seen from the other side, is the negative absurd.

This is the tension, the tension of the life of faith, in which one is to keep himself. But everywhere the tendency is to present faith directly. An attempt in this direction is science or scholarship, which wants to comprehend faith.

x^2 A 592 *n.d.*, 1850

« 9

When, for example, I believe this or that because everything is possible for God, where, then, is the absurd? The absurd is the negative determinant which assures, for example, that I have not overlooked one or another possibility which still lies within the human arena. The absurd is the expression of despair: that humanly it is not possible—but despair is the negative sign of faith.

So it is with offense and faith—offense is the negative criterion which confirms the quality between God and men, but the believer is nevertheless not offended—he expresses just the opposite of offense, yet he always has the possibility of offense as a negative category.

But "faith" has perhaps never before been represented by someone who is just as dialectical as he is immediate. He alone is continually aware that this immediacy of which he speaks is the new immediacy, and precisely this is assured by the negative sign. Take another relationship. Blessedness—and suffering. Here the true expression is: blessedness is in suffering. But it is rarely presented this way. Perhaps a person has suffered indescribably before winning faith—now he has faith; now everything is sheer blessedness. This presentation shows that he is no dialectician, for he has no sign as to *where* his blessedness lies, whether he has not fallen into a delusion. But his presentation pleases men, for with his help they take blessedness in vain and are satisfied with faith at second hand, etc.

x^6 B 78 *n.d.*, 1850

« 10

This can best be ascribed to Anti-Climacus.

I gladly undertake, by way of brief repetition, to emphasize what other pseudonyms have emphasized. The absurd is not the absurd or absurdities without any distinction (wherefore Johannes de Silentio: "How many of our age understand what the absurd is?"[5]). The absurd is a category, and the most developed thought is required to define the Christian absurd accurately and with conceptual correctness. The absurd is a category, the negative criterion, of the divine or of the relationship to the divine. When the believer has faith, the absurd is not the absurd—faith transforms it, but in every weak moment it is again more or less absurd to him. The passion of faith is the only thing which masters the absurd—if not, then faith is not faith in the strictest sense, but a kind of knowledge. The absurd terminates negatively before the sphere of faith, which is a sphere by itself. To a third person the believer relates himself by virtue of the absurd; so must a third person judge, for a third person does not have the passion of faith. Johannes de Silentio has never claimed to be a believer; just the opposite, he has explained that he is not a believer—in order to illuminate faith negatively.

Thus all is in order. The misrelationship is really that Johannes de Silentio is a whole level more penetrating and dialectical and informed than Theophilus Nicolaus, who wants to correct him. Theophilus Nicolaus does not have the dialectical elasticity to assure his faith's passion a negative expression just as high as his supposed faith. That is, his faith is a much lower definition of faith.

The absurd and faith are inseparables, which is necessary if there is to be friendship and if this friendship is to be maintained between two qualities so unlike as God and man.

Therefore, rightly understood, there is nothing at all frightening in the category of the absurd—no, it is the very category of courage and of enthusiasm. Take an analogy. Love makes one blind. Yes, but it is nevertheless a cursed thing to become blind—well, then, you can just diminish the blindness a little so that one does not become entirely blind. But take care—for when you diminish the blindness, you also diminish the love, because true love makes one entirely blind.

And true faith breathes healthfully and blessedly in the absurd. The weaker faith must peer and speculate, just like the weaker love, which does not have the courage to become entirely blind, and for that very reason remains a weaker love, or, because it is a weaker love, it does not become entirely blind.

x^6 B 79 *n.d.*, 1850

« 11

That there is a difference between the absurd in *Fear and Trembling* and the paradox in *Concluding Unscientific Postscript* is quite correct. The first is the purely personal definition of existential faith—the other is faith in relationship to a doctrine.

The author would like to get rid of the absurd—he assumes that faith is by virtue of a higher hint, a higher communication, etc. Look more closely. Johannes de Silentio does not say that he is a believer, but a "higher hint," etc., can very well be nothing less than the absurd for the believer—but for a third person! In the meantime, this is of no help with regard to Abraham, because for him the collision is precisely between two higher hints—God's promise about Isaac and God's demand that he sacrifice Isaac; nothing is said about a third "higher hint."

Moreover, an observation in *Postscript*, p. 193,[6] is of importance.

Also there are the more precise qualifications which Joh. Climacus gives to make sure that the absurd as such is not the absurd in the ordinary sense. P. 437.[7]

The absurd is the negative criterion of that which is higher than human understanding and knowledge. The operations of understanding are to note it as such—and then to submit it to everyone for his belief.

Also important in the *Postscript* is 470, 71, etc.[8]

Finally, it is one thing to believe by virtue of the absurd (the formula only of the passion of faith) and to believe the absurd. The first expression is used by Johannes de Silentio and the second by Johannes Climacus.

x^6 B 80 *n.d.*, 1850

« 12

The objection that there is conflict between the absurd in Johannes de Silentio and in Johannes Climacus is a misunderstanding. In the same way according to the New Testament Abraham is called the father of faith, and yet it is indeed clear that the content of his faith cannot be Christian—that Jesus Christ has been in existence. But Abraham's faith is the formal definition of faith. So it is also with the absurd.

x^6 B 81 *n.d.*, 1850

ACTION

« 13

Action without interest in an idea is like dialectic without interest in knowledge—sophistry—therefore it is extremely interesting that contemporary with the greatest Sophists (in the area of knowledge) lived the greatest Sophists in the area of action, namely, those who practised abstinence through self-torture.

I A 206 July 16, 1836

« 14

God is worshiped not by moods but by action. But this, too, has the problem that it can so easily turn into pettiness and temptation in the form of meritoriousness.

Only the childlike mind or love which wholly loves God can do this rightly.

But I am thinking here particularly of action in the direction of asceticism (for action in the form of witnessing for the truth and against untruth is very simply what one ought to do). For example, a person wants to devote certain days to holy contemplation. He knows of a place, an environment, especially suited to protect this more earnest mood. But this place is remote and it costs a great deal to get there and to stay there. Perhaps it would be true adoration and worship of God to save the money, especially if he is otherwise well advised to do this, and perhaps it is his specific duty to save it, anyway.

Yet it is relevant here that even Christ approves a certain pious prodigality, such as, for example, the lavishing of costly ointment on him. The observation that astringence is corrupting is appropriate here.

x^3 A 342   *n.d.*, 1850

« 15 *Action Expressing Personal Integrity*
never makes a hit at the time; instead it offends people.

But when twenty years have gone by, for example, and the person is still living, and if by this time he has also become a windbag, then he is recognized for that action. But only on the condition that by this time he has become a windbag, for otherwise he will be about to initiate new character-action, and so recognition fails to appear.

x^4 A 71   *n.d.*, 1851

THE ANCIENTS, THE CLASSICAL

« 16

Classical antiquity is the division of the ideal into the actual without a remainder; romanticism always yields a fraction.

I A 135   March, 1836

« 17

The classical is present tense; the romantic is *aorist*.

I A 137   March, 1836

« 18

These words of Plato[9] (spoken by the Egyptian priest to Solon), ’Ω Σόλων, Σόλων Ἕλληνες ἀεὶ παῖδες ἐστέ, γέρων δὲ Ἕλλην οὐκ ἔστιν, are the best and most pregnant aphorism on the essentially Greek.

III A 13   August 10, 1840

« 19 *How Ironical*

The one who demolishes Grecian spontaneous esthetic beauty—Socrates—is the son of—a sculptor and a midwife.

XI^1 A 307   n.d., 1854

ANSELM

« 20 *Amazing Self-Contradiction*

Anselm prays in all inwardness that he might succeed in proving God's existence. He thinks he has succeeded, and he flings himself down in adoration to thank God. Amazing. He does not notice that this prayer and this expression of thanksgiving are infinitely more proof of God's existence than—the proof.

x^5 A 120   *n.d.*, 1853

« 21 *Sunday–Monday*

There is something historical I want to relate.

In the Middle Ages there lived a famous theologian, Anselm, Archbishop of Canterbury. He fell into conflict with the King of England.

Let me first of all briefly give the setting. At that time England had already been Christianized for a long time. There were—yes, I know it is a matter of indifference, so I will make a rough estimate—there were, I suppose, 150 bishops in England. Presumably the bishops did not preach themselves, but every bishop represented—let us take this number—70 priests. This gives us 10,500 priests. Each of these priests recited every Sunday to his congregation (admonishingly, instructively, movingly, grippingly, fascinatingly, upliftingly, charmingly, wonderfully, in quiet modulation, in open jubilation, etc.) that it is blessed, it is blessed to trust God alone, and that it is every man's duty to do it, and that the Christian does it.

Now back to Anselm. He, to repeat, got into a conflict with King William. It looks precarious; he is risking something. So he calls his bishops together to discuss with them. They say: "If, as up until now, you continue to cling to God alone . . . . . then we cannot stay by you."

In margin: See Böhringer, II, pt. 1, p. 295.[10]

> On God alone
> I build all my confidence, etc.

This hymn is found in our authorized hymnbook. Perhaps it is found also in the English hymnbook. We all sing it; and 10,500 pastors preach:

On God alone I build all my confidence—blessed, blessed, blessed it is, blessed, blessed—

—On Monday (the other, you see, was on Sunday; I forgot to mention it) on Monday the bishops say: If, as up until now, you continue to cling to God alone, then we cannot stay by you. There is certainly an element of truth here, for Anselm himself certainly could not in truth properly hold to God alone if all the bishops were to stay by him.

But how can it be that it was a Christian country and a Christian nation with such a difference between Sunday and Monday?

Make your own application, but—something I always suggest—only so that by your own confession you may come into relationship to the truth.

XI^2 A 302   *n.d.*, 1853-54

ANTHROPOLOGY, PHILOSOPHY OF MAN

« 22

How confusing the contemplation of life often is when it appears to us in all its abundance, when we see with amazement the differences in abilities and attitudes, from the person who inwardly has lived so close to the divine that, like John of old, he can be said to rest on God's breast—to the person who with bestial brutality misunderstands and wants to misunderstand every profounder movement in human life; from the person who pierces the course of history with the eyes of a lynx and almost dares to set its hour hand, to the person for whom even the simplest thing is difficult. Or we notice the inequality in rank and position and now enviously feel deprived of what others have been given, and then again with grateful sadness see how much has been given us which is denied to others—and now a cold philosophy will explain the whole thing from preexistence and does not see it as the endless panorama of life with its varied colorfulness and its innumerable nuances.

I A 74   *n.d.*, 1835

« 23

The philosopher can also acknowledge his deficiency in comprehension, but the question remains whether he shall then acknowledge the basis of it to be in his limitation (someone who sits on the periphery of a circle one million miles in diameter will most certainly be able to survey a great expanse, but it does not follow from this that he is marvelously endowed with abilities) or he shall assume that it is rooted in man himself and his sinfulness.

I A 102   *n.d.*, 1835

« 24

Truly, there often is something sad and depressing about someone wanting to communicate something in his lifetime and seeing at the very last that he has communicated nothing at all—but that the person concerned stubbornly continues in his view. But on the other hand there is something great in the fact that the other one and every individual is a world to himself and has his holy of holies where no alien hand can force itself in.

I A 114 January, 1836

« 25

All of human life could well be conceived as a great discourse in which different people come to represent the different parts of speech (this might also be applicable to nations in relation to each other). How many people are merely adjectives, interjections, conjunctions, adverbs; how few are nouns, action words, etc.; how many are copulas.

People in relation to each other are like the irregular verbs in various languages—almost all the verbs are irregular.

I A 126 March, 1836

« 26

It is the tragedy of not having anyone to whom one can make himself intelligible, which is so beautifully expressed in Genesis, where Adam gives all the animals names but finds *none* for himself.

I A 149 March, 1836

« 27

There are human beings who are always *tens* in contrast to the common ordinary *ones*.

I A 199 June 20, 1836

« 28

This is the road we all must walk—over the Bridge of Sighs into eternity.

I A 334 *n.d.*, 1836-37

« 29

There is a contrast of primary significance between Augustine and Pelagius. The former crushes everything in order to rebuild it again. The other addresses himself to man as he is. The first system, therefore, in respect to Christianity, falls into three stages: creation—the fall and a consequent condition of death and impotence; a new creation—whereby man is placed in a position where he can choose; and then, if he chooses —Christianity. —The other system addresses itself to man as he is (Christianity fits into the world). From this is seen the significance of the theory of inspiration for the first system; from this also is seen the relationship between the synergistic and the semipelagian conflict. It is the same question, only that the synergistic struggle has its presupposition in the new creation of the Augustinian system.

I A 101   January 14, 1837

« 30

There are men of whom it cannot be denied that they are human beings (belong within the concept *human being*), but who are more or less defective *casibus*.

II A 162   September 13, 1837

« 31

How profound is the popular legend which supposes that the elf-people play with human beings somewhat as we play with a fish on a line.

II A 646   *n.d.*, 1837

« 32

There are human beings who lack the comparative; generally they are the most interesting.

II A 674   *n.d.*, 1837

« 33

When it is said that in drunkenness men place themselves beneath the animals, there is implicit recognition of a sinfulness which slumbers within man, for otherwise he would simply put himself on an equal level, but now there awakens a hell of impulses.

II A 743   *n.d.*, 1838

« 34

A sorrow just as deep and holy, just as inward and quietly holy as the esthetic sorrow with which Lavater* writes of the defilement by which mankind has distorted the image of God in the countenance, the sonorous expression of the soul, insofar as the image of God shows itself in the face—such a religious-moral sorrow would be the proper grace of Christian sorrow insofar as it comprehends the enormity and profundity of the fall of the human race without falling itself within the qualifications of corruption.

   * See Lavater's *Physiognomonik*.[11]

II A 362   February 11, 1839

« 35

The lyric poetry of our time is different from that of the Middle Ages in that now the idiosyncratic individual gyrates about in his own idiosyncrasy, and therefore the lyrics of one are unintelligible to another. In the Middle Ages, however, lyric poetry was equipped with a complete objectivity—it is not the individual, it is man (Adam, i.e., mankind); every feature is world-historical, this term taken in the ideal sense.

II A 383   March 15, 1839

« 36

Notes appended to H. H. Clausen's Lectures in Dogmatics:[12]
[. . .]

Anthropology

[. . .]

1. *Man's original perfection.*

Clausen thinks that the ideal condition of the human race has been confused with man's first condition, which is described in Genesis and which ought not to be conceived historically. Thus far he agrees with the recent views[13] which render the first condition as the category of pure being, to which life itself is presumably led back, but which nevertheless must not be thought of as existing [*existerende*] as pure being; only the system has this.

2. *Man's immortality* [. . .]

3. *Man's sinfulness* [. . .]

When, in order to explain the significance of Adam's sin for the generations, Clausen appeals, as do other dogmaticians, to the analogy which is found in the individuality of a people; to what extent is this exhaustive, or does he not stop with the category "race and type" instead of reaching the energy of individuality. [. . .]

It is important to note, it seems to me, the synthesis which is found in every New Testament dogma, that this synthesis is maintained only from different sides, either as the divine and human (God-man—Revelation), or as succession and unity (present judgment and future, present resurrection and future), or the spiritual and physical (immortality of the soul—resurrection of the body).

II C 34   n.d., 1839-40

« 37

On the whole one has to say that modern philosophy, even in its most grandiose forms, nevertheless is really only an introduction to making it possible to philosophize. Hegel undeniably completes—but only the development which had its beginning with Kant and was directed toward knowledge. In Hegel one finds in a more profound form, that which earlier philosophy unreflectively assumed as a beginning—that on the whole there is reality in thought. But the whole line of thought proceeding from this assumption (or now happy over this result) entered into genuine anthropological contemplation, which has not yet been undertaken.

See K.K., pp. 20-21.[14]

III A 3 July 5, 1840

« 38

Precisely because a wholly new life arises in a human being through Christianity, it will be impossible to determine anything about the immediacy which precedes and which to all eternity will precede the mediacy and dialectic produced by reflection; likewise the natural birth of the soul must be regarded as being spontaneously related to creative divinity. Thus it is seen that the question about what begins there will remain a purely metaphysical one, and a person reflecting upon it must always be conscious of a relationship to the divine; but for the very reason that spiritual birth itself lies beyond all consciousness, it must lie within the divine, and the fact that the single individual can reflect upon it shows the priority of the divine.

III A 25 n.d., 1840

« 39

The human race pictured as the prodigal son.

There came the moment in the world when the race spoke to God as the son in the gospel spoke to his father: divide and share with us; let us have the inheritance coming to us.

III A 41 n.d., 1840

« 40

In this Leibniz is most certainly right over against Bayle, that by making man the sole measure of all things one gets entangled in contradictions. Bayle, like many others, has given the elemental impression that man has received the distinguished appointment in life to judge everything *et quidem* in relation to this position of man in creation. Leibniz shows that everything is linked together; he establishes a teleology which includes mankind. See para. 119 in *Theodicy*.

IV C 32 n.d., 1842-43

« 41

One cannot deny that there is a weakness in all the answers Leibniz gives Bayle in paragraphs 121, 22 and following; he seeks to avoid difficulty by saying that it is not a question of the individual man but of the whole universe. This is ridiculous, for if there is just one individual man who has valid reason to complain, then the universe* does not help. The answer is that even in sin man is greater, more fortunate, than if it had not appeared, for even the split in man has more significance than immediate innocence.

In margin: He finally takes recourse in analogies from the external world, that God lets it rain, even though low-lying areas are not served thereby. See para. 134.

IV C 33   n.d., 1842-43

« 42

Concerning Sextus Empircus's doubt about criteria of truth.[15]

The first criterion he introduces is man—and here he promptly awakens doubt about what it is to be a man. Socrates is supposed to have said that he does not know whether he is a man or a still more changeable animal than Typhon[16] (see Plato's *Phaedrus*).

It was most discerning of S.E. to use the statement, only like recognizes like,[17] to awaken skepticism (see Tennemann, *Geschichte der Philosophie*,[18] V, pp. 308, 309). The Christian statement, I know to the same degree as I am known, is also of great significance here.

IV C 50   n.d., 1842-43

« 43

What is the universally human, and is there anything universally human?

Is every man an individual, and in the sense that there is not another one like him, like Leibniz's leaves.

Are all men like unto each other as the parts of gold.

IV C 76   n.d., 1842-43

« 44

I know very well that it is not only the poor who hunger, that there is a hunger which all the treasures of the world cannot satisfy, and this hunger still persists after them—I know very well that there is a thirst which all the overflowing streams cannot quench, and this thirst persists after them—I know very well that there is an anxiety, a hidden, private anxiety, about losing—

IV B 173   n.d., 1842-44?

« 45

Even Plato[19] assumes that the genuinely perfect condition of man means no sex distinction (and how strange this is for people like Feuerbach[20] who are so occupied with affirming sex-differentiation, regarding which they would do best to appeal to paganism). He assumes that originally there was only the masculine (and when there is no thought of femininity, sex-distinction is undifferentiated), but through degeneration and corruption the feminine appeared. He assumes that base and cowardly men became women in death, but he still gives them hope of being elevated again to masculinity. He thinks that in the perfect life the masculine, as originally, will be the only sex, that is, that sex-distinction is a matter of indifference.[21] So it is in Plato, and this, the idea of the state notwithstanding, was the culmination of his philosophy. How much more so, then, the Christian view.

v A 14   *n.d.*, 1844

« 46

Basically the situation is such that if a person does not first use all the power given him against himself, thereby destroying himself, he is either a dolt or a coward in spite of all his courage. The power which is given to a man[22] (in possibility) is altogether dialectical, and the only true expression for a true understanding of himself in possibility is precisely that he has the power to destroy himself, because even though he be stronger than the entire world, he nevertheless is not stronger than himself. Once this has been learned, then we can make sufficient room for religiousness and then also for Christianity, for the most radical expression of this powerlessness is sin. For this reason only is Christianity the absolute religion, because it conceives of men as sinners, for no other distinction can in this way recognize man in his difference from God.[23]

v A 16   *n.d.*, 1844

« 47

Reason minimizes everything that imagination and feeling hit upon. This is entirely right for reason, but feeling and imagination do the same thing to reason with the same right. Or do feeling and imagination not belong as essentially to man as reason, or will reason perhaps first undertake to prove that it is the highest, and whom does it want to persuade— itself? Of course, it need not do this. Imagination, feeling? These it cannot. Therefore it is just as arbitrary to exalt reason exclusively as it is to exalt feeling and imagination exclusively. Herein lies the truth in taking reason captive, in abandoning reason to come to the truth; for reason is just as selfish and deceptive as feeling and imagination.

v A 20   *n.d.*, 1844

« 48

Wonder is the natural point of departure for the fear of God. As long as wonder is entirely unreflective, it is also abandoned and can blunder into the most preposterous notions. If Christianity did not regard paganism as sin, if the divine were not so holy to a person that he could not be tempted to want to make the ridiculous misuse and misapprehension of it a subject for comic treatment, it would indeed have happened long ago. Nevertheless, the fact that it has not happened perhaps indicates how stupid the despisers of religion generally are, indicates that they have not spirit enough to understand their task. When the pagan German went into the great forest, when the rays of the sun fell illusively on a tree trunk so that it appeared to be an enormous man, or when the soft light of the moon spiritualized, as it were, such a form—he believed that this was the God. Here was sufficient material for an esthetic conception of the comic in the romantic environment—and now the comic notion that this is the God. If the same person went a little further into the forest and saw an even larger tree which aroused his wonder in a similar manner—then this would be the God.[24]

As soon as reflection enters in, wonder is purified. But now comes reason's enormous error, equally as stupid as superstition, that reflection should eliminate wonder. No! It takes away only that which was the person's own invention, of which superstition still was unaware—but then one stands precisely at the proper point of decision, at the point where absolute wonder corresponds to the truly divine, which reason has not found. Here for the first time faith begins.

VA 25   n.d., 1844

« 49 *This Is the Scale*

The *immediate*. To immediacy all probabilities are simply folly (like falling in love—when Desdemona falls in love with Othello). Most people now live somewhat reflectively and therefore do nothing in pure immediacy but dabble in immediacy and reflection. —When reflection is completely exhausted, then *faith* begins. Here again it is just as foolish to come with probabilities or arguments, because in order to arrive at faith all such temporary devices must be exhausted. Everything which reflection can hit upon, faith has already thought through.

VA 28   n.d., 1844

« 50

... We shall not be so arrogant as to do everything on a grand scale. We shall speak of a single individual human life in the way it can be lived out here on earth. What holds true of the history of the race holds true of such a person. If one can see God in history, one can see him also in the life of the individual; to think that one can do the former and not the latter is to delude himself by yielding, in regard to the historical, to the brutish imbecility which in the observations of nature sees God by being taught that Sirius is 180,000 millions of miles away from the earth. The materialistic man is astounded by this, and when a person has nothing substantial to say it is best to speak of the whole, of the totality, etc. If every single man is not an individual, himself and the race, simply by being human, then everything is lost and it is not worth the trouble to hear about the great world-historical events or the absolute method. But the world wants to be deceived. Now it goes without saying that it is a swindle to get all world history instead of one's own insignificant person —one does not gain in the trade. Yet people are deceived, deceived insofar as they do not come to understand what is made evident by supposing that they have understood the whole world without this. . . .

VB 14:72   n.d., 1844

« 51

Here again one sees a proof that this inquiry [*The Concept of Dread*] is not guilty of any Pelagian soft-headedness, which does not have the power to spin the individuals into the web of the race but lets each individual stick out like the loose end of a thread; but one perceives also that in another sense it protects against the race concept, lest this deprive individuals of power and confuse both individual and race. If by Adam's sin (ἐφ' ᾧ πάντες ἥμαρτον,[25] Romans 5:12) the sinfulness of the race is posited in the same sense that a species of water birds has web-feet, the concept *individual* is abrogated and to this extent also the concept *human race*; for the concept separates itself from the concept *animal* in precisely this way. Protest is made [sic]

VB 53:15   n.d., 1844

« 52

If men had pursued further the ancient idea that man is a synthesis of soul and body, which is constituted by spirit, men would long since have thought more precisely with regard to sin and original sin, its origin and its consequence. Though it can be said that the spirit takes lodging in a defiled body,* and this is the most extreme expression one can em-

* *In margin:* Is this not found in Ecclesiastes or in the Psalms?

ploy, yet it does not follow that the spirit itself is defiled, unless this defilement is again a consequence of that relationship. But even here there is the likeness and unlikeness to Adam, together with the more detailed consideration of the possibility of freedom in the individual.

V B 55:4   n.d., 1844

« 53

To need God is man's highest perfection.

Text

Among those born of women none is greater;[26] yet he who is least in the kingdom of God is greater than he.

If man did not have absolute need of God he could not
(1) know himself—self-knowledge.
(2) be immortal.

V B 196   n.d., 1844

« 54

Man's highest achievement is to let God be able to help him.

V B 198   n.d.,1844

« 55

Who thinks of hitching Pegasus and an old nag together to one carriage for a ride? And yet this is what it is to exist [*existere*] for one compounded of finitude and infinitude!

VI A 102   n.d., 1845

« 56

[27]Evening's leave-taking (from the day and from the one who has experienced the day) is puzzling [*changed from:* has a remarkable ambiguity]; its reminder is like the careful mother's instruction to the child to go home, and its invitation is like an inexplicable hint, as if now for the first time the true life was beginning. Man is blended in approximately the same way—finitude is like the child for whom it is expedient to come home early; infinitude is like the adult who wants to stay out at night—and the evening's leave-taking is puzzling. Sometimes one would like to interpret it as an invitation persuasively insinuated by the night wind as it monotonously repeats itself and searches the forest and fields as if looking for something, persuasively insinuated by the far echo of stillness in oneself (as if he had a presentiment of something), persuasively insinuated by the sublime tranquillity of heaven (as if it were found) and by

the audible silence of the dew, which is evidence of this, and the refreshment of infinitude, the fruitful visit of the quiet night concealed in the lifting fog.

In margin: As if one first found rest by remaining out for a nocturnal rendezvous, not with a woman but, womanlike, with the infinite.

VI B 49   n.d., 1845

« 57

Life in the country does have the gratification that there are approximately ten cows, fifteen sheep, two pigs, and a flock of sparrows to each human being—by which one sees that a human being has some significance. In the urban areas there are about one hundred human beings to one cow—by which one sees that a cow has some significance. But although the human mobs running around in circles in the city are counterfeit money, no one seems concerned about—*becoming* a human being, but instead most men are itching for marriage, and the respective marriages are busily engaged—so that there can *come to be* even more human beings.

VII^1 A 86   n.d., 1846

« 58 *Man*

The Romans[28] took him out of the earth *(homo)*, but the Greeks[29] raised him up ($ἄνθρωπος$.[30])

VII^1 A 171   n.d., 1846

« 59

"Do not fear those who are able to kill the body" (Luke 12:4).

Physically it is true that a man can fall by the hand of another; spiritually it is true that a man can fall only by his own hand—no one can corrupt him but the man himself.

Evil does not corrupt the soul in the sense that sickness corrupts the body, which finally stops, dying of the sickness. But the soul continues to be. It is well known that Socrates[31] based a proof for the immortality of the soul upon this.

VII^1 A 206   n.d., 1846

« 60

. To me it is incomprehensible that any human being *qua* idyllic poet[32] should identify himself or being human with animal life (pastorals in which ducks, geese, and cows are types of a blissful and perfect life). In a purely humorous way the observation of animals can be very enjoyable;

one can stand all day watching them. The stupider they are, the funnier they are—such as ducks, geese, pigs, cows.

VII¹ A 238   n.d., 1845-47

« 61

Men come more and more into kinship with the animals—nowadays we no longer speak of the power of a thousand men but of a thousand horsepower.

VIII¹ A 241   n.d., 1847

« 62

Daub speaks the truth and expresses it very well (in his *Philosophische Anthropologie*; Berlin: 1838; I, p. 25) when he says of the mob, "*dem Alles zur Lebensfrage wird, am Leben Alles und desswegen am Rechte Nichts liegt.*"[33]

VIII¹ A 244   n.d., 1847

« 63

What is humanness [*Menneskelighed*]? It is human equality [*Menneske-Lighed*]. Inequality is the unhuman.[34]

VIII¹ A 268   n.d., 1847

« 64

Yet I could never wish to live at some other time. The knowledge of men, the knowledge of the race which I am acquiring, is not exchangeable for gold, and this is precisely what I needed to illuminate Christianity.

VIII¹ A 454   n.d., 1847

« 65

Just as the expert archer's arrow leaves the bowstring and has no rest before it reaches the target, so the human being is created by God with God as his aim and cannot find rest before he finds rest in God.

VIII¹ A 601   n.d., 1847

« 66

It is customary to assume that there is an analogy between the life of a generation and the life of an individual, to assume that the generation has stages similar to those of an individual. Why not assume, then, that the generation ends by going into second childhood?

VIII¹ A 632   n.d., 1848

« 67 *Something about the Forgiveness of Sins*

To believe the forgiveness of one's sins is the decisive crisis whereby a human being becomes spirit; he who does not believe this is not spirit.

Maturity of the spirit means that spontaneity is completely lost, that a person is not only capable of nothing by himself but is capable only of injury to himself. But how many in truth come in a wholly personal way to understand of themselves that one is brought to this extremity. (Here lies the absurd, offense, the paradox, forgiveness of sins.)

Most men never become spirit, never experience becoming spirit. The stages—child, youth, adult, oldster—they pass through these with no credit to themselves; it is none of their doing, for it is a vegetative or vegetative-animal process. But they never experience becoming spirit.

The forgiveness of sins is not a matter of particulars—as if on the whole one were good (this is childish, for the child always begs forgiveness for some particular thing which it did yesterday and forgets today, etc.; it could never occur to a child, in fact, the child could not even get into its head, that it is actually evil); no, it is just the opposite—it pertains not so much to particulars as to the totality; it pertains to one's whole self, which is sinful and corrupts everything as soon as it comes in slightest contact with it.

Anyone who in truth has experienced and experiences what it is to believe the forgiveness of one's sins has indeed become another person. Everything is forgotten—but still it is not with him as with the child who, after having received pardon, becomes essentially the same child again. No, he has become an eternity older, for he has now become spirit. All spontaneity and its selfishness, its selfish attachment to the world and to himself, have been lost. Now he is, humanly speaking, old, very old, but eternally he is young.

VIII[1] A 673   *n.d.*, 1848

« 68

... if he were not properly composed originally of the temporal and the eternal, he could not despair at all. Thus despair in man is a misrelationship between the temporal and the eternal, of which his nature is composed—but from God's hand in the right relationship.

How does the misrelationship happen, then? From the man himself, who disturbs the relationship, which is precisely to despair. How is this possible? Quite simple. In the composite of the eternal and the temporal, man is a relationship, in this relationship itself and relating itself to itself. God made man a relationship; to be a human being is to be a relationship.[35] But a relationship which, by the very fact that God, as it were, releases it from his hand, or the same moment God, as it were, releases it, is itself, relates itself to itself—this relationship can become in the same moment a misrelationship. To despair is the misrelationship taking place.

VIII^2 B 168:5   *n.d.*, 1848

« 69

There was some truth in regarding heroes, as the Greeks did (for example, Plutarch[36]), as a separate race, different from the human race. It is similar to the Christian qualification: spirit. But humanness consists in this: that every human being is granted the capability of being spirit; it is not that nonsense about a company of brainy people; one often finds a simple man existing within the realm of spirit and a professor a long way away from it.

IX A 76   *n.d.*, 1848

« 70

The real crime, the one people regard as the worst of all and punish cruelly, is to be not like others. This proves precisely that men are animal-creatures. For sparrows have a right to pick to death the sparrow who is not like the others; here the class is superior to the particular—that is, sparrows are animals, neither more nor less. —In respect to men, on the contrary, the qualification is that each one should not be like the others, should have distinctiveness.

Yet every crime is forgiven by men except, in their thinking, the inhuman crime—of being man.

IX A 80   *n.d.*, 1848

« 71

The contrast to the ancient mode, in which the third person is used for oneself because a person's life is merely a fact, is to dare the uttermost in saying *I*, directly to say the most about oneself. This is expressed in the God-man; the God-man would not be the God-man if he were great in such a way that he tended to become third person.

X^2 A 78   *n.d.*, 1849

« 72

We cannot find a better parody of antiquity and its use of the third person than Lamartine's[37] speech in the third person about himself. It is completely improper. Stimulated to the point of lyrical reflection, Lamartine takes up all these things—and yet talks in the third person. This is affectation. Yes, he goes so far—and this has a kind of esthetic worth—as to engage in mimicry. He declares: Thereupon Lamartine said with a look of . . . etc. Here Lamartine has really made a kind of discovery; he has discovered what is absolutely impossible to say in the third person, for one himself cannot possibly know it. It becomes altogether comic and reminds us of Charles in *The First Love*,[38] who also narrates his life in the third person.

To use the third person is either childishness—at a certain age a child talks in the third person, simply because the child is still not a person—or it is an eminence which is more than a person, a person who himself is the event. Anything between the two becomes comic if the third person is used.

x^2 A 79 *n.d.*, 1849

« 73 *The Dialectic Oriented Toward Becoming a Christian*

Socrates did not first of all try to collect some proofs for the immortality of the soul in order then to live, believing by virtue of the proofs. Just the opposite. He said: The possibility of immortality occupies me to the point that I unconditionally venture to wager my whole life unconditionally upon it, as if it were the surest thing of all. And this is the way he lived—and his life is a proof of the immortality of the soul. He did not first of all believe by virtue of the proofs and then live; no, his life is the proof and not until his martyr-death is the proof complete. —You see, this is spirit. It is a little embarrassing for mimics and all those who live second-hand and tenth-hand lives, those who are result-hunters, and those with cowardly, effeminate natures.

Used with discrimination, this may be applied to becoming a Christian.

First of all comes, quite properly, Lessing's[39] doubt that one cannot base an eternal happiness upon something historical.

But here there is [*existerer*] something historical, the story of Jesus Christ.

But is it historically entirely certain? The answer to this must be that even if it were the surest thing in all history, this does not help; no *direct* transition from the historical can be made as the basis for an eternal happiness. This is something qualitatively new.

What do we do now? This— A man says to himself, *a la* Socrates: here is [*existerer*] something historical which teaches me that for my eternal happiness I must turn to Jesus Christ. I must beware of taking the wrong turn into scientific rummaging and reconnoitering to see if it is historically entirely certain; for it surely is historical—that is, if it were ten times as certain even to the minutest detail, it still would not help me—for I cannot be helped *directly*.

Then I say to myself: I choose; the historical here means so much to me that I resolve to venture my whole life on this *if*.* And then he lives on. He lives filled by this thought alone, venturing his life for it; and his life is the proof that he believed. He did not have a few proofs and thereupon he believed and then began to live. No, just the opposite.

This is called *venturing*, and without venturing faith is an impossibility. *Relating oneself to spirit means to be up for examination;*** to believe, to will to believe, means to change one's life, to be up for examination; the daily examination is the tension of faith. —Yet one can preach about this to cowardly, effeminate, unspiritual natures until the end of the world—they do not grasp it, they do not want to grasp it. They actually think it is all very well for someone else to stick his neck out and then they attach themselves to him—and make assurances. But to venture out—no thanks!

But with regard to becoming a Christian there is a dialectical difference from Socrates which must be remembered. Specifically in the relationship to immortality—a person relates himself to himself and the idea—no further. But when a man chooses upon an *if* to believe in Christ —that is, chooses to wager his life upon that, then he has permission to address himself directly to Christ in prayer. Thus the historical is the occasion and still also the object of faith.

But all unspiritual natures turn the matter around. They say: To wager everything upon an *if* is a kind of skepticism; it is fancifulness, not positivity. It is because they will not "venture." And this is the unspiritual crowd which Christianity has taken in tow and which has finally done away with Christianity.

x^2 A 406   *n.d.*, 1850

« 74

* *In margin of 73* (x^2 A 406):
This is to be found in Christ's words[40] as well: If anyone will follow my teaching, that is, live according to it, that is, act according to it, he will experience, etc. This means that there are no advance proofs—nor is he satisfied that accepting his teaching means: I give my word.

x^2 A 407   *n.d.*, 1850

« 75

** *In margin of 73* (x^2 A 406):
This comes from the fact that man is a synthesis of physical-psychical and spirit. But "spirit" establishes the division—whereas in every case the soft character wants to haul along the baser side of life and have its

consent. This explains the anxiety about "venturing." The unspiritual man always wants "probability." But "spirit" will never concede it. "Spirit" is the examination: Will you relinquish probability, will you deny yourself, forsake the world, etc.

x^2 A 408   *n.d.*, 1850

« 76

Julius Müller[41] said it very well: "By creating man, God theomorphizes—precisely therefore man does *not* anthropomorphize when he supposes God as a being resembling man. If one were subjectively compelled to regard everything which man pronounces about God in accordance with his essence as mere anthropomorphism, then God could not have made man more unqualified to know him than by creating him in his image."

x^2 A 491   *n.d.*, 1850

« 77 *Is the Nature of Man, Christianly Understood, a Unity or a Duality?*

There is so much talk about this nowadays; and the philosophers naturally know that human nature is a unity—and my brother Peter gave a little paper on this at the conference; in short, it is certain, something one can appeal to, as to an axiom, that the nature of man is and must be a unity.

When I last spoke with Bishop Mynster, he touched on the same matter in connection with R. Nielsen, of whom he said, in contrast to Stilling who was criticized merely for tone, "I just cannot understand Nielsen; he seems to want to make a dual-entity of man." To which I answered: Well, now, if it is so, your grace, it is also the teaching of Christianity, the battle in every human being between the natural man and the new man, a battle which must in fact continue throughout life.

Then I developed my conception somewhat like this.

The rule for the relationship between man and humanness is: the more I think about it, the better I understand it. In the relationship between man and God, the rule is: the more I think about the divine, the less I understand it. Two heterogeneous qualities can never become homogeneous through continued self-relating to each other; on the contrary, the difference, the qualitative difference, the heterogeneity becomes more obvious. All true religiousness is therefore in a sense a retrogression, that is, it is not direct progress. As a child I think I am very close to God; the older I become, the more I discover that we are infinitely different, the more deeply I feel the distance, and *in casu*: the less I understand God, that is, the more obvious it becomes to me how infinitely exalted he is.

Therefore the more proficient I become in thinking, understanding, and comprehending, the more natural it also becomes for me to want to comprehend and comprehend. But take note of this, I comprehend the divine all the less (on the basis of the relationship between the qualities). And every time this occurs, Christianity comes to me, as it were, and says: Will you now abandon me? To this the believer answers: O, no, certainly not: I will believe. This is the potentiation of faith: the less I can comprehend, if I nevertheless believe, the more intensive the faith.

But Christendom is vain; it wants to avoid the Cross, the humiliation of confessing simply and directly that one has his *life* in what he cannot understand. This is indeed embarrassing for an adult, not least in our speculative age, and the more speculative a person is. And so they substitute profundity and speculation—in order to avoid the Cross.

And Christendom is comfortable—from this comes this tendency toward unity. The Christian categories, valid for the whole of life, are made into something transitory, a thoroughfare. It begins with being incomprehensible, but gradually we smuggle in the natural man's inclination to comprehend and then get unity into its essence—and coziness. For with the coming of this unity, restlessness and striving and fear and trembling, which should obtain for the entire life, go out.

Moreover, that duality belongs to man's nature has prior rootage in this, that God must be an absolute ruler. Consider a domineering person who properly comprehends the pleasure of ruling. I wonder if he is satisfied with ruling directly. No, because in order to enjoy the desire for domination, he establishes a duality in the other person; he transforms himself into the incomprehensible, and precisely by this repulsion he torments the adoration of devotion from the other. In the relationship between man and man this is wickedness. But God cannot do it otherwise. God cannot be the highest superlative of the human: he is qualitatively different. From this at first comes incomprehensibility, which grows with the development of man's understanding—and thereby faith, which believes against understanding, is again potentiated.

Finally, there ought to be Christian unity in the Church; this God wills for the sake of clarity. The pastor ought not say one thing and the professor something else; no, the professor ought to say the same thing but more intensively. When the pastor preaches simply that faith cannot be comprehended, it is not to be assumed that this is a miserable state of affairs and that the professor, on the other hand, comprehends it, presumably so that conceited, cocky men, bold minds, should minimize the pastor and cling to the professor. No, it ought to be thus: if you will not be satisfied with the pastor, then by going to the professor you should arrive at the same thing even more rigorously, for he can comprehend that faith cannot be comprehended; he cannot comprehend anything else, but this he can comprehend with such God-fearing power that he can bring all the stubborn ones who want to comprehend, who want to do business with God on some other basis than that of faith which believes against reason, to their knees.

This makes for tension in life, it is true; but it is also true that it is Christianity. To make man's nature a unity in this life is a drift toward comfortableness, even though one points out a first stage where the duality, the split, was. Christianity has never taught that a human being becomes so perfect in this life that he can repose in such a unity. It is like suffering. Christianly understood, there is no initial stage in which there was suffering, followed by a cessation of suffering already in this life, and a present state of pure happiness. No, Christianly, suffering is the continuing constituent in this life; if suffering disappears, this is not perfection but apostasy from the essentially Christian, corresponding to the kind of security found in the totally secularized man, except that the apostate is even more corrupted.

x^3 A 186   *n.d., 1850*

« 78 *Concerning Bashfulness in Relation to the Sexual*

Montaigne says somewhere that, remarkably enough, what we all owe our existence to is something to be despised. He means that bashfulness here is almost a kind of prudishness. Many strong minds have thought the same thing.

But this requires a reply. It is true in only one sense that a human being owes his existence to the act of procreation; there is also present a creative factor which must be attributed to God. It is not true of the human race, as it is with animals, that each individual is only a particular instance or copy. The person who really becomes spirit, for which he is intended, at some point takes over his entire being (by choosing himself, as it is called in *Either/Or*)[42] and downgrades propagation to a lower level.

What wonder then that there is bashfulness in relation to the sexual! The procreators represent only the lower aspects, just as in the moment of the procreative act itself men are qualified according to the lower aspect of their nature or according to the pole in the synthesis farthest away from spirit. But the very fact that the direction is away from spirit, precisely this is bashfulness; spirit is bashfulness, or the fact that the human being is qualified as spirit is bashfulness. Animals have no bashfulness, nor has bestiality; and the less spirit, the less bashfulness.

x^3 A 501   n.d., 1850

« 79 *The Wedding in Cana*[43]

Christianity changes water into wine; it denies man the earthly, but gives him the eternal; he must die to the world, but then he becomes spirit. Is not the change of animal-creation to "spirit" the same as changing water into wine?

x^4 A 457   n.d., 1852

« 80 *Man*

is a synthesis, and naturally, therefore, if you please, a born hypocrite, or with the possibility of being a hypocrite. And now God's concern with each individual is: Will you be a hypocrite or will you stand in relationship to truth?

Precisely because man is a synthesis, hypocrisy resides close to center. This is why sensuousness in a person takes what spirituality in a person understands and expresses and slips in an entirely different interpretation, although it still appears as if it were the same. Christianity says: I am the joyful news. The spirituality in a person understands in what an infinitely lofty sense this is to be taken—now comes sensuousness and slips in what it understands by joy and gets: Christianity is joy. Consequently there is joy in both cases, but it is understood entirely differently in each case, and hypocrisy consists in giving the appearance of holding to what Christianity says of itself: that it is joy.

This is only an example; there are countless examples, for hypocrisy can be everywhere.

x^4 A 638   n.d., 1852

« 81 *The Collision of Human Existence*

There is a complete, qualitative difference between being spirit-man and merely animal-man.

But physically there is nothing to see in this distinction.

The collision resides in the fact that animal-man rushes in upon spirit-man or is set upon him. If I were to talk in Greek fashion about it, I would have to say that this spectacle amuses the gods in the same way hunting with hounds amuses men. Basically it is also more amusing because that around which everything revolves is physically a nothing. Viewed as hunting with hounds, this battle is also more ambitious than such a hunt usually is, for of what avail are a few hundred hounds compared to legions of animal-men.

Christianly the matter has to be viewed differently. Christianly this collision is the education of the spirit-man, his examination, also his mission, inasmuch as he has the additional task to witness that man is spirit, all of which becomes more and more necessary and also more and more strenuous because of the mounting refined bestiality during the course of hundreds of years.

XI¹ A 225 *n.d.*, 1854

« 82 *The Grand Retort*

The words "Here is the man"[44] ["*See hvilket Menneske,*" literally "See, what a man"] are really the human race's judgment upon itself, the expression for its being prostituted.

Remarkably enough, just as in the different nuances of the Passion story there are to be found one or more suggestive and characteristic expressions for the abominable, the shocking, the cruel, the inhumane, etc. act committed here, if these words "See, what a man" were not there, there would be missing an expression for the fact that the human race, on top of everything else, is also guilty of prostituting itself.

The God-man had never lost patience and turned the relationship about, saying, "I am absolutely not in the human race with you." No, he continued to express that he was in the same human race with them.

But then the family of man could not restrain itself and declared: You are not related to us—see, what a man. The God-man wants to show what it is to be a man, wants to elevate man into relationship with God; the family of man thinks it understands the thing better and declares itself not to be related to him.

This is the prostitution of the human race; in this very instant the family of man is debased beneath what it is to be a man and is essentially animal. A humorist would say that poetic justice requires that man, in memory of the event, be decorated with a tail, and he must insist that this tail stand perpendicularly from the body in such a way that it would be impossible for any tailor's skill to hide it, and also that it could not be chopped off inasmuch as it would have the remarkable capacity of immediately growing out again.

XI¹ A 236 *n.d.*, 1854

« 83 *The Examination and Judgment of Existence*

The question which existence puts to men, if you will, and to which the respective answers divide men into two qualitatively different classes (animal and those related to the divine) is: Do you desire that any one human being should be martyred in every possible anguish so that you can enjoy yourself materially; or are you willing to be sacrificed for others?

He who answers the first question with a "yes" is *eo ipso* an animal. This is just as bestial as Ole Kollerød's sitting at the table and eating with the knife which he used to murder another man.[45] It is animalistic to feed upon and to want to live off another man's anguish and sufferings. This is the enormous mass of perdition. To be sure, this mass is always frightfully huge, but the false teachers are largely responsible for the fact that it is as large as it is.

The second class of men answers "no" to this question. And now it is put to them: Are you yourself willing to be sacrificed for others?

If anyone is unconditionally willing to do this, happily assured that it is out of love that God demands it of him—he is really of the family of God.

But if someone is not so strong that he is willing to be sacrificed for others in this manner, with the top speed of enthusiasm, nevertheless, if there is a willingness in him, then God assuredly helps him to become sacrificed.

If one were to put to a better man the question: Are you willing that another man in all possible anguish be sacrificed for you, he has to answer: If this in any way determines my salvation and blessedness, I accept it, but then I must declare that this other person is completely different from me, qualitatively different from me. I must worship him as superhuman being.

So it is in respect to the God-man.

Analogically to the God-man, even though inferior, the apostles were sacrificed, thus becoming witnesses of the truth. Here Catholicism has in a certain sense been right in wanting to worship the saints, for a saint is a qualitative step superior to someone who is willing to live materially well on another's sacrifice.

Protestantism is the coarsest and most brutal plebeianism. People do not want to know of any qualitative difference between apostles, witnesses of the truth, and themselves, even though someone's existence is completely different from theirs, as different as being eaten is from eating.

With respect to the fact that the God-man is the sacrifice of atonement, it must be remembered that he always demands imitation, so that he does not bear the guilt for this beastly villainy that one person has to be martyred *in order that* others eat and drink, beget children, etc.; and materially enjoy this life.

Man is a synthesis. He is an animal, but there is also a possibility of something divine in him. The answer to this question: Are you willing that another man in all possible anguish be sacrificed in order that you can materially have it good, makes it obvious whether the man concerned is animal or is in family-relationship with the divine.

How animalistic and what a mistake when there lives a man who one realizes is actually being sacrificed for an idea—and then to want to have pity on him and congratulate oneself on not being sacrificed in this way. It is animalistic not to feel oneself called to imitate him, witness for him, fight for him, suffer with him—for the idea. And the pity is a mistake; for since the condition of salvation is bound up with being sacrificed, then he is still the one who draws the longer straw.

XI^1 A 358   n.d.,1854

« 84 *Primitivity* (Primitivet)

Every human being is by nature intended for primitivity, since primitivity is the possibility of "spirit"—God, who has done it, knows this best.

All worldly, temporal, secular cleverness is a murdering of one's primitivity; Christianity means to follow one's primitivity.

Murder your primitivity and materially you will get on very well in the world, perhaps even make a hit—but the eternal rejects you. Follow your primitivity, and you will be wrecked in the temporal, but the eternal accepts you.

XI^1 A 385   n.d., 1854

« 85

In margin of 84 (XI^1 A 385):

By primitivity Christianity naturally does not mean all this intellectual ostentation of being a genius, etc. No, primitivity, spirit, is—first of all, first, first to identify one's life with the kingdom of God. The more literally a man is able to do this, acting, the more primitivity.

XI^1 A 386   n.d., 1854

« 86 *Spirit*

He who has not suffered under the bestiality of man does not become spirit. Man is of such an intended nature [*saaledes . . . lagt an*] that the kind of suffering which is predominantly the suffering "from men" is part of becoming spirit.

XI^1 A 407 *n.d.*, 1854

« 87

In margin of 86 (XI^1 A 407):
Every man is a synthesis, is animal-spirit. In order to get the animal rightly knocked out of him, the person who is to become spirit needs the suffering of being treated bestially by men.

XI^1 A 408 *n.d.*, 1854

« 88 *Vertical Angles*

What Socrates talks about in *Phædo*,[46] namely, that the pleasant and the unpleasant are set together like vertical angles, is the law for everything Christian. Man is a synthesis; but as "spirit" is introduced, the compound of the synthesis is split and is put together like vertical angles. This is why the more spirit there is the stronger do flesh and blood react, and here we have what the apostle really talks about, that which cannot enter into the harmonious synthesis.

XI^1 A 592 *n.d.*, 1854

« 89 *"Man"*

All the extraordinaries who, thinly scattered, have lived through the course of time, have certainly, every one of them, expressed their judgment on "man." One person's report makes out that man is an animal; another's that he is a hypocrite, he is a liar, etc.

I may not be far off if I say: man is nonsense—and he is that with the aid of language.

With the aid of language every man participates in the highest—but to participate in the highest with the aid of language, in the sense of talking about it, is just as ironical as being a spectator in the gallery observing the royal dinner table.

If I were a pagan I would say that an ironical deity had bestowed the gift of speech upon man in order to amuse himself by watching this self-deception.*

By language man distinguishes himself from the animal, the dumb beast—but perhaps the dumb beast still has the advantage, at least it is not—cheated or does not cheat itself out of the highest.

XI^2 A 139 *n.d.*, 1854

« 90

In margin of 89 (XI² A 139):
According to Christianity it is of course out of love that God has bestowed upon man the gift of speech and thereby made it possible for everyone actually to grasp the highest—alas, with what sorrow must God see the result!

XI² A 140 *n.d.*, 1854

ANXIETY (*Angst*), DREAD

« 91

A certain presentiment seems to precede everything which is to happen (cf. a loose sheet*); but, just as it can have a deterring effect, it can also tempt a person to think that he is, as it were, predestined; he sees himself carried on to something as though by consequences beyond his control. Therefore one ought to be very careful with children, never believe the worst and by untimely suspicion or by a chance remark (a flame of hell which ignites the tinder which is in every soul) occasion an anguished consciousness in which innocent but fragile souls can easily be tempted to believe themselves guilty, to despair, and thereby to make the first step toward the goal foreshadowed by the unsettling presentiment —a remark which gives the kingdom of evil, with its stupefying, snake-like eye, an occasion for reducing them to a kind of spiritual paralysis. Of this, too, it may be said: woe unto him by whom the offense comes.

**In margin:* The significance of typology with reference to a theory of presentiment. [See II A 584.]

II A 18   *n.d.*, 1837

« 92

Presentiment is the homesickness of earthly life for the higher, for the perspicuity which man must have had in his paradisic life.

II A 191   November 6, 1837

« 93 *Parenthesis*

To the same degree that there is really anything significant in a person's development, to the same degree that his education comes under the concept of divine upbringing—to that same degree you can save your shouting, your loving nagging, for your voice will have no significance as a signal in his wandering, and the only thing it might accomplish would be that when he stands at a dangerous point he plunges down—as, indeed, unconscious apprehensiveness has at times occasioned the fall of one who otherwise would have stood securely enough.

II A 489   *n.d.*, 1839

« 94

The nature of original sin has often been explained, and still a primary category has been lacking—it is *anxiety* [*Angst*]; this is the essential determinant. Anxiety is a desire for what one fears, a sympathetic antipathy; anxiety is an alien power which grips the individual, and yet one cannot tear himself free from it and does not want to, for one fears, but what he fears he desires. Anxiety makes the individual powerless, and the first sin always occurs in weakness; therefore it apparently lacks accountability, but this lack is the real trap.

III A 233   *n.d.*, 1842

« 95

Addition to 94 (III A 233):
Women are more anxious than men; therefore it was she whom the serpent chose for his attack, and he deceived her through her anxiety.

III A 234   *n.d.*, 1842

« 96

Addition to 94 (III A 233):
In volume VI, p. 194, of his works, Hamann[47] makes an observation which I can use, although he neither understood it as I wish to understand it nor thought further about it: "However, this *Angst* in the world is the only proof of our heterogeneity. If we lacked nothing, we should do no better than the pagans and the transcendental philosophers, who know nothing of God and like fools fall in love with lovely nature, and no homesickness would come over us. This impertinent disquiet, this holy hypochondria. . . . ."

III A 235   *n.d.*, 1842

« 97

To suppose that anxiety is an imperfection merely betrays a straitlaced cowardice, since, to the contrary, the greatness of anxiety is the very prophet of the miracle of perfection, and inability to become anxious is a sign of one's being either an animal or an angel, which according to the teaching of scriptures,[48] is less perfect than being a human being. The additional sensuousness which a woman has is therefore in itself of no consequence and viewed under the orientation of the idea is the expression of perfection, since viewed under the idea it is always regarded as overcome and absorbed in freedom.

V B 53:23   *n.d.*, 1844

« 98

It is quite possible to show that a very precise and correct usage of language links anxiety and the future together. Of course, generally language usage is not particularly scrupulous, presumably because speculation has gradually acquired a language of its own which is not spoken by people other than philosophers. At the same time the art is to be able to use the same words which everyone else uses. Then one can appropriately show his authority as thinker through the clarity of thought in his use of language. The word *anxiety* [*Angst*] has until now been territory open for the taking; we shall attempt to prescribe to it a definite meaning or, better, to affirm it in its definite meaning.

As a new expression, *anxiety* is to designate basically the *discrimen* (ambiguity) of soft subjectivity.

Thus far one easily sees that the future and the possible correspond to it. But when one speaks of being anxious about the past, it seems to conflict with my usage, for the ambiguity of subjectivity has no past. If I now bear in mind that subjectivity is never complete once and for all and that to this extent a recurrence of this ambiguity could be spoken of, it would still not support me if it is really defensible to say: anxiety about the past. But if we now inquire more precisely in what sense we can speak of anxiety about the past, then everything will become clear.

V B 55:10 *n.d.*, 1844

« 99

Just as the gospel about the lilies contains a warning to the poor against pecuniary worries [*Næringssorg*], it also has a word for the corresponding kind of worry which the rich in particular usually have. "No one can add one cubit to his stature." The hypochondriacal concern that one's heart is not beating properly, that one is constipated, etc.

VII[1] A 248 *n.d.*, 1845-47

« 100

Deep within every human being there still lives the anxiety over the possibility of being alone in the world, forgotten by God, overlooked among the millions and millions in this enormous household. One keeps this anxiety at a distance by looking at the many round about who are related to him as kin and friends, but the anxiety is still there, nevertheless, and one hardly dares think of how he would feel if all this were taken away.

VIII[1] A 363 *n.d.*, 1847

« 101

No doubt the reason there is so little preaching about pecuniary worries [*Næringssorg*] is that to talk about it is embarrassing to those who suffer under it, and, secondly, the way the gospel speaks of it seems to them too hard. Poetically (i.e., when personally one has a guaranteed livelihood) what the gospel says is indescribably uplifting. But when it is in earnest, that is, when one is personally in need and want and then is supposed to be uplifted by the freedom from care of the lilies and the birds or by the divine elevation of Christ—this is too lofty and, from a human point of view, too rigorous.

x^1 A 353   *n.d.*, 1849

« 102

Vigilius Haufniensis has quite correctly drawn attention to the concept "anxiety" [*Angst*] as the middle term in relation to temptation. Actually, it is the dialectic of temptation. If a person could be entirely free of anxiety, temptation would not have access to him.

This is how I understand the fact that it was the serpent who tempted Adam and Eve, for the serpent's power is precisely anxiety. It is not so much ingenuity and craftiness as it is the ingenuity which knows how to create anxiety.

And anxiety (as Anti-Climacus[49] correctly observes in respect to immediacy—it is right at the beginning, in the discussion about the universality of despair) is most intense about nothing. This is the way the tempter and the temptation saddle the person who knuckles under with the very discovery of the temptation—for, say the temptation and the tempter: I really said nothing at all. You became anxious over nothing.

Anxiety is the first reflex of possibility, a glimpse, and yet a terrible sorcery.

x^2 A 22   *n.d.*, 1849

« 103

"Anxiety" is actually nothing but impatience.

x^2 A 384   *n.d.*, 1850

« 104 *State of Mind*

The delight which women in particular, and especially the less enlightened, have in terrifying children with all sorts of imaginary notions about a man who comes and takes them, etc. (as today, May 5, out in the neighborhood of Hirschholm, I heard a girl tell a little child that it must not go too near the water, that there was a man in the water who would take it, that merely looking down into the water was enough to be taken—basically a profound observation) hangs together (disregarding that it is a means for getting children to be quiet) with the selfishness which rejoices or is stimulated at the sight of a child anxious about something which one is himself not anxious about, whose nothingness one knows himself.

When a man does something like this, you will see that he is likely to give the whole thing a comic touch. But woman has a secret rapport with anxiety, and she is stimulated by seeing the child's actual anxiety.

x^4 A 288 *n.d.*, 1851

APOSTLE

« 105

A frivolous, vain individual always has an extraordinary conception of an apostle's high honor—i.e., the good fortune, the glory of being an apostle; a humble, profound individual always has an extraordinary conception of an apostle's sufferings.

VI A 14 n.d., 1845

« 106 *An Illusion*

> The supposed humility and modesty
> in admitting that one does not call
> himself an apostle.

Here again is a confusion which appears with the help of "Christendom," which again has turned all Christian concepts topsy-turvy—that is, has prevented them from being what they were originally: turned around.

One is said to be humble and modest if he says: I do not call myself an apostle. Consequently to call oneself an apostle is pride, conceit. That this can be pride and conceit I do not deny; I desire only to illuminate the relationship a little better.

When one speaks this way, the presupposition is that to be an apostle is a distinction; the humility and modesty lie in not claiming distinction. Fine. But like everything Christian, to be an apostle is not a straightforward distinction but a distinction turned around. Here comes a little N.B. In relationship to all direct distinction or distinguishing, the matter is very simple; if it is true that I make no claims, this is being modest, for a direct distinction is without secondary qualifications a direct earthly benefit. But to be an apostle is sheer earthly suffering. Well, if an apostle could be permitted to live again after his teaching had won out, then it could perhaps be an earthly benefit to be an apostle. But while he was living, calling himself an apostle did not help him on the way to honor, respect, or earthly advantage. Precisely this, that he called himself an apostle, was the signal for his having to suffer more than the other adherents, suffer until death.

This is what it means to be an apostle—something quite different from that later conception, which with the help of an illusion takes the apostle in vain.*

But if this is the case, then to ask to be regarded as modest because one does not call himself an apostle becomes questionable, for this can also be worldly ingenuity and effeminacy.

For the confusing word "apostle" (which has subsequently become secularized and identified with the other distinctions of the world) let us substitute a whole lifetime of being laughed at, mocked, persecuted, poor, jailed, and slain. If someone now says: I am not so immodest as to demand to become "His Excellency," etc.—well, this is quite direct. But let someone say: I am not so immodest as to demand to become poor, impoverished, outcast in the world, laughed at, slain—well, this is not quite as direct; for in each generation it is impossible to find ten persons who have courage for this. Consequently it can also be worldly ingenuity and effeminacy which hold one back but also want the advantage of being regarded as humble. This is questionable.

O, if what Christianity is were only kept clearly in mind! That it is not a doctrine but an existence [*Existents*], that what is needed is not professors but witnesses [*Vidner*]—then we would be free of all this self-important scholarliness [*Videnskabelighed*], these show-offs who are scholars—something Christianity now needs. No, if Christ did not need scholars but was satisfied with fishermen, what is needed now is more fishermen. Precisely because Christ was present, the danger would not have been so great if Christianity had fallen into the hands of scholars.

The error is not the studying, but the error is that the accent continually falls on the wrong place—on penetrating and presenting—thus to do something about it becomes ridiculous, a triviality. A simple man, however, has no distractions. Such a man straightway fastens his gaze upon his life, whether it has any meaning or is completely meaningless. But this simplification with regard to drawing up the account is of utmost importance; for then the accent falls on the right place, on existence [*Existentsen*].

x^3 A 96 *n.d.*, 1850

« 107

*In margin of 106 (x^3 A 96):
And it must be remembered that in a certain sense there is nothing we are all more equally close to than to being an apostle, simply because here there is no question of the esthetic difference of being a genius, of having talent, etc. Certainly every human being has the right to order his

life just as an apostle with regard to poverty, suffering for the truth, etc., except that he does not have the right to appeal to divine authority. But he must not feel embarrassed about the first [being like an apostle], least of all out of modesty; that is, if there is to be any question about true modesty, it must be to confess that one is too weak and sensuous, therefore to bring accusation against oneself; it must not be as when I am too modest to ask to become an ambassador, a demigod artist, knight of all the European orders, etc.

x^3 A 97, n.d., 1850

« 108 *The Apostle*

A monstrous knave, which is what the human race is, has a completely unbalanced point of view. "The apostle" has been made into the extraordinary by way of accidental differences (consequently esthetic), and to be an apostle means the extraordinary almost in the sense of the enjoyment of life, instead of "the apostle" as the extraordinary in the ethical sense of what every human being should be, and as the extraordinary in the sense of suffering, a situation everyone wishes to avoid.

So it is that the viewpoint has been unbalanced. Every once in a while there is an arrogant windbag who, assuming that the "apostle" in this misunderstood sense is the extraordinary, has presumptuously wanted to be the extraordinary.

I turn the relationship around completely. I assume that everyone can, yes, ought to be this. Christ[50] himself says that if we had faith as a mountain [should be "mustard seed"] we could move mountains. Consequently, I assume this of everyone; there is only one I do not assume this of—myself. And why? Because I am a coward, a milksop, a sly fellow who does not really have faith, etc. See, this is quite a different story from the hypocritical talk that I am too humble and too modest to will to be this— the ethical extraordinary one.

On the whole I think that one cannot truly speak of Christianity without perpetual self-accusation.

Consequently, I am not the ethical extraordinary. O, God in heaven, what poverty, that there are after all so few who are willing to suffer, who really want to have something to do with you, which means to suffer!

x^4 A 387 n.d., 1851

« 109 *Socrates—"the Apostle"*

It is sheer genial drivel to charge that Socrates was motivated by self-love in acting indirectly, maieutically, in ironic isolation. No, according to Socrates' way of thinking, this is precisely what it is to love. If it is true that every man has to help himself, if it is the ideal to stand alone, then it is entirely valid to prevent the one who is being helped from becoming dependent upon the helper—for in that case he is not helped. This was Socrates' idea, and in addition Socrates is the judge. But he loved men according to a standard of which all these genial drivelers have not the slightest inkling. He loved them in the idea, after first being disciplined by the idea himself to be able to stand unconditionally alone, unconditionally to do without any other man—something the genial drivelers have hardly an inkling of.

"The apostle" is something else. He has another concept of what it is to love, and he has grace to proclaim. But please note that the apostle himself is first and foremost disciplined to be able unconditionally to do without any other man.

Between the Socratic and the apostolic lie the half-measures and finally the nonsense. To be specific, this wanting to win men, this so-called geniality in contrast to Socrates' so-called disagreeableness, can be anything but apostolic, can be a crafty way for the person concerned to express his own need of other men, his need of them because he cannot stand alone (something he does not want to say and instead says hypocritically or stupidly that it is out of love for others), or because he wants to profit from men, or because he does not have the courage to make a stand against the human ambition round about him which wants him to be obliged to express a relationship of dependence upon them.

I began with the Socratic; but I profoundly recognized my inferiority, however, for I had property and thus considerable assistance toward independence from people. Insofar as I now strive to move more directly to myself or to the idea, I regard this as a diminution, an accommodation in a sense, but there is also a movement in the direction of Christianity. Meanwhile I am not foolish enough to say that my way is superior to the Socratic. No, no! Furthermore, it does not lean at all toward the Socratic but toward proclaiming grace, although, naturally, infinitely inferior to the apostolic proclamation.

X^4 A 388 *n.d.*, 1851

« 110 *"The Apostle"*

The condition *sine qua non* for all enjoyment of life is a certain evenness; the person with a most wretched lot also can gain a certain enjoyment if he only has this daily evenness.

But no other situation in life, not one, makes it so impossible to enjoy life as being an apostle. This horrifying life of being tossed in a blanket. At one moment to be brought into direst need, perhaps ravenously hungry, then to be willing—if it be God's will—to die of hunger—and then get a reprimand: You of little faith! Or, in order not to suffer ravenous hunger, to be quite willing to work for his livelihood—and then, just as he is beginning at it, a miracle happens, and he gets a reproof: You of little faith! O, it is a dreadful misery, a kind of conscious madness in all his blessedness, for it is like madness.

Ah, however spoiled and frivolous I am, so much will surely be granted me that I at least have dared venture out far enough to be honest toward the extraordinary and not to take him in vain, at least to have a tolerably true idea of how infinitely the extraordinary has suffered.

X^4 A 418 *n.d.*, 1851

« 111

Serpens, nisi serpentem comederit, non fit Draco.[51]

Further: a rat is trained to bite rats by eating a rat out of hunger.

The reverse: only a person who is bitten by men becomes an apostle; this belongs in order to qualify his passion; an apostle in direct understanding with men is an impossibility.

XI^1 A 173 *n.d.*, 1854

ARISTOTLE

« 112

One can better understand the Aristotelian statement[52] about voluntary action if one remembers that an important distinction is made between Τὸ ἑκούσιον and προαίρεσις (purpose), in such a way that something can be voluntary without being intended. (See Bk. III, ch. 4.)

IV C 20   n.d., 1842-43

« 113

In Book III, chapter 7,[53] Aristotle rejects Socrates' and Plato's idealistic thesis that all sin is ignorance, but he does not remove the difficulty, for he merely ends in a realistic contradiction. This problem is of utmost importance and could very well lend itself to a monograph.

In margin: See Aristotle *Ethics* 7, 3.[54]

IV C 21   n.d., 1842-43

« 114

In the last chapter of Book X of his *Ethics*[55] Aristotle deals with the relation of ethics to politics, as he also begins[56] ἠθικά μεγάλα, saying that ethics is part of politics. Moreover, it is noteworthy that his own dialectic almost annuls this comment, since, indeed, the reflective life is the highest and the inferior happiness lies in the practice of the political virtues. (See 10, 8.) But the contemplative life is isolation.[57]

IV C 27   n.d., 1842-43

« 115 *Paganism—Immortality*

One often learns the most from an occasional remark.

In the *Ethics*, Bk. III, ch. 4,[58] where Aristotle develops the distinction between wishing and moral purpose, he says one cannot make the impossible his moral purpose but one can indeed wish it; "there is such a thing as wishing for the impossible, as for example, for immortality."

X^5 A 31   n.d., 1852

« 116 *Aristotle's* ETHICS

Book VI, ch. 12 to the end:[59] From this it arises that in respect to the νοῦς (i.e., first principles and particular experiences) we should therefore pay no less attention to the undemonstrated assertions and opinions of old and experienced or prudent persons than to demonstrations, for their experience gives their eyes the power of seeing principles directly.

Book VIII, ch. 15 to the end:[60] If there is a being whose nature is simple (not a composite), the one and the same activity would always be pleasant to him. Such a being is the divine, who therefore everlastingly enjoys one single (simple) and unbroken joy. Not all activity is in motion (change); there is also activity in the unchanging. Yes, enjoyment is found more in rest than in motion. According to the poet nothing is more pleasurable to human beings than change, but this arises from his imperfection. The most changeable man is always also the most evil man, and every nature is less perfect the more change it requires; for such a nature is not simple, is not at one with itself—is simply not what it should be.

Book VIII, ch. 16 in the middle:[61] "It is impossible both to get rich at the expense of the state and also to want to get honor for it." Alas, it is being done all the time.

x^5 A 32   *n.d.*, 1852

ART, ARTISTS, ARTISTRY, THE ARTISTIC

« 117

The reason I cannot really say that I positively enjoy *nature* is that I do not quite realize *what* it is that I enjoy. A work of art, on the other hand, I can grasp. I can—if I may put it this way—find that Archimedean point, and as soon as I have found it, everything is readily clear for me. Then I am able to pursue this one main idea and see how all the details serve to illuminate it. I see the author's whole individuality as if it were the sea, in which every single detail is reflected. The author's spirit is kindred to me; he is very probably far superior to me, I am sure, but yet he is limited as I am. The works of the deity are too great for me; I always get lost in the details. This is the reason, too, why people's exclamations on observing nature: It's lovely, tremendous, etc.—are so frivolous. They are all too anthropomorphic; they come to a stop with the external; they are unable to express inwardness, depth. In this connection, also, it seems most remarkable to me that the great geniuses among the poets (such as Ossian and Homer) are represented as blind. Of course, it makes no difference to me whether they actually were blind or not. I only make a point of the fact that people have imagined them to be blind, for this would seem to indicate that what they saw when they sang the beauty of nature was not seen with the external eye but was revealed to their inward intuition. How remarkable that one of the best, yes, the very best writer[62] about bees was blind from early youth. It seems to indicate that however much one believes in the importance of the observation of externals, he had found that [Archimedean] point and now by a purely spiritual activity had deduced from this all the details and had reconstructed them analogously to nature.

I A 8   September 11, 1834

« 118

Doubtless the most sublime tragedy consists in being *misunderstood*. For this reason the life of Christ[63] is supreme tragedy, misunderstood as he was by the people, the Pharisees, the disciples, in short, by everybody, and this in spite of the most exalted ideas which he wished to communicate. This is why Job's life is tragic; surrounded by misunderstanding friends, by a ridiculing wife, he suffers. The situation of the wife in *The Riquebourg Family*[64] is moving precisely because her love for her husband's nephew compels her to conceal herself, and therefore her apparent coolness. This is why the scene in Goethe's *Egmont* (Act V, Scene 1) is so genuinely tragic. Clara is wholly misunderstood by the citizens. No doubt it is for this reason that several of Holberg's comic characters have a tragic effect. Take, for example, the busybody. He sees himself encumbered with an enormous mass of concerns; everyone else smiles at him and sees nothing. The tragedy in the hypochondriac's life also stems from this—and also the tragedy in the character who is seized with a longing for something higher and who then encounters people who do not understand him.

I A 33   November 22, 1834

« 119

It occurs to me that *artists* go forward by going backward, something which I have nothing against intrinsically when it is a reproduced retreat—as is the case with the better artists. But it does not seem right that they stop with the historical themes already given and, so to speak, think that only these are suitable for poetic treatment, because these particular themes, which intrinsically are no more poetic than others, are now again animated and inspired by a great poetic nature. In this case the artists advance by marching on the spot. —Why are modern heroes and the like not just as poetic? Is it because there is so much emphasis on clothing the content in order that the formal aspect can be all the more finished?

I A 86   September 29, 1835

« 120 *Literary Scholarship*

often resembles an impenetrable virgin forest, where one can find a few places where one can ask the way and a family who profess to know the roads in the neighboring province but possess this information by tradition rather than through personal experience. In this literary virgin forest there also live swarms of wild animals *(literary critics)*, which one must keep at bay with all sorts of noise-makers, for example, by falling into step with other critics. The very best, perhaps, would be if one could do with critics as is done with rats: train one to bite the other.

I A 90   October 9, 1835

« 121

There are authors who, like beggars trying to arouse pity by exposing the defects and deformities of their body, strive to make a sensation by exposing the shattered condition of their hearts.

                                            I A 105   November 1, 1835

« 122

There are critics who, completely lacking an eye for the individual, try to regard everything from a universal point of view. Consequently, in order to become as universal as possible, they climb as high as possible until they see essentially nothing at all but a wide horizon—precisely because their viewing-point lies too high.

                                            I A 106   November 2, 1835

« 123

Schiller has properly drawn a boundary between the naive and the sentimental by declaring that the former stirs and moves us by its naturalness, its sensuous objective truth, its living presence. The sentimental, on the other hand, which is generated by reflection upon the impression which the poet himself receives from his object, moves only by reproducing the same reflection in others.

See Molbech, *Forelæsninger*, II, p. 234.[65]

                                            I A 129   n.d., 1836

« 124

All-encompassing—powerlessness—benediction (Serbian folk legend). Stillness, silence, God's side (Mohammed, Pythagoras, Christianity). Strange vibrations quickly round off the past for me in a poetic intuition, and it then seems most interesting to me—soon I feel the unhappiness in it, precisely because (to use a line from *Guldkorset*) the impression is not from anybody else but from myself.

                                            I A 175   n.d., 1836

« 125

Why do we prefer to read comedy in society and tragedy in solitude?

                                            I A 198   June 19, 1836

« 126

What a $\pi\rho o\tau\upsilon\pi o\varsigma$[66] for individual human life lies in the fact that we always see a nation's poetic development begin with the epic and only then does the lyrical follow.

                                            I A 212   August 2, 1836

« 127

In an age when it is the order of the day for one author to plunder another, it is nevertheless pleasant at times to stumble upon men whose individuality so molds and stamps every word with their portrait that it must compel everyone who meets it in a strange place to say to those concerned: "Render unto Caesar what is Caesar's."

I A 234   September 10, 1836

« 128

It is truly remarkable that no one, as far as I know, has had the idea of summoning authors from their graves and having them attend an auction of their immortal works.

I A 245   September 20, 1836

« 129

To be able to write a truly dramatic rejoinder requires considerable clarity and something beyond generality, the vague indeterminate. At an earlier stage what was supposed to be repartee was written together with the parenthetical remarks usually put in small print to indicate how the performer should act, for example, "with deep feeling," "movingly," etc.

II A 15   February 4, 1837

« 130

There are men who talk according to the association of ideas; but more fundamental than this is a level which I would call the *Selbstsucht*[67] of order, where one word carries another word along with it, where words which frequently mingle in the same company seek one another in about the same way as words in a dictionary, if they were to come alive, would place themselves in the same order to which they were accustomed.

II A 583   January 30, 1837

« 131 *A Preface*

Most people usually go about reading a book with a notion of how they themselves would have written it, how someone else has written or would have written, just as if a closely resembling form steps in when they are to see someone for the first time, and as a result very few people really know how the other person looks. Here begins the first possibility of not being able to read a book, which thereupon goes through innumerable nuances until on the highest level—misinterpretation—the two most opposite kinds of readers meet, the most stupid and the most brilliant, who share in common the inability to read a book—the first because of vacuity and the second because of a wealth of ideas. Therefore I have given this work a very ordinary title (it should be called "A Letter") in order to do my part in preventing what is frequently* a loss for the author and sometimes for the readers—misinterpretation.

* *In margin:* I say *frequently*, for it sometimes happens that through misinterpretation one finds good things in a wretched book.

II A 46   n.d., 1837

« 132

The refrain which repeatedly recurs in hero ballads is again one of the very illuminating characteristics of the Middle Ages. The refrain is the as yet not reproduced lyrical rhythm which goes through it, the melodic, or better, the melodious mood—it is the same thing—that appears again when at a later time something is said to be sung to this or that melody, an external token of the musical which has even been carried over into the headings of the hymns (to be sung to this or that melody), only that here the musical is differentiated as a distinct aspect, whereas in the first instance it slumbered within a unity, of which one can say that just as all thought is speaking with oneself (consequently silent) all poetry is singing for oneself, for which we have a word: *humming*. Therefore I believe that the task of the composer of genuine ballad music (as an example I cite the elder Hartmann[68]) is to reproduce the mood of the poet by reciting or rather by chanting the words for himself until this recitation eventuates in music and separates the purely musical from the point of departure for the musical in the lyrical.

II A 636   n.d., 1837

« 133

Earlier I said[69] that Don Juan is musically immediate and thereby indicates the character's infinite immanence in the music, that the actions, character, and text stand in necessary relationship to each other as in no other opera; and I maintained[70] that in Lenau's *Faust* Mephisto begins to play (the musical) when the subordinate sensuous life begins in order to show that the genius of sensuous life is musical—now I find this supported in noting that the demonic in folktales[71] is essentially musical (not only in the dance, which is so light that they dance upon the water and hardly leave a trace on the dewy grass, for what is the dance without music; but what more musical dance can be conceived than one so immaterial that the dance is, so to speak, music, the dance of music, that the dance is the musically sonorous figure, the music visualized, the music captured in a visible medium). Music and dance are the business of nisses, elf-maidens, dwarfs, etc. . . .

II A 180   October 11, 1837

« 134

The Christian must not lack the eye, in a human sense the illuminating light, which for me makes it easier to comprehend a painted landscape than nature; there and in history *he* meets God's eye.

II A 664   *n.d.*, 1837

« 135

When someone wants to express that he comprehends something right away, why does he say that he recognizes a snatch of melody, and why is it that one is far more easily impressed by music than by the word —to what aspect of the psyche does music address itself: imagination?

II A 715   *n.d.*, 1838

« 136

All poetry is a *glorification* (i.e., transfiguration) [*Forklarelse*: transfiguration] of life by way of its clarification [*Forklarelse*] (in that it is explained, illuminated, developed, etc.). It is truly remarkable that language has this ambiguous ambiguity.

II A 352   February 5, 1839

« 137 *The 7th Defense of Anonymity*

Most authors write with so little individuality that almost anyone in the kingdom could be the author of what is written, and since the name becomes a very trivial accessory, one perceives that anonymity has significance also in a poetic sense; on the other hand, authors who have individuality have no need of appending their names.

II A 412   May 6, 1839

« 138

What is expression (style) other than an external birthmark?—and those people who arrive at a result which is not their own are like hens who have hatchery chicks. Every time the idea makes a movement according to its nature (like ducklings taking to water), they become fearful and shuffle their feet, because they know the thought only in a specific form at a specific period of its development. Like unmathematical heads, they are unable to demonstrate the proposition which they previously were able to—now that the figures are changed and other letters are used.

II A 425   May 15, 1839

« 139

Criticism is the most *hypocritical* of all sciences, is really a phony, of which it is written that it strains at a gnat and swallows a camel, useless except as literary baggage inspecting.

II A 539   August 24, 1839

« 140

..... When some people try to write a satire, out of their anxiety to avoid becoming personal they do what Agent Behrendt[72] did when he lost his silk umbrella—lest the finder keep it if he understood that it was made of silk, he advertised saying that the umbrella was made of cambric.

II A 571   n.d., 1839

« 141

That the theater actually was for the pagans what the church is for us is apparent also in the fact that the theater had no admission charge; that it should cost something to go to the theater was just as unthinkable to the pagans as it would be for us to pay admission to go to church. This concept of the theater can, in general, be expanded to a total view of paganism.

III A 110   n.d., 1841

« 142 *Tested Advice for Unwitty Authors*[73]
Price: $5.00

One carelessly writes down his personal observations. Later, by way of all the various proofs, one acquires a fair number of good ideas. Therefore take courage, you who have not yet dared to have something printed; do not despise typographical errors, and do not let on that they are misprints. Besides, no one can wrench your property away from you, since it really belongs to no one. The only problem is that you must have the help of a good friend who knows how to decide what is witty, so that you do not lend your name to new stupidities.

III A 111   n.d., 1841

« 143

Some of the most difficult disputes are all the boundary disputes in the sciences[74]—the boundary between jurisprudence and ethics; moral philosophy and dogmatics—psychology and moral philosophy, etc. Usually a single science is treated by itself; then one has much to say and gives no thought to the possibility of everything suddenly being dissolved if the presupposition must be altered. —This is especially true of esthetics,

ART, ARTISTS, ARTISTRY, THE ARTISTIC   57

which has always been assiduously cultivated, but almost always in isolation. Many of the estheticians are poets. Aristotle is an exception. He easily perceives that it has a relation to rhetoric, ethics, and politics.

IV C 104   n.d., 1842-43

« 144

An observation in Apollonius of Tyana's *Life of Philostratus*,[75] 2, 22 ff., pp. 258 ff. in translation. See also pp. 523 ff. "All poetry is imitation" (Aristotle)—"better or worse than we are."[76] Hence poetry points beyond itself to *actuality* and to the metaphysical ideality. —Where does the poetic center lie—As soon as it is directed toward sympathy—Therefore we cannot say that we sympathize with Christ. Scripture also says the opposite. See Hebrews 4.[77]

IV C 109   n.d., 1842-43

« 145

Literature should not be a nursing home for cripples but a playground for healthy, happy, thriving, smiling, well-developed children of verve, finely formed, whole, satisfied beings, each one of whom is the very image of his mother and has his father's vitality—not the abortions of weak desires, not the refuse of afterbirth.

IV A 130   n.d., 1843

« 146

The law of delicacy by which an author is permitted to use what he has himself experienced is that he never says the truth but keeps the truth for himself and only lets it emerge in different ways.

IV A 161   n.d., 1843

« 147

[*For the title* "The immediate erotic stages,"[78] etc.] What Homer says is true of music: οἶον ἀκούομεν, οὐδέ τι ἴδμεν.[79] *Iliad*, II. 486. One hears it, but he does not know it, does not understand it.
See Longinus in my edition,[80] p. xxxvi., note.

IV A 222   n.d., 1843

« 148

The writing of books in our day becomes very deplorable, and people write about things they have never thought about, much less experienced. I have therefore decided to read the writings of men who have been executed or in some way have been in danger.

IV A 173   n.d., 1844

« 149

The difference between the actor's art and the art of actuality.

The actor should seem to be moved,[81] although he is calm (if he is actually disturbed, this is a mistake). In the realm of actuality one should seem to be calm, although he is moved (if one is not actually moved, this is a mistake, and it is easy enough to be calm).

VA 97 n.d., 1844

« 150

Hitherto, the imperfection in the tragic is that it had to be about great men and great events historically certain.[82] Disbelief in the idea—therefore hitherto the comic has had a higher ideality. We are more inclined to believe that a man is ridiculous than that he is great (see notes on esthetics in tall cupboard nearest the door).

Likewise with the religious prototypes. One who in this connection does not understand *ab posse ad esse valet consequentia* does not at all understand *ab esse ad posse valet consequentia*[83] either, but imagines that he does. Only ideality is the true norm; actuality and historical accuracy are nonsense as a norm.

VB 148:17 n.d., 1844

« 151

Two new books ought to be written:[84]

A Poet's Confessions

His suffering is that he continually wants to be a religious individual and continually goes about it wrongly and becomes a poet—consequently an unhappy love affair with God (dialectical passion in the direction of there being something deceptive, as it were, about God).

VI A 43 n.d., 1845

« 152 **Problem for a Drama**

An actor in his personal existence [*Existents*] is perhaps in our time the only usable figure who is not used. The contradiction of existence and the special difficulty of the actor are dramatically effective. A piece such as *Kean*[85] points this up well, and the old prompter is, at the end, perhaps the best figure in it.

VI A 117 n.d., 1845

« 153

When Erasmus proves that Nille is a stone,[86] we are comically made to see the weakness of the syllogism; when Madame Nielsen (in the

Maid from Lyon[87]), with all the faithful trust of a simple mother, says of her son, who has married an extraordinary lady, that it wasn't so strange after all—For if my son is not a prince, he ought to be a prince, and that is almost just as good—she demonstrates the power of pathos. The very same words spoken in another voice would produce a comic effect because to the understanding that which is spoken is gibberish; but in the pious delusion of humble maternal love the words have enormous pathos.

VI A 118   *n.d.*, 1845

« 154

The concept of literary contemptibility may be characterized as follows: even if it has talent of a sort, it does not have the justification of an idea, has no view of life, is cowardly, servile, avaricious—therefore, to be anonymous comes naturally. To see the distinction properly, think in contrast of the disintegration of Greece and Aristophanes' comedies. Aristophanes has the authority of an idea; he is distinguished by genius and elevated by personal courage. Indeed, it took courage to portray the demagogue Cleon and, when no actor dared do it, to take his role in the play. But just as antiquity could not arrive at the abstraction of modern disintegration, so also—even in the period of its corruption—it had nothing really analagous to the kind of cowardly moral turpitude which anonymity encourages. Admittedly Socrates says in the *Apology* that his real accusers, those who already for many years had accused him, were like shadows no one can grasp, but if town talk and talking between man and man are like shadows, they are still formed in a way by actual human beings, but with anonymity one single person can conjure up a legion of shadows.

VII[1] A 12   *n.d.*, 1846

« 155

In our time everyone is able to write something or other about everything, but no one is able or willing to endure the strenuous labor of thinking through a single thought exhaustively in all its sharpest implications. As a result, the writing of trifles is particularly appreciated in our time, and one who writes a substantial book almost makes himself the object of ridicule. In the old days one read substantial books, and insofar as one read pamphlets and newspapers, one did not care to have it known. Now everyone feels duty-bound to have read what is in the papers and in the pamphlets but is ashamed to have read a substantial book all the way through; he is afraid this will be regarded as a mark of dullness.

VII[1] A 13   *n.d.*, 1846

« 156

Ultimately everything is turned upside-down. Nothing is written in order that anyone should learn something from it—God forbid such rudeness—the reading public knows everything! It is not the reader who needs the author (as the sick need the physician); no, it is the author who needs the reader. In short, an author is a man who is in financial straits—so he writes, and this means to be up for an examination in which the reading public, which knows everything, judges. A person who writes but does not make money is no author; therefore those who write advertisements and insert them in papers are not called authors because they pay out money. —It is the same in art. An actor is not the person who, initiated into the secrets of the art of illusion, with a fine technique seeks to deceive the audience. Heavens, no—for the public can play comedies by itself. It is not the public which needs the actor but the actor who needs the public. An actor is a man who is in financial straits, and when he acts, he is up for examination.—

VII^1 A 51   n.d., 1846

« 157

Every natural phenomenon *calms*, and the more so the longer one looks at it or listens to it. Every production of art provokes impatience. The rule for fireworks will finally come to be that they must be burned up within five minutes—the quicker the better. But the murmuring of the wind, the alternating song of the waves, the sighing of the grass, etc., improve with every five minutes one listens to them.

VII^1 A 93   n.d., 1846

« 158

If, with regard to performances *ubi plurima nitent*,[88] it is pettiness to discover and emphasize one small mistake, then it is also basically mean and petty to pick out and laud one auspicious thought in something otherwise completely insipid. All criticism ought to idealize either by overlooking mistakes which are insignificant compared with the overall excellence or by overlooking the few fortunate passages within the imperfection of the whole.

VII^1 A 159   n.d., 1846

« 159

When the farmer goes to market with his neatly and carefully wrapped food products, it is disgusting to see that the first ones to come up are not the customers who would treat the products decently but rather a few boors who poke and tear at them. So it is with authors in regard to readers—the first ones to come along are some critics.

VII^1 A 242   n.d., 1845-47

« 160

The most thankless existence [*Existents*] is and continues to be that of an author who writes for authors. Authors can be divided into two types: those who write for readers and, the genuine authors, those who write for authors. The reading public cannot understand the latter type but regard such writers as crazy and almost scorn them—meanwhile the second-class authors plunder their writings and achieve a great sensation with what they have stolen and distorted. These second-class authors generally become the worst enemies of the others—it is, of course, important to them that no one finds out about the true relationship.

VIII^1 A 53   n.d., 1847

« 161

All art is essentially involved in a dialectical self-contradiction. The truly eternal cannot be painted or drawn or carved in stone, for it is spirit. But neither can the temporal essentially be painted or drawn or carved in stone, for when it is presented in these ways, it is presented eternally; every picture expresses a fixation of that particular moment. If I paint a man who is lifting a spoon to his mouth or blowing his nose, it is immediately eternalized—the man continues to blow his nose this one time as long as the painting endures.

VIII^1 A 88   n.d., 1847

« 162

The beauty of the antiphonal Amen which the school children sing in Our Savior's Church really lies in the way each individual voice emerges and then, one by one, joins the flock. The flock of voices resembles very much a flock of doves. First each individual dove comes flying out of the dovecote door; thereupon they wheel about joined and united in a flock.

I do not recall this observation except that I must have already written it somewhere. In the meantime I have not been able to locate it, but it still has value for me as a most striking example of the analogy between the audible and the visible. To be sure there is something audible about doves (the individual wing-strokes and the cooing of the flock), but the more immediate analogy is nevertheless to the visible.

VIII^1 A 122   n.d., 1847

« 163

It would be very interesting sometime to develop examples of what is meant esthetically and artistically by eternal images,[89] what basic mood-relationships ought to exist between the particular details of the image in order for them to cohere as an eternal image.

A boat along Kallebro Beach, a boat with a man standing at one end spearing eel, thereby lifting one end of the boat into the air—a finely nuanced gray background—this is an eternal image. An ordinary sailboat along Kallebro Beach is not an eternal image—why not? Because a sailboat has no essential relationship to the special character of Kallebro Beach.

Lake Esrom requires a sailboat—but with women in it.

VIII¹ A 621   n.d., 1848

« 164

The Middle Ages culminates in Raphael, his conception of the Madonna. Protestantism will culminate in the Christ-image; but this will be the flower of the most thorough dialectical development.

IX A 110   n.d., 1848

« 165

What a change! In the old days each drama was usually presented only once; now special performances are on a subscription basis.[90]

Now the presentation of a drama very frequently signifies (in contrast to the old days) that basically interest has passed from the poetry to other objects of attention: the staging, the actors, finally to the scene-painter, the scenery, the hairdresser, the seamstress.

IX A 447   n.d., 1848

« 166

What most people say about a poet's obligation to develop a moral life-view in his work is, of course, nonsense—like everything else the majority say if one inspects it closely. The situation is this: their lives are stuck in mediocrity, they have never become great—not because they did not want to, above all else, even *per nefas*—consequently not because of their moral maturity but because the conditions of their lives did not permit it. Now they want the poet to depict how the "successful" are reduced to wretchedness and nothingness; this is what they mean by developing a moral life-view, and they want this in order, with the help of the poet, to have consolation and compensation in their bourgeois lives, meaning that it would be better to be like us and become a justice of the peace and magistrate, or grocer and captain in the national guard.

A person who really has a moral life-view is quite able to suffer this spectacle in actual life and has nothing against the poet presenting immorality as having great success, becoming great, king, emperor, etc.—his life-view sees through all this and sees the immorality, and this is sufficient for him.

x^1 A 3   *n.d.*, 1849

« 167

"The poet" dreams of exploits which he nevertheless does not carry out himself, and he becomes eloquent. Perhaps he becomes eloquent because he is only an unhappy lover of exploits; whereas the hero is their happy lover—consequently he becomes eloquent because deficiency makes him eloquent. "Deficiency"—O, in their misunderstanding men speak ill of you, as if you were only cruel and not equally compassionate, as if you only took away and never gave—it is deficiency which essentially makes "the poet."

A passage which was not used in the first address in *Lilies of the Field and Birds of the Air.*

x^1 A 198   *n.d.*, 1849

« 168

Humanly understood, it would still be a kind of consolation if a witness to truth dared say to his loved ones at his death: See, now I have suffered—now it will be easy for you. Alas, no, he must say: Now it is your turn.

And so it must and shall be as long as this world lasts.

This world is a world of untruth, of lies, and to live *Christianly* in it means to suffer.

Therefore the most difficult of tasks is this: from "poet" to Christian; for the poet clings fast to this world even though he suffers in it. A poet can endure much in this respect. The one thing he cannot do is to let go of the world as Christianity requires. The poet can become more and more unhappy but nevertheless through imagination continue to relate himself to the world—real renunciation he never achieves.

Alas, in many respects it is as if this had been written about me. Yet there may still be enough of the better in me that at least I have dared venture out far enough so that providence can get hold of me.

x^1 A 346   *n.d.*, 1849

« 169

It is not poetic to live as the lilies and the birds (how stupid of bourgeois philistinism to reproach "the poet" for presumably doing this

—instead of having a job); no, it is simply the true way. But the tragedy is that "the poet" does not do it; only the apostle does this. The poetic way is to earn one's own keep in one way or another and then to preach, speak, poetize about living as the lilies and the birds or as the apostle.

The objection of bourgeois philistinism against the poetic way might have a kind of apparent justification only to a certain extent, namely to the extent that the poetic way might be sheer flightiness. For the apostolic way is to live as the birds and the lilies in respect to livelihood—and then to be filled with the thought of the Eternal, working for eternal goals.

x^1 A 432   *n.d.*, 1849

« 170

In order to defend the reality of art in relationship to religious spirit the argument runs like this: the spirit penetrates a man in such a way that one sees what sort of a man he is—for example, when Luther said: "God help me, Amen," he said this so that people got to see into his inner self, what manner of man he was. This then is something of a concession, although it must be remembered that it must not be taken too literally, for if it transformed a man in this way, then also his enemies might immediately see the same thing. Next, it must be remembered that it does not hold true in respect to the object of "faith," precisely because immediate obviousness is denied in order to test faith and in order that faith can be faith—that is, there can very well have been a human transfiguration (although one should always bear in mind that the enemy did not see it—to take a lower level example, the ones who stoned Stephen did not see his face as the face of an angel), but quite properly there is no corresponding direct immediacy as the token of its being God. And thus the object of faith is not available for artistic presentation. And even in the relations among men, to the extent to which a man in relationship to something may be the object for a kind of faith, to the same extent he cannot be painted or depicted in this relationship. For the fact that there must be accompanying faith signifies precisely that there is no direct immediacy; otherwise everyone would have to see the same thing, also his enemies—who judge exactly the opposite.

But in the midst of Christendom one is hardly ever aware of the Socratic—that the ethical teacher (the pure one, the noble one) was the ugliest of men who looked as if he were capable of all evil—and this is in Christendom which, indeed, relates itself to the God-man, the object of "faith"—and yet people think that all inwardness can be painted, i.e., is directly recognizable. What is "faith," then? Well, of course, nowadays "faith" is this thing and that thing, opinion, and the like—and art is a higher sphere; and then, too, we are all Christians.

x^2 A 380   *n.d.*, 1850

ASCETICISM

« 171

Here will be a place for a complete study of the significance of asceticism as something characteristically Christian.[91]

II A 795   n.d., 1838

« 172

It is ridiculous to hear pastors in our time warn against medieval asceticism[92] (monks and nuns and the like, flagellations, etc.). Münter[93] is particularly zealous in this—alas, in the Nineteenth Century to warn against such things (this is madness)! —And people judge asceticism so stupidly! There was something childish about it; they had a conception then of how terrible it is to bear responsibility and guilt all through life —this eternal continuation, mounting day by day. Thus asceticism was an expression of a life-view something like that of a child, who suffers its punishment on a particular day and then forgetting it all becomes a good child again. It was almost an erotic expression. If a girl in an erotic relationship wrongs the beloved, I wonder if she will not immediately rejoice in his unchanged love and say to him: O, scold me a little! —I wonder, finally, whether everyone in our time, that is, all of the single individuals who in our time have a little religious sensitivity, would not do the same, but in another way, by denying themselves some enjoyment because they are not happy or pleased with themselves and going to church.

—The pastors we now have are the most stupid of all—and yet Bishop Mynster is neglected, the only one who knows what the question is all about.

VI A 39   n.d., 1845

« 173

What Schleiermacher[94] says about asceticism in one of his lectures on religion (no. 2) is, in my estimation, most excellent: every person of depth has his asceticism.

X^2 A 264   n.d., 1849

« 174 *Plain Honesty*

It is my conviction that rigorous as Christianity is (and I have never understood Christianity in any other way), it is also gentle.

It is not given to everyone nor is it unconditionally required of everyone that he must live, in the strictest sense of the words, in poverty and abasement. But he must be honest; he must admit candidly that such a life is too high for him and then rejoice as a child in the more lenient conditions, since ultimately grace is still the same for all.

But one must not reverse the relationship, become conceited, and say: to embrace secularism is more perfect.

I am just as far from considering myself capable of living as an ascetic in the more rigorous sense as I am from ever having seen a single human being whom I could believe to be capable of such a life. O, this alone, the fact that the most trifling matter becomes something of infinite importance in such a life, that everything, everything, even the most insignificant, comes to be relevant to the question of my eternal happiness —O, this is beyond comprehension.

Quite possibly many an ascetic was spiritually puffed up, but it is not for me to judge, since I have to confess that I cannot even reach what for him was the beginning stage.

Secularism has conquered to such a degree that the category "ascetic" is employed as a refinement for flattering oneself in his sensate enjoyment of life with the feeling that Christianly he is superior to the ascetic.

Let the nation's one thousand clergy reassure us that to live as an ascetic is not the highest, although if it were required they would be quite willing—I confess that whether the ascetic is the highest or not the highest, he stands an entire level higher than where I have my life, and, besides, I certainly do not have the right offhandedly to impute spiritual pride to every ascetic; on the contrary, he runs precisely the additional extreme danger of feeling the proximity of that temptation, which by itself would be enough to keep me from venturing upon such a life, even if—which is not the case at all—I thought myself so detached from flesh and blood that I dared venture it. Furthermore, I confess that if I said: If it is required, then I am completely ready and willing—I confess that if I said this it would be a lie in my throat.

Just as my life scarcely resembles that of an ascetic, so have I not in the remotest way required such a life of any man or judged a single man for not undertaking it—I, who only little by little, according to my capacities, have tried on a small scale to pledge myself, and who in any case, aware of this from the beginning, admit that I am without authority. I have no proposal to make concerning the established order, not the slightest. I think that for the sake of the cause it can continue as it is, except that each one before God should make an admission and force himself to remember it.

In my opinion, what has demoralized Christendom, especially

Protestantism, is the fact that the clergy, conformed to secularism in every particular instead of admitting that Christianly this is an indulgence, has reversed the relationship and made this secularity into something Christianly far superior and truer than actual renunciation, than actually living in poverty and abasement. The world has seen through this, and therefore the clergy has no influence.

In this I am wholly in agreement with the world. I find unbearable all this endless drivel and these assurances that if, if—then they would readily give up everything, live unmarried in poverty, etc. This at least is not my situation; I admit that I have neither the powers nor the courage for such a life. This I say directly and then beyond this I praise Christianity with all the capacity given to me.

And yet as an author I have held out as an author proclaiming Christianity on my own, but I have had an inheritance. Among the clergy, as is well known, it is not customary to do something *gratis*. The custom is: FIRST one seeks a salary (which certainly is not seeking first the kingdom of God)—and then gives assurances that if, etc. I have not the slightest objection to the first part; it is quite in order that one makes sure of a job (in the same sense as I have managed by having a little inheritance). But the next part no one, I believe, has the right to say without doing; otherwise it so easily becomes a lot of boasting, which weakens the impression of Christianity. It is not at all dangerous that we get to know that a clergyman is like the rest of us, a human being, no hero; the danger is that he so conveniently gets a reserved seat, with a number, among the heroes—and is a hero also—if that is required. A person can be something—and perhaps also a lieutenant in the national guard if the country gets into war. But to live on as a plain ordinary man, perhaps almost a philistine or bourgeois, and also to be a hero—if—that won't do. It is meaningless to will *also* to be the highest, for one must say to such a person: If it is so easy for you, you really ought to be earnest about it.

In margin: If one is superior in this or that, one can offer assurances that if required he is *also* willing to be inferior in this or that; there is sense in this, for the fact that one is superior guarantees that one can easily be inferior. But when one is inferior, then to offer assurances that if required one is willing to be superior is nonsense, because being inferior is no guarantee, and the other is precisely that *quod erat demonstrandum*.[95]

x^3 A 187   *n.d.*, 1850

« 175 *Asceticism*

What our age would really be most inclined to regard as a counter-

ASCETICISM

part of Don Quixote would be an ascetic in the old sense, an ascetic who fasts and prays and accuses himself of even the slightest sinful thought and imposes punishment upon himself for it—and then we are all Christians!

For someone to live poor and pinched—if he has no other means—is understandable (although the time will come soon when this is not understood, for he could indeed become a Communist), but this is not at all the concept of asceticism. That asceticism is a dialectic of the spirit, has religious meaning for the person himself—this would be considered prodigiously ridiculous—and yet we are all Christians! We are all Christians; and then if one is earnest about existentially expressing Christianity, all would laugh, would find it a ridiculous exaggeration, and the man would be regarded as mad.

x^4 A 150   n.d., 1851

« 176 *Pascal*

Who in modern times has been used by the pastors and professors as Pascal has? They appropriate his thoughts, but they omit the fact that Pascal was an ascetic and went around with a hair shirt and all that. Or else they explain it as birthmarks of the age, of no significance for us.

Excellent! In all other respects Pascal is original—but not here. But was asceticism the usual thing in his day, or had it not already been abolished long before and Pascal had to maintain it in opposition to his age?

But it is like this everywhere, everywhere. This infamous, nauseating cannibalism whereby they (just as Heliogabalus[96] ate ostrich brains) eat the thoughts, opinions, expressions, moods of the dead—but their lives, their personal qualities—no, thank you, they want nothing to do with that.

x^4 A 537   n.d., 1852

« 177 *On Asceticism*

Asceticism can very easily become sophistical. Think of a person who, even though he has not been, as we say, seriously addicted to pleasure, yet considerably—let him give it all up. I wonder if he can stop there. No, soon the same passionate concern will devote itself to the minutest triviality—dare he eat another piece of toast, dare he eat his fill of dry bread, etc.

Thus asceticism can very easily lead a person into either pride or madness.

Incidentally, what in a certain sense supported men in the age when asceticism was really practiced was the fact that they genuinely believed that a limit could be achieved in this respect; they did not have a more developed intellectual conception of the implicit limitlessness.

x⁵ A 94   n.d., 1853

« 178 *The Displacement of the Whole of Christianity*

Christianity was degraded into becoming a state religion. At the same time Christianity thereby became a doctrine—and asceticism arose. Asceticism is *situationless** renunciation. When Christianity battled and suffered persecution, asceticism in this sense was not needed.

* *In margin:* N.B. And again the consequence of this was meritoriousness, super-meritoriousness, also, that there were *extraordinary* Christians and ordinary Christians.

x⁵ A 99   n.d., 1853

AUGUSTINE

« 179

Deus ita artifex in magnis, ut minor non sit in parvis.[97]
                              Augustine
                       VIII^1 A 317   *n.d.*, 1847

« 180

Augustine has nevertheless done incalculable harm. The whole system of doctrine through the centuries relies essentially upon him—and he has confused the concept of "faith."

Quite simply, Augustine has reinstated the Platonic-Aristotelian definition, the whole Greek philosophical pagan definition of faith—and thus he has aided Christianity in about the same way as Saxo Grammaticus, according to Peer Degn's explanation,[98] enriched the Latin language by, for example, bringing in such words as: *a dun horse* [*en blakket Hest*], *equus blakkatus*.

In the Greek view, faith is a concept which belongs in the sphere of the intellectual (it is all splendidly presented, especially in Plato's *Republic*;[99] however, Aristotle's *Rhetoric* also deserves notice). Thus faith is related to probability, and we get the progression: faith—knowledge.

Christianly, faith is at home in the existential [*Existentielle*]—God has not made his appearance in the character of an assistant professor who has a few axioms which one must first believe and afterward understand.

No, "faith" is at home and has its place in the existential and forever has nothing to do with the comparative or the superlative in requiring knowledge.

Faith is the expression for the personality's relationship to personality.

Personality is not a sum of axioms nor is it an immediate accessibility; personality is a bending-into-itself, a *clausum*, a ἄδυτον, a μυστήριον;[100] personality is the "in-there," because of which the word *persona* (*personare*) is suggestive, the in-there to which one, himself a personality, must relate himself believingly. Between personality and personality no other relationship is possible. Consider the two most passionate lovers who have ever lived, whether or not they are, as it is said, one soul in two bodies—nonetheless it can never go beyond one person's believing that the other loves him or her.

In this purely personal relationship between God as personality and the believer as *existing* personality lies the concept of faith.

But already at the time of Augustine, Christianity was much too much at rest, had leisure to enable the scientific or scholarly to rise—with its conceited and misunderstood importance—and then we get pagan philosophy—and this is supposed to be Christian progress....

In margin: Therefore the *obedience* of faith (i.e., Romans 1:5) is the apostolic expression; then faith is oriented toward will, personality, not toward intellectuality.

xi^1 A 237   *n.d.*, 1854

« 181 *Scholarship*

Augustine always turns the matter thus—precisely because Christianity is truth in the form of authority, it is the divine truth; consequently the form of the authority is decisive.

Now we think that scholarship is true only when all authority has been speculated away.

xi^2 A 328   *n.d.*, 1854

AUTHORITY

« 182

What holds true for the apostles, who were very simple men of the poorest class (for in this very way their *authority*[101] was all the more accentuated; they were nothing in themselves, not geniuses, not councilmen or state governors, but fishermen—therefore all of their *authority* was from God), holds true also for the bad Greek of the New Testament. Earlier, Socrates[102] had considered it improper to use the brilliant speech prepared by a young man for his defense, because he, as he said, had grown too old for childish things. How much more unsuitable for God to employ elegant Greek!

VIII^1 A 225   n.d., 1847

« 183

"Authority"[103] does not mean to be a king or to be an emperor or general, to have the power of arms, to be a bishop, or to be a policeman,* but it means by a firm and conscious resolution to be willing to sacrifice everything, one's very life, for his cause; it means to articulate a cause in such a way that a person is at one with himself, needing nothing and fearing nothing. This infinite recklessness** is authority. True authority is present when the truth is the cause. The reason the Pharisees spoke without authority, although they were indeed authorized teachers, was precisely that their talk, like their lives, was in the power of seventeen finite concerns.

In margin: This is the conception of immanental authority, not the paradoxical conception of authority.

***In margin:* Those with authority, therefore, always address themselves to the conscience, not to understanding, intelligence, profundity—to the human being, not to the professor.

VIII^1 A 416   n.d., 1847

« 184

The situation is like this. The one who proclaims Christianity (the clergyman) in a vehemently orthodox way against all heresies, and not without sweat and tears besides, is embarrassed to say of himself and would probably be embarrassed to do it: I have accepted Christianity because I must, because it is God who commands. No, he has accepted Christianity because it is so profound and so elevated. Aha! Now we shall see if the eternal will accept him! All this nonsense about profundity—what else is it but a way "this wicked generation," to which one belongs in intimate fellowship, has of being ashamed of Christianity, of being ashamed of Christ.

They want so very much to win men to the truth. And to accomplish this, they give them an untruth—and, sure enough, they win men. What else is this but to be ashamed of the truth, to be ashamed of standing alone. There is nothing arrogant here, for the simple reason that there is no talk about depth and profundity, which others may not be *able* to understand, but about the willingness to understand the simple *you shall*.

But people are embarrassed by being obedient to the King because he is the King—therefore they obey him *because* he is *clever*. They are embarrassed by obeying God because he is God; and so they obey him—because he is a very great genius, perhaps almost the greatest, greater even than Hegel.

In margin: So it is with all this about depth and profundity and the "matchless."

VIII^1 A 436   *n.d.*, 1847

« 185

It follows of itself that the person who has divine authority can venture out infinitely further than an ordinary man, however gifted he is, because the former always has one secure point, the order from God. The ordinary person gets the dialectical from two sides: the confict with men, and also the relationship to God—do I have the right to venture so far out?

X^1 A 5   *n.d.*, 1849

« 186

If the whole of Christianity were what the pastors preach, then I would have to renounce Christianity. Why? Because it is not elevated enough for me? No, just the opposite, because it would not be and is not simple enough for me. If Christianity is to be accepted because of reasons, then I must ask for something quite different from what the preachers provide. The fact of the matter is that Christianity *must* be accepted. It is that power which is in heaven and on earth which says to every human being: You *shall* believe. See, this is neither too high nor too low, but just right. The preachers' chatter is neither one nor the other.

x^1 A 188   *n.d.*, 1849

« 187 *Christianity and Speculation*

Christianity is an *existence-communication* [*Existens-Meddelelse*], brought into the world by the use of *authority*. *It is not to be an object of speculation*; Christianity is to be kept existentially on the move, and becoming a Christian is to be made more and more difficult.

Take a simple example. An officer says to a disorderly mob: Move on, please—no explaining.

No explaining—why? Because he uses authority.

Is there, then, nothing objective in Christianity or is Christianity not the object of objective knowledge? Indeed, why not? The objective is what he is saying, he, the authority. But no explaining, least of all the kind which, as it were, sneaks behind the back of the authority and finally speculates him away, too, and turns everything into speculation.

How, after all, can a *divine* teaching enter into the world? By God's empowering a few individuals and overpowering them, as it were, to such a degree that at every moment throughout a long life they are willing to act, to endure, to suffer everything for this teaching. This, their unconditioned obedience, is the form of their authority. They use the authority and appeal to God, but they also support it with their unconditioned obedience. If you do not choose the good, well, then we are prepared to suffer everything, and then we will find out who is the strongest. It is like being at an auction. Men want to frighten the one sent from God, show him all the horrors, but he says: I bid just the same because my unconditioned obedience, in which I moreover am self-constrained, makes it possible to outbid you in endurance. He endures, then, and finally he dies. Now he is constraining. Now he constrains the race and thereby brings the divine teaching to bear upon the race. His unconditioned obedience, which was the support, becomes itself an explanation of his having had divine authority, something he himself had said. As long as he is living and striving, he really uses the most unconditioned obedience, because he cannot get a willing ear for his divine authority; but then he dies, and now the authority has all the greater effectiveness.

The two small pieces by H. H. are very instructive.[104]

x^2 A 119   *n.d.*, 1849

« 188

Real self-doubling [Selvfordoblelse] without a constraining third factor outside of oneself is an impossibility and makes any such existing [Existeren] into an illusion or an experiment.

Kant[105] was of the opinion that man is his own law (autonomy)—that is, he binds himself under the law which he himself gives himself. Actually, in a profounder sense, this is how lawlessness or experimentation are established. This is not being rigorously earnest any more than Sancho Panza's self-administered blows to his own bottom were vigorous. It is impossible for me to be really any more rigorous in A than I am or wish to be in B. Constraint there must be if it is going to be in earnest. If I am bound by nothing higher than myself and I am to bind myself, where would I get the rigorousness as A, the binder, which I do not have as B, who is supposed to be bound, when A and B are the same self.

This appears particularly in all religious areas. The transition—which really is from immediacy to spirit—this dying-away-from does not get to be in earnest, becomes an illusion, experimenting, if there is no third factor, the constraining factor which is not the individual himself.

Therefore all the eminent individuals, the real "instruments," are constrained.

The maxim which I give myself is not only not a law, but there is a law which is given me by one higher than myself, and not only that, but this lawgiver takes the liberty of taking a hand in the capacity of tutor and bringing pressure to bear.

Now if a man is never even once willing in his lifetime to act so decisively that this tutor can get hold of him, well, then it happens, then the man is allowed to live on in self-complacent illusion and make-believe and experimentation, but this also means: utterly without grace.

A man can be so rigorous with himself that he is able to understand that all his rigorousness amounts to nothing; I must have the help of someone else who can be that rigorousness, even if he is also mildness.

But to involve oneself with this other one does not mean to give assurances and give assurances; it means to act.

As soon as a person acts decisively and enters into actuality, then existence [Tilværelsen] can get hold of him and providence can bring him up.

It is certainly true that even if a person pampers himself ever so much, it still can occur to providence to take him to task [tage ham i Skole (school)]. But he does not like to do this; this is almost anger. What providence wants is that a man shall believe and believe in him. Providence is no friend of this effeminate coddling, this wanting to play at being autodidactic when at the same time there lives such a remarkable tutor and teacher as our Lord, to whom he can turn.

But in ordinary human circumstances the fact that I am sent to school or seek to enter school means that I go here or there, wherever the teacher lives. Spiritually, this means that I act decisively—and immediately the teacher lives right there. For what is it I want—I want to be brought up to be spirit—and yet I do not want to act decisively? Nonsense!

x^2 A 396   *n.d.*, 1850

« 189

When Christ[106] drove the money changers out of the temple, he fashioned a whip of rope.
This whip he wielded with authority.
The whip of satire is always without authority.

x^3 A 540   *n.d.*, 1850

« 190 *Authority*

Christ preached with authority—this "the clergyman" now also does, for in reserve he has the police and the house of correction.

x^4 A 644   *n.d.*, 1852

«191 *Christianity (the Authority)*

This is the way Christianity came into the world: it was substantiated by authority, its divine authority; consequently the authority is higher.

Now for a long time the relationship has been reversed: men seek on rational grounds to demonstrate, to substantiate the authority.

And yet this is supposed to be the same religion.

This is the way it was when Christianity came into the world: for a long time mankind had despaired of making anything out of this existence [*Tilværelse*], despaired of finding the truth—then came Christianity with divine authority.

Augustine, for example, always turns the whole matter in such a way that the perfection in Christianity is precisely the authority, that Christianity has truth in its most perfect form, the authority, that if one could have the same truth without authority it would be less perfect, for it is precisely the authority which is the perfection. Alas, even Augustine had learned what it is men need: authority, which is precisely what the race, weary of philosophers' doubt and the wretchedness of life, had learned through the entry of Christianity into the world.

Now the situation is turned in this way—a so-called philosophical Christianity finds that authority itself is imperfection, is at most something for the plebeians, that perfection is to get rid of it—to recover the situation as it was before Christianity came into the world.

And theology seeks to substantiate Christianity's authority, to give reasons for it, that is, even worse than any attacker, theology indirectly confesses that it is not authority.

This is the way the situation has been for a long time, from generation to generation—and everything goes along charmingly: students become theological graduates, graduates become pastors or professors, get married, beget children for Christianity, careers are assured in the best manner! O, disgusting!

What they now call Christianity is actually nothing else than making a fool of God.

Ah, but this again is so horrifying to me—will eternity actually discard these generations and millions of people as eternally lost.

XI^1 A 436 *n.d.*, 1854

«192 *That True Christianity*

can be proclaimed only with "authority." Otherwise everything gets turned around, as when "the pastor" proclaims Christianity for—the public.

XI^2 A 404 *n.d.*, 1855

BEING

« 193

τὸ ὄν,[107] the Eleatics (Parmenides), *Pure being* [Væren]—
1. it is universally applicable.
2. most universal. single—immediate.
3. not a distinction as if it were something objective.
4. *copula* without predicate or subject.
    to that extent it is nothing (i.e., nothing is predicated of it).
τὸ ἕτερον (ἕτερον)[108]
Existence [Tilværelsen]—
proceeds out of being—[109]
being presupposes a second, i.e.: existence—boundary.

Every negation implies an affirmation, since otherwise it would itself be completely meaningless—this is what Heiberg[110] calls infinite conclusions.

An abstract beginning is neither something nor nothing, for, if it were nothing, then it would not have begun, and if it were something, it would be more than a beginning.

II C 37   n.d., 1837

« 194

In his lecture today Sibbern[111] made a very good observation about how one must assume a real ideal being [*egl. ideel* Væren], which in itself has being before its expression in actual being [*actuelle* Væren], something one can discern in the fact that in speaking of eternal truths one would not say that they now come to be but that they are now revealed, i.e., in the fullness of time.[112]

II A 305   December 17, 1838

« 195

That thought and being [Væren] are one can be seen in people who suffer under a fixed idea—and here is also proof of the eternity of damnation, since man's more perfect existence must be understood as being free from all distractions, everything momentary and temporal which prevents our feeling the identity of thought and being, not to mention that what is implied by sexual differentiation and the whole historical development which has its point of departure therein must be considered absent, inasmuch as we are to become as angels (neither marry nor be given in marriage); but the Church Fathers teach that the angels' fall is irrevocable, because it occurred in the form of the "true time."

II A 367   February 12, 1839

« 196

Every qualification for which being [Væren] is an essential qualification lies outside of immanental thought, consequently outside of logic.

IV C 88   n.d., 1842-43

« 197 *Concerning the Concepts* ESSE *and* INTER-ESSE[113]

A methodological attempt

The different sciences ought to be ordered according to the different ways in which they accent being [Væren] and how the relationship to being provides reciprocal advantage.

Ontology
Mathematics

The certainty of these is absolute—here thought and being are one, but by the same token these sciences are hypothetical.

Existential science [Existentiel-Videnskab].

IV C 100   n.d., 1842-43

« 198

It is most interesting that Pythagoras supposed that ἕν is both περιττόν and ἄρτιον[114]—it is, as it were, the being [Væren] which is both being and nonbeing—that is, motion.

IV A 38   n.d., 1843

« 199

Very likely what our age needs most to illuminate the relationship between logic and ontology is an examination of the concepts: possibility, actuality, and necessity. It is hoped, meanwhile, that the person who would do something along this line would be influenced by the Greeks. The Greek sobriety is seldom found in the philosophers of our day, and exceptional ingenuity is only a mediocre substitute. Good comments are to be found in Trendlenburg's *Logische Untersuchungen;* but Trendlenburg was also shaped by the Greeks.[115]

VI B 54:21   n.d., 1845

« 200 *Predicate-less Being* {Væren}

Jehovah says: I am who I am;[116] I am. This is the supreme being.

But *to be* in this way is too exalted for us human beings, much too earnest. Therefore we must try to become something; to be *something* is easier.

Roguish, as everything related to humanity is, we express it in this way: earnestness is to be *something*.

Most men, or at least almost everyone, would die of anxiety about himself if his being should be—a tautology; they are more anxious about this kind of being and about themselves than about seeing themselves. So their situation is mitigated. The alleviation might be, for example: I am Chancellor, Knight of Denmark, member of the Cavalry Purchasing Commission, Alderman, Director of the Club. In a deeper sense all this is—diversion. But, to repeat, man is probably not able to bear true earnestness. What I am inveighing against is merely this lying, this making diversion into earnestness. And yet perhaps I am wrong here, too; for generally men would never be able to last it out if they weren't permitted to live in the illusion that this is earnestness; they would die of anxiety about life and about themselves at the mere thought that their earnestness is diversion, without, however, being deprived of this diversion.

But no doubt all these numerous predicates are actually diversions, distractions, which prevent a man from the deepest impression of this *to be*. And how infinitely far men now are from being able to bear the actual impression of earnestness is best seen from the fact that they have even made this predicative being into—Christianity. Nowadays men's inability to bear life's earnestness has gone so far that they must even be permitted to delude themselves that diversion is—Christianity.

XI^1 A 284 *n.d.*, 1854

BERNARD OF CLAIRVAUX

« 201

This is a sample of "Christendom." It is told of Bernard of Clairvaux[117] that parents held back their children and wives their husbands—lest Bernard should persuade them to become Christians in such a way that they actually forsook everything. And so it is always with the vital Christian. He is like the πεισιθάνατος[118] of antiquity to the extent to which he calls a person away from the sensate man's lust of the eye and the pride of life—and yet in Christendom we are all assumed to be Christians! And in our present age, when there lives not even one πεισιθάνατος.

x^2 A 377   n.d., 1850

BIBLE

« 202

It appears to me that on the whole the great mass of interpreters damage the understanding of the New Testament more than they benefit an understanding of it. It becomes necessary to do as one does at a play, where a profusion of spectators and spotlights seeks to prevent, as it were, our enjoyment of the play itself and instead treat us to little incidents— one has to overlook them, if possible, or manage to enter by a passage which is not yet blocked.

I A 54   May 1, 1835

« 203

Following the path of the commentators is often like traveling to London; true, the road leads to London, but if one wants to get there, he has to turn around.[119]

I A 55   n.d., 1835

« 204

It might seem strange that the New Testament ends with a prophecy (Revelation). Could this be a repetition of Judaism so that Christianity, too, finally points beyond itself? Not at all. Rather, it is like a mirror which casts the rays back again into the center of the Christian life; therefore it does not draw attention to something other-worldly but illuminates all the more brightly everything this-worldly. Therefore it is called "a revelation," not a forecast which is obscure until its fulfillment; it is the breath of the Christian life which is exhaled in the rest of the New Testament and now, so to speak, is inhaled again in the book of Revelation.

II A 287   November 1, 1838

« 205

There is something which one always ought to bear in mind while reading the Scriptures, that however much we may attribute to the radical continuity of perception running through the lives of the sacred authors, the temper of mind also had its right and exercised it, in order that this matchless victory over the world which sparkles around their transfigured countenances should not let us completely doubt our likeness, however remote, to these men of God. The deep sorrow, the terrible battles within our attitudes, must not allow us to doubt completely our strength to bear what is our lot to bear. Inasmuch as such instances remind us of the dark and bright hours in our own experience, we shall not lose equilibrium, we shall not imagine that everything is accomplished in one stroke, and we shall not despair when we see that this cannot be done.

II A 479   July 15, 1839

« 206

It is not easy to have both the Old and the New Testament, for the O.T. contains altogether different categories. What, indeed, would the N.T. say about a faith which believes that it is going to be well off in the world, in temporality, instead of giving this up in order to grasp the eternal. Hence the instability of clerical discourse, depending on whether it shows forth the Old or New Testament.

IV A 143   n.d., 1843

« 207

What is essentially Christian and the point in the fifth of the *Christian Discourses*[120] is specifically that the authority of the Bible is affirmed, that it is not something one has thought out but something commanded, something with authority, the command that tribulation is the task. Consequently the analogy of the child of whom the parents require something is continually used: in the same way the Bible, God's word, commands the parents. In an upbuilding or edifying discourse [*opbyggelige Tale*] I could not so rigorously maintain that the Bible says this.

VIII^1 A 20   n.d., 1847

« 208

The Holy Scriptures are the highway signs: Christ is the way.

VIII^1 A 50   n.d., 1847

« 209

In the main a reformation which sets the Bible aside would have just as much validity now as Luther's breaking with the pope. Emphasis on the Bible has brought forth a religiosity of learning and legal chicanery, sheer diversion. A kind of knowledge of this sort has gradually trickled down to the simplest people so that no one can read the Bible humanly any more. But this works irreparable damage; with regard to what it means to exist, its presence is like a fortress of excuses and escapes, etc., for there is always something we have to take care of first, always this illusion that we must first have the doctrine in perfect form before we can begin to live—that is, we never get around to the latter.

The Bible societies, those pale caricatures of the mission, an organization which quite like all the others operates essentially with money and is just as secularly busy about spreading the Bible as other businesses are in their enterprises—the Bible societies have done irreparable damage. Christendom has long needed a religious hero who in fear and trembling had the courage to forbid people to read the Bible. This is something just as necessary as preaching *against* Christianity.[121]

IX A 442   n.d., 1848

« 210 *The Principal Rule*

Above all, read the N.T. without a commentary. Would it ever occur to a lover to read a letter from his beloved with a commentary![122]

In connection with everything which qualitatively makes a claim of having purely personal significance to me, a commentary is a most hazardous meddler.

If the letter from the beloved were in a language I do not understand—well, then I learn the language—but I do not read the letter with the aid of commentaries by others. I read it, and since the thought of my beloved is vividly present and my purpose in everything is to will according to her will and wishes, I understand the letter all right. It is the same with the Scriptures. With the help of God I understand it all right. Every commentary detracts. He who can sit with ten open commentaries and read the Holy Scriptures—well, he probably is writing the eleventh, but he deals with the Scriptures *contra naturam*.

X^2 A 555   n.d., 1850

« 211

In margin of 210 (X^2 A 555):

That is, while reading the letter you are occupied with yourself and your relation to the beloved, but you are not objectively occupied with the beloved's letter, that this passage, for example, may be interpreted in ten ways—oh, no, the important thing for you is to begin to act as soon as possible. Besides, should it not mean something to be the lover, should it not give you what the commentators do not have? Everyone is the best interpreter of his own words, it is said. And next comes the lover, and in relation to God the true believer. *Pereat* the commentators!

X^2 A 556   n.d., 1850

« 212

When a person is almost afraid of tempting God by venturing essentially Christian actions, it is because he is not sure that the Bible is the word of God and that it appears in the word of God.

x^3 A 60   n.d., 1850

« 213 *The Bible—for the "Single Individual"*

Think of two lovers. The lover has written a letter to the beloved. Would it ever occur to the recipient to be concerned about how others will interpret this letter, or will he not read it all alone?

Suppose now that this letter from the lover has the distinctiveness that every human being is the beloved—what then? Is the intention now that they should sit and confer with one another, not to speak of dragging along the scholarly apparatus of countless generations?

No, the intention is that each individual shall read this letter before God solely as an individual, as the single individual who has received this letter by God or from God!

But it was soon forgotten that this letter is from God and entirely forgotten that it is to the single individual. The race has been put in his place. And therefore we have completely lost the impression of the Bible.

x^3 A 348   n.d., 1850

« 214 *The Primitive—the Traditional*

In our time scholarly doubt grows stronger and stronger and takes away one book after another. The orthodox give up hope. Remarkable! They assume that the New Testament is the word of God—but they seem completely to forget that God still exists [*er til*]. But the fact is that they do not believe but mimic history.

Suppose that doubt hit upon and came up with a kind of probability that Paul's letters were not by Paul and that Paul never lived at all—what then? Well, scholarly orthodoxy might give up hope. The believer might quite simply turn to God in prayer, saying: How can all this hang together? I cannot cope with all this scholarship, but I stick to Paul's teaching, and you, my God, will not allow me to live in error, whatever the critics prove about Paul's existence [*Tilværelse*]. I take what I read here in Paul and this I refer to you, O God, and then you will keep me from being led into error through my reading.

I could really be tempted to think that providence permits the scholarly, exegetical, and critical skepticism to get such a strong upper hand because providence is tired of the hypocrisy and all the mimicking which is carried on with the historical and historical proof and it wants to force men out into primitivity again. For primitivity, being obliged to be primitive, alone with God, without having others up front whom one mimics and appeals to—this men do not want at all. And with each century the historical millions and millions grow more and more numerous, and men also become more and more spiritless. Therefore it has pleased God that the critics who are degrading Christianity also get more and more power with the centuries. All spiritlessness is part and parcel of this historical throwing of oneself upon the heap of countless millions who have lived before us.

x^4 A 433   *n.d.*, 1851

« 215 *God's Word*

In order for one to rely upon a person, one requires that he give his word on it: God likewise has given us his word, his word on it—Christ is the Word.

x^4 A 437   *n.d.*, 1851

« 216 *The New Testament*

A young girl "16 summers old"[123]—it is her confirmation day. Among various elegant and beautiful gifts she also receives a beautifully bound New Testament.

Look, this is what they call Christianity! Actually they do not expect her to read it, not any more than the others, of course, or read it in any primitive way. She receives this book as a consolation in her life: Here you will find consolation if you should need it. Of course they do not expect her to read it, no more than the other young girls, and above all not primitively, otherwise she would discover that here are all the terrors, compared to which the ordinary terrors found in the world are almost a jest.

But look, this is Christianity. And this, too, is Christianity, this foolishness with Bible societies which distribute New Testaments by the millions.

No, I could be tempted to make another proposal to Christendom. Let us collect all the New Testaments there are and bring them out to an open place or up on a mountain and then, while we all kneel, let someone talk to God in this manner: Take this book back again. We human beings, such as we are, are not fit to involve ourselves with such a thing; it only makes us unhappy. I suggest that we, like those inhabitants

(Matt. 8:34), beg Christ "to leave the neighborhood." This would be honest and human talk—something different from this nauseating, hypocritical preacher-prattle about life being worthless to us without this priceless good, which is Christianity.

XI^1 A 347 *n.d.*, 1854

BOURGEOIS MENTALITY, PHILISTINISM

« 217

The bourgeois mentality or philistinism is essentially the inability to rise above the absolute reality of time and space and as such can therefore devote itself to the most exalted objects—for example, prayer at certain times and with certain words. This is what Hoffmann has always known how to emphasize so splendidly.[124]

I A 290   n.d., 1836

« 218

The opposite of bourgeois mentality is really Quakerism (in its most abstract sense)—the way in which it encompasses the uncertainty and accidentality found in most lives, on the whole an annihilation of historical development.

I A 301   n.d., 1836

« 219

The *bourgeois* always skip over one part of life, and from this comes their parodying relationship to those who outrank them. [.....]* To them morality is supreme, far more important than intelligence, but they have never felt enthusiasm for the great, for the talented, even in its extraordinary form. Their *morality* is a brief summary of the various police posters; the most important thing for them is to be a useful member of the state and to make after-dinner talk at a club—they have never felt homesickness for an unknown, remote something or for the profundity which is rooted in being nothing at all, in walking through Nørreport with four pennies in one's pocket and a slender cane in one's hand; they have no idea of the view of life[125] (which a gnostic sect made its own): learn to know the world through sin—and yet they too say one must sow his wild oats ("*Wer niemals hat ein Rausch gehabt, er ist kein braver Mann*"),[126] they have never caught a glimpse of the idea which lies underneath when we are pushed through the hidden, mysteri-

* [Omission by editor Barfod in *Efterladte Papirer*, the only extant copy of this entry.]

ous door, open in all its terror only to presentiment, into this dark realm of sighs—when we see the crushed sacrifices of seduction and deception and the coldness of the tempter.

II A 127   July 14, 1837

« 220

In margin of 219 (II A 127):

People reproach others for fearing God too much. Entirely correct, for rightly to *love God* presupposes *having feared* God. The bourgeois' love of God commences when the vegetative life is in full swing, when the hands are comfortably folded over the stomach, when the head is reclining on a soft easy chair, and when a drowsy glance is raised toward the ceiling, toward higher things. Compare the pantheistic "May it do *us* good" [*Velbekom's* (*Velbekomme os*)].

II A 128   n.d., 1837

« 221

In margin of 219 (II A 127):

"One should love his neighbor as himself,"[127] say the bourgeois, and by this they mean the well-brought-up children and now useful members of the state—those who have great susceptibility to every transient emotional flu—for one thing they mean that when someone is asked for a pair of scissors, even though he is some distance away, he will say "Righto!" and get up "with great pleasure" in order to fetch them, and for another that one will remember to pay the proper visits of condolence. But they have never felt what it means to have the whole world give them the cold shoulder, for the whole pack of social herring in which they live naturally does not permit such a relationship to occur; and then when serious help is needed, good common sense tells them that anyone who is in great need of them and in all probability will never be in a position to help them in return—he is not their* neighbor.

II A 130   July 19, 1837

« 222

Addition to 221 (II A 130):

After all, one has no neighbor, for the *I* is simultaneously itself and its neighbor, as illustrated by the expression, "One is closest to himself" (that is, one is his own neighbor).

II A 131   October 7, 1837

« 223

In the everyday life of the world one can scarcely be a success if one is not in the social register or has no honorary degree. But that, again, comes in time, especially if after one's death he is elevated to sainthood. True enough, the age of saints is past; they are not created any more; but Protestantism especially has actually become too conformed to the secular mentality for it to be done without sounding satirical. Take, for example, someone who when alive had been in the social register, honorary doctor, and father of five children (2 boys and 3 girls), of which one was married to Major Marcussen, the other to candlemaker Nielsen, the third unmarried, the one son married to wholesale merchant Jespersen's divorced wife, etc.—this story would be a complete satire. A saint's existence requires significant heterogeneity during his life. But from this one sees in a certain sense how shabby "reality" [*Virkeligheden*] is: having been very involved in it makes one ludicrous to the next generation.

IX A 475 n.d., 1848

« 224

How little resuscitation there is in life, after all, for one almost never gets a clear perception of the idea in an endeavor, but always mixed together with the illusions of finitude.

Let us take Hegel. How does he happen to become the great philosopher-author of seventeen volumes. Well, he probably had a pretty good head on his shoulders, was very industrious, and then he became B.A., M.A., and later professor—and now he begins to work. Now what call to life is there in this—always this triviality in the background: this is the way he makes a living. And then he probably makes money on his books—there we have it again.

To be sure, there is lofty talk that no one thinks about such things—well, maybe so, but it is the world's hypocrisy that at bottom it privately wants to have a shabby explanation of everything—and then talks in lofty tones. Make a test: place an endeavor right in front of people's noses (here in Copenhagen or wherever you want to), but a task which does not have a single illusion in it (neither money, office, honor, nor reputation), a task which, besides this, is so laborious and strenuous that one cannot speak of it as a kind of pleasure: and you will see, if people are encouraged in some way to express themselves completely openly, they will regard this man as crazy or as so peculiar that he teeters on the border of insanity.

There is constant talk in the world about wanting only the *truth*, etc., but something else is always implied. A journal which seeks only the truth: well, this is regarded as all right if the journal has many subscribers; to seek only the truth in this way is understandable. And why? Because the great number of subscribers shows that it is earning a lot of money and that the journal must have a great influence. Think of a journalist who wants only the truth, and consequently, if he originally had many subscribers, they steadily become fewer and fewer; at last he has so few that it is clear that he subsidizes the publication, and still he works just as diligently and industriously as anyone—and you will see that he is ridiculed or at least is regarded as odd.

Woe, woe, woe to these preachers who either are hulks who do not know how it all hangs together or are servile enough not to reveal it, fearing for their wages.

Opportunities come my way to discover this, even where I did not expect it. I can remember saying to Peter a year and a half ago: I believe I will give up being an author for good and start riding horses or something like that—and he answered (and with real earnestness): that would be the best thing to do. So purposeless, then, do my efforts seem to him. Had I become famous as an author, had I earned much money, then he would have said: You are not crazy after all.

IX A 483 n.d., 1848

« 225

Never is that evil, mediocrity, more dangerous than when it is dressed up as "geniality."

X^2 A 358 n.d., 1850

« 226 *The Highest Existentially—and the Lowest Existentially*

Let us begin with the poet. What the poet employs and immortalizes in his songs, in Juliet, for example, killing herself out of sorrow, etc. —this happens rarely in actual life.

Then the ethical-religious comes along and declares esthetic life to be despair and praises just the opposite, in Juliet's case, for example, to will to live.

But then the clergy come along, always accompanied by nonsense. They are not aware that sheer philistinism, regarded only from the outside, has a similarity to the ethical-religious highest. Karen, Maren, Mette, etc. never did kill themselves, although deprived of their respective lovers —these honored ladies, with the assistance of the reverend clergy, advance until they stand far ahead of Juliet.

The clergy do not at all detect the secret: if a life such as the one the "poet" can use is as rare as the poet insists—how rare a truly ethical-religious life must be! No, the pastors canonize philistinism, the bourgeois mentality. And now we Protestants have done away with the Catholic canonization of ascetics, martyrs, etc.—and in their place partners in philistine organizations are canonized, and quite fittingly they are canonized by that last ecclesiastical order to arise in Protestantism: the salaried brethren.

x^3 A 463   *n.d.*, 1850

CALL, CALLING, VOCATION

« 227

The error in the doctrine of predestination, which one will finally find in the N.T. if he is misled by a single word such as πρόθεσιν[128] (for example, Romans 8:28), consists in this: πρόθεσις means a preconceived plan, to be sure, but this is to be interpreted to mean the whole of Christianity, its manifestation in its wholeness was determined from eternity; the individual, on the other hand, is called[129] according to a teaching, of which the whole relationship to time is determined from eternity, but in such a way that it cannot thereby be stated that his call is from eternity.

I C 40   *n.d.*, 1834-35

« 228 *Those Who Were Called at the Eleventh Hour*

(Those who were called in the hour of death, the thief.)

We saw them, those who wandered along the way so carefree, so happy, so full of the joy of life, with the lightheartedness of youth and its lofty expectations; and the young congregated intimately around them and the adults were rejuvenated by the very sight of them. And now there they are, full of days, weary of life—and yet it was not glory and honor nor a striving for a glorious reputation which consumed their power; no, it was the confused enjoyment of pleasures, in whose service they had devoted the courage of their youth, their hope. Or should I describe to you the many who even in their youth lived in the world without the energy to work and without the heart to pray, like shipwrecked people who have lost everything, even faith and confidence in the possibility of beginning once again, the many who lived among us like dead ghosts, and when at times an intimation of power flared up in their souls, they lifted embittered, defiant countenances toward heaven and insolently demanded the return of that which they themselves had dissipated; or, if their disintegration did not vent itself in such a vigorous outburst, a quiet despair brooded over their minds. . . . . yet *these*, too, were called in the eleventh hour; perhaps to them, too, now, came the earnest but gentle voice which created hope within them.

Here one sees the great difference between the world and Christianity. The world is not without feeling; it will shed a tear for them, berate them. . . . . and let them go the way of perdition—but Christianity will not do this. And if now in such a person in the night of his despair the divine call evoked a living hope which flamed up in him with renewed strength, perhaps the world would be struck by this and would tolerate him. But should he fail at times, should the path become too narrow for him and be frequently marked by relapses, then the world would certainly break the staff on him; but if it is obliged to hear that they who are called in the eleventh hour are to have the same wages as those who bore the heat and the toil of the day, it would be *offended*.

But it is not like this with the Christian.

II A 581 *n.d.*, 1839

« 229

Out of life's various occupations. . . . . he called the people to himself, and they flocked to him in the *joyful* times when he lived upon the earth. He proclaimed the heavenly kingdom. Those who still sought the earthly kingdom he sternly dismissed: "Let the dead bury their dead" etc. . . . . . . and he himself went about among men as a shining example of how little a human being needs: "He had nowhere to lay his head; his *bread* was to do his father's will." And if he had then abandoned the earth, if after having taught them he had sent them away saying: Now I have cared for your spiritual well-being; now go away, go on and fill yourselves; I do not recognize these concerns; I scorn them—but he did not do this. I am consumed with pity for the people, he said. . . . . He did not appear in the clouds as an airy form beckoning to men, saying: Forget the cares of the world, forget its joys, and follow me. . . . . but he knew them, for he, too, had *hungered in the desert*. He does not divide, but unites, what God has joined, when he says: Seek ye first the Kingdom of God and his righteousness, and all these things shall be added unto you.

All these things shall be added unto us.

The situation here, we see, was that they had followed Christ in order to be taught, to be guided to find the kingdom of God; they did not demand food from him—and therefore it actually was *added unto* them.

We must note (1) God's caring for us, and if we are content we will find that there is always sufficient, even here in this poor country where one so often hears: How shall we find bread for so many in this barren county; for, as Luther has so well said, one never hears of a Christian dying of hunger.

(2) We must let our minds be led to higher things. Christ censures them later: they came to him not because they saw signs and miraculous acts but because they ate and were satisfied. God's concern for the earthly kingdom should, in fact, lead us to think upon higher things and not make us more and more unreasonable in our desires.

III A 87   n.d., 1841

« 230

..... And when God wants to join someone to himself, he calls upon his most faithful servant, his most reliable messenger, sorrow, and says to him: pursue him, overtake him, do not leave his side ..... and no woman can attach herself more jealously to the man she loves than does sorrow.

III A 191   n.d., 1841

« 231

What is regarded as real earnestness is a kind of training, the trained competence in being a husband, an office-holder, etc. If a person used his time in the service of the highest idea with enormous diligence and every sacrifice, or if a person spent his days on the dance floor and in taverns and dissipated his fortune—both would be regarded in the same way by these ossified bureaucrats. To be a clerk is earnestness, and if one is not a clerk, it makes no difference, absolutely no difference, who one is.

VII[1] A 165   n.d., 1846

« 232

Most men think that *earnestness* means to get an office, to be attentive to openings at a higher level which they can try to get, how they will make the move and what they then will do to adapt themselves. They think it is earnestness to move in exclusive society; they prepare more for luncheon with His Excellency than for communion, and when one sees them on the way they look so serious that it is shocking. All this I can understand well enough; what I cannot understand is that if this is truly earnestness, eternity becomes mere play. For in eternity there is neither promotion nor preferment; nor is there a moving day or luncheon with His Excellency.

VII[1] A 178   n.d., 1846

« 233

No one wants to be a "human being"—this is nothing to be. No one wants to be "a Christian"—this is nothing at all. Such tasks are not regarded as adequate for a life. Yet everyone strives and battles and grubs to become something. But this something is a departmental consultant or a fleet medical officer, etc.

VIII¹ A 368   n.d., 1847

« 234

... Magister Adler's[130] collision with the universal is, therefore, that of a special individual who has a revelation. To want to deny altogether the possibility of this extraordinary experience happening to a man in our age too would certainly have very dubious implications. But if there is nothing new under the sun, neither is there any direct, uniform repetition—there are continually new modifications. Our age is the age of reflection and good sense. It would be all right to assume, then, that the person who in our age is thus called by God would be related to his age. He no doubt would have superior reflective powers as an instrument at his disposal. This, then, would be the apparent difference between the "called" person in our age and one in an older age (for the essential likeness is and remains the call)—namely, that the called person in our age would have as his instrument a serviceable capacity for reflection, before which I, a humble critic, bow seven times, and before his call by revelation seventy times. The called person in our age will not merely be the instrument (spontaneous) but will consciously take possession of his call in quite another sense than what always has been the case in a divine call—to make up his mind about and to understand himself in this extraordinary thing that has happened to him.

To what extent it is possible to comprehend a divine call within human reflection, a joint activity, is a problem which I, a poor menial critic, do not dare presume to answer. The answer would first of all involve the life of the extraordinary person, were such a one to appear. But I can, up to a certain point, dialectically work through the idea until reflection runs aground.

If, then, everything is on the level in this matter of a man being called by a revelation, and he has a superior capacity for reflection at his disposal, he would understand that the ethical accompaniment to this call and this possession of a revelation is an enormous responsibility in all directions, not merely inwardly (that he himself was sure that this extraordinary thing had happened to him and understood himself in it, this we assume), but outwardly in relation to the established order, because in reflection the extraordinary has the dialectic not only of being the supreme salvation but also of being potentially the worst corruption. His responsibility in reflection would then be that he not become the worst misfortune for the established order and that with fear and trembling he see to it, as far as he is able, that no one is harmed by a direct relationship to his extraordinariness. If we now let the serviceable reflection give counsel all by itself, then the final consequence would be that he completely destroys himself, humanly understood, completely destroys his own impression, makes himself as humble and insignificant as possible, almost detestable, because in reflection (where every qualification is indeed dialectical) he properly understands that the extraordinary, beyond the point where it is in truth and is the extraordinary, is and can occasion the most frightful corruption. In the uttermost consistency of reflection he would then transform the fact of revelation itself into his life's deepest secret, which in deathly silence becomes the law of his existence, but which he never communicates directly. —But look, precisely this would be to fail completely in his task, in fact, would be disobedience to God. For the person who is called by a revelation is specifically called to appeal to his revelation; he must, in fact, use *authority* by virtue of being called by a revelation. In a religious revival it is not up to the person who has been awakened in an extraordinary way to go out and preach this to people; on the contrary, it can be completely right and pleasing to God and obedience to God for this to remain the awakened person's secret with God. But if the person who is called by a revelation and to communicate a revelation wants to be silent about the fact of the revelation, then he offends God and reduces God's will to nothing. It is the very fact of the revelation which is decisive; it is this which gives him *divine authority*. It does not depend—as they teach in the confused philosophy of our age—upon the content of the doctrine, but the fact of revelation and the divine authority which follows from it are decisive. If I imagined a letter from heaven, then it is not the contents of the letter, no matter from whom it came, which is the main point. The main point is that it is a letter from heaven. . . .[131]

VIII² B 13:61-63 *n.d.*, 1847

« 235

Youthfulness is looked upon with favor during certain years, but then one is supposed to become earnest—that is, be interested in money and finite things. It goes without notice that just as childlikeness the second time (becoming a child again) is the highest, so also youth and the recklessness of youth the second time are the highest—yes, only this, eternally understood, is earnestness. Temporality cannot possibly know what earnestness is, for earnestness is the relationship to the eternal—and in earnest, i.e., recklessly, absolutely.

IX A 387 n.d., 1848

« 236

The man and the ideal are separated from each other in this way. To be so situated as to be able to live for an idea, to be able to employ all one's time for this, is indeed closer to relating oneself to the ideal—although, of course, when the ideal is Christ there is the infinite qualitative difference between him and one who comes closest to him.

The people, the great majority of men, who must use most of their time in earning a living, in menial work—in regard to them it would be cruel to jack up the price. Here, however, a mildness and a consolation ought to be humanely provided, for the very reason that in such persons the essential concern may be that they are pained by not being able to live for something higher.

Truly, truly I have also always felt and acknowledged this: I have always been indescribably inspired by the fact that before God it is just as important to be a servant-girl, if that is what one is, as to be the most eminent genius. From this comes also my exaggerated sympathy for ordinary people, the common man. And therefore I can be very melancholy and sad about their having been led to ridicule me and thus having been deprived of the one who here at home loved them most sincerely.

No, the cultured and well-to-do class, who if not upper-crust are at least upper-bourgeoisie—they ought to be the targets and for them the price ought to be jacked up in the drawing rooms.

X^1 A 135 n.d., 1849

« 237

In another journal[132] I have drawn attention to the difference between secular advancement, where one continually craves and covets climbing one rung higher yet, and the opposite situation in spiritual advancement, where the man who is called intercedes for himself at every higher step he has to take, since he understands very well how, humanly speaking, the suffering becomes greater and greater.

From this comes the formula of the called life, that when the final race is to be run, the last step to be taken, it is usually with the help of repentance over having wanted to draw back. So it was with the apostle

Peter's denial. If there is a step which is too high for a person and yet has to be reached, this is the last power a man has, this repentance for having wanted to cheat.

x^2 A 194   *n.d.*, 1849

« 238 *The Call from Above—the Call from Below*

Every call from God is always addressed to one person, the single individual; precisely in this lies the rigor and the examination, that the one who is called must stand alone, walk alone, alone with God.

Everything which makes its appearance statistically is not from above; if anyone construes this as a call, you can be sure it is from below. This statistical approach is a slyness which wants to escape from rigorousness, the spirit-rigorousness of being spirit, and, using numbers, operates materialistically.

x^4 A 11   *n.d.*, 1851

« 239 *The Human—the Divine*

When a human sovereign, even if he were the most absolute, needs a person to keep others in line, how does he go about it? Well, he gives this person wine and cakes and sweet words and all earthly glory, etc.—and then says: Now go out and crack down on the others.

It is quite different with God. When he is going to use a person to bring the others in line, how does he go about it? This person is, so to speak, summoned [*kaldt op*]. Then, if I dare put it this way, God takes this person in his own hands and gives him a sound thrashing. And then he says: Go out and bring the rest in line. In the service of God the rule is that no one gets orders to thrash others more than he himself has been thrashed, or a fraction thereof.

Why the difference? Because God is in truth sovereign; God only figuratively "needs" a man, for God needs no one. Every human sovereign needs a man, and therefore he can express sovereignty only in the latter relationship.

x^5 A 22   *n.d.*, 1852

CATEGORY

« 240

What is the historical significance of the category? What is a category?

IV C 90   *n.d.*, 1842-43

« 241

Addition to 240 (IV C 90):
Shall the category be derived from thought or from being?

IV C 91   *n.d.*, 1842-43

CATHOLICISM

« 242

Insofar as the Catholics require (Möhler, Clausen, and Hohlenberg, *Tidsskrift*, II, 1, p. 182) fulfillment of the moral law, they apparently attribute only subordinate value to the Pauline development of man's relationship to the law[133]—that it is impossible for sinful, unregenerate man to fulfill it—and do not realize the far deeper meaning. For, as I see it, either the law must stand before man as something external—and then there is from the outset the implicit impossibility of fulfilling it—or it must have passed over into man completely and have been embodied as a principle; but then it is no longer law.[134]

I A 38   November 26, 1834

« 243

The use of the Latin language in worship within Christianity until now is analogous to the Jews' not daring to pronounce the name of God. There was advance to the point where the clergy could pronounce God's name, but the congregation is not able to do so.

II A 265   September 29, 1838

« 244

The Catholic Church is the contrast to Judaism—there it was God in his majesty who came down to earth and wanted to be clung to in his majesty (thundering on Sinai), and therefore that historical moment, when heaven was upon earth, is kept from reflection; whereas on the other side it was held to as tightly as possible; and just as God is in his majesty, so also the entire practice of worship has, along with the humility arising from the feeling of being nothing before the Lord, this very majesty outwardly—in the Church it is man who gradually ascends, lifted up and raised up by God—God begins with his abasement—Christ took upon himself the form of a servant and the pope still calls himself *servus servorum*. Judaism brings God down from heaven; Christianity brings man up to heaven.

I A 138   March 1836

CAUSE

« 245

The difference between the person who goes to his death out of devotion to an idea and the mimic who seeks a martyrdom is that whereas the first person lives most fully in his idea in death, the second person delights more in the curiously bitter feelings which result from being worsted; the former rejoices in the victory, the latter in his suffering.

I A 138 March 1836

« 246

That Napoleon always had poison in his possession is really an expression of the despairing energy with which he lived. Yet this is something compared to the animal sloth and routine security in which most human beings drowse—until they die. It is not really worth the trouble bothering with others, except those who have sacrificed their lives for a cause or at least have had enough religious or despairing energy to reflect on death every day.

VIII^1 A 168 n.d., 1847

« 247

..... "It is his own fault." Yes, this he has in common with all who have suffered for a conviction—it was their own fault.

VIII^1 A 405 n.d., 1847

« 248

..... It is still true: *it is blessed* to suffer mockery for a good cause; not only can one endure it, but it is blessed.

VIII^1 A 425 n.d., 1847

« 249

When a person voluntarily exposes himself to dangers and loss for the sake of a good cause, people reproachfully say, "It is his own fault," and become angry with him. What are they angry about? It is because of the voluntariness, the fact that he is disinterested, that he scorns what they aspire to as the highest. One can hurt a self-loving person in two ways: as a thief, a robber, gossip, et al., one can take away from him his earthly goods, but one can also by disinterestedness and sacrifice take the value away from those goods, those goods which he values as the highest. Men get just as bitter about the one way as the other. It is also a kind of reduction when that which a person regards as supreme and which he possesses is not actually taken from him but is shown to be empty and worthy of disdain.

VIII^1 A 526 *n.d.*, 1848

« 250 *To Have a Cause*

A. Lower forms

(1) Because it seems good in the eyes of men, a sign of earnestness, etc., one speaks uninterruptedly about having a cause, about wanting to work for the cause, everything for the cause—and he has no cause except that of wanting to please men by this talk about having a cause. Such people have no cause but dress something up, a display mannequin which they coddle as if it were a child.

(2) One has a kind of cause—but the cause, however, is consequential only to the point of gaining one's own advantage by having the cause.

(3) One has a cause but supports it in *every possible way* by clubbing together etc.; one is happy when someone, even through misunderstanding, joins up, for although one has a cause, he wants to spare himself as much as possible, i.e., one wants to have a cause as little as possible.

B. Higher forms

(1) Ethical irony and intellectual, unselfish interest, which have a cause to the degree that it is hidden in order to prevent the misunderstanding in being of help to someone.

(2) The martyrs who suffer for the cause. They need have no fear at all of getting the support of men, because where there is suffering, men flee. But in any case, they are still careful to parry assistance through misunderstanding, if it should be offered, because the cause is to them unconditionally the absolute, the *I* unconditionally nothing. This is what it is to have a cause in the highest sense.

X^4 A 76 *n.d.*, 1851

« 251 *God—God's Cause*

They talk about God's cause, about God's having a cause, about wanting to serve God's cause, etc.

That's all very fine, but the question is: how is this interpreted more precisely? In the long run it is most often interpreted as if God had a cause in the human sense of the word, were an advocate, *interested* in having his cause win and therefore willing to help the person who would serve his cause, etc. This way God actually becomes a somewhat minor character who finally even arrives at the embarrassing dilemma of *needing* human beings, those who honestly will to serve him.

No, no! In this sense God has no cause, is no advocate. For him everything is infinitely nothing. Any second he wills it, everything, everything is nothing—and that includes all opposition to his cause: but *ergo* in this sense he has no cause, is not finitely interested in having it win, etc. Infinite sublimity!

This is why wanting to serve God's cause does not mean the same as coming to his aid—but to be examined. If someone turns to God and says: I want to serve your cause, then it is not God who, so to speak (presumably because he is in hot water for having a cause), becomes hilariously pleased that someone wants to serve him—utter bosh and blasphemy! No, God is infinitely victorious, every moment is infinitely victorious—if someone wants to serve his cause, it is not God who—utter bosh and blasphemy!—who loses his balance and sublimity; no, he fastens his attention upon this volunteer—observantly, and sees how he conducts himself, whether he has integrity, etc. Precisely because God is not finitely interested in causes but is infinitely the conquering Lord, precisely for that reason he can, blessedly, see about it alone.

This is why the more one is involved with God the more rigorous everything becomes—it is God's infinite sublimity and still out of his infinite love that he wants to involve himself with a human being. The very fact that God permits evil people to thrive in this world is his infinite sublimity—O, you do not understand it, but God understands it—frightful punishment, that God overlooks them!—But he is rigorous and more rigorous with the good: O, we do not understand how blessed it ought to be for a man that God wants to involve himself with him, but God understands it.

Usually a person thinks that when he, as they say, honestly wants to serve God's cause, then God should also help along—well, how? In a material way? By successful outcome, prosperity, earthly advantage, etc.? But in that case everything goes backward and remains no longer God's cause but a finite cause like other causes—and maybe I was a cunning fellow, after all, who really did not want to serve God's cause but in a genteel way beguile God to my advantage—for (yes, it must certainly be because God is in hot water by having, in a finite sense, a cause) he became so happy that I wanted to serve his cause that he made a bargain. Utter bosh and blasphemy! No, God is spirit—and a man's task is to be transformed to spirit; but spirit is opposed precisely to being related to God by way of external evidence. This is God's sublimity. And it seems as if a poor human being must expire in this sublimity—and yet this is nevertheless the infinite love of God!

Yes, infinite love, infinite—that you desire to involve yourself with a human being, weak, foolish, carnal hearts who—because God indeed said of himself that he was love, as if he were love in a finite sense—try to make him into a nice uncle, a really fine grandfather whom we men can make good use of. The more sensate we are, the less we are of desire to be spirit.

Yet here also God is infinite love in that he does not suddenly all at once overpower a man and demand that he shall be spirit—in that case a man must perish. No, he handles him so gently; it is a long operation, an upbringing. There come times when one puffs a little and God strengthens the patient by finite means—but then on again. And there is one thing God requires unconditionally at every moment—integrity, that one does not reverse the relationship and prove his relationship to God or the truth of his cause by good fortune, prosperity, etc., but *on the contrary* understands that this happened because of his weakness, is an accommodation on God's part, very likely something he will omit at some later date—in order to make progress. It is further required of the patient every moment that he have the integrity every time he uses his wits to manage a little alleviation, a little relief, to record this immediately as a debit in his relationship to God, that he must not, for the sake of God in heaven, get conceited because of his brilliance—for then the relationship to God terminates altogether, and he probably becomes one of the most unhappy persons alive, one of those for whom everything succeeds in this world—because God's punishment is upon him in the fact that God has nothing more to do with him.

X^4 A 473   *n.d.,* 1852

CERTAINTY

« 252

Just as there is an a priori certainty in comparison with which every empirical fact is ephemeral, just so faith (according to Protestant doctrine) is the a priori certainty before which all the empiricism of works vanishes.

It is remarkable, however, in this regard that it is the Catholics who teach that one can have faith although he is in mortal sin; whereas the Protestants deny it (See *Apology* for the *Augsburg Confession*).[135]

I A 316   *n.d.*, 1837

« 253

What is this life, where the only certainty is the only thing one cannot with any certainty learn anything about: death; for when I am, death is not, and when death is, I am not.

IV A 187   *n.d.*, 1844

« 254

The same doubts which, in the contemplation of the world, nature, one's self, the course of events, line themselves up against belief in God—the same doubts may find a place in regard to Christianity. In respect to Christianity I cannot ask for a greater and different certainty than that which I have with respect to assurance about the existence [*Tilværelse*] of God. —It would be worthwhile, perhaps, to pursue this parallel sometime.[136]

VI A 9   *n.d.*, 1844-45

« 255 N.B.

Here again is one of the most important points concerning the God-relationship.

If a person could have empirical certainty that God wanted to use him as an instrument (as a king, a cabinet member)—how easily he would be able to submit to everything in every sacrifice. But is it possible to have an empirical or even a purely immediate certainty of a relationship to God? God is spirit. To a spiritual being it is impossible to have a relationship other than a spiritual relationship; but a spiritual relationship is *eo ipso* dialectical. —How then does an apostle understand that he has been called by a revelation and the like and has an immediate certainty which is not at all dialectical? I do not understand him—but this can be believed.

As far as an ordinary man's relationship to God and to Christ is concerned, this I understand Socratically. Socrates did not know definitely that there is immortality.[137] (O, the rascal, for the fact is that he knew that immortality is a qualification of the spirit and *eo ipso* dialectical and on the yonder side of all immediate certainty. Even though he did not know to what extent he was immortal—which so many dunces know positively—he nevertheless did know what he said.) But his life expresses that there is immortality and that he is immortal. Immortality, he says, preoccupies me so infinitely that I put everything into this *if*.

The relationship to Christ is this—a person tests for himself whether Christ is everything to him, and then says, I put everything into this. But I cannot get an immediate certainty about my relationship to Christ. I cannot get an immediate certainty about whether I have faith, for to have faith is this very dialectical suspension which is continually in fear and trembling and yet never despairs; faith is precisely this infinite self-concern which keeps one awake in risking everything, this self-concern about whether one really has faith—and precisely this self-concern is faith.

But what has brought such enormous confusion into Christianity is that preaching is done dialectically at one time and at another time as if faith were the immediate, the immediate certainty.

Alas, and all this, on which I could continue to work and ponder year in and year out—what do men care about it—not the slightest. And this shallowness is Christianity—and I, who in fear and trembling hardly dare call myself a Christian—I am mad, an eccentric.

IX A 32 *n.d.*, 1848

« 256 *A Different Kind of Certainty*

That Jesus Christ has lived here upon earth, by his suffering and death has saved the believers—that this is certain was once expressed by the fact that a person was sacrificed for it, died for it—it was that certain.

Now they get married for it—so certain is it—but is it really that certain?

XI^2 A 330 *n.d.*, 1854

CHANGE, COMING INTO EXISTENCE

« 257

Dec. 1, 1841-42.

In what Werder has covered so far, there are two points which I believe must have significance for every undertaking in dogmatics. The one is the transition from *Werden* to *Daseyn*;[138] the other is the transition from changeableness to unchangeableness, finitude to infinitude. *Entstehen* (*Nichts in Seyn*) and *Vergehen*[139] (*Seyn in Nichts*) are in each other: this expressed as rest, as product, is consequently not *werden* but *was geworden ist*, i.e., *Daseyn*.[140] This sounds good enough, but it involves sheer play with the concept of time, which is not given and which I think cannot be given in logic anyway. *Etwas* and *Anderes*[141] are not merely in each other, but *Etwas* is only insofar as it is *Anderes*, and *Anderes* only insofar as it is *Etwas*; they fashion each other. The movement is a redoubling [*fordobler sig*]. On one side *Etwas*. As an *sich*[142] it is *Etwas*; as a being for another it is *Anderes*—*Anderes* is *an sich Anderes*; as a being for another it is *Etwas*. But thereby *Etwas* consequently is— through *Anderes*; and consequently *Etwas* is not only *Anderes* but *nur Anderes*, and this is expressed by *Andersseyn*,[143] but this expressed as unity is change. —Finitude is what *am Ende ist*;[144] consequently the finite is *was gewesen ist*.[145] But infinitude? It is finitude which is not itself (nonfinitude—both); consequently it is infinitude: *was nicht gewesen ist*. Insofar as this is to be the expression for the significance of finitude, it manifestly has not received its due.

III C 30   December 1, 1841-42

« 258

The transition from possibility to actuality is a change—thus Tennemann translates κίνησις;[146] if this is correct, this sentence is of utmost importance (see p. 127).

κίνησις is difficult to define, because it belongs neither to possibility nor to actuality, is more than possibility and less than actuality (see p. 128).

Continuation and decay are not κίνησις.

There are three kinds of κίνησις:
  with respect to quantity
     αὔξησις–φθίσις[147] (decrease)
  with respect to quality or accidental characteristics
     ἀλλοίωσις[148]
  with respect to place
     φορά[149]

             IV C 47 n.d., 1842-43

« 259

In margin of 258 (IV C 47):
All this deserves attention with respect to movements in logic.

             IV C 48 n.d., 1842-43

« 260

Hegel has never done justice to the category of transition. It would be significant to compare it with the Aristotelian teaching about κίνησις.

In margin: see Tennemann III, p. 125; he translates the word κίνησις as *change*.

             IV C 80 n.d., 1842-43

« 261

Can there be a transition from quantitative qualification to a qualitative one without a leap? And does not the whole of life rest in that?[150]

             IV C 87 n.d., 1842-43

« 262

What has happened has happened[151] and cannot be undone—only to this extent is the past changed, but this change is not a change into necessity, which would indeed be a contradiction, since what was not previously necessary would become necessary (i.e., everything necessary presupposed as necessary); it never becomes necessary, since only that can become necessary which was necessary, but consequently was necessary before it became necessary. Therefore, the necessary cannot come into existence [*blive til*], for this is the same proposition that nothing by its coming into existence [*tilbliven*] or in its coming into existence can become the necessary.

What has happened has happened as it has happened, but could it therefore not have happened otherwise?[152]

In what sense is there change in that which comes into existence; that is, what is the nature of the change of coming into existence; for all other change presupposes the existence [*at det . . . er til*] of that which changes, even when the change consists in ceasing to exist [*at være til*]. That which comes into existence [*det tilblivende*] certainly does not do this by becoming greater or lesser or, if it consists of parts, by way of some change taking place in these, in their relationship, and thereby in the whole, etc.; for if the subject of coming into existence does not itself remain unchanged in the change of coming into existence, it is not *this* subject of coming into existence which comes into existence but something else, whereby the question is only postponed and is not answered. The subject of coming into existence remains unchanged, therefore, or only suffers or takes upon itself the change of coming into existence, but what is this? Thus if my plan, for example, is changed in coming into existence [in being fulfilled or carried out], it is then no longer my plan and it is another plan which comes into existence, but if it comes into existence unchanged, then it is my plan which comes into existence; this constitutes the unchanged, but coming into existence is also a change. This change is from not being to being [*ikke at være til at være*]. But this non-being from which it is changed must also be a kind of being [*en Art af Væren*], because otherwise we could not say that the subject of coming into existence remains unchanged in coming into existence. But such a being which is nevertheless a non-being we certainly could call possibility, and the being into which the subject of coming into existence goes by coming into existence is *actuality* [*Virkeligheden*]. Therefore the change of coming into existence is the change of actuality. In coming into existence the possible becomes the actual. But could it not also become the necessary? Not at all, and therefore we still maintain that coming into existence is a change, but that the necessary cannot be changed, that it is always related to itself in the same way. Therefore everything which can come into existence shows in this very way that it is not the necessary. The necessary* is by no means a change in being, as is actuality in relationship to possibility, where the essence continues essentially unchanged. But if the possible by becoming the actual did become the necessary, its essence would become changed, and thus one can understand that it cannot become the necessary, for if it became the necessary, it would no longer be itself. The necessary is therefore not a qualification of being, and one says, even though he expresses himself somewhat differently, one says not that it is necessary but that the neces-

* *Obliquely in margin:* Necessity is the unity of possibility and actuality.

sary is; one does not say that because it is, it is the necessary, but that since it is necessary, therefore it is.*

* *In margin:* Nothing ever comes into existence by necessity, and if, for example, the world must have come into existence by necessity, it would never have come into existence. (This has significance for creation —repentance in ethics.)

VB 15:1   *n.d.*, 1844

« 263

The difference is misunderstood in the newest philosophy (when Trendlenburg quite properly points out that we ought to begin with κίνησις), as if the question were merely whether we should *begin* with being or with becoming. No, the question about becoming, about movement, comes again at every point; if we do not begin by presupposing κίνησις, we do not move from the spot with *seyn*; if, however, we assume motion, then we can bring it to a halt at every point, because getting away from the initial spot already involved κίνησις.[153]

X^2 A 324   *n.d.*, 1849-50

« 264

On the subject of pilgrimages, Gregory of Nyssa says most excellently: "One does not come closer to God by changing one's place."[154] Oh no, it is all too clear that this is done only by changing oneself.

X^2 A 561   *n.d.*, 1850

CHILDHOOD, CHILDREN

« 265

If after reading the essay someone were to say that I do indeed speak of *the art of storytelling*[155] but in the entire essay seem rather to rant *against it*, I would not *wholly* agree, inasmuch as I have spoken only against misuse, and I would also point out that I have used the expression *storytelling* in a more comprehensive sense involving everything with which one occupies a child's mind outside of formal schooling, not all of which can accurately be called play, and in which, of course, storytelling does play a major role.

That so many people are engaged in telling stories to children is a natural consequence of the fact that there are a great number of children and that children have a deeply rooted desire to hear stories, and yet there are very few people who have talent for storytelling. As a result much harm is done. There are two recommended ways of telling stories to children, but between these two there is a multiplicity of wrong ways.

First, there is the way which children's nurses (and others who may be so categorized) unconsciously follow. They open up a whole world of fantasy to the child, and the fact that they are sincerely convinced of the truth of their stories* must instill a salutary tranquillity in the child, no matter how fantastic the content itself may be. Only when the child himself detects that the teller does not believe stories are the stories damaging—yet not because of the content itself but because of the untruth in regard to the teller—because of the mistrust and suspiciousness which the child gradually develops.

The *second* way can be followed only by someone who in perfect clarity has reproduced the life of childhood, who knows what this life requires, who knows what is good for it and now from this vantage point offers children intellectual-emotional nourishment which is beneficial for them, who knows *how to be* a child; whereas the nursemaids basically *are* children. (Fortunately, children are able to derive good from both ways, and following the second way certainly does not exclude appreciation of

---

* "Nursery-tales"—this expression implies just as much about the mode of telling the tales as it does about the content.

the first. On the other hand, the semieducated usually eliminate the process of development valued by one who has a mature view of life.)

The preparation is not elaborate. The husband comes home from the busy office, puts on his slippers, gets his pipe, kisses mother on the cheek and says, "Well, my dear" (this is to accustom the children to affectionate behavior)—and now we see a scene common to most children's books—"Uncle Frank," who tells the stories which the children have eagerly anticipated all day, and little Fritz and Mary coming on the run, clapping their hands: "Uncle Frank* is going to tell stories!" The mother clusters the children around her, with the smallest in her arms, and says, "Listen nicely, now, to what your dear uncle is telling!"

As for the procedure for the storytelling, for our storytellers—all general pursuits on behalf of children outside of formal instruction, and this, too, as much as possible, should be *Socratic*. One should arouse in children a desire to *ask*, instead of fending off a reasonable question, which perhaps goes beyond Uncle Frank's general information or in some other way inconveniences him, with the words: "Stupid child! Can't he keep still while I am telling the story?" To prevent more serious scenes, the mother assures that "he will not do it any more." The whole point is *to bring the poetic into touch with their lives in every way*, to exercise a power of enchantment, to let a glimpse appear at the most unexpected moment and then vanish. One should not schedule the poetic for certain hours and certain days. Children do not jump around such a person like loutish calves with dangling legs and clap their hands because they *are going to hear* a story. *Him* they approach in an open, free, confident way, entrust themselves to him, initiate him into many little secrets, tell him about their play, and he knows how to join in, also knows how to give the game a more serious side. The children never distress him or pester him, for they have too much respect and esteem for him.**

---

* Unfortunately there is a reason for its always being *an uncle* who appears as the central figure, for the parents' activity is usually limited to making their appearance on the monthly day-of-reckoning as chief administrators or presenters of prizes for noble deeds—in both cases with the precise and punctual conscience of a bookkeeper. If, then, there were any uncles, there would undoubtedly be plenty for them to do.

** *We ourselves ought to learn from children*, from their marvelous creativity, which—unlike certain self-important tutors—we ought to allow to prevail, remembering Christ's words when he was twelve years old, "Did you not know that I must be about my father's business?" —(I believe I have read something similar in one of Mynster's sermons.)[156] It is better not to be quick with the prosaic switch, as was the schoolteacher in *Alferne*,[157] because children have deep feelings—and in this way one avoids, among other things, (O divine nemesis!) falling 1400 yards down beneath the earth and becoming—a ninny.

He knows what they are doing in school. He does not do their homework with them but quietly inquires about their lessons, masters them, not in order to quiz them, not to take a particular part and dramatize it for them, not to give them an opportunity to show off if there are others around—but rather to let a glimpse suddenly leap forth, to connect it in a special way to what usually occupies them, yet entirely *en passant*, so that the child's soul is electrified and feels, as it were, the omnipresence of something poetic, which is indeed precious to him but which he nevertheless dares not approach too closely.* *In this way* an intellectual-emotional mobility is constantly nurtured, a continuing attentiveness to what they hear and see, an attentiveness which otherwise has to be produced by *external* means, for example, by having the children come from a dimly lighted room into a brightly lighted room, where "Uncle Frank" is sitting, by wearying them the whole day by talking about "how wonderful" it is to hear Uncle Frank tell stories—etc.

However, even though clarity prevails, a certain sentimentality can easily intrude if one forgets that adulthood has what childhood promised. We are inclined, however, to think that it promised a lot more, especially when dealing with exceptionally alert children, and so we intervene alarmingly in their lives (anxiety can actually stem from this cause and not always from trivial complaining). Those daily assurances, "You are happy now, but wait until you are older**—then the troubles will come," etc., have a *harmful effect*, inasmuch as they strike at the roots of the child and instill a peculiar anxiety as to how long he can continue to be happy (and in this way they *are* already unhappy). If this continuous Jeremiad makes no impression, it naturally has the same harmful effect as all other misplaced chatter.

This indefiniteness [in the Socratic approach] might seem to militate against a certain very proper demand for rigor and clear limitation; this should rather be represented in the schoolroom in the personality of the teacher (here we are concerned with free time). He who in childhood has never been under the *gospel* but only under law never becomes free†

---

* Children are not deeply interested in Greek mythology, at least not in that which in more mature years is regarded as the most magnificent (yet Hercules, possibly—N.B. extraordinary deeds).

** Many begin this so early, while the children are still very small, that occasionally it occurs to such a child to do as the baby Abraham St. Clara tells about, who saw the miserableness of the world so vividly at the time of birth that it ran back into its mother's womb again. —Is this a way to *strengthen* a child for life? Does this not enervate the child's whole life by depriving it of *enthusiasm's perpetuum-mobile*?

† A *state* becomes in a sense unfree in that it gives itself law.

—maybe this is wrong, but there is something noble in it; whereas the more the law is propounded, the more minor mischief germinates, and nothing is more capable of producing enervation. The eye has a power to call forth sprouts of the good and to crush the evil—but misinterpreted rigor and discipline, a daughter of indolence, almost permits one generation to take revenge upon the next for the thrashing it received itself and for the mishandling it has suffered—by treating the next generation in like manner.

But then shouldn't one tell stories? Certainly, mythology and good fairy stories are what the child needs. Or the child is allowed to read them himself and tell them and is then Socratically corrected (gradually correcting by questioning in such a manner that the child is by no means set straight under the coercion of a tutor but seems rather to be correcting others—and anyone who otherwise understands how to handle children will certainly not be in danger of encouraging arrogance). But above all let this be impromptu, not at a set time and place; children should experience early in life that happiness is a fortunate constellation which one should enjoy with gratitude but also know how to discontinue in good time; and above all one should not forget *the point of the story*. (A mistake I can only touch upon here, although it comes up again later, is this: continually and almost all day long to tell trashy, empty stories and thereby manufacture these readers of novels who devour a volume a day, one after the other, without any specific impression.) Furthermore, one evokes a certain self-activity (drawing and the like) because the story, told in various ways, becomes related to a child's familiar environment.

Now comes the question: *what significance* does childhood really have? Is it a stage with significance only because it conditions, in a way, the following stages—or does it have independent value? Some have expanded the latter position to the point where they assume childhood to be fundamentally the highest level attainable by human beings and that everything beyond it is progressive degeneration. The first position has had the practical result that people try to make time pass by*—and if children could be shut up in the dark and force-fed on an accelerated schedule like chickens, everything would certainly be organized to this end. Another consequence has been to use this "tiresome time of childhood" primarily for caring for children's physical well-being. In this view the supreme rule of upbringing runs something like this: "The child who does not clean up his plate gets no dessert."—(How frequently children's

---

* This is rooted in the haste of the times, which basically misunderstands every age because it believes that each age-level exists merely for the sake of the next.

lives, particularly girls', are embittered by hearing continually that they are good for nothing, etc.)

The *mistaken ways* come about because one passes beyond the nursemaid's position but does not go the whole way and thus remains stationary at the halfway point.

First stage. Those who have gone beyond the stage of spontaneity, instead of now in their mature years assimilating childhood transfigured, as would be natural, decay into "being children" (compare *fountain-of-youth*), those overgrown puppies who are so innocent and naive, who would give anything if their beards never grew enough to require a shave so that they could remain downy, bare-necked youths, who have become children again to such a degree that they talk as children, use all the childish expressions, and who would like ultimately to get all of us to talk as children and write as children talk—a caricature which will surely come to be as soon as the opposite, that children want to be grown-ups, which is common now, has been outlived. It is a tragic-comic sight to see these gangly, childish jumping-jacks leaping around the floor and riding the hobby-horse with the sweet little ones and to hear their dull stories about "innocent and happy childhood."* (Compare their behavior with that of adolescent girls who want to be grown-up: they parody one another.)

Their stories "for children and childlike souls"—poetic rinse-water! If this error is found most often among youth, there is also a similar mistaken way among adults who "descend" to children out of the conviction that childhood in itself is so empty and devoid of content that they wish, as it were, to breathe fullness into it. Basically both points of view must presuppose the emptiness of childhood, for otherwise the former would not permit itself to undertake anything so loathsome, something a sound nature would immediately censure, and the other would not undertake to breathe the spirit of life into it.

After a story has been told, it is important not to destroy the entire

---

* Compare Hamann, *Fünf Hirtenbriefe, das Schuldrama betreffend, Sämtl. Werke,* II, pp. 412 ff. But here his all too polemical irony goes too far; basically he maintains that one should learn everything from children in the strictest sense, and therefore his motto reads: "*Es ist ein Knabe hier, der hat fünf Gerstenbrot,*"[158] which obviously says too much. But this is again consistent with his whole tendency, for no doubt he says this not because he himself believes it but in order to humble the world. It is quite different with Socrates—to question as a child—something Hamann also demands; but it is that peculiar polemic which makes him prefer hearing wisdom from Balaam's ass rather than from the wisest man, from a Pharisee against his will than from an apostle or an angel (as he himself says somewhere). His polemic goes too far and is at times, it seems to me, somewhat blasphemous, as if he wanted "to tempt God." —Otherwise there are, of course, excellent things in these five letters.

impression by ending with a "But you do understand, don't you, that it was *only* a fairy tale?" This sort of thing reappears later in people who have absolutely no sense for the poetic and consequently spoil the impression of every anecdote, etc., by probing its factual truth.

The fantastic and lopsided tendency which storytelling has assumed. It has been considered unreasonable and damaging later to overstock the child's imagination with such stories. On the other hand, it has been considered quite all right to tell something to while away the time and amuse the children. Since it was merely for diversion and they did not want to spend time in preparation,* they started those interminable silly tales about the dog and the cat, etc., telling them with the most horrible monotony. The children, once they are spoiled, continually demand more and more editions of the same, always returning** to the stereotype with one or more important alterations (for example, that once it was a red dog, then a black one).

In the meantime this view was discovered to be wrong, since, indeed, the time could be utilized better, could be used for something better even in the form of jest and play. Two procedures evolved from this—*either* educate the children morally, as it is called, *or* impart some useful knowledge. The consequence of the second path I shall touch upon slightly. There came as if by magic a plague of natural history, not textbooks but

---

    * Those clever people who think it is not an art to speak with children—to them I say with Hamann: *"Kindern zu antworten ist in der That ein Examen rigorosum; auch Kindern durch Fragen anzuholen und zu witzigen ist ein Meisterstück, weil eben Unwissenheit der grosse Sophist bleibt, der so viele Narren zu starken Geistern krönt—et addit cornua pauperi.*¹⁵⁹ (Horace, Ode III, 21.)

    ** Once in a while such people accidentally remember a more fanciful story from their childhood, but they tell it in order to answer the question which comes up as soon as they are finished—"Are there mermaids like that?"—with a "No, mermaids are just something people imagine." Is the fairy tale then *so* meaningless that one must immediately destroy the story and its impression, that one must promptly break the glittering soap bubble in order to show that all its glory was nothing more than soapy water? Children crave fairy stories, and this alone is sufficient proof of their value. —Now the question arises—to what extent *should the storyteller himself believe these stories?* If the storyteller himself believes the stories, then I do not think the question will arise for the children as to whether or not it is true. The story should simultaneously exercise such an overwhelming and tranquilizing effect that it never occurs to the children. Not to tell children such exciting imaginative stories and tales leaves an unfilled space for an anxiety which, when not moderated by such stories, returns again all the stronger (compare Tieck, *Die Verlobung*; Dresden: 1823; pp. 63-65). Compare also the artless, simple story in *Nordisk Kjæmpehistorier* II, ed. Rafn; Copenhagen: 1827 (N.B. naturally the story is not by Rafn), especially the end, p. 9: "Can it be that someone who hears these stories will find that the mighty events and great deeds of the sagas do not square with his experience and for that reason will minimize them"—right: *hinc illæ lacrymæ!*

reading books and all kinds of picture books to impart to the children the vocabularies of modern languages, and "Uncle Frank" told of his travels in Africa and designated the plants and animals by their scientific names, and parents and others asked: "What is *nose* in French?" etc. Or one taught them to pick out a simple piece on the piano. (If one really wishes by such things to keep children from being embarrassed by being conspicuous, then on the other hand one really ought not make children eager to be conspicuous.)

Out of all this there developed a completely atomized knowledge which did not enter into a deeper relationship to children and their existence [*Existents*], which was not *appropriated* in an intellectual-emotional way, and which was thus deprived of any possible standard. As a result people fell into the presumption that they were great natural scientists and linguists. If only details are decisive, it is naturally quite incidental how many or how few are required for mastery. Out of this arises seductive opportunism—and the busy Martha's who forget the one thing needful. Of such atomized knowledge it is not true that what is assimilated in youth is never forgotten in old age.

With regard to the *mode* in which I believe it is necessary for all instruction and upbringing to allow the child *to bring forth the life within him in all stillness*, I find a good observation in reading Steffen's *4 Nordmænd*. Regrettably I have only the Danish translation, the Steen edition. The passage is in Part II, p. 250-52.

I remember an example of how in such a life everything becomes engendering, how everything the children read in the classics became reflected; when they read of ostracism, they introduced it at once into their play, etc.

And now those children's books for "well-behaved, industrious, obedient, lovable, innocent, unspoiled" children—consequently by presenting them with a copy one says to them that *they are such*, since otherwise it would be a misunderstanding to give them the book.*

II A 12   *n.d.*, 1837

« 266

Childhood is the paradigmatic part of life; adulthood its syntax.—

II A 41   *n.d.*, 1837

* I note a *good title* in the latest catalog: Blumauer, *die kleinen Enkel auf dem Schoosse der erzählenden Grossmutter, ein Gegenstück der kleinen Enkel am Kniz des erzählenden Grossvaters*.[160] (Exhibition catalog for July, 1836—January, 1837, p. 27, top.)

« 267

It is a dreadful thing if a person's consciousness from childhood on has been under a pressure which all the resilience of the soul and all the energy of freedom cannot remove. Sorrow in life can certainly oppress the consciousness, but if the sorrow comes for the first time in later years it does not have time to become essentially formative; it remains a historical element, not something which encompasses, as it were, the consciousness itself. One who has such pressure from childhood is like a child who is plucked from his mother's womb with forceps and always has a reminder of the mother's pain. Such a pressure cannot be removed, but one does not therefore need to despair, for it can be borne with humility. It is undeniably one of the most difficult tasks, for it is very difficult to include it within the category of guilt. There was a time when, for fear of becoming proud of my sufferings, I formulated the thesis that basically everybody suffers equally. Yet this, after all, is a kind of Stoicism, which by abstraction annuls the more concrete conception of providence. Pontoppidan says in his *Explanation* that particular persons are tried in unusual sufferings, but at some time this will benefit their souls. This is far more beautiful.

IV A 60   *n.d.*, 1843

« 268

When one is a child and has no toys, one is well provided for, because then imagination takes over. I still remember with amazement my childhood top, the only toy I had—what acquaintance was as interesting as this one? Yet it did not belong wholly to me. It had, so to say, its official duties as an actual top, and only then in its leisure did it become my diversion. In our day there are complaints that an official holds too many offices, but this one encompassed all.

V A 2   *n.d.*, 1844

« 269

Fundamentally everyone is born to rule. This is best seen in children. Today I saw a little girl in her nurse's arms. They met some acquaintances of the child's family. The nurse held a flower in her hand, and now everybody, each and all, very submissively had to smell the flower and say, "Achoo!" This was repeated several times. If the nurse wanted to skip someone, the little girl noticed it at once and gave her to understand that she had to do everything exactly right. And then the little female sovereign bestowed with a smile her highest favor upon the one who sneezed exactly right.

Then the nurse wanted her to walk, but she leaned out a bit from the nurse's arms, dropped her head coyly, and rewarded the nurse with a kiss from beneath—affectedly, and yet with a childlikeness.

VI A 96 *n.d.,* 1845

« 270

Take a child who has not been spoiled by chatter and by letting him memorize that Christ was crucified; take such a child, place in front of him several different pictures—a man with a three-cornered hat on a horse, etc., Alexander, Napoleon, and the like—and place among them a picture of the crucified one. The child, with this picture as with every one of the others, asks: Who is it? Say to the child: That was the most loving man who ever lived—then the child will ask: But who killed him and why did they kill him?

O, even though one has become an adult but still has retained some childlikeness—how gripping it can be when walking by a store with Nürnberg pictures in the window he sees this picture among all the others.[161]

IX A 395 *n.d.,* 1848

« 271

On the words of Paul:
> When I was a child, I spoke like a child, I thought like a child, I reasoned like a child; when I became a man, I gave up childish ways.[162]

one could speak on the theme:
> *what judgment do you make on your childhood and youth?* Do you judge that it was foolishness and fancies? Or do you judge that you were at that time closest to the Most High?

Just tell me how you judge your childhood and your youth, and I will tell you who you are. Say it to yourself how you judge, in order that you might come unto wisdom, for wisdom is nothing else than to judge childhood and youth rightly, together with expressing it in one's life that he judges rightly.

X^2 A 97 *n.d.,* 1849

« 272

The Sunday between Christmas and New Year, Epistle: Gal. 4:1-7. Theme: God's upbringing or our upbringing by God.

1) First we are slaves under the law, 2) then we become children, 3) then children who cry Abba, Father, and co-heirs of Christ.

Consequently there is an increasing openness in relation to God. But it is not like the relationship between adults and children, in which the openness comes after the child has grown up; here it is the reverse—one does not begin as a child but as a slave, and the openness increases as one becomes more and more a child.

As I have noted in another journal,[163] the increase of inwardness in the relationship to God is indicated by the fact that it goes backward for a person; one does not come closer to God *directly*; on the contrary, one discovers more and more deeply the infinite distance. Therefore one does not begin by being a child and then become progressively more intimate as he grows older; no, one becomes more and more a child.

x^2 A 320   *n.d.*, 1849

CHRIST

« 273

Christ's whole life in all its aspects must supply the norm for the life of the following Christian and thus for the life of the whole Church. One has to take every particular aspect of Christ's life straight from his baptism to his resurrection and show correspondence in the Church.—Moreover, it is natural that with regard to the view that Christ existed simply to act (a view which, after all, I naturally do not insist upon, and all the less so since the preaching of the Word continues in the Church and consequently must be regarded as corresponding to Christ's teaching), it is, I say, natural that a great many people should object considerably—in part those who believe that Christ really was sent to communicate a perfect morality to mankind, in part the Catholics, for example, who believe that they still are able to fulfill the law. In spite of all this I believe that his activity was the principal thing, because that life which he enjoins (Matt. 5) cannot blossom forth before regeneration; consequently this is the *conditio sine qua non*; and, on the other hand, this life must necessarily unfold in him who is truly regenerated.

I Corinthians 5:7; Ephesians 5:2; Romans 3:25.

I A 28   November 26, 1834

« 274

What the Jews and many others later demanded of Christ, that he should prove his divinity, is unreasonable, for if he really *were* God's son, proving it would be a farce, just as ridiculous as if a human being were to prove his existence [*Tilvær*], since in this case Christ's existence [*Tilværen*] and his divinity [*Gudværen*] are the same—and if he were a fraud, he most certainly would have been able to play the role well enough to perceive that just when he proved his divinity he would contradict himself.

I A 53   April 19, 1835

« 275

I also think that one might be able to present entirely a priori a proof of Christ's actual death, for it surely must be accepted as belonging to his truly human development.

I A 210   n.d., 1836

« 276

The thesis that it cannot be true that Christ was born of a virgin because something similar is said of Hercules, etc., and in Indian mythology, etc., which is not true, is rather curious, since in a certain respect the opposite conclusion seems more correct: precisely because they say this about so many other great men for whom it was not true—for this very reason it must be true of Christ, for the fact that it has been said so often points to man's need for it. If, with regard to a new direction which would manifest itself and which people at times declared had emerged, without its being therefore true, if someone concluded from this that it would never take place, might he not come to an erroneous conclusion, and might not someone who now expected it be more right?

I A 232   September 9, 1836

« 277

It is really remarkable that Christ came to be precisely 33 years old, the number of years which according to general reckoning denotes a generation, so that here too there is something normal, in that whatever goes over this number is accidental.[164]

I A 325   January 22, 1837

« 278

When God had created the whole world, he looked at it and—behold, it was very *good*;[165] when Christ died upon the cross, he said—"It is *finished*."[166]

II A 93   June 9, 1837

« 279

It is certainly true, as Daub says (Bauer's *Tidsskrift*),[167] that the whole story of Christ's life is contained in three statements: Did you not know that I must be in my Father's house?[168] I must work the works of him who sent me, while it is day; night comes when no one can work.[169] It is finished.[170] But one should not forget three others: And the child grew and became strong, filled with wisdom (Luke 2:40). He is tempted.[171] My God, my God, why have you forsaken me?[172]

II A 97   June 12, 1837

« 280

People rant so much against anthropomorphism and forget that Christ's birth is the greatest and the most significant anthropomorphism.

II A 133   July 15, 1837

« 281

Christ did not go in for writing—he wrote only in sand.

II A 675   October 2, 1837

« 282

Even though in an inverted way, a true token of the true Christ would nevertheless be the same as of the true Eve: this is flesh of my flesh and bone of my bone.

II A 197   November 23, 1837

« 283

The birth of Christ is an event not only on earth but also in heaven, but our justification is also an event not only on earth but also in heaven.

II A 594   n.d., 1837

« 284

At every moment Christ is God just as much as he is man—just as the sky seems to be as deep in the sea as it is high above the sea.[173]

II A 595   n.d., 1837

« 285

Christ walks in history as he walked in life (his earthly life)—between two robbers: one of whom hardens his heart, the other repents.

II A 713   April, 12, 1838

« 286

One of the exclamations in which the humanity of Christ appears most forcefully is his remark to Judas:[174] What you are going to do, do quickly; and the opposite is just as forceful, for in his foreknowledge he knew that Judas would betray him (which is specifically noted above); but this human uneasiness, this wavering when the decisive moment was approaching, nevertheless also had its place, and it will be a consolation to many when they remember this in their hour of need.

In margin: See page 9 in this book [II A 97].

II A 258   September 11, 1838

« 287

The profundity of Christianity is that Christ is both our redeemer and our judge, not that one is our redeemer and another is our judge, for then we certainly come under judgment, but that the redeemer and the judge are one and the same.¹⁷⁵

II A 261   September 12, 1838

« 288

Here again one can discern a difference between the Orient and the Occident. Both have had a print of Christ conveyed in an incomprehensible, mysteriously human way: the Orient in the famous portrait of Christ to King Abgarus, the Occident in the five wounds of Christ on the body of St. Francis.

II A 276   October 13, 1838

« 289

Christ also feeds people with five loaves and three fish¹⁷⁶ as far as his teaching is concerned, if one notes how the most insignificant external events give him occasion for the most profound interpretation—how far this is from elaborate preparations, from all pretentious apparatus!

II A 284   October 30, 1838

« 290 *Prayer*

Lord, be near to us with your power, so that we may feel the heart's glad assurance that You are not far away from us, but that we live, move, and have our being in You!¹⁷⁷

II A 295   n.d., 1838

« 291

It is clear that modern philosophy¹⁷⁸ makes the historical Christ a kind of *natural son*, at most an *adopted* son.

II A 765   n.d., 1838

« 292

The divine and the diabolic are the only genuine mysteries, but the mystery of God is *revealed* in Christ—whereas the mystery of the devil (*mysterium impietatis*) will first become visible in a corresponding manifestation: the anti-Christ.

II A 767   n.d., 1838

« 293

The Lord comes, even though we must wait for him; he comes, even though we become as old as Anna,¹⁷⁹ as gray as Simeon¹⁸⁰ (this Noah the second); but we must wait for him in *his house*.¹⁸¹

« 294   II A 316   December 31, 1838

The most fulfilled prophecy there has ever been was Christ's when he said: It is good for you that I go away,¹⁸² since this was the moment when Christ's earthly existence [*Tilværelse*] had reached its maturity, when his body was *dried up* like fruit when its time is past, when the whole fullness of divinity could no longer be contained in earthly form as *individual* existence [*Existents*].

              II A 369   February 13, 1839

« 295

In the Passion story there comes a point which indicates not only that the law has been fulfilled but that there is something more, for when Christ had drunk the vinegar which was offered to him, he said: It is finished,¹⁸³ that is, now the law is fulfilled, but these were not Christ's last words—he also prayed for his enemies,¹⁸⁴ and this is of the gospel.

              II A 388   March 28, 1839

« 296

Just as Christ's entrance into the world of the spirit is what creation is in the physical world—so also the Holy Spirit is the sustenance in the world of the spirit, i.e., the concept of sustenance.

              II A 419   May 12, 1839

« 297

It is quite remarkable that the address in Matthew 5 and following is called *The Sermon on the Mount* and thereby typically brings to mind (just as it does in a deeper sense by its contents) the great *mountain sermon from Sinai*, except with the difference that on Mt. Sinai Jehovah is not seen, but Moses climbed the *mountain summit* in order to speak with him. Here, on the other hand, Christ, in the likeness of God, sat *at the foot* of the mountain and thereby suggested typically that Christ was the fulfilling of the law and that this fulfilling of the law was now made possible *on earth*.

              II A 473   July 7, 1839

« 298

He spared Abraham's firstborn and only tested the patriarch's faith;¹⁸⁵ he spared not his only begotten son.

              II A 569   September 13, 1839

« 299 *On Christ's Sacrificial Life among Us*

Christ's suffering has been variously understood at various times—the great physical pain, etc., but you have certainly noticed that however excruciating the sorrow of contrition may be, the sorrow which grips us when we suffer innocently, when we must bear the consequences of another's guilt, is even deeper. So it was with Christ's sorrow. Yet in all this suffering, he was not one to think of himself or let the burden of his sorrow fall upon others. With good reason he could have said to the sorrowing ones who sought comfort from him: Do you not see how much I am suffering, what a heavy burden rests upon my shoulders—and yet he was always willing at all times to hear the complaints and sufferings of others in order to give comfort.[186]

III C 6   n.d., 1840-41

« 300

..... and Christ does not always *sit* at the Father's right hand, but when dangers threaten, he *arises*, he stands erect, just as Stephen saw him standing at the right hand of the Father.[187]

III C 20   n.d., 1840-41

« 301

The more superior one person is to another whom he loves, the more he will feel tempted (humanly speaking) to draw the other up to himself, but (divinely speaking) the more he will feel moved to come down to him. This is the dialectic of love.[188] Strange that people have not seen this in Christianity but always speak of Christ's becoming man as compassion or necessity.

IV A 33   n.d., 1843

« 302

The most terrible expression of the way Christ was misunderstood would not have been that he had been completely ignored—no, but that he became the object of curiosity to the unthinking crowd, so that the eternal truth walked about in life and street-urchins ran after him and house-maids poured into the streets to stare at him—but no one, not one, thought about what he was or gained some impression.

VII^1 A 79   n.d., 1846

« 303

"The good shepherd lays down his life for the sheep."[189] From a distance, this seems peaceful enough. One envisions the sheep gathered around the shepherd, and now come the wolves. Ah, but just suppose that the sheep themselves are stupid enough to side with the wolves in putting the shepherd to death.

VIII^1 A 72 *n.d.*, 1847

« 304

When I consider the death of Christ, the sight (regarded as the prototype) is scarcely upbuilding or edifying. (1) There is little edification in seeing that the holy and innocent one has to suffer in this way, consequently that the world is so corrupted. (2) What upbuilding is there for me (the guilty) in the innocent one's suffering in this way? But it[190] is the atonement. Therefore, at the same time that he thrusts me away from himself as if to say: What fellowship is there between you and me? —at the same time he draws me to himself by the atonement.

VIII^1 A 83 *n.d.*, 1847

« 305

Rarely does one make a real attempt to understand how it was that Christ (whose life in one sense could not possibly have collided with anyone since it had no earthly aims) ended his life by being crucified. Perhaps one fears getting to know anything of the implicit proof of the existence of evil in the world. So one pretends as if Christ himself and God's providence ordained it this way. (Here one also learns the meaning of all the chatter that one ought not venture out in decisions but ought to wait until they come to him, since the former is—to tempt God. I wonder then if Christ's life was not the one and only attempt to tempt God!) But the truth of the matter is twofold. The fact that Christ was willing to sacrifice his life does not at all signify that he sought death or forced the Jews to kill him. Christ's willingness to offer his life simply means a conception of the world as being so evil that the Holy One unconditionally had to die—unless he wanted to become a sinner or a mediocrity in order to be a success in the world. It is unbelievable how meager a conception of an essential view of existence [*Tilværelsen*] men have. They live out their lives in tomfoolery. They go out into life saying: Perhaps I shall become a somebody, perhaps I'll be a nobody, perhaps I shall even be persecuted. What foolishness! Please, simply choose, and you do not need to guess; the specific conditions of existence can be calculated very well. If you will unconditionally risk everything for the good—then you will be persecuted, unconditionally persecuted, *tertium non datur*. If you compromise, well, then you will certainly come to live in the ambiguity of tomfoolery, for then it is possible that you will become a somebody, but the opposite is also possible. Therefore all you prudent pastors ought to say forthrightly: We have omitted and set aside the most important view of existence; what we preach is a prudential life and a philistine-bourgeois gospel especially inspiring to lottery-players.

The death of Christ is the result of two factors—the Jews' responsibility plus a complete demonstration of the world's evil. Since Christ was the God-man, his crucifixion cannot signify that the Jews at this time were, by chance, demoralized and that Christ came, if I may put it this way, at an unfortunate time. No, Christ's fate is an eternal fate; given the specific gravity of the human race, Christ would undergo the same treatment at any time. Christ can never be the expression of something accidental.

Well, now, it would be appropriate right here to show how the Jews could become so enraged. But, as said, we shrink from doing this. Maybe we are afraid of getting to know too much—for example, that being high up on the world's totem pole might in itself constitute a case against a man.

Distance Theology

VIII^1 A 145 *n.d.*, 1847

« 306

Wonderful! The contemporary generation hates and persecutes and crucifies Christ—and then that very generation benefits from Christ's death. In this way Christ never did, as it were, get justice from men. But this is not what he wanted at all—he wanted to save them. Usually the innocent victim can still say: My death will become your punishment—but Christ's death became a salvation for them. It was not Christ who said: My blood be upon you; it was the people.

VIII^1 A 330 *n.d.*, 1847

« 307

It is so heartbreaking that Christ, who is the teacher of love, is betrayed—with a kiss.[191]

VIII^1 A 343 *n.d.*, 1847

« 308

From the beginning Christ knew that he would suffer and die. How grueling, before it actually comes, hoping at one moment to escape it and dreading the next. That is, Christ's suffering was a choice.

VIII^1 A 344 *n.d.*, 1847

« 309

His self-abasement was in earnest. It was not like a pope's washing the feet of the poor, when everyone knows that it is the pope—then he has a double gain: his papal status and also the status of humility.

VIII¹ A 345   n.d., 1847

« 310

How much we appreciate in this life not only to have someone who does favors for us—but the friend who gave his life for us, the friend who for my sake also let himself be mocked—to him we do not give a thought.

VIII¹ A 346   n.d., 1847

« 311 *Friday Sermon*

John 12:32

And I, when I am lifted up from the earth, will draw all men to myself.

When a ship is to put to sea, the end of a cable is cast out and fastened to a tugboat—and in this way the ship is drawn. When a human life is to be commenced and continued without too much dependence upon the temporal, a cable must be cast out. In this a dead loved one can be helpful. But Christ above all is the drawing power from eternity to all eternity.

He is lifted up—he has to be if he is to draw—lifted up with the Father*

and He draws to himself.

In this hour he is indeed closer to earth, present at the altar, but this, again, is only in order to draw.

Yes, draw us wholly unto yourself
Let thoughts, etc. (from an old hymn).

There is so much which resists and holds us back (diverts); therefore You draw us.[192]

VIII¹ A 371   n.d., 1847

« 312

* *Addition to 311* (VIII¹ A 371):

Yet in his exaltation He is neither indifferent nor inactive. He is always ready to appear before us with unspeakable sighs. Nor does he sit down, for when the danger is great, he rises up—as Stephen saw him.[193]

VIII¹ A 374   n.d., 1847

« 313

Christ is God's right hand.

VIII¹ A 377   n.d., 1847

« 314

If Christ were to examine us, we should perish, for this would exanimate us.

VIII¹ A 378   n.d., 1847

« 315

..... for "He" did not go to meet his suffering the way a man does who at every moment has the possibility of avoiding it and even of having everything turn out well. He knew it in advance; he knew it when the people rejoiced and cried hosanna when he appeared. —In this way the weight of suffering was infinitely increased.

VIII¹ A 391   n.d., 1847

« 316

See journal notebook¹¹, pp. 33 ff., pp. 166 ff. [VIII¹ A 145:271-76].
How was it even possible that Christ could be crucified.*

There was once a man who as a child had been piously instilled by his parents with faith in Jesus Christ—but as he grew older, he could understand it less and less. "I understand very well," he said, "that he was willing to sacrifice his life for the truth and that He, if He sacrificed his life, sacrificed it for the truth. But what I do not understand is that He, who was love, did not out of love for men prevent men from committing the worst of all crimes: murdering him."

The fact of the matter is: Christ is not love, and least of all according to the human notion of love. He was *the truth*, absolute truth; therefore he could not simply defend himself, but he had to permit men to become guilty of his death—that is, to reveal the truth in a radical way (the opposite would have been not to defend himself because of weakness).

* *In margin*: the book will be pseudonymous.

VIII¹ A 469   n.d., 1847

« 317

When secular sensibleness has permeated the whole world as it has now begun to do, then the only remaining conception of what it is to be Christian will be the portrayal of Christ, the disciples, and others as comic figures. They will be counterparts of Don Quixote, a man who had a firm notion that the world is evil, that what the world honors is mediocrity or even worse. But things have not yet sunk so deep. Men crucified Christ and called him an enthusiast, etc.—but to make a comic figure of him! Yet this is unquestionably the only logical possibility, the only one, which will satisfy the demands of the age once the secular mentality has conquered. Efforts are being made in this direction—for the world progresses!

VIII[1] A 519 *n.d.*, 1848

« 318

One who truly believes that Christ was and is God (here is the main impact of offense), who prays to him repeatedly every day, who finds all his joy in association with him and in thinking of him—such a person does indeed come to terms with the historical. How silly to be upset if one gospel-writer said one thing and a second another; he can turn to Christ in prayer and say: This disturbs me, but is it not true that you still are and remain with me? It is nonsense that the significance of historical details should be decisive with respect to faith in Him who is present with one and with whom one speaks daily and to whom one turns.

The sequence is this: a person first must gain some knowledge of Christ. But if we start with all these scholarly nonessentials, the next part never takes place. The next step is that one now resolves to turn himself prayerfully to Christ. Yet Christ is actually treated as if he were merely a historical figure who lived 1,800 years ago.

Christ says:[194] Where two or three are gathered together in my name, that is, are praying to me, calling upon me, believing in me, there I am. Here there is none of all this ungodly, weak, frivolous talk about the-book-or-the-symbol.

Believe that Christ is God—then call upon him, pray to him, and the rest comes by itself. When the fact that he is present [*er til*] is more intimately and inwardly certain than all historical information—then you will come out all right with the details of His historical existence— whether the wedding was at Cana or perhaps somewhere else, whether there were two disciples or only one.

A merely historical person, a human being, is present only historically—therefore every detail is of great importance. It certainly does not help me to pray to Socrates: what I am to know about him I must learn from history or shape it out of my own head. But Christ is present in an entirely different way. Once again it is seen how strict orthodoxy really downgrades Christ. For however paradoxical it is, it is true and it is Christian that with regard to Christ the historical details are not nearly so important as with Socrates and the like, simply because Christ is Christ, an eternally present one [*en evig Nærværende*] for he is true God.

VIII¹ A 565   n.d., 1848

« 319

What a moving expression of human forsakenness there is in Christ's saying three times to Peter:[195] Do you love me? O, He who is ringed about by a world of enemies, He who lives in such a way that whatever misfortune befalls him seems a joke to his contemporaries, whatever evil can be said of him seems to be a delight, whatever injustice and injury can be inflicted upon him seems to be a theatrical diversion—he learns to ask his only friend three times: "Do you love me?"—his only friend, yet, no, for this friend too denied him.

VIII¹ A 583   n.d., 1848

« 320

If the one who says these words: Come to me, all who labor and are heavy-laden,[196] is himself surrounded by all the favors of temporality, is healthy, handsome, rich, powerful, distinguished, etc.—then the words are taken in vain, Christianity is taken in vain. People very much want to hear it; they think that if the speaker, the one who is saying this, looks like this, then it certainly is worth listening to and perhaps we, too, may be helped in the same way. But in connection with what is Christian, there always stands an awkward N.B. Christ is the one who says it—not this fantastic nonsense such as Christ is in Christendom, no, a persecuted, despised, and much-avoided man, a man of whom it must be said: Look at the sort of man he is. Then no one wants to listen to these words, people become afraid of the speaker and think that if he wants to comfort them, he is crazy—never listen to him, for he probably wants his listeners first to become just as wretched as he is, before the consolation comes.

IX A 16   n.d., 1848

« 321

The real issue is that Jesus Christ be presented as he walked and tarried and lived 1,800 years ago. Only in this way is he present and wills to be here upon earth; in eternity he will come again in glory.

With Jesus Christ it is quite different than with a man who perhaps did live despised, looked down upon, socially inferior, poor, misunderstood, and then died—and men discovered that there was something great in him, and now he is that great man. Now men do not ask anymore about his social inferiority—never mind that; at most this has historical interest; now he is and continues to be the great man he was. This means that social inferiority is not essentially related to him.

It is quite different with Jesus Christ. He is the paradox. Social inferiority belongs to him absolutely essentially; he is this very paradox, the compounding of God and a socially insignificant man.

But this is not the way men do it. They regard Jesus Christ as a great man who lived misunderstood as long as he lived, but after his death he became a great somebody and this is how he is regarded now.

Aha! This is why all Christianity is nonsense. All the danger in Christianity is taken away. It is flirtation and blathering consolation and the like.

No, Jesus Christ is the sign of offense and the object of faith. Only in eternity is he in his glory. Here upon earth he must never be presented any other way than in his social insignificance—so that everyone can be offended or believe.

To regard Christ as something great in the way cited above is blasphemy. If at every moment the greatest possible human danger is not unconditionally bound together with being a Christian—as it once was —then Christianity is abolished.

IX A 57 *n.d.*, 1848

« 322

In regard to Columbus, for example, it is proper merely to speak about his greatness and let it be forgotten that men regarded him as mad, that children were taught (this is historical) to point to their heads when they went past him, signifying that he was mad.

It is different with Christ—the fact that he *willed* to be the socially insignificant one, the fact that he descended from heaven to take upon himself the form of a servant—this is not an accidental something which now is to be thrust into the background and forgotten.

Columbus goes forward; he was regarded as mad—and now lives in history as a great man.

Jesus Christ will not live in history in any other way than as Jesus Christ; he *wills* to be the sign of offense and the object of faith.

This means that the eternal in Columbus is his greatness, but the eternal in Jesus Christ is this compounding of insignificance and being God.

But how do we manage in this respect? Certainly we cannot keep men from the knowledge they have privately. Quite simple. Every true follower of Christ must approximately express existentially the very same thing—that insignificance and offense are inseparable from being a Christian. Christ shall be preached, indeed, but always in such a way that he is presented existentially. As soon as the least bit of secular advantage is gained by preaching Christ, then the fox is in the chicken house. The preacher must thrust this away from himself—and then people will become angry, look upon it as pride—and then the matter is set right again.

Christ is the very opposite of Columbus and the like. Columbus wanted very much to be a great man, he was conscious of being it, but *injuria temporum* he did not become it. Christ *wanted* to be insignificant. What impudence to make someone great who wants to be insignificant! And he wills to be insignificant in order to save men, but this salvation is also the judgment. Christ did not come to the world in order to judge it but in order to save it; but by the very fact that He came to save it the world becomes judged.

The whole appeal to these 1,800 years as proof of the truth of Christianity is the most mendacious of all. The truth of Christianity must not be proved, not for all the world. No, Christ must be presented as he was, what he himself would be—the Savior, but the sign of offense. It was no *injuria temporum* that it turned out bad for Christ in the world; he does not need the rehabilitation of history—merciful God, what nonsense and blasphemy! No, he wants to save you—but also test you. The life of Christ has nothing to do with history, does not garrulously join up with history, remains outside of history as the eternal sign by which every generation shall be judged.

IX A 59 n.d., 1848

« 323

The words "My God, my God, why hast thou forsaken me"[197] were understood as Nemesis, that he who had had so much in his power had not been smart enough to assure his own future, etc. If I were to talk purely humanly about it, it is as if Christ in his human nature had become so lost in the God-relationship that everything else was forgotten. It is an expression of being extremely close to consummation, this feeling for the last time of the chasmic depth of separation between being man and being with God; therefore, it is the final expression for what comes next—being blessedly with God.

IX A 103 n.d., 1848

« 324

From a purely historical point of view (therefore not as the object of faith) the point where Christ's heterogeneity with every human being reveals itself most vividly is perhaps this, that the nation to whom he belonged was destroyed. Usually the relationship is such that the nation appropriates to itself the most eminent among them, even if he died as a martyr. But this probably never occurred to the Jews with regard to Jesus. Therefore the nation was destroyed: this is the expression for Christ's being the single individual who is more than the whole generation. And the nation was destroyed and thus disappeared from history —no, it remains standing in the situation of ruin, giving expression to that ruin: this is (*ad modum* of military honor) divine honor to Christ in history. All the consequences of his life are dialectically not nearly so noteworthy as this consequence. How marvelous and gripping that providence has to watch continuously to hold a nation at the same point of ruin, century after century, as if in an eternal refrain repeating the expression of respect for Christ.

IX A 249   *n.d.*, 1848

« 325

The passage in John 10: 1-10 is noteworthy because Christ compares himself with the door and says that the good shepherd (the true teacher) goes through the door; whereas he later likens himself to the shepherd and says he is the good shepherd. It is like his being the truth and the way—he is both the door and the shepherd.

IX A 368   *n.d.*, 1848

« 326

Luke 10:23: Blessed are the eyes which see what you see.

This is the passage which pandering pastors and currying Christendom have misused to secularize Christ, as if this were something to see *directly*. It certainly is a misuse; but let us see if the Bible has not done everything to prevent it.

Christ is talking *especially* to the disciples (then turning to the disciples he spoke privately). Strangely enough, in the passages in the Sermon on the Mount where Christ talks about what is required of the Christians, the pastors are very attentive to the fact that it says he was speaking especially to the disciples. But here the sermon finds it most convenient to overlook this.

Therefore he spoke especially to the disciples. The whole chapter explains this, for Christ complains about the sluggishness and wickedness of the others, that they saw nothing (12, 13, 14, 15). In exact contrast to this, to this human sluggishness and sensuousness, Jesus becomes aware of his infinite significance or his God-consciousness, and it is then that he says this to the disciples.

This means, then, that all this gloriousness is only for faith.

IX A 440 *n.d.*, 1848

« 327

Christ veritably relates tangentially to the earth (the divine cannot relate in any other way): He had no place where he could lay his head. A tangent is a straight line which touches the circle at only one single point.

X^1 A 49 *n.d.*, 1849

« 328

There is a remarkable doubleness in all the answers Christ gave to the tempter, in that we understand each of them differently if we consider that Christ, the one speaking, is himself God.

X^1 A 127 *n.d.*, 1849

« 329

What contributed, humanly speaking, to Christ's being killed is quite clearly the fact that he unremittingly kept the people in tension. Humanly speaking, he could have spared the people by living in seclusion for a few years, for example, and then coming forth again. This would naturally have been untruth. But no doubt it was precisely this which precipitated his downfall, the fact that it took such a short time, and yet the people at no time were permitted, as it were, to exhale. The whole thing is like one breath. With jubilation they receive the extraordinary one, and almost in the same moment there is such a heavy pressure upon them that the downfall is already intimated. This is the dialectic of the extraordinary person, compressed together. The conception [of Christ] is reversed. The first impression comes again a second time, and then the cry of jubilation is transformed into the cry: Crucify, crucify.

If we forget for a moment that Christ did come into the world to suffer and to die, and if we assume that he had lived as a teacher for thirty years instead of three and also that he had inserted, humanly speaking, a suitable interval to give people time to breathe—then it is possible that he would not have been killed. But to introduce such a suitable interval would indeed have been a false accommodation. With a human being it is another matter, because he usually is himself con-

« 330

Just take a very close look at the fact that the prototype is called a "lamb." This is already an offense to the natural man; no one wants to be a lamb.

x^1 A 204   n.d., 1849

« 331

It is really a kind of cruelty that I (a believer) should rejoice over Christ's suffering and death.

x^1 A 232   n.d., 1849

« 332

Pilate's wife had been much troubled by her dream that day and therefore advised against the conviction of Christ.[198] But Pilate did not dream by day; he understood that if he did not convict Christ, he would be no friend of the emperor—and he condemned him. The really amazing thing was that Pilate's wife, who dreamed by day, was more awake than Pilate, who did not dream by day.

x^1 A 243   n.d., 1849

« 333

There is a heartbreaking inversion of all human categories[199] when they are applied to the God-man; if one could speak about Christ in an entirely human way, one might say that the words "My God, my God, why hast thou forsaken me"[200] are impatient and untrue. Only when God says them can they be true, and therefore also when the God-man says them. And truly, since they are true, this is grief at its maximum.

x^1 A 245   n.d., 1849

« 334

I constantly return to this dialectic: Christ comes into the world in order to save men, to make them eternally happy; the angels sing[201] at his birth: Glory to God in the highest, and on earth peace among men with whom he is pleased—and yet Christianity itself teaches that to be a true Christian is, humanly speaking, to be the most wretched of all, that consequently Christianity makes a person, humanly speaking, more wretched than he otherwise would ever be.

This I have understood only in this way, that there is a collision between the divine and the human qualities, that Christ understands every-

---

strained to this for his own sake, since he cannot hold out incessantly.

x^1 A 201   n.d., 1849

thing in the divine sense, but precisely this, that one is to be drawn up so high, is for a human being the greatest possible suffering, just as it would be for an animal if it were treated as a human being or if it were required to be a human being.

Yet it must be firmly maintained that Christ has not come to the world only to set an example [*Exempel*] for us. In that case we would have law and works-righteousness again. He comes to save us and to present the example. This very example should humble us, teach us how infinitely far away we are from resembling the ideal. When we humble ourselves, then Christ is pure compassion. And in our striving to approach the prototype [*Forbilledet*], the prototype itself is again our very help. It alternates; when we are striving, then he is the prototype; and when we stumble, lose courage, etc., then he is the love which helps us up, and then he is the prototype again.

It would be the most fearful anguish for a person if he understood Christ in such a way that he only became his prototype and now by his own efforts he would resemble the prototype. Christ is simultaneously "the prototype," and precisely because he is that absolutely he is also the prototype who can be approached through the help of the prototype himself.

Moreover, it must be remembered—something I constantly drive home—that to be a Christian, humanly speaking, is the greatest wretchedness in order that the accent can fall infinitely upon the fact that only sin can drive a human being to Christ, that Christ shall not be taken in vain in the usual preacher-chatter about a heavenly friend, gentle lessons about truth, profundity, the satisfaction of profound longings, and other sweets which silk-robed preachers serve to silk-clad listeners.

x^1 A 279   n.d., 1849

« 335

Christ was silent. There are two reasons for being completely silent: either because he did not have a single word to say in his defense or that it would have been a most atrocious falsehood to say a single word in his defense.

x^1 A 285   n.d., 1849

« 336

There is a beautiful verse which concludes each station of the so-called *Kreuzweg-Andacht* (pp. 654 ff.) by A. Liguori: [202]

> Süsser Jesus, um zu sterben,
> Gehst Du hin, aus Lieb' zu mir;

> Um das Leben zu erwerben,
> Lass mich sterben, Herr! mit Dir!

and then it is altered from the twelfth station on:

> Süsser Jesus, schon gestorben
> Bist Du nun, aus Lieb' zu mir:
> Hast das Leben mir erworben,
> Ach lass sterben mich mit Dir.

x^1 A 352 *n.d.*, 1849

« 337

Christ was wrapped in rags and laid in a manger, but he was buried in a new grave.[203]

(And in a grave which belonged to another person, which Luther regards as an allusion to the symbol that Christ is dead for us.)[204]

Yet burial in this way is an exception to degradation.

Burial in the new grave and with the greatest possible solicitude is connected with the Resurrection. Suppose, for example, that Christ's body had been cremated, since he was indeed a criminal, and the ashes strewn to the four winds—yes, of course this is inconsequential, because the Resurrection is essentially still the same miracle, but there would nevertheless be something offensive to the weaker ones.

x^1 A 354 *n.d.*, 1849

« 338

It should be remembered that Christ did not turn Nicodemus away, consequently that he was patient with him—but he never did become a real disciple, although John calls him a secret disciple, but where? I cannot remember the passage; I know I have read Luther's reference[205] to it in the Gospel-text for Good Friday.

x^1 A 355 *n.d.*, 1849

« 339

Christ has almost been upbraided for irresponsibility for making a treasurer of a man like Judas, who had thieving inclinations. On the other hand, one could rather say: What trust and love on the part of Christ, for the best and boldest way to save such a person is simply and readily to show him unconditional confidence; if this does not help, then as a rule there is no help for him.

x^1 A 364 *n.d.*, 1849

« 340

The whole problem of Christ's second coming prophesied as approaching but still not fulfilled I explain by pointing out that it is a subjectively true expression. Not only must Christ speak in this way and after him the apostles, as was the case, but every true Christian must also speak this way. That is, to be a true Christian is so agonizing that it would not be endurable if one did not continually expect Christ's second coming as imminent. Agony, suffering, nourish a necessary illusion. Therefore the opposite can be said, that everyone who does not speak this way but some other way, who expects Christ's coming sometime many centuries hence, or everyone who is busy showing that events have not happened as Christ predicted, is no true Christian. One is not a true Christian except in the pain and agony of being a true Christian in this world; and if one is in this pain and agony, then this illusion is a necessity.

Think of a girl in love who is separated from her beloved. The more in love she is and consequently the more she feels the pain of separation, the closer this pain brings her the hope of meeting him again. She hopes for reunion very soon, and yet she perhaps lives on for many years but continually hopes for reunion very soon. As soon as she begins to talk about a reunion sometime, after many years, etc., this means that she is no longer in love; generally it means that she wants to arrange for a new marriage.

It is wonderful that in the [Danish] language the word *nourishment* [Næring] is related to *near* [nær]. To the degree that the need is greater, the nourishment is nearer; the nourishment is in the need, and even if it is not the need, it still is the nearest. If the lover is really in love, the reunion is very near to her; if she is not entirely in love—then the reunion is a remote prospect.

The only form of polemic one can use against objections is to fall upon the objector from behind. When a girl has the look of being in love and says: I long for my beloved, for the sight of him again, but this is a remote prospect—then one does not argue with her but says: Well, my girl, from this I see that you are not in love. So also when objections are raised regarding Christ's declaration about the imminent second coming. One says to him: You must declare yourself either not to be a believer or to be a believer. If you say the first, then I reply: What concern is the whole matter to you; it concerns you no more than love concerns a third party. If you say that you are a believer, you who nevertheless make such objections, then I say to you that you are not a believer—this I prove from the way in which you speak.

x¹ A 447   n.d., 1849

« 341

It is as if Christ said to the soul: How can you be anxious about me and become more anxious in my presence; I am in fact your very Savior. Believe me that I am. This is not an assurance, this is infinitely more than an assurance; I let myself be crucified for you; if this cannot convince you, then it is impossible.

x¹ A 503   n.d., 1849

« 342

Christ had the certainty that what He suffered was atonement for all, unconditionally for all, and the confidence that with his every step, his every word, "the Scriptures were fulfilled."[206] He was the Scriptures given life.

x¹ A 587   n.d., 1849

« 343

In a certain human sense the matter must be put the very opposite to what is usually done. It is generally found to be quite natural that the disciples felt themselves forsaken upon Christ's departure, that a miracle was needed to strengthen them, that it was easy for them to be strong as long as Christ was with them, and the like.

What simple human experience teaches is forgotten. In a certain sense the disciple leads a timorous existence [*Existents*] as long as the master lives with him. In a certain sense the disciple cannot be himself, vacillates between being apprehensive every moment over the teacher's judgment, which is right at hand, and wanting every moment to be propped up by him.

The law is always this: precisely in order to reach his full strength, a person must not have visible but only invisible help. The same divine help which when invisible is absolute help is in a certain sense, humanly speaking, an impediment when it is visible.

Certainly this is the meaning of Christ's words that it is profitable for them that he go away, for otherwise the spirit cannot come.

x¹ A 624   n.d., 1849

« 344

Christ is born in a stable, wrapped in rags, laid in a manger—so unimportant is this child apparently, so meagerly valued. And immediately afterward this child is already so valuable that it costs the lives of the children in Bethlehem. Such is the squandering which can take place in connection with this child.

x^2 A 38   n.d., 1849

« 345 *Texts for Friday's Sermon*

Some of the words which were mockingly spoken to him when he was crucified could be used, but with a different meaning.

No. I.

Matthew 27:40. "You who would destroy the temple and build it in three days, save yourself."

> They say the very opposite; if he had saved himself, then the temple would not have been destroyed.
>
> *In margin:* If he saves himself, he does not destroy the temple.
>
> Save yourself—O, no, the Christian must say; do not save yourself, you who are the Savior of the world, for then the world would be lost.
>
> In this way one can learn something from mockery as well.

No. II.

Matthew 27:40. "If you are the Son of God, come down from the cross."

> No, just because he was the Son of God, he remained upon the cross, or just because he remained upon the cross he showed that he was the Son of God.
>
> But men do not comprehend that which is of God; they demonstrate and draw conclusions inversely; they want to conclude that he is the Son of God from the fact that he descends from the cross—but then the Son of God is precisely what he would not be.

No. III.

Matthew 27:42. "He saved others; he cannot save himself."

> No wonder—if he would save himself, he could not save others; it is precisely in order to save others that he will not save himself.
>
> Here again the mockery says something entirely different from what it seems to say.

x^2 A 73   n.d., 1849

« 346

One could also understand the gospel about the wedding celebration in Cana as follows: it is the first miracle simply because it is the motto for Christ's entire life: first of all suffering, then glorification. Christ's reply to Mary:[207] O woman, what have you to do with me, also has a certain distant resemblance to his reply to Peter:[208] Get behind me, Satan! You are a hindrance to me. At that moment Mary also has some of that earthly impatience which wants to be helped immediately.

x^2 A 85   *n.d.*, 1849

« 347

It certainly must never be forgotten that Christ helped also in temporal and earthly needs. It is also possible falsely to make Christ so spiritual that he becomes sheer cruelty. After all "spirit," absolute spirit, is the greatest of cruelties for us poor men.

Consequently Christ also relieved earthly suffering, healed the sick, the lepers, the deranged; he fed people, changed water into wine, calmed the sea, etc.—but, says the pastor, we dare not expect such assistance nowadays—and so it is dropped, and Christ becomes almost more cruel toward us than toward his contemporaries.

The answer to this has to be "No." Please note that since the striving involved in becoming and being a Christian is in proportion to contemporaneity with a Christian in the strictest sense of the word, then contemporaneity with an apostle is so rigorous that none of us will get to experience it. And now contemporaneity with Christ himself. The miracle, the miracles of compassion for earthly need and suffering are still somewhat alleviating and the altogether indispensable alleviation—otherwise it would have been impossible to live with Christ. If for only one single day Christ had expressed what it is to be absolute spirit, the human race would have blown up.

But we who are living 1,800 years afterward—we are content to regard the horror through the imagination, and on the other hand we are all too inclined to turn everything into human sympathy—this way, you see, our situation becomes far easier than that of the contemporaries, who had the miracles to hold on to.

x^2 A 86   *n.d.*, 1849

« 348

Even a human being can approximately understand that a man does not live by bread alone but by every word which proceeds from the mouth of God—although these words and the context in which they were used (namely, the temptation story, where the contrast is with having fasted for forty days and nights) are superhuman, for a human being is certainly not such pure spirit that he can live literally on the word of God instead of on food and drink.

O, but a person can live on for a long, long time, year after year, suffering and perhaps tormenting himself under a particular conception of some specific Christian point—and then suddenly the lights go on for him and he comes to see the same matter from another side and he feels a relief comparable to that which a hungry man feels when he gets food, or a fainting person when he is restored.

Think of a person who is deeply conscious of being a sinner, has tormented himself by being able to conceive of Christ only as the Holy One and therefore only shrinks from him, although he continues to stick by him. What a transformation when it really becomes clear to him that Christ is the Savior, is like a physician upon whom one calls in his weakest moment; whereas, in the very opposite way, he had dared turn to the Holy One only in his best moment.

x^2 A 136   *n.d.*, 1849

« 349

Galatians 2:19 (for I through the law died to the law) corresponds exactly to the presentation I usually give of our relationship to "the prototype." "The prototype" must be presented as the requirement, and then it crushes you. "The prototype," which is Christ, then changes into something else, to grace and compassion, and it is he himself who reaches out to support you. In this way through the prototype you have died to the prototype.

x^2 A 170   *n.d.*, 1849

« 350

What self-contradicting anguish in Christ's relationship to the disciples! He, the master, He who demanded adoration, He sees that the disciples, humanly speaking, really suffer by being His disciples, so that, humanly speaking, it was almost as if He ought to thank them for remaining faithful to him.

And what a singular kind of value-dialectic—to know oneself to be God and then to be so unable to assure his trusting disciples of a tiny little bit of esteem, that on the contrary they have to suffer debasement just because of their relationship to him—and then still to maintain the image of infinite worth.

Is this not as it is everywhere—that what is essentially Christian can be illustrated only analogously by madness. A deranged person can continue maintaining the delusion that he is a king, in spite of the protest of the whole world. Yes, but when a person is not mad, and then to maintain the thought that he really is the infinitely exalted one when everything expresses contempt and mockery, to maintain this before the disciples who, humanly speaking, instead of adoringly giving thanks for the possibility of being disciples, would rather, humanly speaking, have been right to let him feel that it was he who should thank them, he who still in a certain sense cannot even do without them, for he has to have and use a few men—this is superhuman!

x^2 A 311   n.d., 1849

« 351

When Christ is compared with the bridegroom and the believer with the bride, it must be remembered that the first part of this figure does not fit; for certainly it is not the bride who chooses the bridegroom but the bridegroom who chooses the bride by making an offer of marriage; but he courts her and is at that very moment subordinate. It is not this way with Christ. However, it may still remain a weak analogy; for just as it is precisely the man's conscious superiority which makes him courteously express this to the weaker woman by humbling himself (and therefore it would be very inconsiderate for a girl, who is actually the weaker one, to make the proposal, since it would become pure begging, simply because she is not strengthened by the supporting truth that she is in truth the stronger one), so is it also the mark of infinite superiority in a superior person that he practically presents himself as the one who requests the devotion of the other. This is the considerateness of superiority; and the reason why infinite superiority can do it is precisely that it is infinite superiority.

x^2 A 319   n.d., 1849

« 352

Even the chosen apostle, and thus everyone without exception, is qualitatively different from the God-man in this way—the apostle must be constrained; the God-man is the only one who has pure ideality and therefore voluntarily does the maximum.

x^2 A 422   n.d., 1850

« 353

It is frequently said that if Christ were to come again now he would once more be slain. This is perfectly true; but qualified more precisely, it would have to be added that he would be sentenced to death and slain because what he proclaimed was NOT CHRISTIANITY but a lunatic, wicked, blasphemous, misanthropic exaggeration and caricature of that gentle doctrine, Christianity, the true Christianity, which is found in Christendom and whose founder was Jesus Christ.

x^3 A 257   n.d., 1850

« 354

Today in a communion sermon Pastor Smith said something which struck me: Christ has not only spoken to us by his life but has also spoken for us by his death.

x^3 A 354   n.d., 1850

« 355

As a man is, so is his Christ-image. Mynster could not imagine him except at a certain polite distance from actuality; Martensen could not imagine him doing anything but discoursing, etc.

x^3 A 427   n.d., 1850

« 356 *Distraction*

The rigorous interrogator knows that the most drastic examination obliges the person being investigated to look steadily at a single point, for example, at a joint in the wall; but it is a saving distraction, the only saving distraction (which is Christianity), to gaze upon another, upon Christ, to forget everything, each one his presumed crumb of perfection, but also each one his cares and wretchedness and guilt, by gazing upon him.

x^3 A 655   n.d., 1850

« 357 *The Storm Arises—Christ Sleeps*[209]

Thus the highest is similar to the lowest. Only a child, especially a very little child, or an animal, can lie very quietly and sleep in a storm. The rest of us cannot do this. But the God-man can.

And what do the rest of us have to do? Yes, just what the disciples did: they called upon Christ.

x^4 A 50   n.d., 1851

« 358 *The Crucifixion of Christ*

Never has bitterness directed at any man been like that toward Christ. The one corresponds to the other—that he had declared the maximum about himself, said it so specifically of himself, is precisely what returns inverted in the passion of bitterness against him.

For a moment let us think of one whom I otherwise do not regard as an analogy: Socrates. That Socrates ironically puts everything off, decisively says nothing decisive about himself, results first of all in his not being able to arouse the highest passion of admiration among his contemporaries, but inversely it also turns out as a good for him, for neither can the passion of bitterness be so strong. In order really to arouse bitterness against oneself, a man must have said unconditionally the maximum about himself. To speak of some divinity is not enough to arouse the passion of bitterness (when admiration is displaced by bitterness) as compared to declaring unconditionally and without the slightest reservation that one is himself God. From this one can prove that human bitterness has never raged as it did against Christ.

x^4 A 506   n.d., 1852

« 359 *Joseph of Arimathea*[210]—*Christendom*

This man is a symbol of Christendom: he went to Pilate and asked that he might have the body of Christ—and he buried it.

In the same way Christendom honors Christ by burying him; it is just as important to Christendom as to the high priests to know for sure that he is dead—but then Christendom buries him, with great pomp and glory, the final honor.

x^4 A 507   n.d., 1852

« 360 *The Story of the Passion*

The divine can also be recognized by the fact that (1) everything that happens, that is spoken, or that goes on, etc., is an omen; the facts continually change to *mean* something infinitely higher, and in this way everything is elevated a whole quality above the human. The high priest says:[211] It is better that one person suffer, etc.—and he prophesies. It is a declaration of secular prudence, but look, it is a prophetic voice. —The high priest's demand[212] that Pilate have the grave guarded to make sure that Christ did not rise—and it is precisely the presence of the guard which becomes testimony to his having risen. —Pilate writes: King of the Jews—and says:[213] What I wrote I wrote—yes, he was right, too, but he did not suspect how.

(2) Almost all the remarks give an inverted echo, become true when heard inversely. The mob stands by the cross mocking, all are mocking— and speaking out of their human discernment demand that Christ, if they are to believe that he is Christ, do the very thing which, if he did it, would in the divine order prove precisely that he is not God's son. "Come down from the cross;[214] help yourself; let us see if God will help him,"

etc. And yet it is true that if he had come down from the cross, if he had helped himself, saved his life, if he had summoned the legions of 12,000 angels,[215] etc., he would, on the contrary, not have been the son of God.

X^4 A 514   n.d., 1852

« 361 *The Way—the Way*

Whenever I observe a man who by proclaiming Christianity has acquired all the worldly enjoyment possible, all worldly goods—I do not deny that there is a way which leads to this; I merely deny that the way does this, the way of which Christ speaks when he says: I am the way.[216]

If I meet a man walking on Amager going in the direction of, let us say, Dragør, and he says it is the way which leads to Roskilde—I do not deny there is a way leading to Dragør, I merely deny this is the way leading to Roskilde. Likewise I do not deny that there is a way—it is old, to be sure, an old, well-known, well-traveled way—which leads to worldly goods, but I deny that it is the way Christ is talking about when he says: I am the way—for otherwise Christ himself has taken the wrong road, which, however, is impossible because he himself is the way.

He is himself the way—this is so that no fraud may be perpetrated about there being many ways. There were not many ways, of which Christ took one—no, Christ is the way.

X^4 A 659   n.d., 1852

« 362 *"Truly, Truly"*

How divine to say upon the cross that which Christ says to the thief.[217] All, all, all, even God in heaven by whom he "was forsaken," witness against him—but he, completely unchanged, with the same trustworthiness as ever, says from the cross: "Truly, I say to you, today you will be with me in paradise."

X^5 A 131   n.d., 1853

« 363 *Therefore!*

"I find no guilt in this man; *therefore* I will chastise him." What a curious *therefore!*

"Pilate said *three* times:[218] I find no guilt in this man, THEREFORE I will chastise him."

XI^1 A 13   April 14, 1854

« 364

"And a sword will pierce through your own soul also."

Luke 2: 34, 35. These parenthetical words, which were spoken in the context of the statement about Christ's being a sign which shall reveal the thoughts of many hearts, should certainly not be interpreted simply as pain at the sight of her [Mary's] son's death—no, it must be interpreted to mean that the moment, the moment of pain, the moment of agony, will come to her when, at the vision of her son's suffering, she will *doubt*—was not the whole thing a dream, a delusion, the whole affair of Gabriel being sent by God proclaiming her to be the chosen one, etc.

Just as Christ cries out:[219] My God, my God, why have you forsaken me—so Mary must suffer through something similar on the human level.

A sword will pierce through your soul—and reveal the thoughts of your heart, yours also, if you still dare believe, are still humble enough to believe, that you truly are the chosen among women, the one who has found grace before God.

XI^1 A 45   *n.d.*, 1854

« 365 *The Idea*

In this world of temporality and sensuousness and, as Christianity teaches, in this world of sin, the idea can actually be only in suffering.

Only once has the idea been unconditional, in Christ; his life was therefore unconditional, absolute suffering.

XI^1 A 280   *n.d.*, 1854

« 366 *What Indirect Mockery of the World!*

The attack upon the Savior of the world is made—anonymously. Glory be to the human race!

XI^1 A 483   *n.d.*, 1854

« 367 *The Savior of the World*

Whenever I think of the insipid, mawkish, syrupy concept of the Savior of the world which Christendom adores and offers for sale, reading his own words[220] about himself has a strange effect: "I have come to set afire," come to produce a split which can tear the most holy bonds, the bonds God himself has sanctified, the bonds between father and son, wife and husband, parents and children, etc.

XI^2 A 15   *n.d.*, 1854

« 368 *Baptism*

If Christ had agreed to regard baptism as Christendom regards it today, as analogous to circumcision, an *opus operatum*, he would hardly have used the word *baptism* figuratively, as, for example, when he speaks[221] of being baptized with a baptism—"Are you able to be baptized with the baptism with which I am baptized?"—an expression which refers to his suffering.

XI^2 A 25   *n.d.*, 1854

« 369 *Mark 15:39*

The centurion says: Truly this man was the son of God. He has obviously heard wrong, just as did all the bystanders, and believed that Christ called upon Elijah. And yet Christ is saying something entirely different.

But is this not singular, stirring, that precisely these most suffering words of Christ, to which the bystanders, if they had heard correctly, would have had to reply: Look, he gave himself up—that these words are heard wrongly by the bystanders. The bystanders hear the words in such a way that they see them as proof of his being the son of God.

There is a deep, mysterious coherence in this; for precisely the enduring of suffering to the uttermost, precisely this was, before God, the expression of his being the son of God. But the wonderful thing is that those around him heard wrongly—and still in a far deeper sense heard correctly. It is as if God spoke through them—by means of letting them hear wrongly.

xi^2 A 95   *n.d.*, 1854

« 370 *Let the Little Children Come to Me*[222]

Yes, absolutely right—Christ is the Savior of the world, and the infant, too, by its existence [*Tilværelse*] belongs to the lost race.

But to interpret this passage in the way it has already been repeated millions and trillions of times: Now let us simply have children, for Christ says, "Let the little children come to me"—this is either stupid animalism or insolence, impudence.

In Christendom they have managed to make Christ over into a good fellow, the one who provides wine at the banquet, almost as if Christ had not come into the world to save a lost people but in order to stand as God-father to the children of the world.

However, the matter is as simple as this—we have heard all too much about saving the race (which means *the race* is lost); the main question has to do with being saved *out* of the race, and obviously the first step must be to quarantine the race.

Christ did not come in order to become the founder of a new race, descending from him. Yet this is exactly how Christendom wants to rewrite Christianity, instead of letting it remain as it stands in the New Testament: The race is lost, Christ wants to save; not: Christ wants to become the point of departure for a new race.

xi^2 A 164   *n.d.*, 1854

CHRISTENDOM

« 371

How the world does retrogress! In the oldest Christian times they "who staunchly confessed Christianity at the risk of losing possessions and life" were called "confessors" (*confessores*).[223] Nowadays we learn in every geography book that this or that country has so and so many confessing Christians.[224]

II A 236 July 11, 1838

« 372

Much of the love for Christ in our so-called Christendom is like that of a child playing in a pleasant sun-filled room with all the conveniences and answering his mother's question: Whom do you love most of all? by saying: Mother. But this is not Christianity at all. They have, as they say, given a lot of thought to the problem and have reflected on the contemporary scene, etc. But this is not at all the way Christ relates himself to a believer. Get into the thick of it! There is a kind of Christian sentimentality which is only a refined Epicureanism. In order to keep at a distance the question whether they really have the right, whether any man has the right, to enjoy such a soft pleasant life, they give thanks, as they call it, for all this good fortune. Can this really be Christianity?

VIII^1 A 392 n.d., 1847

« 373 **N.B.**

Can there be the slightest doubt that what Christendom needs is another Socrates, who with the same dialectical, cunning simplicity is able to express ignorance or, as it may be stated in this case: I cannot understand anything at all about faith, but I do believe. It is this everlasting understanding which has been the misfortune. At various times true teachers have arisen in Christendom, teachers who in simplicity have held to the faith. But these teachers have never been dialecticians in the strict sense. Now that science and scholarship have developed more and more, such simple persons are no longer able to penetrate. Consequently, a dialectician is now needed, and this eminent dialectician in particular must be the simple one.

VIII^1 A 547 n.d., 1848

« 374

I understand people less and less. What is preached in the churches is really not Christianity.[225] On the one hand the governmental officials and clergy seem interested in having the country regarded as being Christian, and on the other hand people themselves seem to have a dim notion that after all it might be a good thing to be a Christian, and therefore they still want to carry the name and want others to prove that this is what they are, but nothing really remains of Christianity. What the clergy preach is not far removed from blasphemy. Everywhere in life's trivialities they find analogies to the highest. Someone has had a loss, and presto!—the preacher refers to it as the Isaac whom Abraham *sacrifices*. What nonsense! Is a loss a *sacrifice?* To sacrifice means voluntarily to bring a loss upon oneself. A man is sick, presto!—it is the thorn in the flesh. *Pro dii immortales!* Life is carried on as in paganism, where they also aspired to a certain external righteousness and then provided for earthly needs whereby they got consolation. But in Christendom they immediately talk about Gethsemane.

Therefore one can easily be put to death for proclaiming Christianity. For men *want* to be Christians, but they do not want to hear what Christianity in truth is. They fight to be called Christians, and therefore hate the person who makes it strenuous for them to be Christians.

VIII^1 A 629   *n.d.*, 1848

« 375

"In truth" (this is the way a scoffer would talk, greatly exaggerating, to be sure, but perhaps it is still beneficial that it be heard, even though I neither could nor would talk so untruthfully or so mockingly), "established Christendom is an epigram upon itself, and this becomes very obvious and the epigram most biting every time anyone inconsistently seeks to act in the interest of the sacred. A new Sunday ordinance is passed and is strictly observed. Charming! If the Sunday ordinance were to be strictly observed, the churches first and foremost ought to be locked up on Sunday. After all, being a pastor is a means of living and the church is the pastor's shop; why, then, should the pastor be the only businessman permitted to stay open on Sunday?" To transfer the church service to market-day and to list pastors in the census under the title of innkeeper would be less epigrammatic than a Sunday ordinance and more in the spirit of Christendom.

VIII^2 B 171:15   *n.d.*, 1848

CHRISTENDOM 155

« 376

If all Europe were to declare itself honestly and openly regarding the existing state of Christendom, it would have to pronounce the existence [*Existents*] of Christ a fantasy, exaggeration, and so on.

Yet this is all wrong. It is the result of an established Christendom, of making a living, etc.

Room must be made. It should not and must not be the highest and most earnest aim to get a secure position in the state church and make a living. No, because of human frailty everyone should be allowed to find security for himself in this way—but this certainly ought to be admitted.

Right here lies Mynster's basic heresy. This business about going along with the established order of things, getting a secure position—all of which may be all right—if this is going to be life's highest earnestness, then Christ, the apostles, all Christians in the strictest sense of the word—are impractical visionaries.

But this is the way it always is with secular-mindedness—you win in two ways: first security and comfort and a good income and assured advancement—and then in addition honor and reputation as a genuinely earnest person.

IX A 60 *n.d.*, 1848

« 377

The defect in the life of Christendom is neither in the form of government nor in anything of this sort—no, the error is that people on the various levels of that life live too remote from one another. In the absence of close acquaintance with others, everything becomes too much a matter of comparison and too rigid in its comparativeness. This is true especially of the clergy. In Copenhagen there really are no clergy at all. For this reason it has been possible for a city like Copenhagen to become so appallingly demoralized, and not one person has felt authorized to witness against it.

IX A 199 *n.d.*, 1848

« 378

The only Christianity there is in Christendom is really Judaism. Rightly so, for Christianity thought about in repose (established) is Judaism; Christianity in motion is Christianity.

IX A 301 *nd.*, 1848

« 379

The kind of respect with which most people in Christendom talk

156 CHRISTENDOM

about Christ is nothing but affectation and goes together with the fact that in a deeper sense they are not involved with him at all. The person who in earnestness is involved with him at all. The person who in earnestness is involved with God or Christ in such a way that he understands it applies to his life, that he pledges himself to submit in all things, to give his whole life in service whatever the sacrifice—he speaks in quite a different way. From those quasi-Christians one hears, of course, not an impatient word—well, I can believe that—they really have nothing at all to do with Christ or God. But even from the apostles is heard the impatience of the purely human.

IX A 308 n.d., 1848

« 380

Like children playing war games (in the security of the living-room), so all of Christendom (or the preachers insofar as they are the actors) plays at Christianity; in the security of worldliness they play the game that the Christian is persecuted (but no one persecutes him, the speaker), that the truth is crucified (but the speaker himself already ranks with the court justices). The Middle Ages was more honest in its divine comedies. If I myself live in security, then I (if I am to be esthetically scrupulous) should at most talk humorously about the truth being persecuted; as far as I am concerned, men see the opposite. Therefore, either what I say is a lie or it is a lie that I say it, a contradiction, without question a highly satirical contradiction.

IX A 405 n.d., 1848

« 381

It would be a frightful satire on Christendom if one published a work like Blosius's *Consolatium Pusillanimium*, in order to show what a pastor as spiritual adviser found necessary to say in former days, naturally, because then it was something in which to exist. Nowadays there are no longer pastors as spiritual advisers but only as mere spectators, naturally, because it is not lived any more.

X^1 A 7 n.d., 1849

« 382

A question which one of our distinguished men, who also makes a claim to being a Christian, wants answered.

(1) That the most practical way to live is to live hidden, entrenched behind illusion, acquainted with only the best people, that this is most practical, the only practical way—this I know and this I knew very early

—but now comes the question: does one have the *Christian right* to do this, isn't this secularism's lie and falsification, for which one will be called to account on judgment day quite differently than for common crimes, for particular crimes are one thing and the fact that one's whole life has daily deserved condemnation is another, that one's life from beginning to end has been a consistent carrying out of this untruth?

(2) To venture to make the mass of men aware of the truth and to eliminate the distance of illusions and to deal with the mass in such a way that this must be judged to be a dangerous business, a sure road to martyrdom, and humanly speaking, madness to do it—but now comes the question: does one have the right to shirk, won't one be called to account on judgment day first of all on the basis, so to speak, of the total structure of his entire life?

(3) When one orders his life in such a way that he Christianly forsakes the prudence of the secular mentality, risks a bloodless martyrdom —and suffers it—how can there be any sense in calling such a place or such a country Christian where such things happen, or is there a trace of sense in becoming a martyr—in Christendom—because one expresses what is essentially Christian? Does this situation not prove that it is an untruth, when a place where such things happen calls itself Christian?

x^1 A 249   *n.d.*, 1849

« 383

The situation could, however, easily become fatal.

The situation is neither more nor less than that Christianity has been abolished in Christendom, and that Christendom nevertheless will still not give up the claim of being Christian.

If I were to fight over doctrines—O, it is not likely the conflict would become so dangerous, at least in our time when tolerance is so broad or when indifference is honored in the name of tolerance.

No, what is involved in Christendom's abolition of Christianity is: self-denial, renunciation of the world, etc.—about such things it does not want to hear a word and yet wishes to be Christian.

And to have to speak of this could easily become fatal. For what else does a man love as he loves the secular, his profit, honor, esteem, the community of mutual self-love, etc. If he is allowed to continue along this line, then he is quite ready to accept Christianity as a doctrine.

But the movement which must be made in order to lead Christendom back to Christianity again is a movement of inwardness. It is as if a lawyer came to an estate and in a certain sense found everything entirely in order—except that the occupants had got the idea that the property belonged to them and not to the benevolent master. What is to be done, then? It would not be his business to fire the blacksmith or the pastor or the foreman, etc. no, everyone is permitted to keep his place, except that a legal document is drawn with all concerned and covering everything on the estate whereby it is made known publicly that the estate belongs to the benevolent master.

Christendom has repeated the parable of the vineyard workers[226] who killed the lord's messengers and finally also his son, "because this is our vineyard." We think we might just as well be a Christian—who knows, it might be prudent. But there is no ear for what Christianity requires regarding self-denial, renunciation, and seeking *first* the Kingdom of God. And then once in a while someone comes along who either is a true Christian or is so concerned for the truth that he makes no secret of what is understood by being a true Christian. He is shouted down as a traitor, *an odium totius Christianitatis* (*ad modum odium generis humanum*, as the earliest Christians were called[227]), and killed. It is also treason to disclose this whole web of lies by being honest. Therefore they kill him. They say, as did those in the vineyard: "Let us kill him, since the vineyard is ours."

Humanly speaking, it is a thankless task; first to constrain oneself to self-denial (good Lord, one is still flesh and blood!) and then to be hated, cursed, and treated as inhuman because one does this.

This is Christianity, this is the "gentle doctrine of truth" in "quiet moments" in "holy places."

x^1 A 460 *n.d.*, 1849

« 384

"Gold and silver I do not have, but I give you what I have; stand up and walk," said Peter.[228] Later on the clergy were saying: Gold and silver we have—but we have nothing to give.

This was prompted by reading in Rudelbach[229] (on the constitution of the church) that a prelate, while showing a magnificent bowl, is supposed to have said that it is now no longer true to say: Gold and silver we do not have. The epigram has greater force the way I have edited it.

x^1 A 672 *n.d.*, 1849

« 385

Christianity does not really exist [*er ikke til*]. At least I have not seen a single Christian existence [*Existents*] in the more rigorous sense, and this applies to me. Is it, after all, anything but a frightful mockery that a whole nation is Christian and one thousand men live off the whole nation's being Christian.

Christianity does not really exist. The relationship to original Christianity is like that between a delicate, sentimental engagement and a marriage. They maintain a relationship of possibility to Christianity—perhaps with death in mind, but otherwise they do not put it on existentially [*existentielt*]. No one boldly ventures, so to speak, to leap existentially into the ethical.

The essentially Christian does not exist. Everything is merely *about* Christianity, which *is* not.

x^2 A 16   *n.d.*, 1849

‹ 386

Here is another peculiarity in Christendom. If Christianity relates to anyone in particular, then it may especially be said to belong to the suffering, the poor, the sick, the leprous, the mentally ill, and so on, to sinners, criminals. Now see what they have done to them in Christendom, see how they have been removed from life so as not to disturb—earnest Christendom. Rarely do they have a pastor, and then he is a mediocre one. Christ did not separate them in this way; it was for them especially that he was a pastor. The pastors, however, go on living in secular security; there they decorate life; "they assuage the sorrows and ennoble the joys" —this they do, and, most curious of all, they do it according to a fixed price.

Christianity in Christendom fares as a weak child who is given something and then a couple of stronger children come and grab it. These all too intensely secularized people whose entire life and way of thinking are secular, they take possession of Christianity, grab all its consolation served up in the form of human sympathy—and those unfortunate persons who especially ought to have the benefit of Christianity are shoved aside.

x^2 A 27   *n.d.*, 1849

‹ 387

In margin: Matthew 16:23.

In her relationship to the man (erotic love—marriage) it is really true that the woman—and this is her special charm—"understands only the things of men" (Matthew 16:23): sparing the beloved, taking care of him, adorning his life for him, etc., which is directly opposite to the truly divine prodigality, which is the impetuosity of martyrdom, which is to be sensitive to what belongs to God. —What is true of the woman holds true also of the friend as commonly understood.

From this it is readily seen that "the martyr" in his lifetime will be accused, hated, and cursed for egotism, vanity, misanthropy, and so on.

From this it is also readily seen how right I am in my basic contention against Christendom, that Jewish piety has been slyly substituted for Christian piety. Jewish piety is an attachment to this life and is an understanding of the things of men—Christianity means to be sensitive to the things of God. The sermon-address basically suppresses Christianity and dresses up Judaism. They organize themselves cozily in this life with Jewish piety—and then with the help of Christianity add atonement and eternity. Until now this has been the most convenient kind of religion ever invented.

x^2 A 58 *n.d.*, 1849

« 388

It is the concept of "Christendom" which must be reformed; what has to be done is the dialectical opposite of introducing Christianity and yet in another sense rather similar: to introduce *Christianity—into Christendom.*

The illusion that all are Christians has reached its peak—well, then, there can be no talk about introducing Christianity—therefore examination in Christianity is required; through a presentation of Christianity a test must be made of what is really meant by saying that all are Christians. This is analagous to Socratic questioning. Just as he began with the Sophists, who claimed to be Christians [*sic*],[230] and then emptied them by questioning, so we begin here with the claims of those who say they are Christians. And just as he was the ignorant one, so the examiner here must be someone who says that he is not himself a Christian. And just as the fruit of the Socratic questioning was a sharper definition of knowledge, the fruit here is a sharper definition of what it is to be a Christian.

x^2 A 135 *n.d.*, 1849

« 389

As for the objection raised against appealing to the N.T. in defense of the polemical factor in Christianity, the objection which says: Yes, so it was then, but now, in Christendom—well, all right, let us take Luther, who certainly lived in Christendom. Read, for example, his sermon on the gospel [John 16:16]: A little while, and you will see me no more; again a little while, and you will see me.

No, the situation in Christendom is infinitely worse and more dangerous than when Christianity lived *vis à vis* paganism, precisely because of the mendacious illusion of Christendom. This is why the polemical factor should, if possible, be even stronger.

x^2 A 139   n.d., 1849

* 390 *"Christendom"*

This is the enormous illusion which actually has abolished Christianity. One can get completely dizzy staring into the dreadful confusion of concepts which in this way has arisen with regard to what is Christian.

In brief, the confusion is this, but it is continued from generation to generation by millions upon millions: they enter into Christianity all wrong. Instead of entering as an individual, one comes along with the others. The others are Christians—*ergo*, I am, too, and am a Christian in the same sense as the others are.

It makes me think of old Socrates. He was concerned with what it is to be human, for in his age to be a human being was comparable to what it is to be a Christian nowadays. The individual *qua* individual was not a human being—but since the others are human beings, I am also.

But that confusion was still nothing compared to this one in Christendom, because being a Christian should be the most mature and most self-conscious decision.

x^2 A 453   n.d., 1850

* 391 *Proportions*

In these times the majority of people (thousands upon thousands) are automatically Christians simply by being human beings. The greatest possible exception to this would be a demon who with the aid of Christianity aspired to become a human being. He might advantageously revise the illusions in established Christendom.

x^2 A 462   n.d., 1850

* 392 *Text for a Lenten Sermon*

For this I shall use the words of the Passion story: Now Judas, who betrayed him, also *knew* the place.[231] And then show that this is the treason of all "Christendom"—it knows Christianity, is informed about it, but by means of this becomes treasonable.

In addition, every single human being has a constant inclination toward this treason: to be satisfied with knowing the place—the betrayer also knew the place.

x^2 A 514   n.d., 1850

* 393 *The Calamity of Christianity in Christendom*

There has not been one single objection to Christianity, not even from the most raging rationalist and the most scandalized, to which the "real Christian" cannot calmly answer: yes, it is so.

But the fact of the matter is: those people in Christendom who want to be Christians are coddled, are spoiled by having and getting Christianity on conditions all too cheap, and therefore they are not able to resist.

x^2 A 593   n.d., 1850

« 394

O, do not believe that what Christ and the apostles have sanctified and made into the highest dignity is beneath your dignity, but strive to understand that it is the ungodly secular *dignity*, brought into the world by a secularized clergy, which confuses the concepts.

x^3 A 137   n.d., 1850

« 395 *A Misgiving*

There are so and so many children baptized every year, so and so many confirmed, so many become theological professors; there are a thousand pastors; there are theological professors, bishops, deans, custodians, sub-custodians—everything is as it should be—if only Christianity also existed.

x^3 A 192   n.d., 1850

« 396

In margin of 395 (x^3 A 192):

See p. 43 [i.e., x^3 A 286].

There is a lot of sly talk in Christendom. It is said that Christianity is the highest and greatest good, but there is silence on how this is to be understood more specifically, that Christianity is the highest good in the sense of the eternal; whereas in the temporal sense it makes a man unhappy. —It is said that the Christian is blessed, but it is not specified in what sense he is blessed, that according to Christianity it is in the sense of the eternal; whereas in the earthly sense he is a tormented man. —It is said that Christianity is healing for suffering, but it is not specified what the sufferings are, that Christianity has in mind the anguish of conscience, fear of judgment, and so on; whereas in return for saving a person from these sufferings Christianity lays upon him earthly sufferings, the sufferings of temporality.

x^3 A 282   n.d., 1850

« 397

It is the other and really decisive side of Christianity which has been abolished in Christendom. Christianity has become a doctrine; but conversion, rebirth, imitation, dying away from this world, renunciation, self-denial, etc.—they are as if blown away.

x^3 A 420 n.d., 1850

ˣ 398 *The Difficulty of Becoming a Christian— in Christendom*

The difficulty is that having been brought up in this religion from childhood, one has had a continuous impression of its mildness and treats it almost as a kind of mythology—and now when he is older he has to discover for the first time how rigorous it is. Where pagans are involved, pagans who are to become Christians, the first impression is one of rigorousness, on the whole repelling—and not until then mildness.

An enormous problem arises from being spoiled by the supposition that this doctrine is sheer mildness, almost a kind of human confection.

But, of course, most men do not ever get involved in this problem (of having to become aware of the rigorousness for the first time later in life) because they have a few childhood impressions of great things, and when they have become adults they really have no time to spend on the question of becoming Christians.

x^3 A 505 n.d., 1850

ᶜ 399 *Basil*

Even then he described the situation in Christendom when he declared: "Our troubles are oppressive, and yet martyrdom is an impossibility—because our persecutors bear the same name as we do."

See Böhringer, I, pt. 2, p. 190.[232]

x^4 A 147 n.d., 1851

ᵉ 400 *The Disciple*

There was a time when one could almost be afraid to call himself a disciple [*Discipel*] of Christ, because it meant so much. Now one can do it with complete ease, because it means nothing at all.

x^4 A 200 n.d., 1851

« 401 *Christendom*

The more I think about it, the clearer it is to me that a person who is brought up in Christianity from childhood will never be able to achieve the rigorousness which is necessary to introduce Christianity again, i.e., to introduce Christianity into Christendom. This mildness of childhood will always make this impossible for him—the fact that nevertheless —and in the perception of a child—all is grace.

If Christianity is to be reintroduced into Christendom, it must again be proclaimed unconditionally as imitation, as law, so Christianity does not become the conjunctive (which sanctifies all our cherished relationships and our earthly fortune and striving) but the disjunctive: to let go of everything, to hate one's father and mother and oneself.

It is conceivable that if this is to be realized (which in a certain sense can be realized only by the God-man himself), it could happen in this way that Christianity is proclaimed to Jews, pagans, and among these there could be a person who, not having been spoiled by being a Christian from childhood, becomes the missionary, the missionary to Christendom.

x^5 A 42   *n.d.*, 1852

« 402 *Epigram*

Christianity has become complete nonsense. We are all Christians by birth—in "Christendom" a child is not merely born in sin but also in nonsense.

x^5 A 107   *n.d.*, 1853

« 403 *Epigram*

It is told of a Swedish pastor that having moved everybody to tears by his—it must surely have been—masterly, magnificent speaking, he reassuringly added, presumably himself shaken by the sight of the effect he had produced: "Don't cry, my children; it may all be a lie." Why don't pastors add this in our time? Why not?

Answer: it is not necessary. The congregation knows it—but therefore their tears could be just as much in earnest, or aren't the tears which fall in the theater in earnest, where, to be sure, the congregation or Christian public knows that it is all a lie.

x^5 A 110   *n.d.*, 1853

« 404 *Christendom*

Are a thousand women disguised as men a thousand men?

Likewise all Christendom is a disguise—but Christianity does not exist at all [*er slet ikke til*].

xi^1 A 245   *n.d.*, 1854

« 405 *The Corruption of Christianity*

I dare claim *a priori* that this corruption is without analogy in the history of religion: the corruption consists in this—that Christianity continues to survive after it has been made into the opposite of what it is to be Christian (especially in Protestantism, especially in Denmark).

Furthermore, there is inherent in this kind of corruption and in the fact that it is exclusively Christian an indirect expression of respect for the fact that Christianity is the true religion. They do not dare abolish it; neither do the preachers ridicule it privately while they recite it to the people—no, they sneakily make it into something else, something opposite; with all their might they strive to delude themselves that this is Christianity—to this extent they have real respect for Christianity.

XI^1 A 308   n.d., 1854

« 406   *Christendom's 1,800 Years*

What if providence thought as follows: I have now established Christianity—from now on it is turned over to men; I send no one to represent it in the divine interest; I want to see how men manage it and what becomes of it. And God, who in love is infinitely concerned for each and every individual, in another sense majestically squanders millions and centuries of time.

This accounts for the fact that in the course of 1,800 years since the time of the apostles there is no one to be found who really represents Christianity in God's interest, hating being a man, hating himself, and in this hate loving God, unconditionally serving the unconditional; on the contrary there is great human integrity—but always in the direction of human interests.

This can be linked with Christ's words: When I come again, I wonder if I shall find faith on earth.

What if this were providence's idea—to use 1,800 years to look things over—and not until the maximum confusion is reached, not until then to interfere by again raising up individuals who in God's power and might express Christianity in the interest of God.

XI^1 A 309   n.d., 1854

« 407   *Ridiculous!*

A man's whole life is secularized, his every thought from morning until evening, his waking and dreaming.

In addition he is, *of course*, a Christian, for he lives, to be sure, in "Christendom."

And in the capacity of being a Christian he is "a stranger and exile in this world."

This is just as ridiculous as savages' making themselves elegant with a single piece of European clothing—for example, the savage who comes on board stark naked except for the epaulets of a general on his shoulders.

XI^1 A 503   n.d., 1854

« 408 *Christendom*

is a disguise. All this business about the preachers and professors gives the appearance of being labor for the infinite, but it is finitude, purely and simply like all other trades. It is just the same as when Martin Fredriksen,[233] playing the part of a Russian officer, shows up in fine society—yet without disavowing his borrowed role—but suddenly a policeman becomes aware of him and says: Ha! It's Martin Fredriksen! It is the same with the preachers and professors who are disguised as servants of the infinite and the idea—the police know them immediately and know that they are disguised bacon peddlers and hotel managers.

XI^1 A 529 *n.d.*, 1854

« 409 *Christendom*

To be a Christian in Christendom in plain and simple conformity is just as impossible as doing gymnastics in a straitjacket.

XI^2 A 349 *n.d.*, 1854

CHRISTIANITY

« 410

I am surprised that none of the theologians who otherwise have observed often enough that Christianity in the New Testament still has a strong flavor of Judaism has also treated the doctrine of unrestricted grace in the same manner. If, for example, we observe that particularism appeared in its strongest possible form in the Jews, in such a way that it even bordered on fetishism (see Schleiermacher[234]), then it would certainly be reasonable that the tendency toward universalism in Christianity would not please the Jews. Examples of such dissatisfaction are numerous in Acts.[235] At the same time this very essential element in Christianity (its universalism) had to assert itself. Then the Jewish Christians advanced a step further (at first they believed that one should be circumcised, etc.) in that they believed that other Christians were also the object of divine care, but yet in such a way that Jewish Christians had to have some prerogatives. This, then, was the situation with the Jewish Christians. But how easy it was for them to infect the Christian gentiles. However, since in relation to the Jews they were always in the habit of regarding themselves as a whole, their particularism was not modified according to nation and geography, as with the Jews. And since they also acknowledged the Jews to be their equals, they believed that this particularism was not limited in that way; but they nevertheless supposed that within the larger whole there were a few individuals who stood out above others.

I A 4 July 8, 1834

« 411

ἄφεσις τῶν παραπτωμάτων.[236] This expression is always used where justification is discussed. Consequently it does not seem to signify the remission of sins as much as it signifies the loosening of sins. That is—by the act of justification man is placed in the right relationship; in this way the relationship to his sins is, so to speak, cut off. But man can still very well continue to feel their after-effects.

I A 6 August 19, 1834

« 412

Christian dogmatics, it seems to me, must grow out of Christ's activity, and all the more so because Christ did not establish any doctrine; he acted. He *did not teach* that there was redemption for men, but *he redeemed men*. A Mohammedan dogmatics *(sit venia verbo)* would grow out of Mohammed's teaching, but a Christian dogmatics grows out of Christ's activity. Through Christ's activity (which actually was the main thing) his nature was also given; Christ's relationship to God, man, nature, and the human situation *was conditioned by his activity*. Everything else is to be regarded only as introduction.

I A 27   November 5, 1834

« 413

It seems to me that the idea of the damnation of the pagans must have consequences, specifically with respect to Christianity, quite opposite to what has been expected by the defenders of this doctrine, for in this way the worth of Christianity is obviously reduced, since it then no longer appears as a universal divine plan, as a point of rest for all, but as a plan calculated according to time and place. But, of course, on this theory Christianity cannot bestow eternal salvation on man but only a temporal one, and Christianity is put on the same level as Mohammed's teaching, etc., in which the pagans, those who do not know this doctrine, are clearly excluded from the salvation that Mohammed will provide for man, only with the difference that Mohammed and Moses, etc., recognized the temporal in their plan and therefore did not regard it as entering the picture in eternity.

I A 40   December 2, 1834

« 414

It seems to me that the question of the perfectibility of Christianity can be answered simply by considering that it is attached to Judaism. Since Christianity itself acknowledges Judaism as being only relatively true and attaches itself to this, it can never be absolute truth itself; for it would never be able to acknowledge the relative and least of all attach itself to it.

I A 46   February 3, 1835

« 415

It is the same with Christianity or with becoming a Christian as it is with all radical cures. One postpones it as long as possible.

I A 89   October 9, 1835

« 416

With all his life and faith, the Christian may yet easily be taken for a person with a particular fixed idea. Before he succeeds (this is what the Christians tell us when we pay attention to the distinctive phenomena of this religion; I shall here consider primarily those Christians who have not so much sought to bring Christianity into the world as to take themselves out of the world in order to live in Christ; I refer to those edifying writings which are drawn out of a completely Christian life and consequently are not merely observations about the life of a particular individual but have served to strengthen a great number of devout Christians in their Christianity)—before he succeeds in arriving at the Christian conviction, he is confronted by many struggles and much spiritual suffering when doubt arises. When, finally, he achieves conviction, he undergoes spiritual trial [Anfægtelse], i.e., reason asserts its claims once more before it finally subsides. But the Christian has advance knowledge of these objections and problems, before he has heard them, that they proceed from the devil; therefore all his skill consists in following the commendable scheme recommended earlier by Ulysses with regard to the sirens: plugging the ears, since one must not allow himself in any way to have dealings with them as coming from the devil, for it was thought that the objections were taken care of in this way, just as in our day we think we have taken care of an opponent when we have attacked his morality. Therefore I regard all this talk about the devil as a great Christian evasion. —The reason why these doubts are able to appear a second time (for that which appears now, a second time, under the name of spiritual trial, is what we in the first instance called doubt) is that they were not dismissed in the first place through debate but through displacement by another force or growth. The reason these spiritual trials do not continue throughout a Christian's life is not because they have been struggled with, for we clearly saw that they do not want to get involved with them, but one can benumb himself in a certain respect, one can become spiritually deaf in one ear so that it is impossible to arouse him. Finally, then, the Christian has finished and points proudly to his last hour and speaks with a certain arrogance about the tranquillity with which he looks death in the eye—but no wonder. When a person has occupied his whole life with living into a particular idea, no wonder if he then sees it in the same way as a person with defective vision sees sparks everywhere in front of his eyes. Is there any wonder that these sparks or specks prevent his seeing what actually lies in front of him? It takes on the appearance of happy madness. To be sure, one can point to the many brilliant minds and deep thinkers who have been Christians, but I must in part reserve for myself one or another little heresy about these most distinguished names, partly because some of us have already seen pople who in a fixed idea have manifested an unparalleled brilliance, just as one of the most capital things about Don Quixote, it seems to me, was the ease with which he discovered that it must have been the evil demons who always followed on his heels, when, for example, he mistakenly took windmills for giants. And I wonder if at any time he doubted his knightly resolution? I wonder if he lacked peace and tranquillity? And yet it is *this* which Christians appeal to especially and insist that in order to judge them we should first become Christians ourselves.

I A 95   October 19, 1835

« 417

When I look at a goodly number of particular instances of the Christian life, it seems to me that Christianity, instead of pouring out strength upon them—yes, in fact, in contrast to paganism—such individuals are robbed of their manhood by Christianity and are now like the gelding compared to the stallion.

I A 96   n.d., 1835

« 418

Christianity was an impressive figure when it stepped forcefully into the world expressing itself, but from the moment it sought to stake out boundaries through a pope or to hit the people over the head with the Bible or lately with the Apostle's Creed, it resembled an old man who believes that he has lived long enough in the world and wants to wind things up. Naturally, therefore, some of its illegitimate children (the rationalists) have set about declaring it incapable of managing its own affairs and in need of a guardian; whereas its true children believe that in the critical moment and to the world's astonishment it will rise up like Sophocles[237] in full power. —The voice is indeed the voice of Jacob, but the hands are Esau's.

I A 97   n.d., 1835

« 419

Christianity is essentially the consciousness of the mediated relationship through which man must always approach the divine—thus, for example, to pray in Jesus' name, that is, to pray in a way that involves the consciousness that each one of us is a link in the development of a race, for only in this way can a person place himself in relationship to God, whether he acts or prays. For this reason almost all nations have had someone or other in whose name they prayed. But it was limited to them, because the consciousness of the whole world did not merge in them, but only a national consciousness, a local consciousness—thus praying through the saints, the Catholics praying through the mother of God, are cases in point.[238]

I A 172   June 12, 1836 (Josty)[239]

« 420

Conversion goes slowly. As Franz Baader[240] rightly observes, one has to walk back by the same road he came out on earlier. It is easy to become impatient: if it cannot happen at once, one may just as well let it go, begin tomorrow, and enjoy today; this is the temptation. —Is *this* not the meaning of the words: to take God's kingdom by force—?[241]

This is why we are told to work out our salvation in fear and trembling,[242] for it is not finished or completed; backsliding is a possibility. —No doubt it was in part this unrest which drove people to seek so zealously to become martyrs, in order to make the test as brief and momentarily intense as possible, a test which is always easier to endure than a prolonged one.

I A 174   June 13, 1836

« 421

Insofar as Christianity holds to the doctrine of the God-man θεάνθρωπος, it is to this degree not romantic; it is this aspect which Hegel has emphasized especially.

I A 215   August 4, 1836

« 422

Christianity has a certain settling power by affirming the highest degree of relativity, by presenting an idea, an ideal, which is so great that all others disappear alongside it (the romantic and humorous aspect of Christianity). Therefore, it is always far more enjoyable to converse with a Christian, because he has a criterion which is definite; he has a fullness in comparison with which the infinite differences in capacities, occupations, etc., are nothing. From this comes the stance which, if it does not degenerate into arrogance, is very worthy of respect.

II A 30   n.d., 1837

« 423

They forget that profound observation about the cross: that the cross belongs in the realm of the stars.

II A 82   n.d., 1837

« 424

This is the road Christianity has always traveled through the world —between two thieves (for this is what we all are)—except that one was penitent and said that he suffered the punishment he deserved.

II A 83 n.d., 1837

« 425

What is the nourishment offered one by all the world's knowledge in comparison to what is given by Christianity, which pours out the very body and blood of its founder.

II A 606 n.d., 1837

« 426

Postponing baptism until the end, until the deathbed, was also a way of uniting life and Christianity (just as in a later period, the romantic, one entered a monastery.)

II A 628 June 12, 1837

« 427

All other religions are oblique; the founder steps aside and introduces another who speaks; therefore, they themselves belong under the religion —Christianity alone is direct address (I am the truth).[243]

II A 184 October 29, 1837

« 428

It is remarkable that Justin Martyr,[244] who was in such sharp contrast to the paganism which conditioned the brief historical development of Christianity, nevertheless does not conceive of the world nearly so polemically as does the newer orthodoxy.

II A 217 n.d., 1838

« 429

It would make excellent *tragic* material: the young man who, persecuted by Marcus Aurelius, inspired by the courage of Polycarp and men like him in the hour of their death, also wanted to be a martyr, but when confronted by horrible torture became afraid and cursed Christ as the pagans demanded. —From this one sees that it is the same in Christianity as it is in earthly life: one must first *grow* before God and men, and even though in our time we are not exposed to such great temptations which in a horrible way destroy everything, nevertheless embryonic theologians, for example, ought to take care that, by beginning to preach too early, they do not *talk* themselves *into* rather than *identify* themselves with Christianity and take the consequences.

II A 234 July 11, 1838

CHRISTIANITY 173

« 430

In our Christian times Christianity is on the way to becoming paganism—at least the big cities have long since given it up.[245]

II A 245 August 11, 1838

« 431

Christianity's universal character is discernible also in this—that with Christianity all national distinctions cease as transcended elements. The only distinction which might seem to remain is that between the Orient and the Occident, although this is on a far greater scale and is based essentially on contrasts of dogma as such, whereas the other distinctions were only secondary and were based on national contrasts. The remaining contrasts (Catholic—Protestant, etc.) are often within national similarities and *simply* are based upon the objective qualifications of the idea.

II A 249 August 21, 1838

« 432

The Greek perfection of development in earthly development, the ascent of the infinite in the finite, recurs also in oriental Christianity in that the Greek cross,* , limits, as it were, the heavenly striving; whereas the Roman cross, , strives into the infinite.

II A 250 August 22, 1838

« 433

*In margin of 432 (II A 250):
Heaven is closed, as it were, to those whose striving has limits.

II A 251 n.d., 1838

« 434

There are these two elements in the Christian life which need to be united: (a) an unshakable sureness, an unshakable certainty about one's relationship to God, about God's mercy and love, which, however, must not be conceived abstractly, whereby through a long line of modifications one finally is led almost to sin in order to be certain of one's salvation; and (b) an empirical development, which, however, must not lose itself in disparate parts, lest the individual be tossed about on stormy seas—(cast them into the desert, as it says in the Augsburg Confession[246]).

II A 252 August 23, 1838

« 435

The union of Law and Gospel is found in the beautiful prayer:

174   CHRISTIANITY

Infinite Wisdom, you dwell not only in the high and holy* place[247] but also with him who is of a contrite and humble spirit, in order to make** the contrite and humble spirit alive in Christ Jesus our Lord.***

In margin: *Law; **Gospel; ***See Romans 1:16, δύναμις γὰρ θεοῦ ἐστιν.[248]

II A 277   October 15, 1838

« 436

We are tempted in the desert!
(Sermon on the temptation story)
There may come a moment before the hour when no help is to be found on earth, a moment in which you feel yourself alone, when you are tempted in the desert, so that even if you cried to the whole earth, no voice would answer you that would be able to console you—except for the voice of the Omnipresent One, which the Old Testament has portrayed so terrifyingly: If I take the wings of the morning, ... Thou art there[249]—the voice that precisely to the Christian is so consoling.

II A 293   November 11, 1838

« 437

In margin of 436 (II A 293):

Later this is repeated in Christ's life when he is tempted in solitude, when the apostles are sleeping. It is the same for us in the moment when it seems as if all those to whom we could turn sleep securely and soundly, unavailable to us in our need—then a higher consolation needs to be found.

II A 294   *n.d.*, 1838

« 438

Paul is the *spiritus asper* of the Christian life; John its *spiritus lenis*.

II A 307   December 22, 1838

« 439

The same miracle which amazed the contemporaries at the wedding in Cana[250] repeats itself in the life of every Christian: you have served the poor wine first and then the good wine—particularly anyone who has experienced how the world serves first the good wine and then the poor will agree with this.

II A 317   January 1, 1839

« 440

Do you think that just as the Jews brought Jehovah a tenth of the fruits of the earth and of the flocks you are to bring him only one-tenth of your heart, or that just as the Jews labored six days out of the week and rested on the seventh, you are to think about the world and its activities six days but about God on the seventh? No, the *Christian's* tenth and the Christian's sacrifice is his whole heart, and the Christian's holy day is the whole of his life. And if you bring God a tenth, watch out lest God open his window, as the prophet says, and look down and see you.

II A 329   January 17, 1839

« 441

The first impression one gets of Christianity is salutary and powerful enough immediately to transform* our whole mind, so much so that it is no wonder that along with the disciples we wish to remain on the mountain and pitch our tents there (see Matthew 9:5, etc.); but, like the disciples, we have to descend from the mountain, and down below there frequently awaits us as difficult a testing as the demonic was for the disciples (see Mark 9:11, etc.).

In margin: See Luke 9:29.

II A 333   January 18, 1839

« 442

..... only when the heart's anxious or arrogant hypocrisy is dislodged does the word ring for us, just as Christ did not speak his word to his disciples from the fullness of his heart until the Pharisees were silenced and had departed.

II A 338   January 27, 1839

« 443

The profoundly penetrating significance of original sin is shown in the fact that all Christianity in the single individual begins with grief—*godly grief*.[251]

II A 360   February 10, 1839

« 444

..... Christianity has a battle greater than any conflict ever fought in the world, for Christianity battles with the world. But if you have seen an army inspired in the moment of attack by the commander's speech, how much more should the Christian be inflamed by his battle-cry: If God is for us, who can be against us—a battle-cry which in truth contains not only an unmistakable note of differentiation from the enemy but a gospel for every warrior. Or shouldn't the Christian be encouraged to fight under a commander who himself had overcome the enemy, to fight a battle in which victory is certain, the reward an eternity.[252] —Christianity has also its peace, a peace which has overcome the world—and Christianity has also its joy,[253] a joy which does not hide at the bottom of a bitter cup and which only shows itself more clearly in proportion as the cup becomes more bitter.[254]

II A 365   February 11, 1839

« 445

Christianity (in comparison with Judaism) involves a much greater cleavage with the world, just as the words of Christ to his apostles ("Whoever does not hate his father and mother for my sake is not worthy of me")[255] are more profound than the words which were spoken to man in the beginning ("He shall forsake his father and mother"[256]), and as a result the union is all the more inward. See p. 27 [i.e., II A 469-70].

II A 376   February 25, 1839

« 446

The Christian consciousness presupposes an entire preceding human consciousness (in the sense of both the world-historical consciousness and the individual consciousness in the single individual), and while the Christian, therefore, has the consciousness of a flood[257] which has annihilated the preceding existence [*Tilvær*], the philosopher believes that existence begins here.

II A 443   May 24, 1839

« 447

When one views the historical roles of the religions on their journey through the world, the relationship is as follows: Christianity is the actual proprietor who sits in the carriage; Judaism is the coachman; Mohammedanism is a groom who does not sit with the coachman but behind.

II A 499   n.d., 1839

« 448

As Jewish women regarded being without children as a disgrace,[258] so the Christian ought to regard being without tears (which, like children, are the gift of God) as a disgrace and pray and pray, as did Rachel,[259] that God will open the womb[260] and viscera of the spiritual man and in the inward movements of the heart give proof of its having become pregnant.

II A 547   August 29, 1839

« 449

CHRISTIANITY INTENDS TO BE EVERYTHING TO US.

When people think about the world in this way, Christianity reveals itself in its magnificent elevating form, and they feel that it is, after all, the most splendid and the most profound of all and they say to themselves: "My thoughts will often return to these lofty considerations. When anxious doubts about man and his significance come into my fearful mind, I shall look to this divine picture in order to assure myself as to what man nevertheless is; I shall recall it in my best moments in order that thought, since it is expanded, can also be strengthened. I shall not allow myself to be disturbed by the many disturbing concerns of earthly life which so easily make life wretched for us; I shall forget everything else in order to identify myself with these perceptions which, even if they were only a dream, would still be the most blessed" . . . . .

But Christianity is opposed to being treated in this way. Just as it never found any day too bad for it to enter with gladness, no human being too insignificant for it to take up residence in his heart, so also it has never repudiated its divine authority. It comes to us in humble insignificance in order not to distress us with its magnificence, but it also comes in heavenly magnificence as that in whose name every knee shall bow in heaven and on earth. Only when it becomes the way, the truth, and the life for you, only then does it become everything to you, and it must be *all or nothing* for you. But when its mighty voice speaks to you and says: I will be everything to you; I will be your God and establish my covenant with you; I shall no longer be merely a poem which inspires you in a happy moment and perhaps vanishes when uneasiness darkens your mind; I shall be with you even though at times you were to stray away from yourself; even though at times you were to forget me, I nevertheless shall not forget you; I shall warn and admonish you, call upon you at the opportune time in order that you may remain close to me, and when you feel weak and demolished you will feel the heavenly powers moving within you, and when you doubt, you will at the opportune time feel the heavenly assurance—in the heat of conflict God's grace will shade you

II A 577   n.d., 1839

« 450 *On Communion*

You find it to be a beautiful token of the brotherhood which should exist among all human beings . . . . . or even more, you feel the elevation of its being also a token of the brotherhood which should exist between Christ and us, which is the condition for our brotherhood with men.

But should it not be something more? —I want to ask you a question: What is the basis of the practice of offering it also to the dying? It certainly is a practice which you would by no means consider superfluous, meaningless, or a practice which ought to be abolished, for you also wish to have it offered to you in your final hour. But is there any moment in life when we feel that we stand alone in the world more than in the moment of death? Even if they surrounded our deathbed in great numbers, all our friends and relatives, they would stand there powerless to do anything for us, perhaps unaware of what moves within us at that moment, what gives us uneasiness, or what consolingly smiles upon us. And yet, in this moment, you desire to participate in the most sacred sacrament. Would it be because even in this last hour you would, as in a farewell, be reminded of the brotherhood of which you are now to take leave, because once again you want to let this beautiful thought stream through your soul? Or is it not because your thoughts turn toward your God, stray beyond earthly relationships and cannot find rest, because you feel that just as you were and are a link in the great chain, so you are also surely an object of God's attentiveness, accountable to him for your conduct and your striving? Therefore you want to be assured of your reconciliation with God, and this ought to have taken place already—this, therefore, is the preeminent significance of communion. But the other meaning, the corollary, should also have its place, because you can be a member of a brotherhood only because you are an independent being, and you can be a worthy and contributing member only insofar as you in yourself and with yourself are assured of your reconciliation with God.

But as we prepare ourselves for the holy communion, we must take care that nothing which could seem meritorious insinuates itself, as if by our preparation, by our repentance of sins, by our contrition, we were made worthy of grace. But the assurance of the forgiveness of sins and of our community with Christ, which are here declared to us, are not a reward but a gift of grace, and the all too great uneasiness about going to the Lord's table can often have its roots in one's wanting to take as little as possible as grace.[261]

II A 579   n.d., 1839

« 451

The lines found in Philostratus the Elder's *Hero-tales*[262] could be a little epigram on the relation between paganism and Christianity: on wild trees the blossoms are fragrant; on cultivated trees, the fruits.²⁶³

IV A 27   n.d., 1842-43

« 452

If Christianity could become naturalized²⁶⁴ in the world, then every child need not be baptized, since the child who is born of Christian parents would already be a Christian by birth. The consciousness of sin is and continues to be the *conditio sine qua non* for all Christianity, and if one could somehow be released from this, he could not be a Christian. And this is the very proof of Christianity's being the highest religion, that none other has given such a profound and lofty expression of man's significance—that he is a sinner. It is this consciousness which paganism lacks.

V A 10   n.d., 1844

« 453

The task is not, as human stupidity believes it is: to justify Christianity to men, but rather to justify oneself to Christianity.

V A 23   n.d., 1844

« 454

It is really comical (a task for irony) to say that a king has "introduced" Christianity into his kingdom, just as one introduces improved sheep breeding. Christianity is precisely the one thing that cannot be introduced.

V A 26   n.d., 1844

« 455   *A Proof of the Truth of Christianity*

This proof is that many times its most zealous enemies have become its most zealous defenders. With philosophers and others like them the opposite often happens, that the closest adherent becomes an enemy and falls away. The double relationship in Christianity is the very thing that demonstrates its absolute truth, the fact that it goads just as intensely as it attracts. Generally an adherent's first relationship is immediately defined as that of a friend, not of an enemy; he becomes charmed (he is repulsed by Christianity), and then he becomes bored. It is just the opposite with Christianity. It is so full of meaning that it first repels and then attracts, and the repulsion of the contrast is the dynamometer of the inwardness.

VI A 109   n.d., 1845

« 456

No wonder that it can be taken for granted that we are all Christians. I recall an incident from my own experience. Once in my youth I was in a group where the young people suddenly had a gay notion of wanting to dance. Music was produced and everything was unusually lively and gay. Unfortunately, I cannot dance, and therefore I withdrew. A young lady came into the room where I was in the company of an elderly gentleman and obviously wanted to embarrass me. She invited me to dance—and I had to say that I could not dance.[265] And yet to be able to dance is an accomplishment, but to be a Christian is something so easy, so completely gratuitous, that it must be frightfully disgraceful to admit that one is not a Christian when everybody else is—*ergo*, we are all Christians.

VI B 27: 2   *n.d.*, 1845

« 457

Yes, it certainly is wonderful to be a child: to slumber on its mother's breast and then to wake up and see mother—to be a child and know only mother and toys. We exalt the happiness of childhood; the vision of childhood soothes with its smile*—and the person who is granted happiness does not forget it through the years. Nevertheless, praise God, things are not such that this is supposed to be the highest; it can be omitted without losing the highest; it can be lacking without having lost the highest.[266]

Of course it is splendid to be young: unable to sleep because of the turbulence of happy thoughts, and having slept to awaken early amid the singing of birds to a continuation of cheerfulness! We exalt the happiness of youth; we rejoice in its joy; we wish youth gratitude for its happiness and for the future we wish youth gratitude for the past—but, praise God, things are not such that this is supposed to be the highest. It can be omitted without losing the highest; it can be lacking without losing the highest; it can be lacking without having lost the highest.

Certainly it is blessed to be in love: to have only one desire even though everything else is fulfilled or denied, one desire—the beloved; one longing—the beloved; one possession—the beloved! We exalt the happiness of erotic love—O that the happy one might be faithful in the daily discernment of domestic life; O that he who was happy might be faithful in the enduring discernment of memory—but, God be praised, things are not such that this is supposed to be the highest, for this can be omitted without losing the highest; it can be lacking without having lost the highest.

Why is it, I wonder, that the Bible has a predilection for the halt

* *In margin:* with smile to smile.

and the lame, the blind and the crippled?²⁶⁷ Is it because the divine wants to be in association only with them? Is it because the divine thinks of itself as so inadequate that it wants to be only a part, something which is not for everyone? Is it because the divine is envious of the happy ones? O, no, for then the divine would be at variance with itself, then it would do wrong in giving them the best, the one true good instead of giving the suffering ones a compensation. No, the real reason is that the person who has the good things is very easily satisfied by these and therefore, with greater difficulty, becomes aware of the eternal. Not only while dancing or sitting at the banquet table, but even in church, men usually are very reluctant to listen to such things.

But let us consider such an unfortunate person from the time of his birth.²⁶⁸ Alas, he had no happy childhood. Maternal love is no doubt faithful and tender, but even a mother is a human being. He lay upon his mother's breast and saw that she was grieved; she did not look on him with joy but rather with sorrow. Sometimes when he awakened he saw her weeping. Among adults it is often the case that when they are all sitting around despondent and then he comes in the door, the happy one with a light heart and gay spirit, saying, "Here I am," then things begin to be cheerful and the clouds of care are lifted. A person with such endowments is uncommon, but what does even the most gifted of all accomplish compared to the child when in the agonizing pains of the birth hour he opens the door and says, "Here I am," and then things begin to be cheerful. O, the good fortune of childhood, to be so welcome!

Thus did he grow in the days of youth, but he never played with the others, and if someone asked, "Why do you not want to play with the others?" he might well have replied, "You know well enough; do not sadden me by asking." —So he drew apart, yet not to die, for he was still only a youth. —Then came the season of love, but no one loved him. Of course there were a few who were friendly toward him; but it was out of compassion and sympathy. —Then he became a man, but he did not sit in the assembly—and then he died, but he was not missed. The little band of mourners all said it was a blessing that God took him away, and the pastor said the same. Thus he died—and thus he was forgotten.*
There was no joy and jubilation when he was born, only fearful dismay; there was no grief or pain when he died, only a quiet melancholy joy. So passed his life or, more accurately, so passes his life, because, my listener, this is not an old fairy tale I am telling, this is not something that hap-

---

* *In margin:* and all his useless sufferings.

pened to an individual in bygone days; the same things happen every day and for many, even though superficiality and sensuousness, worldly cleverness and godlessness, wish to remain ignorant of it. He took part in life—by living, but there was one thing in life with which he was unfamiliar, something which in all the situations of life is happiness, as in the passion of erotic love—namely, like for like—this he never received and this he could not give, for he was a suffering object of sympathy and compassion. No, like for like he never received; so as a child he did not make his mother glad; if others had made his mother sad, he did not make her happy merely by smiling as he awakened. No, he never received like for like, for he loved his playmates in a different way than they loved him. No, like for like he never received, and therefore he had no spouse; he could not respond as a husband, and therefore he stayed at home and was lonely. In death he did not receive like for like: to be missed as he missed the loved ones. He died, but no matter what the mourners and the pastor said, God be praised, it is not true that he was thereby excluded from the highest. On the contrary, his life can properly teach us what the highest is.

When a child, perhaps because of parents who are too strict, does not get permission to join in with other children, and then a friendly old man comes along and, feeling sorry for the child, says to him, 'Come, my child, and we shall play together"—at first sight this seems to be a poor substitute. But look, that friendly old man knows how to engage the child, little by little, so that finally the child longs for him, for him alone, longs more intensely for him than the happy child longs for his playmates. So it is with the religious life. The religious life is not sympathy in the sense of compassion; it is first of all true equality for the fortunate, the rich and powerful, and for the halt, the blind, and the lame.

My reader, you call yourself Christian. Consequently, the one for whom you are named when you are called by your most significant name, he it was of whom a Roman governor,[269] in order to awaken compassion and sympathy, said: Here is the man! I wonder if there is anything the sensuous man would be more reluctant to have said to him than these words when they are spoken to awaken sympathy: Here is the man, see him standing there, abandoned, he who would rebuild the temple in three days, he whose tall talk now returns to mock him. See how forsaken he is, he who calls himself a king! See how helpless he is, he who would help others! What an object of ridicule he is, when even the person who wants to save him can say nothing in his defense except the poor words of pity: See, here is the man! I shall not lead your thoughts, my listener, to what you already know of his suffering and death; but even his earlier life was the very last kind of life a secular mentality could desire. Not only in death was he nailed to the cross, but in life he bore the heavy cross of misunderstanding, the sort of misunderstanding which made his whole life seem in vain, as if he came into the world in vain, if his death were not precisely the intention. He who in sorrow over a fallen race bore the sin of the whole world—around him flocked the curious crowd. Can a more horrible misunderstanding be imagined than curiosity, street-rioting—and this is the earnestness of the eternal. And so he walked, alone and forsaken, forsaken by men even as in death he was forsaken by God. He who brings only one thing, but the one thing needful—he who will be only one thing, that which he is, the only necessary one—from him men wish to receive everything else: food and drink and wine at the wedding—men wish to turn him into everything possible!* He is unacquainted with friendship, for this certainly is not friendship when the one loves and loves until the end while the friend changes, drops away in the time of need, dozes in the time of spiritual trial [*Anfægtelse*], and denies in the time of ridicule. The mockery was surely in dead earnest. Do not let your thoughts allow you to forget too quickly that you know who he was. No, the mockery was in dead earnest —at that time when no one wanted to assert it, when even the single individual who had a perception of it did not want to be aware of it. It was earnestness when the scribe dared to visit only in secret, hidden in the night, for he knew very well that if he were to walk the forbidden way of scorn in the sight of all, he ran the risk of himself becoming an object of scorn.

In margin: into a king, into a malefactor.

VII¹ A 144 n.d., 1846

« 458 *The Gospel about the Son of the Widow of Nain*

He was raised from the dead. Christ said: Arise.
But it also says in the Gospel that the people said:
God has *raised* a great prophet among us.

                          consequently—the dead man
                          rose up, and thereby a prophet
                          was *raised* among the people.

VII¹ A 239 n.d., 1845-47

« 459 *The Gospel about the Tax Coin*

Theme: God's image in us
                and
              Caesar's image on the coin.

In the Epistle for the same Sunday (Philippians 3) it says: Our citizenship is in heaven.

VII¹ A 243 *n.d.*, 1845-47

« 460

I know very well that for ecclesiastical vestments some pastors use broadcloth, others silk, velvet, a silk-cotton cloth, etc. But I wonder if this is the genuine vestment. I wonder if the Christian vestment is not rather to be detested for a good cause, to be derided and spat upon, and that this should be the rule for establishing rank and precedence. Christ certainly was not a suicide; consequently, it is self-evident that the guilt of the world was made known in the crucifixion. Yet how much better has the world really become? But then in silk and finery to go preaching about this in the crush of curiosity-seekers! Revolting!

VIII¹ A 102 *n.d.*, 1847

« 461

People are always *busy* in order to win adherents. And it is extremely important (to them, that is) that it happens immediately. They rush to employ every means and to reject everyone who declines. God wins his adherents patiently; he wins them at the last moment. This is why a man's adherents fall away—at the last moment; but God's adherents persevere.*

VIII¹ A 129 *n.d.*, 1847

« 462

*In margin of 461 (VIII¹ A 129):

This is precisely the way Christ won Peter,²⁷⁰ that time when he denied him—consequently at the last moment. A witness was needed, a witness before whose thought the crucified and risen one could hover day and night. Peter became this witness. The memory of that most shocking sight might not have been able to arouse his zeal adequately. But Peter had one more memory—the denial, which reminded him of the same thing. What he had seen and experienced could not possibly ever be forgotten. It was quite impossible that Peter's testimony to it could ever be silenced. But that look of love which overtook Peter on the path of perdition reminded him day and night of what he had to make up for.²⁷¹

VIII¹ A 130 *n.d.*, 1847

« 463

But to what purpose is all this? First of all in human self-denial to renounce everything of body and of mind which a human being otherwise holds dear and then in Christian self-denial to reap scorn, disdain, persecution, and death as a reward—is this not madness? What can this lead to, why is it done, what is to be gained? Alas, it is all too clear that contemporary Christianity has utterly lost its basis in the eternal; or, as a painter would say, it lacks priming, everything has become flat. The most paltry of the fixed ideas lazily lodged in all men is that we are all going to be saved, somehow or other. If I were to say, "Do you not believe there is an eternal damnation?" the prompt answer would be that only an arrogant person can believe that he will be eternally blessed and another will be damned. If I then say, "Christ does say this," then they get rid of the Bible with the cooperation of the critics.

Then what shall I say? I would say to the single individual: Make this experiment—shut your eyes; do not let yourself be disturbed by any man's talking or thinking; then think of the eternal, God, your own guilt, and you will see that you will get no peace before you are willing to suffer everything, sacrifice everything; it will become clear to you that *you* must needs become eternally unblessed if you do not do this.—"I cannot do otherwise" is ultimately the only thing there is to say. Whether all are blessed or not, whether all who possess the treasures of earth and have a gay life of it become blessed or not, I cannot do otherwise.

But if anyone says that it is actually self-torment to close one's eyes in this way when one might be comfortable and also be blessed, that it is indeed really self-torment to develop the highest conception within oneself, because it does make life burdensome, to this I answer: Claim this to be a self-contradiction, but it can never be self-torment to develop within oneself the highest conception. And finally I answer: I cannot do otherwise.

VIII^1 A 157   n.d., 1847

« 464 *The Gospel about the Unfaithful Steward*^{272}

Suppose that the steward himself owns everything—then it is commendable that he sits down and writes receipts canceling one-half of the bills. But this would be madness, the world says. Right. But nevertheless this is what Christ intends us to learn from the steward—to jest with one's means and with the accounts just as lightly as the steward did with the owner's property. The owner is usually scrupulous about giving nothing away, but the steward made friends for himself by being lenient—do the same yourself, but out of your own holdings.^{273}

VIII^1 A 214   n.d., 1847

« 465

*In margin of 464 (VIII^1 A 214):
"The unrighteous mammon"^{274} must by no means be understood as

unrighteously gained mammon. No, "money" is unrighteous, for it makes no difference to money whether its owner is a thief or an honest man.

VIII¹ A 215 *n.d.*, 1847

« 466

It is a familiar fact that police do not use people with the best records as their trusted agents. This is the way God does it too. More often than not he fetches the ones he uses from the paths of perdition, some of them from far along the way. God is able to use such people because they dare not argue or demand an easy life but have to submit to everything and thank God for it. But the police do not worry about their trusted agents' becoming even more degenerate—if only they continue to be shrewd, inventive, and thorough-going. God, on the other hand, also educates the lost whom he uses in this manner as his agents.

VIII¹ A 238 *n.d.*, 1847

« 467 *Text for a Friday Sermon*[275]

II Timothy 2:13-13.
If we *deny* him, he also will deny us; if we are *faithless*, he remains faithful, for he cannot deny himself.
The difference between denying and being faithless, which every believer is more or less, weakness, etc.
Here, then, are the Law and the Gospel.

VIII¹ A 267 *n.d.*, 1847

« 468

Here, in the temporal world, Christianity cannot be and ought not be viewed complacently. If there were a spot where there lived none but true Christians, they would have to be missionaries. And this is a question everyone must face before he is done.

But nowadays there is none at all; there is nothing but mimicry [*Efteraberie*], one mimicking the other.

VIII¹ A 325 *n.d.*, 1847

« 469

The foolish virgins[276] are not presented as having completely forgotten the bridegroom's coming; they are instead represented as having gone to purchase a new supply of oil—and yet they were excluded. Therefore one is not to excuse himself because he is, after all, doing something, occasionally thinking about the salvation of his soul, waiting for the publication of a new book, etc.

VIII¹ A 357   n.d., 1847

« 470

It is very difficult to know how a Christian who actually acknowledges his faith would look today, how he would be judged. The Christians who most closely approximate this are, of course, the clergy. But the trouble here is the presence of that unholy middle category—the fact that it is their paid occupation; they are officeholders. This means that people get no pure impression at all of a person who chooses to dedicate his time and his life to obeying Christ, occupied with the divine; they find it entirely in order that everyone seeks a paid occupation for himself and consequently one person becomes a clergyman, another a businessman, etc.[277]

VIII¹ A 365   n.d., 1847

« 471

The entire confusion and tragedy of the modern age can be expressed in one sentence: it has taken Christianity in vain.[278] Just as a cursing sailor gives little thought to the name of God he utters, just so do we give little thought to being a Christian, which we say we are. The clergy preach and they are listened to just about as much as the town-crier—and the town-criers also proclaim Christianity. The eventual fruit of the Reformation will be to abolish the clergy completely and be satisfied with town-criers.

VIII¹ A 435   n.d., 1847

« 472

This is the idea of Christianity: that the most unfortunate person, the one who suffers most, is the very one who is to bring consolation to others. This is the very expression of the infinitude of his suffering, that it is not a matter of anyone's consoling him, but only that he is to console others—so inconsolable, in a certain sense, is his suffering!

This is poetry and dialectic. The grounds of consolation which the preachers sweep together are nonsense and at best can be of help only to those who really have nothing in particular to whimper about.

VIII¹ A 493   n.d., 1847

« 473

A few people bunch together and persuade each other that they are the only true Christians and are then to associate only with each other. Excellent! It must be admitted that by doing so they avoid the inconvenience of making men aware and of all the attendant danger. But could it also be Christian to insist that there are but so few Christians and then not do everything, even to risk one's life if needed, in order to make men aware? To insist that the Christians are so few and then not become missionaries is an unchristian self-contradiction.

VIII[1] A 528 n.d., 1848

« 474

It is easy enough to show how false and basically traitorous, even though unconscious, all this defense of Christianity is—yes, even the very form which discourse about Christianity ordinarily takes. The fact of the matter is that pastors and scholars, etc., do not believe in Christianity at all. If a person himself firmly believes that the good he is discoursing about is the highest good, if he almost sags under the impression of its exceedingly abundant blessedness—how in all the world could he ever come to defend it, to conduct a defense of its really being a good, or even to talk in the following manner: This is a great good for three reasons—this supreme good, this good which makes the wisest of men's understanding dizzy and reduces it to tiny sparrow-like understanding, this is a great good—for three reasons. What an anticlimax! Imagine a lover. Yes, he can keep on talking day in and day out about the gloriousness of his beloved. But if anyone demands him to prove it with three reasons, or even defend it—I wonder if he would not regard this as a demented proposal; or if he were a bit more sagacious, he no doubt would say to the person who suggested this to him: Oho, you do not know what it is to be in love at all, and you half believe that I am not either.

IX A 2 n.d., 1848

« 475

To hate father and mother, etc., for the sake of Christ is also the expression of the pure spirit-qualification of being a Christian. Christ's declaration that he who hears the word and acts accordingly is my brother, etc., means that all immediate qualifications of kinship and the like are nothing if they are in opposition to Christ.

IX A 5 n.d., 1848

« 476

There is something almost cruel about the Christian's being placed in a world which in every way wants to pressure him to do the opposite of what God bids him to do with fear and trembling in his innermost being. It would be something like the cruelty of parents if they were to

CHRISTIANITY 189

threaten and sternly order their child to do thus and so—and then place the child together with the kind of children who would pressure him in every way to do just the opposite.

IX A 6   n.d., 1848

× 477

"Seek first the kingdom of God"—these words[279] could be presented in such a way that one negatively examines everything else and shows that this is what one should not do, or in such a way that one shows that the first manifestation of seeking God's kingdom first is, in a certain sense, to do nothing; for to seek the kingdom of God first is at first the same as to renounce everything.

IX A 13   n.d., 1848

« 478

In margin of 477 (IX A 13):
Seek first the kingdom of God. But what am I supposed to do? Shall I seek an office in order to be influential? No, first you shall seek God's kingdom. Shall I give all my fortune to the poor? No, first you shall seek God's kingdom and his righteousness. Shall I go out in the world as an apostle and proclaim this? No, first you shall seek God's kingdom. But isn't this in a certain sense doing nothing at all? Yes, to be sure, in a certain sense this is what it is.

IX A 14   n.d., 1848

« 479

John 16:20. (The gospel for the third Sunday after Easter.)
"Truly, truly, I say to you, you will weep and lament, but the world will rejoice; you will be sorrowful, but your sorrow will turn into joy."

This is the relationship between the Christian life and the secular mentality. In the first race it seems that secularity wins (the world will rejoice—you will weep and lament); but in the second race—yes, it is really only in Christianity that there is talk about a second race; the secular mentality is too empty and vain to run more than once, which is nothing at all. The Christian life really means a second time (just as "spirit" means a second time), and then sorrow will be turned into joy.

IX A 20   n.d., 1848

« 480

After all, many people think that the Christian message (i.e., to love one's neighbor as oneself) is purposely a little too rigorous—something like the household alarm clock which runs a half-hour fast so that one does not get up too late in the morning.

IX A 28 *n.d.*, 1848

« 481

Being a Christian is neither more nor less, without a doubt neither more nor less, than being a martyr; every Christian, that is, every true Christian, is a martyr.

But I hear one of those shabby pastors (by shabby I mean one of those who is shabby enough to accept two or three thousand rix-dollars a year, prestige with decorations, etc.—in order to betray Christianity) say: But, of course, we cannot all be martyrs. To this God would reply: Stupid man, do you not think I know how I have arranged the world. Fear only that it will never happen that all become Christians, that only 1/10, only 1/1000 become Christians.

The point is this—becoming a Christian is an examination given by God. But for this very reason in every age (year 1 and year 1848) it must continually be equally difficult to become a Christian. In a certain sense God has squandered so much upon existence [*Tilværelsen*] that at any and every moment there will be thousands upon thousands in abundance to persecute the true Christians—and yet in another sense it continues to be possible for every one of these thousands also to become a Christian.

The purpose (and this will also be the end of the matter) of Christendom's suddenly being called out for inspection is that in a more serious way all the sweat will be tormented out of all those shabby, profusely sweating clergymen.

Let us then once again in a noble Christian sense get shabby pastors, poor men who walk about in poor clothing, despised men whom all ridicule, mock, and spit upon. I hope and believe that with the assistance of God I would be able to preach fearlessly even if someone spat in my face as I climbed the stairs to the pulpit. But if I were to be dressed up in a velvet cloak with stars and ribbons and then name the name of Christ—I would die of shame.

IX A 51 *n.d.*, 1848

« 482

Christianity should not be lectured about. This is why Christ says,[280] my teaching is food—this is to show that it ought to be existed in [*der skal existeres deri*].

IX A 105 *n.d.*, 1848

« 483

But if Christ came into the world not to take away suffering, so that we can be comfortable, but to bring new suffering, does not this supposition make his coming into the world futile? Not at all. He came into the world to remake men in such a way that all these human sufferings (poverty, wretchedness, sickness, loss of status, etc.) would become childishness to be reckoned as nothing. Christ wants to remake the man partly by teaching him greater fear, fear of sin, partly by the salvation he promises, therefore by hope.

This is Christianity—but with the slightest diminution of the dialectical, it is no longer Christianity.

IX A 147 *n.d.*, 1848

« 484

On the whole there are two decisive mistakes with regard to Christianity.

(1) Christianity is not a doctrine (its being regarded as a doctrine accounts for all the disorders of orthodoxy, with strife over this and that, while existence [*Existentsen*] remains entirely unchanged, so that men quarrel over what is essentially Christian just as they quarrel over what is Platonic philosophy and so on) but an existential-communication [*Existents-Meddelelse*]. For this reason it begins over again with every generation. All the scholarship about the preceding generations is essentially superfluous, not to be scorned when it understands itself and its limitations, yet extremely dangerous when it does not.

(2) Consequently (since Christianity is not a doctrine), it is not a matter of indifference—as with a doctrine—who presents it if he only says objectively the right thing. No, Christ has not appointed assistant-professors—but imitators or followers [*Efterfølgere*]. When Christianity (precisely because it is not a doctrine) does not reduplicate itself in the one who presents it, he does not present Christianity; for Christianity is an existential-communication and can only be presented—by existing. Basically, to exist therein [*at existere deri*], to express it in one's existence etc.—this is what it means to reduplicate.

IX A 207 *n.d.*, 1848

« 485

Yes, right here is the real conflict between Christianity and man— the fact that Christianity is the absolute, or teaches that there is some absolute, and demands of the Christian that his life express that there is an absolute. It is in *this* sense that I say that I have not known a Christian; I have never seen any man whose life expressed *this*. The Christianity of Christians is profession and profession, an accent upon orthodoxy and an attack upon heterodoxy, etc., but their lives, just exactly like the pagans', express that men live in relativities. Their lives are nothing but relativities.

IX A 284   *n.d.*, 1848

« 486

It is Christianity's absolute character, the fact that what ought to help makes everything worse, which really brings reason to a standstill and constitutes the possibility of offense; people were better able to escape this in Luther's time. Actually, Luther here moves in the direction of imagination. Now the devil appears. Luther explains the contradiction to which reason points as being instigated by the devil. That means the matter does not become dialectical. The dialectical is this: here consolation is offered—and behold, the consolation is worse than what one otherwise suffers. Luther says of Christianity: Here is consolation. But then he does not dialectically place the next part together with it, but says: When one is ready to permit Christianity to help him, the devil is immediately there and from him come all the sufferings. This is entirely undialectical. The fact of the matter is that Christianity helps absolutely, but in its initial form the absolute means suffering for the relative man.

Luther's approach is similar to one's teaching a child to attribute everything good to God—evil comes from evil men, a bad man, etc. This is undialectical.

It is the same with Luther's understanding of Christianity. He distributes: the good is credited to Christianity; all sufferings, spiritual trial, etc., come from the devil. Dialectically one must say: both the consolation and the suffering come with Christianity, for this is the dialectic of the absolute, and Christianity is the absolute.

Luther smuggles away the real objection. Human reason, from its point of view, quite rightly says: What do I want with doctrine or help which makes the matter worse than it was before. To this Luther answers: What silly talk; Christianity is the help, sheer consolation and healing; all the disturbance comes from the devil.

This, to repeat, is undialectical. Upon closer examination one will also see that it does not explain anything; for then reason says: If what you say is so, why does not Christianity secure itself once and for all against the devil?

Dialectically the matter must be formulated this way: Christianity is the absolute; therein is found both the one and the other. Absolute help (it is found in the category-relationships themselves, since the actual relationship is lacking) is first of all suffering for one whose life is in the relative. But man as man lives in the relative.

For this reason Christianity cannot answer the question: Why? For in the absolute sense, "Why?" cannot be asked. The absolute is the absolute. But if "Why?" is asked relatively, Christianity cannot answer a relative *why*. In the one case it cannot be asked; in the other it cannot be answered. If I am absolutely seized by Christianity I cannot ask: Why is this doctrine? If I am living in the relative and ask *why*, Christianity cannot answer.

IX A 292 *n.d.*, 1848

« 487 *The Rarity of a True* CHRISTIAN

The rarity of a true Christian can be calculated as simply as an algebraic problem.

The first requirement is a man who in one way or another is desiring, seeking, possessing, etc., wholeheartedly—or, absolutely with passion or with absolute passion. Secondly, this desire, etc., is denied him, that is, his absolute passion gets an absolutely mortal wound (which, again, can only happen because he is absolutely in passion)—and then the question is whether he chooses faith.

The poet may be used as the deputy-auditor and examiner. For the poet can use a man who is absolutely in passion (and this is the first step in relation to becoming Christian). But how rare is such a person! The poet witnesses to the fact that there are scarcely ten in any generation. As for becoming a Christian, which consequently begins there where the poet leaves off—the poet finds practically no one.

But does not Christianity relate itself, then, to the common man? Yes, and this the poetic does too. It is poetically true that all are equal in passions, that a servant-girl and a princess, a shoemaker and a count, etc., are absolutely equal in being able to fall in love. Yet the poet teaches and insists that the poetic (absolute passion) is prodigiously rare. Then what about becoming a Christian?

The curious thing is that men actually are not offended when the poet protests that men's lives are poetically usable, all too prosaic; yet, on the other hand, they are enraged with the person who submits this protest in the name of Christianity. Here one sees (indirectly) what the situation is in Christendom, that in Christendom the poetic is really regarded as something far higher than being a Christian, so that in a country with one million Christians or, to put it more strictly(!), 100,000 Christians—there are scarcely ten poetically usable human beings.

What gibberish this established Christendom is!

IX A 297 *n.d.*, 1848

« 488

The same passion which, when God-fearingly tightened, leads to martyrdom, the same passion, when it is humanly relaxed along the way, changes into human sympathy, which spreads itself about and gets to be loved, esteemed by men.

This is or can be a spiritual trial [*Anfægtelse*] which comes in weak moments when the soul cannot hold to the absolute: "But then you can do a little for others" (just as if sacrifice in the service of truth were not doing something for others), "You could knock off a little; there are so many everywhere who know less than you, so many sick you could comfort," etc. If this temporary interruption is victorious, then essential Christianity is reduced to a merely human sympathy. The essentially Christian and the absolute are unconditionally one: absolute recklessness. Christ says: [281] Let the dead bury their dead.

More particularly, the spiritual trial is: to the question "Why?" one has no *why*—this is precisely the absolute.

IX A 300 *n.d.*, 1848

« 489

Yes, humanly speaking, there is something cruel about Christianity. But this is not due to Christianity; it is due to the fact that it has to exist [*existere*] in a sinful world, manifest itself and expand in a sinful world. The cruelty is not Christianity but what happens to Christianity. Christianity itself is gentleness and love, or love itself or itself love.

Yes, humanly speaking, there is something cruel in what is required of the Christian—yet, no, not in what is required of him but in what happens to him, for this is not due to Christianity—it is due partly to the fact that he himself is a sinner, partly to the fact that the world in which he has to live is sinful. Christianity requires simply that he should love men with his whole heart; it is not the fault of Christianity that this is rewarded with persecution. But answer this question honestly: Could you wish that Christianity did not require as much, not quite as much, wish that it compromised and thus made life a little more comfortable for you—could you then love Christianity as much? It is your own weakness which in a weak moment might wish that Christianity were different, and were it then to be different, you would disapprove of it. It is the same as when a young girl in love requests out of weakness something from her beloved which she afterward basically regrets, partly because he has gone down in her estimation, must go down in her estimation because of his indulging her—and yet she is weak enough to ask.

Remember the eternal—and that tale in A *Thousand and One Nights*. A poor couple who only by scraping and scratching can make a living implore heaven again and again for help. One night a precious gem falls down to them. Thus they are helped. But then the woman dreams one night that she is in heaven where she sees gorgeous thrones inlaid with precious gems for all the righteous. She asks if there isn't one for her husband. They show it to her—but it lacks that precious gem. Then she reflects—better to lack a little in this world than to go through all eternity sitting on a throne which lacks the precious gem. So they ask God to take that precious stone back again.

IX A 329   *n.d.*, 1848

« 490

This beats all, this humble objection to Christianity: that Christianity seems too lofty. O, one himself feels all too keenly that he is far from being good—and then to have to be good in such a way that he is persecuted for it. When one considers human life, sees how demanding it is merely to keep in line with civil justice, if then one ponders the moral demands upon a man's innermost being if he is to be considered good—which no one, however, is, not even Christ wanted to be called that—and then to be good in such a way that one suffers *for it*. That this was the case with Christ is something entirely different. So it seems that Christianity really is suitable only for Christ.

But to this must be answered that this is the way it is as soon as a man or a Christian turns toward God; but he must let himself be instructed by Christianity that the world is so evil that one needs to approach the good only at a remote distance before one begins to suffer some persecution.

And yet, I dare not leave the impression that I suffer because I am good. What is to be done, then, if this is the way it is—that if I do not want to abandon the good, I must carry the distinction of suffering for it. There is nothing else to do than constantly, as much as is possible, to turn one's gaze inward so that I am before God, where I shall not be troubled by the thought that I am so good, and on the other hand, if possible, be as if absentminded about the sufferings which the world inflicts upon me.

At the same time it can also be an untrue weakness if a God-fearing man, because he is in awe before God, almost makes it appear that those who do him wrong are justified. A Christian should have the confident courage freely and positively to witness against the world; in suffering he should not get away with the *erhabne Lüge* that the others are right. To be patient in this way is not godly.

What is to be done then? This—that a Christian remembers every day that Rome was not built in a day, that in one year he may perhaps accomplish what he does not accomplish today, if only he is honest before God. If he is so overwhelmed by his God-relationship that his patience is pretty close to committing the untruth that the others who are doing wrong are in the right—then he should hope and believe that he will get sufficient confident courage in time.

IX A 350 *n.d.*, 1848

« 491

The fact of the matter is that Christianity is really all too joyous, and therefore really to stick to Christianity a man must be brought to madness by suffering. Most men, therefore, will be able to get a real impression of Christianity only in the moment of their death, because death actually takes away from them what must be surrendered in order to get an impression of Christianity.

IX A 360 *n.d.*, 1848

« 492

It is still unconditionally certain and true that if a man in all earnestness would comply with the words:[282] Whatever you wish that men would do to you, do so to them, and if God impinged upon a man so powerfully in the God-relationship that with his gaze only upon God he became blind to everything else and acted according to these words—then his contemporaries would at the very least burst into laughter. For the wisdom of the secular mind is always a relativism; in doing well I should also be relative: be careful, differentiate between a person of status and a simple man and a beggar, etc., and organize my well-doing in proportion to this relativity. If I forget this relativity, then the comical appears. And no one will care about my acting out of fear and trembling before God. It is absolutely impossible, absolutely, for a Christian not to make himself laughable. For what is more laughable than the absolute in this world, which is a world of relativity (the category determination is dialectically accurate), but the true Christian fears God absolutely. He dares not be content with relatively expressing that he finds a certain relative likeness between himself and a poor man; no, he expresses what before God is the truth, absolute likeness—and then it is altogether impossible to avoid the world's laughter, and esthetically the world is completely justified in this laughter, for it is quite according to the rules of esthetics.

This, again, here as everywhere else, is not anything I have hit upon and perhaps make a big noise about—that the world is like this, so evil, now. No, it was this way in the year 1, the year 335, and the year 1848— and it will be just the same in the year 10,008.

IX A 394 *n.d.*, 1848

« 493 N.B.   N.B.

To be a Christian involves a double danger.

First, all the intense internal suffering involved in becoming a Christian, this losing human reason and being crucified on the paradox. —This is the issue *Concluding Postscript* presents as ideally as possible.

Then the danger of the Christian's having to live in the world of secularity and here express that he is a Christian. Here belongs all the later productivity, which will culminate in what I have ready at present and which could be published under the title: *Collected Works of Consummation* (cf. this journal, p. 21) [i.e., IX A 390].

When this has been done, the question bursts forth as with elemental power: But how can it occur to a human being to want to subject himself to all this, why should he be a Christian when it is so demanding? The first answer might be: Hold your tongue; Christianity is the absolute, you shall. But another answer may also be given: Because the consciousness of sin within him allows him no rest anywhere; its grief strengthens him to endure everything else if he can only find reconciliation.

This means that the grief of sin must be very deep within a person, and therefore Christianity must be presented as the difficult thing it is, so that it may become entirely clear that Christianity only is related to the consciousness of sin. To want to be involved in becoming a Christian for any other reason is literally foolishness—and so it must be.

IX A 414 *n.d.*, 1848

« 494

Infant baptism can very well stand, but confirmation ought to be postponed to the twenty-fifth year.

IX A 461 *n.d.*, 1848

« 495

It is really Christianity's discovery that the sin of the world or that sin is a double lie: first, the lie of regarding it as madness, untruth, and then the lie of wanting this to be right, to be honored for doing this. It is a lie of the first magnitude: to get earthly advantages through the communication of truth—the next lie is that getting advantages in this way is supposed to be earnestness, is honored as earnestness, as wisdom in contrast to dreams.

x^1 A 178   n.d., 1849

« 496 *For Life*

My friend, you have now lived for a time in the world, in the world of men, and will perhaps live many more years in this world where men naturally have unqualified superiority over you, a single human being, and you dare not count on God's direct intervention for your sake. If, then, you expect in a human sense to see happy and pleasant days, then never let yourself become involved in Christianity *in earnest*—in earnest, for you can easily do it in the ordinary preacher-way. Yes, do not even speak of it. If you do it [become involved in earnest], you will find out how it will go with you, how busy the clergy will be in preserving the congregations' cherished illusions in which they are so cozily ensconced and which also protect the pastors' paid occupations.

If in any way your life expresses that you love God in earnest (consequently according to God's conception), you will be badly treated by men, and in the same degree, and worse in the very same degree as your life more and more expresses that you more truly love God. To dabble in human sympathy, to haggle, is not Christianity. If this were Christianity, then Christ's own life was not Christianity and no paradigm at all. Do not even speak of this, for it points again to the illusion of trillions of Christians and then to the illusion of "paid occupation."

Humanly speaking, there is an almost mad self-contradiction in Christianity's requirement, which is the anguish of being a Christian. It sets a task and says: In the same degree as you succeed, you will come to suffer more and more. You will continually think: "But, Lord God, if I rightly love men—then . . . . ." The Christian answer to this must be: Stupid man, or presumptuous man, did not the Savior of the world rightly love men, and he was mocked, spit upon, etc.; has it not been this way for all true Christians, and if not, it merely indicates that they were not Christians, for the prototype settles everything.

This contradiction in what Christianity requires and predicts is like a father's saying to his child, "This and this is what you are to do, this is the task, this you shall do—do you understand me?—If not, then shake in your boots,"and then adding, "This, then, is the task, but to the same degree, precisely to the same degree that you exert yourself more and more and are more diligent, more vigilant, etc., and to the same degree that you succeed better in the task, you will also come to suffer more." If a father were to talk to his child in this way, it indeed would seem madness to the child, and the child would be right (disregarding the confusion of suffering and suffering the same thing but as punishment), if he said: In that case it is better not to begin at all, since I come out just as well, and therefore I am better off sparing myself all the trouble and effort.

But this is the way Christianity speaks to a person (as that father to the child)—this is Christianity. But then Christianity adds: But remember that there is an eternity.

Yes, but this means: if you desire, humanly speaking, pleasant and happy days, then never get involved *in earnest* with Christianity.

If you do, there is humanly only one consolation for you: death, for which you will learn to long more impatiently than the most amorous girl longs to see her lover again. Yet death is no consolation either. But truly there is, there is one consolation—the eternal. Love the eternal, then you hate this life—this is Christianity. Love God, then you hate this world—this is Christianity. Love Christ, then you are hated by all men—this is Christianity.

See, this is Christianity. If you are not conscious of being a sinner to the degree that in the anxiety of the anguished conscience you do not dare anything other than to commit yourself to Christ—then you never will become a Christian. Only the agony of the consciousness of sin can explain the fact that a person will submit to this radical cure. To become a Christian is the most fearful operation of all, of all. Just as unlikely as it is for a person who merely feels a little indisposed to think of submitting to the most painful operation, just as unlikely is it for a man to think of getting involved with Christianity if sin did not pain him inordinately— if, note well, he then knows what Christianity is and has not been talked into some nonsense about Christianity's gentle, life-beautifying, and ennobling ground of comfort.

X^1 A 190   *n.d.*, 1849

« 497

There is only one consistent conception of Christianity, and that is to be slain for the sake of truth, to become a martyr, naturally not helter-skelter, the sooner the better, but with the most thorough-going reflection as an aid.

Suicide, occasioned by not being able to endure the tedious preparatory work of the martyr, is a misinterpretation of this only true and consistent conception of Christianity (every other view is secular, temporal, earthly, cowardly, or stupid delay).

x^1 A 217   *n.d.*, 1849

« 498

All human religiousness, and also Judaism, culminates in the words of Solomon (or David):[283] I have been young, and now am old, yet I have not seen the righteous forsaken by God.

Compassionate God—and then it is Christ who says:[284] My God, my God, why have you forsaken me, and it is Christianity which makes this whole earthly existence [*Tilværelse*] into suffering, crucifixion.

Then how do you get a mild morality out of Christianity!

x^1 A 301   *n.d.*, 1849

« 499

A tragic result of the completely mistaken, twisted, totally unchristian view, the majority view that truth is where the majority is—a tragic result of this is that people are always talking as if Christianity had become more true because there are now so many millions of Christians. They say that when Christianity came into the world miracles were needed because there were so few Christians; now that there are so many Christians, indeed, almost all are Christians, now miracles are not needed. Well, thanks for that, but it seems to me that miracles are needed now more than ever. They do not maintain that Christianity is a militant teaching, is a polemic, that it posits eternal enmity between God and the world, and then they turn the relationship around and say it—this polemical view—wins (according to men's quite scatterbrained notion of winning) because the majority assume it.

Moreover, there is something objectionable to me in all this talk about miracles being needed at that time, just as if human reason were subsequently competent to see through God's tactics, which reason understands neither before nor afterward. But we are vain; we want so very much to comprehend or appear to comprehend; we want so very much to fraternize with God.

To put it very simply—miracles happened at that time; therefore, they may well have been needed—but I do not allow myself to speculate about how they were needed.

It is this disastrous impertinence of scholarship toward God which is all too difficult to root out.

X^1 A 399   n.d., 1849

« 500

It is not difficult for men to understand Christianity, but what is difficult for them is to understand the degree of self-overcoming and renunciation which Christianity demands. Established Christendom promotes this situation by brilliantly proving that one can be a Christian —and also as secular-minded as anyone.

It is dangerous to have to tighten the screw of essentially Christian self-renunciation—and thus contend with men who insist that they know very well what Christianity is.

X^1 A 427   n.d., 1849

«501

Humanly understood, things look like this. This earthly life has sorrows and misfortunes in great number (sickness, poverty, etc.). Let us help one another as well as we are able; honor and praise to anyone who hits upon new means and methods—and then comes Christianity and brings only a new occasion for need and wretchedness: the truth—to be obliged to suffer for the truth.

X^1 A 438   n.d., 1849

« 502

All the objections to Christianity—what are they, after all, to the person who in truth is conscious of being a sinner and in truth has experienced belief in the forgiveness of sins in this name and in this faith is saved from his former sin.

The only conceivable objection would be: Yes, but it was still possible that you could have been saved in some other way. But to this he cannot reply. It is just like a person in love. If someone were to say: Yes, but you could perhaps have fallen in love with another girl—then he must answer: To this I cannot reply, for I know only one thing, that this is my beloved. As soon as the person who is in love can reply to this objection, he is then *eo ipso* not in love. And as soon as a believer can reply to this objection, he is *eo ipso* not a believer.

X^1 A 443   n.d., 1849

« 503

There is only one, and quite rightly pathological, proof of the truth of Christianity—when the anxiety of sin and the burdened conscience constrain a man to cross the narrow line between despair unto madness—and Christianity.

There lies Christianity.

x¹ A 467 *n.d.*, 1849

« 504

Perhaps it is not required at all that you should let yourself be slain for Christianity or bring many sacrifices, but you must have offered yourself absolutely. But then can anyone observe whether or not a person has done this? No, nor is he supposed to be able to do this; yet it must be remembered that one can get a kind of suspicion about a man's whole life when one puts together all the external data. Even if you are altogether pure, you will have to submit to this as your cross; you will have to endure this misunderstanding, as if in all inwardness you had not offered absolutely—this is the least you can suffer in recompense for not coming into the dangers of actuality.

x¹ A 471 *n.d.*, 1849

« 505

Christ halted Paul and said:²⁸⁵ Saul, Saul, why do you persecute me? It is perhaps a more common shattering conversion when Christ halts a person and says: Saul, Saul, why do you run away from me, why are you afraid of me; I am in fact your savior. This is the transition-crisis in becoming a Christian, that is, the person who is to become a Christian is first of all anxious before Christ, although he relates himself to him.

x¹ A 472 *n.d.*, 1849

« 506

In margin of 505 (x¹ A 472):

The words of the angel to Mary Magdalene at the grave²⁸⁶ could be used here: Do not be afraid; for I know that you seek Jesus of Nazareth; because until confidence in his grace and compassion appears, the person who seeks Jesus at first actually experiences fear before him, before his holiness.

x¹ A 473 *n.d.*, 1849

« 507

To the natural man the Christian view of life must seem to be a hatred toward life, and the pagans were justified as pagans in calling Christians: *odium generis humani.*

"Established Christendom" has messed the whole thing up with human sympathy, and therefore the natural man is almost highly pleased with—yes, with Christendom, which, of course, is not Christianity.

In margin: And besides, when the sum total of religiousness is nothing more than the solemnity of Sunday in quiet hours, from whence should the possibility of offense come? The possibility of offense lies precisely in this, that the solemnity should be in the everyday.

x¹ A 547   n.d., 1849

« 508

Christianity tends above all toward actuality, toward being made actuality, the only medium to which it truly is related. It is not to be possessed in any way other than by being made actual; it is not communicated except to or in upbuilding and awakening. It must always be assumed that there are some who do not have it or who are still lagging far behind—therefore there must be labor on their behalf. But Christianity dare not be communicated in the medium of tranquillity (less so because one who does this ventures to affirm that now all are Christians). Therefore, Christianly understood, the artistic, the poetic, the speculative, the scientific, the pedagogical are sin—how do I dare give myself the tranquillity to sit this way and piddle with it!

Martensen, whose activity is to find half-terms and definitions, also says²⁸⁷ that Christianity must be a life, an actual life—and now come the assertions—a genuinely actual life, a completely genuine, actual life in us; one must not relate himself to Christianity by way of imagination. Good. But Martensen's own existence—what does this express? It expresses that he wants to be a success in the world, have great honor and regard, be in a high office, etc.—is this the actualization of Christianity?

As a philosopher, Martensen makes assertions and is not at all dialectical, and as a Christian, he also merely makes assertions. Generally the categories are purely rhetorical—which can very well beguile a person.

I am a little more than a poet to the extent that I nevertheless have had the courage to expose myself to ridicule and endure it. But I have had the advantage of a living. I do not believe I achieve any more. I withdraw, but with God's help I shall keep an enthusiastic vision of those who achieved more.

x¹ A 558   n.d., 1849

« 509

Christ as the God-man could, of course, have continued as long as required; it cannot be assumed that suffering consumed him; but otherwise it is quite typical that he did not go beyond his thirty-fourth year. If being a Christian in the most rigorous sense is to be endured from childhood on (whereby the overwhelming impression of Christianity—if it is rigorous Christianity which is communicated—promptly overstrains the child) and is continued more rigorously without becoming a kind of illusion: such a person can hardly live more than thirty-four years.

x^1 A 649   *n.d.*, 1849

« 510

In margin: About "The decline"

"The decline" which Christianity predicts[288] before the consummation of everything probably will come, indirectly, from Christianity itself.

The deepest confusion of Christianity is the profane, frivolous way in which Christianity has been identified with the world and all are made Christians as a matter of course—in short, the greatest deterioration has been the concept "Christendom," which in our time is simply synonymous with mankind.

Now if Christianity again rises up and regains its tension, this Christian-world will become furious; now comes the decision—and the decision will probably be that if this business of being a Christian is going to get so serious, then they will give it up.

We must not forget that "the decline" can come from the world, from the offended, the demonic, the free-thinkers, and the like, but also, as shown here, dialectically and indirectly from Christianity itself.

The world's greatest offense at Christianity was indeed when Christ lived. Then the whole world repudiated Christianity. That was not a decline, for the world at that time was not shamming Christianity.

All this sloppy optimism that all are to become Christians has no place in Christianity; Christ himself says:[289] When the Son of man comes, will he find faith on earth?

"The decline" will carry greater guilt than did the first offense at Christianity, because the basis of "the decline" is that men have pretended to be Christians.

x^2 A 37   *n.d.*, 1849

« 511 *Christianity in the Situation of Possibility—
and in the Situation of Actuality*

As soon as I take Christianity as a doctrine and then apply my acumen or my profundity or my eloquence or my imagination to presenting it, people think it is fine and I am regarded as an earnest Christian, I am esteemed, etc.

As soon as I will express existentially [*existentielt*] what I say, consequently situate Christianity in actuality—then it is exactly as if I had blown up the world. People are immediately scandalized.

Take the rich young man—let me then preach [*in margin*: But remember one thing, preaching must be your job and your living; job and livelihood are the genuinely popular; even the most abstruse philosophy becomes almost popular when people know that it is a person's livelihood] about his not being perfect, that he could not bring himself to giving everything to the poor, but that the true Christian is always willing to give everything. Let me preach this way, and people are deeply moved and I am esteemed. But if I were a rich young man and went and gave all my possessions to the poor—then people would be scandalized. They would find it a ridiculous exaggeration. —Take Mary Magdalene. Let me preach about her deep consciousness of sin, the passion which becomes indifferent to everything but her sin, which goes out to the Savior, opening herself up to all kinds of ridicule, etc. I concentrate on moving people to tears, and I the speaker (note—if preaching happens to be my job, for otherwise the affair would appear to men to be exaggerated) will be regarded as an earnest Christian, I will be esteemed. If, however, I myself, conscious of being a sinner, if suddenly I actually step forward with a public confession of sin, offense arises immediately, people will consider it vanity and ridiculous exaggeration. —To preach that the true Christian consults God in everything is moving (naturally, if it is your job to preach; otherwise it would be disturbing)—if in actuality a man does step forward and refers to his having consulted God, this is censured as presumption, pride, exaggeration, madness. —Picture those quiet spirits who, remote from life, filled their souls with only the thought of God—it will move to tears (but naturally, preaching must be your job; otherwise people would not accept it; you yourself become an exaggeration to them). But let someone really do it and he becomes an object of ridicule. People almost regard it as their duty to ridicule and laugh at him.

x^2 A 141   *n.d.*, 1849

« 512

Christianity has been changed too much into a consolation, and we have forgotten that it is a *requirement*. Woe unto you, you flabby preachers! The result is that it becomes so much more frightfully costly for the person who is to proclaim Christianity again.

x^2 A 187   *n.d.*, 1849

« 513 *A Proposal to Put an End to All the Nonsense about How One Enters into Christianity*

In regard to all existential [*existentiel*] knowing, the main thing is to bring about the situation. This is what people have completely forgotten, and for this reason they cannot get an impression of Christianity.

I am thinking of a man who so far does not have any impression of Christianity and is not deeply gripped by the sense of his sin but lives on in the comfortable notion that he is still going to be saved.

Let him then take and read the New Testament. No one can deny that the ethical teaching presented here is such that it moves the imagination of every man.

Well, now, let him begin there. He carries out his intention to realize Christianity; for the present, he says, it makes no difference whether Christ has existed [*har været til*] or not, who wrote the New Testament, etc.

And so he carries it out. But look, because he carries it out, he will in a Christian way collide with the world; he will be abused as an egotist just when he acts more disinterestedly, etc.

Now the pinch comes, now he cannot hold out alone—now he must have religious help. In order to hold out against the surrounding world he must have religious help. But not for this reason alone—he must also have it to hold out against himself. Simply because the world squeezes him so strongly, he must—in order to hold out by himself—be entirely sure at every moment that the error is not in him, that he perfectly realizes the good.

See, now the matter is in full swing; now he needs grace; now he needs Christ.

This is Christianity. Let a person just begin seriously to will to realize it and he will soon learn to need Christ. Let him literally give all his fortune to the poor, literally love his neighbor, etc. and he will soon learn to need Christ. Christianity is a suit which at first glance and to the imagination seems attractive enough, but as soon as one actually puts it on—then one must have Christ's help in order to be able to live in it.

It seems to me that this is very simple. But this aspect of Christianity people have completely abolished. And yet this aspect is suggested in Christ's words:[290] If anyone wills to do what I say, he shall experience etc.; he shall experience—yes, it is almost ironical, he shall first of all experience that he needs the help of Christ.

X^2 A 284   *n.d.*, 1849

« 514 *An Objection to Christianity Poetic*

This objection may be conceived in a particular way so that it does not have any of the impudence which objections usually have.

It might go something like this:

Why, O God, did you wish to do so much for men that you gave them Christianity, which really makes them unhappy.

No doubt you did it out of love, but you do not seem to have considered that a very humble and insignificant person can come to suffer very much simply by becoming the object of a very superior person's love. The very superior person promptly lays down his standard—he does what he does out of love, but the fact that he employs his standard cannot be avoided, since he is who he is. But what does he do? He actually makes the other unhappy.

It is the same with Christianity! It is your standard, O God, which is Christianity; in Christianity you really related yourself to yourself. To be sure, you say it is out of love, that you do it for our sake. But the standard is still yours.* How in the world could it occur to a man that sin was something so terrible that in order for your wrath to be appeased, your own Son, the Holy One, had to suffer cruel death. This is too high for a man. It is you who are appeased, but what sets you at rest is too high for man and therefore is precisely the thing that disturbs him.

Suppose a girl is loved by a man who is decidedly superior to her; the more sincerely he loves her, the unhappier he will make her—and out of love. He applies his standard; he cannot do otherwise; he loves her sincerely; and what happens—the very thing which he regards as the strongest expression for his love, precisely this will be too high for her and will disturb her.

This objection is an odd one. But it takes a completely different view of the matter than the usual objections against Christianity.

Here one sees, by the way, the necessity for the unconditional *thou shalt* in order to pull through.

x^2 A 420   *n.d.*, 1850

« 515

* *In margin of 514* (x^2 A 420):

In the same way original sin as guilt is also an expression of God's using his standard; for God sees everything *in uno*; and therefore the merely human understanding finds it so difficult.

x^2 A 421   *n.d.*, 1850

« 516

The use made of the "Church" is also an indulgence from the crucial decisions related to becoming a Christian. What a difference between the time when there was no Christianity but a beginning had to be made, and the weight of the world fell with almost crushing impact upon "the single individual's" decision to become a Christian—and now when the accumulation of 1,800 years of colossal illusions has changed it almost into a kind of trick, something one becomes but knows not quite how.

These 1,800 years are so far from being a proof of the truth of Christianity that one could (in a religious way, even though it is irreligious inasmuch as it is mutinous) rather convert it to an argument against Christianity—that providence has allowed Christianity to sink so far down in an illusion. But it must not be forgotten that it is the fault of the Christians; then Christianity almost changes into the most frightful charge against the human race, that after Christianity was implanted, it let it degenerate to such an extent that it has become meaningless, unrecognizable in a colossal delusion.

If this battle is to be fought through, it will be more horrible than when Christianity came into the world; with intensified passion it will call true Christianity the *odium totius generis humani*. After the world has established itself in Christianity, taken possession of it—then to want to take Christianity away, that is, make Christianity what it was—then the world will really let loose. The martyrs will not bleed as formerly because they are Christians—no, it is almost insane!—they will be put to death because they are *not* Christians. Frightful drama! And how alone the martyr will stand! Simply because the contrast then was so glaringly obvious and qualitative, it was far easier to choose either/or decisively. But now the illusion has enervated the contrast. If someone ventures out and barely meets any opposition, the illusion is promptly at his service with a new little refinement, and he recedes again. In the beginning the world pressured the Christian into character; nowadays the illusion, inexhaustibly inventive, continually rips him out of character. To find footing was not the problem when Christianity fought against paganism, for the qualitative opposition of mutual contrasts provided the footing; nowadays it takes almost superhuman powers merely to find footing, for day in and day out the illusion continually slips in. Let a man be condemned for life because of conviction—well, that is a test; but if that settles the matter, it can still be coped with. But suppose that every eight days the punishment is intensified by a new interrogation and that a document is placed before him—if he will sign it, he is free—this is a frightful intensification. And yet if it is word for word the same formulation—it can be coped with. But let him be interrogated every other hour—and a new formulation repeatedly be laid before him—if he signs it, he is free—this is beyond human powers. This is what battling an illusion is like. At every moment the illusion is perfectible; it counterfeits, but in illusion, the position of the witness-of-truth, and says: Good Lord, we are agreed—why do you want to make yourself unhappy and disturb the rest of us. This is torture.

Paganism truly did not claim to possess Christianity, but the illusion is not willing at any price to be done out of the notion that it possesses Christianity. The illusion is willing at any moment to bid differently—all in proportion to the resources of the witness-of-truth; but it does not want decision. The illusion is willing to make concessions to a remarkable degree (as in bidding at an auction)—but one thing is certain: it sticks basically to tradition.

To move ahead in this kind of battle, the witness-of-truth must have not only an almost superhuman cunning but an almost superhuman cunningness in being cruel to himself. One weak moment—that is enough—then the illusion swallows him; then he himself does not know inside from out—and so he makes the task for the next witness-of-truth 50 per cent more difficult.

The most terrible battle does not occur when one idea opposes another; no, the most terrible battle occurs when two men say one and the same thing—and the battle is over the interpretation, and the interpretation nevertheless constitutes a qualitative difference. Instead of letting the interpretation be the focus of battle, the deluder is interested in keeping the first notion meaningless in the foreground: we are saying one and the same thing.

Everything has become reversed. There was a time when the world wanted to fight—then Christianity fought. Now the world is in fraudulent possession of Christianity, and its tactics therefore are: with all its power, at any price, to prevent a showdown. It is as when a swindler has misgivings—if the matter goes to court, he has lost—and therefore all his tactics are directed toward keeping it from going to court. In the realm of the spirit this is far easier than in the actuality of civil life, for the technique consists in continually counterfeiting the other party's position so that to a certain extent they are saying the same thing—but good God, then we are agreed!

Then suppose someone asserts that the world has progressed since that time: then, when it persecuted the Christians with fire and sword, and now—when with all the power of the liar it battles for the appearance of being Christian.

But what is the struggle about, then? To be a Christian requires so much self-denial that it cannot be particularly inviting to the world. Right—but the world regards Christianity in another way. It has a fixed idea that somehow in this teaching there is nevertheless an insurance for eternity, and therefore it is imprudent to give it up. To give up this make-believe in order really to become a Christian is, of course, just as imprudent, for then the insurance is too high-priced. It would be crazy for anyone to pay his whole fortune in order to insure—yes, what would there be left to insure? No, one pays a certain percentage—thus no prudent man would be without insurance. And this is the way the world wants to have its Christianity. It is impossible to make clear that Christianity cannot be had in this way; because the world does not want to understand this, does not want to take the matter so much in earnest. But that someone should compel it to surrender the name of Christian and consequently to step out of the insurance company—no, never! The person who works for that is not only the enemy of man but also of God.

Influenced as the world has been by Christianity in a volatized tradition, the world's impression is somewhat as follows: there is still the question of eternal life—a prudent man does something about it for safety's sake; he insures himself and pays a certain percentage a year. One insures himself—only then is he at peace. Now he can enjoy life; now for the first time—as "the pastor" [changed from "Mynster"] so beautifully puts it—the joys of life have their true taste. What joys? Well, let us not talk about that (nor about their "true" taste). He gets himself insured; now he has something which—as "the pastor" [changed from "Mynster"] so beautifully puts it—can alleviate the cares and sufferings of life. Ah, yes! if one is "earnest" enough to be able to free himself completely from the worry that this whole business of insurance might possibly be irregular, that it might possibly be a bubble, so that what is most needed is an insurance company to guarantee the insurance. But, to be sure, this we have; we have the clergy. Look to them, and you will readily see, drawing the conclusion from their security, the security with which you can insure yourself with them—and on much cheaper and more favorable terms. Just listen to their reasons and proofs—yes, no insurance salesman knows how to recommend his company in this way; it is as obvious as $2 + 2 = 4$ that insurance here does not in the slightest way mean "risking" anything, that it is rather the most prudent of all calculated moves, to secure for oneself at a bargain-basement price the most inestimable of all goods, the true good, "which for the first time gives the joys of life their true taste and gently alleviates the cares." They do the whole thing for you with no fuss at all. All you have to do is give your name, which the church secretary then places in "the Book of Life," and thus you are recorded. And in order that externals should not disturb you in any way, the clergy—who could easily look too earnest since they alone are responsible for this serious matter of insuring for eternity—have done everything in order externally etc. to be just like you.

And if anyone (who is registered with and known to the secretary and consequently—it amounts to the same thing—to heaven) says to "the pastor," "But is it entirely certain that there is an immortality?" (that he is certain that there are immortality and eternal happiness, of that there is no doubt; his doubt is whether it is certain that there are an immortality and an eternal salvation), then he answers, "Nothing is more certain; if there should prove to be—for a moment let us suppose the preposterous—no immortality, then see to it you get hold of me in the next life and you will get your money back, and you will also have the right to call me a deceiver—yes, and if you want to, you can put me to death. But one thing you will not in all fairness be able to upbraid me for, neither here nor in the next life (and least of all in that final place where you will find with glad surprise that you have received 'the eternal weight of glory beyond all comparison,' as Paul says),[291] that we are too high-priced; for it can be mathematically illustrated with precise accuracy that the Lutheran Church in Denmark offers just about the lowest price, while its insurance in all respects is just as safe, yes, probably even more secure, than that of Catholicism and other confessions, which, however, make greater demands on the policy-holders."

X^2 A 460 n.d., 1850

« 517 *Has a Christian the right to use cleverness, except inversely, not to make his life easy but to make it difficult, not to avoid danger but to enter into it?*

Granted that Christianity is a doctrine (as it objectively is called), that consequently it is a sum of doctrinal statements. It is now clear that this same thing can be said in many different ways and still *qua* doctrine remain the same. For example, the difference can be that one person (aided by his how of saying it) gains extraordinary good fortune; another (aided by his how of saying the same thing) is persecuted—is it then the same thing, the same Christianity, and has a Christian the right to use his cleverness in the direction of the first *how?*

Note. Incidentally, we see here how foolish it is to call Christianity a doctrine, for then the difference of one person's gaining good fortune by proclaiming the same thing for which the other must suffer would be completely unessential if they actually were saying the same thing. Thus, with respect to Plato's philosophy, for example, if two people are actually declaring the identical truth, then if one uses his cleverness to achieve success as well and the other scorns this cleverness and becomes persecuted—this difference is essentially of no consequence.

But Christianity is not a doctrine; it is an existence-communication [*Existents-Meddelelse*].

x^2 A 603   *n.d.*, 1850

« 518 *The Essential Relationship of Reduplication to Christianity*

It would be a very strange idea, thought, view, and the like, if one were enthusiastic about Christianity and employed all his powers directly to winning men to it and then would not be able to enlist a few for it.

But this direct relationship is really not Christianity. The essentially Christian is the rigorousness of the reduplication [*Reduplicationens*] with which the teacher, even more cruel toward himself in serving the idea, watches lest the winning of men develop into an illusion for them, lest it become something they say, etc., also lest the cause very gradually go backward, lest it be held to the center less than originally, which usually is the case the more there are who join up.

x^3 A 100   *n.d.*, 1850

« 519 *Christianity—the Human*

How far Christianity is from being related directly to being a human being, so that only a little eloquence is needed to get people to enter into it, is best seen in that the genuine proclaimers of Christianity have had to be constrained against their will and *qua* human beings would rather be free.

But we are spoiled by being brought up in Christianity from childhood. This is the way we live: we make life for ourselves as self-indulgent as possible, and then we have the consolation of having Christianity in reserve, but this is not really Christianity.

x^3 A 134   *n.d.*, 1850

« 520 *My Conception of Christianity*

When it is introduced, a great cry will go up that it is an exaggeration, that I really want to abolish Christianity or frighten people away from it, etc.

To that, this answer. When from generation to generation these thousands and millions have been permitted unchallenged to diminish and to diminish [Christianity]—well, then the reversal certainly must appear to be a frightful exaggeration, especially since (for the simple reason that the error has been continued for such a long time) it must be taken, if possible, to a qualitative extreme so that the reversal itself does not finally become conformed to the error.

But in such a case the mistake does not lie in the reversal but in the earlier error.

x^3 A 172   *n.d.*, 1850

« 521 *My Opinion*

is that it is entirely in order that a teacher of Christianity be paid by those who learn; on the other hand, I also think that in all eternity it is not right to alter Christianity in order to make people more willing to pay the teacher—for what then is really not Christianity. If this is what they prefer, fine, but then let them quit calling it Christianity.

x^3 A 173   *n.d.*, 1850

« 522

My activity with regard to the essentially Christian.

It is to nail down the Christian qualifications in such a way that no doubt, no reflection, shall be able to get hold of them. It is like locking the door and throwing away the key; thus the Christian qualifications are made inaccessible to reflection. Only the choice remains: will you believe or will you not believe, but the chatter of reflection cannot get hold of it.

x^3 A 209   *n.d.*, 1850

« 523 *To Dispute with Men about What Christianity Is*

is a misunderstanding, because with rare exceptions their tactic is specifically directed to defending themselves against understanding or getting to know what Christianity is, because they have a suspicion that it is rather easy to understand, but that it would disturb their lives.

x^3 A 285   *n.d.*, 1850

« 524 *That Christianity Does Not Fit into the World*

is proved perfectly by Christ's own life.

Nowadays, as the saying goes, Christianity has spread all over—yes, but one pays no attention to the fact that perhaps it should first be demonstrated that what has spread all over is Christianity; on the other hand, no proof is needed that what Christ proclaimed was Christianity.

They boast that nowadays all are Christians and do not note how satirical it is that when Christ proclaimed Christianity, all fled—therefore the tremendous propagation is very likely due to the fact that it is not Christianity which is being proclaimed.

x^3 A 362   n.d., 1850

« 525 *Ordinary Christians—Extraordinary Christians*

The Sophists automatically present this distinction as one of their fixed ideas: the great requirements are not for all of us. Rather than that there shall be only one kind of Christian and that we are all measured by the criterion of the ideal—in order to learn humility and also the elevation—rather than this, the self-satisfaction which appears when one [is measured] only according to his given relativities.

The best example of such consequent sophistry and indulgence is *La devotion aisée*, the comfortable piety (Paris: 1652), by Le Moine, a Jesuit. (Selections are found in Reuchlin's *Life of Pascal*, p. 296 *et passim*). Here a system is developed and mediocrity is completely legitimized.

The whole book deserves to be presented, because it corresponds so well to the way of preaching customary now. And if one did this, without mentioning the title or that its author was a Jesuit, most of the clergy would consider it to be true Christianity.

x^3 A 649   n.d., 1850

« 526

..... One becomes a Christian—without Christianity.

x^3 A 733   n.d., 1851

« 527

Humanly speaking, the greatest thing of all is to be so competent that one is indispensable to a whole society, a whole nation perhaps.

Divinely understood, it is even greater to have just as great abilities, just as great energy—and yet be superfluous in the world, minimized by all the practical people, for what is superfluous in this way is essentially to the glory of God.

x^3 A 738   n.d., 1851

« 528 *Existential Proportions*

When perhaps through very severe sufferings and temptations one is brought to Christianity, it still does not follow unconditionally that he must make it just as rigorous for others. For then the aim of providence is not really achieved with respect to the influence of the individual upon others, upon the whole. No, the thrust is propagated and becomes weaker in others, and there is indeed an infinite relativity difference between man and man.

In this regard there is actually a misunderstanding zeal for the idea, which can be so zealous that it simply hinders the idea from coming into the world and keeps it in a merely tangential relationship to the world.

x^4 A 28   n.d., 1851

« 529 *Science and Politics*

are two detours for Christianity, and the latter is the more dangerous because it can become so popular.

x^4 A 78   n.d., 1851

« 530 *One Thesis*

Luther nailed ninety-five on the church door; that was a battle over doctrine. Today one could insert one single solitary thesis in the newspaper: Christianity does not exist at all [*er slet ikke til*], and offer to debate it with all the preachers and professors.

x^4 A 115   n.d., 1851

« 531 *Basil*

We can flee evil either out of fear for punishment—like slaves, or out of hope for reward—like hirelings, or out of love of God—like children.

See Böhringer,[292] I, pt. 2, p. 258.

x^4 A 149   n.d., 1851

« 532 *Anselm*

Böhringer[293] (II, pt. 1, page 429) reproaches Anselm because in his theory of satisfaction the fact that it is for man's salvation comes at the very end, almost tag-end, and that the relationship is primarily regarded as a restitution with respect to God's honor.

Here is a point I have often stressed in the journals.

We human beings have now ventured almost egotistically to take over Christianity. We do not bear in mind (what Anselm and the ancients remembered) that Christianity is God's invention and, in a good sense, God's interest.

We forget that egotism [*Egoisme*] is one thing and I-ness or subjectivity [*Egoitet*] is another, and that although God is infinitely far from being an egotist, he nevertheless is the infinite subjectivity (he cannot be otherwise).

What I have often stressed as the most difficult aspect of Christianity for us human beings is specifically this—that it is in the interest of God on a grand scale. We human beings are pained to understand that sin should be something so frightful, God's righteousness so rigorous, etc. But out of love God wants to be reconciled. Yet if he is to be reconciled, then his standard must be applied—and all the while it is out of love for us men—but the standard is so great that this assistance almost seems to be the greatest misery, because it is so great.

Take some human analogies. When a person of vastly superior intellect is going to be together with far less endowed people—he perhaps does everything (let us suppose) out of love, but he uses his standard (he cannot do otherwise without demolishing himself), and it is so great, much too great for the others, that his assistance, his love, almost becomes an affliction to them.

In Christianity the possibility of offense lies right at this point.

Alas, but Christianity is not presented at all any more; to that extent it has become meaninglessness, a thing of habit. The fact that Christianity is the divine combat of divine passion with itself, so that in a sense we human beings disappear like ants (although it still is infinite love for us)— this is forgotten; God is made into a lenient something or other which is neither God nor man.

X^4 A 212 *n.d.*, 1851

« 533 *Divine Compassion*

Think of a lenient master. Yes, say his subordinates, he does everything for us, 'tis true—but really to put himself in our shoes, this he cannot do. He has never been in our shoes; he cannot help us all the way.

Here is Christianity. God decided to become man in order really to be able to have compassion for men.

X^4 A 452 *n.d.*, 1852

« 534 *Christianity-Christendom*

Not until a person has become so wretched that in the strictest sense it is true of him that his only wish, his only consolation, is to die—not until then does Christianity begin.

When this is a person's situation, then *eo ipso* in relationship to this, his only consolation, there awakens a concern, his *only* concern—do I dare hope to be eternally happy? And what could possibly stand in the way? Sin and sins. And, *here* Christianity genuinely begins. For what does Christianity want? It wants to help a person to die eternally happy.

Inasmuch as such a person does not die but remains alive, his life will be oriented toward suffering, suffering for the teaching, etc., but not in the direction of enjoying life.

But in *Christendom* Christianity has been employed as a stimulant oriented toward enjoying life, as a new, intensified stimulation of life-enjoyment. Therefore Christendom is: refined life-enjoyment, dreadfully refined, for in paganism's enjoyment there was always a bad conscience. But in Christendom an attempt has been made to eliminate conscience by introducing atonement in the following manner: You have a God who has atoned—now you may really enjoy life.

This is the greatest possible relapse.

x^4 A 470 *n.d.*, 1852

« 535 *The Perpetual Chatter and Conversation of the "Awakened" about Their Christianity and Christianity*

As soon as the awakened get together they immediately chatter about nothing else but Christianity.

This is disgusting frivolousness. But didn't the first Christians do it? Indeed. Why was it not frivolousness then? Because the sword of persecution hung over their heads every hour, because it was constantly a matter of life and death, because everything was event and action, so that it was impossible to talk about anything else than that, just as it is impossible to talk about anything else than a fire—as long as it lasts.

But the awakened nowadays suffer nothing, do nothing—and that is why this continual chatter is frivolousness.

x^4 A 516 *n.d.*, 1852

« 536 *Being-in-and-for-Itself—and My Task*

I take out the New Testament (previously I became more closely acquainted with classical antiquity, but I have not let the first Christian centuries go unheeded) and ask: How are we human beings and the human race now related to the whole concept of life contained in the N.T.? Compared with this, has there not been a complete qualitative change in the race and in what it means to be a man?

Indeed there has, and nothing is easier to see.

What is this change? It is that being-in-and-for-itself, the unconditional, has completely gone out of life, and "reason" has been substituted, so that being-in-and-for-itself, the unconditional, has not merely gone out but has become ludicrous to men, a comic extravaganza such as Don Quixote, which we would laugh at if we got to see it, but we never get to see it, for it has gone out of life.

Being-in-and-for-itself and reason relate to each other inversely—where the one is the other is not. When reason has completely penetrated all relationships and everything, being-in-and-for-itself will have completely gone out.

And that is about where we are now. Reason everywhere: instead of unconditionally being in love—a marriage of convenience; instead of unconditional obedience—obedience by virtue of reasons; instead of faith—knowledge of foundations; instead of trust—guarantees; instead of venturing—probability and shrewd calculation; instead of action—incidents; instead of the single individual—a group; instead of personality—impersonal objectivity, etc.

But the N.T. represents precisely being-in-and-for-itself, purely and simply being-in-and-for-itself. And so I ask now: What does it mean that we continue as if it were quite all right to call ourselves Christians according to the N.T. when it is as if the nerve in the N.T., being-in-and-for-itself, has gone out of life.

Many others have also been aware of the fact that there is a tremendous incongruity here. They would like to give it the twist: the race had grown beyond Christianity.

I think it is just the opposite: the race has gone backward [*in margin:* is not a marriage of convenience (even if there were 170,000 of the loveliest reasons for it) a step backward compared with falling in love?]; such men as Christianity is intended for do not exist; in general there has been advancement in the human race, but there are no more individuals who are able to be bearers of Christianity.

And so I propose that we—in recognition of this fact—humble ourselves in such a way that we (there is not the remotest thought that we are the ones who have grown beyond Christianity) confess that we are able to manifest only an approximation of Christianity.

Here, I believe, is where we are now. It is my belief that the race must go through reason to the unconditional again. But truth must touch us where we are.

It is easy to see that what concerns me is not a conflict with this person or that, that he is not a true Christian—no, what concerns me is the change which has clearly happened to the whole race compared with the whole N.T. (It would be easy to demonstrate in similar fashion that even the most zealous of the old orthodox themselves are immersed in reason and do not express being-in-and-for-itself.) . . . . .

x⁴ A 581   n.d., 1852

« 537 *Infant Baptism*

If people absolutely insist on infant baptism, then they ought all the more vigorously see to it that rebirth becomes a decisive determinant in becoming a Christian.

x⁴ A 616   n.d., 1852

« 538 *God Is Love—To Die to the World*

If a man really honestly says: God is love, then this man *eo ipso* has only one desire, to love God (who is love) with all his heart and all his strength.

And when God discovers that this is the way it is with a man, that he has this desire, God says: Yes, yes, my dear child, if this is the case, I shall help you, I shall help you die to the world, for otherwise you cannot love me.—Take a purely human relationship. If the lover is not able to speak the beloved's language, he or she must learn it, however difficult it may seem to them—otherwise, if they cannot talk together, there cannot be a happy relationship. It is the same with dying to the world in order to be able to love God. God is spirit—only one who has died to the world can speak this language at all. If you do not wish to die to the world, then you cannot love God either; you are talking about entirely different matters than he is.

It is also evident that in Christianity it is not even the law which orders you to die to the world; it is love which says: Do you not love me, then? And if the answer is: Yes, then it follows as a matter of course that you must die to the world.

But the human race has egotistically as possible turned Christianity completely around.

Christianity does not preach the law; on the contrary, it preaches what God in infinite love has done for man. To God it must appear to be so great that it would move stones. Here the proclamation stops, as it were; there comes a pause, for God does not want to command what comes next, but still he waits for what should come next—specifically, that this so moves man, that he resolves to love God. But if he resolves to do this, he also resolves *ipso facto* to die to the world.

But in the way Christianity has now been turned, we men have ingeniously turned God into humbug. We talk about the fact that God is love, that we love God (who does not love God, what inhumanity not to love God, etc.) and finally we even count on making him—with all this continual talk that God is love and that we love him—unable ever to see that our relationship to him is purely and simply a natural egotism, the kind of love which conists of loving oneself—for the love which genuinely loves expresses the fact by doing the will of the beloved, consequently by forsaking the world, if this is what is desired; whereas we try to get this loving God's assistance (and to this end also love him, as it is called) in order, if possible, to lead a right cozy and enjoyable life.

O, just to be a loving man—you shall see how human egotism knows how to take advantage of that—but then God let it be known that He is love—now that was something for human egotism!

O, true enough, this loving God is very deeply grieved: ah, is it possible that there is no one who is saddened over misusing God's love, saddened over pretending he did not understand what God wished him to do, how God wants him to express his love for Him.

Yet take care, whoever you are, visited by such thoughts; this God does not sit in heaven at a loss for someone to comply with his will and to love him. Then if someone, moved by God's love, honestly says: I will love God—he takes care, for his life will become suffering, which is the very sign that God looks upon him with favor.

In Christianity, then, God has, as it were (I shall speak in human terms), wooed us men in order to win our love. He gave us all this—a gift of love—and then thought: Now man cannot possibly do anything else than love me. But we human beings, we were and are Satan's bright boys: we took and we take the gifts of God—and we call it loving God when we live according to our own fancies and then say a "thank-you" to God. Think of a father. There was something he wished the child to do (the child knows what it is); so the father thought: I will figure out something which will really please my child and give it to him (ah, it is far too much I am doing for the child)—and then, I am sure, he will love me also in return. "He will love me in return"—by this the father understands that the child will now do the father's will. But the child—well, he was one of Satan's bright boys—the child took the gift but did not do the father's will; on the contrary the child thanked again and again and said "Many thanks!" and said, "He is an affectionate father"; but the child got his own way.

And so it is with us human beings in relationship to God. When he became love, we availed ourselves of it and now pretend as if it is loving of us to go our own way, but nevertheless we dance before him and clap our hands and blow the horn and with tears in our eyes say: God is love; who could help loving this affectionate God?

x^4 A 624   n.d., 1852

« 539 *To Become a Christian*

Most people leave Christianity entirely undecided.

Those who do relate themselves to it, however, behave in such a way that they let Christ worry, as it were, about their eternal salvation in the sense that they themselves have nothing to do with it at all and spend their time and energy enjoying this life.

Thus they transfer into eternity what it is really to become a Christian—alas, in eternity it is impossible to become a Christian; there the settlement comes, and the settlement has to do with whether one has been a Christian.

x^4 A 648   n.d., 1852

« 540 *How Can All This Hang Together?*

Nowadays all of us expect to be saved—and Christ, who certainly is best informed, says:[294] Only few will be saved.

Nowadays we are all going along the way which leads to life; we recognize the way precisely because everyone is taking it—and Christ, who certainly is best informed, says: Only a few find the way—and the way is recognized precisely because only a few take it.

Nowadays the way is easy; it goes faster than on a train; the whole thing is quickly decided in a minute, yes, without any inconvenience at all to ourselves. The whole thing consists of being sprinkled with a little water as an infant, and then they say: Please move on—and Christ, who certainly is best informed, says of the few who go along the right way that they press on along the narrow way!

x^4 A 658   n.d., 1852

« 541 *Christianity as Consolation in the* TRIVIAL *Sense*

Christianity is trivially applied in Christendom simply as consolation, consolation that in earthly respects things will surely get better, etc.

But note what Christianity is according to the New Testament! Christianity, becoming and being a Christian, is accompanied by suffering to such a degree that in order to endure these sufferings they are promised a "Spirit" which shall make the whole conversion easy for them, since otherwise, according to the New Testament's own teaching, it could not be endured.

x^5 A 36   n.d., 1852

« 542 *The Perfectibility of Christianity*

It is this πρῶτον ψεῦδος²⁹⁵ which contains the germs of and has also given rise to all of the confusions in "Christendom."

Christianity is perfectible—what does this mean? It actually wants to say that Christianity is just like anything else human, perhaps a superlative superlative of the human, but nevertheless human. And the law for things human is: development is perfectibility.

But Christianity is divine, the *opposite* of the human; it is so far from being perfectible in time that it retrogresses in time, is moderated, declines.

But even the unconditionally most consistent and most Christianly two-edged of all the Church fathers, Tertullian, even he who had so rightly conceived that the faith, *fides objectiva eller quae creditur*, unconditionally remains unchanged, even he assumes that there is a perfectibility in discipline and conduct (see Böhringer, p. 362).

No, Christianity is as far as possible from being perfectible in time; and the point is also to prevent the transposing of Christianity from the present over into the past so one gets all this historical nonsense to lug along. Tertullian rightly perceived this, although it was in some measure proclaimed to be heresy, Montanism.

It seems to me that it ought to be illuminating for anyone who will reflect upon it once it is said—that Christianity cannot be perfectible, yes, that to assert its perfectibility is high treason against Christ and the apostles. Alas, and yet how long propounding the perfectibility of Christianity has passed for earnestness and wisdom!

x^5 A 98   *n.d.*, 1853

« 543 *An Earlier Christianity, Contemporary Christianity, the Achievement of an Inversion*

If I were to sketch the difference with one single parallel, this alone is enough: early Christendom postponed baptism as long as possible; contemporary Christendom introduces it as early as possible.*

And why? Because early Christendom regarded baptism primarily as commitment, responsibility (baptism also atoned only for the past; later sins had to be atoned for by good works; "good works were supplemental to the sacraments"—Cyprian); contemporary Christendom regards baptism only as a prize which one should get his hands on, the sooner the better. There is much truth and pertinence in what Pascal says, that later Christianity with the help of some sacraments excuses itself from loving God.

It is everywhere apparent that God has been tricked out of Christianity, that it has been rearranged and interpreted *in toto* in man's interest; whereas originally it was in God's interest, even though out of love.

x^5 A 144   n.d., 1853

« 544

* *In margin of 543* (x^5 A 144):
Therefore the Christmas celebration was unknown in the early Church; Easter was regarded as the greatest festival. Now, however, Christmas has become the "most beautiful Christian holiday," and Christianity has become Christmas chatter.

x^5 A 145   n.d., 1853

« 545

"I am come to save the lost"[296]—to bring up the child in Christianity to become a Christian as a tiny infant.

Yet what nonsense Christianity becomes when they take away the foreground or the background of Christianity. Christ says: I am come to save the lost—see, this is the background; on this Christianity can be placed.

Now we bungle everything by passing off the tiny infant as Christian.

Yet nonsense is what man feels the deepest need for and as the sole necessity; only in nonsense is man happy and well.

XI^1 A 39   n.d., 1854

« 546 *A Frightful Discovery—the Orthodox Church
     —Playing at Christianity*

From the earliest Church originates this contrast: the orthodox Church—heretics, schismatics.

Pay close attention to one thing—the orthodox Church was really the believing Church, was a community of men who were more or less in the character of faith; yes, even the external circumstances constrained them into the *character* of faith.

Let us see if everything in our time is not frightfully confused. In our time, also, we maintain this contrast: the orthodox Church—heretics, schismatics; we boast of belonging to the orthodox Church, we speak as if everything would be splendid if there were not those heretics and schismatics, who are not, God knows, after all, so numerous or important.

But let us see if the actual situation is not an extremely dismaying discovery: whether what one understands by the truly believing Church, the orthodox Church, whether it is not a society of men who are not guilty of any heresies or schism—no—but who play at Christianity. Is not the official orthodoxy in our time *playing at Christianity?* The congregation is not in the character of Christianity but shoves this upon the preacher. The preacher is just as little in the character of Christianity but proclaims the doctrine *objectively.*

In this way the orthodox Church is far more dangerous to Christianity than any heresy or schism.

We play at Christianity. We use all the orthodox Christian terminology—but everything, everything without character. Yes, we are not fit at all to shape a heresy or a schism, for which some character is always necessary, after all.

No, the whole thing survives: the Christian sacraments and customs, the Christian terminology—but it is all decoration, a way of speaking, the preacher-actor, the artist.

But then Christianity is nothing but mythology, poetry—and the difference between the orthodox clergyman and the free-thinker is this—the free-thinker comes out and says it, but the orthodox clergyman says: For the sake of God in heaven let's not talk about it, let's just keep our ears open—otherwise the whole thing goes to pot.

There is something frightful in the fact that the most dangerous thing of all, playing at Christianity, is never included in the list of heresies and schisms. Still, of course, it is too frightful to be included this way on a list with other heresies. No, this frightful thing has to have a rubric for itself. The question is whether this is not precisely what the New Testament means by "the fall from Christianity."

XI^1 A 70   *n.d.,* 1854

« 547 *Earnestness*

Christianity is the frightful earnestness that your eternity is decided in this life.

What has been called Christianity for many generations of Protestantism and what millions call Christianity is: playing at it *afterwards*, playing at it after men have lived for whom this life was decisive for their eternity—this is their Christianity.

Even these millions do not keep out of the game, as it is called, no, but they do not become earnest in the game. They do not become earnest because that which concerns them has been decided almost before they were born—that they are Christians and assured of an eternal happiness.

Yes, if they could cut a three-month old fetus from a dead mother, I believe "the preacher" would gladly baptize it and declare it a true Christian; the more, the better; the earlier, the better—by both methods it is best guaranteed that Christianity becomes tomfoolery.

XI¹ A 91   n.d., 1854

« 548 *The Little Children*

One nevertheless notices that it is not Christ who addresses himself to the little children[297] or orders them to be brought to him. No, but when the disciples want to push them and their mothers away—then he says: Let them come to me.

Christ does not deny that the disciples are right in thinking that Christianity is really not for infants—but he also admonishes the disciples to become themselves like children.

XI¹ A 123   n.d., 1854

« 549 *The Christianity of the Majority*

consists approximately of these two statements, which actually could properly be called Christianity's most questionable extremes or, as the pastor says, the foundation one must have to hold on to in life and in death: first, the statement about the infants, that one becomes a Christian as a child, that to such belongs the kingdom of God; the other is the thief on the cross.

Men live out their lives on the strength of the first statement—and in death rely on the example of the thief for consolation.

This is what all their Christianity amounts to; and if one were to describe it accurately, it is a mixture of childishness and crime.

XI¹ A 124   n.d., 1854

« 550 *The Lord's Supper*

One could propose the question whether one dares take part in the Lord's Supper without committing himself to dying for the doctrine; for the act was something like this in the New Testament.

XI¹ A 222   n.d., 1854

« 551 *Christian Observation*

Christianity and what Christianity is should be adhered to in such a way that when, for example, a king or a millionaire wants to be a Christian, the preacher is so far from being pleased as punch over it that, on the contrary, he regards it with utmost suspicion, fearful of the enormous illusion which so easily goes along with this.

But for a long time Christianity has been preached this way, amid illusion but exultantly, when a king becomes a Christian, or a millionaire; there was rejoicing over the King's power to provide entrée for Christianity and over the millionaire's money.

Christianly, there is joy much less mixed and much more exalted when a farm-hand, a poor man, becomes a Christian, for here there is no occasion for creating an illusion.

XI^1 A 264   n.d., 1854

« 552

* *In margin of 551 (XI^1 A 264):*

They think it is perhaps a highway for getting Christianity spread more widely; alas, it is all too easily the wrong way, which in the name of spreading Christianity abolishes Christianity, when spreading becomes synonymous with preaching, just as when a person increases his wine supply by diluting it with water and probably gets a far greater number of flasks of—wine and water—and finally a countless number of flasks—of water.

XI^1 A 265   n.d., 1854

« 553 *The Future*

It will cost a frightful struggle if Christianity is to be introduced once again.

For Christianity is related to the human not only as that which did not arise in any human heart, consequently something alien. No, with the frightful keen-sightedness of the divine it is calculated on the most appalling scale to irritate and embitter man—if he cannot humble himself—for Christianity is the sovereignty of God.

And alas, Christendom, which is coddled by this nonsense that the Christian's God is such an inoffensive pedant, a good fellow, a special friend of female gossip and childbearing!

XI^1 A 293   n.d., 1854

« 554 *Christianity*

Take 1/10 of the essentially Christian, add this ingredient to what man has invented—and you will find (what thousands and thousands of clergymen and professors of lies have found) that this kind of "Christianity" tastes so sweet to men, so delicious, so indescribably delightful, that they do not know what they should concoct in return as a treat for such a professor or preacher.

Take Christianity whole—and you will find (what you, glorious martyrs and witnesses of the truth, have found!) that even the most good-natured man becomes as if he were infuriated, furiously embittered, by this kind of "Christianity," that it is a matter of life and death.

Alas, but God knows man, and since, according to the New Testament, to love God is to hate the world, God has intentionally established Christianity in such a way that it completely shocks those who, merely humanly speaking, might be called the most good-natured of men, as well as the most obstinate of men. For God wants no man to have direct transition into being a Christian. Men do not, according to Christianity, live in a pretty world which God loves—in such a case to become a Christian could be a direct transition for natural human goodness and kindness. No, born in sin, every man, according to Christianity, lives in a sinful world which God hates, and to become a Christian is anything but direct transition; Christianly, this so-called natural human goodness and kindness is just as bad as defiance, etc., and this shows up, also, as soon as Christianity in its truth is brought into contact with this natural human goodness and kindness, for then it becomes just as infuriated with Christianity as defiance, etc.

XI^1 A 324   n.d., 1854

× 555 *The Freethinkers—the Christian Rebuttal*

The freethinker says: If only there were no clergy with their Christianity.

The Christian rebuttal: If only there were no clergy with their Christianity—which makes Christianity impossible.

XI^1 A 332   n.d., 1854

× 556

In margin of 555 (XI^1 A 332):

The freethinkers want to do away with the clergy, thinking thereby to get rid of Christianity. You shortsighted people with your superficial observation—the truth of the matter is that the clergy do not stand in such an intimate relationship to Christianity. No, the Christian rebuttal understands the matter better—it wants to be rid of the clergy—in order to get Christianity.

XI^1 A 333   n.d., 1854

× 557 *Christianity a Fortress*

Imagine a fortress, absolutely impregnable, supplied with provisions for an eternity.

Then a new commandant comes. He gets the idea that the right thing to do is to build bridges over the ditches—in order to be able to attack the besiegers.

Charming! He transformed the fortress into a village—and the enemy captured it, naturally.

So it is with Christianity. They changed the method—and the world conquered, naturally.

XI^1 A 349   n.d., 1854

« 558 *Being Christian: a Race*

The first race is: trusting in God, loving God, to risk being abandoned by men.

When a person has finished this race so that it finds grace and favor before God, *the second race* begins: abandoned by men and also abandoned by God—something men then mockingly appropriate as recompense. But still believe it, believe it, believe that God suffers in love with such a man more than he does: O infinite love!

The world has invented something new—to be a Christian is to live like these millions of people in Christian countries. Ridiculous—that such an existence [*Tilværelse*] is supposed to be called a race, a race in which men not only do not move from the spot but only sink deeper into the mire. Still more ridiculous—that this supposedly is what it means to be a Christian.

XI^1 A 444   n.d., 1854

« 559 *Sanguis Martyrum Est Semen Ecclesiae*[298]

If this means that for every blood-witness more and more are added —who will not lay down their lives—then the statement is actually false from a Christian point of view. The martyrs are the true Church; the others become the envelope. But then the Church does not grow, but the envelope.

Already in these words the idea of expansion is too dominant. It looks as if Christianity is a human affair related to expansion instead of being a divine matter related to intensity.

But how infinitely easy it is for a man to be carried away so that he does not hold to this—that to be sacrificed has intrinsic value—but defines it teleologically, that it has value in preventing others from becoming sacrificed, that in this way many, many more may be added, so that in the end, instead of being sacrificed, one gets money for being a Christian —and thus Christianity is completely transposed into the merely human and the very opposite of the New Testament.

XI^2 A 47   n.d., 1854

« 560 *To Be a Christian*

is an ideality, yes, the highest.

Isn't it folly, then, to have hit upon the notion that all people, by the millions, are supposed to be Christians.

Take a far inferior ideality—that of being a poet—what would the upshot be if it became commonplace in the world to assume that all are poets.

And yet something very much like this could be done the way it has been done with Christianity. Let the state pay 1,000 civil servants whose job it is to make people imagine, to say, and to declare that they are poets, and to say to them: Only believe it and you are that, only believe it, have nothing to do with experimenting to see whether you are a poet or not, such as by wanting to produce poetic works—no, no, just believe it—that is, make yourself believe it and then you are it, and finally, be careful to stay away from any attempt to prove whether you are that; such thoughts are temptations which will confuse the belief.

This is the way Christianity is proclaimed. Only believe that you are Christian—fill your life with earthly busy-ness. Never attempt anything which might let you find out whether you actually believe—no, no, leave it alone, abhor such thoughts, it is temptation; only believe, that is, imagine that you are Christian—and use every power to entrench yourself in the notion and it in you.

In this way the highest—to believe, in a Christian sense to believe—has become imagining something—and in this way we have all become Christians.

XI^2 A 49 *n.d.*, 1854

« 561 *Playing at Christianity*

The more I look at it, the clearer it becomes to me that the guilt of Christendom is actually this—instead of what the New Testament understands by Christianity, Christendom has hit upon—playing at Christianity, of course as boldly and inexhaustibly as the human imagination can be.

Playing at Christianity is always recognizable by the partitioning of life so that in practical life, in the actual world, one lets life go the way it is going—and then one is a Christian.

What the God of Christianity wanted was a world-transformation, but a transformation of the actual, the practical world.

To that end he let his will be proclaimed, and as much as said: Begin now; I am sitting and waiting, willing to be involved with you.

Everyone who is Christian in such a way that he says: In hidden inwardness or on Sunday in church I evoke these exalted thoughts, but in practical life, I know very well things don't go that way, and so in practical life I do just as the practical world does—he plays at Christianity, and he makes a fool of God. For it is making a fool of God to let him sit and wait, willing to join in—when, please note, the Christian really ventures out.

When it sometimes is said of a child that he continues too long with this playing—it is probably a matter of a year or two at most, and the child is, to be sure, only one child—but that this can go on in such a fashion for hundreds of years with millions of people playing at Christianity—this is frightful! The proportions of existence [*Tilværelsens*] are so frightening that one becomes dizzy—fortunately the individual, in the Christian sense, has only to take care of himself.

XI^2 A 102   *n.d.*, 1854

« 562 *The Problem*

I could be tempted to pose the problem thus: Is it at all possible for a man, without in one way or another failing, to endure the act of separation which is the condition for becoming Christian according to the understanding of the New Testament; is it possible for a man, without failing in one way or another, to be separated even more violently than death separates, to be separated by dying-away and then to live; is it possible to endure being at every moment before God?

And then there are Christians by the millions!

XI^2 110   *n.d.*, 1854

« 563 *Christianity Is Fire*

Just as that fire was guarded by virgins, so it is also appropriate to fire-setting which Christ consummated that the Christian be—solitary.

XI^2 A 315   *n.d.*, 1854

« 564

Have you seen people at a fire? How do they look? Is it not true that everyone in death-anxiety thinks only of saving himself.

But according to the Christian view a man lives at every moment in far greater danger than in the most raging fire, in danger of forfeiting an eternity: do they look like it?

XI^2 A 315   *n.d.*, 1854

« 565 *Flesh and Blood*

Christianity in the New Testament is on one hand *duty toward God*. Yet we have realized for a long time that there are not duties toward

God—and go on being Christians—that is, we are Christians after having abolished Christianity.

On the other hand, Christianity in the New Testament is *the battle of the spirit with flesh and blood*. Yet this is also totally abolished; all those frightful battles and spiritual trials [Anfægtelser] no longer appear these days, and why is this? Well, it is quite simple, because as we now live, flesh and blood is really sovereign. But like every tyrant flesh and blood is both clever and cautious and also agreeable—flesh and blood knows how to put up with all and sundry if only it is assured of dominion. And this is the way we are living. Truly, a fine cultured man in our day, who probably considers himself master of flesh and blood by having "refined" it, would, I think, experience something else if he were to fight with flesh and blood and die to it, etc. in the old Christian sense.

But then there live among us a few who understand "the resurrection of the body"[299] to mean the wildest debauchery—and yet we continue to call them Christians and to treat them as Christians: thus the rest of us profit from this in treating our life and activity as the spirituality which the New Testament demands. No, if a Christian from early times were to judge us, he would have to say of each and every one of us: Here, indeed, flesh and blood rules.

To make this refinement of flesh and blood appear to be dying-to-the-world—since it surely is a conjured up hypocritical pose—is even farther away from what it is to die-to-the-world than the wildest debauchery.

XI^2 A 375   *n.d.*, 1844-55

CHRISTMAS

« 566

Christmas is certainly a real children's festival, and the whole pandering concept of the advantages of childhood in regard to becoming a Christian has its stronghold in this holiday with all its spurious emotionality and sentimentality. Please note that the Christmas festival was first introduced in the Fourth Christian Century and that it did not occur at all to the earlier Christians to do this. The culmination of their life view was that death is birth unto life.

> Regarding the historical aspects of this, see Lisco's *Kirkenjahr*, I, p. 9, para. 17-18.[300]

But, as I have said in *Concluding Postscript*, everything Christian has been dislocated by this *orthodox* sentimentality.[301]

VII^1 A 161   *n.d.*, 1846

« 567

In margin of 556 (VII^1 A 161):
One can state the change in this way: instead of remaining conscious of being in conflict, Christianity makes itself comfortable, settles down comfortably and cozily in existence [*Tilværelsen*]. When this is the case, Christmas becomes "the most beautiful holiday."

VII^1 A 162   *n.d.*, 1846

« 568

Second Christmas Day
Theme: the Kingdom of God is not of this world.
(St. Stephen's Day)

Second Christmas Day contains a more precise interpretation of first Christmas Day, the meaning of Christ's being born—in order that the natural man should die.

In so-called Christendom, Christmas has been made into a great festival. This is completely untrue and was not at all the case in the earliest Church. To be a Christian is confused with being a child—this unholy sentimentality of peanut-brittle and the Christmas-baby.

"And gazing at him, all who sat in the council saw that his face was like the face of an angel."[302] According to human understanding we speak of a child looking like an angel, but Christianly it is a dying person who looks like an angel.

To die is to be born.

VIII[1] A 470   n.d., 1847

« 569

In margin: N.B.

Without a doubt Johannes Climacus[303] is right in everything he says about the sentimentality of this so-called childlike Christianity. The Christmas celebration is really a heresy—that is, as it is now observed. It goes together with the whole enormous illusion of an established Christendom. How reassured I am (for I have long had a suspicion in this direction but have not quite dared to express it) that the Christmas festival first came into existence in the third and fourth centuries—and as a substitute for a pagan festival.

IX A 460   n.d., 1848

« 570

In margin: N.B.

Christmas as it is now celebrated in so-called Christendom is pure paganism, mythology. Its idea or thought is this: a child is the Savior [*in margin:* as it says in the hymnbook, number 573, second stanza: the little child on its mother's breast] or to become father and mother means life a second time, purification, ennoblement. The earnestness of life (which is psychical) properly begins when one himself establishes a new generation and now really for the first time in a deeper sense comes to live in love to one's offspring, in responsibility for its upbringing, etc. But this idea is not specifically Christian; it is a pagan, sexual-psychical sentimentality.

Here again all of Christianity has been pulled backward a dialectical step. Jesus was born of a virgin and thus, if we are going to talk about Christmas, is not related to marriage and the nursery and all this which is actually ingratiating about Christmas for most people, to the extent they regard it as the supreme Christian festival and become sentimental at the thought of becoming children again, interpreting this to be dancing around the Christmas tree, having the urge to play games and eat fruitcake. No, the Christ-child is related to the spiritual qualification of what it is to be a human being and consequently is not related to marriage, father, mother, child, but to every single individual human being *qua* spirit.

IX A 472 n.d., 1848

« 571 *First Day of Christmas*

Today a Savior is born to you—and yet it was night when he was born.

It is an eternal metaphor: night it must be—and it becomes day in the middle of the night when the Savior is born.

Today—it is a declaration of eternal time, just as when God says: Today, and just like the books which come out "in that year." It is repeated from generation to generation, for every individual among those millions—and every time anyone in truth becomes a Christian it says: Today a Savior is born to you.

X^2 A 283 n.d., 1849

« 572

It might be very good for Christianity to be represented by an unmarried person also for this reason. Ultimately all of Christendom's little morsel of Christianity is swallowed up in Christmas and its Christmas cookies. The little baby Jesus—this kind of Christianity is far remote from stressing the concept of imitation [*Efterfølgelse*]. It is certainly not the task to become a child oneself—no, the Savior of the world himself is neither more nor less than a child, and this is just about where it all remains; and father and mother regard their little Sophie also as a little God-child. Sheer effeminacy! For the most part this is the one and only emphasis of Christmas, turning Christianity completely upside-down. Christmas appeared for the first time in the fourth century; but in this respect orthodoxy is not eager to abide by the first three hundred years.

X^2 A 305 n.d., 1849

« 573 *Christmas*

Why did the Savior of the world become a child?

The strongest expression for our being saved entirely by grace, that we are able to do nothing, is the fact that the Savior is a child. Here there can be no talk at all about imitation [*Efterfølgelse*].

Nevertheless, we must above all be careful not to take this path and make Christianity into mythology. The Christmas festival did not appear until the fourth century.

X^4 A 439 n.d., 1851

CHRYSOSTOM

« 574 *Chrysostom*

When lay people objected that they did not have time to read the Bible, that they were so busy with their secular businesses, and that Bible reading was really something for monks and hermits, Chrysostom answered: No, just the reverse, just because you move about so much in the secular, for that very reason you need to read the Bible even more than the monks and hermits.

Neander, *Chrys.*[304] I, 192.

x³ A 755 *n.d.*, 1851

« 575 *Chrysostom*

He once heard a Christian debate with a pagan who was proud of pagan science and art, and then the Christian wanted to prove that Paul surpassed Plato in eloquence as well as in learning. Chrysostom censured the Christian's conduct, because he had attacked the very thing that was most advantageous to his cause. The very fact that the apostles were not learned and eloquent and still had been able to overturn the systems of paganism was itself proof that Christianity was not human wisdom but God's cause.

Neander, *Chrys.* I, 227-28.

How correctly Chrysostom grasped the issue! But what is all modernity if not the very retrogression which this Christian displayed. Christianity is presented in direct categories—far deeper, more profound, higher, etc. than Plato, etc.—rather than in the category of being foolishness to reason, the absurd.

x³ A 760 *n.d.*, 1851

« 576 *Faith Does All*

Without faith one stumbles over pieces of straw (Peter becomes afraid of a girl—and denies Christ);[305] with faith one moves mountains.

The remark about Peter's becoming afraid of a girl and denying is by Chrysostom.[306]

x³ A 765 *n.d.*, 1851

« 577 *Chrysostom*

says superbly: The house did not fall because the storms came—but because it was built on sand.[307]

x⁴ A 49 *n.d.*, 1851

CHURCH

« 578

The subjectivity which I think must be central for the Church—since the same objections which have been directed properly against the Bible can be brought against every new norm one wants to establish for the Church—is already prefigured in the fact that the most objective part of the creed[308] begins in this way: *I believe.*

I A 56   *n.d.*, 1835

« 579

I am conscious that I exist [*existerer*] (K.)[309] not whether I have existed or how
  consistent development introduction to the apostolic *symbolum* [*sic*]

I A 57   *n.d.*, 1835

« 580

In a certain sense it is quite correct for the orthodox to say that the Church may be immediately conscious of its existence [*Existents*]; I find it just as correct as to say that every human being is immediately conscious of his existence [*Existents*]. But just as it would be unreasonable for a person to say: "I am conscious that I exist [*er til*], ergo, I existed [*var til*] yesterday"—for he is not conscious of the latter—it is equally unreasonable for the Church to say: I am conscious of my existence [*Existents*], ergo, I am the original apostolic Church. It must undertake to demonstrate and prove this latter determination, since it is a historical question.

I A 58   *n.d.*, 1835

« 581 *Is the Church Justified To Write a Bible at a Particular Moment in Time?*

For a long time attention has been called to the enormous advantage the apostles had over all later Christians. It is true, I suppose, that the one who stands closest to the source must also receive the strongest and most immediate impression. But does it necessarily follow that it is the most pure? I find it necessary to call attention here to a most essential fact, that now after 1,800 years Christianity has pervaded all life so that the whole life of the Christian Church is essentially impregnated by what is Christian (Christian philosophy, Christian esthetics, Christian history), and then call attention to the fact that possibly it ought to be easier now to find out what is essentially Christian. One should not study the plant in the bud but in the bloom.[310]

Have the apostolic Church and the Bible prefigured the Christian Church and its doctrine? No! It is no prefiguration (an assumption which could lead to the assumption of inspiration; just as inspiration consequently leads to this assumption); it is the first stage of development; and the Bible is our first telegraph message.—

I believe, therefore, since I in part must go along with those who want to sharpen the boundary and knead the bricks for the building of the church wall by recognizing the worthlessness and delapidation of the existing boundaries (The Bible constitutes the Church? No, the Church constitutes the Bible, which presumably is demonstrated by this fact, among others, that it is written for Christians. Protestants regard the Bible as hovering over the Church just as Mohammed's coffin hovers between the four magnets.) —I believe that the gates must be opened, that Christianity can possibly stand some fresh air, and that there will still be true Christians in the world even though such a high-unto-heaven wall (I am justified in calling it this since the Christians will in no case permit entry into heaven without the required entry-ticket) no longer hides them from the eyes of the world. I also think I know liberals and liberalism, although I cannot point to a community somewhere which has drawn up such a creed, still less to one which is supposed to have attempted to maintain such a creed not as the direct expression of what lives and moves in the community but as a customs tariff for determining which commodities may come across the borders and also how long a quarantine period they should endure.

I A 108   November 3, 1835

« 582

The tendency of the Greek Church toward stagnation is discernible also in its inability to retain the peoples given to it by developments. The northern nations were all Arians first and later Orthodox—the nations converted by the Greek Church later went over to Rome. Strange to say, the Greek Church had fathers one hundred and fifty years longer than the Roman Church, but it had all the fewer sons.[311]

II A 269 October 6, 1838

« 583

The most noble Avenue of the Church Fathers, in whose shade I still at times can find rest.

II A 750 n.d., 1838

« 584

The strong advance of the liturgical service centered at the altar in the Middle Ages was a return to paganism, classical antiquity, the abdominal processes—however, the sermon permitted the head to play a role again.

II A 792 October 22, 1838

« 585

In the development of Christianity it holds true that the disciple is not greater than the master; in the development of the world this is not the case—therefore we ought to honor *what is transmitted from the Fathers.*

II A 315 December 31, 1838

« 586

And if we did not know that the Church has always regarded the Lord's Supper as belonging to the *disciplina arcana*, might we not feel it with that terrifying simplicity of the report of the world's treachery when it says: Our Lord Jesus Christ in the *night in which he was betrayed*[312]—might not the thought of that night (to be compared only with the night out of which day emerged) squeeze the Church together, make it anxiously reconnoitre for the threat of another night of betrayal and with fear and trembling watch over its children to keep them from betraying their Lord and Master.

II A 522 July 28, 1839

« 587 *The Relationship of the Congregation to Christ in the Metaphor of the Bride and the Bridegroom*

This might even seem improper . . . . . in our day the divine has been elevated too high to be satisfied with such a metaphor—this both good and bad, and one should never overlook the meaning of the metaphor . . . . . one ought not play or *flirt with such metaphors* . . . . . Or is the reason for our not being fond of this metaphor, when it is understood literally, that love in our time is not very sacrificial, not very inspired, not very persevering? Here we must remember that all of life is a time of betrothal, the grave is the bridal chamber, heaven ..... Or is this not the case if we think of the blessed moment when the believer, after many mistakes, many misunderstandings, after having overcome much trouble and many temptations, now finally sinks into the arms of his Savior?

III C 15   n.d., 1840-41

« 588

Right now, when there is talk of reorganizing the Church, it is obvious how little Christianity there is, or what Christendom is. The Church and the state are treated exactly alike; men completely forget that the Christian Church is a historical concept. When individuals at a stated time all together or through representation agree on this and that constitution for the state, they are within their rights. When, on the other hand, individuals at a stated time agree to introduce divine worship —for example, adoring and worshiping the Round Tower—well, it still cannot be denied that this is the worship of that nation. But that it is supposed to be the Christian Church surely must be a lie. But the fact is that we confuse what it is to be a Christian and what it is to be a man (and this is the unholy illusion of Christendom); we automatically make them identical. But the Christian Church is a purely historical concept.

IX A 264   n.d., 1848

« 589

The day a boy is confirmed the pastor calls him—a young Christian. This is unmitigated affectation or a way of covering up the inadmissibility of letting such a boy bind himself by a holy promise. How strange that the custom of having the confirmand wear a false beard has not been introduced so that he might look like a man—and that there be meaning in extracting such a promise from him. Confirmation, which ought to be the most solemn act, is nothing more than a game in which children play grown-ups.

X^1 A 38   n.d., 1849

« 590

If you have not sensed today that God is present here and that you are before him, your coming into God's house is in vain, because whatever else you have seen and heard is of no consequence—if I simply name it, you will recognize how inconsequential it is. It will perhaps seem to you that I desecrate this holy place by speaking of such things, but this is not so, for the person who does that is the one who has no impression of being before God and only hears and sees such [inconsequential] things. Then you could just as well—yes, perhaps better—have stayed at home, so that your coming here would not be a sin; as David says: The prayer of the ungodly shall be counted as sin (Psalms 109:7). On the other hand, at home, *in your own house,* you could in a truly vital way be aware that God is present and that you are before him. Thus in another sense you could very well have stayed at home. Surely this place is God's house, but the task is precisely that your own house should become a house of God. Surely this place is a holy place, but the task is precisely that your living room should also become a holy place. The relationship to the holy is not so much that you take off after it [*tager ud*] as that you take it home to yourself [*tager til*]. As far as entertainment and diversion are concerned, it can be in order that you take off after them, and it is not advantageous to have them home with you, but in relation to the divine, it is not so much that you should take off after it, and in every case when you do this, you should strive to take [*at tage med*] it home with you.

x^1 A 212   *n.d.,* 1849

« 591

The secular mind asks, "Who preached today?" In a godly spirit one would not ask about such things. For here, in God's house, whether the pastor preaches or the sexton, the most renowned pastor or the least-known student, there is always One who preaches, always one and the same—God in heaven. That God is present, this is the sermon; and that you are before God, this is the content of the sermon.

x^1 A 271   *n.d.,* 1849

« 592

It is not church management and the like which ought to be reformed in our time—but the concept: Christendom.

x^1 A 537   *n.d.,* 1849

« 593

"The Church" should really represent "becoming" [*Vorden*]; "the state," on the other hand, "the established" [*Bestaaen*]. Therefore it is very dangerous when state and Church grow together and are identified. For "the state" it holds true that even if one institution or another is not very successful—if it is part of the established—one must be very circumspect about abolishing it, simply because the idea of "the state" is "the established"; and we are perhaps better served by vigorously maintaining a less successful establishment than by reforming it prematurely. In "the Church" the opposite holds true, since its idea is becoming. "Becoming" is more spiritual than "the established." Therefore the servants of the Church ought not be officials, perhaps not married, but those implementers qualified to serve "becoming."

x^1 A 552   n.d., 1849

« 594

Even our churches express how superficial and externalized everything becomes. When one enters one of the old churches with those closed pews, with the old gallery, one unconsciously gets an impression of how much can lie hidden in a man's deep inwardness—of which those closed pews were indeed a symbol.

But now everything is a lounge; churches are also built this way nowadays. It is awkward and bad taste for someone to have an interior life of his own; it is an affectation—"Why should he have something like that for himself"—no, we are a public.

x^1 A 579   n.d., 1849

« 595 *For the Accounting*[313]

..... And insofar as there is the religious "community" or "congregation" [*Menighed*], this is a concept which lies on the other side of "the single individual"; "the single individual" must have intervened with ethical decisiveness as the middle term in order to make sure that "community" and "congregation" are not taken in vain as synonymous with public, the crowd, etc.; and the familiar fact must still be kept in mind that it is not the single individual's relationship to the community or congregation which determines his relationship to God, but his relationship to God which determines his relationship to the congregation. Then, too, there is—this should be included—the highest relationship of all, in which "the single individual" is absolutely higher than "congregation," the single individual κατ' ἐξοχήν,[314] the God-man, the judge in the O.T., the apostle in the N.T., although these reverently confess that they have their divine authority in order to serve the congregation. —Consequently, from a religious point of view, there is only the single individual (in contrast to "public," "crowd," etc., which can have their validity politically). To me, the edifying author, it was, therefore, a genuine joy, etc.

x^5 B 245   n.d., 1849-50

« 596

Solomon's judgment may be applied to the Church. It was clear that the *true* mother was the one who would rather give up the child than have half. So it is with the Church, the true mother: it would rather let go of the individual, let him still live, than have half of him—and spiritually it is just as impossible to have a half person as it is physically.

Hamann says it well (III, p. 72):³¹⁵ *mit einem getheilten Kinde ist einer wahren Mutter nicht gedient.*

x^3 A 54   *n.d.*, 1850

« 597 *High-Ranking Clergy*

If there have to be high-ranking clergy, then such a clergyman, if he is going to be Christianly consistent, will have to express and bear the label of dissimilarity from secularity all the more strongly the higher he goes—for example, by asceticism and the like; then his high rank, his distinction, etc. turn out to be simply for guiding and leading.

x^3 A 521   *n.d.*, 1850

« 598 *The Abolition of Confession*

the joint action of congregation and clergy. The congregation became afraid of going to confession; the confessional box brought matters too close to home. The clergy became afraid of hearing confession; things became much too earnest.

And the whole proclamation of Christianity became oratorical eloquence, the art of speaking, which quite rightly omitted the decisively Christian element: the application, the single individual.

x^3 A 697   *n.d.*, 1850

« 599 *The Emancipation of the Church*

If the Church *is* free from the state—well, that's fine— I will immediately find my way in the given situation.

But if the Church *must* be emancipated, then I need to ask: In what way, by what means.

A religious movement must be served religiously—otherwise it is a forgery. Consequently this emancipation must come by means of martyrs, with or without bloodshed.

However, in a secular way to vote with a secular mentality on the emancipation of the Church (and voting is secularity), this certainly is secularity, yes, a bad secularity.

It is merely secularity in a new form; for this reason people do not immediately recognize it. And while they (even the patriots) piously roar against this frightful secularity of being perhaps a saint and also his excellency—a secularity which is probably not so dangerous and in any case, with a little concession, can be quite all right, a concession which the person concerned has piously made, which is precisely why such a form can be suitable—they forget that this voting on the emancipation of the Church is much more dangerous. The first form of secularity—if in a particular individual it is worldliness really deserving of punishment—deserves only the damnation of the individual, Christianly understood. The other deserves the damnation of Christianity, if this were possible.

"Freedom of the Church from all secularity?" Yes, that is an exalted Christian thought—to be sure. [*In margin:* It is an exalted thought, Luther's thought—just think what Luther would say if he were to hear that it should take place by means of an election.] But it is so exalted that for this very reason it is incompatible that such loftiness is to be achieved by shabby means like an election.

In the realm of the spirit the price is the purchase.

But those who want to achieve the emancipation of the Church in this way (sparing themselves martyrdom) have introduced a purely secularized concept of tolerance (tolerance identical with indifference), and this is the most appalling insult to Christianity.

"But only when the Church is free can things be better." Perhaps so, but who taught you that such profane means are admissible for this end—and that this is supposed to be Christianity?

And even if you win, Christianity loses, for in that moment Christianity will actually have lost its cause—will have given up its sovereignty and be downgraded to wanting to live on equal terms with Judaism, paganism, and every other religion. Great God! Then Christ is not the Savior of the world if his followers could live to such a degree at peace with this assurance, a peace which would bring shudders to the crowd of witnesses, those who did not want to live at peace in this manner.

Truly, Christianity does not want to force anyone. No, but Christianity wants its followers, suffering, to force the world to become Christian.

If a follower cannot achieve this, if he dare not sing so high a note, then he can pray for himself. This is something entirely different. But such a follower will also feel too humble to dare become involved in wanting to influence, yes, to "reform" the Church. Thankful for grace he will live in quiet inwardness.

But it was the "only true Christians in Denmark," they were just the ones for whom it became clear that this great good could be achieved —by voting.

x^4 A 22   *n.d.*, 1851

« 600 *"The Church"*

The definition of "Church" found in the Augsburg Confession, that it is the communion [*Samfund*] of saints where the word is rightly taught and the sacraments rightly administered, this quite correctly (that is, not correctly) grasped only the two points about doctrine and sacraments and has overlooked the first, the communion of saints (in which there is the qualification in the direction of the existential [*Existentielle*]). Thus the Church is made into a communion of indifferent existences [*Existentser*] (or where the existential is a matter of indifference)—but the "doctrine" is correct and the sacraments are rightly administered. This is really paganism.

x^4 A 246   *n.d.*, 1851

« 601 *Christ*
   Paul—James
   Peter—John, etc.

This means that the God-man is the only individual who alone expresses Christianity. If it is not the God-man, it always requires at least two to express Christianity.

x^4 A 594   *n.d.*, 1852

« 602 *Infant Baptism*

It is easy to see that this really belongs together with the rascally cunning by means of which the race has tried to trick God out of Christianity and turn it into Epicureanism.

Take away the make-believe of child baptism and we immediately have the true Christian collisions—to be father and mother, themselves Christian, hoping for eternal blessedness—but having to leave it to the child whether in due time he wills it himself.

This exertion, this tensing exertion, which would both make men a little less inclined to marriage and marriage more earnest, this exertion which Christianity simply will not do away with—this we want with all our might to do away with.

So they invented infant baptism, and now litttle infant Christians are practically bred; everything about eternity is automatically in order; one can quite properly hanker to enjoy idyllically the pleasures and joys of family life.

Oh, it is loathsome to have falsified Christianity so villainously! Of late it has become so inverted that its destiny seems to be to give men the desire to have children.

xi^1 A 546   *n.d.*, 1854

« 603 *The Church*

The Forgery.

Christianity is constituted in such a way that it relates itself to the individual [*Individ*]. Precisely here is the tremendous ideality but also the strenuousness of being a Christian, relating oneself as individual to God, not cloaked in any abstraction, which, you may say, wards off the blow or, like colored glass, moderates the fire of the sun's rays.

But what the wholly human tends toward is—to get rid of God.

This is the common element. The method is twofold (just as one speaks of genteel and crude suicides). The one is to rebel against God or deny that there is a God. I am not speaking of this.

The other, the more genteel, is to get an abstraction between God and oneself, and on the very pretext of zeal for God and the cause of God.

Such an abstraction today is "the Church." Men have hit upon making it into a person, and by first of all talking brilliantly about it as person, about its birth, its career, etc., finally getting into the habit of regarding the Church as the Christian—in another sense there are no Christians.

The Christians, then, vacation behind this abstraction. Solemnly, profoundly, brilliantly they talk about the Church—but single individual Christians, of them there is none—or, if you will, there are plenty of them, millions of them, so that a million Christians more or less means no more than one sausage more or less during the butchering season. Presumably it is as Schleiermacher says somewhere, that it certainly is not man's idea in the discovery of lightning rods to sit securely behind them and laugh at God, who thunders and lightnings, and similarly it is not the intention of the parties concerned to make a fool of God by the discovery of the Church, by substituting, as Peter Mikkelsen did, a straw man for his person—but as a matter of fact it is still making a fool of God and of Christianity. The Church, this abstraction, is the folding screen behind which the Christian evades the real strenuousness of being a Christian.

XI^2 A 229 *n.d.*, 1854

COLLISION, CONFLICT, ADVERSITY

« 604

It is to a man's advantage to be bent over a little by adversity in life, just as a candlewick is sometimes bent over—then it trims itself all evening long.

V A 5   n.d., 1844

« 605

When I was young and saw an attack upon a man and also saw that many hurried to stop it, I thought (then when I was young): By Jove, that must be a real scrap. Now that I have grown a bit older, when I see an attack upon a man and also see many hurrying to stop it, I think: Ah, the attack is not so dangerous after all since there are many to stop it. —When in my youth I heard a man under attack say of the attack: It is a vile, scurvy thing, then I thought (in my youth) —If only he can hold out. But when I heard such a one say of the attack: It is nothing, then I thought (this was in my youth), He can get along all right. Now I think the opposite. Only when a man knows he is secure does he acknowledge the violence of the attack. It is precisely when he is most afraid that he minimizes the attack. When he is sure of being the stronger, he says: It is a scurvy attack; but when he feels weak, he says: It is nothing—that is, he shams.

VII[1] A 211   n.d., 1846

« 606

It is the grace of God toward a man when he, like a rare instrument, shows himself especially in adversity to be so excellently constructed that with each new adversity the strings not only are not damaged, but he gains one more new string!

VIII[1] A 128   n.d., 1847

« 607

The Jews' desire to make Christ King was in itself a part of his being crucified. When a fire is to be lighted, there must be a draft; but spiritually understood, a draft is a double-movement. A person who immediately comes into conflict with men does not easily become a sacrifice. But the very person of whom men have been appreciatively aware—when he turns against them, when his will is not their will: this is what fans the fire and fans it to flame.

See this book, pp. 160 ff. [i.e., VIII¹ A 271-76].

VIII¹ A 307   n.d., 1847

« 608

It is one thing to become a person of distinction in the world by birth and something else again to work one's way up. One can do nothing about the former, but the latter cannot be achieved without making one concession or another to evil at various points—being silent when one should have spoken and speaking when one should have been silent, bowing when one should have been proud and the reverse, etc.

VIII¹ A 354   n.d., 1847

« 609

If one is going to live among fools, he had better be prepared to be scoffed at—if he is not willing to deceive them, for then they make him king and worship him.

VIII¹ A 423   n.d., 1847

« 610 *A Remarkable Dialectical Collision*

An individual who is tried in the most critical decisions, who earnestly (i.e., is himself willing to act accordingly) occupies himself with the thought of offering his life for an idea or something similar in which there is a real risk, will, far along in the course of things, experience the spiritual trial [*Anfægtelse*]: Have I not arrogated too much to myself? Should I not have discussed this matter with others? Remarkable! If he had talked to others about it, if he talks, then nothing ever comes of it; that very moment he gets discharged from the highest and gets off on cheaper terms—every communication of this kind is *eo ipso* ennervating. And the spiritual trial will sound like this: Do I have the right to do it, should I not discuss it? This spiritual trial is only a humbling so that he may not become arrogant. Any time he wants to, God can turn to him and say: Why have you not talked to other men, sought their confidence —and yet, yet, is it not perhaps just in spite of this spiritual trial that he is to go forward?

IX A 21   n.d., 1848

« 611

Christ himself says[316] that he has not come to bring peace but discord; only to his own will he give peace. This is quite correctly the polemical relationship: Christianity is discord with the world, but in the Christian is the peace of Christ.

IX A 56   n.d., 1848

« 612

This is the teaching of Christianity. There is an eternal happiness in expectation, a happiness which transcends all understanding, and which a person can already partially experience during this life in the blessedness of faith—but as for the rest, let's go on, now comes the next thing. Absolutely and literally no one, no thief, robber, or swindler can be said to plunge into certain ruin in the way a Christian does. No one, no one is hated in the same way. For the world does not hate the robber et al., who express that the world is better than they. The world does not hate the thief, who expresses just as forcefully as a miser that money is a great good. Only the Christian is *hated*; he must be destroyed and in the basest way, as no criminal is destroyed. If not, the secular mentality gets no peace and joy from things of the world, whose influence is weakened by the Christian, he who expresses that erotic love is self-love, that friendship is self-love, that honor and such are nothing and money less than nothing. Is this not mutiny, is this not the basest atrocity, should not Barrabas and all the others be released, almost honored and respected in comparison to such a vile criminal as a true Christian? For the secular mentality is not so secular that it cares about things of the world in and for themselves if they are not joined to the conception that it is earnestness and integrity to make money and gain honor and esteem—but it is precisely this idea which the Christian takes away. Nor would anyone care very much for friendship if he had to confess publicly that it is self-love—no, but the appearance that this relationship is true love, this appearance the world wants—and it is this very appearance which the Christian takes away.

In fact, the more truly one is Christian, the greater will the opposition become, increase, until the end. If the opposition fails to come, the explanation must be that he has spared himself in one way or another, evaded it.

This is Christianity. The terrible thing is the increase and inescapability [of opposition] guaranteed by the fact that to avoid suffering is an indictment against oneself.

X^2 A 57   n.d., 1849

« 613

The more a man gets in the habit of participating to the point of going along with everything, the more the spirit is curtailed in him—and the more of a hit he will make in the world.

x^2 A 397 n.d., 1850

« 614 *Christianity Is a Kingdom Not of This World*

Yet it wants to have a place in this world—right here is the paradox and the collision; it wants to have a place, but again not as a kingdom of this world.

This is the way it is in the New Testament. Christendom naturally has not been able to go along with this; it was all too strenuous. Therefore they have *either* made it into a kingdom of this world (Catholicism) whereby the Christian collisions vanish, and direct recognizability, which is pleasing to men, becomes the rule, or they have transposed Christianity into hidden inwardness, an adequate form, if you will, of not being a kingdom of this world, but yet not the Christian form, not the paradox, and again they avoid the Christian collisions. It is easy enough to see that hidden inwardness corresponds very closely as an adequate form to a kingdom which is not of this world, for hidden inwardness is a negative like this *not of this world*. But then one notes again the paradox of Christianity—namely, that a kingdom which is not of this world still wants to have a place, a visible discernible place, therefore paradoxically wants to have a place in this world, constantly vigilant so that it remains paradoxical, so that it is not transformed into becoming a kingdom of this world.

One sees here also an example of how this is related to all of Christendom's so-called progress. For all this about hidden inwardness as the true existence-form of true Christianity, all this which has even been proclaimed as superior and truer than early Christianity, is purely and simply an inferior form. Christianity as it is in the New Testament no doubt has as much hidden inwardness as at any time in Protestantism, but it will not be satisfied with that, it wants to have the paradoxical recognizability, and it is only through this that all the Christian collisions are produced.

xi^2 A 80 n.d., 1854

« 615 *Catastrophe*

How does catastrophe come about in the relationship of the spirit? Quite simply—by leaving out some intermediate links, by producing a conclusion and not giving the premises, by drawing a conclusion without first showing that from which it is a consequence, etc.—then the collision between the person acting in this manner and the contemporaries can become a catastrophe.

For example, let the one who actually is a bearer of whatever idea there is in the age, let him work silently for a few years. During all this time he will himself develop more and more, thereby becoming more and more alienated from his contemporaries; let him then take the very latest stage, and with the most intense brevity begin with that—then it can become a catastrophe. On the other hand, it would not become a catastrophe if he had successively communicated the prior stages, and it will not become a catastrophe, either, if he begins with the earliest.

It has happened frequently that an individual has collided with his contemporaries to the point where it became a catastrophe. But this has been spontaneous. The individual in question has actually had no idea of how far his contemporaries were from being able to understand him, to what extent they lacked the intermediate links, the premises.

This is the catastrophic collision of geniuses.

The conscious arranger of catastrophe is altogether different—to be so clear that one can measure with the eyes that the distance must now be so great that it must become a catastrophic collision, consciously to design the whole thing. This consciousness, however, is really only the Christian consciousness, the really Christian concept of being sacrificed, a voluntary sacrifice.

But here I stop again and am tempted to ask: Does a man have the right to this? Is it not harshness toward others?

One seeks illumination in vain in Christendom. As far as the New Testament is concerned, this after all is the God-man, and the God-man is qualitatively different from every human being.

On the other hand, it is not possible to put an end to lack of character, sophistry, and the nonsense of reflection without catastrophe. Catastrophe is the real μετάβασις εἰς ἄλλο γένος;[317] what the sign of the cross is for the devil, catastrophe is for reflection.

But to begin with the conclusion, to leave out the premises and the like—and then to say one does it to bring on the catastrophe is, again, to prevent the catastrophe; for in this explanation there is again a rapprochement which reduces the contemporaries' distance, and then the collision does not become catastrophic.

XI^2 A 263 *n.d.*, 1854

« 616 *To Be a Christian, To Confess Christ*

The New Testament presents it in the following manner: one can be Christian only in opposition, can confess Christ only in opposition—

that is, there must be something or someone in opposition to whom one is a Christian and confesses to being a Christian, for, according to the New Testament, there is danger bound up with confessing Christ. (Tertullian also says very correctly: Confession takes place only where there is persecution. See Böhringer.)

In "Christendom" we are all Christians. Consequently here one cannot be a Christian in opposition; neither can one confess Christianity in opposition—but according to the New Testament the presence of opposition goes together with confessing.

What is the result of this? The result is *either* that the whole business of Christendom is pure nonsense, that one must comply with the New Testament and in opposition to Christendom confess Christ, precisely because "Christendom" is the place where one least of all (except in opposition) can be Christian, since "Christendom" is a lie perpetuated from generation to generation, *or* that this Christendom is quite in order and we are all Christians, but in this case the New Testament will no longer be able to furnish the rule for being a Christian, since the situation is completely changed, and all relationships are exactly the opposite of the New Testament's, and consequently we must, I suppose, pray God for a new revelation in order to get instructions on being a Christian in "Christendom."

XI^2 A 341   *n.d.,* 1854

COMMUNICATION

« 617

There must, after all, be something which is so holy that it cannot be expressed in words—otherwise how did those men to whom something absolutely tremendous was revealed become: dumb?

In a highest stage the senses blend. Just as Lemming stroking the guitar almost made sound visible, so also in the moonlight the glints of color on the surface of the water become almost audible.

I A 327   January, 1837

« 618

There are observations and feelings which are expressed in such a medium that they are perceived only upon being kindled by the warmth of sympathy and the flame of inspiration, just as the writing on a certain kind of paper becomes visible only when it is held up to the light.

II A 620   n.d., 1837

« 619

Daub's sentences[318] are true labyrinths; one needs Ariadne's thread to read them—that is, love and inspiration.

II A 624   June 9, 1837

« 620

It is genuinely upbuilding to see the instinctive confidence with which simple people appropriate God's word to themselves, how often they go away with a true blessing from a sermon which they are far from understanding; like birds of the heavens they neither sow nor reap, and yet their heavenly father feeds them.[319]

II A 393   April 7, 1839

« 621

Among the selfish pretensions in preaching there is a point of view which is identical to the Pharisee's moral position when he said: I thank God that I am not like other men, a point of view which believes that talent and virtuosity in delivery bring one closer to the divine.

II A 463   June 30, 1839

« 622

What an enormous conceptual confusion in our time! This is most obvious in preacher prattle. Preachers have become so erudite, always talk about the sweep of world history, and then perhaps in conclusion a little about the individual in his uniqueness. And their categories! I heard a pastor preaching on a text about the Ascension.[320] He wanted to emphasize the historical aspect, the historical event, and then he constructed a beautiful climax: the apostles had not only seen this with the eyes of faith [*Tro*] (naturally, to avoid implications of superstition [*Overtro*], this was handled in such a way that it did not become anything out of the ordinary) but also with their physical eyes (competent physical gesticulations). He pounded the pulpit so that the congregation at least heard it (the pounding, that is);—yes, and the congregation was persuaded. What inexhaustible gibberish! His climax was in fact developed backwards; and in the meantime the idea roars with laughter at him because his sermon does not ascend but descends (goes from the higher to the lower), his gesticulating correspondingly increases as if he were proceeding from the lower to the higher. That the cæsura in poetry can come at the wrong place and disturb the idea is forgivable; but such a contradiction as this—how abundantly comical! Alas, alas, but people concern themselves so little with the spiritual that they do not even notice this.

V A 18   *n.d.*, 1844

« 623

Men do not seem to have acquired speech in order to conceal their thoughts (Talleyrand,[321] and before him Young in *Night Thoughts*[322]), but in order to conceal the fact that they have no thoughts.

V A 19   *n.d.*, 1844

« 624

Have I, after all (however much I should like to have someone share my point of view), the right to use my art in order to win over a person, is it not still a mode of deception? When he sees me moved, inspired, etc., he accepts my view, consequently for a reason entirely different from mine, and an unsound reason.

The majority presumably do not understand the discussion at all —if one has any art, he ought to use it; yes, anyone who does not use it in this way is an immoral person who does not recognize his duty, lacks earnestness, is self-centered, etc. Answer: Bah![323]

V A 47   *n.d.*, 1844

« 625

What is said in the text [*Stages on Life's Way*, p. 421] is not my own but the religious position; here, however, I want to do what the religious person probably would not do—in order to illuminate a bit more the illusory positivity with regard to the religious,* to sketch a speculative and historicizing sermon in order to see what the positive is.

(A) *The Speculative Sermon*

Let the theme be: Christian joy. The text is read, the theme is off to a proper start, by means of, for example, the contrasting movement but this is unimportant—now the discourse begins. In the first place, Christian joy is not (1) the world's joy. This is developed rhetorically in proportion to the speaker's talents, yet not very rigorously, for he is not talking to criminals and adulterers but to cultured people and distinguished sinners. One does not dare move them with the demonic passions. One comes to the conclusion of this point in a pleasant, almost complacent, mood. (2) Christian joy is not the satisfaction which poetry and art confer. Here is something for the cultured; they do not have time themselves to read the system, so they get it in church, and it is always something for the preacher's annual gratuity. But the clergyman does not have a splendid leisure, and what he knows here is soon used up. The fact that he does not have leisure, even though praiseworthy, is nothing to joke about, but the one who knows what scholarship is never dabbles in the subject in the pulpit. The satisfaction of poetry and art is *appearance*. The point here is to get this word introduced—it is so speculative. If one wishes to talk still more speculatively, one says: *the external appearance*. This is found even in children's reading books. In a long series of such books there has been a story called: *Appearances are Deceiving* —an English crime story. In a more recent speculative reading book, probably published under the direction of such a clergyman, the title is *External Appearances are Deceiving*. (3) Christian joy is not the spirit's repose in itself which scholarship bestows upon its cultivators. Knowing a little bit about ways of speaking, one could, if the clergyman had time, point out to him especially many passages in Aristotle[324] where there is discussion of the blessedness of the gods—these lend themselves excellently to use in a pagan address, and in our time also in a sermon.

In margin: and pertaining to the determinants: fear and compassion.

—But let us see what time it is. Good gracious, it is eleven o'clock! So there are only a few moments left. Attention, please, ladies and gentlemen—now comes the positive: the Christian joy is higher than all this. Amen. This is positive speculation in the pulpit. The theme has not even been talked about.* If anyone says that the Christian joy is unutterable—well, then this is what is to be discussed, and the theme becomes *the unutterable joy*. It is even a beautiful theme, but then there must be discussion of the unutterable, why it is unutterable, etc. On the other hand, one does not discuss the unutterable by talking about something else which is so easy to express that one can even say it by rote. To talk about the unutterable in this manner is similar to the language in Behrent's advertisement: when he had lost a silk umbrella and out of fear that someone would keep it if he came to know that it was made of silk, he advertised that a linen umbrella had been lost. This kind of positive talk is an outright waste of the listener's time. He who has anything to do with scholarship does not wish to hear such a one-shilling course, and he who does not have anything to do with scholarship does not understand it anyway, and a good listener wishes first and last the simple biblical teaching. If the clergyman still ventures the incredible, he says the following in the pulpit: *the innermost center*—but this is not particularly gripping for the person who is accustomed to move about in such scholarly phrases, and a respectable citizen who sits in a church is disturbed because he only knows these words from target-practice in the national guard.

That which really should be accentuated in religious joy is suffering and the idea that is the hinge of the category, namely, that the joy of poetry, art, and scholarship stands in an accidental relationship to suffering, because one person becomes a poet without suffering, another by suffering, a thinker without suffering (as a genius), another by suffering,

In margin: In order quite perfectly and genuinely speculatively to conceal this irregularity, the speaker would need only to say: Yet this is not the place to talk about it (but, to be sure, about the art, poetry, and scholarship). This category, this is not the place, must be regarded as the system's main cornerstone, which holds up the enormous construction, which one can never storm—because this is not the place—just as the man who obtained the royal dispensation to choose the manner of his death was never executed because he very kindly explained regarding each particular manner of death that this was not the place or this was not the way he would choose.

but religious joy is in the danger. From here on it is easy to show why it is unutterable.

VI B 10   n.d., 1844-45

« 626
Continuation of 625 (VI B 10):

B. *A Historicizing Sermon*

In this sphere grammar, dialectic, plan, design, consistency, train of thought, and everything which constrains are cast off together with the Roman yoke. The free spirit naturally has free speech, and free speech is thereby different from ordinary speech in that whereas one usually has a beginning, an intention for the thought which is clear in the beginning and achieved in the conclusion (the speculative address perhaps has the defect of merely beginning), free speech is remarkable in the fact that it begins by virtue of an event so that the beginning comes upon the speaker just like Christmas Eve. But once begun, free speech is again remarkable in that there is no compelling reason for it to stop. Just as that worthy performer in the Dyrehave carnival draws the rope out of himself, just so free speech rushes on, and to such an extent two performers could be necessary: the speaker, who produces the continuous web of free speech and the clerk who measures with an authorized yardstick and clips it off when the piece has gotten so long that it is a sermon. Remember what Pastor Grundtvig[325] so rightly said in the preface to his sermons: "to preach is not to write with pen and ink," from which it would also follow that every child who no longer writes on a slate but in a tablet (consequently with pen and ink) had been preaching. But even if this is so, even if—because of this matchless discovery—the staff is broken on all who write and everything written, it still does not follow that every ever so noisy sound issued by a Peder Ruus[326] is therefore a sermon.

Therefore, even though it is with pen and ink, let us make an attempt. Let the theme be: The Word of the Church. One goes back quite a few centuries, one gropes about in the darkness of the Middle Ages, the intolerable Roman yoke which papal power pressed upon consciences with nightmare attacks, until Martin Luther, the man of the word, made a visual demonstration of the thick darkness in which the papists groped and won the decision on the church door in Wittenberg, where he shut the mouth of the excessively erudite tongue-thrashers and word-distorters. But then the darkness fell again for three centuries, until the matchless discovery here in the North, when the living word was set free and installed in its rightful place as the most beautiful field and meadow of Denmark's mother tongue, in spite of German schoolmasters. And the folk-mouth and the folk-tongue shall not be bound, but all shall talk in the spirit when the golden age arrives, the matchless future of which the seer catches a glimpse with a hawk's eye and proclaims on a mouth harp when the living word, the Church's word, God's word, which was from the beginning, sounds in Denmark. May this come to pass! Amen, amen, in all eternity, amen.

Such an address is no sermon, even in its best form; yes, even if a genius opened his purse-strings and scooped information out of the horn of plenty. Clarified by occasional glints of thought, at times stirred in mood, this is a historical lecture. In relation to the religious, it holds true that all historical knowledge is negative. In relation to the religious, all historical presentation is a diversion. The listener forgets himself over the papists and the twilight, over Luther and the sunrise, over the matchless discovery which was made in Copenhagen. But in relation to the religious it is precisely negative to forget oneself.* A religious speaker must not be different from his listeners as the teachers *ex cathedra* are different. The richer in spirit and the more knowledgeable the religious speaker is, the greater is the self-possession required in order to achieve unity with the listener. The religious speaker should be distinguished by his having existentially made sure of what the simplest of men also knows. A hawk's-eye view of world history does not replace a sober insight into oneself; the most matchless discoveries, even the discovery of gunpowder, do not compensate as a substitute for a lack of self-knowledge and of maieutic skill in relation to others.

*In margin: and the positive is to be made self-active.

VI B 11   n.d., 1844-45

« 627

A new science must be introduced: the Christian art of speaking, to be constructed *admodum* Aristotle's *Rhetoric*. Dogmatics as a whole is a misunderstanding, especially as it now has been developed.

In margin: N.B.

VI A 17   n.d., 1845

« 628

In margin of 627 (VI A 17):
Aristotle places the art of speaking and the media for awakening faith ($\pi \iota \sigma \tau \iota s$) in relationship to probability,[327] so that it is concerned (in

contrast to knowledge) with what can be relevant in another way. Christian eloquence will be distinguished from the Greek in that it is concerned only with *improbability*, with showing that it is improbable, in order that one can then *believe* it. Here probability is to be rejected just as much as improbability in the other, but both have in common the distinction from knowledge.

VI A 19 n.d., 1845

« 629

It is certainly remarkable that the abstract expression in a rhetorical presentation is sometimes more effective than concrete description. For example, if a pastor were to say, "I do not know your life, my listener, I do not know what lies most heavily on your mind, what your secret sorrow is," he would very likely draw tears from one who would sit unmoved if the pastor actually described his particularized sorrow. Just as the lyric in the Middle Ages often consists of the universal—for example, instead of talking about himself the sufferer talks about universal man (this lyrical objectivizing)—in the same way the abstract also has something engaging about it, a breeze, as it were, from the universal which passes over the listener's head and stirs him precisely because he is not being talked about in particular.

VI A 115 n.d., 1845

« 630

See journal p. 158n., p. 130 [i.e., VI A 1, V A 47].
1) A little about the contradictions in the upbuilding or edifying address.
    The relationship to scholarship—which categories may be used.
        Here a little about my edifying discourses,[328] that they were not sermons. (Objections have been made to this without bearing in mind that for this reason the title was not put that way—but edifying discourses.)
    It is of equal merit to be a good speaker and a good listener:
        in scholarship as many results as possible,
        in religious address as few results as possible,
        just as strong in the immediate as the reflective, and one must above all have existed [*existeret*] in both.
    The one is a work of art; the other a work of scholarship.
        Situation: that Hegel in punishment for his attack upon the religious would have to deliver an edifying discourse.

VI A 147 n.d., 1845

« 631 *Something about Religious Eloquence*³²⁹

Illustrations:

They say, for example, that there are two ways—the way of desire and the way of virtue—they describe the first as strewn with flowers, etc.; the other as rigorous in the beginning, but little by little . . . . . here the preacher suddenly forgets himself and virtue's narrow way, for his description of virtue's way little by little becomes seductive. What then? The result is that a sensualist is not only crazy for not choosing the way of virtue but that he is a crazy sensualist for not choosing the way of virtue —if it is as the preacher says. —So the discourse is a disappointment, for it brings the rewards into the foreground instead of saying what the task is, without entering upon the reward here and beyond. One gladly listens to such a discourse, for it prevents acting.

VI A 149   n.d., 1845

« 632

Double-reflection³³⁰ is already present in the communication itself, in the fact that the subjectivity (who wants to express the life of the eternal*) existing [*existerende*] in isolation wants to communicate himself, something he cannot possibly do directly, since it is a contradiction.

One may very well want to communicate himself, like the person in love, but always indirectly.

Every finite certainty is simply a deception; to demand this of God is only to make a fool of him. It is like the unfaithfulness in an erotic relationship which consists not in one's loving another girl but in having lost the idea.**

VI B 38   n.d., 1845

« 633

Later I again found illumination of the meaning of the experiment as the form of communication.³³³

If existence [*Existents*] is the essential and truth is inwardness, if it is precisely the dubiousness of speculation to have overlooked this, if the misfortune it brings upon men is precisely that life becomes meaningless to them unless perhaps they take two or three years to read the system,

---

*Where all sociality and all communication are inconceivable, because motion is inconceivable. Trendlenburg's contribution³³¹ to the category; the passage in the conclusion³³² about Isis and Osiris, which are noted in my copies.

**If such a girl were to long for the wedding day because it would give finite certainty, if she wanted me to understand that now she was certain, I would deplore her unfaithfulness, for then she would have lost the idea of love.

and even if one has entertained himself with it for a long time, it nevertheless still makes individual existence [*Existents*] meaningless to the existing individual [*existerende Individualitet*] himself—then it is always good that this be said, but then it is also good that it be said in the right way. But this right way is precisely the art which makes being such an author very difficult; therefore it pleases me that the pseudonymous authors have overcome the difficulties which I had almost despaired over. If this is communicated in a direct form, then the point is missed; then the reader is led into misunderstanding—he gets something more to know, that to exist [*at existere*] also has its meaning, but he receives it as knowledge so that he keeps right on sitting in the *status quo*. [Portion omitted is essentially the same as S.V., VII, p. 210, lines 23-37.³³⁴] Thus the system, too, is well disposed; it says: Heavens, there is room enough; we can readily take it up into the system.* Alas, yes, in the system there is plenty of room.

VI B 40:45 n.d., 1845

« 634

Insofar as the religious address is confused with worldly wisdom or with the doctrine of calculation and results, it is to be regarded as an estheticizing lecture on the ethical. In a strict sense it is not even ethical, much less religious. It is by no means my opinion that a religious speaker should pooh-pooh what he in so many ways must naturally be occupied with, but he should never dare to forget the totality-category of his sphere,³³⁷ and that this is what he should use and have with him throughout, however mildly he admonishes the happy one that the religious lives within man and that suffering will also come if he is religious, and speaks likewise to the unhappy one. But if he becomes so complexly involved in the traffic of finitude that he forgets suffering as essentially different from the dialectic of happiness and unhappiness, then he also transforms³³⁸ the church, if not into a robber's den then into a stock-exchange building. This is the reason that the religious address³³⁹ in these times treats happiness, unhappiness, duty, the seven last words, uses the name of God and of Christ—and almost never draws attention to trials [*Anfægtelser*]. Trials belong to the inwardness of religiousness, and inwardness belongs to religiousness; trials belong to the individual's absolute relationship to the absolute τέλος. What temptation [*Fristelse*] is

---

* This happened to Hamann, for example, in Michelet.³³⁵ Jacobi is also in paragraphs in the system.³³⁶

outwardly, trial is inwardly. I will permit myself a psychological experiment.

VI B 60:2   n.d., 1845

« 635 *Malpractices in the Oratorical Address*

> They say Paul is one of the *most remarkable* of the apostles, which means that there are esthetic categories together with the dogmatic categories.

One admires an expression such as the figure of a race at the racetrack.³⁴⁰ Even if one does not admire it as foolishly as Münter³⁴¹ did the other day, the esthetic is a mistake. —The apostolic quality is authority—not brilliance, for I, too, can toss off just as striking a figure, to say nothing of the Greeks.

God knows what one would really think if a man begins to admire the matchlessness of such an expression.

VI B 129   n.d., 1845

« 636

It is, on the whole, a big question to what extent it is permissible to bring purely personal influence to bear, as in saying one is rescued in a miraculous manner. In any case one must avoid producing an imaginary effect. One must state very accurately and specifically the nature of one's error and sin; otherwise one can very easily arouse anxiety in the more innocent by a horrifying representation of evil. —In addition, sometimes there is danger also in the opposite, when a man is completely silent about his own life but shows such descriptive powers that one involuntarily comes to some conclusions about his own life. One can himself have made such a terrifying acquaintance with evil that he can listen to such descriptions in sermons unscathed, but a person can also be made anxious by them. And evil can well-meaningly be described so shockingly that the anxiety [*Angesten*] is thereby coaxed into a young person's soul.

VII¹ A 91   n.d., 1846

« 637

It seems to be quite forgotten that to be an author is action.³⁴² This is why no one dares move ahead slowly, because every author regards himself as one who is up for examination; he fears that someone will think that he does not know much. Since existence [*Tilværelsen*] itself is dialectical, it is a matter of situating every element in such a way that it makes its impression. In order to grasp the forgiveness of sins, I must first and foremost have the impression of consciousness of sin in confession of sin. Now the point here is to do this with penetrating relevance, and then not a word more. But the speaker or the thinker fears or is ashamed that someone might think that he does not know very much, and therefore he must say it all at once. In this way the whole impression is vitiated.

VII^1 A 123   n.d., 1846

« 638 *The Difference between Christian Discourse and Sermon*[343]

A Christian discourse deals to a certain extent with doubt—a sermon operates absolutely and solely on the basis of authority, that of Scripture and of Christ's apostles. Therefore, it is neither more nor less than heresy to deal with doubt in a sermon, however well one might be able to deal with it.

The preface to my *Christian Discourses*, therefore, contains the phrase: if a sufferer who also has *run wild in many thoughts*.

A sermon presupposes a pastor (ordination); Christian discourse can be by a layman.

VIII^1 A 6   n.d., 1847

« 639

It would perhaps be all right for once to give a few sermons which attempt to grasp men on the tender side.[344] For example, describing heart-rendingly Christ's sacrifice, his self-denial—and then the exhortation: Would you now as a matter of course brush this all off as nothing at all, sit in your comfort, made secure by all this, indolently and dully call him your benefactor without feeling the slightest need to resemble him, to say nothing of sacrificing something, etc.

The art is to achieve once again the sweep which has been tricked out of Christianity by this unsanctified stupidity that we will all be saved just as we are, etc. —To thunder is no longer of any avail; it merely embitters men. Yet sermons of this sort might still accomplish something. The main thing would be to individualize so sharply that the listener could not imagine that it is some other "you" who is being addressed.

But the clergy who ought to be helping men out into the stream are the ones who are teaching men all these delusions, for the clergy themselves are not out in the stream and do not wish to be out there. Again, the most dangerous thing of all is not merely that the congregation itself is indolent but that it lies at anchor to boot—thanks to the clergy.

VIII^1 A 243   n.d., 1847

COMMUNICATION   263

« 640

Ecclesiastes 5:1: "Guard your steps when you go to the house of God" could very well be used in a sermon as contrast to the nondescript mode of preaching concerned primarily with getting people into church. Beware of entering there. It is your responsibility if you do not act according to what is preached. And if the preaching is as it should be, you might perhaps get an impression which you can never live down, an impression of what God requires of you—self-denial, etc.—therefore beware!

VIII^1 A 256   *n.d.*, 1847

« 641 *The Difference between an Upbuilding Discourse and Reflections*[345]

Reflections [*Overveielse*] do not presuppose the qualifying concepts as given and understood; therefore, they must not so much move, mollify, reassure, persuade, as *awaken* and provoke men and sharpen thought. The time for reflections is indeed before action, and their purpose therefore is to rightly set all the elements into motion. Reflections ought to be a "gadfly"; therefore their tone ought to be quite different from that of upbuilding [*opbyggelige*] or edifying discourse, which rests in mood, but reflections ought in the good sense to be impatient, high-spirited in mood. Irony is necessary here and the even more significant ingredient of the comic. One may very well even laugh once in a while, if only to make the thought clearer and more striking. An upbuilding discourse about love presupposes that men know essentially what love is and seeks to win them to it, to move them. But this is in fact not the case. Therefore the "reflections" must first fetch them up out of the cellar, call to them, turn their comfortable way of thinking topsy-turvy with the dialectic of truth.

VIII^1 A 293   *n.d.*, 1847

« 642

In margin of 641 (VIII^1 A 293):
The difference can be seen expressed in the preface: that single individual . . . . . kindly reflect whether, etc. The preface to an upbuilding or edifying discourse could never read like that.

VIII^1 A 294   *n.d.*, 1847

« 643

Generally an introduction to a talk to be delivered is simply a hindrance. The audience is assembled, the setting has its own influence

—then the art is simply to move straightway into the subject. In a discourse to be read an introduction is of importance. The readers come to the work with all kinds of heterogeneous impressions, and therefore the introduction must be a kind of striptease in order to get them to come along. Therefore an introduction needs to be engaging, striking, interesting—in short, it should be enthralling.

VIII^1 A 362   n.d., 1847

« 644 *Concerning the Hypocrisy of Current Preaching*

It is not unusual to hear someone say that this or that pastor is a hypocrite. Such a thing does not really concern another person. The point to be discussed here is something else, the hypocrisy inherent simply in the objective qualifications of current preaching. The question is not whether a particular clergyman means what he says, but the point is that generally there is no existential meaning in present preaching, that to exist [*at existere*] in accordance with it is an impossibility, because it is nonsense. But then it is hypocrisy, because preaching should have of all things the very closest relationship to existing.

VIII^1 A 448   n.d., 1847

« 645

When in a matter of communicating something it is entirely clear what communication means, when it is so self-evident that not a moment needs to be wasted in speaking about it, when it is the sort of presupposition which does not even need to be mentioned, then, if one has something to communicate, it goes as easily as putting one's foot in a stocking. But if an author has his own distinctive conception of communication, if all his distinctiveness and the reality of his historical significance are perhaps focused precisely in this, well, then it will be a long-drawn-out affair—O, school of patience. Before there can be any mention of understanding something of what he has communicated, one must first understand him in his distinctive dialectic of communication and in this light understand everything which one understands. And this, his distinctive dialectic of communication, he cannot, however, communicate in the traditional dialectic of communication. The age, of course, will demand just this of him, which naturally is nonsensical. O, it is a long way home to being understood—O, school of patience. And the more a person understands himself in what he understands, the more readily he discovers that he is not understood—only people who themselves understand nothing at all can through delusion succeed in believing themselves understood by all. O, the sadness of having understood something true—

and then to find oneself only misunderstood. O, the sadness—for in the secrecy of inwardness what is irony but sadness. The sadness is in being alone in having understood something true, and as soon as one is in the company of others, with those who misunderstand, this sadness is irony.

VIII[1] A 466 n.d., 1847

« 646 N.B.

Presumably I could this moment rather easily procure someone or other who would teach my ideas; it would also be easy for me to be helpful to such a one in this respect, and it would be a relief for me not to stand entirely alone. I am completely clear about this, and I will now make an account of what I am doing.

The fact of the matter is that there ought not to be teaching; what I have to say may not be taught; by being taught it turns into something entirely different. What I need is a man who does not gesticulate with his arms up in a pulpit or with his fingers upon a podium, but a person who gesticulates with his entire personal existence [*Existents*], with the willingness in every danger to will to express in action precisely what he teaches. An assistant professor, that is, someone with seventeen concerns, wants to have a paid occupation, wants to get married, wants to be well thought of, wants to satisfy the times, etc. What I have expressed, when delivered in a lecture by such a professor, becomes *eo ipso* something entirely different. Precisely this is the profound untruth in all modern teaching, that there is no notion at all of how thought is influenced by the fact that the one presenting it does not dare to express it in action, that in this very way the flower of the thought or the heart of the thought vanishes and the power of the thought disappears.

It is true that if I died at this moment, I certainly could not prevent its being taught. True enough. But neither can my obligation be extended beyond my life. Moreover, if I keep the enterprise pure as long as I live, I give the tension which may possibly effect the awakening of someone or another.

The basic flaw of the age is this teaching which leaves a person's inwardness completely secure. Just as novelists and their kind weep buckets over one or another remarkable character (just as the shadows in the underworld sucked the blood of the living to continue living, so novelists *et al.* are unreal, shadows), in the same way the assistant professors want to swallow an existential thinker in order to obtain blood and life-warmth in paragraphs for a while. This shadow-existence is the secret of the system, *knowing about,* not being.

This is how I have understood myself. And, as always, I regard as my duty to do what I can understand, convinced of God's support. Consequently, I do not provide myself with a couple of lecturers to whom I then teach this difficulty—no, I remain silent and act.

It is strenuous, and it certainly becomes more and more strenuous, but it is endurable when I scrupulously hold to the divine regulation not to be concerned about tomorrow[346] but to thank God every day that he today gives me sufficient power. All exhaustion comes particularly from squandering away time, from thinking about many years, etc. instead of saying: Can you not hold out for today? And when the answer is Yes, then one holds out and believes for tomorrow.

Moreover, there is still a circumstance which makes all direct communication or talk about my activity as an author uncomfortable. I am aware of how much has been granted to me. But lest I become proud or arrogant about this, I carry about in a concerned consciousness an enormous responsibility, heavy, heavy memories, many, many trials. Of all these things I cannot speak. If I were to speak with someone simply about my activity as an author, I would speak only about big things. I cannot speak directly to another person of how before God I feel less than a sparrow, or just as insignificant. In conversation among men we use human standards, and by human standards I have a great superiority. But to speak in this way is extremely painful to me and afterward it grieves my spirit;[347] it is to me as if I deceived God.

Therefore I am silent and keep going. If God permits the appearance of a contemporary who independently and with responsibility toward God declares himself at one with me, I thank God for it. But I am not permitted to make my position easier by placing someone in a direct, that is, an untrue relationship to me. I have no responsibility, as if I would keep the truth to myself. My books lie before the eyes of the world; they are *publici juris*; but I have no right to help anyone with personal prattle to cheaper terms than I myself have been helped—this would be to deceive him. If anyone wishes to call this self-love, I shall call what he calls love effeminacy.

VIII^1 A 554   *n.d.*, 1848

« 647 *From Thoughts Which Wound from Behind for Upbuilding*

Discourse VI

. . . Just like a child who, about to get a licking, puts a towel under his pants unbeknownst to the teacher so that he will not feel the blows, so, alas, is even the preacher of law, who for good reasons gives the congregation a helping hand by surreptitiously slipping in another figure which is now punished—to the upbuilding, contentment, and enjoyment of the congregation. For good reasons—for in the case of the child there is no danger involved in being the teacher who is to administer the caning, but truly to be a preacher of law—yes, here the concept turns about, for it means not so much to spank others as to be spanked oneself. The more beatings the preacher of law gets, the better he is. Therefore a so-called preacher of law does not dare actually to administer a beating, because he knows very well and all too well understands that those before him are not children, that the others, the ones he is supposed to beat, that these people together with these thousands of others who at this moment are the honored, respected, and lauded ones through serving the passions of the moment—these people are by far the strongest, they will *actually* strike back, perhaps beat him to death; for to be a preacher of the law is to be put to death. Consequently the preacher of the law restricts himself to—beating the pulpit. (In this way he achieves his ridiculous purpose, to become the most ridiculous of all monstrosities—a preacher of the law who is honored and respected, greeted with applause!)

VIII^1 A 564   n.d., 1848

« 648

THE DIALECTIC
OF ETHICAL AND ETHICAL-RELIGIOUS COMMUNICATION[348]

A Little Sketch

As far as I recall this is from 1847. In any case, it is not later than the March publication of *Christian Discourses*, which was in the Spring of 1848.[349]

VIII^2 B 79   n.d., 1847

« 649

1

INTRODUCTION

If one were to concentrate in one single descriptive word the delusion and confusion of modern science and scholarship—or essentially the delusion and confusion of the modern age, especially since the abandonment of Kant's honorable way and giving the well-known 100 dollars in order to become theocentric, then one might say: It is dishonest.

Dishonesty—Lack of naïveté—

2

More specifically
> that science and scholarship have become *fantastic* (pure knowledge) and in addition always *learned*—the ridiculous combinations:
>> in the same book to treat pure thought *sub specie æterni* and an instructor's little dissertation.

3

More specifically
> that what it means to be a human being has been forgotten.
>> The Greeks—how humanly they remembered this—and toward God—no Sophist, not the most high-flying, was theocentric—which we are now by custom to such a degree that no one censures it.

4

In margin of 81:3:
The powers of the human world have been fantastically extracted and a book world has been produced (one now becomes an author simply and solely by becoming a reader—instead of by primitivity, just as one now becomes a man simply and solely by aping "the others," instead of by primitivity), a public of fantastic abstractions. As soon as one writes, he is no longer a single individual human being himself, nor is the reader that to him, either.

5

More specifically
> that the distinction between art and science has been forgotten.
>> Everything has become science and scholarship, and art is understood only esthetically as fine art.

But there is a whole aspect of art which science and scholarship have taken possession of—or wish to take possession of—this is the ethical.

The ethical is indifferently related to knowledge; that is, it assumes that every human being knows it.

The confusion when that which ought to be communicated as scholarship and science is communicated as art (scholasticism is an example), but also when that which should be communicated as art is communicated as science and scholarship, and this is the confusion of the modern age, that the ethical is communicated as scholarship and science.

Let me illustrate with an example. The military assumes that every country lad who comes into military service possesses the necessary capacities to be able to stick it out. Therefore he is first of all examined so that there be no difficulties in this respect (in the same way the ethical assumes that everyone knows what the ethical is). Now the communication begins. The corporal does not explain to the soldier what it is to drill, etc.; he communicates it to him as an art, he teaches him to use militarily the abilities and the potential competence he already has.

And this is the way the ethical must be communicated. If one begins first of all with a course to instill the ethical into the individual, then the communication never becomes ethical and the relationship is disturbed from the beginning.

The communication here implies luring the ethical out of the individual, because it is *in* the individual. The corporal begins essentially by regarding the farm boy as a soldier, because he is that κατὰ δύναμιν.

Corresponding to the corporal (apart from all the disparity in the military system of subordination) is an EXISTING ETHICIST, who remains conscious of himself and in reflection returns into himself to be that which he teaches, and he presupposes—that every human being is the same κατὰ δύναμιν.

The whole modern science of ethics is, ethically understood, an evasion.

On the whole, ethics has come to be neglected in modern science and scholarship—but there is especially the total lack of an existing ethicist. And that is why ultimately men have forgotten completely what earnestness is and in all earnestness regard as nonsense that which leads to self-knowledge, turns a person out of his delusions, etc.; whereas every communication of knowledge is regarded as earnestness—and yet every new communication of knowledge only nourishes sickness. In a certain sense there is something horrible about contemplating the whole mob of publishers, book-sellers, journalists, authors—all of them working day and night in the service of confusion, because men will not become sober and understand that relatively little knowledge is needed to be truly human —but all the more self-knowledge.

6

In margin of 81:5:
Science probably can be pounded into a person, but the ethical has

to be pounded out of him—just as the corporal, precisely because he sees the soldier in the farm boy, might say: I certainly will have to pound the soldier out of him; on the other hand, with respect to the manual of field tactics (what an army is, what sentry duty is, etc.) the corporal might say: Well, that will have to be pounded into him.

7

COMMUNICATOR—RECEIVER
THE OBJECT

As soon as I think of communication, there is at once a division into these three categories.
    Brief general observation about this
    (that "receiver" is an active word,
    that we have no passive word).
(Generally there is teacher—pupil—

                                          object of teaching.)
Will attempt to find the ethical by dialectically transforming these three relationships.

8

THE OBJECT

The object must be a knowledge.
All knowledge is
either knowledge about something (to be carried out—reference to the Greeks—and to the moderns—all the way from the empirical to the highest sciences) (even the so-called knowledge about knowledge is knowledge *about something*),
or self-knowledge (not fantastically the pure self-consciousness and the pure I).
Let us suppose that a person has pressed to the highest level in self-knowledge; consequently he knows completely who and what he is, but he is what he is in any case. —The irony and the earnestness in this. We are all immortal—if someone immerses himself in this thought, lives in it, he does not thereby become more immortal than the rest of us.

Even in self-knowledge difficulties appear with respect to the dialectic of communication.

9

Let us now make an experiment and assume that there is an object or a knowledge which we all have. What would the implications be for the dialectical in communication?

From this it would follow: (1) the object drops out, for if we all know it, one person cannot communicate it to another; (2) the concept communicator drops out; and (3) the receiver. The only communicator remaining would be the one who had given all men this knowledge and inasmuch as everyone is a receiver, the concept receiver is abrogated.

In this way the dialectic of communication is essentially changed.

10

But is the very thing we are talking about the ethical?

What, specifically, is the ethical? —Well, if I put the question in this manner, I am asking unethically about the ethical, I am putting the question just as the whole confusion of the modern age does, and then I cannot put a stop to it. The ethical presupposes that every person knows what the ethical is, and why? Because the ethical demands that every man shall realize it at every moment, but then he surely has to know it.* The ethical does not begin with ignorance which is to be changed to knowledge but begins with a knowledge and demands a realization. Here it is a matter of being unconditionally consistent. The slightest uncertainty in attitude—and then the modern confusion has gotten hold of us. If someone were to say: I must first know what the ethical is—how plausible—especially since from childhood we are accustomed to being arguers. But the ethical answers altogether consistently: Scoundrel, you want to make excuses and look for excuses. If someone were to say: There are quite different concepts of the ethical in different countries and in different ages. How is this doubt halted? It can result in scholarly folios and still not stop, but the ethical seizes the doubter with ethical consistency and says, what concern is it of yours? You shall do the ethical at every moment, and you are ethically responsible for every moment you waste.

11

So it is with the ethical. Every human being knows the ethical. How, then, is the dialectic of communication changed?

---

* *In margin:* Prometheus, who gave all men the ethical equally.[350]

1. The object drops out, for since we all know it, there is no object to communicate—to want to make an attempt to communicate the ethical in this way is precisely unethical.
2. The communicator drops out—for if everyone knows it, one person cannot communicate it to another.
3. The receiver drops out—for if the communicator drops out, the receiver goes also.

There remains only one communicator: God.

12

We have now thought through the dialectic of communication as knowledge and have seen that it is done away with. Now follows a new conception of communication.

> The difference between communicating something as an art and communicating as a science.

13

The ethical must be communicated as an art, simply because everyone knows it.

> The Corporal and the Farm Lad

The object of the communication is consequently not a knowledge but a realization.

14

In margin of 81:13:

An example of the misunderstanding through conceiving instruction aimed at capability as instruction in knowledge. A sergeant in the National Guard says to a recruit, "You, there, stand up straight." Recruit: "Sure enough." Sergeant: "Yes, and don't talk during drill." Recruit: "All right, I won't if you'll just tell me." Sergeant: "What the devil! You are not supposed to talk during drill!" Recruit: "Well, don't get so mad. If I know I'm not supposed to, I'll quit talking during drill."

15

In regard to the communication of an art, it is either competence which makes the teacher or *authority*, also.

16

In regard to the ethical, one person cannot have authority in relation to another because, ethically, God is the master-teacher and every man is an apprentice. If someone were to say to men: You ought to act ethically, it is as if God were heard speaking simultaneously to this important man: Nonsense, my friend, it is you who must do it.

In margin: Like Petro to the castle superintendent: Get out, get out —ah, it is he who should get out.

17

In regard to the ethical, proficiency cannot make a master-teacher either. A person can become so proficient in a human art that it is something to talk about, but ethically every man relates himself as an apprentice to God, who is the master-teacher, and always has the task of his own development.

18

If, however, there is to be any question of instruction in the ethical as in an art, the dialectic of communication must have one extension more, and then everything is in order again.

INDIRECT COMMUNICATION[351]
DOUBLE REFLECTION[352]
THE MAIEUTIC[353]

19

In margin of 81:18:

Socrates said he could not give birth but could only be a midwife. That is, every man possesses the ethical and the one who has been born cannot be born again[354] (here the Christian rebirth enters in—as a relationship not between man and man but between God and man, a new creation).

20

INDIRECT COMMUNICATION

(The object, as was shown, is not a knowledge but an art, a realization.)

The communicator always dares influence only indirectly, (1) because he must always express that he himself is not a master-teacher but an apprentice and that God, on the other hand, is his and every man's master-teacher, (2) because he must express that the receiver himself knows it, (3) because ethically the task is precisely this—that every man comes to stand alone in the God-relationship.

Consequently the receiver can never become an apprentice [to the indirect communicator], for he already knows; nor can he buy in on the communicator, for ethically this is an atrocity.

21

DOUBLE-REFLECTION

Since ethically there is no direct relationship, all communication must go through a double-reflection; the first is the reflection in which the communication is made, and the second is that in which it is recaptured.

Docendo discimus, a gymnastic teacher himself exercises in teaching others; but it is not in this sense. One cannot, for example say that God is the true teacher in gymnastics or in Latin and Greek. But in the ethical God is the only teacher, and therefore the so-called master-teacher *shall* himself practice what he teaches.

22

THE MAIEUTIC

All indirect communication is different from direct communication in that indirect communication first of all involves a deception[355]— simply because an attempt to communicate the ethical directly would mean to deceive.

23

Irony—the highest earnestness. Earnestness is that I as an individual relate myself to God and thus with every human being. —People stupidly think it is earnestness to have many followers who are willing if necessary to die for me. —Stupidity—To help a man relate himself to God as an individual is earnestness. But it must be done indirectly, for otherwise I become a hindrance to the one who is helped.

24

The maieutic art—the dialectical consequences of the deception—the moral character which is needed in order to be a maieutic—ataraxy—true heroism—true humanity—that men are altogether unconscious of it.

In margin: this deception signifies that the communicator first and foremost does not seem to be an earnest man. There is really nothing people want to do more than to mimic—one can never mimic an ironist, for he is a Proteus who incessantly alters the deception.

25

The more precise dialectical determination of all communication in relation to the medium in which the communication takes place.

26

THE MEDIUM OF IMAGINATION

The deceptive in instructing young people in the medium of imagination or fantasy; whereas everything looks just the opposite in the medium of actuality.

27

THE MEDIUM OF ACTUALITY

Recognizable by the fact that the communicator himself is and always strives to be that which he communicates.

28

In margin of 81:26 and 81:27:
All communication of knowledge is in the medium of imagination, the communication of an art less so, inasmuch as it is an execution. But the communication in the ethical can be given only in actuality, in such a way that the communicator or teacher himself exists [*existerer*] in it and in the situation of actuality, is himself in the situation of actuality that which he teaches. When someone instructs in ataraxy—from a platform—it is not ethically true. No, the situation must be such that he himself demonstrates ataraxy simultaneously as he instructs in ataraxy. For example, if someone is instructing in ataraxy while surrounded by a crowd of people who are insulting him—this is a genuine situation of actuality.

29

To what extent is it permissible to win men[356] instead of thrusting them away from oneself in order to win them for the truth. But the thrust must have an energetic expression in the action (the qualitative dialectic).

30

To what extent must the receiver first be cleansed—the negative in the maieutic. To communicate can mean tricking out of, a kind of communication which is very dangerous for the communicator, for Socrates does say[357] that men could become so angry with him that they would gladly have bitten him—when he tricked them out of a stupidity or two.

31

The dialectical in that the communicator must work against himself.³⁵⁸

32

The dialectical in that the communicator must have eyes in the back of his head with regard to the actual appropriation of the communication.

33

In margin of 81:32:
The giddiness and the unethical in being so busy about communicating that one forgets to be what one teaches. God is not in a fix. This confusion comes from observing existence in an imaginary way.

34

The pathos-filled and the dialectical transition.

VIII² B 81   *n.d.*, 1847

« 650

[*Expanded sketch and elaborations:*]

1
FIRST LECTURE

2

The DISHONESTY of the Modern Age (dishonesty—self-deception—perplexity—).

The lack of naïveté (the naïve and the acquired. It is not maturity to have ceased to be naïve or never to have been that. Naïveté must be preserved. For example, to distinguish between what one understands and what one does not understand—the preponderance of the generation. A generation is an abstract concretion and can never be naïve).

The lack of primitivity* (the primitive and the traditional, *das Herkomliche*).

literary
viewed from the time when there was only one learned language—vernacular languages—periodicals—all media have become sciences.

social
the increasing culture—growing necessities—life in the great cities.**

3

In margin of 82:2.

Every human being *ought* to be naïve. —Naïveté rescues from illusions of the imagination, but also from the shallowness of acquired knowledge.

4

In margin of 82:2:

Nowadays one becomes an author by reading—not by his primitivity, just as one becomes a man by mimicking others—not by his primitivity. One does not know by himself that he is a human being but arrives at this conclusion because he is like the others. God knows if any one of us is! And in our age, which otherwise doubts everything, no one ever thinks of doubtingly asking—but God knows if any one of us actually is human.

5

In margin of 82:2:

The tryanny of the daily press, periodicals, brochures, which are written for "the many," who understand nothing, and by those who understand how to write—for the many.

6

Addition to 82:2:

* A genuine primitive genius is the true general-examiner. Every primitive existence contains also a reexamination of the universally human. And every existence ought to have some of this reexamining quality. It is dishonest to lack the quality of reexamination altogether and automatically to accept everything as custom and habit and to let custom and habit be sufficient.

7

Addition to 82:2:

** One lives in the moment and at best with the next moment as perspective. One cannot get distance.

8

Modern philosophical science has become imaginary or
    fantastic (pure knowledge) †
    and confusingly learned (the apparatus).

† *In margin:* Especially since abandoning Kant's honorable way and giving, if I dare say so, the well-known 100 dollars to become theocentric.

Mad combinations of this: in the same book to treat pure thought *sub specie æterni* and afterwards to regret that one has not gotten around to consider an assistant professor's little discussion in a newspaper.*

9

What it means to be a human being has been forgotten. The Greeks[359]—it echoes in their poetry, their philosophy—the sorrowful—the humane—the godliness therein—even the most inflated Sophist was not theocentric—something we now all are without ever thinking about it—what a Greek would think of our age.

Instead of men, everywhere fantastic abstractions. Book-world—the public—as soon as one writes he is no longer an individual human being himself, nor does he think of a reader as an individual human being, either—here the means of communication is at fault; it is much too ambitious.

10

In margin:
If someone wanting to speak had a speaking-trumpet so strong that it could be heard throughout the whole country, he would soon create the impression that he was not a single person (but something much more—for example, the voice of the age, etc., an abstraction) and that he was not talking to an individual or to individual human beings but to the whole world (the race, etc., an abstraction). Thus with the invention of the art of printing and especially its growth. Communication is as if through an enormous trumpet, *ergo*—yes, even if it is utterly unimportant, completely stupid, even if it is the shouting of *prosit*, the communicator becomes self-important and has a fantastic notion of who it is he is talking to.

And now anonymity. Antiquity's *persona—per sonare—* to intensify the voice of the individual, while it still is the voice of the individual—but anonymity and then the press. What madness!

---

* *In margin:* The historicizing method.

11

Everything has become objective.

Physiologists have observed that modern man is an inhuman, abnormal development of the stomach and brain—in the same way there is an abnormality in this becoming objective without correspondingly becoming subjective, and thus all the mental phenomena which correspond to abdominal difficulties, which end in apoplexy.

12

In regard to the ethical and the ethical-religious, the genuine communication and instruction is *training* or *upbringing*. By upbringing a person becomes that which he is essentially regarded to be (a horse, if it is trained and the trainer has good sense, becomes precisely a horse). Upbringing begins with regarding the one who is going to be brought up as being κατὰ δύναμιν that which he shall become, and by regarding him from this point of view brings it out of him. He *brings* or *draws it up*, consequently—it is there—(to "up-nurture" a plant, to "up-bring" the child).

Therefore the rule for the method in upbringing is that the one who is being brought up does as well as he can at every moment. Confusion arises when the upbringer instead of upbringing teaches as if he were imparting knowledge. It becomes sophistry when one thinks: What good is it for me to do it now since I am doing it so poorly; I must first get to know much more, etc.—but this is nothing but escapism and heresy. The rule is to do it as well as one can at every moment, and then again to do it as well as one can the next moment, and so on further, in order continually to get to know it better and better. If, on the other hand, the upbringing is communicated as knowledge, one never receives an upbringing but is always getting merely something to know.

13

The difference between upbringing in the ethical and upbringing in the ethical-religious is simply this—that the ethical is the universally human itself, but religious (Christian) upbringing must first of all communicate a knowledge. Ethically man as such knows about the ethical, but man as such does not know about the religious in the Christian sense. Here there must be the communication of a little knowledge first of all—but then the same relationship as in the ethical enters in. The instruction, the communication, must not be as of a knowledge, but upbringing, practising, art-instruction.

My service in using pseudonyms consists in having discovered, Christianly, the maieutic method.

> Until now, from generation to generation, men have taught Christianity as a knowledge (the first course) and then the next course, again, as a knowledge.
>
> Together with having placed *I*'s into the middle of life. It is completely lacking in our age for someone to say: *I*. Strictly speaking, these *I*'s are now only poetic *I*'s, but that is always something, nevertheless.

14

I myself feel the difficulties all too well. Here it is not a matter of an error which one clears up in the twinkling of an eye and then it is gone. Here it is a matter of an error which has entrenched itself from generation to generation, in which we are brought up, completely coalesced in it, by virtue of which our whole language-expression is formed. Here the exact opposite will happen. When the error has been brought out and one has understood it, he will immediately return to himself and not understand it any more, for everything, everything, be it little or big, reminds him of the error and forces it upon him, but nothing of the truth. (It is just like the earth moving and the sun standing still.) I know it myself from experience, even though I have been engrossed in it for a long time.

15

To stand—by another's help alone
and
    To stand alone—by another's help.[360]

> The latter is the maieutic relationship; therefore there is also the ironical in the formulation; whereas the first formulation is a direct relationship and a direct statement. There is therefore no reason to use a dash in the first formulation, since it all belongs together. But, to stand alone—by another's help, this is a formula for irony. The first statement says one thing, and that which comes after the dash ironically slips in the opposite as the explanation. To stand alone is not to stand by another's help, but the maieutic's help is hidden, and therefore the ironical "to stand alone—by another's help." But if he is going to

stand alone—by another's help, then he must by no means have any conception of this other as advantageous, for this advantageous idea usually becomes a hindrance to his standing alone.

VIII² B 82   *n.d.*, 1847

« 651

When I think of communicating, I think of four parts: (1) the OBJECT, (2) the COMMUNICATOR, (3) the RECEIVER, (4) the COMMUNICATION.

First Distinction

When "the object" is reflected upon

"the object"	no "object"
The communication of knowledge [*Videns Meddelse*]	*The communication of capability* [*Kunnens Meddelse*]
	In regard to the communication of capability it holds that there is no object. What that means. But this, that there is no object, demonstrates that there is reflection and consequently also a distinction in the direction of "the object," namely, negative in the direction of "the object," or away from "the object."
	The division of capability
	Esthetic capability
	Ethical capability or oughtness-capability (where there is unconditionally no object)
	Religious capability or oughtness-capability (where there is an object insofar as there is at first a communication of knowledge).

Second Distinction

When "the communication" is reflected upon

A. "The communication" in the sense of "the medium"

The medium of imagination or fantasy	*The medium of actuality*

All communication of knowledge is in the medium of imagination (possibility).	The communication of capability is in the medium of actuality.
	    esthetic capability not unconditional
	    ethical capability unconditional
	    religious capability not unconditional insofar as there is here a communication of knowledge.

B. When the "communication" is reflected upon

Direct communication	*Indirect communication*
All communication of knowledge is direct communication.	All communication of capability is indirect communication. 1) The communication of esthetic capability is direct communication, but the direct communication of capability, consequently indirect communication. 2) The communication of ethical capability is unconditionally indirect communication. 3) The communication of religious capability is direct communication insofar as there is at first a communication of knowledge, but essentially indirect communication.

Third Distinction

When (in reflection upon the communication, within the definition of the communication of capability) reflection is upon

The communicator	The Receiver

A. When the emphasis is equally upon the communicator and the receiver:

the communication of esthetic capability

B. When the emphasis is predominantly upon the receiver:
> the communication of ethical capability (maieutic; the communicator in a sense disappears, steps aside)

C. When the emphasis is predominantly upon the communicator:
> the communication of religious capability (the communicator has authority with respect to the communication of knowledge, which here comes first)

VIII^2 B 83 n.d., 1847

« 652

Addition to 651 (VIII^2 B 83):
N.B. The second and third distinctions are really not in relation to the communication of knowledge, which, being objective, reflects exclusively on "the object," therefore also tends toward the impersonal. Generally, where there is reflection on the communication, the communicator, the receiver, there is also in one form or another communication of capability, and here the orientation is toward personality.

VIII^2 B 84 n.d., 1847

« 653

Outline and sketch:

1

Part I
                          Direct Communication
The Communication of Knowledge
"The object" is reflected upon.
This is apparent from the lowest empirical knowledge to the highest. It is always "the object" which is reflected upon. "The communicator," "the receiver," "the communication" are completely in the background. (The objective.)

2

In margin of 85:1:
Here the receiver is presupposed to have a sensitiveness, to have a predisposition, but the main emphasis does not fall on the fact that he has it but on the fact that he receives *the object*.

Mathematics is related, for example, to imaginative intuition.
Historical knowledge to memory.
Philosophic knowledge.

3
Part II

The Communication of Capability
                              Indirect Communication
               Chapter I [crossed out]
What it means to say that there is no "object."

4

In margin of 85:3:
Here "the teacher" has competence, virtuosity.
   The rule for the communication of capability is: begin immediately to do it. If the learner says: I can't, the teacher answers: Nonsense, do it as well as you can. With that the instruction begins. Its end result is: to be able. But it is not knowledge which is communicated.

5

In margin of 85:3:
(This is a problem which is suggested on a piece of paper lying in the tall cupboard, in which there are older papers.)
   Concerning the difference between a dialectical and pathos-filled transition (the leap).
   In the communication of knowledge there is only the dialectical transition (therein the truth of immanent necessity); in capability, especially in ethical capability and the religious, the transition is pathos-filled. (Faith is thus the pathos-filled transition.)

6
Chapter I

The Communication of Capability in the ordinary sense
                    Esthetic capability
                         Indirect communication as a
                         border region of direct communication.

7

In margin of 85:6:
Here "the teacher" has competence, virtuosity.
   physical competence (military exercises, dancing, etc.)

physical-intellectual competence: to calculate, for example
the higher arts: for example, acting.

8

Chapter II

Ethical Communication (in strictest sense indirect communication)
Ethical capability or oughtness-capability
In what sense there is here, even more accurately, no "object."*

9

In margin of 85:8:
Here "the teacher" has earnestness.
Since the emphasis must fall absolutely upon "You shall," there can be no communication of knowledge at all here; for if I am supposed to get to know something first of all, then this "shall" is not foremost, not absolute.

10

In margin of 85:8:
Instruction in esthetic capability is communication of competence, in ethical capability [communication] is essentially upbringing.
The ancient Greek[361] on whether or not virtue can be learned; here, perhaps, a few dialogues by Plato could be studied.

11

Addition to 85:8:
* It may be that science can be pounded *into* a person, but as far as esthetic capability is concerned (simply because there is no object) and even more so with the ethical (simply because here in the strictest sense of the word there is no object), one has to pound it *out* of him. The corporal sees the soldier κατὰ δύναμιν[362] in the farm boy and therefore says: I will have to pound the soldier out of him. On the other hand the soldier studies a manual of field tactics; in regard to the instruction contained therein, the corporal might say: I will have to pound this into him.

12

Part 1

Concerning "situation" and the essential connection of situation with ethical communication

13

Already in relation to the communication of esthetic capability the teacher and the learner form a situation. In relation to the communication of knowledge, where everything is objective, there is no situation.

14
Part 2

Concerning "the medium"
the medium of imagination—the medium of actuality.
All communication of knowledge is in the medium actuality; however, esthetic capability, not in the actuality; however, esthetic capability, not in the strictest sense, but ethical capability, in the strictest sense.

15

In margin of 85:14:
Esthetic capability is not in the strictest sense in the medium of actuality, inasmuch as this capability is not to be realized in the existential [*Existentielle*] of the everyday.

The confusion which arises by communicating the ethical in the medium of imagination. (The rhetorical.)

16
Part 3

Concerning the situation of "actuality" as essential, as the real *conditio sine qua non* for ethical communication
That the ethical cannot be taught didactically, for to teach it didactically is to communicate it unethically.

17

In margin of 85:16:
"Actuality" is the existential reduplication of what is said. To teach in actuality that the truth is ridiculed, etc., means to teach it as one ridiculed and scoffed at himself. To teach poverty in actuality means to teach it as one who is himself poor (profiting—in the sense of advancing a science, an art, not in the sense of having profit from it). To that extent all instruction ends in a kind of silence; for when I existentially express it, it is not necessary for my speaking to be audible.

But here one sees the relationship of the truth to actuality. Suppose someone lectures and has 1,000 adherents; if he were to do the same in actuality, he would probably get not one; this would be regarded as "overdoing it."

As far as "actuality" is concerned, almost all men have a kind of fear of water. They want the teacher to be related to them as the swimming instructor who in a safe and "quiet hour" explains the motions of swimming to them; but when he says: Let us now dive in, they say: No thanks.

18

In "achieving actuality" there is also something which both antiquity and original Christianity thought about and followed through—to be present for the mass, to live and learn on the street. Luther[363] was absolutely right in saying that preaching really should not be done in churches but on the street. The whole modern concept of a pastor who preaches in a church is pure hallucination, really a poet-relationship, the existential situation is represented at most by an assurance "that if it is demanded—then . . . . . ." Not until the ethical and again the Christian are made actual in this way (and every other communication is unethical, consequently an unethical communication of the ethical) does that which I am always talking about also appear: *the double-danger*.[364]

19

Part 4

Concerning "reduplication"
                          To be what one teaches.
                          The existential.

Has one the right to "win" men.

20

Much more is understood by reduplication that what holds in respect to all education: *docendo discimus*.

21

Part 5

Concerning double-reflection

22

Part 6

Concerning "the deception"

23

The "earnest" communicator must not have the appearance of earnestness. To appear to be earnest is direct earnestness but is not earnestness in the deepest sense. Earnestness is that the other becomes earnest (and here the accent lies), but it is well to note that this is not by way of immediate impression and by mimicking, but by oneself—and that is precisely why the communicator must not appear to be earnest.

24

Addition to Part 6 "Concerning the Deception"

To "deceive" belongs essentially to the essentially ethical-religious communication. "To deceive into the truth." That it is a deception is also the expression for the reduplication, in which the teacher and the learner are separated from each other in order to exist [*existere*] therein. Ethical communication in character always begins with placing a "deception" in between, and the art consists in enduring everything while remaining faithful to character in the deception and faithful to the ethical. But here again you will see the reduplication. Here in these lectures I really do not follow this through; I show you in a direct way how one behaves, but I am not in character; to do that, I would have to relate myself maieutically to you,* and this I am not doing. In a sense I am lecturing.

25

Part 7

Concerning the maieutic

26

Part 8

Concerning indirect communication, how far a man has the right to use it, whether or not there is anything demonic in it

Much to be found in last summer's journals about this [i.e., 1849].

27

Chapter III

Ethical-religious communication

(Direct-indirect communication)

---

* Use purely indirect forms.

28

Here "the teacher" has authority
with respect to the element of knowledge which is communicated.

29

Religious capability or religious oughtness-capability

Here is an element of knowledge and to that extent an object. But it is only a first thing. The communication is still not essentially of knowledge but a communication of capability. That there is an element of knowledge is particularly true for Christianity; a knowledge about Christianity must certainly be communicated in advance. But it is only a preliminary.

30

Insofar as the ethical could be said to have a knowledge in itself, it is "self-knowledge," but this is improperly regarded as a knowledge.

31

Appendix

That the fundamental modern confusion is not only to have forgotten that there is something called communication of capability but without consideration of meaning to have transformed the communication of capability and oughtness-capability into the communication of knowledge.

The existential [*Existentielle*] has disappeared.

32

They tell a story about an army recruit who was supposed to learn to drill. The sergeant said to him: You, there, stand up straight. R.: Sure enough. Sgt.: Yes, and don't talk during drill. R.: All right, I won't do that. Sgt.: No, you are not supposed to talk during drill. R.: Yes, yes, if I just know it. The recruit's mistake is that he continually wants to transform an ability-communication into a communication of knowledge. But the mistake in the modern period is that the ethical and the ethical-religious have been taught, people have been given information about them.

The pastor says: The Christian seeks first the kingdom of God. Yes, this is well enough, but if you and I are Christians, we do not talk about that; you and I shall seek first the kingdom of God. Scholarship says it does not stop with faith—good, but if you and I are believers, that you and I ought to be believers is not talked about.

VIII² B 85 *n.d.*, 1847

« 654

INTRODUCTION

If one were to concentrate in a single descriptive word the confusion of the newer philosophy, especially since the time when it—if I may refresh your memory about a catchword—left Kant's "honorable way" and, if I dare say so, gave the well-known 100 dollars[365] in order to become theocentric: then I know of no more descriptive word than that it is *dishonest*. And if science or scholarship is going to be the generation's eye,[366] what confusion there must then be in the generation if the eye is confused. But if one would describe the confusion of the modern age, again I know no more descriptive word than: *it is dishonest*.

Dishonesty! Yet I wish to make it immediately clear how this is to be understood and with what right it can be said. By dishonesty one very likely thinks first of deliberate deception. And in this sense one could not really call the age dishonest; it is more a question of whether the age is not confused to such a degree that deliberate deception—and truth—have really gone out of use. Shallow people, novel-readers, and young girls of a certain age usually have a fantastic notion that all around one in life there are ill-natured fellows, hypocrites, Jesuits, seducers, etc. Most often this notion is fantasy. A real hypocrite is a rare sight in these times, for a real hypocrite is a man of character. On the other hand, there flourishes another kind of deception, a self-deception, about which not very much is said.

To describe self-deception as dishonesty is certainly linguistically quite in order. The hypocrite can give himself good account of his dishonesty, but the self-deceived person is bewildered, and since one is never blamelessly in the bewilderment of self-deception in and about himself, then it is perfectly correct to use the word *dishonesty* about it. Let us imagine someone who could be called a slipshod individual, who has begun seventeen things but completed none, knows vaguely about everything possible but knows nothing useful, has made up his mind about his purpose in life seventeen times and has changed it seventeen times, and by this constant vacillation—for he was, nevertheless, originally gifted and many times had worked zealously and busily—managed to be able to talk about everything possible and very often in such a way that it was well worth hearing: thus we have in such an individual an example of the most terrible and tragic and yet apparently innocent, yes, such brilliant dishonesty.

A life can be begun within many presuppositions, and then these can quickly be combined in such extremely intricate combinations that it is impossible to make head or tail of it—such a life is also dishonesty. It is in this sense that one may speak of the dishonesty of the modern age, and we can therefore also until later replace it with another milder expression: *the modern age's lack of naïveté*. It is by no means a sign of maturity that one has completely ceased to be naïve; still less is it a natural human existence never to have been that. A healthy and honest human existence possesses a certain element of naïveté to the very last.*

Yet one may well say: Yes, but how does this apply to a whole generation? The ancient period was naïve, but obviously the modern age cannot be that. But right here we come to the dishonesty of the modern age. The newer science has wanted to teach us—and we have all learned all too much from it—to abolish the category of the individual and set up the generation. It is this πρῶτον ψεῦδος which has brought about an unrest, a hastiness, into existence [*Tilværelsen*], which makes an appalling bewilderment inescapable, and to that extent also dishonesty.

But what sounds like the bitterest epigram over the dishonesty of the modern age is the fact that it is precisely this age which—in order to put more heat under the kettle of confusion—has hit upon wanting to have the merit of beginning without any presuppositions at all. There is nothing more dangerous than the thief passing himself off as a policeman, nothing more dangerous than a radical cure miscarrying and contributing to the disease, nothing more dangerous than being stuck in something and saying: Now I will make a desperate extreme effort to get loose—and then by this attempt proceeding to get all the more stuck. The fact that before Hegel presuppositions had grown beyond men's control is clear enough; but then with the assistance of this grandiose enterprise to bring the confusion of presuppositions to a still higher level—this

---

In margin: The naïve and the traditional; the acquired. Thus the naïve belongs in order at every age in life to be able to make the Socratic distinction between what one understands and what one does not understand.

is the most corrupting of all, partly because the confusion increased and partly because men concealed it from themselves by imagining and deluding themselves into thinking that now they had once and for all gotten the better of the bewilderment of presuppositions. There is certainly nothing more terrible than an amazing, gigantic program of disease eradication which turns out to nourish the disease—and Hegel's enormous exertion to master the presuppositions was especially affected by the thought of the presuppositions themselves, was a quantitative annihilation instead of a qualitative one. In relation to the confusion of thinking by self-reflection, ethics is the only salvation and Hegel simply did not understand ethics. But all other medicines are only welcome to the disease, since they nourish it.

Instead of saying that the dishonesty of the modern age is a lack of naïveté, one could also say it is a lack of primitivity, and I would like to dwell upon this word.

If I were to imagine a human being who was brought up in such a manner and lived out his life in such a manner that he never got any impression of himself but always lived by adaptation and comparison—this would be an example of dishonesty. And this is precisely the state of affairs in modern times. The history of the generation runs its course, it is true, but every single individual should still have his primitive impression of existence [*Tilværelse*]—in order to be a human being. And as it is with every human being, so also with every thinker—in order to be a thinker. But the thinker who sacrifices his primitivity or aborts a fetus in order to be understood by his contemporaries, to acquire a little influence in a hurry, to board the train of the generation hastily just as it is pulling out—he is worse than a girl who sacrifices her virtue for base gain, and he actually sins against God, and this is just as detestable and just as inhuman as a mother who performs an abortion.

Indeed, if this is the case, then the watchword is given, dishonesty is let loose, and the confusion increases every second. It has become especially horrible since Hegel, for he discovered the historicizing method, which completely abolished all primitivity and actually merely arranges. What haste, what confusion—as if by an earthquake! Young people, even children, are aware of how fraudulent everything is and what nothingness it is to be a human being, how everything depends on clinging to the generation, following the demands of the age, which nevertheless are always changing. Thus the life of the generation hisses and fizzes uninterruptedly; although everything is a whirlwind, a signal-shot is heard, the ringing of bells, signifying to the individual that now, this very second, hurry, throw everything away, reflection, quiet meditation, reassuring thoughts of the eternal, or if you come too late you will not go along on the generation's expedition, which is just pulling out—and then, then, how terrible! Ah, yes, how terrible! And yet everything, everything is calculated to nourish this confusion, the unholy haste of this wild hunt. The means of communication become more and more excellent, printing can be done more and more rapidly, with incredible speed—but the communications become more and more hurried and more and more confusing. And if anyone dares, both in the name of primitivity and of God, to resist it—woe unto him! Just as the individual is seized by the whirlwind of impatience to be understood immediately, so a generation domineeringly craves to understand the individual at once.

This produces dishonesty; concepts cease, the language is confused, men fight each other in all directions. There could never be more suitable conditions for all prattle-peddlers, for the universal confusion conceals their own confusion. It is a golden age for prattle-peddlers.

VIII² B 86   *n.d.*, 1847

« 655

THE PRIMITIVE—THE TRADITIONAL

Now, from a somewhat more distant point of departure, let us try to present a conception, step by step, in a crescendo, of this confusion.

There was a time when there was only one scholarly language in Europe. Even though this had its drawbacks, it was still a great good. First and foremost it was thereby assured that not everybody could get into the literature; next, that reciprocal communication was made easy, that there was hope for a more or less standing and permanent terminology which gave continuity with antiquity; and, finally, that the years of a man's life in which his primitivity should develop were not all-toomuch overburdened with apparatus.

National individualities came to consciousness; the mother tongue was installed in its rightful place. But since that vanished age men have not forgotten the idea of a European literature or a knowledge of European literature. This they still would not surrender, and now the task is at least foursquared, consequently 64 times as great. First of all, much of the best time for the composure of primitivity has to be utilized in learning approximately 3 or 4 languages. But one never learns a foreign language quite like his mother tongue; whereas, on the other hand, everyone, with respect to the language which is his mother tongue, believes himself far more entitled to do just as he likes (a universal scholarly but dead language, on the other hand, provided equality for all). If one now turns to rediscover and follow up concepts in the nuances which they have in the many different languages, one is naturally enriched in a certain sense with an extraordinary wealth of reflections—but this comes to be the very problem, because a consistent terminology from now on is almost unthinkable. Since the communication increases foursquared, there is only an increase of confusion, for the more that is communicated, if nothing remains fixed, the more appalling becomes the confusion, the more inhuman and the more superhuman the task which is put before the individual.

This was the first step in developing extensively instead of intensively.

Then they made the glorious discovery in Europe that something had to be done to maintain the perspective. That is to say, they themselves realized that confusion was prevalent and they hoped by one discovery or another, which was in the service of the confusion, to make an end to it. Imagine an office where one begins to keep records but watches them swell up so that a new office has to be found which contains a file; in the meantime one feels that even this is not sufficient—what does one do then—one gets a new office which contains a file of the file, etc., and every time one does something like that he does it— to maintain perspective—but does not observe that with every step it becomes more and more impossible.

As a consequence *the scholarly periodicals* arose.

The idea of the periodicals was to aid in perspective, but then the periodicals proceeded to become an independent literature. This is from beginning to end the modern age's misfortune. The periodicals became more and more ephemeral; ultimately the demands of the age became the demands of the moment. Then the daily press drags along a mass of people who have only a hindering relationship to literature. But this mass becomes arbitrary, and finally the real literature has to make the concessions. (It is precisely the same as the conflict between patricians and plebeians.) Along with the periodicals arose the second-class authors, that is, the non-authors, people who, so to speak, to a certain degree understand everything but nothing thoroughly, the most dreadful of all types. Nevertheless, the journal has the power of the moment and the power of circulation. Because of the publisher's financial interest, real literature has to make concessions. Now, finally, the relationship is reversed. Journal literature abandons criticism and writes for the mass. The mass understands nothing, and the journalists understand how to write for the mass. This creates despondency in genuine author-literature. The author despairs of penetrating, sees the shabbiness in this order of things but does not have the strength to hold out—so he writes brochures in order also to come as near as possible to the moment; he publishes his books in sections; he indicates far in advance what he intends to do in order to be sure that he gets noticed.* Every protest in the name of true literature against this odious system avails nothing—the journalist defiantly points to his thousands of subscribers and his power at the moment. Nor is there a redeeming outlook for the near future, for the journalist has become a type; the individual dies but the journalist never dies—there only get to be more and more of them. One thinks of the superhuman work which the already developed world situation has laid upon an author, and then in all this he has to see how existence [*Tilværelsen*] is confused. It all becomes overwhelming.

So it goes with literature. But it is just the same with society. While superficial education and culture increase, people are squeezed together in the big cities. From his very infancy a man receives no impression of himself. In the big cities one has a greater impression of a cow than of a man, for in the country there are two, three, or more cows to one man, whereas in the big cities there are 1,000 men to one cow.

So it is with the confusion of the modern age; appallingly it drags the weight of traditions along with itself; the generation is trapped in the perplexity of existence [*Tilværelsens*] as never before. This is the dishonesty of this age. If I were to describe it more wittily, I would say that it is like scurvy—and what means are there to prevent it? Only one— green primitivity. But the enormous task of drilling an artesian well is not as difficult as obtaining primitivity in such an age and getting it to penetrate through. It demands sacrifices, and it will come to be by way of the most tortured martyrdoms. Have men ever been so immersed in the sophism—what is the use of one individual's trying? What can one person do? O, ye gods! This sophism is so entrenched at present that without the slightest exaggeration it is the same as madness under these circumstances to want to believe in God and primitivity, and yet it is this very primitivity which is needed, consequently the single individual [*den*

---

* *In margin:* Now a new potentiation has been added; everything which before was merely a medium has now become science (language has become science—the N.T. is no longer a medium but is made critically dialectical in all possible respects, etc., so that another comparative science arises which treats the relationship between these sciences about media —so one gets an idea of the superhuman task.

Enkelte]. And no haggling, none at all. Let us suppose that an eminent genius perceived this, but instead of being faithful to God and wanting to make the sacrifice to the uttermost, he erred and in human prudence wanted to do just a little. No one could do greater damage than he, simply because he was so near to the truth and became the most dangerous of all the Sophists. The individual who wants to believe in being able to penetrate through must get the impression that he is going mad; on the other hand the contemporary age will also discover it and, if possible, will use every means to smother him—not with power, because for this it has no passion, but with stupidity and envy and indolence and scorn, etc.

VIII^2 B 87   *n.d.*, 1847

« 656

FIRST LECTURE

In a certain sense the person who relates himself as a matter of course to the scientific spirit of a given age is lucky, lucky if he merely has to read and study the given, then present it, at one point or another modified by his thinking, to others, who immediately join in, since they essentially relate themselves to the same line of thought and method of representation. In a certain sense he is lucky. He is completely free from what I would call the pangs of delay which are connected with more primitive thinking, which first of all stays far out in the quiet depths, isolated at the very outset, with no foothold in the given, often discouraged almost to despair, anxiously observing how easy it is for others to communicate and be understood. When he finally gets to the point where he thinks he is able to try to communicate, he is promptly, with the first word he utters, doomed to fear the tedious tag of the eccentric, the freak, which makes people disinclined to get involved with him, for eccentricity and freakishness immediately indicate to them either that nothing is there or that a certain resignation and a certain effort are required, and for this they probably have no desire.

If I may say so, I number myself among these unlucky more primitive thinkers, unfortunately the worse for me. That this is a fact, you, my listener, will promptly know for sure with the very first words in this introductory lecture. But truly, I dare claim that for a number of years I have with great patience done some sustained thinking; I beg you, my listener, to have patience for a few hours.

I begin this enterprise not without many doubts and much hesitation. I am thinking here not only of what every assistant professor will think of—whether or not he will succeed generally in satisfying his audience, himself, and the subject. No, just because I want to concern myself, essentially, with presenting the kind of communication of which, either unconditionally or even conditionally, it is true that there is no object—that this dialectically is the case and whatever dialectical content it has, whatever follows dialectically from it, is simply the total thought of these lectures—I promptly begin to wonder whether this, the fact that now from a podium I begin to lecture about what I intend to lecture about, is not contradictory to what I am to lecture about. That is, I am preoccupied with and therefore am aware of the subject of the intended lecture: namely, that to apprehend ethical and ethical-religious truth in particular requires a situation, and the same is true of communicating ethical and ethical-religious truth—and now arises the misgiving: is a podium the adequate situation? I am preoccupied with, therefore am aware of, the subject of the intended lecture: namely, that truly to apprehend ethical and ethical-religious truth means to reduplicate existentially what is known—and now arises the misgiving: does a lecture *ex cathedra* involve a reduplication, can it involve such a reduplication? The misgiving is that if the whole undertaking itself existentially reduplicates everything I have to say, then I do not in a single lecture get a chance to treat what reduplication is and its close relationship to the professing of ethical and ethical-religious truth and the communication of truth, but the whole undertaking reduplicates what is going to be lectured about.

This in a certain sense can serve to pull you *in medias res*, because the misgivings are related to the total thought of the whole undertaking. Later, more than once, there will also come a point where you yourself will become aware of the discrepancy which has occasioned my misgivings; then you will remember that I myself at the outset on the very first day pointed this out to you. But enough of this. During the rest of this hour I intend to use the time for various remarks concerning the whole undertaking and myself in general.

In the first place I solicit your attention to an observation I have felt the need of making for a long time, even though presumably I am known to most of you as an author. *That which in life is regarded as pride can also be the fear of God.* It *can* be the fear of God—more I do not say. Let me illuminate this in the following way. Everyone will certainly agree with me that a man is duty-bound to God to present the truth in its truest form. Fine. But it holds true for every man that in the same degree to which he has the ability to render truer the form of truth—if he then does this—to that same degree he will win fewer men.

(This is illustrated by showing the difference between the communication of ethical-religious truth in the form of possibility and in the form of actuality or making it into actuality—yet very briefly, for this will be developed in detail in its proper place.) Now if a man does not have an essential relationship to God, a daily, present relationship, he lets his prudence be in control. He says: It cannot lead to anything. Acquaintance with practical life teaches me that I must adapt. So he adapts, uses the less true form, says the same thing but in the less true form—and wins many. If, on the other hand, he has an essential God-relationship, it will seem to him as if God says to him: Stupid man, what is he thinking? Does he want to play providence? Is he merely concerned with doing his nicely calculated duty? Every witness of the truth who has been misunderstood by his contemporaries, harshly judged, even put to death, has experienced this collision: by giving the truth a less true form and apparently saying the same thing, he has had it in his power to gain happiness in the world, to win men—or, by being unconditionally obedient to God, expressing that God's providence shall rule and not his providence, to become misunderstood and judged. Consequently he does not adapt; he stretches himself and as mightily as he can—of course, he wins what amounts to none at all and is accused of pride. Here you immediately have an example of reduplication. If I say what I have said here in this way to an audience, it may affect one or two, and why? Because this is direct communication, I do not reduplicate, I do not execute what I am lecturing about, I am not what I am saying, I do not give the truth I am presenting the truest form so that I am existentially that which is spoken. I talk *about* it. As soon as I execute it, reduplicate it existentially, I alienate, and somebody or other says—it is pride. In the one case I confide to the others that I am perplexed, set between two alternatives, whether I shall absolutely, unconditionally hold to God or whether I shall accommodate myself to them—this is already the admission which proves that I do not unconditionally hold to God—and this one and the other, or more exactly, the mass, think this is all right. In the other case I am in earnest about holding unconditionally to God and therefore give the truest form to the truth which is granted me to understand—and the crowd says: This is shocking pride. What is the basic confusion in modern life if it is not this—that in every communication of truth they consider man to be the authority rather than that God is the authority, especially in ethical-religious communication. Thereby they have given the whole of ethical-religious communication a wrong form: they are completely spoiled by the fact that if there is going to be any adapting, it must be in the direction of God's demand, and if any admissions are going to be made, then in regard to human authority.

And since this is the way it is and has been for a long, long time, it is not so easy to avoid making the mistake in life of regarding as pride that which perhaps is the fear of God. This is what I have wanted to draw attention to. In the lecture itself there probably will be places where it would be possible for me to win you over to my presentation by adapting the form somewhat, but where I dare not do this—and immediately someone or another will probably judge me and find me odd or proud. But I have another doubt: I have doubted whether I have even any right at all to say what I am saying, whether I have the right to say it is from the fear of God that I do what I do. For already this is an attempt to make men the authority, to appease them so that they travel along with me more easily. Whereas unconditional obedience would be not to say a word about it but to act.* And truly if a man, believing every moment, could cling to the thought that God is very near to him, he would also do likewise. But as soon as it seems that God is very far away and one has to help himself, he immediately yields; and if God is infinitely far off, then man—in the modern style, without further ado, makes man the authority.

Consequently, what in the world is regarded as pride can be the fear of God.

Next I wish to give you, very briefly, an idea of what you can expect from these lectures, in order, if possible, to make you more receptive and in any case prevent, if possible, too many and too deeply disappointed expectations.

In the strictest sense, this will not be a lecture ex cathedra; if there

---

* *In margin:* Not to be afraid of men (making men the authority is actually the expression for the fear of men), something which is regarded as pride, can also be an even greater fear of God, because to such a one it is as if God said to him: How dare you be afraid of men if you desire only to be alone before me and afraid only of me? Is it not like a father saying to his child:[367] How dare you be afraid of your playmates if you simply understand that you fear me and me alone? It does not necessarily follow that the child is, for all that, not afraid of his playmates, but he does not dare express this—from fear of his father. Strict upbringing! The playmates become angry with him and say it is pride and do not let his pride go unpunished—alas, and from fear of his father he dares not be afraid of them!

is any resemblance, it will at times be most like a physics lecture in which experiments are also presented. Now and then I will endeavor to let the presentation happen before you; at one point I shall probably permit myself to involve you very slightly in the development in a more dramatic way; I ask your consent for this in advance. —The lecture will try as far as possible to make everything *present*, if possible, to convey the impression to you that at one and the same time you have the most contradictory thoughts. Therefore it will not have the simplicity of the more strictly academic lecture, which has a definite place for the discussion of each particular point, about which there is no discussion either before or after. No, the lecture will constantly, if I dare say so, be haunted by the memory of what was said on other points; the reflections will constantly traverse the points at issue in order to call to mind the past and the future, in order to maintain, if possible, the impression that everything is present at one and the same time, which in a certain sense is more than the usual academic lecture can do to keep the listener aware, but which probably can also disturb and weary him, almost making him angry. The intention, of course, is not that I shall incessantly persist in mishmashing all the individual terms together tumultuously or kaleidoscopically so that there is no logical place in the sequence where each concept finds its more exact and detailed development; the intention is only that every point will, if possible, carry the marks of what is said on other points, so that, if possible, everything continuously brings about the contemporaneity of being present. Nothing (even after its detailed presentation) is to be regarded as entirely finished to the extent that there should be no more discussion or recollection of it; on the contrary, the references to it will directly or by contradiction endeavor to call it to mind and in any case, the manner in which the next point is discussed will, if possible, be an indirect discussion of that which is completed. You will also see that the fact that I have set myself this task is not strange. For the whole thing I intend to lecture about is one idea, and I will not invest it with the slightest scholarly apparatus.

More direct communication (what is to be understood by that and by its opposite, indirect communication, will be given in detail in the lecture itself) will be employed, although the subject, for the most part, is about indirect communication or that which essentially or in part can be communicated only by indirect communication. That which in the strictest form can be communicated only in the situation of actuality and in character (indirect communication)—this I am going to show you in a more direct form, how it occurs; I am going to use direct communication to make you aware of indirect communication.

The lecture will not lack earnestness, but the nature of the earnestness, something which lies in the relationship itself, will be something different from the earnestness of the more strictly academic lecture. The more strictly academic lecture is usually regarded as real earnestness. And so it is when it is a matter of communicating mathematics, philology, history, philosophical scholarship, etc. In short, it is entirely correct to say this of those subjects which usually are lectured about *ex cathedra.* But in relation to different things earnestness is also different, and I willingly concede that it is also out of order for me to lecture *ex cathedra* about what I have to present. Earnestness in relation to ethical and ethical-religious communication, which in a certain sense cannot be communicated *ex cathedra,* is something else entirely. The ethical and the ethical-religious have to be communicated existentially [*existentielt*] and in the direction of the existential [*Existentielle*]. The right kind of earnestness (absolutely in respect to ethical communication, and partially in respect to ethical-religious communication), merely to mention it, contains much more irony and what belongs to irony than I dare allow in the presentation in these lectures. The really right kind of earnestness, especially as regards ethical communication, would certainly appear to most people to be jesting, but be as it may, they probably would still find something earnest in the presentation in these lectures.* But this is not the situation. The lecture will take somewhat a middle course between the more strictly academic lecture and the earnestness related to ethical communication strictly understood, which cannot be otherwise as soon as I begin to speak from a podium. In pseudonymous books published by me the earnestness is more vigorous, particularly in those passages in which the presentation will appear to most people as nothing but jest. This, as far as I know, has not previously been understood at all. Perhaps in the kind of lecture I intend to use I will succeed in contributing something to the better understanding of this. But, to repeat, this is achieved not by a more earnest lecture but precisely by its having less of the more rigorous earnestness.

I must excuse myself for the manner in which I use "I" in these

* *In margin:* It is unconditionally true of the ethical that it cannot be taught. The instructive lecture deals with an object—and ethically there simply is no object (more about this in the lecture itself). There is discussion *about* this object. But the lecture itself does not existentially [*existentielt*] express that the teacher exists [*existerer*] in it; nor does it occasion the listeners to exist in it. But the lectures themselves will deal with all this.

lectures. Yet I must add that, however willingly I make this excuse, it is, from my standpoint, an accommodation. In my opinion it is my weakness and imperfection, partly a consequence of my groaning under the weight of the past, that I do not more boldly venture to use my "I." One of the tragedies of modern times is precisely this—to have abolished the "I," the personal "I." For this very reason real ethical-religious communication is as if vanished from the world. For ethical-religious truth is related essentially to personality and can only be communicated by an *I* to an *I*. As soon as the communication becomes objective in this realm, the truth has become untruth. Personality is what we need. Therefore I regard it as my service that by bringing poetized personalities who say *I* (my pseudonyms) into the center of life's actuality I have contributed, if possible, to familiarizing the contemporary age again to hearing an *I*, a personal *I* speak (not that fantastic pure *I* and its ventriloquism). But precisely because the whole development of the world has been as far as possible from this acknowledgment of personality, this has to be done poetically. The poetic personality always has a something which makes him more bearable for a world which is quite unaccustomed to hearing an *I*. Beyond this I admittedly do not go. I never venture to use quite directly my own *I*. But I am convinced that the time will come when an *I* stands up in the world, someone who says *I* directly and speaks in the first person. Then, for the first time, he will also in the strictest sense rightly communicate ethical and ethical-religious truth.

If anyone were to ask me how I regard these lectures in relationship to my whole effort as an author, I would answer: I regard them as a necessary concession, for which I intend to bear responsibility. You will remember what was said at the beginning of the hour, that in respect to the truth he has understood, every man is duty-bound to God, if he wants to communicate it, to communicate it in its truest form. If it seems to him that he thereby produces no effect, then it can very likely be his duty, at least by way of experiment, to choose another form, but maybe it is also only his impatience to demand quick results instead of having faith. He thereby incurs a responsibility; and in any case it becomes his duty, if he now quickly produces a great effect by that other form he chose, to remember that there is a "please note" here, since it was because he used the less rigorous form. Especially in the communication of ethical truth and partially in the communication of ethical-religious truth, the indirect method is the most rigorous form. Yet a more direct form which runs parallel to this can also be necessary in order to support that by which in another sense it is itself supported. This I have understood right from the beginning of my activity as an author. Therefore along with the pseudonyms there always was direct communication in the guise of the upbuilding or edifying discourses, and the last few years I have used direct communication almost exclusively. And these lectures are also in the form of direct communication (and in a certain sense are to be regarded as an even greater concession). But in a stricter sense I am not a lecturer or professor; that would be too, too satirical: an appointed lecturer in ethical-religious communication, i.e., in something which neither can nor should be taught because it must not become science and scholarship but must relate itself to existence [*Existents*]. If I were to call myself anything, I would rather declare that I am a kind of teacher in the ancient style; and if an auditorium were suitable for it, I would not have anything against sometimes converting the lecture to conversation.

But however many, however great, and however dialectically developed the problems which are involved in this undertaking, I believe I dare say that I know them. And one thing I believe I dare promise the listener definitely—if he gives me his attention, at the conclusion of these lectures he will be aware of and acquainted with problems as he has never been before. This seems a little provocative—especially in respect to what in our times is customarily promised philosophically and announced *ex cathedra*—and yet it probably is for all that provocative and inspiring; for as a pseudonym[368] has said: The task must be made difficult, for only the difficult inspires the noble-hearted, or, as he more explicitly says it: What our age needs is an honest earnestness which affectionately preserves the tasks, which does not alarm people into wanting to rush pellmell into the highest but keeps the tasks young and beautiful and lovely to look at and beckoning to all and yet for all that difficult and inspiring to the noble, for the noble nature is inspired only by what is difficult. My listener, how did I dare be so impolite as to doubt that I shall succeed in inspiring you—for I have the difficulties all ready.

VIII^2 B 88   *n.d.*, 1847

« 657

SECOND LECTURE

THE COMMUNICATION OF KNOWLEDGE

AND

THE COMMUNICATION OF CAPABILITY

Here as everywhere I feel myself abandoned to my own thoughts. Wherever I look I meet the sciences. As far as I can judge, I observe that they, every one of them, are extraordinarily developed, in almost every case have enormous apparatus which is gone over and remodeled again and again.

But I also find everywhere that men are preoccupied with the WHAT which is to be communicated.

What occupies me, on the other hand, is: what does it mean to communicate—of this I know I have really read nothing at all in the productions of the modern period, nor have I heard anything spoken about it. Once long ago, in antiquity, primarily in Greece, I find that men occupied themselves with this problem.

The modern age has—and I regard this as its basic damage—abolished personality and made everything objective. Therefore men do not come to dwell upon the thought of what does it mean to communicate but hasten immediately to the *what* they wish to communicate. And since almost every such *what*, even at first glance, reveals itself to be something very prolix, there is in the passage of time even less of an opportunity or place for considering what it means to communicate. A philosopher, a dogmatician, a pastor, etc.—they all begin immediately with the *what* they wish to communicate, with studies and preliminary sketches of it. And since, to repeat, there is everywhere an enormous apparatus, this practically overwhelms them, and in any case they soon get a tremendous amount to communicate.

They are, to recall an expression from the previous hour, "happily saved from the pangs of delay."

When everything, instead of becoming objective, becomes personal, then the delay begins. And when everything becomes personal, the accent immediately falls upon what it means to communicate.

There is, again, a fate which hovers over more primitive thought, namely, that it appears so impoverished. Allow me to refer to myself. I also know something of what every educated person knows about China, Eastern philosophy, Greek philosophy, modern philosophy from Descartes to Hegel, the modern Germans from Kant to the younger Fichte. If I want to talk about this, I have much to say.

But this problem of delay, what it means to communicate, about which not a single book has been written, yes, it certainly appears impoverished. It looks impoverished, also, when—instead of lecturing on the history of nations and of the human race—someone gets the ludicrous idea of occupying himself with the problem of what it is to be a human being, whether we really are human beings, whether you and I are really human beings.

There is a fate which hovers over more primitive thought—namely, that it works at certain fundamental questions which otherwise are usually so taken for granted that it does not occur to anybody to dwell upon them. The primitive is far from being what men might think—that it is before other men—rather it is continually far behind. Let us take examples from other relationships. A man in whom there is not much primitivity will come to consider the question of which girl he should marry. He will reflect: There is a choice, and the question is—which girl? The more primitive person perhaps will so immerse himself in the question of what reality there is in marrying that he never gets married. A man who does not have much primitivity will perhaps reflect on which public office he should seek or, if he has chosen a certain career, which appointment he should seek, whether in Jutland or in Fyn or in the capital. The more primitive man perhaps will so immerse himself in the question of whether this mode of existence is essential for man that he never gets a position. Someone who has not much primitivity usually will assume that he is a Christian as a matter or course and now occupies himself with the problem of straightening out the Church. A more primitive man† perhaps will so immerse himself in the question of whether or not he should accept Christianity that he gets no time to reform the Church. Take the ultimate. How would it go in life with the person who only moderately seriously took Christ's command to seek *first* the kingdom of God.³⁶⁹ I wonder if he would not soon come to stand as if abandoned and infinitely far, far behind all the others! For the others** scramble for the take; everyone takes his share of the finite and usually takes it *first*; but poor pious poky Peter, he immerses himself more and more in this "first the kingdom of God." And even if he does not take hold of God's kingdom, it will always have the result that his life becomes tried in the spiritual trials of Christianity. For soon, soon he will be ridiculed, pitied, laughed at, he who became nothing at all—and this one becomes for sure by taking seriously seeking *first* the kingdom of God—and wins nothing, that is, nothing finite—and this he can be completely certain of if he takes seriously seeking God's kingdom first. —But this seeking first the kingdom of God is nevertheless real primitivity.

** *In margin:* As the old saying goes: Everyone takes his, so I take mine, and so the others get nothing—only here it turns out that the others get theirs and the primitive gets nothing.

† The primitive does not lie before but behind.

But just as the basic trouble with the modern age is that it makes everything objective, so it is the basic misfortune of the modern age that it lacks primitivity; from which it naturally follows that the genuinely primitive questions never arise. And herein lies what I would call the *dishonesty of the modern age*. It is undeniably the safest and most comfortable thing to join up thoroughly with tradition, to do as the others, to believe, think, and talk as the others and prefer to go out after finite goals. But providence never intended it to be this way. Every human existence [*Existents*] ought to have primitivity. But the primitive existence always contains a reexamination of the fundamental. This one sees most clearly in a primitive genius. What is the significance of a primitive genius? It is not so much to produce something absolutely new, for there really is nothing new under the sun, as it is to reexamine the universally human, the fundamental questions. This is honesty in the deepest sense. Completely to lack primitivity and consequently reexamination, to accept everything automatically as common practice and let it suffice that it is common practice, consequently to evade responsibility for doing likewise—*this is dishonesty*.

And thus I regard it as dishonesty also that the question *what does it mean to communicate* never comes up at all.

I now intend to proceed as simply as possible with this poor, little question.

When I think of communicating, I think of four parts: 1) *the object*, 2) *the communicator*, 3) *the receiver*, 4) *the communication*.

With the help of these points I shall now show you the complete structure of the lectures, for differentiating commences as reflection falls variously on each of these four points.

In the main, I make the division according to reflection upon the *object* or reflection upon *communication*. This distinction is decisive for my whole project, since, as has been developed, it is the basic error of modern times that everywhere people are occupied with the *what* they are to communicate—not with *what communication is*.

If it is the object which is reflected upon, then we have the communication of KNOWLEDGE [*Videns*].

If, on the other hand, there is no "object" (how this is to be understood will be developed), then there can be no reflection upon the object, but if the communication is reflected upon, then we have in contrast to the communication of knowledge the communication of CAPABILITY [*Kunnens*].

And this, again, is the error of modern times, to have forgotten completely that there is a communication which is called the communication of capability, that this has been completely abolished, or what should be communicated as capability has even been meaninglessly communicated as knowledge (all this remains to be developed).

We proceed now to a closer definition of the communication of capability. Actually, this is what the whole lecture is about, the complement to the modern view, which has completely forgotten this.

THE COMMUNICATION OF *Capability*

When in reflection upon the communication the communicator and the receiver* are reflected upon equally, then we have in the ordinary sense the communication of capability, instruction in art, and whatever belongs to it.**

When in reflection upon the communication the receiver is reflected upon, then we have ethical communication.† The maieutic. The communicator disappears, as it were, makes himself serve only to help the other to become.

Ethical communication is the communication of capability, even more specifically, *oughtness-capability*, but the communication is not in the direction of knowledge but of capability.

When the ethical communication also contains initially an element of knowledge, we have the ethical-religious,‡ specifically Christian communication. By this element of knowledge it is separated from ethical communication in the stricter sense, but in the main it is not classified under the communication of knowledge but under the communication of capability, more specifically under oughtness-capability. The communication is not in the direction of knowledge but of capability; the knowledge which is communicated in this communication is a preliminary.

The main classifications, corresponding to the main classifications of the communication of knowledge and the communication of capability, are:

* *In margin:* the receiver and the communicator stand equally before each other—for example, the teacher in an art and the learner.
** *In margin:* the communication of esthetic capability.
† *In margin:* ethical capability.
‡ *In margin:* religious capability.

THE DIRECT METHOD and THE INDIRECT METHOD

All communication of knowledge is direct communication.

All communication of capability is more or less indirect communication.*

First of all comes what I have called genuine art-communication; it is indirect or at least essentially indirect.

Then ethical communication; this is unconditionally indirect.

Then ethical-religious communication, namely, Christian; this is direct-indirect.

* *In margin:* Here again it is naturally the error of the modern period that all communication is direct, that it has forgotten that there is such a thing as indirect communication.

VIII^2 B 89   *n.d.*, 1847

« 658

It is very dangerous (and very seductive for those concerned) if a religious speaker capable of exercising a great influence upon others does not himself in the deepest sense give the impression of being bound by the same with which he binds others. And yet this is often what men want, and why? Because this relationship indirectly preaches indulgence. But it is so dangerous for the speaker that, instead of giving the humble impression of one who earnestly feels himself bound and fearful before God, he proudly exercises power over men.

IX A 79   *n.d.*, 1848

« 659

Sermons should be preached first and foremost in the following manner: *why has Christianity come into the world?* (In order to put a stop to and get rid of all this human nonsense about its being a consolation, which it certainly is, but this is not its *telos*.) Because it is the absolute.

Next, that it *must be believed*. Here is the Bible passage:[370] he who does not believe makes God a liar. (To put an end to all this impudence of proving.)

Finally. Have *you* believed? That is—let us see whether your life expresses that *you* have believed, for this is the only proof. (To put an end to the baleful importance of being an orthodox, who loathes the Baptists, etc., and yet has no more faith than the back of my hand.)

IX A 127   *n.d.*, 1848

« 660

The balefulness of the situation in Christendom is really all this preaching and the fact that one can constantly see indirectly that the preacher does not exist [*existerer*] at all in that which he is preaching about. I have never heard a single preacher preach about prayer or read a sermon by him about prayer without promising myself to demonstrate as 2 plus 2 equals 4—but indirectly—that the preacher himself hardly ever makes the practice of praying definitely once every day, whatever he says about praying constantly for the presence of God in everything. This is why the sermon-discourse today constantly and unconditionally only moves about in degrees of simple comparison: pray, pray zealously, constantly, every day, every moment. Charming! One sees in the very way it is said that the preacher is a long way from having made a beginning in such things: for otherwise he would have to have it on his fingertips that here begin the spiritual trials [*Anfægtelserne*], the horror that a man cannot possibly do it because he will experience almost insane collisions if he is going to take God along in even the least thing he does, going for a haircut, buying a new hat, making a visit, etc.

The sermon-discourse these days is therefore essentially nothing but a lie. The preachers are like gymnastics coaches who cannot swim themselves and then instruct people in swimming, even standing on the dock and shouting: Just strike out briskly with your arms—as if one could not strike out all too briskly with his arms, something every swimmer knows.

But the fact of the matter is that it cannot be demonstrated directly, for the doctrinal concept is altogether orthodox. Therefore this, too, is a part of the superficial sanctity of the modern age: when a preacher prides himself on teaching what is orthodox or when he is busy looking for still more precise definitions against those who believe in another way. Oh, you masterful scoundrels, in this way you have diverted attention away from what is decisive, from the power which Christianity should and would exercise in life so that it might transform life and not be itself turned into artificial ornamentation.

IX A 198 *n.d.*, 1848

« 661

Another one of the disastrous results of Christendom's having become part of the established order is that the language has become meaningless or topsy-turvy. In contrast to paganism, which placed all its honor and pride in self-esteem, in the early days of Christianity it could be a significant and true expression for the opposite to speak of everything as being by the grace of God. But now in Christendom the expression: By the help of God's grace, it is not I who do it, it is God's grace—this has become a hackneyed phrase which everybody uses and consequently there is no opposition. Or this expression also comes to be understood as pretentious piety, because this grinding away at grace is a triviality, but when someone places special accent upon it, then he must want to be regarded as especially pious. The meaninglessness arises from the fact that the attackers use the same language. The pagans never talked about anything being by grace; in contrast to this was Christianity's speaking of grace; the pagans did not call themselves Christians at all; in contrast to this there were the Christians, etc.

IX A 232 *n.d.*, 1848

« 662

The difference between direct and indirect communication. If a teacher who was an artist as well were to say to another who claimed to understand him perfectly: Well, that's fine. I am happy, and so we shall live in this mutual understanding, but I give you advance notice that there will come moments when both for your sake and for my own and for the sake of truth (lest by continuous use of the direct method the truth become lazy, a self-spreading delusion) and in fear and trembling before God (all the greater as I become more fond of you—but it must be this way in order to make proper room for God, lest men relate to each other without each one's being related to God individually)—consequently there will come moments when I (certainly not from my own inclination but prompted by something higher) must set between ourselves the awakening of misunderstanding. At that time I myself will suffer most of all, but it must be this way. And there will come moments for you when you will bitterly regret having become involved with me. When a teacher who is also an artist does this, the other one understands this perfectly, thinks almost even more of the teacher than before. He understands it—and why? Because it is direct communication, because he basically thinks highly of the teacher. But when the moment comes, what then? Well, then the teacher naturally practices deception, uses all his skill to keep it up, devises the most irritating and wounding means— otherwise he is a really poor artist. And then—well, if the other one is not just as sure of himself as the teacher, then he cannot understand it, then it is as if every prediction that it would go this way had been forgotten.

With me it is the same as with that teacher, except that I do not call myself a teacher. I am the person who is being brought up—but by

God. And there is nothing arrogant in saying this; indeed, every Sunday the preacher says that every human being is brought up by God—but the sad thing is that no one gives it a thought. No wonder, then, that they are so badly brought up!

IX A 233 *n.d.*, 1848

« 663

The whole concept of a pastor as a speaker is *eo ipso* the abandonment of Christianity. This is then hidden in a still deeper confusion when it is assiduously explained that the pastor should be simple—in his expression, avoiding the use of many artificial words. Never mind this—besides, it is based on accidental circumstances. No, the fact of the matter is that the pastor should not be a speaker; the proclaimer of Christianity should not be an orator but a proclaimer by proclaiming as an existing person.

This useful conception of a pastor automatically demoralizes the congregation. There one sits in a cozy church, surrounded by beauty and magnificence (yes, as in a theater)—then a man steps forward, an artist (let us not deceive; indeed he says that he is simple, but this means he has perfected himself in the art—for true simplicity is that one's life expresses what one proclaims), a man dressed in fine clothes, possessing all of life's favors—and he speaks about the highest, about sacrificing everything. O, it looks lovely, quite different from losing the littlest bit in earnest. O, terrible seduction, what refinement, to have everything—and then to do all this artistically.

This is the reason men cannot recognize it. Take Paul when he was in chains—how many saw the loftiness in him. No, the majority, the great majority saw an enthusiast for whom they had a little pity at most. But when Bishop Mynster in the Castle Church, where everything breathes security and peace and everything is beauty and magnificence—when he, powerful as he is in his personal presence, steps back a pace in the pulpit, displays the full stature of his person, great as he is *qua* artist—when he describes [Paul] in this manner, we all understand it—we are not far from confusing Bishop Mynster with such a one, an apostle. O, this is enormously demoralizing.

And yet I regard Bishop Mynster very highly, and not simply because the memory of my father links me to him. No, M. expresses the purely human in the most masterful way I have ever seen. On the other hand, he is certainly so alien to the decisively Christian that if he were to speak his mind on it he might say: It is the demonic.

IX A 240 *n.d.*, 1848

« 664

Indirect earnestness is in a certain sense (dialectical) far more earnest (the dialectical in fear and trembling). Once it is all settled that this is earnestness and that this man is earnest, illusion becomes the support. Precisely for this reason courage and self-denial are necessary to abolish this kind of assistance and indolence.

The misunderstanding can be twofold—the one which endangers truth is that with the assistance of illusions men fancy themselves to be earnest. This is the misunderstanding of laziness, which meanwhile is profitable for the communicator, who enjoys honor and esteem as earnestness personified, and for the receivers, who imagine themselves to be in earnest, something they enjoy immensely.

The other misunderstanding is in an egotistical sense dangerous for the communicator, that men judge him not to be earnest, that he is a flighty bird or, indeed, even a scandal. One seldom has the courage to expose himself to this danger.

The fact of the matter is that most people have not the slightest intimation of this kind of earnestness. As soon as the one regarded as earnest establishes the misunderstanding, they actually believe that he has become a joker. They do not suspect what a terrible strenuousness it is to be truly earnest in this way.

IX A 257 n.d., 1848

« 665

It is just another blind pretext which has been invented—namely, this conflict about preaching grandiloquently or simply, that is, about using more pretentious words which only a few can understand or more simple ones. No, simplicity is to do what one says; to act is to make simple; what I carry out in action is simple, for it cannot be done otherwise. On the other hand, to use the most simple words—and then not do what one says, to talk about suffering degradation in simple words while longing for superiority oneself—this also is grandiloquence.

IX A 439 n.d., 1848

« 666

What I frequently developed in an earlier journal (summer, 1848)[371] about reduplication and absolute indirect communication being nevertheless somewhat demonic in the relationship between man and man is in a sense true. The question is: does a human being have the right to that extent to take sides with God against man; is it not treason toward men and forwardness toward God? Here the life of Christ is not illuminating, because he himself was God. But if a person is to remain among men, we get no further than the religiosity of human sympathy.

Here as everywhere I see only one way out: if a person is going to cling to God in this way, it must not be in the direct superexcellence of humanness but inversely through the misery of being subordinated under the universally human, put outside it, and thus as a sufferer constrained to relate himself absolutely to God as his only possibility.

x^1 A 122   n.d., 1849

« 667 *Situation*

A theologian but not appointed. Through a period of years he has worked in such a way that he has achieved a fame which will unquestionably guarantee that people will stream to church to hear him, especially all the people of distinction, etc.

He has it announced that he will preach, and he chooses the most prominent, most beautiful church in the national capital.

Everybody is there in the church, including the King and Queen.

He enters the pulpit and prays; he reads his text about Jesus driving the money changers out of the temple.

Immediately he begins in the following manner.

So let the word be declared, the word which I have to say to the world and for which I have prepared myself throughout my whole life: to preach Christianity in these surroundings is not Christianity; be it ever so Christian, it is not Christianity—Christianity can be preached only in actual life. And I hereby transform this building into actuality. I am now in your power, I, a solitary human being, but now I shall speak —and thereby this is actuality. I shall speak on the theme: Christianity can be preached only in actual life.

Away with this whole elegant church and this elegant congregation. Christ was not an elegant man who preached to an elegant assembly in an elegant church about suffering for the truth—the *actuality* was that they did spit upon him.

An uproar breaks out in the whole church; men shout: Down with him, out of the church! But he raises a thundering voice which deafens them all and says: Now this is right; now I am preaching Christianity. If my intention had been suspected I would have been kept out of this pulpit or everyone would have stayed home. But here I stand and I am speaking, and I charge you in responsibility toward God to listen to me, for it is the truth which I speak.

This would be an awakening.

x^1 A 136   n.d., 1849

« 668

Nowadays the preaching almost always fails in this way: to occasion the listener to apply what he has heard at that very moment, to get him to begin, to pledge himself at that very moment to a very specific task. (I have read in a Catholic writer, who understands these things, that one ought never go to communion without pledging himself to something very specific for a very specific end.) But the situation is that the pastors do not themselves live in the religious; therefore they are almost afraid that their sermon might have the effect of someone's taking it in earnest right at that very moment. The pastors are like a person who stands on dry land and gives swimming lessons—he does not dare let it become decisive; yes, he would be anxious and afraid if one of the listeners took it seriously and sprang into the water, for the swimming instructor (the pastor) would not know how to help him at all in this case, so confused would he be simply at the sight of someone *actually* diving into the water.

With one thousand such swimming instructors a nation will go far in Christianity!

x^1 A 185 *n.d.*, 1849

« 669

A new practical training course ought to be introduced for theologians (something I have noted in one [VI A 17] of the earliest journals): practice in the Christian art of address, specifically not in the art of preaching, rhetoric, and everything belonging to it, but in the art of being able to preach—Christianity. For with respect to communication Christianity has a singularity which brings entirely unique categories into force.

x^1 A 216 *n.d.*, 1849

« 670

WITNESSING is still the form of communication which strikes the truest mean between direct and indirect communication. Witnessing is direct communication, but nevertheless it does not make one's contemporaries the *authority*. While the witness's "communication" addresses itself to the contemporaries, the "witness" himself addresses God and makes him the authority.

x^1 A 235 *n.d.*, 1849

« 671

To communicate truth is *to suffer*—if not, then neither do you communicate truth.

x^1 A 345 *n.d.*, 1849

« 672

I John 2:21 should be the principle for the proclamation of Christianity in Christendom: I write to you, *not* because you *do not know* the truth (that is, in relation to pagans), but because you know it.

x^1 A 480   *n.d.*, 1849

« 673

All personal communication and all individuality have disappeared; no one says *I* or speaks to a *you*.

It is said that "faith" is primary, is the basic condition, is the presupposition for comprehending: this is true; but whether I have faith, whether I actually have faith—there is no question at all about this.

It is said that rebirth must come first—then follows this and that; but whether or not I myself am reborn, whether I am actually reborn or not—about this there is no question. And so it is throughout. People diligently put off such matters; public opinion regards it as bad taste to question in this way, to ask whether the professor is actually a believer, whether he can answer: yes or no.

In Martensen's whole dogmatics, at least in the portion I have read so far, there is not a single sentence which is a plain *yes* or *no*. It is the old sophistry of being able to talk—but of not holding a dialogue. For dialogue immediately posits: *you* and *I*, and such questions as require: *yes* and *no*. But the speaker develops one side and then the other, and meanwhile the reader or listener is so distracted that he no longer notices that essentially he has learned nothing.

x^1 A 566   *n.d.*, 1849

« 674

Just as the Draconian laws achieved nothing because they were too abstractly cruel, so it is with the idealized nonsense of the priestly-lecture —it is not made concrete, and the existing actuality [*Existentielle*] remains untouched by the essentially Christian.

x^2 A 12   *n.d.*, 1849

« 675

There is really something tragically true in the fact that it would be better if Christianity were not proclaimed at all than that it be done as it is now. It amounts to being elevated for an hour once a week just as in the theater, and the disaster is that people get used to hearing everything without having the remotest notion of doing something.

x^2 A 19   *n.d.*, 1849

« 676

What is true of actors, artists, and poets is also esthetically true of "speakers"—antithesis is usually the condition for or corresponds to the presentation; personal existence [*personlige Existents*] is commonly the opposite of what the presentation expresses; for it is the very longing growing out of the antithesis which produces fire in the imagination, out of which the presentation proceeds.

From this one sees how hopeless it is to let Christianity be represented by "speakers" only. One single ascetic walking about among us—he preaches altogether differently than twenty such speakers.

This is, after all, the best proof that people have completely transferred Christianity from being an existence-communication [*Existents-Meddelelse*] to being a doctrine—that people have substituted speakers, assistant professors, and the like for the ascetics.

Nowadays it is so easy to dismiss all this by promptly dishing up all this business about flagellants and the like. But the matter is not really dismissed thereby, and in talking this way people only show that they would rather forget the whole matter.

Let the welfare office decide how much a man needs to live on—and let that be the wage. There is nothing at all extravagant in the concept of asceticism. Christ was also an ascetic. Look in the N.T. and see how much he needed to live on. Paul, too. The true concept of asceticism is to reduce the requirements of life to a minimum and then, of course, as far as the rest is concerned, not to mistreat oneself by floggings or such things. O, this is very easy to understand; and the reason why people are so slow to understand is also very easy to understand.

I can understand it, too, but I will not propose it, for my existence [*Existents*] does not reach out so far; I am tried only by way of mistreatment by contemporaries.

x^2 A 146   *n.d.*, 1849

« 677

Christ continued with the indirect method until the last, for the fact that he was incognito, in the guise of a servant, makes all his direct communication nevertheless indirect (as Anti-Climacus correctly notes someplace in *Training in Christianity*, II).[372] But then his life has a phase which is otherwise denied—the Resurrection from the dead, the Ascension—here is really his first direct communication.

x^2 A 367   *n.d.*, 1850

« 678 *What and—How*

The distinguishing characteristic in life is not what is said but how it is said. In regard to the *what*, it is the same thing which was said before, perhaps many times previously—and so the old saying is true: there is nothing new under the sun, this old saying which nevertheless always remains new.

But *how* it is said—this is what is new. Understood in this way, it is true that everything is new. It is still new—even when someone out of prudence joins the chorus, even when a mimic repeats one or another old proverb with utmost carelessness. The new thing is that the old has become nonsense, a triviality.

The eye for this *how* really belongs to the spirit. On the other hand there is among other things a scholarship lacking in spirit, and its secret is to say: This new thing is the same as this and that in the Seventeenth Century and that again is the same as this and that in the Middle Ages, etc.

This is the intellectual distinction: *what* and *how*.

Again, the ethical-religious distinction is: *what* is said and *how*.

The words: I know nothing except Christ and Him crucified[373]— spoken by an apostle, they cost him his life; spoken by a witness of the truth, they bring persecution; spoken by a lesser person, by me, for example, they result in a kind of suffering; spoken by a poet—they bring good fortune; spoken by a declaiming pastor, they bring not only good fortune, but he becomes venerated almost as a saint for his earnestness.

"The single individual"—this thought spoken by a witness of the truth in a strict sense—means death. Spoken by an imperfect one, by me, for example, it is nevertheless a crucial break with the world and with what belongs to the world, thus something of a sacrifice; spoken by a declaiming speaker, it brings good fortune.

How is there not the esthetic, the rhetorical, whether spoken in flowery language or in a simple style, whether with euphonious organ tones or with a scratchy voice, whether drily and unemotionally or with tears in the eyes, etc.—no, the distinction is whether one *speaks* or whether one *acts* by speaking, whether one uses the voice, facial expression, arm-gestures, a single word thrice, perhaps ten times underscored, etc., for emphasis in order to make an impression or whether one uses his life, his existence [*Existents*], every hour of his day, sacrifices, etc., for emphasis. This emphasis is the elevated emphasis which transforms what is spoken into something entirely different, even though a speaker says literally the same thing.

There is, as I said today to His Excellency Ørsted, there is an infinite difference in ways of putting one's thoughts into the world, between being issued as a one-dollar, a ten-dollar, or a hundred-dollar note. Two men may say the same thing, perhaps word for word, but which one says it—this is not the same—no, this is the infinite distinction.

What abominable guilt, illustrated so often in our time, that when a shrewd fellow notices someone else whose life bears the marks of being sacrificed in order to express one truth or another, and then this shrewd fellow says the same thing—and it brings him good fortune. He says the same thing; yes, he may even defend himself against the other by saying, "I am saying the same thing word for word." You hypocrite! Certainly you are saying the same, but you do not act by speaking; you just talk, and that is how you make it into something completely different, so that it brings you good fortune—by saying literally the same thing.

Truly the eternal will take this kind of guilt most seriously. There are not many crimes of this magnitude, and not very many who have disgraced the truth as have such shrewd fellows.

x^2 A 466   n.d., 1850

« 679

In margin: Anti-Climacus is not indirect communication.

Anti-Climacus is not indirect communication, inasmuch as there is a foreword by me.

Indirect communication is a placing together of dialectical contrasts —and then not a single word of personal understanding.*

The mitigation in more direct communication is, among other things, that the communicator has a need to be understood personally, has a fear of being misunderstood. Indirect communication is sheer tension.

x^3 A 624   n.d., 1850

« 680

In margin of 679 (x^3 A 624):
* But, of course, although this is not indirect communication as such, it may (since the secrecy consists in its being such a little foreword that one perhaps does not have time to see it, even less to see what it contains) very well occasion the question to the established order: What do you think of what is said here; is this opposition which you must

reject or is it precisely some truth which you need so that each one comes to make an admission before God.

x^3 A 625   n.d., 1850

« 681 *Christian Eloquence*

In his *Spirit of Christianity* Chateaubriand speaks of Christian eloquence as something which distinguishes Christianity from paganism, something which paganism did not have—and Tzschirner[374] in his *Letters to Ch.*; Leipzig: 1828) agrees.

It must be said that this is an error. For, Christianly understood, the whole notion of Christian "eloquence" is in many ways a mistake, an indirect proof that Christianity is set apart in the realm of practical activity [*existentielle*]; for eloquence increases in proportion [to decline]; all political analogies show that eloquence flourished at the time of the dissolution of states. To that extent it is perhaps rather a proof of paganism's greater proficiency in practical activity that it was ignorant of ecclesiastical eloquence. And if paganism had an analogy to Christian eloquence, it was the eloquence of the Sophists. To a large degree eloquence is essentially sophistic; sophistry consists in the displacement of appropriate action by eloquence.[375]

x^3 A 648   n.d., 1850

CONSCIENCE

« 682

Just as one who has ears to hear also has the ability to ask questions, so God has it also. He questions you more diligently than anyone else; he questions you, for what is conscience but a question; he questions you in the manifold destinies of your life—and when he has asked, he turns his ear, so to speak, to you, but you will not answer.

III A 196 *n.d.*, 1841-42

« 683

In the secular world the King is unconditionally the only one who is bound by the relationship of conscience.[376] It is his preeminence that he alone is responsible only to God and his conscience. —But in the spiritual world, how completely different. Paul says, "Therefore one must be subject, not only to avoid God's wrath but also for the sake of conscience." Consequently it is a relationship of conscience. A poor woman who weeds the gardens of the rich can say: "I am doing this work for a dollar a day, but I do it very carefully for the sake of conscience." In truth, these are kingly words! But one must remember that he must have such words for himself—with God. This is real magnificence. For this reason it is very foolish to want to make the poorer class impatient with their condition. The small worldly alteration which may be achieved is nevertheless as nothing, but this phrase and this thought—*for the sake of conscience*—is a transformation of language, is the Archimedean point outside the world, and with this, when it is in deep inward silence before God, the weeder-woman can say that she moves heaven and earth.

VIII^1 A 60 *n.d.*, 1847

« 684

It is presupposed and stated that every human being has a conscience —yet there is no accomplishment (neither in the physical, like dancing, singing, etc., nor in the mental, such as thinking and the like) which requires such an extensive and rigorous schooling as is required before one can genuinely be said to have a conscience. Just as gold in its original state is found alloyed with all sorts of worthless and miscellaneous components, so it is with conscience in its immediate state, which contains elements which are the very opposite of the conscience.

Herein lies the truth of what Hegel[377] says about conscience being a form of the evil. But in another sense Hegel says this without justification. He ought rather have said: What many, indeed most, people call conscience is not conscience at all, but moods, stomach reflexes, vagrant impulses, etc.—the conscience of a bailiff.

One is compelled to say that eternity, when everyone is to be judged, will first and foremost require that every human being has equipped himself with a conscience. This, then, is the basic judgment: Have you or have you not had a conscience—but note that if you have had none, you are condemned.

x^1 A 51   n.d., 1849

« 685

Do you employ your cleverness to spare yourself. If you are weak, nevertheless simply venture; confess all your weakness before God, how anxious you are; then he manages everything so that you can bear it, and you still save your conscience by having ventured.

x^3 A 344   n.d., 1850

« 686 *A Matter of Conscience*

Someone says: This or that is to me really a matter of conscience, and I am ready to sacrifice various things for it. Nonsense! How can it then be a matter of conscience—only what one risks everything for is a matter of conscience.

One sees here again that the existential is the genuinely expressive. Let a man be silent, but let his life express that in relationship to the religious life he has ventured everything—then it would be a matter of conscience.

But we, as we are, are much too puny and skinny to have a matter of conscience, to be able to endure having a matter of conscience. You see, we must say this about ourselves, confess this to ourselves and to God, and humble ourselves.

x^4 A 24   n.d., 1851

« 687 *The Mental Marks of Having a Matter of Conscience*

The distinguishing feature is this: someone who has a matter of conscience does not seek earthly help, nor does he avoid dangers, nor does he seek "the most convenient way"—no, he seeks dangers, creates difficulties for himself, discovers the most difficult way. For him there is one concern: that he has not made a mistake, that it was not a matter of conscience, and dangers help to make this become clear.

Where this symptom is not present, there is no matter of conscience in the stricter sense.

As calmly as a bank clerk looks at a bank note and says: It lacks a dot over the *i*; this bill is counterfeit. One dot, to everyone else it seems a trifle, yet it is enough to indicate that it is a counterfeit bill. As calmly as a broker considers a bond and says: A flourish is missing here; this is counterfeit. As calmly as a physician says: The illness is not this, for the symptom is lacking. Just as calmly I say: Where this symptom is absent, there is no matter of conscience. But I do not say: Where this symptom is present, there is a matter of conscience, it is absolutely sure—no, this I do not say.

X^4 A 34   *n.d.*, 1851

« 688 *Conscience*

After all, to have a conscience before men does not reach much farther than having a conscience (con-sciousness) with men. Thus, even taking an oath—look more closely and you will see what creeps in: Well, I'll swear in the same way, with the same implications, as all the others.

How many people really have a conscience with God?

XI^2 A 260   *n.d.*, 1854

CONTEMPORANEITY

« 689

In developing the concept of inspiration they talk about the close relationship in which the apostles stood to Christ as a basis for their interpretation being correct above all others—but they do not remember that on the other hand those who are living after Christianity has existed for 1,800 years have a great advantage because Christianity has asserted itself in all life relationships, has developed more and more; whereas, on the other hand, the apostles had to battle much abuse, misunderstanding, etc., simply because Christianity was just beginning to develop.[378]

I A 50   February 5, 1835

« 690

The disciple [*Discipel*] at second hand[379] is indeed the noncontemporary, and this all the subsequent generations have in common over against the contemporary—that they are not contemporary.

In margin: You did not answer my question but elicited a new one.

V B 18   *n.d.*, 1844

« 691

Out with history. In with the situation of contemporaneity. This is the criterion: as I judge anything contemporaneously, so am I. All this subsequent chatter is a delusion.

This is really the direction in which my whole productivity has tended. This is why I use experiments instead of *actual* histories.

Luther's mistake was that he did not go back far enough, did not make a person contemporary enough with Christ.

The possibility of offense then becomes that which is to judge Christendom.

Alas, alas, Christianity has been taken in vain. How would one judge a country claiming to have a million lovers like Romeo and Juliet—and yet this is what men are fancied to be in Christendom, that all are Christians; whereas a true Christian is more rare than Romeo and Juliet.

IX A 95   *n.d.*, 1848

« 692

By becoming contemporaneous with Christ (the prototype), you simply discover that you are not like it at all, not even in what you call your best moment; for in such a moment you are not in the corresponding tension of actuality but are spectating. The result is that you effectively learn to flee to faith in grace. The prototype is that which requires itself from you; alas, and you feel the unlikeness horribly; then you flee to the prototype that he may have compassion upon you. In this way the prototype is simultaneously the one who infinitely judges you most severely—and also the one who has compassion upon you.

IX A 153   n.d., 1848

« 693

With regard to contemporaneity with Christ, an observation must still be made about making it the criterion for being a Christian.

What I have developed in various works about contemporaneity as the criterion is poetically, historically, and ethically absolutely true, has thus its validity and to that extent also its validity with respect to Christ as a historical, actual person.

But Christ is also the dogmatical. Here is the distinction. His death is indeed the atonement.

Here the category takes a qualitative turn. From the death of a witness to the truth I am to learn to will to die for the truth as he did, to will to resemble him. But in relationship to Christ's death, I cannot will in this way. For Christ's death is not a task for imitation [*Efterfølgelse*] but is the atonement—I do not dare regard or consider Christ as a merely historical person. When I am reflecting upon his life and his death, I think or I ought to be thinking that I am a sinner.

It must also be said that in one sense it has become easier for men to become and to be Christians after the death of Christ than during his lifetime. Indeed, his atoning death must be valued as a means to this end. Besides, while He lived He himself had the task of expressing the prototype [*Forbilledet*] and compelling the praise of truth until they murdered Him. But after his death he can also aid the Christian.

Therefore it is not simply a matter of Christ's being the prototype and that I simply ought to will to resemble him. In the first place I need His help in order to be able to resemble Him, and, secondly, insofar as he is the Savior and Reconciler of the race, I cannot in fact resemble him.

The medieval conception of Christ as the prototype, its beautiful zeal to resemble him—this is youthfulness which wants to get along right away.

But the older one becomes, the deeper becomes the qualitative distinction between the ideal and the man who wants to resemble it. Therefore Luther actually fought against a too zealous and too enthusiastic desire to make Christ only the prototype—and now it appears all the more that the prototype is also something else, is the Atoner whom we cannot resemble, who can only help us. Finally, this was emphasized so much that His being the prototype almost evaporated as something altogether too transcendent. This, however, must not be done.

x^1 A 132   *n.d.*, 1849

« 694

On closer inspection all this talk about wishing to have been contemporary with Christ is presumptuous; for what is it but fancying oneself to be good enough to be an apostle. And even the apostles fell away, and they had to be equipped with extraordinary divine powers in order to be, that is, to be able to keep on being, contemporary with him—the best evidence that no one can keep on being contemporary with him all by himself.

But those who talk this way about contemporaneity do not know what they are saying; it is the usual thing: they take the glory and leave out the difficulty. It is flirtation.

And as I have noted somewhere else in a journal [i.e, x^1 A 132]— Christ's life has another meaning as well; it is atonement. If Christ were only the prototype, then it was cruel of Him to force the issue to such an extreme; but He had to die—in order to save the world.

x^2 A 253   *n.d.*, 1849

« 695 *Contemporaneity with Christ—Being a Disciple*

In those portions where Christ himself defines the demand so infinitely high, it is in relationship to someone who wanted to be a disciple and therefore himself asked to become a disciple.

Otherwise Christ acted benevolently to the multitude of sick and wretched—without asking that they should leave everything and follow him or become disciples. Therefore he did not require more than their faith and their gratitude.

Yet one must remember that contemporaneity with Christ is always a prodigious exertion.

But now contemporaneity has been removed; therefore the milder relationship (that of gratitude, which, be it noted, does not express itself by imitating him) easily becomes too mild and is easily taken in vain. Therefore it ought to be enjoined (also in order that gratitude can become all the greater) that the criterion is to become a disciple, except that one should not take himself by surprise and venture stupidly, but if one is not called in this way, he becomes all the more grateful.

It is this which Anti-Climacus has done.

x^3 A 653   *n.d.*, 1850

« 696 *The Basic Confusion—Contemporaneity*

The basic confusion lies in getting Christianity transformed into the historical, into having a history, not to mention the blasphemy of being perfectible by accommodation.

In one generation alone it can be confusing enough with these many millions (for the whole question is one of getting hold of "the individual"), but now to tow along these many millions of the centuries—how in all the world is it going to be possible to get an unconditional impression of the unconditional.

No, it begins with every generation—and with the New Testament.

XI^1 A 38   *n.d.*, 1854

« 697 *Contemporaneity*

The God-man lives on earth—contemporaneously there is not a single person, literally not a single one, who remains true to him; the thousands hate, mock, spit upon, curse him; the intellectuals lay a snare for him; the crowds help them topple him over as the greatest curse, and his few disciples flee, even the most loyal desert him.

—— and then he dies.

And then centuries later—when, please note, Christianity has become common practice, habit, custom—then millions go on pilgrimage on their knees to see the places where he lived—and among all these millions there naturally was not a single person, literally not one, who contemporaneously would not have taken to his heels the best he could and also have been along to insult, mock, spit upon, laugh at him.

Ah, how loathsome!

But really loathsome, however, are those lying teachers, preachers, and professors who strengthen the somewhat more innocent throng of men in their pure fancy that mimicking without danger and game-playing are the same as being a Christian.

XI^1 A 59   *n.d.*, 1854

« 698 *God—We Human Beings*

We human beings think as follows: this business of Adam's fall, that happened a long, long time ago and is forgotten, and nowadays we are nice people—for God this happens with Adam today.

We human beings make ourselves believe that this business of Christ being put to death, this villainy of the human race, that all this happened 1,800 years ago, long ago, and is forgotten; now we are nice people—for God this happens today.

XI^1 A 362 *n.d.*, 1854

CONTRADICTION

« 699

The fact that Christianity has not outgrown the principle of contradiction demonstrates precisely its romantic character. What is it that Goethe wanted to illuminate in his *Faust* but this very thesis?

I A 324   January 22, 1837

« 700

Generally speaking, the imperfection in everything human is that its aspirations are achieved only by way of their opposites.[380] I shall not discuss the variety of formations which can give a psychologist plenty to do (the melancholy have the best sense of the comic, the most opulent the best sense of the rustic, the dissolute the best sense of the moral, the doubter often the best sense of the religious), but it is through sin that one gets a first glimpse of blessedness. Therefore the imperfection consists not so much in the opposite as in one's not being able to see one thing and its opposite *simultaneously*.

III A 112   n.d., 1841

« 701

Old age accomplishes the presentiments of youth. Yes, indeed, one sees this in Swift: in his youth he built an insane asylum; in his old age he himself entered it.[381]

III A 123   n.d., 1841

« 702

Which view contains the deepest interpretation of life: that contrasts unite men—or oneness and likeness? Heraclitus taught that only those things which oppose each other are useful to each other; Empedocles, that only like attracts like.

See Aristotle's *Ethics*, 8, 2.[382]

IV A 5   n.d., 1842-43

« 703

That the principle of unity has abolished the principle of contradiction can be said only in the same sense as Pythagoras taught[383] that *one* is not a number. *One* is prior to discrimination and counting begins first with discrimination. Unity is prior to contradiction, and existence [*Tilværelsen*] first begins with contradiction.

In margin: Or in the same sense as Zeno the Eleatic said: μηδὲν τῶν ὄντων ἐστι τὸ ἕν.³⁸⁴

See Tennemann, I, p. 264 f.n.

IV A 57   n.d., 1843

« 704

The view which sees life's doubleness (dualism) is higher and deeper than that which seeks unity or "pursues studies toward unity" (an expression from Hegel³⁸⁵ about all the endeavors of philosophy); the view which sees the eternal as τέλος, and the teleological view in general, is higher than all immanence or all talk about *causa sufficiens*. The passion which saw paganism as sin and assumed eternal torment in hell is greater than the *summa summarum* of the thoughtlessness (which is disheveled) which sees everything within immanence.

IV A 192   n.d., 1844

« 705 **N.B.**

It is not difficult to comprehend that in a certain sense the principle of identity is higher than the principle of contradiction and the basis for it. But the principle of identity is only the limit for human thought; it is like the blue mountains, like the line the etchers call the base—the drawing is the main thing. As long as I live in time, the principle of identity is only an abstraction. Therefore nothing is easier than to delude oneself and others into thinking the identity of all by abandoning diversity. Nevertheless one might ask such a person how he conducts himself with regard to living, since in identity I am beyond time. Suicide is therefore the only ethical consequence of the identity-principle adhered to in time. The confusion arises only from living in categories different from those used in writing books—O, wretched book-writing!

As long as I live, I live in contradiction, for life is contradiction. On the one side I have eternal truth, on the other side manifold existence [*Tilværelse*], which human beings as such cannot penetrate, for then we would have to be omniscient.³⁸⁶

The uniting link is therefore faith.

V A 68   n.d., 1844

« 706

Addition to 705 [v a 68]:
Identity can never become *terminus a quo* but is *terminus ad quem*;[387] one always comes to it only through abstraction.

v a 69   n.d., 1844

CORRECTIVE

« 707

In margin: To supply the corrective.

To supply the corrective is essentially a task of resignation.

At first, when one begins, the dominating misconception abroad in the world looks haughtily down on the poor corrective: "It is antiquated, obsolete," etc.

When the corrective, through its slow but quiet and deeper influence, by its threatening stance, gradually has taken the courage out of this misconception, people surreptitiously utilize the corrective and pretend as if they themselves had said it. Or they circumspectly allow a certain amount of time to elapse, as long—so to speak—as the corrective's operation lasts. During that time there is official silence; that is, they do not write. If they detect that the corrective has power, they advance and covertly utilize the corrective—and then appropriate to themselves the honor of exemplifying moderation. If this is successful, they go a step further. Since they take only part of the corrective and, on the other hand, the corrective in order to be effective has to control by means of the excitement of the paradox—they abandon the corrective as an exaggeration.

Cowardly sneaking—that is what Martensen is capable of.

x^1 A 658   *n.d.*, 1849

« 708 *My Task*

has continually been to provide the existential-corrective by poetically presenting the ideals and inciting people about the established order, with which I collaborate by criticizing all the false reformers and the opposition, who simply are evil—and whom only ideals can halt.

x^4 A 15   *n.d.*, 1851

« 709 *"The Sacrificed Ones," the Correctives*

Just as a skilled cook says of a dish which already has a good many ingredients mixed into it, "It has to have a little dash of cinnamon" (the rest of us probably could scarcely taste that this little dash of cinnamon was added, but she knows for sure why and how it tastefully blends in with the whole mixture); just as the artist says of the whole painting's color-tone, which is composed of many, many colors, "A little bit of red has to be introduced here and there, at this little point" (and the rest of us probably could scarcely discover the red, the artist having shaded it so well, whereas he knows exactly why it should be introduced): just as with the cook and the artist, so also with providence.

The administration of the world is [like running] an enormous household, [like making] an immense painting. Yet it is the same for him, the Master, God in heaven, as it is for the cook and the artist. He says: "There must be a little dash of cinnamon now; a little bit of red must be introduced." We have no idea why, we can hardly detect it since the little smidge vanishes in the whole, but God knows why.

A little dash of cinnamon! This means: here a man must be sacrificed; he must be added to give the rest a specific taste.

These are the correctives. It is an unhappy mistake if the person who is used to introduce the corrective becomes impatient and wants to make the corrective normative for the others, an attempt which will confuse everything.

A little dash of cinnamon! Humanly speaking, how painful to be sacrificed in this manner—to be a little dash of cinnamon! But on the other hand God knows very well whom he chooses to be used in this manner, and he knows with most intimate understanding how to make it blessed for him to be sacrificed so that among the thousands of heterogeneous voices which everywhere express each in its own way the same thing, his voice is also heard, and perhaps his in particular is truly heard *de profundis*—that God is love. The bird on the twig, the lily in the field, the deer in the forest, the fish in the sea, the countless crowds of happy humans jubilate: God is love. But underneath, supporting, as it were, all these sopranos as the bass part does, sounds the *de profundis* from the sacrificed ones: God is love.

x^4 A 596   *n.d.*, 1852

« 710 *To Hate Oneself*

All development is always dialectical; the "next generation" will always need the "opposite" as corrective.

Everyone, then, who in giving expression to the religious chooses the side which is omitted from the viewpoint, from the contemporaries' viewpoint—such a one hates himself. The person who chooses the side supported by the contemporaries' viewpoint really loves himself, even if the contemporaries' viewpoint were—to fast, to scourge oneself, and in this way to hate oneself.

x^5 A 106   *n.d.*, 1853

« 711 *Luther's Emphasis*

Luther's emphasis is a corrective—but a corrective made into the normative, into the sum total, is *eo ipso* confusing in another generation (where that for which it was a corrective does not exist). And with every generation that goes by in this way, it must become worse, until the end result is that this corrective, which has independently established itself, produces characteristics exactly the opposite of the original.

And this has been the case. Luther's corrective, when it independently is supposed to be the sum total of Christianity, produces the most refined kind of secularism and paganism.

XI^1 A 28   *n.d.*, 1854

DEATH

« 712

When in the hour of death it grows dark for a true Christian, it is because the sunlight of eternal happiness shines too brightly in his eyes.

II A 213   n.d., 1837

« 713

Generally it is regarded as the wisdom of life to live as if one were about to die. I knew a man who became very unhappy precisely because he continually believed that he would die—this robbed him of all patience to live.

III B 181:9   n.d., 1841-42

« 714

There is indeed a shocking eloquence (even though shocking in a different sense than the voice of Abel's blood, which cries out to heaven[388]) when one reads the brief words which a deceased person has had placed over his grave, the last words, his final testament, the last cry, into which he has poured his whole soul. What is all preacher-prattle compared with this commentary. In the lower part of the Church of the Holy Spirit there are some small basement windows with iron bars. A skull is depicted there, together with a brief inscription. Thus does the grave call out to one. —Death's last struggle, when there is no time anymore to select widely or to chatter about categories or about the difference between paganism and Christianity.

V A 36   n.d., 1844

« 715

My reader, it is very curious, but not everyone gets to become an author in this life—for that various talents are required. Ah, but go out into the graveyard and look at the graves[389] and you will see that occasionally someone has become an author without even giving it the slightest thought. Those brief inscriptions, a pious saying, an admonition—for example, remembrance of the God-fearing is a benediction—out there everything preaches; for just as nature declares God, so every grave preaches. There is a gravestone with the bust of a young girl. No doubt she was beautiful at one time, and now the stone has sunk and nettles grow over the grave. She seems to have had no family. Here is the grave of a soldier; his helmet and sword lie upon the coffin and beneath it says that his memory shall never be forgotten. Yet, alas, the top of the railing is already torn down and one is tempted to seize his sword to defend him, since he is doing it no longer—and those who mourned him thought that his memory would never be forgotten!

V A 56 n.d., 1844

« 716

There is a beautiful expression which the common man uses about dying: that God or our Lord "brightens" for him. Accordingly, at the very time everything becomes darkest— for what is as dark as the grave— God "brightens."

V A 63 n.d., 1844

« 717

It is difficult to make a comparison between different periods, and a speaker who frequently does this easily confuses, because in the interest of eloquence he emphasizes one side and therefore easily becomes involved in contradictions. But there can still be at times an easily recognizable trend. If you pay attention to the way death is spoken of in our time, you will note a great change in comparison with that of an earlier time. Almost universally you will hear it said nowadays that a quick and sudden death is to be desired. What does this mean? It means that we want to shove away the thought of death and shove death out of life as much as possible. Men desire to live as if there were no death, and when it has to come, then let it come quickly and suddenly, so that it may be almost as if it were not. Strange human sophistication about life, how ingeniously you think you fool death—and how horribly you deceive yourself: for eternity is neither sudden nor quick. On the other hand, in the old collect of the Church, which is even now to be recommended, among the various evils the believer prays God he may be spared from is the evil of a sudden death. The person who is to take a long road is better served in this way. In respect to what is over in a moment, it may very well be best at times to close one's eyes and leap—but with regard to the beginning of what is longer than anything else—eternity—there the prudential leap is not only foolishness but the most appalling self-deception.

VII^1 A 145 n.d., 1846

« 718 *At the Cemetery*

..... And if you go out there earlier in the morning, when the sun peeps vivaciously through the branches, you will find everything so nicely decorated. The small families each have their own little plot for themselves, approximately the same size. To be sure, in life it happens that a family is forced to stint, but in death all must do so. In life an influential man can manage to spread himself around, but in death all must restrict themselves. Yet there is a minor distinction, like a droll reminder of the distinction which was so enormous in the world; if there is a distinction here, it is a matter of inches for one to have more than the other. Having a flower on one's grave already amounts to a big difference, and having a tree is prosperity—alas, thus life returns in death, for in childhood owning a flower was already a big thing, and to own a tree extraordinary.

Even in the middle of an earnest contemplation of death, one has to smile—not at the equality of all, but that there still continue to be distinctions.[390]

VII^1 A 232 *n.d.*, 1845-47

« 719

Over against sickness, all physical suffering and the distressing misrelationships between soul and body rooted therein, there is this consolation: death is the sickness which puts an end to all the others.[391]

VIII^1 A 87 *n.d.*, 1847

« 720 *Poetice*

The reply of individuality:
"As the captive animal paces around its cage every day for the sake of movement or measures the length of its chain, so I measure the length of my chain every day by turning to the thought of death—for the sake of movement and in order to endure living."

VIII^1 A 406 *n.d.*, 1847

« 721

In talk about death there is a mistaken leap from the ethical to the esthetic when it is phrased: Not our own death or the fact that we ourselves shall die—for this is not the most painful—but the death of our friends. For the only earnestness is that *I* shall die and then go up for judgment. One must first unethically falsify the point about death before arriving at this nonsense about whether it is more painful to lose another or to die oneself.

X^1 A 233 *n.d.*, 1849

« 722

Which is worse: to be executed or to be slowly trampled to death by geese?

x^2 A 434   n.d., 1850

« 723 *Point of View in Christendom*

The usual thing nowadays is to wish for a quick death—and in one of the collects of the Church there is the petition that God will save us from—along with other evils—a sudden death.

That a person is consoled by death, longs to be out of this life, is judged to be a fault, to be unchristian. But I am grateful that it is Christianity! Christianity means precisely that death is a person's essential consolation, his death-day is his birth-day, and the longing for eternity becomes greater and greater. But the fact is that people idolize a sensuous clinging to life and interpret longing for death as the position of one who scarcely assumes immortality at all. And this is in Christendom, where we all are Christians.

x^3 A 250   n.d., 1850

« 724

"To die to" means to regard everything as one will see it at the moment of death and consequently to bring death as close as possible. Even the most dazzling and enchanting pleasure—in the moment of death, will it not be a matter of complete unconcern whether you enjoyed it or not? On the other hand, every good work—yes, for God in heaven's sake, do not neglect to do it—in the hour of death it will be of utmost urgency that you did not neglect it. —Alas, who has achieved this!

x^3 A 340   n.d., 1850

« 725

The situation of confession has a similarity to that of death: to be entirely alone—before God.

We avoid as much as possible the thought of death; we do not want to be disturbed by it—and Christianity wants to bring us as close to it as possible.

Confess that this is the way we live: in our relationship to Christianity we are like the person who deposits a sum with a burial society, a relationship of possibility, and reckon to become Christians in death—but as you live, so do you die.

x^3 A 710   n.d., 1851

« 726 *Death*

Scriver says[392] that it is good to have business with death—the advantage is ours ("to die is gain").

This is a more splendid way of tricking death than that of Epicurus:[393] Death cannot get hold of me, because when I am, death is not, and when death is, I am not.

x^4 A 60   *n.d.,* 1851

« 727 *Fear of Death*

Christianity took away the fear of death and replaced it with the fear of judgment; this is a sharpening but is a step forward as well. We cannot sufficiently get it into our heads that spiritually a genuine step forward is recognizable by its being a sharpening. Spiritually no step forward is truly made in which the matter becomes easier; no, what makes the matter easier is *eo ipso* not a step forward, no matter how much it is trumpeted as being this.

XI^1 A 479   *n.d.,* 1854

« 728 *The Zest for Life*

Everything, everything arouses man and the race to maintain zest for life.

And if a man is genuinely to have anything to do with God, to be loved and to love, to become spirit, the zest for life must first of all be ousted, death-longing.

How painful this can be for a man God knows best, and he is therefore willing to grieve with him; but he does not change it.

But look, in Christendom we have managed to turn Christianity around in such a way that it is Christianity's particular service to animate and inflame the zest for life (Judaism or paganism).

For this reason I am anxious about [*angest for*] getting involved with anybody in particular, for I am not yet so strong that I feel keenly the pains of dying-to-the-world, and I am quite willing to go back to a zest for life; and I know that every man will assist me in this respect—that is, corrupt my cause for me.

XI^1 A 565   *n.d.,* 1854

« 729 *Life's Entrance and Exit*

Listen to the newborn infant's cry in the hour of birth—see the death struggle in the final hour—and then declare whether what begins and ends in this way can be intended to be enjoyment.

True enough, we human beings do everything as fast as possible to get away from these two points, hurry as fast as possible to forget the birth-cry and change it to delight in having given a being life. And when someone dies, we immediately say: Softly and gently he slept away, death is a sleep, a quiet sleep—something we do not say for the sake of the one who died, for our talking cannot help him, but for our own sake, in order not to lose any of the zest for life, in order to change everything to serve an increase in the zest for life during the interval between the birth-cry and the death-wail, between the mother's shriek and the child's repetition of it, when the child at some time dies.*

Imagine somewhere a great and splendid hall where everything is done to produce nothing but joy and merriment—but the entrance to this room is a nasty, muddy humble stairway and it is impossible to pass without getting disgustingly soiled, and admission is paid by prostituting oneself, and when day dawns the merriment is over and all ends with one's being kicked out again—but the whole night through everything is done to keep up and inflame the merriment and pleasure!

What is reflection? Simply to reflect on these two questions: How did I get into this and this and how do I get out of it again, how does it end? What is thoughtlessness? To muster everything in order to drown all this about entrance and exist in forgetfulness, to muster everything to re-explain and explain away entrance and exit, simply lost in the interval between the birth cry and the repetition of this cry when the one who is born expires in the death struggle.

XI² A 199   n.d., 1854

« 730

Addition to 729 (XI² A 199), in margin:
Notation
The birth cry—the death cry

It is the mother who cries out, but the question is whether the child does not have more reason to cry out. The mother *does exist* [*er til*]; consequently her pain is only a pain in existence [*Tilværelse*]; but the child *comes into existence* [*bliver til*], comes into existence to the pain of existence. But if the child does not cry out immediately, then it surely will come—the death cry is indeed the shriek over being born.

XI² A 200   n.d., 1854

« 731 *To Be a Christian*

July 2.

To be a Christian is the most appalling of all agonies; it is, so it must be, to have one's hell here on earth.

What does a man shrink from most of all? From dying, to be sure, and most of all from the death-struggle, which one therefore wishes to be as short as possible.

But to be Christian means to be a dying man in the state of dying (you must die to yourself, hate yourself)—and then to live, perhaps 40 years in this state!*

And not merely this, there comes an added sharpening. Those who stand around a dying man's bed usually do not grin at him because he groans in the struggle of death. Neither do they hate, curse, loathe him —because he lies in the struggle of death. But this suffering belongs to being a Christian, comes of itself if true Christianity is to be expressed in this world.

And then the spiritual trial [Anfægtelse], in which the possibility of offense is present at every moment and will make the most of the moment, the possibility of offense—that this is supposed to be God's love, that this is supposed to be that God of love about whom one has learned everything but this from childhood on!

And yet he is love, infinite love (but he can love you only if you are a dying one); and this nevertheless is grace, infinite grace, infinite grace, to get eternal suffering transformed into temporal suffering.

But woe to these mobs of oath-bound liars, woe to them for having taken the key to the kingdom of heaven, and not only do they themselves not go in, but they also hinder others from entering.

*In margin: We shrink from reading about what an animal used for vivisection has to suffer; yet this is only a short-lived picture of the suffering of being a Christian: to be kept alive in the state of death.

XI^2 A 422   n.d., 1855

DEMONIC

« 732

The leap with which Bournonville, in his role of Mephistopheles,[394] always enters and bounds into a motionless pose is commendable. This leap is an element which ought to be noted in an understanding of the demonic. The demonic[395] is, namely, the sudden.

Another aspect of the demonic is the tedious, as little Winsløv[396] so excellently interpreted it, whereby it passes over into the comic (the way in which, as Pepin in *Charlemagne*, he said, "Patience"—. See his Klister in *De Uadskillelige*.

IV A 94 n.d., 1843

« 733 *The Demonic*

He who has an ear for the speech of a demoniac has often experienced that what the demoniac says is of such a nature that the truth is present as soon as the meaning is inverted.

A demonic feminine or masculine willfulness shouts: There is one thing I cannot bear, and that is to have someone rule over me. Interpret this inversely and you have the law for his cure, the thing he needs; what he simply cannot endure but precisely what he stands in need of is someone to rule over him.

This no doubt is because the demoniac himself knows—at least with a kind of clairvoyance—what the remedy is; but as a demoniac he loves his sickness and is afraid of the remedy, and this is why he shouts that this very thing (the remedy) is the only thing he cannot bear—it would be utterly fatal to me.

XI^1 A 270 n.d., 1854

DESCARTES

« 734

He[397] had already been struck by Hegel's[398] and Spinoza's saying that Descartes did not doubt like a skeptic *for the sake of* doubting, but *for the sake of* finding truth . . . . . this *for the sake of*. —And why do these men talk about it as if they themselves had not done it? Has Descartes[399] done it for all of us in the same way Christ was crucified—is this a scientific question—or a practical one—. It certainly must be that for Descartes.[400]

IV B 2:16 *n.d.*, 1842-43

«735

Descartes teaches that wonder [*Forundring*] (*admiratio*) is the only passion of the soul which has no contradiction—therefore one sees how right it is to make this the point of departure of all philosophy.

IV B 13:23 *n.d.*, 1842-43

« 736

It is splendid to see the honest earnestness with which Descartes has grasped the idea of doubting everything, how he will not upset anything established, will not draw others into the same doubt. There are examples enough of this in his *Discourse on Method*. I have noted them in my copy. One gets a quite different impression of Descartes by reading him oneself. Descartes thinks a divine revelation should be believed even if it teaches *quod naturali lumini contrarium*.[401]

IV C 14 *n.d.*, 1842-43

DESPAIR

« 737

The present age is the age of despair,[402] the age of the wandering Jew (many reforming Jews)—
I A 181 n.d., 1836

« 738

Caligula's idea[403] of wanting all heads on one neck is nothing else than premeditated, cowardly suicide. It is the counterpart of suicide. Both are equally desperate world views.
II A 409 May 4, 1839

« 739

What in a certain sense is called "spleen" and what the mystics knew by the designation "the arid moments," the Middle Ages knew as *acedia* (αχηδια, aridity).[404] Gregory, *Moralia in Job*,[405] XIII, p. 435: *Virum solitarium ubique comitatur acedia . . . . . est animi remissio, mentis enervatio, neglectus religiosae exercitationis, odium professionis, laudatrix rerum secularium.**[406] That Gregory should emphasize *virum solitarium* points to experience, since it is a sickness to which the isolated person [is exposed] at his highest pinnacle (the humorous), and the sickness is most accurately described and rightly emphasized as *odium professionis*, and if we consider this symptom in a somewhat ordinary sense (not in the sense of churchly confession of sins, by which we would have to include the indifferent church member as *solitarius*) of a self-expression, experience will not leave us in the lurch if examples are required.
July 20, 1839

The ancient moralists show a deep insight into human nature in regarding *tristitia*[407] among the *septem vitia principalia*.[408] Thus Isidorus Hisp. See de Wette [*Lærebog i den christelige Sædelære* (Copenhagen: 1835)], p. 139.
II A 484 n.d., 1839

« 740

* *In margin of 739* (II A 484):
This is what my father called: A *quiet despair*.[409]
II A 485 n.d., 1839

« 741

Or do you think that your sorrow is so terrible that what until now has been held as true is disproved by your life—that God cares for every human being with fatherly concern and does not leave himself without witness! Think of that! If that eternal law in the world of the spirit, more beautiful and powerful than the law in nature which holds the heavenly bodies in their definite, measured course, if that law, then, is abrogated, then everything must collapse in a despair more terrible than if the heavenly bodies collided in frightful chaos. If what you maintain were the truth, if you really were discriminated against in this way and could truthfully say such things—I am no coward, but I would nevertheless say to you: Hide yourself from men, hide your wisdom, let them live in this beautiful faith in a fatherly providence. But it is not so, and I do not need to ask you to flee, but I say: Step forward and proclaim your high-flying wisdom—I am not afraid. Like Simon the magician, mentioned in Scripture, who wished to fly in the air—the apostles bowed down to earth and prayed, and he fell down.

III A 195   n.d., 1841

« 742

..... When everything is lost, when that which to you is dearest of all is denied you, when there is not one remaining doubt which can keep the soul breathing, when it wants to sink down in stagnation and death "because there is nothing left to do"—could there really be absolutely nothing left? I do know of one thing still—before you lay yourself down to die, even though you keep on living, ask yourself: Do I still love God as deeply as before? If you have to admit that you do not, then your soul will not have time to fall asleep but will have much to do; and if you sense that you do, then you will be so happy that you will feel more alive than ever.

III A 238   n.d., 1842

« 743

..... And when you had become utterly weary of the world, when you wanted to give your passion the outlet of one single statement, you perhaps said: "Let the world pass away and the lust thereof."[410] But at the same moment your soul was reminded of an old saying, and involuntarily you began to repeat what was almost a childhood memory: God's word endures forever. At first you said it quite indifferently, but finally it became everything to you.

III A 241   n.d., 1842

« 744

There is, however, nothing to be done with the age before it experiences far deeper convulsions. The whole age can be divided into those who write and those who do not write. Those who write represent despair, and those who read disapprove of it and believe that they have a superior wisdom—and yet, if they were able to write, they would write the same thing. Basically they are all equally despairing, but when one does not have the opportunity to become important with his despair, then it is hardly worth the trouble to despair and show it. Is this what it is to have conquered despair? —Those lines in *Die deutsche Theologie*[411] can really be regarded as a motto for the times (perhaps according to the author the German words do not have this precise meaning—he has no intimation of the ultimate of despair): "If we are no longer spiritually rich, we forget God and take pride in being lost" (see chapter 10, p. 41). It is this commendation, so to speak, the age wants to have before God. This is the way the despair of the age shows that it cannot dispense with God, for the clue to its despair is precisely this: that there is a God. It is like the girl who, when she cannot get her way with the beloved, spites him by falling in love with another. She only proves thereby her dependence on him, and the clue to her first love is precisely her relationship to the first one. In the very same way the age wishes to become self-important in the eyes of God. It treats him in the same way Emmeline in *The First Love* treats the father. If she cannot get her will, she will get sick and die "and then, when I am dead, then it is too late."—Presumably the age is of the opinion that in like manner God will be in trouble.

IV A 165 *n.d.*, 1843-44

« 745 *Quiet Despair*[412]
A Narrative

In his early years the Englishman Swift[413] established an insane asylum, which he himself entered in his old age. Here he is said[414] to have observed himself frequently in a mirror and to have exclaimed: Poor old man!

There were a father and a son. Both were highly endowed intellectually and both were witty, especially the father. Everyone who knew their home was certain to find a visit very entertaining. Usually they discussed only between themselves and entertained each other as two good minds without the distinction between father and son. On one rare occasion when the father looked at the son and saw that he was very troubled, he stood quietly before him and said: Poor child, you live in quiet despair. But he never questioned him more closely—alas, he could not, for he, too, lived in quiet despair. Beyond this not a word was exchanged on the subject. But the father and the son were perhaps two of the most melancholy human beings who ever lived in the memory of man.

From this originates the phrase: quiet despair. It is never used otherwise, for generally people have a different conception of despair. Whenever the son merely said these words to himself, quiet despair, he always broke into tears, partly because it was so inexplicably moving, and partly because he was reminded of his father's agitated voice, since like all melancholics he was laconic but also had the pithiness of the melancholic.

And the father believed that he was responsible for his son's melancholy, and the son believed that he was responsible for his father's melancholy; therefore they never raised the subject. That outburst by the father was an outburst of his own melancholy; therefore when he said this, he spoke more to himself than to the son.

V A 33   n.d., 1844

« 746

How things have changed since the time the prophet declared:[415] Rend your hearts and not your garments—now most men have broken hearts and fine clothes (elegant and refined despair), without having rent hearts in the biblical sense.

VIII^1 A 28   n.d., 1847

« 747

He[416] calls this: to despair. The fact that to despair means something else entirely, that it means to lose the eternal, not to lose the earthly or anything earthly, that consequently, viewed in the light of truth, he lost infinitely much more, inflicted upon himself a loss in comparison with which the loss he talks about, the loss he suffers, is child's play—this is completely hidden from him.

In margin: Consequently, while he stands lamenting the loss of the earthly and despairs (but to lose the earthly is by no means to despair), he loses something else completely different, the eternal, which is to despair; he consequently loses something completely different and infinitely more than what he is talking about; strangely enough, without despairing, he inflicts upon himself a loss in comparison with which the loss he talks about is child's play.

VIII^2 B 154:3   n.d., 1848

« 748

Thus it appears that much of what is embellished in the world under the name of resignation is often this kind of *despair* (such as suffering or a situation occasioning suffering): in despair to will to be oneself, in despair to want to comfort oneself by becoming more and more abstract, in despair to will to let the eternal suffice and thereby to be able to defy the earthly and the temporal.

VIII² B 159:4   *n.d.*, 1848

« 749 *Despair Is Like Being Dizzy or Dizziness, Yet Essentially (Qualitatively) Different*[417]

1. The possibility of dizziness lies in the composite of the psychical and the physical, an ambiguous joint boundary between the psychical and the physical.... Thus dizziness is an interplay of the psychical and the physical, even where it is easier to decide which is primarily active, although in many cases it is very difficult to decide.

2. What dizziness is with respect to the composite of the psychical and the physical, despair is in things of the spirit, with respect to that composite of the finite and the infinite, freedom and necessity, the divine and the human in a relation which is [reflectively and responsibly] for itself [*for sig*]. The relation between the psychical and the physical, although a relation, is not (like despair) a relation which is for itself. This is how it happens, as was shown, that the despairing person who, like the dizzy person in the moment of dizziness, is not himself master in the moment of despair, yet is responsible for his position in despair, something the one who is dizzy cannot in the same way be said to be.

With respect to despair, just as with respect to dizziness, it is sometimes easier to show which of the composites is primarily active, sometimes very difficult. But in all despair there is an interplay of finitude and infinitude, of the divine and the human, of freedom and necessity. Thus, to take an example of what will be developed later, a man despairs over [*over*] necessity, that is, when despair makes its appearance, necessity has become apparent to him in all its iciness. But nevertheless he despairs by virtue of freedom; it is, indeed, freedom which despairs. But now suppose that he despairs of [*om*] his freedom. Well, the interplay is there just the same; for in despairing of his freedom, necessity in one form or another must have become apparent to him. And yet it is by virtue of freedom that he despairs—of freedom. Consequently in all despair there is an interplay, since it [despair] is a misrelation in that which has a relation to each other [to itself] or that which is in a relation to each other [to itself] or that which is the relation to each other [the relation of a composite to itself], only that this misrelation is always responsible. A person can be afflicted with dizziness but never with despair.

3. In observing a person who is afflicted with dizziness, one will note, as is known, something remarkable in his appearance (symptomatic). A person thus afflicted often complains that something has fallen upon him, that it is as if he had a weight to bear, etc. This pressure, this weight, is not anything external; it is, as one says of an optical and an acoustical delusion, a nervous delusion, it is an inverse reflection of something internal; the sufferer feels an inward pressure as something external. It is the same with despair. The despairing person understands his despair as a suffering—instead of its being a guilt. This belongs so essentially to all despair, simply as a more extreme (but of course responsible) result of becoming and being in the state of despair that it is a sign of healing and the beginning of deliverance, if the despairing person learns to understand this differently. But as a neurotic complains about that external pressure, so the despairing person complains about despair and does not hear that it is—a self-accusation.

4. If one were to follow up the countless expressions of dizziness, he would always find that which corresponds to despair, he would always find in dizziness a similarity to despair. And many times this similarity can excellently illustrate and illuminate—indeed, in describing his situation, the person who despairs often resorts to expressions which are related to dizziness. It is only a similarity. The difference is infinite; the difference is that despair is related to spirit, to freedom, to responsibility.

5. In a healthy state or when there is equilibrium between the psychical and the physical, a man is never dizzy. It is the same with despair. If a man in relating himself to himself relates himself absolutely to God, there is no despair at all; but at every moment when this is not the case, there is also some despair. Consequently when a man in relating himself to himself absolutely relates himself to God, then all despair is annihilated. To an extent this differs from dizziness, because dizziness is a qualification of the human being psychically defined and is only a question of an equilibrium in the relation between the psychical and the physical, or, where this is disturbed, a question of bringing it about, whether the physical is primarily affected or the psychical, but where it is not a question of this relation's being for itself and thus also not a question of this relation's relating itself to a third. In the relation between two the relation is in a certain sense a third; but if this relation is not

for itself, then the relation is the third, but the relation is not a relation to a third. On the other hand, with respect to despair it is not a matter merely of equilibrium between the two, or, more accurately, the human being as spirit simply cannot have equilibrium in himself. He is, as the composite (the synthesis), a relation, but a relation which relates itself to itself. Yet he has not established himself as a relation; the relation which he is, even though a relation for itself, is established by another. Only by the relation to this other can he be in equilibrium. As soon as there is a misrelation in the relation there is despair, but as soon as he does not in the relation relate himself to the other, there is also despair.

This last formula for despair does not merely indicate a special kind; on the contrary, all despair can ultimately be resolved in this, can be traced back to this. If the person who despairs is, as he believes, aware of his despair, he no longer speaks senselessly about it as something which happens to him, and now with all his might he will fight against it, but if he is not aware that the sickness lies still deeper, that the misrelation in him also reflects itself infinitely in the misrelation to the power which established him as a relation—then he is still in the despair, and with all his supposed labor he only works himself into an even deeper despair; he loses himself in despair and is again guilty and responsible for it.

Thus despair is essentially (qualitatively) different from dizziness. Yet perhaps this comparison, which neither depends upon a vagabond whim nor presents merely a fugitive resemblance but is as well considered as it is pregnant with analogies, probably has its deeper meaning.

VIII² B 168:6   n.d., 1848

« 750

To despair over oneself, in despair not to will to be oneself, in despair to will to be rid of oneself, in despair to will to devour oneself is the formula for all despair, to which also the other form of despair, in despair to will to be oneself, can be traced back, just as above, in the despair not to will to be oneself, to will to be rid of oneself, is traced back to: in despair to will to be oneself.[418]

VIII² B 168:8   n.d., 1848

DIALECTIC, DIALECTICAL

« 751

The various ways of conceiving the dialectic of life—for example, battle against wild animals and monsters in the ballads and tales of the Middle Ages, an examination in China, doubt in the Church (travels in Greece, Pythagoras, Homer).

I A 113 January, 1836

« 752

Just as it is necessary to have a shadow, so it is necessary for every man to have a specific object for his life-polemic, a Haman[419] whom he can cudgel at every opportunity—but the remarkable thing is the innumerable variations, from those who polemicize against a particular person in the same area, in the same profession (for example, Pryssing[420]), or those who polemicize against a single concept, to those who polemicize against a whole corporation, against nations, against worlds, against eternities.

II A 654 n.d., 1837

« 753

Every truth is nevertheless truth only to a certain degree; when it goes beyond, the counterpoint appears, and it becomes untruth.

II A 751 n.d., 1838

« 754

It was only by way of an accidental and arbitrary use of his own principle that Socrates did not become positive but remained negative, for the art of questioning is simply the dialectical aspect of the art of answering (and if it is said that a fool can ask more questions than seven wise men can answer, the wise men deserve the apology explaining that they cannot answer because the fool cannot question), but Socrates used his art only polemically in order to show that John Doe could not answer. In this respect it could be a very interesting project to show how the words of Socrates,[421] where he speaks of immortality and the assumed association with Homer in the other life, etc., were also part of his wishing to question them; for either this was for the purpose of showing that they knew nothing and thus to plunge every ὕψωμα⁴²² into the *einfache* empty infinitude of ignorance, or here the positive plays an important role—questioning for the purpose of learning something. What modern philosophy has been so preoccupied with—to get all presuppositions removed in order to begin with nothing—Socrates did in his own way, in order to end with nothing.

III A 7   July 10, 1840

« 755

Scholastic dialectic is curiously reminiscent of the Gothic style, in which, amid all the apparent richness, there still is a dominant poverty, since the same poor means are used throughout, but they are combined very richly (the same syllogistic process). Incidentally, it is remarkable that the Gothic is an art form which pays most attention to mathematical relationships and yet is romantic, and the scholastic dialectic is the most subtle and yet is romantic. Thus one sees that the romantic resides in the dialectical, in the *infinite wrestling*.

III A 92   n.d., 1841

« 756

"Either/Or"⁴²³ is a talisman with which the whole world can be demolished.

III B 179:27   n.d., 1842

« 757

Even here the dialectical is present (with regard to the inwardness of religion). A person becomes apprehensively alarmed that the most frightening thing of all is going to happen. What now? Shall he beseech this thought to get out and not bother him? If he does, he is determining the religious by finite categories, which is irreligious. Shall he open himself to it? How do we stop the dialectical? (See p. 182 [i.e., VI A 46].) Shall he say, "Not my will but yours"? If this pleading expression is to be genuine and not a fraudulent phrase in the service of finite categories, he must really have considered the possibility of the very worst, but this thought is fully as bad as the actuality of the suffering. Or shall we say, perhaps, that the happiness of mankind also belongs with the religious: therefore we should banish these dark thoughts. God wants us to be happy. To be sure, but how does he want us to be happy? Now the dialectic begins again. Shall we not be happy by keeping God and losing everything—that is, not merely tolerating it but enthusiastically shouting: "Look! Here is the only, the one and only joy, the one and only happiness."

VI A 51   n.d., 1845

« 758

See pp. 182, 189 [i.e., VI A 46, VI A 51].

Even here the dialectical is present in relation to the religious. For example, if a man pleadingly tells God that he still has not completely appropriated Christianity, that he still has some doubts, and would God therefore give him time to conquer them (and thus it is always sometime later), then the dialectical seizes him at once, for this utilization of time instantaneously becomes infinitely dialectical (suppose that he dies tomorrow, and Christianity is the only salvation, and he is outside of it), because the eternal decision makes its demand with infinite haste. This proves once more how difficult it is to get a historical point of departure[424] in time for an eternal happiness.

VI A 60   n.d., 1845

« 759

Everything turns upon making the distinction absolute between quantitative dialectic and qualitative dialectic. All logic is quantitative dialectic or modal dialectic, for everything is and the whole is one and the same. Qualitative dialectic belongs in existence [*Tilværelsen*].

VII^1 A 84   n.d., 1846

« 760 *Inverted Dialectic*

If you believe that you "gain everything," then not only do you lose nothing (the theme of VI of "Exultant Notes in the Conflict of Suffering," Part II of *Christian Discourses*), but the loss itself is a gain, so that losing is not simply losing something, not simply losing nothing, but is a gaining. The everything you lose may very well be a counterfeit everything, for of the everything you win you lose nothing, but the everything you win is the true everything. And to lose a counterfeit everything is not only not losing anything, is not only losing nothing or losing nothing at all, but is a gaining.* If you completely lose all of secular man's understanding of the world and what the world is, if you lose even the slightest susceptibility to every worldly illusion, if you become as forgetful in this respect as a weak old man, if you forget everything as one who has never known it, if you are changed in the same way as a person who in a foreign country has lost all facility in his mother tongue and speaks unintelligibly, if you lose everything in this way—every such loss, if you believe that you gain everything, is a gain. Furthermore, if you lose all understanding of these sham connections, all taste for these doubtful

* *In margin:* As the butterfly *gains* by *losing* its cocoon.

benefits—if you believe that you win everything, then this loss is also a gain. Consequently, to lose is to gain. Straightforwardly, to lose is to lose; inversely, to lose is to gain.

VIII¹ A 492 *n.d.*, 1847

« 761

The point of the essentially Christian is that it is presence [*det Nærværende*]. For this reason no poet and no speaker can portray it, for they use too much imagination. This again is the very reason (this error) that the poet and speaker themselves come to be loved and esteemed. For it is *at a distance* that Christianity appears lovable in men's eyes.

Only a dialectician can portray Christianity, because by continuously taking away all illusions he drills it, so to speak, into the present. Consequently it will go hard with such a dialectical person, for Christianity which is *wholly present* is hateful and disturbing.

IX A 114 *n.d.*, 1848

« 762

The dialectical always ends in some way with pathos (this among other things was my thought regarding a problem which lies somewhere in my papers:[425] the difference between a dialectical transition and one of pathos). In the Middle Ages this appeared in a strange way in that where the dialectical ended the fantastic commenced.

An instance was provided today by Rosenvinge,[426] which prompted my thinking about it again. The question about the permissible degrees of blood-relationship in marriage naturally gave enormous impetus to medieval dialectic. The discussion finally became so involved that it could not stop, and then it was stopped—at the seventh level. Why? Can you guess? asked Rosenvinge. I answered: Because God rested on the seventh day. Precisely, replied Rosenvinge. Now I do have a kind of rapport with the Middle Ages, but oddly enough, what I really had said as a quip was right.

But here one sees pathos in the form of the fantastic, and so it always was in the Middle Ages; it was the necessary knot which had to be tied in the dialectical thread.

X¹ A 219 *n.d.*, 1849

« 763

Throughout Christendom the dialectical element has been abolished. The doctrine of "grace" is moved a whole stage too high. Christianity has demanded the genuine renunciation of the worldly, has demanded the voluntary, and then, on top of this, one is to acknowledge that he is nothing, that all is grace. Christendom removes the former entirely—and then lets grace move up; it grafts "grace," if you will, directly onto the secular mind.

x^2 A 132   n.d., 1849

« 764 *Third Sunday in Advent (Matthew 11:2-10)*

Here is a special kind of dialectic, a dialectic of quality. The most likely way to think of it is that the predecessor (John the Baptist) certifies that Jesus is the expected one. But this, dialectically, is improper subordination, because in order to certify the certifier must be superior. Therefore it is John the Baptist who sends disciples to Christ to ask him whether he is the expected one—and then it is Christ who, after having answered the disciples, concludes by certifying John the Baptist as the legitimate forerunner. It is not Christ who props himself up with the authority of the predecessor (which is a paralogism)—no, it is he who draws the predecessor within his authority and by virtue of his authority certifies him to be the legitimate predecessor. Now for the first time the predecessor's words to the believers that Christ is the expected one really have authority, now when Christ has certified that the predecessor really is the predecessor.

This seems to be a circle, but it is as far as possible from that; it is the one and only consistency within the dialectic of authority.

x^2 A 271   n.d., 1849

DISCONTINUITY, CONTINUITY

« 765

The crucial point which, if carried through, will become the classical of our time, will be the continuity of attitude rather than the continuity of concept, rooted in its necessary relationship to a literary and scientific development beginning with the Greek view or even earlier and which moves along the path of intelligence rather than that of feeling (for example, love between the sexes will not advance but, instead, what Hamann[427] calls "spiritual pederasty").

II A 661   n.d., 1837

« 766

With respect to continuity of attitude the aphorism is like the singular expressions in a language (for example, the Latin word *oppido*) which are memorials to an entire previous formation; some aphorisms are really antediluvian fossils and like such words are petrified in a particular case.

II A 709   n.d., 1838

« 767

Is there, then, no eternal agreement (*harmonia præstabilita*[428]) concluded between the heavenly and the earthly?

V A 41   n.d., 1844

« 768

The dialectic of beginning[429] is quite commonplace; yet one side is forgotten—that the beginning must be a breaking off, and therefore it presupposes a whole line of thought in order to make a beginning; for if something else is not presupposed, the act whereby I abstract from everything is presupposed. But this I cannot do, I cannot get around to making a beginning since I am using all my powers in order to abstract from everything.

V A 70   n.d., 1844

DON JUAN

«769

Don Juan has never become as popular as Faust—why?

II A 55   *n.d.*, 1837

DON QUIXOTE

« 770

I believe it could be a very interesting idea to work out a comic novel, "A Literary *Don Quixote*." A complete misunderstanding of the significance of books has developed in the learned world. Instead of their being regarded as a necessary supplement to life, primary stress is placed on reading as many as possible. The comic would then lie in the hopeless struggle to "go along with this" and, paralleling this, in the absolute failure, nevertheless, of accomplishing anything in the world, because the learned people are forever producing learned works and losing themselves in footnotes. There should be a fine irony together with the simple, unpretentious impression given by the writing—for example, a book by Claudius—who still knew how to make the whole tantalizing endeavor fruitful reading. Accompanying this, also, could be the irony which consists of his always being the one who followed along behind and picked up, like the girl who follows the harvesters. Everytime he would say something which *he thought* was something new but eventually turned out to be something old he had read (this aspect also could be very interesting), someone else would already have said it. —A whole raft of comic ideas (which would cast additional light on him) could evolve from this.

It might also be a very good feature for such a man to get the notion of writing for the common people (*Dansk Folkeblad*).[430]

I A 146   March, 1836

« 771

It is a sad mistake for Cervantes to end *Don Quixote* by making him sensible and then letting him die. Cervantes, who himself had the superb idea of having him become a shepherd! It ought to have ended there. That is, Don Quixote should not come to an end; he ought to be presented as going full speed, so that he opens vistas upon an infinite series of new fixed ideas. Don Quixote is endlessly perfectible in madness, but the one thing he cannot become (for otherwise he could become everything and anything) is sensible. Cervantes seems not to have been dialectical enough to bring it to this romantic conclusion (that there is no conclusion).

VIII¹ A 59   *n.d.*, 1847

DOUBT

« 772

Now I suppose I understand what Erdmann[431] means in saying that the eccentricity of the later position is conditioned by its transition to the essentially speculative, whereby its own presupposition (faith) is drawn along within the doubt; consequently one discovers within the immediate an element which now constrains the later position as a tendency in the totality to doubt its own presupposition. To this extent naturalism is involved, because it is a doubting of a positive position and consequently has this as its presupposition, while the content of this position is the object of its doubting.

II C 47   November 26, 1837

« 773

A condition for the unity of the divine and the human given in faith is the doubt (which corresponds to the doubt prior to the unity of the divine and the human, of the infinite and the finite, given in knowledge) whether sinful humanity, after the original relationship has been altered, is able to return to unity with God—a doubt or, a more pathos-filled and concrete expression, a *concern* (which, like everything Christian, is a concretion).

III A 4   July 5, 1840

« 774

What the skeptics should really be caught in is the ethical. Since Descartes[432] they have all thought that during the period in which they doubted they dared not express anything definite with regard to knowledge, but on the other hand they dared to act, because in this respect they could be satisfied with probability. What an enormous contradiction! As if it were not far more dreadful to do something about which one is doubtful (thereby incurring responsibility) than to make a statement. Or was it because the ethical is in itself certain? But then there was something which doubt could not reach!

IV A 72   *n.d.*, 1843

DOUBT 359

« 775

The method of beginning with doubt in order to philosophize seems as appropriate as having a soldier slouch in order to get him to stand erect.

IV A 150   n.d., 1843

« 776

Genuine skeptics do not doubt for the sake of doubting—the immanental, which ordinarily is recommended—but in order to doubt one must will it—the factor of willing must be taken away if one is to halt it—consequently one must will to stop it, but then doubt is not at all conquered by knowledge.[433]

IV B 5:13   n.d., 1842-43

« 777

Retiring Doubt
ἐποχή
(a passage in Diogenes Laertius[434] which I marked in my edition).
Inquiring Doubt
This is really not doubt, at least not *about everything*, since I rather know everything and only doubt how I shall order it, just like the poet before he catches the intimately known powers of the piece in the poetic idea.

In freedom I can emerge only from that into which I have entered in freedom or in doubt I must be presupposed to have entered. If am going to emerge from doubt in freedom, I must enter into doubt in freedom. (Act of will.)

IV B 13:21   n.d., 1842-43

« 778

It is claimed[435] that arguments against Christianity arise out of doubt. This is a total misunderstanding. The arguments against Christianity arise out of insubordination, reluctance to obey, mutiny against all authority.[436] Therefore, until now the battle against objections has been shadow-boxing, because it has been intellectual combat with doubt instead of being ethical combat against mutiny.

VIII[1] A 7   n.d., 1847

« 779

It must always be remembered that one has a responsibility in communicating doubt (sickness) when he himself does not possess the remedy. It is my theory that a person should never begin to communicate doubt before he has the remedy and should never communicate more doubt than he can put a stop to.

x^2 A 386   n.d., 1850

« 780 *The Religious—Doubt*

Official preaching has untruthfully represented the religious, Christianity, as sheer consolation, happiness, etc. Doubt has thereby won the advantage by being able to say loftily: I do not care to be made happy by an illusion.

If Christianity were truthfully represented as suffering, greater as one advances in the faith, then doubt would be disarmed, and in any case there would be no occasion to act superior—in case one wished to be spared—from suffering.

x^4 A 234   n.d., 1851

DREAMS

« 781

Men must have lived in a far simpler manner in those days when they believed that God divulged his will in dreams. Even in respect to diet they must have lived far more simply. The idyllic life of a shepherd, and living partly on vegetables—then there is a possibility. But imagine life in the great cities and the manner of life there—no wonder people attribute dreams to the devil or to demons. —Moreover, the slight significance attributed to dreams in our era is consistent with the spiritualism which constantly emphasizes consciousness; whereas that more simple era piously believed that the unconscious life in man is both the paramount and the most profound aspect.

x^2 A 258   *n.d.*, 1849

EDUCATION, UPBRINGING

« 782

All knowledge tending toward seductive opportunism is of the contemporary-practical [*realistisk*] kind. "Do you see those blue-eyed boys?" "Who knows what *nose* is called in French?" Parents must, then, make up for the lost time of their childhood and take quick correspondence courses which cover in fifty hours what otherwise takes three years; and then on occasion they can with certainty say something in German, French, or English which can just as well be said in Danish, all according to the vocabulary they learned in the latest lesson in one or another of these languages; whereas the classicists generally use their dead languages only when they cannot express themselves as felicitously or beautifully or pungently in the native language. —Those children's books[437] about child-types are also of the contemporary-practical kind; for example, those about naughty Peter would never interest children if they were as they should be and by and large do not interest them—those naughty Peter's who then become successful businessmen, or those sensible Emily's and Mary's who get happily married and enrich the world with new editions of the same kind instead of dying as spinsters for the good of the world.

II A 4   *n.d.*, 1837

« 783

When the question of education emphasizing the humanities or the contemporary-practical has once been taken up, it could perhaps turn out that instead of moving toward modern languages, natural science, etc., one will move back through Greek to Sanskrit, since education should be directed toward letting the individual traverse the stages of life in the outside world, which the world has previously traversed, until his own cue appears.

II A 5   *n.d.*, 1837

« 784

Contemporary-practical education makes people into fractional human beings like the Russian trumpeters[438] who were here. Furthermore, it occurred to me that their music approximated the sounds of nature.

II A 6   n.d., 1837

« 785

There are men who say with a certain pride: I am indebted to no other human being; I am self-taught. There are others who say: This great philosopher is my teacher, this outstanding general, and I count it an honor to be his disciple, to have fought under him—but what would you think if a person were to say: God in heaven is my teacher, and I count it an honor to be his disciple, that he educated me.[439]

III A 231   n.d., 1842

« 786

It might be worthwhile sometime to present the modern educational system—all these weighty matters in the newspapers about programs which the *Berlingske Tidende* finds so interesting, etc.: Bartholin,[440] who planned to satisfy the demands of the times by adding window ventilators, etc.! and then to present as a contrast to this the old schooling when the school was an enclosed place, when there was a certain pathos in speaking about "behind the school walls" (akin to: behind the monastery wall) instead of the school's being a throughway (Per Madsen's alley, the passageway), the time when even the parents were afraid of the schoolmaster, the great unknown, whom the pupils found terrifying when they merely entertained the thought of being sent to him, as a lamb being sent to the wolves—and now there is tea talk and coffee cackle. (One could idyllically-romantically depict a scene from the first day in school.) —The modern hypocrisy with respect to the whole educational system and upbringing—instead of working in earnest, parents and teachers assure one another how important this matter is and what they are doing—in order to get new window ventilators.

But the entire first section of the article must be done with pathos ("Our age is the age of the Reformers," etc.) in the most serious mood; otherwise one will not get the people to join in because immediately they become stubborn.

The world ultimately forces one to become so ironical that he does not even dare let irony peek through.

VIII^1 A 257   n.d., 1847

« 787

We can readily agree that everyone who can produce the children can also bring up his young (just as animals do), but to bring up human beings is a very rare gift. Yet here, too, is leveling, and the basis of this leveling is the sophism that everyone who can produce children also understands the bringing up of human beings. Perhaps in no area or development does the confusion of our age appear more ludicrous than in the educational system. In the next generation the parents will probably be so mediocre that they themselves will be very much in need of upbringing—and they are the ones who are supposed to aid the schoolmaster in bringing up the children! Especially when Grundtvig prevails and introduces the new education: proverb-games, *Saxo* and *Snørre*, the mother tongue. When the time comes, I trust I shall be dead, although I could wish that Grundtvig might still be living then.

VIII^1 A 258   n.d., 1847

« 788

There are two kinds of education. The one is Socratic—to question in order to starve out hollow knowledge. The other is the opposite: the learner asks the questions. Grundtvig really made an invaluable observation when he said once in a conversation that instruction by questioning the child is wrong; it is the child who should be permitted to question.

X^1 A 647   n.d., 1849

« 789

And so one sees what a dubious thing it is to bring up a child in Christianity. Christianity presupposes the actuality of a conviction of sin; it is the glad news that God in Christ accepts sinners; Christ is the sinner's friend—happy news for every sinner, happier in the same degree that he has become more and more deeply aware of the power of sin and the anguish of repentance.

But now the child: he has no actual consciousness of sin. What then? Well, all that talk about how good God and Christ are—the child must have his own thoughts about that—he notices that an *aber* is included: if one has sinned.

Take an analogy. Describe the family physician to a child as a very rare and lovable man, etc. What happens? The child thinks something like this: yes, it is very possible that there is such a rare man. I would gladly believe it, but I would also rather stay clear of him, for the fact that I become the object of his special love means that I am sick—and to be sick is no fun; and therefore I am far from being happy at the thought that he has been called. Suppose there is a sickly person in the family who never stops praising the physician's love; the child then thinks: yes, that's all right—if one is sick.

When one is actually sick and the sickness is serious, then one is very happy that there is a physician, but when one is not sick, has no idea at all of what it is to be sick—then "the physician" is really a disagreeable thought.

In the relation of Christianity to the child, either what is really Christian must be left out, and what does upbringing in Christianity mean then! —or it must be said, and then the child is prompted more to be afraid of Christianity than to be happy for it.

People by the millions ought to be made aware of this, if the whole matter of the multitude of Christians and the upbringing of their children in Christianity is not to be humbug. Scholarship and science want to make Christianity into mythology—and then there is an outcry. We do not notice that what generally passes for upbringing in Christianity now is really mythology.

X^2 A 455 *n.d.*, 1850

ENTHUSIASM

« 790

There nevertheless has to be a limit to enthusiasm; moreover, there are things which are so inferior that they are utterly unworthy of enthusiasm; one ought rather be chastised for enthusiasm. —Even if Pythagoras[441] was permitted to run naked through the streets crying "Eureka," we would certainly be very surprised if someone were to do the same thing upon finding a pin.

I A 197   n.d., 1836

« 791 *The Difficulty with Our Age*

On the other side of "intellect" lies enthusiasm: that is what should be fought for.

But, alas, there is no intimation of any context in the contemporary age for the person who is going to stir up this enthusiasm. Everywhere [there are] only these half-ripe and very blasé individuals who when they were very young may have had a flush of enthusiasm but soon thereafter became "reasonable." They are now so far from letting themselves be carried away that they, on the contrary, instantaneously raise the opposition of envy, and instead of taking part—think they should relate themselves to the enthusiast as a "spectator," hoping that it will all end with his becoming sensible also or getting into a mess.

Have you seen a ship aground in a spongy bog (for example, at high tide)? It is almost impossible to get it afloat again because it is impossible to drive piles; no pile reaches ground firm enough so that one can rely on it. In just the same way the whole generation is stuck fast in the spongy bog of reason; and there is no grief over it—no, there is self-satisfaction and conceit, which always accompanies reason and the sin of reason. O, the sins of the heart, the sins of passion—how much closer they are to salvation than the sin of intellect!

X^4 A 550   n.d., 1852

ENVY

« 792

Imagine an enthusiastic artist, but a young one. He produces an excellent piece of work, but see, it receives only opposition and attack. He considers it to be a rather severe judgment but nevertheless just. What does he do, then? He expands himself again and achieves an even more excellent work. But see, the opposition becomes still greater. Alas, he does not detect that it is envy[442] he is contending with, that envy is working against him, and that the opposition therefore would surely enough increase if his achievement became even more excellent. The noble, enthusiastic young man cannot understand this. This is splendid of him, and we praise him for it; unfortunately we can easily explain it, and we dare not suppress it if we were to counsel him.   VIII^1 A 155   *n.d.*, 1847

« 793 *Nonsense Breeds Nonsense*

When someone who knows something about something enters a group discussing this particular subject, conversation stops; people become silent, let him talk, and become hostile toward him because they sense his superiority. On the other hand, if someone joining the group promptly betrays by opening his mouth that he knows no more than the others, then there is lively conversation.

So it goes also in the larger areas. In literature a real achievement is never discussed, is not reviewed, but what stands no higher than the average gets big space in all the periodicals—and the real achievement becomes merely an object of silent envy.   X^3 A 729   *n.d.*, 1851

« 794 *Surprising Self-Contradiction*

There is nothing, of course, which human envy assails the way it assails the extraordinary.

And yet no one becomes a true extraordinary except through the mistreatment of men.

Consequently, envy will mistreat a person in order to prevent him from becoming the extraordinary, and no one becomes the extraordinary except through human mistreatment—consequently envy produces the extraordinary.   XI^1 A 410   *n.d.*, 1854

ESTHETICISM, THE ESTHETIC

« 795

Representing life in its three tendencies, as it were, outside of religion, there are three great ideas (Don Juan, Faust, and the Wandering Jew), and not until these ideas are mediated and embraced in life by the single individual, not until then do the moral and the religious appear. In relation to my position in dogmatics, this is the way I view these three ideas.

I A 150   March, 1836

« 796

There are certain things which never grow dull by repetition, such as when during a walk in the woods one hears the sound of reapers cutting grass in a nearby field and then they all pause at the same time to sharpen their scythes—a sound which recurs montonously as the refrain in ballads, a kind of prayer and invocation.

II A 632   n.d., 1837

« 797

Christianity does not at all emphasize the idea of earthly beauty, which was everything to the Greeks; on the contrary, in a flight of genuine humor Paul speaks about the earthenware pots in which the spirit dwells. It is a real problem: to what extent should Christ be portrayed as an ideal of human beauty—and strangely enough, although many other kinds of similarities have been discerned between Christ and Socrates, no one has thought at all about this aspect, for Socrates was, as is well known, uglier than original sin.

II A 791   n.d., 1838

« 798

It is deplorable that happiness in a later time of misfortune is like the 7 fat years in the 7 lean years, according to Joseph's interpretation of Pharoah's dream: and after them there will arise 7 years of famine, and all the plenty will *be forgotten* in the land of Egypt (Genesis 41:30), except that the phenomenon recurs not in the course of 7 years but in the course of a few days, even hours.

II A 553   August 31, 1839

« 799

..... Being with nature is just the opposite of being with people. A particular region grows in value for a person the more often he visits it, even though the moment of enjoyment becomes shorter each time; it gives increasing satisfaction because the beholder's uncertain fumbling among objects gradually ceases and he grasps the essential beauty with greater sureness, and because what he enjoys and seeks to enjoy in nature is its sameness, that which has endured from the first happy moment. In men we seek the changeable (not in the sense in which, regrettably, all men are changeable: unstable), i.e., the eternally young life, and when it is not to be found, people are boring all the more that we have anything to do with them.

III A 10   July 15, 1840

« 800

When one understands Brorson's words

> When the heart is most oppressed
> Then the harp of joy is tuned

not religiously, as they were written, but esthetically, then he has in them a motto for all poet-existence, which necessarily must be unhappy.[443]

III A 12   August 9, 1840

« 801

I have the courage to doubt, I believe, everything; I have the courage to fight, I believe, against everything; but I do not have the courage to acknowledge anything, the courage to possess, to own anything. Most people complain that the world is so prosaic that things do not go in life as in novels, where the lovers are fortunate. I complain that life is not as it is in novels, where one has hardhearted fathers to struggle against, maidens' bowers to force open, convent walls to storm. I have only the pale, bloodless, tenacious-of-life nocturnal forms to struggle against, to which I myself give life and existence.[444]

III A 218   November 16, 1840

« 802

There are animals that cannot eat as long as anyone is watching them, animals that get their nourishment in the most amazing and cunning ways—so it is with my moods: what I seem to despise, I absorb secretly and unnoticed.

III A 219   *n.d.*, 1840

« 803

The genuine moment of enjoyment also involves the mounting destruction of conditions around one. This is why the dinner scene in *Don Juan* is so interesting, for everything is taken away from him, his expensive apartment, leaving him only a little anteroom. The hypochondriac's enjoyment consists precisely in hovering this way over the wreckage and gathering together again all the power of the imagination. The hypochondriac's enjoyment is an infinite interfusing of actual and imagined pleasure. But the imagined pleasure satiates even more than the actual, and I believe that a Don Juan does not become weary nearly so quickly as a hypochondriac.[445]

III A 94 *n.d.*, 1841

« 804

Dreaming rises to ever higher powers; thus a dream within a dream-existence (whereby it becomes transformed into a kind of actuality) has an infinitely volatilizing effect. With what infinite ardor a youth can read the words of P. Møller's poem, "The Old Lover":

> Then, to my easy-chair, comes a dream from my youth
> A heartfelt longing comes over me for you
> O thou sun of women.[446]

Here the dream is in the second power for the youth; he first of all dreams that he is old in order to suck in through the funnel of a whole life the most aromatic moment of his earliest youth.

III A 95 *n.d.*, 1841

« 805

There are, as we know, insects that die in the very moment of fertilization; so it is, after all, with all joy—life's highest, most splendid moment of enjoyment—is accompanied by death.[447]

III A 96 *n.d.*, 1841

« 806

A bad conscience is capable of making life interesting; no wonder that persons in despair clutch at the very last means of diversion.[448]

III B 45:1 *n.d.*, 1841-42

« 807

He was like one of those long-legged spiders—briskly and easily and with shrewd eyes, he hurried across life.

III B 45:5 *n.d.*, 1841-42

« 808

The relation between esthetics and ethics—the transition—pathos-filled,* not dialectical—there a qualitatively different dialectic begins. To what extent are poetry and art reconcilable with life—something is true in esthetics—something else in ethics?

See Curtius, p. 388.[449]

* *In margin:* Martensen?

IV C 105 *n.d.*, 1842-43

« 809

In what relationship ought a lyrical poet stand to his poetry?

IV C 106 *n.d.*, 1842-43

« 810

This is also one of the misinterpreted climaxes that have been developed with respect to Christianity. Christ is delineated in words and descriptive phrases, and then it is said: All by itself such an idea, to say nothing of the actuality, must move every man. The fact is that it is far easier and much less dangerous for understanding to admire the idea than to believe the actuality. The result is that the essential point remains ambiguous: that this is the god [*Guden*].

As an example, a portion of Claudius, cited by Jacobi, *Collected Works*,[450] III, p. 252, may be mentioned.

V A 35 *n.d.*, 1844

« 811 *From a Possible Preface To My Occasional Discourses*

..... I wonder if a woman who embroiders a cloth for sacramental use does not make every stitch as carefully as possible and perhaps begin over again many times. Yet I wonder if it would not distress her if someone viewed it in the wrong way and looked at the embroidered pearls instead of at the altar cloth, or saw a defect instead of the altar cloth? She found her priceless joy in doing everything as carefully as possible simply because this work has no significance and ought to have none; the seamstress is unable to stitch the significance into the cloth—the significance lies within the one who looks.[451]

VI A 25 *n.d.*, 1845

« 812

Among the annoyances of life there are certain things which, although unimportant, can be quite tiresome. Among these I include: drafts, smoke, bedbugs, and chatter.

VII^1 A 59 *n.d.*, 1846

« 813

Merely to be admired by men is not stirring; this admiration becomes a supine habit, and even if what the person admired has to say is brilliant, he is not greatly benefited. But to have an opportunity to scoff at someone, to vent their evil passions against him—if they finally do get their eyes open—this is stirring. By this very scoffing they have achieved a far more inward relationship to such a person than by continuous supine admiration.

VIII^1 A 270   n.d., 1847

« 814

If I were a father or had responsibility for someone and gave an order and the person who should obey immediately went around saying that what I had said was beautiful, extraordinarily beautiful, so profoundly and supremely beautiful—I would say, "Go to blazes! Shut up and obey!" But this is the way certain orthodox people actually treat God and Christ—always this chatter about beautiful and beautiful, all this theatrical and festive dancing around. It seems to me that God and Christ must finally become weary of it and say, "Be human beings, period. Obey, fear, love, and none of this nonsense."

VIII^1 A 530   n.d., 1848

« 815

They say that preaching Christianity (even though in a mediocre and confused way) is better, after all, than nothing at all: that is, than silence. O, they are mistaken. This unfortunate preaching and preaching tends to weaken scruples in the sphere of action. As soon as a person begins to make a profession of all this preaching about lofty virtues, he continually slips backward, and the same thing happens to the hearers. The one who has silently kept to himself what was bestowed upon him has nevertheless advanced a little farther. The one who has once experienced declaiming, even to the point of crying and getting his listeners to cry, yet without doing something about it—that one is lost.

IX A 289   n.d., 1848

« 816

The difference between the distance of esthetic presentation and the actual utterance in a concrete situation is always like this: when Christ said (Luke 8:52), "The girl is not dead but sleeping [sover]," they laughed at him—when the pastor preaches about the beauty and consolation in the thought that death is a sleep, we weep. In the church there is no dead person present of whom it is said: He is not dead, he is sleeping—for we are all alive. In a situation with an actually dead person, the comic enters. As far as we are concerned, we must also remember that the expression has become for us a triviality.

Moreover, there is a remarkable distinction regarding the biblical expression *to fall asleep* [*at hensove*], which Luther also notes (Epistle for the twenty-fifth Sunday after Trinity) in I Thessalonians 4:15.

In margin: "Paul does not say: We shall not all die, but—we shall not all fall asleep [*hensove*]. For he distinguishes between dying and sleeping." Luther.

x^1 A 248 *n.d.*, 1849

« 817

There is a striking passage in the beginning of Tertullian's book about patience (translated by Ferd. Fenger in *Nyt theol. Bibliothek*, J. Møller, 1830; XVI, pp. 64 ff.). I acknowledge before the Lord God that in a somewhat rash and perhaps even shameless way I have presumed to write about patience—I, who myself am so very deficient.

This reminds me of my own collision: to what extent should a person dare present the ideal of the Christian although he himself is so far from it? A poet-existence which is not at all related in striving to the ideal, but merely presents it, is one thing; it is something else actually to strive oneself, but then poetically to present the ideal which he himself is far from being.

x^1 A 502 *n.d.*, 1849

« 818

How fraudulent all this eloquence is in relation to Christianity appears even in the otherwise noble Fénelon (*Works*,[452] translated by Claudius, II, 208, the essay on the time of fasting, confession, and prayer and the one on All Saints Day). In the first there is lamentation over those who do not press on in the God-relationship to become as a child in his mother's arms. In the second there is discussion about the saints, how in constant hand-to-hand combat with themselves they never for a moment become confident.

By and large it is the most disastrous notion in the world that "eloquence" has become the medium for the proclamation of Christianity. Sarcasm, irony, humor lie far closer to the existential in Christianity.

x^1 A 523 *n.d.*, 1849

« 819

Even though a poet suffers actual persecution from his contemporaries, he reproduces and transforms even his actual suffering into a work of art and gives his contemporaries occasion—for new enjoyment. An ethicist goes about it in earnest, actualizes it, and says: It is you, my contemporaries, of whom I speak. He does not publish plays, does not poetically hold the matter at a distance.

In a certain sense the poet is more resigned; he does not actually demand justice; he abandons his case with actual people and transposes the whole scene into the medium of imagination. But the poet lacks courage. His imagination terrifies him; so he does not dare attack the actuality directly; he distills something poetic out of it and holds himself back.

It would probably be one of the most interesting tasks to present a poet who was developed to such a degree and had come along so far that he himself really began to understand that he should make a $\mu\epsilon\tau\acute{\alpha}\beta\alpha\sigma\iota\varsigma$ $\epsilon\grave{\iota}\varsigma$ $\check{\alpha}\lambda\lambda o$ $\gamma\acute{\epsilon}\nu o\varsigma$,[453] that is, go over into the ethical, the heroic—but still could not convince himself of this and become dialectical at that point.

x^2 A 137 *n.d.*, 1849

« 820

That Victor Hugo! Pampered and practiced for years in the kind of debauchery which novelists engage in by flirting poetically with feelings that are the opposite of what their lives express—how he attacks the clerical party in a "brilliant lecture."[454]

One can imagine his anticipatory pleasure in thinking about the situation—to play "witness-to-the-truth" in this manner and to be admired, honored, and respected for it.

I support the clerical party—its cause is in the minority, and the natural sciences have conquered. And now he dishes it out! Who denies that the natural sciences also have had their martyrs; but Victor Hugo seems to have forgotten completely that their names are not from recent times, because these very sciences are now triumphant.

What tyrant, what idol is he worshiping with this speech? It is "the crowd," "voting," and the like. And has it claimed no sacrifices? It claimed Christ and Socrates and "the host of martyrs."

What about the example of what Christian religiousness is? The fool, wanting to talk about things he does not understand at all! The examples he employs are generally great and good actions, not at all specifically religious, let alone specifically Christian—paganism has the very same examples. Such great and noble deeds are honored in the world, but Christ and his followers certainly were just as practiced in high-mindedness and the like, and yet they were persecuted and put to death for it.

If I might give advice, Victor Hugo would be set aside for half a year to learn the lessons of Christianity.

To repeat, what a find for "the poet"! One can imagine the other poets being quite jealous of him since they are not members of the court. One thinks of Eugene Süe, who has written his way to being a millionaire by describing the poverty and wretchedness of actual life. Indeed, I am grateful that he was in a position to give 50 dollars to the poor, that he was the lucky person to whom this enviable opportunity was offered—to play the hero, witness-to-the-truth, with applause and laurel leaves.

x^2 A 392   n.d., 1850

« 821

Imagine the beautiful church, the festive gathering, the young women with almost childlike piety, etc. —now the organ dies away, the speaker steps forward; he talks enthusiastically about self-denial; he is moved, actually moved (this happens also to the "poet," the true poet); he moves everyone; he says, and he believes it (just as does the true poet; this is the very condition for the truth of the poem), that even if everything were demanded of him, he would be willing (perhaps we have just previously sung hymn 595 in the hymnbook) to sacrifice everything— and all are blissfully moved.

O my friend, my friend, do it—make it an actuality—and everything is changed. No longer do you charm others, but all flee from you. You only make the girls anxious and cause men to avoid you. You inspire no one, hardly get permission to enter a pulpit—in Christendom, where all are Christians and that presentation is admired, that poet-presentation.

x^3 A 151   n.d., 1850

« 822 *Pathos in Relation To Having a Conviction*

When a person is in love, he is not satisfied with saying "I am in love," declaiming it in every key, with tears in his eyes, etc. It is not even enough to say it to his beloved. He suddenly undergoes an emotional μετάβασις εἰς ἄλλο γένος* in pathos, asks to kiss the beloved and for whatever erotic love can hit upon.

It is the same with having a conviction. The person who really has no conviction, but plays at having such a thing, loves to formulate this conviction of his verbally in quiet hours, practices great art in facial ex-

* See note 453.

pressions, gestures, and voice, is even esthetically moved to tears. In short, the game has a certain esthetic truth.

But the person who really has a conviction properly undergoes a μετάβασις εἰς ἄλλο γένος; he places this conviction of his in action squarely in the center of actuality, and as a lover begs to kiss the beloved, so he feels the need to suffer for his conviction, and it satisfies the pathos in him to suffer for his conviction.

x^4 A 222   n.d., 1851

« 823 *Possibility—Actuality*

The law is: that which in possibility stirs us, awakens our admiration, etc.—the same thing in actuality we hate, curse, persecute.

x^4 A 580   n.d., 1852

« 824 *Christianity—Eloquence*

All the ancients (Plato—many places in *Phaedrus, Gorgias,* etc.; Aristotle in *Rhetoric*; the later ancients after Plato and Aristotle) were unanimous, as were other later ones who thought about the matter, that the potency of eloquence is based upon probability.

Christianity is the paradox. When it came into the world there was no eloquence (for the apostles and martyrs were far from being eloquent speakers; their lives were paradoxes and their words paradoxes just as Chistianity is).

But now Christianity has produced an effect in this world. This effect, whatever else it is, should not be confused with Christianity itself, is not Christianity itself.

This effect (the shadow of the paradox of Christianity) comes within the category of probability.

Christianity is now made probable—and so *eo ipso* the rhetoricians flourish. With reasons upon reasons, they are able to depict and depict and bellow and make all Christianity so probable, so probable—that it most likely is no longer Christianity.

At first it happened *bona fide*, with good intentions—in our time the rhetoricians know well enough that it is wrong, but they think, let us just keep on.

Christianity as probability—and served by rhetoricians—thus Christianity is abolished.

x^4 A 633   n.d., 1852

« 825

This form of Christian wilting can appear essentially only in Protestantism, for it is a taking in vain of the inwardness principle, which that honest man Luther introduced into the world, and it will appear most easily in a Protestant country that does not have the counterweight of Catholicism in the same country. Furthermore, it will appear most readily in a small country, which by being small is only too close to pettiness, mediocrity, spiritlessness; and, again, it will appear most readily in this little land if it has its own language entirely by itself and does not even through its language participate in possible movements elsewhere. It will most readily appear in such a small country if the people are prosperous, have no great differences in life, and have a common and regularized abundance, which is related all too easily to secular security. It will most readily appear in or show itself as the fruits of good days of peace—under a church leadership which fears nothing more than what Christianity has understood by "spirit": unrest, awakening, movement, but on the other hand, to use the mildest terms, it *artistically* loves tranquillity, which is the condition for being able to enjoy life. It mistakes (the better it does this, the more dangerous it is) the artistic for the Christian, human upbringing for Christian character, human cleverness for Christian recklessness, human superiority for Chistian worth, the charming magnificence of appearance for the plain everyday dress of truth, a secular, not to say pagan, Sunday-Christianity for New Testament Monday-Christianity; it mistakes artistic seriousness in playing Christianity for the real earnestness of Christianity, the idyllic enjoyment of quiet hours for New Testament painful decision; it mistakes enjoyment for suffering, winning the world for renunciation of the world, heightening life's enjoyment for painfully dying to the world; it mistakes playing over a past event for—what is Christian—making it contemporary, which means that the danger becomes actual and the suffering becomes actual and the offering which is brought is actual, and which means that it does not become, artistically accomplished, an appearance, while the actuality becomes advantage, salary, profit, pride of life, secular-mindedness.

x^6 B 233 *n.d.*, 1853

« 826 *Change of Setting (Christianity—Christendom)*

The Savior of the world, Jesus Christ, puts everything, everything, everything, both in heaven and on earth, in motion in order to make "actuality" the setting—and this he calls Christianity.

Christendom gets everything, everything, everything man can devise to prevent actuality from being the setting, devises everything possible to shift the setting, to put it at an artistic distance from *actuality*.

The one really means ushering Christianity *into* the world; the other, ushering Christianity *out* of the world.

XI¹ A 394 *n.d.*, 1854

« 827 *Symptom*

When something is about to go out of life or has gone out, the change is recognizable by the fact that the passing actuality evokes another kind of interest—for example, speculative, esthetic, artistic.

Thus it is characteristic of our age that a more and more common theme for novels (here among us even Goldschmidt[455]) is the struggle of the genius with actuality. This indicates that no one ever thinks of realizing these things in actuality (Goethe, for example, openly adulterated his genius into talent). But just the same, we have to have the struggles of genius around, and the novels supply them.

Shortsighted people make the mistake of thinking that it nevertheless is always a good thing that something is introduced this way; they even believe that in this manner it comes nearer to us or that we draw closer to it—ah, they are mistaken, this mode signifies that the actuality is becoming more distant. Thus the more artistically finished the novel becomes, the less it enters into life, the more it merely pampers and coddles people by dealing enjoyably with such things in the realm of the imagination. To believe that the artistic helps one into actuality is just as mistaken as to believe that the more artistically complete the sermon, the more it must influence the transformation of life—alas, no, the more it influences life esthetically, the more it influences away from the existential.

XI¹ A 570 *n.d.*, 1854

« 828

..... But then there is an eternity, in which there is no winter cold or summer heat, no violent storms, or the numberless mosquito bites of the thousand plagues; neither is there that which tortures just as much —human envy and pettiness and chatter and wretchedness. Nor that which probably tortures even more—well-intentioned misunderstanding. There, what you did out of love does not appear as cruelty—no, there it is clearly understood that it was love—blessed peace! There, what you did in humility does not look like pride—no, there it is clearly understood that it was humility—God be praised! There, what you did in self-denial does not look like a crime, is not punished as a crime—no, there it is decisively, clearly understood that it was self-denial—blessed reward! I ask no greater!

Yes, so it is. But if anyone happens to read this, you yourself, perhaps, he will say to himself, are they not two different things altogether: to be inflamed by the poetic beauty of such a discourse, and to be warmed by the thought itself? As I have said so often, the poetic is a dangerous gift both for the man himself and for others, lest that which ought to be a character transformation becomes an esthetic flash-fire.

And yet the situation in Christendom is such that people would regard it as surpassing every requirement if it were true that every pastor in the country is as eloquent as this—and if this were the case, it would by no means follow that there would be a single Christian.

XI^2 A 48 *n.d.*, 1854

« 829 *Hypocrisy*

A hymn, after all, is the production of a poet, and the process no doubt goes something like this: the poet is seized by a mood, and he surrenders to it.

Let us now assume that the content of such a hymn is love for his Savior, how the soul loves him, gives up the whole world to have him, etc., and this is set forth in the most glowing expressions.

That may be enough. But this hymn is supposed to be sung by the congregation. It always says *I* in the hymn; consequently, it is I who am singing. [*In margin:* for example, hymn 595 in Mynster's supplement, v. 2.[456]] Am I able to say such a thing about myself—even in the remotest manner? No; therefore either I must sit without thinking so that I notice nothing at all, or I must be forced into hypocrisy.

Generally the law for all religious communication is that it be true. Why? Because religiously there should be a turning in the direction of acting, doing accordingly, and it is precisely this turning which distinguishes the religious from the esthetic. The esthetic leads into the wild blue yonder, comes like a sneeze and goes like a sneeze. The esthetic is the moment and is in the moment; religiously, it is precisely the next moment which is decisive, for then I am supposed to act, and if I do not attend to that, I have changed that moment in the church or in the hymn singing into esthetic enjoyment.

Therefore it is very important that everything that is said and sung in church should be true, not that it should be beautiful, great, glorious, ravishing, etc., not that I start to cry while my heart beats violently—no, the question is whether I am primarily related to all this in terms of acting accordingly.

In church there is rarely straightforward talk of how things go in actuality. "But it is improper"—what?—the way things go in actuality? —this I admit. But this is precisely why it should be talked about in church, in order that things may be different. The law is always: the truer, the better—not, the more ceremonious, the better. Religiously, ceremony is "doing accordingly"; ceremony with trombone and trumpet, or ceremony in silk and velvet is, religiously, a misunderstanding, a ceremoniousness which seems to be neither a product of nor an aid to an understanding of the fact that God is spirit.

As soon as we move in the direction of getting a ceremony appropriate for what is fitting to talk about in church or, more correctly, for expressions which are suitable in church, expressions ceremonious enough to be used in church, we very easily end in shadow-boxing or in hypocrisy. For God knows that life outside does not proceed very ceremoniously at all, and nevertheless this is what should be aimed at.

XI^2 A 280   n.d., 1853-54

« 830 *The Measure of Distance*

In the early Church the most profound earnestness was encompassed by the highest pathos: by the fall of the angels the number became diminished and this then became the infinitely elevated goal for the Christian's striving—they thought that by properly utilizing this life it is possible for one to step into the place of a fallen angel. Alas, no one knew the number of these fallen angels; admittedly it was not large; and they could not agree on the extent to which God would raise the number in proportion to the original plan. But that it consequently still was possible to become an angel, that this life properly used was commensurate to this eternal decision: yes, this was the Christian's deepest earnestness, this was his highest pathos. Therefore he was willing to renounce everything, willing to suffer everything, willing to be sacrificed, and therefore every minute of the precious time was infinitely important, and he constantly called himself to account for his every deed, for every word he spoke, every thought in his mind, every look on his countenance, that he not be guilty of missing what occupied him with the highest pathos.

Now we live in such a way, especially in Protestantism, especially in Denmark, that (as sure as I am writing this) there does not live one single man who would seriously think of doing the least bit, the very least, about this conception of relating oneself with pathos to the decision to become *an angel.*

Ordinarily this matter of becoming an angel appears ridiculous to us. If anyone were to declare seriously that he was trying to become an angel, we would all laugh. When a farm lad in a comedy sings: For I am an angel with snow-white wings—we all laugh. At most we put up with a child saying to his mother sorrowing over the father's death: You must not cry; father is well off now—he has become an angel. We acquiesce to this, find it childishly beautiful. In like manner we acquiesce to a poet speaking emotionally in this way.

But if this is done in earnest, then we all laugh. We would scarcely find it as ridiculous if someone assumed that after death man becomes a camel.

Although this is how things are now, it is assumed that this same teaching of the ancient Church, still unchanged, is the religion of the country; 1,000 men have no misgivings about getting married, together with their families making a living from the teaching, and keeping up the appearance that it is the same teaching—the same teaching but with the difference that its highest pathos has become funny.

Take another aspect. In a fear and trembling of which we have hardly an inkling, the first Christians related themselves to the thought of an eternal accounting and judgment, that life was meant to be a test —frightful strenuousness—with the conclusion eternal salvation or eternal damnation.

Nowadays there is not a single man who seriously believes this talk about an accounting; it almost never appears in sermons; in daily talk a person relates to it ironically; only poets (consequently it has only poetic reality) relate themselves in esthetic earnestness to this idea: and yet it is claimed that the same teaching as in the first days of Christianity is still the religion of the country, and 1,000 men have no misgivings about getting married and making a living from it as though it were the same teaching.

It so happens that the alteration, which is the abolition of Christianity, naturally goes together with the meaningless propagation of Christianity: that all are Christians.

We are all Christians—but then we must, indeed, all become angels. Absolutely right—then it becomes ridiculous, as it has become; it would be less ridiculous if we all became camels.

We are all Christians, *ergo*, we all become blessed. Already as infants we are Christians—*ergo*, this matter of accounting and judgment becomes ridiculous. Absolutely right, it does become ridiculous, as it has become.

The only thing remaining—or, more correctly, it appeared later, but it is the only thing which is not regarded as ridiculous—this one and only thing is: making a living. xi^2 A 331   *n.d.* 1854

ETERNITY, THE ETERNAL

« 831

There is a most remarkable saying, I know not where, but one which bears the inward stamp of being the kind of utterance which, so to speak, is spoken with the mouth of a whole people. A desperate sinner wakes up in hell and cries out, "What time is it?" The devil answers, "Eternity."

I C 80   n.d., 1836

« 832

The romantic Middle Ages comprehended only one side of eternity —the vanishing of time (cf. poetry of the Middle Ages, many examples —The Seven Sleepers, etc.), but not, as the Jews, the other aspect, the closeness of time to eternity. The Middle Ages said properly: 1,000 years are but as a day; but not, one day is as 1,000 years, because although in its striving it certainly had a moment of blessedness, it did not have the blessedness of eternity. After all, there is more than a simple parallelism in the words: 1,000 years are for God as one day, and one day is as 1,000 years;[457] it is much more than a speculative statement, since it neither abolishes nor demolishes the concept of time but rather fulfills it.

II A 100   June 30, 1837

« 833

The divine can very well move in an earthly context, and it does not require the annihilation of the earthly as a condition for its own appearance, just as the spirit of God revealed itself to Moses in the burning bush, which burned *without being consumed.*

II A 351   February 3, 1839

« 834

The relationship between time and eternity is such as is found in the Hebrew word עַד, which first means *transitus* and then *eternity*, except that the eternal must not be understood merely as a denominator of *transitus* but also as a continuous state of fulfillment.

II A 570   September 13, 1839

« 835

Many people are afraid of eternity—if we can only endure time, certainly we can be ready for eternity. Therefore when one hears the lovers swear mutual love for all eternity, it does not mean nearly as much as when they pledge their love for time, because one who pledges love for eternity can always answer: You will have to excuse me for time.[458]

III A 124 *n.d.*, 1841

« 836

If a man is going to be a rural pastor for a few years, for social reasons he inquires in advance what sort of families live in the area. Should it not be even more important to consider what kind of persons one will live with in eternity and to be concerned beforehand about trying to get into good company?

VIII^1 A 10 *n.d.*, 1847

« 837 *The Gospel for the Second Day of Easter*
[Luke 24:13-35. April 15, 1847.]

Salvation invisibly accompanies the sorrowing ones along the way. Fundamentally this is always the case. The highest is always very near to a man—but his eyes are closed. So it is that eternity and the highest accompany a human being through the various ages of life; he does not become quite aware of this; he does not look closely enough, but he desires, he hankers, he is busy. Just as one can tell time by the shadow an object casts, so can one determine a person's maturity according to how close to him he thinks the highest is. Youth and adulthood run their course; it is not until evening comes and days decline that one understands that the highest is closer than all else to a man and has walked beside him all his life although he has not appreciated it—would to God that it might also "abide with him."

VIII^1 A 56 *n.d.*, 1847

« 838

A person is out upon the deep only when the eternal is his sole support.[459] Frequently a person wants to be noble but within the very same temporality over which he nobly wishes to elevate himself. This is a delusion. He wants to bring a sacrifice to the good, but he wishes to be understood by others. This is a delusion. This is precisely not to bring a sacrifice to the good.

VIII^1 A 73 *n.d.*, 1847

« 839

In margin of 838 (VIII¹ A 73):
Yet it is very tempting at the time to win support in the world.[460] Let us imagine a person who with talent and cleverness attacks the wrongs of the age—whereupon his friends and well-wishers readily say of him that *everybody* recognizes his noble character, etc.—but then the polemic is pure nonsense, for in such a case the age is indeed good.

VIII¹ A 74   n.d., 1847

« 840 *An Old Scrap*

How abstractly the eternal may be conceived is illustrated by the fact that pathos-filled speaking about the eternal and eternal life, about the hereafter, omits the names of those addressed or spoken about, because such concreteness would be disturbing. (Names like Socrates would be all right, but imagine, for example, bartender Joe Johnson!) In a funeral sermon one says: the deceased—not his name. A funeral poem can produce a comic effect by using the man's name in the verse itself. In a certain sense, a proper name is the least significant of all. Of course, everyone has a name, Joe Johnson included. But to use a name with pathos demands a great deal. —In funeral address and in a discourse about the eternal, one seeks to place the single individual under common categories, under the universal: to be a human being, to undergo something human, etc., and therefore the proper name is omitted. A pastor can begin thus: "We are gathered here to give to the grave that which belongs to the grave." If he were to begin this way: "We are gathered here to bury Joe Johnson," then it would be comical. A speaker can say: to live in this way, the deceased considered . . . . . —not, to live in this way Joe Johnson considered . . . . .

VIII¹ A 221   n.d., 1847

« 841 *Life-View: a Double Test*

Imagine a young person and how he would like *to live*—but let us make a test. Imagine a dying person, how he would like *to have lived*—and you will discover that you arrive at the very opposite result. Who then is right? Certainly the dying person. Because the young person desires for this life (these seventy years); the dying person desires for eternity or that he had lived for eternity.

VIII¹ A 543   n.d., 1848

« 842

In respect to every finite object there must be a moment when in circumnavigating it one *has* circumnavigated it, and from then on it appears smaller. It is different with the infinite. This is the reason why God grows away from most people as their conception of the infinite gradually develops. The longer and the more intensively a person is concerned with the infinite, the more he discovers how infinite it is, i.e., no matter how many relativities he puts behind himself, the infinite is still not emptied. Therefore one is almost tempted to say that for this very reason a person does not come closer to God in eternity, since the law of the relation is just the opposite—the infinite becomes more and more infinite and the person himself disappears more and more. But in eternity a person is not in the succession of time, and being *eterno modo* is the most intensive punctuality.

x^1 A 48 *n.d.*, 1849

« 843

We appropriate from Judaism everything connected with promises, promises for this life; we teach that like a Jew one is to pursue them, and, like a Jew, to see the proof of God's grace in the fact that one is rich, happily married, blessed in an earthly sense. And if this fails, then we take the other dose—Christianity's promises for eternity. And this mixture is Christianity! We completely forget that Christianity's promise of eternity is glowing because it requires such a complete forsaking of temporality, and further, that Christianity teaches specifically that to suffer in the temporal is the very mark of God's grace. We forget that Judaism's conception of eternity was weak because it promised so much in this life.

Take the gospel story about the rich man.[461] The only omission (yet this needs to be pointed out in order to illuminate the essentially Christian) is that he felt perfectly assured of being in the grace of God. Why? Because he was successful in everything. Luther[462] also makes this observation in his sermon on the gospel account of the rich man and the poor man.

The fact is that the Jews and men in general make God too small and not spirit enough. He repays the weak and the sensuous immediately; he expresses his wrath and displeasure immediately. With the superior one he does not contend in this way; "spirit" does not contend in this fashion. "Spirit" must express that the earthly is the indifferent and express this precisely by suffering as the mark of the God-fearing man and success in everything here in the world as the mark of the ungodly man. Everything comes his way as if he were in a state of enchantment; he becomes more and more confident and finally entirely confident in the delusion of being in the grace of God, of being God's favorite—and then he dies and goes to hell. Humanly speaking, it is almost as if God were too cruel to the ungodly man by letting him have success in everything this way.

x^1 A 426   *n.d.*, 1849

« 844 *Christianity Wants To Make Eternity Easy, but Makes This Life Hard*

Christianity really presupposes that eternity engages a man absolutely. Christianity knows the remedy for this concern.

But in the ordinary course of living we never dream that eternity is supposed to have any significance for us: we are all going to be saved—no question about that.

Therefore Christianity is to be accommodated within this life, as an aid in this life. But this it simply cannot be; it can only make this life as strenuous as possible.

Christianity assumes the concern for everything to go well for one in eternity to be so great that in order to find peace in this respect one finds joy in—yes, gives thanks for, God's making this life somewhat more, yes, infinitely more strenuous than it is when a person does not get involved with Christianity.

By itself, to have a genuine concern for one's eternal salvation (as Christianity requires), this alone is an enormous weight compared to the manner of living that leaves the eternal an open question.

x^2 A 617   *n.d.*, 1850

« 845 *Human Dishonesty*

Often there is lament over the great amount of dishonesty in trade and business, etc.

Ah, the tragedy is that in no relationship is there so much dishonesty as in the most important one, which concerns the soul's salvation, eternal happiness, Christianity—that here even the most honest person of all is somewhat dishonest. And why is he like this; what is the source of this? It comes from the fact that every man is afraid of eternity, of its enormous power, afraid of getting involved in earnest with it. And just because we human beings are all afraid, we share a kind of mutual human honesty—we all stick together in being dishonest.

XI^1 A 326   *n.d.*, 1854

« 846 *The Terms of Salvation. Change. That They Are Unchanged.*

Let me talk figuratively. Think of a fisherman. He owns a splendid net which he has inherited from his father.

Year after year he puts out his net—but gets no fish.

What is the matter? What can it be? "Sure enough, I know," says the fisherman: "The fish have changed; in the course of time they have decreased in size; if I want to catch them, I must get hold of a net which is not made for large fish."

The net, however, totally disinterested in whether fish are caught or not, is quietly aware of being a splendid net and consequently could not dream of changing because the fish have changed.

Now think about eternity and the terms of salvation.

From generation to generation, steadily, incessantly, the cost of being Christian has become cheaper and cheaper, the terms of salvation have become easier and easier. A generation of jubilant millions, served by huckster clergy, has replaced the other and is not merely happy over the easy terms gained but proud of it, because this process of rendering Christianity worthless or of taking Christianity in vain has occurred in the name of perfecting Christianity.

Eternity has quietly looked on and observed: I am catching no one.

But—eternity is not subjective like the fisherman, does not need men—this is an inept comment. It is men who need eternity, to be caught is to be saved—also an inept comment. In being subjectively objective like the net, eternity is just as objective as it is subjective, or eternity is at one and the same time the fisherman and the net—consequently it does not change; consequently man has succeeded only in fooling himself.

XI^3 B 124   *n.d.*, 1855

« 847

As far as Christianity is concerned, it is not at all eternity's intention to want to catch men in the egotistical sense that the fisherman wants to catch fish. Eternity wants to save men. So it does not alter itself because men prefer to fool themselves and to be fooled.

The Moral

The fisherman needs the fish; *ergo*, he changes the net. If, on the contrary, it is the fish that need to be caught—and this is the Christian way—to be caught is to be saved—then there is nothing else to be done, the fish must change, which is impossible as far as the metaphor is concerned but not in respect to what the metaphor signifies.

By becoming smaller the fish can fool the fisherman if he does not decide to change the net; by changing the terms of salvation man succeeds only in fooling himself—because eternity does not change the terms. The fish is right and behaves sensibly in doing everything to avoid being caught; man is self-deceived when he tries in every way to avoid being caught, is happy at not being caught, or is happy at being caught in a way that is not the right way—he is self-deceived, for to be caught is to be saved.

XI^3 B 125:8 *n.d.*, 1855

THE ETHICAL, THE ETHICAL CONSCIOUSNESS

« 848

There are people who, when they really want to accomplish something, take such grandiose steps that they completely miss the mark, just like the dwarf in the fairy story who, when he wanted to pursue the fleeing princess and prince, put on seven-league boots. Not until he reached Turkey did he remember that the runaways probably did not use the same kind of transportation.[463]

I A 84 n.d., 1835

« 849

It is odd that our age, which is so enthusiastic about utility, does not go so far, for example, that it abolishes all funerals and piety regarding the dead and recommends burning the bodies. Surely artificial fertilizer could be made in this way.

I A 124 February, 1836

« 850

It is remarkable to see how in all life-relationships and movements (political, religious, etc., also in small matters) a point of view has developed called the middle way, but which I would rather call *life's neuter gender*. This certainly is the most tiresome kind of person one can have anything to do with. Such people are pure hermaphrodites.

I A 141 March, 1836

« 851

The relationship between law as the purely external, objectively given, and its adoption within the individual can be seen, by way of example, in a doctor's dietetic prescriptions: first, it is almost impossible to follow them, since the doctor really ought to be there every moment to tell the patient what he should do, and also, even if the patient could follow them, they bring no "salvation" because improvement depends basically upon whether he assimilates the diet essentially and then with consummate discretion judges particular situations.

I A 152 April, 1835

« 852

Antiquity does not have an ideal to strive for; the romantic, on the other hand, does have. This is because antiquity must disapprove every endeavor which goes beyond the world of actuality, since perfection, or at least the most perfect that is possible in the world (which here are conflated, because otherwise men would have to be counseled to strive beyond the actual) is in the realm of actuality. It has no ideal, neither moral, intellectual, nor esthetic. It has no ideal—or, what amounts to the same thing—it has an ideal attainable in this world. The moral ideal is replaced by adaptation to whatever the conventional structure of a particular time indicates as appropriate for a contemporary. The ideal of knowledge is replaced by the indigent perception of the contemporary mind as the highest for a contemporary (an illustration of a striving for the ideal of knowledge may be seen in the zeal of the orthodox for a divine word—no matter how it twists and turns, eternally and immutably raised above all time and the vicissitudes of time. Yes, even if it is not entirely his in this life, the orthodox believes that it will come in the next: but, take note, as an ideal, something the Hegelians, for example, can never conceive; they think that in the course of time will come a greater intelligence but never as ideal, neither in respect to the level of knowledge of bygone time, which [sic]   I A 221   n.d., 1836

« 853

..... The esthetic ideal is replaced by national taste, yes, town-and-class taste, and the most correct copy of it.   I A 222   August 11, 1836

« 854

The marvelous way in which something that happened long ago can suddenly leap into the consciousness is really remarkable—for example, the memory of something wrong, something one was scarcely conscious of in the moment of action—a flash of lightning which intimates a great thunderstorm. It does not step forward but actually leaps forward with tremendous power and claims to be heard. And that, broadly speaking, is the way we should understand that passage in the gospels which says that a man will be held accountable on the day of judgment for every improper word he has spoken.[464]

I A 254   October 8, 1836

« 855

Outline for a sermon. "Why do you think evil in your hearts?"[465] —Introduction: this fits the whole life of the Pharisees—their external holiness—are not thoughts, then, duty-free—no, on the contrary, they pay sin a much higher duty than words and deeds. They invite self-excuse—in connection with words and deeds we hear more rarely the excuse: I couldn't help it because it is in my nature. They invite continuation, because they can be kept hidden. —They hinder conversion far more than anything else, because we escape the punishment and suffering and humiliation here in the world, which are also a call from God.

II A 13   n.d., 1837

« 856

It has often amazed me to see otherwise strict Christians tempted so easily by little things that others would never begin to regard as an obstacle to be overcome. (I have seen them craving a little bit of the forbidden food, have seen them willing to pay three hours of pain for one moment's sensuous enjoyment of something, have seen them making it an object of extensive investigation and then imagining a great victory when they restricted the enjoyment considerably.)

How can this happen? Most likely because from the ordinary point of view we regard it as a matter of indifference, which therefore does not tempt, or when participating in such things we regard them as insignificant and do not share the common Christian view that the devil tempts them precisely in such things. To this extent there may be something to the proof, often used by Catholics, of the idea that pagans cannot be saved in spite of the fact that they are moral people, as has been argued in their defense—since Satan was sure of them he did not tempt them.

II A 39   n.d., 1837

« 857

How typical of the story of the human heart is the tendency of the Jews, when things went wrong for them in the world, to shift their hope for a savior to expectation of an earthly messiah! How reminiscent of the many daydreams of money which is going to cure and comfort, of a prosperous marriage, of appointment to a particular public office, etc.

II A 150   August 31, 1837

« 858

In margin of 857 (II A 150):
Every Christian has also had his earthly messiah.

II A 151   n.d., 1837

« 859

It is always the Moses in our life (our whole, full, poetic life-power) who does not enter the Promised Land; it is only the Joshua in our life who enters; as Moses is related to Joshua, so the poetic morning-dream of our life is related to its actuality.[466]

II A 165   Sept. 23, 1837

« 860

There is something curiously farcical in reading that a brownie (a kind of elf; see Grimm, *Irische Elfenmärchen*, p. xlix) appreciates most of all a piece of cast-off clothing.* It is curious enough to read of their hankering after something to eat (which the brownies have in common with many other similar beings), but to see such a character walking around in cast-off clothing must be truly laughable.

II A 173   October 8, 1837

« 861

* *In margin of 860* (II A 173):
Thus in memory one often turns back in deep melancholy to the threadbare actuality of childhood and, dead to the world, wraps himself in it as in a shroud.

II A 174   June 8, 1839

« 862

Why are strict Christians, unlike the rest of us, easily tempted by little things (food and drink)?

II A 593   n.d., 1837

« 863

Happy is he in whom the sense of the universal relationship of responsibility has not yet awakened, who acknowledges another person as master—therefore the boyhood years are so happy—one makes a racket, gets a licking,[467] etc., and tries to trick his teacher.

II A 671   n.d., 1837

« 864

This is how one knows that he has become a Christian—he acts toward another as did Rebecca: I shall not only give you water to drink but your camels also.

II A 759   July 18, 1838

« 865

On the basis of the *a priori* which lies in purpose as compared to temporal, successive development, intentions toward the good are very tempting and often contain a kind of narcotic that develops an opinion and not an elasticity that generates energy.

II A 303　December 2, 1838

« 866

It is noteworthy to see in the pietistic controversies after Spener's death that the orthodox tried to maintain that there is a host of moral adiaphora; whereas the pietistic movement maintained particularly that there is a host of intellectual adiaphora. Christ's declaration:[468] Let what you say be simply "Yes" or "No"; anything more than this comes from evil—certainly holds true, yet not only with respect to the moral but also to the intellectual.

II A 306　December 18, 1838

« 867

The confusing thing about us is that we are simultaneously the Pharisee and the publican.

II A 322　January 7, 1839

« 868

Only when a life-view is no longer a thought-experiment among other thought-experiments,* but rather an outlook which precisely by being this has a *drive* (an inner, immanental power) requiring actualization and because of this posits itself at every moment, only then does the true cleavage in a man appear. Only then does one feel that he battles not with a volatile phantom but with a power, a body, a body of sin (Romans 7) which one must get torn out, whatever the cost; that it is a dying-away-from (which like every death occasions tears in the beginning, bitter because we must be separated from something in which we have lived and which we often have an unreasonably hard time to forget, but soon mild and quiet because we feel the Lord's consolation, soon tears of joy, when we see the end draw near); that it is a divine kingdom, a *gegliedert* order of things that cannot be taken by force, in which we should be placed.

* *In margin:* not a "Now you can *choose.*"

II A 430　May 17, 1839

« 869

According to the way the reformers enjoin faith, it follows that good works ought have the same relationship to man as charity according to Christ's command—the right hand is not to know what the left hand is doing.[469]

II A 447　May 28, 1839

« 870

There is a view of life which is achieved with tears but which is also stronger than iron, like that shirt:[470] *"wenn sie ihn unter Thränen spinnt, mit Thränen bleicht, ein Hemde draus unter Thränen näht, schützt mich des besser als alles Eisen, es ist undurchdringlich."*[471] But unlike that shirt, this view of life protects only him who himself has prepared it, not everyone, as did that iron shirt.

See *Magyarische Sagen*, by Graf Mailath, p. 152. [472]

II A 449   May 29, 1839

« 871

The position of Christianity in relation to the universally human position is like that of the Church to the state: it does not deny the state except insofar as the state seeks to encroach upon it.

II A 450   June 5, 1839

« 872

If for a moment I were to employ de Wette's*[473] terminology, I would say that moral obligation is the truth of obligation to law; moral obligation is the invisible church within the visible church of lawful obligations, and because of this legal obligations can be suspended although moral obligations are realized.

* *In margin:* the German Uvette, usually called de Wette.

II A 465   July 3, 1839

« 873

By this we can see that love has overcome the world—that it repays evil with good.

II A 501   n.d., 1839

« 874

In the sense that true Christian love has no enemies (love your enemies)[474] and thus to that extent is all in all (as the relationship of the genitive and dative), in the same sense God is all in all in the relationship of the nominative and accusative, but the reality of evil is not hereby denied—yet with this difference, that the element of humbly dispensing with judging the world, which is in part the basis for love to enemies, is of course not found in God.

II A 502   n.d., 1839

« 875

It is still the greatest, the *roomiest** part of the world, although spatially the smallest, this kingdom of love in which we can all be landholders without the need of one person's holding crowding another's—yes, it rather extends another's holdings (out of the eater came something to eat[475]). On the other hand, the kingdom of anger and hate—how small it is in its egotistic isolation and how great the space it demands—the whole world is not spacious enough, because it has no room *for others.*

II A 513   July 25, 1839

« 876

* *In margin of 875* (II A 513):
Just as we sometimes hear people say that it is inconceivable that all thoughts can be *contained in one head.*

II A 514   *n.d.*, 1839

« 877

The Christian can certainly be unhappy in the world, can sorrow over it; yet this is not a sorrow which he carries alone, but God helps him with it if he is not too proud to take God into it. It is as Kingo says:
>   Weep, my eyes, but let your tears
>   flow onto Jesus' breast,

for this is the true temple poor-box into which the Christian, poorer even than the poor widow, puts down the only thing he has, for, as Peter said, gold and silver has he none.[476]

II A 530   August 8, 1839

« 878

Out of the eater came something to eat[477]—just as we say upon seeing a certain kind of sea plant: There are tench and eel here, etc., but do not reason that because these plants are present, the fish are there, but rather, because these fish are present, therefore there are these plants—so also in spiritual things all receptivity is productivity.

II A 536   August 8, 1839

« 879 *On Perseverance in Expectations*

The world, too, teaches this and censures the childish impatience that wants to reap just when it sows.
We need to ask: What is the object of your expectations?
If it was something earthly and perishable, then of course the fulfillment could come too late and your impatience could be reasonable. If it was honor, power, and earthly domination that your youth thirsted for, then of course it could come too late; for what good is it to you when your arm is feeble, when with dismay your age more and more loudly

reminds you that everything earthly is vanity, what good is it to you that you are offered the scepter which you cannot wield? —Or was it pleasure's gaudy diversions that deluded you in your youth, that your soul thirsted for; yes, of course, they could come too late, for you would almost take it as mockery if in your feeble old age you are offered the cup of intoxication for which in your youth you vainly reached.

But if your expectation is oriented toward the imperishable, the heavenly, the eternal, then the fulfillment can never come too late, for even though you might grow as old as Anna,[478] as gray-haired as Simeon, even though you might become as unfortunate in the world as Lazarus, the hope of God's glory will nevertheless pour its blessing upon you, if not before, nevertheless in the hour of death. (Paul, II Corinthians 5.)

II A 578   *n.d.*, 1839

« 880

Semi-pelagianism is no position at all; it runs out into the infinite details of particular phenomena *semper numularii instar deum computatione instruit, semper inter arma nunquam neque beatitatem pacis neque lætitiam vitcoriæ reportat, semper anxie!**[479] It maintains that perhaps one individual needs it and another does not need it. If we ask why not, it can answer nothing but merely says: Perhaps that is the way things are. If we ask why that is, it may answer: Because things are factually thus and so, or because a greater depravity requires it. Then if the question is raised about how great this needs to be, there is no answer at all—

* *semper indagans, verbosus garrulus nunquam propositi potitus habeant, valeant vivant cum illa—*[480]

III A 23   *n.d.*, 1840

« 881

On good works—
Shade—the right hand does not know what the left hand is doing.

III A 28   *n.d.*, 1840

« 882

It is not deficiency which awakens true ideal longings in men, but superabundance; for a deficiency still has within it an earthly skepticism.[481]

III A 63   *n.d.*, 1840

« 883

The negative, polemical relationship in which the pagan world placed future existence [*Existents*] and present existence is apparent in their belief that everyone upon arrival in Elysium had to drink from the river Lethe.[482] The Christian view teaches that a man must make an accounting of every improper word, which among other things certainly implies the total presence of the past, even though another Lethe will take away that which gnaws and corrodes.

III A 214   n.d., 1840

« 884

How beautiful, how true, and how profound is what J. Boehme says somewhere:[483] In the moment of spiritual trial [Anfægtelse] the important thing is not to have many thoughts but to hold fast to *one*. God, give me the strength for this.

III A 125   n.d., 1841

« 885

Everyone who bases his life upon something accidental[484] leads a robber-existence [Røverexistents], be it upon beauty, wealth, background, science, art—in short, upon anything which cannot be every man's fate. And even if you are successful in carrying this out—and if then a young person turns to you with all the confidence and prerogative of youth, and you cannot deny youth the prerogative of asking you how you have grounded your life—would you not be ashamed, for you would not be able to divulge to him all your cunning and craft, would you?

III A 135   n.d., 1841

« 886

It is really good once in a while for a person to feel that he is in God's hands and not everlastingly and always sneaking around in the familiar nooks and crannies of the town, where he always knows a way out.

III A 154   n.d., 1841

« 887

It is curious: in the gospel story about the good Samaritan, Christ gives his own definition of the word *neighbor*. Generally one believes that one's neighbor is the one from whom he can most immediately get something. Christ seems to suggest that a person should not try to have many people whom he can call *neighbor* as much as himself to be a neighbor to many, for he says: Who is his neighbor?—and the answer is: He who helped him. That is, not the one he could most immediately have counted on but the one who himself became a neighbor.

III A 184   n.d., 1841

« 888

Passion is still the main thing; it is the real dynamometer for men. Our age is so shabby because it has no passion. If my good Jonas Olson[485] really could hate as no one has ever hated before, as he wrote in that memorable letter, I should count myself fortunate to be his contemporary, fortunate to be the object of this hate—this is still a battle.

III A 185   n.d., 1841

« 889

The main point is still that one should not be diverted by the external.[486] When, in order to subvert the position that there is an absolute in morality, an appeal is made to variations in custom and use and such shocking examples as savages putting their parents to death, attention is centered merely upon the external. That is to say, if it could be proved that savages maintain that a person ought to hate his parents, it would be quite another matter; but this is not their thought; they believe that one should love them, and the error is only in the way of expressing it. For it is clear that the savages do not intend to harm their parents but to do good to them.

III A 202   n.d., 1842

« 890

It certainly would not be appalling that I should suffer punishment which I deserved because I had done wrong; but it would be appalling if I or any man should be able to do wrong and no one punished it. It would not be appalling that I should wake up in anxiety and horror to the deceit of my heart; it would be appalling if I or any man should be able to deceive his heart in such a way that no power could awaken it ..... I will conduct myself at this moment as I consider best, but then I beseech you, O God, that, if I have acted wrongly, your declaration of punishment will not give me peace until I have realized my delusion, for it is not important that I go free but that the truth take place. It is not that I would hide or hide my action from myself; I know and I want to know what I have done; and even if I awakened in the middle of the night I still would want to be able to say definitely what I had done. I do not want to deceive myself; I want to know clearly and specifically what will at some later time be either to my shame, yes, to my horror, or to my peace and joy.

III A 230   n.d., 1842

« 891

Doubt is produced EITHER by bringing reality into relation with ideality.
    this is the act of cognition.
    insofar as interest is involved, there is at most a third in which I am interested—for example, the truth.
OR by bringing ideality into relation with reality.
    this is the ethical.
    that in which I am interested is myself.
    it is really Christianity which has brought this doubt into the world, for in Christianity this self received its meaning. —Doubt is conquered not by the system but by faith, just as it is faith which has brought doubt into the world. If the system is to set doubt at rest, then it is by standing higher than both doubt and faith, but in that case doubt must first and foremost be conquered by faith, for a leap over a middle link is not possible.

In a *stricter sense* doubt is the beginning of the ethical, for as soon as I am to act, the interest lies with me inasmuch as I assume the responsibility and thereby acquire significance.

                                IV B 13:18, 19   *n.d.*, 1842-43

« 892

The thesis that virtue is the way of moderation Aristotle maintains[487] only with respect to the so-called moral virtues. Here the observation is entirely right, because what they have to do battle with is neither good nor evil, for inclination and disinclination are in and for themselves neither good nor evil.

In margin: the moral virtues have to do only with the irrational part of the soul. See Bk. VI, ch. 1 and 10:8.

                                      IV C 16   *n.d.*, 1842-43

« 893

In margin of 892 (IV C 16):
That he does not believe virtue to be the postulated midpoint at all times can be seen in his distinction between virtue and voluntary acts. The voluntary act is the discreet; virtue is the continuous. He therefore says[488] most profoundly that free action lies totally in a man's power; virtue does not, except with respect to the beginning, because it is a competence (continuity) 3:8.

                                      IV C 17   *n.d.*, 1842-43

« 894

Is the good good because God wills it, or is it good in and for itself?
  Hobbes and the Englishman King.[489]
If the good is good in and for itself, how then is God free in relation to it; how [then, is there] human freedom?

IV C 72   n.d., 1842-43

« 895

Generally every ethical[490] teaching, including pure philosophy (in contrast to that which deceitfully has blended with Christianity) comes to the same point—that knowledge (wisdom) is virtue.[491] Socrates presented this thesis; later, all Socratics. —Christian teaching is the opposite—that virtue is knowledge. From this comes the expression—to do the truth. —At the same time it is still always a problem for Christianity to establish on the basis of spirit an existence [*Existents*] which is indifferent with respect to knowledge so that one could be perfect although completely ignorant. The question is whether knowledge is accented first or last. But even then a very dialectical deliberation is necessary.

IV C 86   n.d., 1842-43

« 896

Every individual life is incommensurable for conceptualization; the highest therefore cannot be to live as a philosopher—In what is this incommensurability resolved? —In action—That in which all men are one is passion. Therefore everything religious is passion, hope, faith, and love. —Greatness is to have one's life in that which is essential for all and therein to have a difference of degree. —To be a philosopher is a distinction just as much as to be a poet.

IV C 96   n.d., 1842-43

« 897

Christ hid something from his disciples because they could not bear it. He did it out of love, but is it ethical? This is one of the most difficult ethical doubts—if by suppressing something I can save another from pain, do I have the right to do it, or am I not trespassing on his human existence [*Existents*]?[492]

In margin: Right here lies the paradox of my life; in relation to God I am always in the wrong, but is it a crime in relation to men?

IV A 73   n.d., 1843

THE ETHICAL, THE ETHICAL CONSCIOUSNESS 401

« 898

The more a man is able to forget, the more metamorphoses his life can pass through; the more he is able to remember, the more divine his life becomes.[493]

IV A 82 n.d., 1843

« 899

One ought to be so developed esthetically that he is able to grasp ethical problems esthetically[494]—otherwise it goes badly with the ethical. How many are able to do this? Daub[495] says somewhere that when a soldier stands alone with a loaded rifle at his post near a powder magazine on a stormy night turbulent with thunder and lightning, he thinks thoughts others do not think. Quite possibly—if he is developed enough esthetically; quite possibly, if he is esthetically developed enough not to forget. How many people could be told about the ascetic who lived in solitude and drank only dew and rain and who, the moment he forsook solitude, got a taste of wine and took to drink—how many could hear this but find nothing more in it than a curiosity? How many are there who feel the anxiety and trembling, who comprehend the ethical problem?

IV A 92 n.d., 1843

« 900

The other sermon[496] could also be planned in another way. It could begin with the words:[497] If you then, who are evil, know how to give good gifts to your children, how much more will God know it. It should then begin with doubt as to whether a man really knows how to give good gifts. This doubt should be carried to the paradoxical extreme where even love (purely human love) becomes a doubtful good gift. It would turn out, then, that Christ's words were more a kind of irony than we commonly understand them to be. After that the development should proceed.

IV A 98 n.d., 1843

« 901

In margin of 900 (IV A 98):

People have little understanding of what constitutes the good. They are informed about weather and wind (see, for example, a place in the gospel:[498] When the sky is red, you say it will be stormy). Job 28:1-11. v. 12.

IV A 100 n.d., 1843

« 902

The highest expression of an ethical view of life is repentance, and I must always repent—but precisely this is a self-contradiction of the ethical, whereby the paradox of the religious breaks through, that is, atonement, to which faith corresponds. Speaking purely ethically I must say that even the best that I do is only sin; consequently I will repent of it, but then I cannot actually get around to acting, because I must repent.[499]

IV A 112   n.d., 1843

« 903

It certainly is no sophistical observation to say that a person holds in his soul at every moment the possibility that God at this very moment can still make everything good. If he does not sustain this possibility, he makes himself impotent in despair and is not even in a position to accept the good when it actually is offered.

IV A 131   n.d., 1843

« 904

The main thing is nevertheless that one is entirely honest toward God, does not seek to get away with anything, but drives through until he himself gives the explanation; whether or not it is as one might like to be, it is still the best.

IV A 134   n.d., 1843

« 905

Life first begins to be difficult when the life-task itself becomes dialectical: i.e., when the previous dialectic must constitute the task. This is the case whenever freedom enters the discussion. A man is mentally unhinged; human power and the freedom of will can indeed work against it —here the problem is: shall he persecute himself, as it were, and perhaps go mad over his inability to overcome it, or shall he humble himself under it? And yet is not this humility weakness? Shame on them who whimper when the task itself is not dialectical.

[<i>A page removed from the journal.</i>]

IV A 149   n.d., 1843

« 906

It is really a defect in personality if a person can give himself to another in such a way that he keeps himself in reserve. A truly mature personality belongs to itself as a dove belongs to its familiar dovecote—sell it to as many as one will, it always comes back to the dovecote.

IV A 155 n.d., 1843

« 907

The first part[500] contains melancholy (egotistic-sympathetic) and despair (in reason and passion). The second part therefore teaches despair and choosing oneself. Even the essay on Don Juan has melancholy, an enthusiasm which robs him of understanding, a dreaming, almost deranged, reveling in fantasy. The first part is therefore essentially paradoxical—that is, it does not contain this or that paradoxical thought, but it is sheer passion, and this is always paradoxical and must not be destroyed; for the paradox is the passion of thought. The motto[501] also suggests that it is sheer passion in its arbitrariness.

The first part continually gets stranded on time. This is why the second part strongly affirms it, since it is shown in the first discussion that the esthetic is broken upon time, and in the second discussion it is shown that the meaning of finitude and temporality is to be able to become history, to gain a history.[502]

Fantasy like this always creates melancholy; therefore the first part is melancholy.

IV A 213 n.d., 1843

« 908

The point in the whole story lies in Abraham's being genuinely assured that he loves Isaac more than himself. This doubt is dreadful; who decides it; assurances to the Cherethites and Pelethites are of no use; here it is a question of the God-consciousness in an individual; then the outward manifestation itself, the deed, is in contradiction to it. If Abraham does it and then becomes uncertain about himself, he can be certain that no one will understand him, that he either will go mad or will win God-consciousness within himself again. If he sacrifices him because of duty, it is less significant, for placed in the context of duty his son has the position of a single human being (in the same way as when that Roman allowed his son to be executed because he had committed an offense); but if he violates duty and the whole thing appears in the context of a test, then it is of extreme importance. He who denies himself, sacrifices himself out of duty, and gives up the finite in order to grasp the infinite is safe enough, and he must always be understood within the universal, for duty is the universal; but the one who gives up duty in order to grasp something still higher, if he is in error, what salvation is there for him? —The terrifying thing in the collision is this—that it is not a collision between God's command and man's command but between God's command and God's command.

IV B 67 n.d., 1843

« 909

You believe that God is love and that he guides everything into good for you. But what image do you have of this, what instructive representation of this love, if you yourself do not develop your life accordingly. If you are not moved by the pleas of the destitute, if you can walk past him and forget, is it not as if in that moment God forgot you, that it must go with you in the world the very same way you let it go with others?

IV B 170 n.d., 1843-44

« 910

Whenever I really want to convince myself how deplorable it is to want to influence people in the sense of expecting to make a visible harvest at some time, I read the scene in Shakespeare's *Julius Caesar*[503] where Brutus and Anthony hold conversation over Caesar's corpse.

IV A 172 n.d., 1844

« 911

..... It is only the day-laborers in life who, like factory workers, require pay every Saturday night and cannot possibly wait any longer (which is not so strange, after all, because that for which they work would become all too meaningless if they were to wait long for it), but the mature soul has the courage to make all of temporality into a week of work without pay.

IV A 179 n.d., 1844

« 912

A beginning is always a resolution, but a resolution is really eternal (for otherwise it is only nonsense and something which under later scrunity will appear as skepticism). For example, I decide to study logic. I put my whole life into it. Otherwise it is no good, and I am studying only for the next examination. At the same time the doubt arises whether this can be life's definition and whether it is justifiable to use one's whole life for this. If I do not have this reflection or something similar, then I do not begin by virtue of a resolution but by virtue of a capacity or talent (or the foolishness of a fad, etc., in order to be along) and consequently make a beginning spontaneously, which explains nothing at all.

Why have modern science and scholarship been so deceitful and remained silent about how the individual goes about this? No one can understand them, because they do not know how they themselves did it. Thus even significant writings often conceal an untruth, because the writer has not understood himself but has, of course, understood a certain area of learning—the latter is much easier than the former.

V A 72   n.d., 1844

« 913

To make health the highest good is an animal principle;[504] this is the way an animal is regarded—if it is not in good health, it is not worth anything. But man is spirit. To enunciate this principle is sin against the Holy Spirit, the most terrible revolt against fellow-feeling.

V B 148:38   n.d., 1844

« 914

..... but did not know himself in relation to himself.

In margin: there can be changes and thereby one is changed (another becomes the strongest, the most handsome, the richest, etc.: basically there are implicit in this person's self-relationship to his environment all of the sophistic positions Socrates fought against, that the strongest is the just, etc.).

V B 207:3   n.d., 1844

« 915

The thinnest beer can effervesce just as much as the strongest, but the difference is that the thin beer holds its foam a minute at most and the strong beer holds it in proportion to its strength. It is the same with men. The difference is not that some are able to effervesce and others are not; they all have a time for that. The question is—how long does it hold?

VI A 7   n.d., 1844-45

« 916

Of all the brilliant sins, affected virtues are the worst.

VI A 27   n.d., 1845

« 917

Sometimes a person becomes impatient because he is not more successful in willing the good, but this impatience is still not sorrow over his sins but an act of violence against God and a lack of sincerity.

VI A 34   n.d., 1845

« 918

Addition to 917 (VI A 34):
The first and foremost ingredient of all reformation is a humble recollection of one's weakness, what it was like. Then at times a person may have an experience similar to that of a released criminal when a runaway prisoner, like a frightening memory, passes or approaches him—in much the same way there comes at times the memory of something put away long ago and he is made anxious. He becomes impatient and will not acknowledge this; he has lost out. Then he whines, thinks it unjust to be reminded of it, instead of being humbly grateful that he is now better.[505]

VI A 35 *n.d.*, 1845

« 919

Two housemaids, one arm in arm with her sweetheart, all dressed up (it was Sunday), stood and talked, and the one without a sweetheart said: Well, a person must be satisfied to have his reward within himself—and then the hereafter. This is a housemaid speaking—most likely she is not sure of a job for one month or six months or of good wages—she is engaged eternally—how moving!

VI A 70 *n.d.*, 1845

« 920

Cowardly dogs that do not bite bark immediately when they see a stranger; when he has gone by, they are silent. Dangerous dogs are completely silent when someone goes by; they follow him a few steps, bark once or twice, and then bite. Men are like this in their responses to the events of life; the lower natures bark at once; the more earnest ones walk slowly behind and conceal everything.

VI A 72 *n.d.*, 1845

« 921

Martensen has most penetratingly demonstrated[506] that there is nothing which is indifferent, but something is indifferent merely because we have not grasped its ethical significance. Magister Hagen has even taken the opportunity to cite this in his thesis,[507] in order, I suppose, to cite Prof. Martensen. It is the kind of extremely profound observation by which mediocre heads are especially astonished and with which they astonish others. As soon as the individual is alive, exists [*existerer*], the indifferent is present and is rooted in the alternation of existence itself. Regarded eternally, everything is posited as completed, so it is quite natural that there is nothing indifferent. The indifferent is conceivable only in connection with existence [*Existents*] and becoming [Vorden]. As soon as there is completion, eternal completion, the metaphysical gets mastery in such a way that there is nothing ethically indifferent—because the metaphysical is.⁵⁰⁸ That which is indifferent is related to becoming, and therefore all of Martensen's wisdom is parallel to the position that the past is more necessary than the future.⁵⁰⁹

VI A 92 n.d., 1845

« 922

Ethical consciousness is decisive in life.⁵¹⁰ It is the authorization and the aim and the measure of human existence [*Existenses*]. As for the rest, the differences can be what they are—whether a merchant measures out millions of yards a year and a poor widow only a few hundred, this difference is of no consequence, but they both measure with the authorized yard.⁵¹¹

VI A 113 n.d., 1845

« 923

Like plants which not only give a beneficial yield but also purify and improve the earth in which they grow, thus, far from exhausting its richness, improve it—so it is with every good striving:⁵¹² it not only bears fruit but it also purifies the soil of the mind.

VI A 122 n.d., 1845

« 924

For a man engaged in saving himself there is something dreadful about seeing another person go down because of the very same error (this is touched upon in "Guilty/Not Guilty," in Frater Taciturnus's discussion of sympathetic repentance).⁵¹³ But if it is true that I do not have the right to compare⁵¹⁴ myself with others in order to praise and exalt myself but need only to relate myself to the ideal, then it is also true that I do not have the right to compare myself with others in order to despair over myself, but here again I must keep to myself and to the truth and never permit myself either proudly or sympathetically to want to understand the truth through the fate of a third person whom I can never know; instead I must grasp the eternal truth.

VI A 137 n.d., 1845

« 925

If it is taken for granted in this way that Hegel* lacked a sense of

* *Obliquely in margin:* abstract thinkers.

the comic, then this is *eo ipso* proof that all his thought is but the feat of a talent which has simply followed its talent. The ethical act of reflection is in the last analysis decisive. However great, however glorious everything else is, it does not help. Everything higher than the universal must first have tested itself in the ethical act of reflection, which is the measure of the universal. Briskly to follow a talent, to choose a brilliant distinction, even if one amazes the world ten times over, means to remain behind. Ethical reflection is the authorization; if it is secured, then the distinction can be celebrated. If a merchant sells yardgoods by the thousands of yards and a poor widow measures out only a single yard once in a while—the decisive thing is the authorized yard which legally makes the sale a lawful sale. Similarly, ethical reflection and going through the universal involved in it first makes each human existence a truly authentic existence. The distinction of talents is in itself a sad affair.

VI B 54:3   *n.d.*, 1845

« 926

There is such deep and beautiful truth in what Socrates says to Crito (in *Phaedo*), when in the solemn moment of taking leave he asks with spontaneous intimacy if there is anything the dying one in the moment of departure wishes him to do. Socrates answers: Nothing—only that you attend to your own selves, even if you promise me nothing now; but if you are indifferent to your own selves and do not follow in life the track of what has been set forth now and at other times, then you achieve nothing at all even though you promised ever so much and ever so solemnly. (See para. 115 in *Phaedo*.)

VI B 98:46   *n.d.*, 1845

« 927

Finally, just as metaphysics has supplanted theology, it will end with physics supplanting ethics. The whole modern statistical approach to morality contributes to this.[515]

VII^1 A 15   *n.d.*, 1846

« 928

The very thing which makes scholarly work difficult is completely overlooked. It is assumed that everyone, and thus also the scientist and the scholar, knows what he ought (ethically) to do in the world—and now he sacrifices himself for his science and scholarship. But the ethical reflection itself should be the first concern—and then perhaps all scholarship would run aground. The scientist and scholar has his personal life in categories quite different from those of his professional life, but it is precisely the first which are the most important.* He prays, for example —and then his entire effort is preoccupied with proving the existence of God. But how can he pray fervently in this way when his being is fragmented in this self-contradiction. And if he prays fervently, then the question arises, how does he cross over from praying to being busy with his scholarship. The question is: how does he as a professional man of learning understand himself in prayer, and how does he as worshipper understand himself as a professional man of learning.

VII^1 A 28   n.d., 1846

« 929

* *In margin of 928* (VII^1 A 28):
Thus begins a little piece by Spinoza[516] (*De Emendatione Intellectus*, p. 495), very naturally and simply.

VII^1 A 29   n.d., 1846

« 930

When a man wants to work to the utmost of his abilities but always adds that he does not insist on achieving anything, he is regarded as an egotist. If he works half as much but always declares that he wants to achieve something, etc., he is praised for being altruistic. Why? Because this kind of behavior ingratiates the mass, which is flattered by his being so occupied with them. In many ways there is a tendency toward this inversion of things. An author subordinates himself to the public, begs for lenient judgment by the public, etc.; this flatters the public, and finally an author becomes only a hired servant and every bacon-peddler the public.

VII^1 A 30   n.d., 1846

« 931

I have now read Spinoza's *Ethics* through. It is very curious to construct an ethic upon such an indeterminate, although correct, principle as this, *suum esse conservare*,[517] and to maintain it with such ambiguity that it signifies the physical, the egotistic, just as much as it signifies the highest resignation in intellectual love.

Nevertheless, it is a contradiction to discuss how,[518] by what means, one attains perfection in the mastery of emotions, the way to this perfection (cf. p. 430—end), and then to present it as an immanental view, for the way is precisely a teleological dialectic. I take this or that way, do this or that, *in order to*—but this *in order to* certainly distinguishes between the way and the goal.

vII¹ A 35   *n.d.*, 1846

« 932

The conception in which Christianity differs perhaps most specifically from the ancients is the conception of the good. The Greek could not comprehend the good without the beautiful (the outward direction). In Christianity the essential expression of the good is suffering (the inward direction, for suffering lies precisely in this: that the outward direction is negated—the world's sin).

vII¹ A 73   *n.d.*, 1846

« 933

Affectation is best translated into Danish by *Tillyvelse* [sham]. An affected person does not lie [*lyver*], but he falsely ascribes [*tillyver*] something to himself, either directly or by doing the opposite or by omitting something.

vII¹ A 89   *n.d.*, 1846

« 934

. . . . . It is true that in a moment of crucial danger a person is able to do many things he otherwise would not do, that on many decisive, solemn occasions he has thoughts he otherwise does not have—yet without indisputable proof that this was thereby the right thing, was precisely the thing he ought to do when the situation is different, in the ordinary situations of life. But again, on the other hand, neither does it follow that the viewpoint of great decision should not be the fundamental one with regard to existence [*Tilværelse*]. Only the physical-temporal urgency of actuality and the implicit possibility of easy error and of doing something completely insignificant and accidental—only this must be warned against, and the postponing of the decisive view of life until what is decided is as good as past. If, however, a person can experience in possibility the essential impression of decision (where there is no more diversion, no escapes, no occasion to go out and mix among people or to gather a clique around one and console oneself by being like others, or to invent new projects to pass the time—for the crucial danger is precisely in this, that the time is past)—then this is the right decision. If in the most decisive moment of actual life-danger there is only one name a person could desire to name, the name of Christ, one consolation he would seek, Jesus Christ, one single vision of the next world in which he would put all his trust—here then is proof that it is the right decision. And it is also proof that all understanding and speculation and conceptualizing are unessential, because it takes good time for such things. But the decisive view of life ought to be that very one which can satisfy when there is no time left. When the thief on the cross gathered his whole soul in that one wish—that Christ would think of him in his kingdom[519]—this then was the eternal decision of inwardness which did not require a long time of understanding, so much the less since this long time of understanding is a seductive invention. The task now is to hold fast to this decision in time, preserving the impression of the decision.

VII¹ A 138 *n.d.*, 1846

« 935

..... Yes, certainly virtue and the good have their reward; it is certain, eternally certain, nothing is so certain and nothing is more certain than that God is, for this is the same thing. It has its own reward—but when and how—surely not in an earthly sense. Virtue, it should be noted, has its reward in ingratitude, but this is not the reward we are speaking about when we say it is certain that virtue has its reward, but the reward of ingratitude comes first. Virtue does have its reward—it is rewarded with death. This is not the reward we are speaking about when we say it is certain that virtue has its reward; nevertheless this is virtue's reward and it comes first.

VII¹ A 146 *n.d.*, 1846

« 936

Every human being would be infinitely powerful if he did not need to use two-thirds of his energy in finding his task. Therefore a child has so much energy, because the father sets the task, and the child has only to obey. It is the dialectics of the task which really enervates.

VII¹ A 172 *n.d.*, 1846

« 937

Not only do men themselves discard all ideas and higher thoughts, but when they are not quite able to do so, they even become envious of the person who pursues something higher. As long as he is living, they cannot stand him, because as their contemporary he expresses: You too, should be doing the same. When he is dead, they idolize him—and remain just as stupid as before.

VII¹ A 179 *n.d.*, 1846

« 938

The demoralized conception of the ethical as being custom and use, the demand of the times, etc. is expressed in the old Sophist motto: τὸ δικαίον καὶ τὸ αἰσχρόν οὔ φύσαει ἀλλὰ νόμῳ[520] because by νόμος was here understood the finite element, whatever was the accepted custom and usage in the city, where one lived—in short, the trivialized deification of a majority and an opinion, not merely by a simple majority, as we say, but by a wretched majority. This is similar to what is said now about satisfying the public.

See Ritter, *Geschichte der alten Phil.*,[521] I, p. 581.

VII[1] A 251   *n.d.*, 1846

« 939

The difference in all instruction is essentially only this—in what medium is the instruction to be communicated? Children and young people are instructed in the medium of the ideality of imagination. What is said there is true. And yet this very truth can become a trap in the medium of actuality. It is taught that one ought to love the good. Inasmuch as we all learn this, if we all acted accordingly, the medium of actuality would be just as ideal as the medium of imagination. But this is not the case. Then comes the last instruction. It teaches exactly the same thing as was taught to the young, but in addition it teaches how things go in the medium of actuality—that the good is persecuted, is punished as if it were evil, that when the insolent person gets away with his insolence, it is not this insolence men are afraid to be associated with, but the good whom the insolent one persecutes.[522]

VIII[1] A 62   *n.d.*, 1847

« 940

The gospel for the first Sunday after Pentecost (John 14:27-29) reads: And now I have told you before it takes place, so that when it does take place, you may believe.

> The theme could be
> *The relation between the first and the last instruction in life.*

The first instruction is really only a prediction of what will happen. This is instruction in the medium of imagination, which simply teaches the good but is not particularly attentive to the dialectic introduced when the medium itself (actuality) becomes dialectical.

The final instruction is in the medium of actuality, in the dangers of actuality, etc.

VIII¹ A 143 *n.d.*, 1847

« 941

Patience, faith, humility, etc., in short, all the Christian virtues in non-actual dangers (for example, when a person shirks making the right decisions, refuses to take the showerbath of actuality so that he is *actually* scoffed at, is actually destitute, is actually hated by the world, etc.) are like heroism in peacetime. It is as if a soldier on the drill ground in a peaceful military exercise to capture a peewit-house assumed a martial air like that of Daniel Rantzau in battle. What is comical about it is the martial air—and the danger is pure nonsense, make-believe, a stage setting. Children play soldier, in peacetime men play war, and most men play at religion.

VIII¹ A 144 *n.d.*, 1847

« 942

What Socrates[523] says about loving the ugly is really the Christian doctrine of love to the neighbor. The ugly is the reflected, consequently the ethical object; whereas the beautiful is the immediate object which all of us therefore most willingly love. In this sense "the neighbor" is the "ugly."

VIII¹ A 189 *n.d.*, 1847

« 943

Here the discourse has paused at the point it wishes to make the object of consideration. The command that one shall love the neighbor appears to be synonymous with the command to love oneself. Our aim has not been to talk about love to the neighbor. On the contrary, we wish to talk about
    THAT LOVE IS DUTY, *that*
    we SHALL LOVE *the neighbor*;
for the distinguishing characteristic of Christian love is the very fact that it contains this apparent contradiction—that to love is duty. And yet it is only this kind of love which finds out that the neighbor exists [*er til*] and—it is one and the same—that everyone is that. If it were not a duty to love, then there could not be any question of loving the neighbor; for the concept "neighbor" corresponds to loving as a duty. Neither romantic love nor friendship nor any other kind of love corresponds to the concept —the neighbor—to this corresponds only the love that is duty.[524]

VIII² B 30:4 *n.d.*, 1847

414   THE ETHICAL, THE ETHICAL CONSCIOUSNESS

« 944

But love is *the fulfillment of the law*. The fact that other men want to exempt you from having duties, that they are willing to call it love in you if you permit them to idolize you, adore you, coddle you, does not exempt you. In these circumstances genuine love will be recognizable by the fact that it does the opposite of what is demanded of it. And precisely this will be the sacrifice. It is by no means love to indulge human weakness. Neither is it human judgment as such which is to determine what sacrifice is, for God is to determine this, and human judgment is only valid when it judges in accordance with God's judgment. God's requirement is that love shall be sacrificial, but how this is to be interpreted more specifically in the particular case, God, again, must determine.

Love is the fulfilling of the law, this is the eternal demand which you dare not cheat or pare down in any way in compromising with men, for it . . . . .

VIII^2 B 34:7   n.d., 1847

« 945

"Beloved, let us love one another." This kind of speaking is the proper intermediary tone. If you want to test the words, weigh them; you will see that you do not find the rigorousness of duty, nor do you find the rigorousness of the eternal as command and order, but neither do you find the intensity of poetic passion and of inclination. It is like a sadness, a sadness which, agitated by life and mitigated by the eternal, says: "Lord God, what does life have to give, etc.—let us therefore love. Certainly it is a command and order of the eternal, but, Lord God, it is also the only blessed consolation both here and in the next world." A confession of faith is not enough to indicate whether one is a Christian. "Thereby shall it be known that you are my disciples if you love one another."[525]

VIII^2 B 58:14   n.d., 1847

« 946

In the crucial dangers of life people can come to some devout resolutions. But when the dangers are past, they think that they could just as well get the same thing at a little cheaper price—without noticing that when they do this they do not get the same thing at all. How is it that such a change occurs, unless it is that they no longer have the conception of the eternal and absolute validity of the devout resolution as

THE ETHICAL, THE ETHICAL CONSCIOUSNESS   415

before. But they will say: No one can endure being in crucial danger constantly. Why not, if this is the condition for holding fast to the devout resolution?

VIII¹ A 223 n.d., 1847

« 947

Pleasure can be pleasant enough at the time. Ah, but there is nothing more blessed to remember than suffering, that is, suffering for a good cause.

In margin: One has at most seventy years for enjoyment—but an eternity for remembering. And pleasure does not show up at all well in memory.

VIII¹ A 236 n.d., 1847

« 948

To lie, as an earlier writer has said so well,[526] is to denounce oneself, to despise God, and to fear men. Montaigne points out very well this repulsive inversion—instead of fearing God and, if necessary, of despising men.

VIII¹ A 291 n.d., 1847

« 949

To exist [*existere*] Christianly is a compound of the eternal and of the temporal. But now in these times the eternal is never supposed to gain decisive expression in the external world—therefore the whole thing may easily become a deception, a fancy. One acts as worldly as possible, clings to this earthly existence [*Tilværelse*]—but is also, as they say, inwardly a true Christian. No doubt it is possible on rare occasions to find someone who truly achieves the astonishing harmony of the secular mentality and Christianity. Usually it is the Christian part which is left out, almost as if it were supposed to be merely an assimilated element of the secular mentality.

In any case, it is of great importance for life that in every generation there be a few existences [*Existentser*] who simply give expression to the dialectical element. There are enough existences who express the purely secular—but we lack completely the one-sided and absolutely consistent expression of the purely sacred. Nevertheless, this is extremely important in order that a little control may still be maintained with this so-called sacred existence [*Existents*], which probably has solved problems here that even Christ did not solve, for Christ was not preoccupied with becoming cabinet member or with making a living; neither was he an apostle, an aspirant to orders and titles—and then also in his inward being a good Christian.

Just as the poetry in life has been completely banished with the aid of the lie about assimilated elements (every girl sorrows just as deeply as Juliet, but, in addition, she understands how to bear it and then gets engaged again—lies! Pure lies!)—in the same way Christianity is banished by the fraud that the highest is not to forsake or give up the worldly, etc., but to remain in it and in one's hidden inwardness to be a Christian.

VIII¹ A 312 n.d., 1847

« 950

In the Sermon on the Mount (either the fifth [47] or sixth chapter in Matthew) there is a line which has superb application to modern life: And if you salute only your brethren, do not the heathen do the same?

VIII¹ A 316 n.d., 1847

« 951

..... Let us understand each other. You are afraid that this and this will happen to you if you do this and this—which, however, you still do regard as your duty to do, but you are simply perplexed about whether duty can require so much of you. Now perform a thought-experiment. Think of the most fearful of all things—and then think of God as the Almighty. You do not want to venture this and this because of fear of this and this—but now suppose that the Almighty brings this and this upon you as punishment for your disobedience. You fear that by doing this and this you will expose yourself to the mockery of the world —but now suppose that God, even though you did not do it, arranged things in such a way that you nevertheless are exposed to the world's mockery. What security do you have against the Almighty—when you, with all the ingenuity you possess, schemed to escape this and this, and then God brought it upon you, perhaps in a completely different manner. No, there is only one security and assurance in relation to the Almighty —namely, to obey him unconditionally.

Let us think of Moses and in this way. He says to himself: I do not dare go to Pharoah; he will kill me, so I shall stay at home. So Moses stays home. But now why should not God, who is omnipotent, turn things in such a way that Moses is picked up by Pharoah's guard (through a misunderstanding, an unfortunate misunderstanding; of course, it was a misunderstanding, since Moses was entirely innocent, but Pharoah had gotten an idea into his head and no one could get him out of it) as an insurrectionist.

The fact is, most men lack the imagination to understand concretely what the Almighty is capable of.

As far as I am concerned, when out of fear of this and this I avoid doing something which I nevertheless regard as God's will, when I want to sneak out of it, the Almighty brings upon me as punishment precisely that which I feared.

VIII^1 A 319 *n.d.*, 1847

« 952

No one can serve two masters.[527] This does not mean only the vacillating, irresolute person who does not quite know what to choose. No, the person who defiantly breaks with God and heaven in order to serve his desires and drives also serves two masters, something no one can do—for he has to serve God whether he wants to or not. The situation is not this simple: choose one of the two. The situation is rather this: there is only one choice if one is actually going to serve only one master, and that is God.

VIII^1 A 359 *n.d.*, 1847

« 953

Ethics has been completely transformed into the esthetic. We see it and admire it in the theater, in the medium of imagination, but in life it has no home—there it is ridiculous to will even to try to actualize anything of the ethical. In the same way the religious, Christianity, is transposed into the medium of imagination, but to do something about it in life is ridiculous.

VIII^1 A 398 *n.d.*, 1847

« 954

Live in such a way that if your life were to be put on the stage the audience would weep in ecstasy. If you live your life this way in actuality, you will—in proportion to how far you go in expressing the ideal—be persecuted, derided, spit upon, and ostracized. It is easy to understand— it is the human self-defense against the rigors of ideality.

VIII^1 A 410 *n.d.*, 1847

« 955

..... in these times, when the meaning of obedience has been forgotten, especially obedience toward God, nowadays when the clergy know so well how to penetrate and fathom God's being and the validity of men's relationship to God (but do not know how to preach), when they say that "praying" is beneficial for three basic reasons. Truly, if praying has no more worth than that, praying is not worth anything.

VIII^1 A 413   n.d., 1847

« 956

Young man, if you are extraordinarily gifted, there are two ways for you. Either use these gifts of yours to strengthen men in their darling stupidities and errors—yet, please note, with the appearance of helping them toward truth and clarity—and you will be idolized, earn honor and lots and lots of money, be poetized and praised, and at your grave many a eulogy will be drooled by the grief-stricken mourners. Or before God, aware of your responsibility, resolve by every sacrifice really to help them, if possible, at least a little along the way to clarity—then take care. This will be rewarded unreservedly with scorn and indignities (out of stupidity and envy, the most dangerous collusion in the earthly sense, when the stupid do not understand you and those who are able to understand you collaborate with the stupid out of envy)—perhaps even with your life.

VIII^1 A 494   n.d., 1847

« 957

Have faith, and the rest is of no consequence. Every other good is dialectical in such a way that there is always an *aber* about it, so that seen from another side it perhaps is not a good. Faith is the good which is dialectical in such a way that even if the greatest misfortune were to happen to me, faith would still allow me to regard it as a good.

VIII^1 A 509   n.d., 1848

« 958

People do indeed speak sometimes of truly extraordinary persons who lived in various periods and who were not persecuted but rather were honored and esteemed. Perhaps. But let us look at the matter a little more closely. It does not follow from the fact that a person is great —for example, an artist, a poet, an actor, an orator, etc.—that he is ethically great. Perhaps, in spite of his esthetic greatness, he was weak enough to want to be honored and esteemed in the world in an inauthentic way; perhaps he also knew how to flatter the evil or at least knew how to avoid dangers which he should have risked. This, please note, is something different. Imagine a poet. I do not deny that he is truly great as a poet, but it is probably not for this reason that he becomes so highly regarded and admired by his contemporaries. No, he is also a weak character, cowardly; he maintains good public relations with the voices of envy, bolstering himself with good connections, etc.—therefore he lives honored and esteemed.

The fact still remains that never has anyone of ethical greatness been honored and esteemed as long as he was living, because then the world would also have to be good. It is only by debasing himself that one actually succeeds in being honored and esteemed while he is living. The fact that someone is actually a genius does not help. If that poet had also been an ethicist, he would not be honored and esteemed.

VIII¹ A 671   n.d., 1848

« 959

"Even Peter denied."[528] What concern is that of mine? When Peter does the good, then Peter is Peter, and I try to learn from him. When Peter does wrong, then I have nothing to do with him, for I shall not learn this from him.

IX A 104   n.d., 1848

« 960

The best in life is a discovery. Sometimes we seek and find; sometimes we find although we have not sought. He who finds a pearl[529] he has not looked for nevertheless finds it; but if he then gives up everything in order to possess it, he inversely expresses that he sought it; for having gotten it and then to *acquire* possession of it in this way is *inversely* the very same as to seek.

IX A 111   n.d., 1848

« 961

The only ethical relationship to the great (thus also to Christ) is contemporaneity. To relate oneself to a great person who is dead is an esthetic relationship; his life has lost its sting, does not judge my life, permits me to admire him and even to live in completely different categories, does not compel me decisively to judge . . . . .

IX A 314   n.d., 1848

« 962

It is said that a golden key opens up everything. But certainly determination, decision also open up, and therefore it is also called resolving; with resolution or in the resolution the best powers of the soul open up.

IX A 346   n.d., 1848

« 963

This way it went with Socrates and also, proportionately, with Christ: they had many admirers and among those many admirers also some who knew how to admire—but of imitators they had very few. The difference between an admirer and an imitator is that the imitator is ethically what the admirer is esthetically. An admirer is himself a being different from the one admired; an imitator is himself the admired. And this is the only true admiration. —The truth of admiration depends on or corresponds to the power it exercises over the one who admires. Its maximum power is itself to be or to resemble the admired. On the other hand, it is not true that a person truly admires that which has no influence upon or power over him so as to change him into likeness to the admired. Such admiration is a forgery. In a pinch he can understand the admired, all right, or what it is that he admires, but he does not understand himself or does not understand himself in admiring. If he understood this, he would then understand that his own lack of change is like a satire over his admiration and at every moment makes it a lie. But such an admirer does not think of this. He declaims more and more vehemently: the *bravo* and *bravissimo* of admiration rise in intensity— ah, now I know, confound it, that he does in fact admire—alas, but the satire which he is upon himself only grows more sarcastic.

Generally people seem to forget completely that there is after all a limit to the pathos of making assurances, that this limit lies where the pathos of action should begin. And when this is lacking, the pathos of verbal assurances only becomes, the more vehement and shrill they are, all the more a declaration that what is said is a lie in the assurer's throat.

But woe to the man who has understood existence [*Tilværelsen*] so profoundly and truly expresses that he does not want admirers but is satisfied with one or two imitators. For admirers can always be had—but their price is the truth; and to call for imitators makes life much too strenuous for men.

To admire is most often a softness for which many men feel a need. And if someone then permits himself to be admired, it is good; then the admirers pet him as one pets a bird-dog which has an exceptionally rare color and, so extraordinarily rare, a single white spot on the forehead.

IX A 372 *n.d.*, 1848

« 964

If there were any question about my having gone a little bit too far out (that is, I have not gone far out yet; it is still in my power to turn aside, but I consider the possibility of going that far out), then it would be with regard to the necessity of suffering, of succumbing, i.e., that I do not remain in suspension, leaving it to an ambiguous determination as to whether or not I am just as likely to win out or at least come out somehow, etc.

The situation is that the ideal must necessarily suffer, succumb, become a sacrifice in this world; here is the unconditional necessity, for in relationship to the ideal the circumstances of existence [*Tilværelses*] can be calculated purely dialectically. But no human being is sheer ideality or the ideal, and of course I am not that at all. For this very reason there has been for me the possibility of variation with respect to the outcome of my striving—but this is obviously no perfection on my part; it is my imperfection.

Moreover, the ideal does nothing at all in order to enter into suffering, for suffering comes necessarily because it is the ideal—and because it must be in the world of reality. However, if an individual human being who is not the ideal were to think that he should do nothing at all in order to enter into suffering (i.e., to venture), perhaps in order not to tempt God—then existence [*Tilværelsen*] cannot get hold of him, that is, cannot test him in spiritual trial [*Anfægtelse*], for spiritual trial is precisely the suffering of the voluntary or the suffering of whether one has not ventured too much.

IX A 392 *n.d.*, 1848

« 965

That the essentially Christian, the true Christian, must become a sacrifice in the world is easy to see in the manner in which everybody in daily life, on weekdays, speaks unconditionally about how things go and must go and ought to go in *practical life*.[530] Practical life is decisive. It is generally considered that the emotions of a Romeo and a Juliet belong on the stage—in practical life one gets married three times. Similarly it is generally considered that the Christian requirements for what it means to exist [*existere*] belong in the pulpit—but in practical life it is madness. Yes, to be sure. But what is Christianity? Christianity is these very requirements executed in practical life: *ergo*, Christianity is madness. Christianity means that the ideal and ideality must be kept alive in practical life.

But practical life is spoken about with unbelievable unembarrassment. I can remember Bishop Mynster once saying to me: "Well, you will see, as soon as you enter into practical life, it will surely disappear."

What? Ideality. And I vow that at the time Mynster said this he meant it as sincerely as possible and it was his conviction—this is the whole trouble, especially if one thinks this way on Sunday.

IX A 418 n.d., 1848

« 966

It is said that the good gives strength. This is all very true, but it is a very refined and sensitive strength. Evil, on the other hand, gives robust strength. Otherwise how does it happen that when someone has done the good, he then suffers, suffers much more—unless it is because the good has also in an ennobling way made him refined and sensitive. One can try it on himself. When he has done some wrong—the evil will straightway help him by giving him strength, for the fact is that he must now pull himself together simply because he has done wrong. In comparison the good is weak. This is why despairing individuals who believe neither in God nor in eternity usually appear to be so strong in this life —they are entirely unacquainted with the sensitivity which the eternal gives. Therefore the old saying correctly says: Weeds never die.

That the good gives strength remains just as certain, but it gives the kind of strength which is not advantageous in the world.

IX A 419 n.d., 1848

« 967

The abolition of moral guarantees in order to substitute legal guarantees was an invention of conceited and suspicious human ingenuity; but it was also something else, an attempt to abolish God or to make of God a blockhead, he who on the one hand is beggarly enough to be satisfied for his part with the moral guarantees and on the other hand is the guarantor of all the moral guarantees.

IX A 443 n.d., 1848

« 968

Even though everyone had a pair of seven-mile boots,[531] not everyone would be capable of using them. The suddenness of being transported seven miles in a second would make this step a very serious step, for which we scarcely have the courage. Man is intended for gradualness, anyway.

IX A 464 n.d., 1848

« 969

A person cannot have two fixed points, for then he is unable to move. Therefore either the one point remains fixed: that this is the

THE ETHICAL, THE ETHICAL CONSCIOUSNESS 423

truth—and then he gesticulates with the whole of his personal existing [*Existeren*] in making sacrifices. Or he fixes the other point: My job, my good name and reputation, my advancement, etc. must not be touched—and then he gesticulates by means of abridging the truth.

x^1 A 208   *n.d.*, 1849

« 970

It cannot really be said that the world does not have knowledge of the good; indeed, it is men of the world who most frequently have a highly developed eye for what nobility, disinterestedness, etc. really are. As soon as they spot a man who, they must admit, strives in this way, envy mobilizes all their observational ability in order to judge him as severely as possible; yes, they try to put every possible obstacle in his way so that he might stumble and become self-interested, etc. They say: Why should he be better than we are. Thus they do not really hate the good, but in their envy they do not want anyone to be what they themselves are not.

This is approximately Scribe's[532] frame of mind: he does not hate the good; on the contrary, he presumably holds it in high honor, even with a certain abstract enthusiasm, but he does not want anyone to be good; his enviousness does not want such a thing, since he himself does not strive in the good.

When the angels spot a person who sincerely wills the good, even though in weakness, they hasten to help him along. God help the man who the world discovers actually is willing the good, who is still striving.

x^1 A 321   *n.d.*, 1849

« 971

The earthliness of earthly goods—which proves that they are not goods in and for themselves—is that they are goods only through the conception of others that they are goods. The first mark of the goods of the spirit, whereby they are recognized as goods in and for themselves, is that it is a matter of indifference whether or not others regard them as goods. Take money, take any earthly good whatsoever—if you live in a country where this is not regarded as a good, if there were no place to which you could travel where these things are regarded as a good, then money is not a good at all. So it is with all earthly goods. If, then, someone who possesses an earthly good, *si ita dicere licet*,[533] lives in an area where no one else regards it as a good, he would be regarded as mad, and he certainly would be. It is quite different with someone who possesses a good of the spirit which no one else regards as a good; it is a good nevertheless and fully as much so; he is indeed regarded as mad, but it is he who is the wise one.

x^1 A 327   *n.d.*, 1849

« 972

No doubt immediacy can be attained again—but the nonsense of "The System" is the contention that it is attained again without a break.

Immediacy is attained again only ethically; immediacy itself becomes the task—you *shall* attain it.

During the most developed period of the most intellectual nation Socrates attained ignorance (ignorance, with which one begins in order to know more and more) and how? Because in radical ethicality he took his task to be that of preserving himself in ignorance, so that no temptation [*Fristelse*] without and no temptation within would ever trick him into admitting that he knew something, he who nevertheless in another sense did know something.

People who have no conception of spirit talk in this way: When immediacy is lost, one can never recover it. And in order to illustrate it properly (thereby also revealing how they confuse the spiritual and the sensuous), they add: A girl can lose her innocence but she never recovers it. But spiritually the following is true: if I cannot recover innocence, then all is lost from the beginning, because the primary fact is simply that I and everyone have lost innocence.

If for a moment I omit all the more specifically dogmatic aspects of the cooperation of the spirit, etc., I can define rebirth in this way: it is immediacy won ethically.

Ethics or, better, the ethical, is the turning point and from here the movement is into the dogmatic.

x^1 A 360   *n.d.*, 1849

« 973

Just as that which is esthetically valued depends on the power to wish, the courage and foolhardiness to wish (therefore Aladdin is the poet's hero, and the poet himself is an Aladdin—give the ring to another and he does not have the courage to wish), so in the same way the ethical norm for the individual is the power to demand actuality, the power to achieve presentness, the power to minimize the medium of imagination and to will to have only the medium of existence [*Existents-Mediet*].

Most men have a conception of greatness, but however they turn and rotate it, a false image slips in—it was that way long ago, or this one and that one were great, or this one and that one are great—but that one himself be this, that the task is intended for existence [*Existents*], this escapes them.

An essentially ethical individual immediately converts greatness to contemporaneity. He says—to himself—this is what I will. Quite possibly I cannot reach it, but this is what I will. If cannot reach it immediately, then I will creep; if in my whole lifetime I cannot do any more than creep along, then I shall creep along my whole life—but this is the direction. He does not let go of it; he is like a pilgrim who perhaps has vowed to walk on his knees to Jerusalem—and he died on the way; but from the point of view of the idea he has reached Jerusalem. And in this way the true ethical individual must reach the highest—he must reach it, if not before, then in eternity.

But this is why all esthetic and sensuous men have anxiety about living contemporaneously with such an ethical individual—simply because he transforms everything into actuality: what he understands, he does.

x^1 A 393 *n.d.*, 1849

« 974

There is really much truth in what Lessing somewhere (in *Letters to Mendelssohn*)[534] develops, that essentially we cannot admire the heroic—to do so makes us feel alien. This is entirely true. What admiration insinuates itself into, where it sees, so to speak, its opportunity, is the *suffering* of the great man, but it is precisely suffering which the heroic does not have. Admiration is therefore made a fool of, in a way. Human admiration is self-love—when the great man suffers, admiration promptly comes forward. But the heroic is not seen to suffer; it is stronger than suffering—therefore admiration fails to appear. Men are almost chilled by the heroic when it is contemporary and estranged when it is past.

(My own life can illuminate this to a degree. If I, *suffering*, were to have become an object of attack by mob-vulgarity, how admiration for me would have increased. But the fact that I myself demanded it shocked men. They felt alienated by anything that went over their heads. What I could reasonably claim, esteem for the nobility, the disinterestedness, the sacrifice in my position—well, it perhaps would be unreasonable to claim it, for the whole thing is over their heads, for them it borders on madness.)

Another question is to what extent the essentially Christian has the heroic. This I deny and have pointed it out elsewhere (for example, in

The Gospel of Suffering [Joyful Notes in the Strife of Suffering], VII).⁵³⁵ No doubt there is heroism in the suffering Christian, or he is not seen to suffer; but his God-relationship means that he nevertheless is to be regarded as suffering. He contends ultimately with God—the responsibility—and there he suffers, suffers in fear and trembling. If there were no God-relationship, the essentially Christian would be the heroic. Thus the essentially Christian is not subordinated to the heroic but is above it, is first of all the heroic and then also suffering. But watch out for this dialectic; otherwise one prattles about it in the same way the clergy so readily do, which makes Christianity into whimpering and howling.

x^1 A 412   *n.d.*, 1849

« 975

In the realm of genius, the realm of natural qualifications, the realm of the esthetic, what counts is: to be able. In the realm of the ethical: to be obliged. Therefore the ethical is related to the universally human; whereas the esthetic is related to the differences between man and man. It would be a contradiction of the ethical to speak of *being obliged* if every human being did not have the conditions for being able if he himself only wills.

In connection with the ethical there are, therefore, no conditions; it is the unconditional ought which tolerates no conditions because it presupposes no conditions.

The esthetic presupposes the conditions and is unconditional only where the condition is unconditionally present; whereas the ethical is unconditional in that there is no condition and thus is unconditional everywhere or unconditionally unconditioned.

x^1 A 430   *n.d.*, 1849

« 976

When James⁵³⁶ says: The body apart from the spirit is dead, so faith apart from works is dead—we could rather turn the figure around and say: So works apart from faith are dead, for faith corresponds more to spirit and works more to the body than the other way around.

x^1 A 457   *n.d.*, 1849

« 977

Most men continually have their lives only in the particular; men who have an essential ideality always relate themselves to a principle.

For example, the majority of men deliberate over which girl to marry, whether her or her (the particular). For more ideal persons a girl, for example, is the occasion for reflecting upon what it means to marry, upon the reality of marriage.

And so it is on all points.

That is why the more ideal natures always appear to be stragglers—because they relate themselves to principles instead of dealing immediately with the particular.

It is true, as I have noted elsewhere in a journal, that every genius is a scruting of one or more of the principle questions in existence [*Tilværelsen*]. For most men everything is tradition, only the particular is new. It is the tradition, and thus automatically taken for granted, that one gets married—the only question asked is: to whom?

x^1 A 580   n.d., 1849

« 978

All Christian knowledge and generally all ethical knowledge is not what it essentially is when it is separated from its situation.

A situation (actuality, that is, or that a person expresses in actuality what he knows) is the *conditio sine qua non* for ethical knowledge.

This point is also made at the end of the work, "Come unto Me all Ye Who Labor and Are heavy-laden."537

x^1 A 610   n.d., 1849

« 979

Alas, it should be that the thought of God delights a person so much that his entire life after that moment, its every hour, is in God's service. As for us, alas, all we really want is that God should love us. —I admit it—the thought that a human being dares to say, "I love you" to God, even this seems to me to be almost too exalted.

x^2 A 23   n.d., 1849

« 980

The ethical expression for the distinction which an artist, a thinker, a teacher of ethics claims is that he himself surrender the money motive. Insofar as the money motive controls, I cannot make sense of the prudishness about the great difference between them and every other tradesman. Yet art and science and scholarship are indeed differentiated; a difference between them and other trades can be granted to the extent that one profession is more attractive than another. But a teacher of ethics is not characterized by differences; the more money-motivated he becomes, the more he becomes even less than an out-and-out tradesman.

x^2 A 142   n.d., 1849

« 981

How suggestive in Christian meaning are the words: to become sober.[538] How seldom a person is found who became sober in such a way that he understood (in the sense of acting accordingly) that the very least actual self-denial is far greater from the Christian point of view than the boldest enterprise of the most eminent genius, even in connection with the spreading of Christianity and the like.

The fact of the matter is that we are unable to form properly for ourselves an idea of God's sublimity. We always bog down in our esthetic quantifying—the amazing, the tremendous, the very influential, etc.—whereas God is so infinitely elevated that the only thing he considers is the ethical.

x^2 A 178   *n.d.*, 1849

« 982

If, instead of personally protesting to the public and positing the single individual, I had lectured, talked, written something about "the single individual" to the public, it would have gone over with the people.

Here one sees the difference between ethical reduplication and lecturing. Ethical reduplication transforms into action; therefore it requires a sacrifice. A person who lectures apparently says the very same thing—and makes a hit.

x^2 A 201   *n.d.*, 1849

« 983

The relation of Christ as redeemer to the believer is, I think, somewhat like that of an adult to children when the adult says: Now I will take care of everything; just be very calm and trust me—and then he becomes angry when the children, instead of being happy and letting him take care of things, want to do it themselves. I believe that Christ as redeemer is angered in the same way when the believer in any manner occupies himself with making restitution for his sin. No! The atonement is the decisive thing. Then, on the other side, precisely out of joy over the reconciliation, comes an honest striving, which he himself, it is well to note, nevertheless understands almost as a jest, however honest and earnest his striving is, as a jest if in any shape or manner it is supposed to be a restitution.

It is by no means man's effort which brings atonement, but it is the joy over the reconciliation, over the fact that atonement has been made, it is the joy which produces an honest striving. It is somewhat as Luther says: It is not good works which make a good man but the good man who does good works, that is, the man is the character, that which is more than all the individual acts. And, according to Luther,[539] one becomes a good man by faith. Consequently, faith first of all. It is not by a good life, good works, and the like that one achieves faith. No, it is faith which works that one does truly good works.

x^2 A 208   n.d., 1849

« 984

The fact that grace is free finds its absolutely right expression in the New Testament. An heir has no merit, not the remotest whatsoever. Everything is the bequeather's benefaction to him.

Now if the matter is viewed purely externally, namely, that the heir has the right to do whatever he likes with the inheritance, then the whole thing is taken in vain. In the realm of the spirit—where the inheritance is not something external, and "faith" therefore is the condition for becoming, for becoming aware that one *is the heir*—it is essential that a person have a relationship of responsibility toward the inheritance. Here, again, is the concept of striving.

x^2 A 224   n.d., 1849

« 985

Just as men who do not have much ideality cannot understand an idea, a joke, an anecdote, etc. without finding out "about whom they are talking" (the name), so it is with men who do not have much ideality in regard to work. They do not succeed, in silence and through the work of ideality, in transforming themselves into points of intensity. As soon as they get just a random thought, it immediately has to be imparted to actual people, to this one and to that one (the name), or they must immediately attack this one and that one (the name, the external actuality). So there comes to be a sensation, a little riot and mob scene, alarm in the camp, a racket; it looks as if they produced an effect completely different from that of the points of intensity. Why? Because they use weaker means. "At the moment" the most intensive means always appear to have accomplished absolutely nothing, to have set nothing in motion; on the other hand, the weakest means, that is, the least intensive, those which are most akin to the immediate moment, are more moving simply because in the deepest sense they do not move at all. Specifically, there is no point beyond, which dialectically is necessary, however, in order truly to move; it is movement in the moment itself. It has no heterogeneity at all; anyone can immediately enter into it or immediately understand it, and so names are named, names of the followers, names

« 986

Through incessant voting ethical concepts will ultimately vanish from the race. The power of ethical concepts is the context of conscience; but voting externalizes everything.

Many people still live in the comfortable idea that the world will never get so bad that stealing, for example, becomes a virtue. Who knows that? Look at France! How many would there be in this instance who dare maintain that stealing is a sin. In such a case there would certainly be a Christian collision. Whereas all steal, one himself suffers by being robbed without venturing to steal in return; and then one suffers again by acknowledging the conviction that stealing is sin.

How many are there who in this moment *dare* to witness against balloting! At most a "profound prophet" would propose at a meeting (after a brilliant lecture, "gripping and moving," describing the moral and religious dangers in balloting) that a vote should be taken on refraining from voting. Of course this deep insight will be admired as the deepest wisdom and the purest morality. Refined lack of character is the glittering sin of our age, the way to "success and power."

x^2 A 419   *n.d.*, 1850

« 987 *The Measurement of Distance*

At one time in the conception of distance from the ideal there was the idea of enormous effort and self-denial, etc.

Nowadays the distance is much more than doubled, for now in between (between the ideal and striving for it) there lies the reflection of a most distinguished and refined reason which finds the whole attempt ridiculous, completely ridiculous, a childish immaturity, and also the sure way (besides all the exertion and all the self-denial, etc.) to expose oneself to the most frightful thing of all—to make oneself ridiculous.

O, the distance between the rich man and Lazarus was not more dreadful than the distance between the ideal and striving for it nowadays.

There is no one to be seen, really, I have seen no one, not one single person, who launches out on ideality; they all navigate by calculation: relative aims, either relative aims pure and simple or relative aims like interpretation for the sake of security—probably (even such a level of striving is very seldom found) in order to avoid the laughter.

These relative aims—they are clothing; the ideal endeavor is like going stark naked—offensively striking, ridiculous.

To be an individual human being, sheer striving with one's sight upon the ideal—no, they would die of shame (of course, the shame is rather misplaced here, for it is the relative aims one should be ashamed of) or die of fear of becoming ridiculous.

The mint standard of being an individual human being is set appallingly low. Therefore all seek to dress up with one abstraction or another: *we, our age, the public*, and for the sake of "earnestness," in order not to become ridiculous, stick to relative aims.

x^2 A 546   *n.d.,* 1850

« 988 *Meritoriousness*

To avoid meritoriousness in the following way—not to get involved at all in the essential requirements of Christianity, to live on in the best possible way according to the secular standard of living, and then to introduce "grace" and think that God is certainly a pleasant fellow—this is not the intention of Christianity at all; this actually abolishes Christianity.

x^3 A 66   *n.d.,* 1850

« 989 *Human Deceit*

This form of deceit appears frequently in ordinary life—when ethical tasks are stressed and someone is prodded a bit to act, he answers: I do not have the capacity for it. The deceit is to transform the ethical task into a task according to differences. The question is not at all about capacities but about will—the simplest man has capacities, if he wills. But in this way one parries and also profits by seeming to be modest. Well, thanks for that. Let us take the most rigorous ethics, the commandments. If the thief were to say, when one tells him to quit stealing: Yes, that is all right for those who have capacities for such things, but I do not have such capacities—would this not be strange talk? But this is the way it always is with the ethical. The ethical requirement for a man to witness for the truth is not a matter of intellectuality but a matter of will. The requirement is not that he become a genius—O, no, it is very simple; but it is hard on flesh and blood, and so one tries to slip out of it by making it a matter of esthetic differences and says *modestly*: Such capacities I do not have. Thereby one lies in yet another way, for one weakens the impression of the true ethicist, as if he is able to do something easily because he has such and such capacities—but it is not a question of capacities. But people are afraid of the true ethicist and would rather protect themselves against him by making him out to be unusually gifted so that his life loses the power of being a requirement, for if it depends upon capacities, then it is nonsense to require of a person what has not been given to him.

x^3 A 104   n.d., 1850

« 990 *Ethical Ideality*

In respect to the highest which one has not yet fulfilled, it is a completely confused use of language to say: I cannot—as if it were a matter of talent, etc. To use *can* here, one must remember, is so far from being an excuse that it is a self-accusation. Paul does not say:[540] I cannot be perfect; he says: But I press on to make it my own. When someone says: I cannot—it usually means that he wants to turn aside and take it easy.

x^3 A 248   n.d., 1850

« 991 *A Conception of Christianity*

One can say that Christianity did not enter the world in order to develop the great virtues in the individual—on the contrary, the great virtues and the heroic were prominent in paganism.

But then the situation was such that simply because the "ideal" κατ' ἐξοχήν was not known in paganism, the individual was prompted to imagine that he himself could be approximately the ideal and to pride himself over it, so that the contrast became one between the heroes and the rest of humanity who were almost animals.

Then the true ideal appears. The true ideal makes it clear that all need grace and humbles everyone. Selfish distinctions cannot stand up—because in relation to the ideal the strongest stand in need of grace just as much as the weakest. And in a certain sublime sense the ideal transforms all distinctions in perfection between man and man into a jest.

Christianity did not come in order to develop the heroic virtues in the individual but rather to remove selfishness and establish love—"Let us love one another." Time and energy are not to be used for improving oneself up to a certain maximum, which can so easily be selfishness, as much as for working for others.

But this, again, can be taken in vain so that one completely forgets his own development in activity for others. Then the intensity must be accentuated again.

Yet it is always dangerous to stress markedly the distinction between true and false Christianity if the mark of the first is presented as being more heroic and the like, because this can easily become paganism.

Therefore I have always urged that Christianity is properly for poor people who perhaps toil and sweat the whole day and are scarcely able to make a daily living. The greater the advantages the more difficult it is to become a Christian, for reflection can so very easily take a wrong turn.

My desire has always been to preach to the common man. But when the journalism of mob vulgarity did everything to present me to the common man as being demented, I had to give up the desire for a time, but I shall return to it again.

x^3 A 714   n.d., 1851

« 992 *Has a Man the Right to Intend His Own Destruction?*

No. Why not? Because this sort of thing either has its basis in life-weariness, etc.—and then one ought to combat it—or it is wanting to be more than human. True enough, there are situations in which human reasonableness can perceive that here a sacrifice would have an enormous effect, would really clear the way. Nevertheless, to intend one's own destruction is too exalted for a human being.

To intend one's own destruction is so exalted that only the divine can have this intention in perfect purity. In every human being who might intend such a thing, there would always be an admixture of melancholy. Here, then, lies the mistake. Perhaps it is a repressed desire, etc., something over which he nevertheless despairs arbitrarily (because for God everything is possible), and his passion throws itself into this sort of heroism.

But this is not permissible. A human being must acknowledge his desires before God, humanly try to get them fulfilled, pray God to do it—and then turn over to God the possibility of his meeting his destruction in this particular way. In short, a human being ought to be a human being.

x^3 A 715   n.d., 1851

« 993 *The Christian Emphasis*

Christianly the emphasis does not fall so much upon to what extent or how far a person succeeds in meeting or fulfilling the requirement, if he actually is striving, as it is upon his getting an impression of the requirement in all its infinitude so that he rightly learns to be humbled and to rely upon grace.

To pare down the requirement in order to fulfill it better (as if this were earnestness, that now it can all the more easily *appear* that one is earnest about wanting to fulfill the requirement)—to this Christianity in its deepest essence is opposed.

434   THE ETHICAL, THE ETHICAL CONSCIOUSNESS

No, infinite humiliation and grace, and then a striving born of gratitude—this is Christianity.

x^3 A 734   *n.d.*, 1851

« 994 *The Way to Christianity*

is not that another person by coaxing, etc., undertakes to lead you to it.

No, you must go through this "You *shall*"; this is the condition for *unconditional* respect. And behind this *you shall* lies grace, and there everything smiles, there all is gentleness.

x^3 A 737   *n.d.*, 1851

« 995 *Rumford*

It is modern and devoid of character—the inventor of Rumford soup is rewarded by being elevated to the nobility, probably got rich to boot.

People would have been upset over a thing like this in antiquity and the Middle Ages. But our day or the modern age finds nothing wrong with this lack of reduplication. Eugene Sue complains about the plight of the poor[541]—and earns a half a million thereby. Well, of course, they say, he would be crazy to do otherwise. This is not the way people would have conducted themselves in antiquity or the Middle Ages. There was much more feeling and ethical respect for existential transparency.

It is this modern hypocrisy about the objective, about doctrine, about the cause, etc. that has completely abolished Christianity. It appears to be something, this extensive work of protesting the plight of the poor—and if the originator becomes a rich man thereby, it makes no difference. Alas, no, my friend. This lack of reduplication makes the whole enterprise an illusory movement; nothing is really done for the poor, but a new way is discovered for getting rich.

Ethical reduplication makes it seem at first glance as if the individual failed in great and far-reaching effectiveness—but he works fundamentally, and above there is a providence which keeps its eye on every honest person like that. At the time all the activity of the other one looks like something—but it is like a desert mirage.

And thus it is that the whole of modernity is nothing but a confusing mirage, because it lacks ethical reduplication.

In margin: Instead of history and characters we now have a fog of all sorts of impersonality and lack of character. History is fundamentally past, and people do not believe in the eternal—and humanity is like a school where the record book has disappeared. They comfort themselves nowadays with the thought that everything may be written in the book of forgetfulness.

x^4 A 176   n.d., 1851

« 996 *That I Am Supposed To Be an Eccentric Sort of a Fellow*

This is, however, really a hilarious satire upon the age. I express on a small scale, such as it is, a little ethical unselfishness in relationship to an idea. God knows that measured by the ideal this is sheer paltriness. But, humanly speaking, it still is a little—and, please note, every one of us *should* express the ethical. The average is down so low that I am shuffled aside as an eccentric, and even Bishop Mynster does this.

An odd eccentric fellow! I should be grateful if there appeared a genuine existential ethicist—what odd eccentricity this would be!

The ethical is always requirement—and consequently it is the greatest possible backwardness and distance from the ethical to regard it as peculiar, as eccentricity, that is, as something especially for that particular individual.

x^4 A 184   n.d., 1851

« 997 *Productivity*

Ethicists like Socrates, the religiously committed in the more rigorous sense, show no evidence of actual productivity—for this they have no time; they are completely dedicated to the energetic or intensive; they are completely oriented teleologically and are continually pressing into the existential.

x^4 A 320   n.d., 1851

« 998 *The Ethical Hierarchy*

The ethical begins straightway with this requirement to every person: you *shall* be perfect; if you are not, it is immediately charged to you as guilt.

In this way an end is made to all the chatter about wanting to be, wanting so very much to be—. No, in relation to the ethical you can speak only in self-accusation. If you are not perfect, you ought not have the audacity to chatter about wanting so very much to be, but you must admit humbly and at once: It is my fault; if I am not perfect, it is my own fault. Ethically, I myself am the only one who prevents me from being perfect, I, myself, who do not will rightly. To say that I would like very much to be, but that there is something else which prevents me, is to insult God and providence, is high treason against the ethical, is insidious hypocrisy.

x⁴ A 362   n.d., 1851

« 999 *Sophistry*

What makes the difference is not whether one person earns money by reading books, by painting, drawing, etc., another by making shoes, driving a taxi; no, the difference is whether one person renounces profit and money, the other does not.

This is Christianity's intention. It arranges everything ethically. All are equal; only the ethical determines the difference.

But sophistry has classified in such a way that the ethical concept of value, laudability, is transferred to certain aristocratic arts, which aristocratically reap benefits and accept money and are remunerated with advantages—as if the essence of aristocracy were not rather to renounce the advantages.

x⁴ A 549   n.d., 1852

« 1000 *Conservatism*

The very same thing which can be explained as something ethical in a man can also have its ground in a dominant addiction to pleasure—namely, this wanting to hang on to the old, the established state of things.

Precisely those men who are preoccupied with the desire to enjoy life, make a brilliant career in the world, precisely those men find it of utmost importance that there be no movement whatsoever in the religious. As soon as "the spirit" begins to move, existence [*Tilværelsen*] becomes so uneasy that a person cannot pull himself together and make a career in the world. Therefore it is very important that everything stay the same, that the religious should be appropriated from the previous generation exactly as it was, at most with only a few minor modifications. For the Epicurean always goes by the old Epicurean statement: *nil beatum nisi quietum.*[542]

x⁴ A 563   n.d., 1852

« 1001 *"And Also"*

About the most laughable thing one can imagine is to be a public official, social leader, honorary-degree holder, father, member of friends of societies—and also—"a reformer"!

But the category of "good sense" is precisely this "and also"—that one can be everything possible and also this and that.

"Character" is simply to be only "one thing." Thus one perceives that "good sense" has made everything characterless. The infinite is essentially abolished. In the realm of the finite, it holds, as good sense says, that one can join many things, can be the "and also." But infinitely one can be only one thing, or to be only one thing is to be infinite. And this is "character."

But both character and Christianity, etc., have been abolished. On the other hand there remains the machine with 1,000 jobs buzzing cozily. "Spiritually" such things can be done very nicely. The loss of an arm or a leg cannot go unnoticed, but "spirit" can very nicely disappear—and the machine continues to go on.

x^4 A 571   *n.d.*, 1852

« 1002 *Rule*

With regard to desire and everything involved in it, the rule is: procrastinate a little. Even if you do not believe yourself capable of complete victory over it, just try to manage to wait an hour, a day, etc., according to the circumstances.

As far as the good is concerned, the rule is: for every moment of delay more difficulties arise, and the spirit, which would incite you, is grieved, and you get into a prattling state which can engender the most demoralizing of all, either obtuseness or a desperate impatience.

x^4 A 669   *n.d.*, 1852

« 1003 *Christianity as a Regulating Weight*

Christianity has been abolished somewhat as follows. Men have entrenched themselves more and more firmly in the fixed idea that Christianity's meaning should be in a trivial sense to make life easier and easier, the temporal easier and easier, something which again is consistent with the fact that the preaching of Christianity has for a long time been, in a trivial sense, an occupation, so these rascally preachers, for the sake of profit, have administered Christianity just as shopkeepers or journalists—nothing better on the market—and therefore the meaning of Christianity becomes in the trivial sense: to make life easier.

Thereby they have succeeded in completely abolishing Christianity, for Christianity is not some physical externality which remains even though untrue affirmations are made about it; no, Christianity is an inwardness which is transformed by the affirmations.

And since Christianity has been abolished this way, the whole realm of the temporal has also come to be muddled, with the result that it is no longer a question of a revolution once in a while, but underneath everything is a revolution which can explode at any moment.

And this is consistent with the fact that we have abolished Christianity as the regulating weight, as weight, of course, but as regulating weight.

It certainly is true, as I have pointed out somewhere else, that the more meaningless we make life, the easier it is, and therefore that life in one sense has actually become easier, not, as the pastors falsify, by means of Christianity, but by abolishing Christianity. But, on the other hand, this nevertheless has its difficulty; when a man or when a generation must live in and for merely finite ends, life becomes a whirlpool, meaninglessness, and either a despairing arrogance or a despairing disconsolateness.

There must be weight—just as the clock or the clock's works need a heavy weight in order to run properly, and the ship needs ballast.

Christianity would furnish this weight, this regulating weight, by making it every individual's life-meaning that whether he becomes eternally saved is decided for him in this life. Consequently Christianity puts eternity at stake. Into the middle of all these finite goals, which merely confuse when they are supposed to be everything, Christianity introduced weight, and this weight was intended to regulate temporal life, both its good days and its bad days, etc.

And because the weight has vanished—the clock cannot run, the ship steers wildly—and for this reason human life is a whirlpool.

XI^1 A 252 *n.d.*, 1854

« 1004 *Duty to God—Duty to Oneself*

Concurrently as duty to God disappeared, duty to oneself made its appearance.

It is quite characteristic. Duty to God intends to strain man in the direction of the unconditional, undeniably the most inconvenient—so enough of that.

In compensation for this a new kind of duties arose, duties to the individual himself, or there was an advancement of all the baseness, the egotism in man; they advanced and became—duties to oneself. Strange, incidentally, that it took so long for this discovery to be made; after all, it lies so very close—one is closest of all to himself.

Some examples of duties to oneself. Suppose someone falls into the water. Another person comes walking by. Now it has always been the case that this second person does not have the courage to want to save the first one, but before the discovery of duties to oneself it went like this: the second one sneaked away and himself understood that he was a coward. Now, on the other hand, one does not sneak way, no, one withdraws with dignity—this is a duty to oneself. —To eat and to drink surely has always been custom and habit, but after that discovery it has come to mean something else: it is a duty to oneself. No doubt to be concerned about scraping money together was always the usual thing to do, but now it is in addition something meritorious—it is a duty to oneself.

In brief, such duty-people as we have nowadays were never found before. Their whole life is nothing but fulfillment of duty. Glorious invention: duties to the individual himself! What previous moral systems tried in vain to do by presenting the duty and getting men to do it has now been achieved by making into duty what men are inclined to do and what one does anyway.

My proposal is this: now that duty to God has vanished, duty to the neighbor should also be abolished and all of ethics should be treated under the heading: duties to oneself.

XI^1 A 451   n.d., 1854

« 1005 *To Live—To Die*

There are only two views of life which correspond to the duality that is man: animal and spirit.

According to the one the task is to live, to enjoy life, and to put everything into this.

The other view is: the meaning of life is to die.

XI^1 A 528   n.d., 1854

« 1006 *To See God Is To Die*

(*to die to*)

What paganism and Hebraism, too, maintained, namely, that to see God is to die, or at least to become blind, dumb, etc., Christianity expresses ethically as the task—to die to [the world] is the condition for seeing God.

In both situations there is the expression of majesty—that we cannot see God in the same sense as we see everything else, we cannot go on living and to see Peter and Paul—and also God. No, to see God (immediately) is to be set *in pausa*. And ethically the task is to die to the world in order to see God.

XI^2 A 113   n.d., 1854

« 1007 *Ironically Enough!*

There is nothing of which every man is so afraid as getting to know how enormously much he is capable of. You are capable of—do you want to know?—you are capable of living in poverty; you are capable of enduring almost all possible mistreatment, etc. But is it not true that you do not wish to get to know this; you would become enraged at the person who would tell you this, and you regard as a friend only the one who helps you to confirm yourself in the idea "I am not capable of enduring, it is beyond my power, etc."

XI^2 A 381   *n.d.*, 1854-55

EQUALITY

A *still-life*

« 1008 *The Two Brothers*

Once upon a time there were two brothers. They looked exactly alike, except for the difference that there was one pearl button more on the handle of one brother's black silk-umbrella than on the other's. And so they looked exactly alike—the brothers exactly, the umbrellas almost. If the umbrellas were excluded, they would have looked exactly alike.

VII^1 A 245 *n.d.*, 1845-47

« 1009

..... So it goes—God gives one person great joy in life and makes him speechless, and to another God denies joy in life and makes him eloquent—now isn't that equality! God makes one person great in the world and makes him envied; he makes another poor in the world and makes him blessed—now isn't that equality! God gives one person the beloved, but she distorts the image; he denies another the beloved, but lets him keep the image—now isn't that equality! God gives one person honor in the world and, see, he appropriates it to himself; God makes another despised in the world and, see, he, the despised one, gives God the glory—is this not, then, equality! Yet someone perhaps says: "This isn't the way it is, there is something phony about this equality; a note of sadness even creeps into the voice of the speaker." Yes, no doubt there is a sadness, and it should be there, because all consideration of human life on earth, if it is not accompanied by sadness, has no ring to it or is out of tune. Yes, there is sadness in it, to be sure, because the speaker, too, has dreamed his youthful fairy tale, the old, familiar tale which children tell in the evening, that far off in the woods he saw an old castle where a princess lived—and he did not find the world to be just like this; but neither did he find equality in the fairy tale.

VII^1 A 134 *n.d.*, 1846

« 1010

For the single individual there is something very humbling and yet at the same time infinitely elevating in the fact that God concerns himself just as much, absolutely just as much, with the least of men as with the greatest of them. But we human beings prefer to live in illusion. Alas, this is precisely why worldly fame and status are such dangerous traps (dangerous just as wealth tempts one in the direction of losing faith in providential care), because being the object of attention by the many, having the fate of all these people in one's hands, can so very easily lead to the erroneous conclusion that he is more important to God as well.

VII^1 A 180   n.d., 1846

« 1011

It is very moving to preach on Sundays about Christ's associating with sinners and tax-collectors—but on Mondays it is a crime to speak with an ordinary man, with a servant girl. It is, as they say, imprudently stupid to involve oneself in this manner with people instead of avoiding them and keeping out of sight. How stupid Christ must have been.

VIII^1 A 314   n.d., 1847

« 1012

Consequently even in Christendom the distinctions of earthly life all too easily come to assert themselves unchristianly. Yet the love command, which commands loving the neighbor, watches over this Christian equality between man and man. Every man, in Christendom as well, is assigned a place in one of the distinctions of earthly life where he particularly belongs by birth, rank, circumstance, education, condition of life, for no one of us is the purely human. Christianity has nothing against this distinction; Christianity is too earnest to romanticize about the purely human; no, it simply does not want a man to damage his soul by falling in love with this distinction, so that he either foolishly believes he has it so glorious and good here on earth that he would gladly let God keep heaven, if only he may keep all his glory, or so embittered by his oppressive lot here on earth, his wretchedness and misery that he foolishly will listen to nothing about the blessedness of heaven. This is what Christianity wants to prevent, and it will not be deceived. Because Christianity has conquered and eradicated the crying-to-heaven and horribly obvious abominations of earthly distinctions, because Christendom at first glance appears to be Christian, Christianity therefore sees very clearly how damnation and detestableness can dwell in a person's inwardness, only more concealed. It sees, surely with grief, that earthly busy-ness and the false prophets of secularism have made it appear as if only people of consequence can fall in love with the distinctions of earthly life, as if insignificant people were entitled to do everything in order to achieve equality—only not by way of becoming Christian in earnestness and truth. Now men seem to want to reverse the relationship; once upon a time it was the person of consequence who did not want to recognize his neighbor in the insignificant man, and now the insignificant man is to be taught to see in the person of consequence only—his enemy; I wonder if we come closer to Christian equality along this way?[543]

VIII² B 31:20 *n.d.,* 1847

« 1013

Let us think of another distinction in earthly life—that which exists between the learned man and the layman.[544] The times are past when the learned man arrogantly insisted that it be perfectly clear that compared to him everyone else was stupid. But I wonder if this same depravity, only more hidden and subtle, cannot still dwell in a man. Thus the learned depravity teaches that there still is and remains a yawning abyss between the knowledgeable and the ignorant; the knowledgeable ones are human beings, the others are numbers, the superfluous, the waste products of existence [*Tilværelsen*], necessary to a degree as substratum. This is the secret. But be careful, they say, don't express this too obviously lest you incite people, and these days one must not run the risk of such things happening. So this learned depravity wants to make the learned man believe that he should associate only with the intellectuals, should exist [*være til*] only for them, should have nothing to do with other men, should not be known by them. Yet he must not say such things out loud; it could be dangerous. The art of it is to sneak away from every contact and admission of relationship with other human beings in such a way that they do not become aware of it at all. It is no use getting involved with them, and so it is best that they never find out that one exists. Closed up within himself in this way, associating only with his fellows and those of the same synagogue, to other men he is supposed to be a momentary transient vision, seldom seen, soon forgotten. Ah, yes, the world has changed since those days when the learned ones showed themselves to the astonished throng in a splendid procession and accepted its adoration. The world has changed—and depravity along with it; and yet everything has remained the same.

And if there were a learned man (whose life consequently belonged particularly to the community of the learned) who could not find it in him to do this, who loathed this secret, who would rather admit openly that scholarship is not everybody's affair but on the other hand would rather not accept it as the basis of distinction between man and man—

444   EQUALITY

such a scholar would certainly run a double danger. His ranking associates would look upon him as a traitor, and the less important people would perhaps misunderstand him and mock him. Yes, if he had chosen to head a revolt of ignorance against everything pertaining to art, science, and scholarship, then they probably would have honored him, but that he would not do. And when he then stood accused by his own and ridiculed by the unimportant people—then the learned depravity would triumph. And many better ones among the learned would perhaps not be able to avoid taking part in the mockery. Many a better one—perhaps the better ones were constantly in the company of the learned or in an environment which insured them their distinction as scholars—would be enthusiastically willing to champion the statement that essentially all men are equal. But to champion equality in this manner is still, fundamentally, a confirmation of the distinction.

VIII² B 31:22   *n.d.*, 1847

« 1014

I have always maintained that all men have equal access to passion and feeling; this has been my consolation. But yet one also sees the hazards. A bustling oaf like Pastor Boiesen blasts⁵⁴⁵ at Dr. Rudelbach's scholarship, etc., for he (Boiesen) is a patriot! Bravo, what an enormous lie. Merely by being a patriot, merely by shouting about it, one becomes somebody. I had thought that by being a patriot one was a patriot and that was that.

VIII¹ A 665   *n.d.*, 1848

« 1015

Fundamentally every generation goes equally far, partly because one generation cannot depend upon the communication of another generation, which providence has no doubt arranged in order to protect itself. What enormous, gigantic strides the race would make if one could depend upon the communications, if what is put in writing were entirely true, if every author, especially every thinker, said outright wholly and precisely what he meant. But this conventional lying, especially the clergy's—how it has damaged spiritual life and the cause of Christianity!

IX A 44   *n.d.*, 1848

« 1016

It is still a comfort, a relief, if what one has to communicate is not related to the distinctions between man and man. If this is not the case, then there is still perhaps the consolation of being able to find among common men an honest person who can and will understand and can be used. It is precisely among ordinary people that the best capacities are to be found. At first glance the temptation might be to consider this to be the suffering in Christ's life, and in a certain sense it was this—that he had to look for his disciples among the common people. But what a consolation it nevertheless was, for him who was compelled to feel his heterogeneity with the established order as deeply as he did—that the common man was nevertheless related to him as a possibility.

But the person whose communication is related to the distinctions between man and man is deprived of this final, consoling access. A presentation in which the dialectical is the very point cannot address itself to the common man. Consequently in his search he is limited to the established order of things. He must seek these presuppositions of talents and knowledge—and then a categorical honesty. What wonder, then, if he seeks in vain. For this last qualification in particular is found, most likely, in a common man, who makes only a few demands upon life and has not been initiated into dangerous refinement.

IX A 340 *n.d.*, 1848

« 1017

To become sober![546] From a Christian point of view, this thought is so gigantic in its simplicity that we can become almost completely confused by it. How many, after all, have existed [*existeret*] who, existentially [*existentielt*] in their personal lives, even though equipped with extraordinary abilities, have understood that the very least actual self-denial, even if it were in a most insignificant aspect of daily life, has more value than a world-historical achievement which, interpreted externally, even religiously transforms a whole country or a world! How many have existed who, existentially in their personal lives, even though they were millionaires, have understood that the widow gave more than they did when they gave 900,000 dollars! It really makes a man shudder to think of the infinite unchangeableness of spirit with which God makes this distinction, God, for whom only the ethical and the ethical-religious have value.

There is a problem in connection with the simple person which I have often thought about. Imagine a young man who, for example, is a student; he becomes ill, can accomplish nothing, and is deeply troubled. Now if I were to console him—and how gladly I would do it—I would say: Consider that in the eyes of God your life, in spite of everything, is unconditionally just as important and full of meaning as the life of someone who astonishes the world and transforms it with his thinking. Yes, but in order truly to rest in this exaltation, is it not necessary, again, to have a good head, considerable intellectual power? So we are right where we started.

But I cannot escape the thought that every man, unconditionally every man, no matter how simple he is or how suffering, nevertheless can comprehend the highest, specifically, the religious. If this is not so, then Christianity is really nonsense. For me it is frightful to see the recklessness with which philosophers and the like introduce differentiating categories like genius, talent, etc., into religion. They have no intimation that religion is thereby abolished. Only one consolation have I had, the blessed one that I know something which can console, blessedly console every human being, unconditionally every single one. Take this consolation away, and I would rather not live, then I am splenetic.

Think of the highest, think of Christ—suppose that He came into the world in order to save a few clever people, for others could not understand Him. Detestable! Disgusting! He is not nauseated by any human suffering, by anyone's stupidity—but the society of clever people: yes, that would have nauseated Him.

I have had a deep sympathy for simply and solely being human, especially the suffering, unhappy, handicapped, and the like. I have learned to thank God for this sympathy as a gift of grace. God knows I have become a sacrifice because of this very sympathy, for without it I would never have involved myself so much with the common man and would never have exposed myself to vulgarity, which I did in sympathy for the many, the many who suffer innocently in the vilest manner.—It is still my constant prayer that God will keep me in this sympathy and increase it more and more.

Here at once is an example of the nonsense that voluntarily to expose oneself to danger is to tempt God and that one must not pray God to be tried in life. Do I not have the right, then, to pray God to grant that in a truly Christian sense, in a truly Christian sense, I may love men, love the neighbor? I should think so. But it is eternally sure that if I succeed only in some measure to love the neighbor in a truly Christian way, then suffering is unavoidable (this is Christianity's own teaching, and I have had the opportunity to be eternally and absolutely convinced of its truth); but then my prayer will carry the implication of running into danger.

X^2 A 348 *n.d.,* 1850

« 1018

There are many distinctions—yes, and of course the eternal can really remove all other distinctions. But there is one distinction between man and man which the eternal cannot take away—the distinction of the eternal: Have you lived in such a way that truth was in you, that there was something higher for which you actually suffered? Or did you live in such a way that your life revolved around profitable returns? The fact that you got along well only makes the matter worse.

This distinction the eternal cannot and will not take away: it will not contradict itself; two such men can never in all eternity come to an understanding with each other.

All other distinctions—of abilities, circumstances, fate, sex, age, etc.—the eternal must be able to remove and be able to bring about understanding and equality between these many distinctions in the temporal—but this other distinction it cannot remove.

What a satire, then, if someone whose life is profitable returns, a preacher or the like, speaks in fanatical expressions about being gathered together with Christ and the saints, yes, almost makes himself believe it, looks forward with longing to this gathering—what a satire, for it would surely be the most severe punishment for him to have to live in this company.

XI^2 A 122   *n.d.*, 1854

EXIST, EXISTENCE, EXISTENTIAL

« 1019

There appears at times a phenomenon which spiritually is quite comparable to a vegetative, digestive dozing off into a pleasant convalescent feeling. Consciousness appears as an overarching moon reaching from the front of the stage to the back. One dozes, as it were, in the totality of things (a pantheistic element, without producing strength as does the religious) in an oriental revery in the infinite, in which everything appears to be fiction—and one is reconciled as in a grand poem: the being of the whole world, the being of God, and my own being are poetry in which all the multiplicity, the wretched disparities of life, indigestible for human thought, are reconciled in a misty, dreamy existence [*Tilværelse*]. But then, regrettably, I wake up again, and the very same tragic relativity in everything begins worse than ever, the endless questions about *what I am*, about my joys and other people's interest in me, in what I am doing, and at the same time perhaps millions are doing exactly the same thing.

II A 125   n.d., 1837

« 1020

How intimately and essentially the measure of how much one knows himself depends on the measure of how much he believes he is known can be seen in the fact that nearsighted people do not believe that others some distance away can see them. Likewise the nearsighted sinner does not believe that God sees his straying; whereas the devout Christian, since he is known by God, now also recognizes his own frailty with a clarity that can be supplied only by sharing the prophetic eye of the spirit which scrutinizes the kidneys.[547]

II A 235   July 11, 1838

« 1021

Most men think, speak, and write the way they sleep, eat, and drink, without any question ever arising as to their relationship to the idea; with very few does this happen, and then this decisive moment has either

EXIST, EXISTENCE, EXISTENTIAL 449

an extraordinary propulsive power (the genius), or through apprehensiveness it paralyzes the individual (irony).

II A 556 September 6, 1839

« 1022

A sigh as great as the sound of ice in winter when the lake water is drained away.

II A 610 *n.d.*, 1837

« 1023

One has achieved tranquillity when, like the Alcidæ [*Alcedo ispida*] (Ice-birds),[548] he can build his nest upon the sea.[549]

II A 612 *n.d.*, 1837

« 1024

Life is like musical pitch; true pitch hovers between true and false and therein lies the beauty; true pitch in the more restricted sense, like logic, ontology, or abstract morality—here the mathematical—would be false for the musician.

II A 711 April 11, 1838

« 1025

Life can be interpreted only after it has been experienced, just as Christ did not begin to expound the Scriptures and show how they taught of him until after his Resurrection.[550]

II A 725 April 15, 1838

« 1026

When the individual has given up every effort to find himself outside of himself in existence [*Existentsen*], in relationships and the environment, and then after this shipwreck turns toward the highest, the absolute [*det Absolute*] increases not only in its fullness for him after this vacuum but also in the responsibility which he feels he has.

III A 26 *n.d.*, 1840

« 1027

It is a curiously sad feeling which grips one when he sees the poetic making its appearance in the development of an individual. For the poetic is the divine woof of the purely human existence [*Existents*]; it is the cord through which the divine holds fast to existence. Therefore one could believe that they are the blessed, those gifted individuals, those living telegraph wires between God and men. But this is most certainly not true. Madness is their lot; yes, and envy, lostness, in short, the annihilation of their personal existence as being incapable of enduring the touch of the divine. And thus they go through the world misunderstood, neglected, criticized (can anything more ridiculous be imagined!) —yes, misunderstood, for must not everyone who understands the poet also undergo the same experience of being burned? And this is the glory of the world; this is the highest and the best on earth: the poet—this illustrious name to which one attaches the most elevated conceptions, the most lofty expectations—and yet this is his fate: to know a thirst which is never satisfied. The poetic life in the personality is the unconscious sacrifice,* the *molimina* of the divine, because it is first in the religious** that the sacrifice becomes conscious and the misrelationship is removed.

III A 62   n.d., 1840

« 1028

What is the relation between the speculating subject and historical existence [*Existents*]?551 What is continuity? What is primitivity?

IV C 92   n.d., 1842-43

« 1029

*Nullum exstitit magnum ingenium sine aliqua dementia*552—this is the secular expression for the religious thesis: one whom God blesses religiously he *eo ipso* execrates in a secular way. So it must be: the first has its basis in the boundaries of existence [*Tilværelse*] and the second in the doubleness [*Duplicitet*] of existence [*Tilværelsens*].

IV A 148   n.d., 1843

« 1030

Philosophy is perfectly right in saying that life must be understood backwards. But then one forgets the other clause—that it must be lived forwards.553 The more one thinks through this clause, the more one concludes that life in temporality never becomes properly understandable, simply because never at any time does one get perfect repose to take a stance: backwards.

IV A 164   n.d., 1843

---

* Just as for the Jews fertility was the epitome of the highest blessedness, so is the poetic for every man in whom something higher stirs, and yet Rachel deservedly unbraided God, saying: If this is what being pregnant means, why did I get this way?

** Therefore Goethe is less appealing, because he is too self-confident to be a sacrifice and not profound enough to want to be.

« 1031

What is happiness? A ghost which is only when it has been. What is hope? A persistent tormentor one cannot get rid of, a shrewd swindler who holds out even longer than honesty, a quarrelsome friend who always retains his rights, even when the emperor has lost his. What is memory? A burdensome consoler, a knave who wounds from behind, a shadow one cannot sell even if someone would buy it! What is bliss? A desire one gives to whoever will have it. What is faith? A rope by which one gets hung if he does not hang himself. What is truth? A secret the dying take with them. What is friendship? One plague more! What is expectation? A flying arrow which does not take off. What is fulfillment? An arrow which misses the mark.[554]

IV A 188 *n.d.*, 1844

« 1032

That I exist [*er til*] was the eternal presupposition of the ancient world; that I am a sinner is the new spontaneity of the Christian consciousness; the one can be demonstrated no more than the other.[555]

V A 6 *n.d.*, 1844

« 1033

From the logical point of view, the Cartesian formulation: I think, therefore I am [*er*]—is a play on words, because the "I am" logically signifies nothing other than " I am thinking" or "I think."[556]

Cf. Jacobi S.W., II, p. 102n.

V A 30 *n.d.*, 1844

« 1034

When *an existence* [*Existents*] is genuinely considered *under the aspect of the eternal, the result is*, eo ipso, *isolation*. The desperate thing about it is that one never gets to know anything concerning this among the thinkers; they leap over such things. But take for example (in Weil, *Biblische Legenden der Muselmänner*; Frankfort a.M., 1845; p. 277), that on the last day Adam will shout: Oh Lord, just save my soul, I'm not concerned about either Eve or Abel; all of Christ's utterances about the fall of Jerusalem, where the meaning is precisely that the God-relationship in its eternal validity will neutralize every relationship, where he says (Mark 13:9): But take heed to yourselves—then what becomes of all the busy world-historical social categories?

VI A 65 *n.d.*, 1845

« 1035

You stand as if on the mountain of transfiguration and would be off and away—but then finitude's little demands and petty debts to the grocer, shoemaker, and tailor get hold of you, and the sum of it all—you remain on earth and the transformation does not take place in you but in the mount of transfiguration, which becomes a manure pile. It is as if a man wants to go from Per Madsen's Alley to the castle, but he meets so many conflicts of finitude before he gets off this street that he cannot appear at court and stays home. Existence [*Tilværelse*] is always a tragedy in the beginning and turns into a vaudeville act.

* *In margin:* something will certainly come of it. The meaning is either that someone could teach something by being a witness, for to be a witness is in no way direct communication, or that it becomes clear that there is no schoolmaster.

VI A 101   *n.d.*, 1845

« 1036

If there were no earthquakes, no volcanic eruptions, no plagues, wars, etc., to teach men the uncertainty of all things, then for daily use the religious address would effectively do the job. Yes, there you get it.

VI A 136   *n.d.*, 1845

« 1037

This would be a suitable humorous line for a married man to his pregnant wife: "Now listen, little mother, couldn't you see about speeding up a little with this piece of work?" A humorist comes easily by impatience, but the course of nature is a satire over human haste and human slowness.

VI A 139   *n.d.*, 1845

« 1038 *Concluding Simple Postscript*

The meaning of the last section in the Introduction (or if it comes to be in the Appendix): "For if I say so myself, I am anything but a devilish good fellow," etc.,[557] is that on the whole there can be no schoolmaster, strictly understood, in the art of existing [*at existere*]. This is said often enough in the book, but it is said here in such a way that many will understand it straightforwardly, and yet probably no one will raise an objection. Barbs bristle in the words: "the ambiguous art"* and farther on, "be this a joyful or a sorrowful sign," joyful, namely, that there is no one, because he who will straightforwardly be this is a fool, and finally, "far be it from me, the vain and empty thought of wanting to be such a teacher" (vain here in the biblical sense). —With respect to existing, there is only the learner, for anyone who fancies that he is in this respect finished, that he can teach others and on top of that himself forgets to exist and to learn, is a fool. In relation to existing there is for all existing persons one schoolmaster—existence itself.

VI A 140   n.d., 1845

« 1039

That an abstract thinker in our age does not think about such things [existing and abstraction] is irrelevant, but the Greeks were at any rate aware and their skeptical ataraxia was at any rate a serious attempt to abstract from existing [at existere], completely different from unthinkingly not becoming aware of it at all and continuing to live in this manner because lack of awareness has become habit and custom. If I did not exist [existerede], my thought would never add to existence [Existents]; on the contrary, it subtracts from it. The being [Væren] which specifically is the being of thought is within possibility, is possibility's representation of actual being, but it is not the being which relates itself as actuality to the whole sphere of abstraction as possibility. The annulled being Hegel himself calls essence [Væsen], and the medium of thought is not being but essence.

VI B 54:10   n.d., 1845

« 1040

If a couple thousand years are not suddenly sliced away for men and this bridge demolished in order to teach men to begin with the problems of actual life and existence [Tilværelse], everything is unhinged. We confuse the existential [existentielle] problem itself with its reflex in the consciousness of all the generations of the learned. The main issue in regard to every existential [existentielt] problem is its significance to me; after that I can see whether or not I am fit to discuss it learnedly.

VII[1] A 33   n.d., 1846

« 1041

There is a very good observation by Ritter[558] (in Introduction to Vol. I*) regarding the idea of structuring, that it is easier to structure a complete world-history than the history of the earth or of man, easier to structure the history of man than the history of philosophy—at the

---

* In margin: p. 23.

same time it fortunately has never occurred to anyone to want to structure the history of a single individual human being. This is properly satirical and quite sound. The idea of structuring is imaginative, and for this very reason it is embarrassed by the concrete. Thus, general surveys conceal man's ignorance (which is why the half-educated, especially, excel in this kind of thing), and a little concreteness makes this clear.

VII^1 A 48   n.d., 1846

« 1042

The difficulty in thinking something through increases in proportion to the existential [*existentielt*] use a person is to make of what he thinks about. One who sits with anguished conscience and at every moment could use the alleviation of believing in the forgiveness of sins— if he is to think it through, he is hard pressed. But ordinarily philosophers (Hegel and all the rest), as most men, in daily affairs basically exist [*existere*] in categories entirely different from those in which they speculate, and they console themselves with something entirely different from what they solemnly discuss. Out of this come the untruthfulness and confusion prevalent in science and scholarship.

VII^1 A 80   n.d., 1846

« 1043

The reason so-called immanental thinking has become so fashionable, practically among bartenders, too, is that it so splendidly encourages thoughtlessness in existence [*Existents*] and yet flatters it so profusely. Once in a while one thinks something in imaginative distance, a compound of abstraction *sub specie æterni*, which wipes out all distinctions —and for daily use exists [*existerer*] in animal categories (vegetates comfortably, discreetly chats a little with neighbors and the fellow next door, etc.). How infinitely remote most men's so-called thinking usually is from their existence; how rarely does even one single person get any reflective transparency with regard to his thought-existence [*Tanke-Existents*]; how rare is even the one who is simply aware of this.

VII^1 A 140   n.d., 1846

« 1044

That even Poul Møller[559] was tried in all sorts of doubt is at times apparent in some quite accidental expression. In an aphorism he speaks of fanatical pastors who speak glowingly and do not detect that all their religiosity is accelerated circulation of the blood. Alas, this is just where the knot binds. How many man live so transparently that they really know what's what? They think in entirely different categories from those in which they live. They speak in religious categories and live in categories of sensuousness, the categories of immediate well-being.

VII^1 A 216 n.d., 1847

« 1045

In margin of 1044 (VII^1 A 216):
If it is to become apparent that a sufferer has faith, then faith must appear simultaneously along with the suffering. But what happens—as pain, misfortune, and opposition are gradually taken away, his life as interpreted by the secular mind becomes healthier and happier—and he thinks this is due to faith; whereas, on the contrary, it takes place through the restored vitality of immediacy.

VII^1 A 217 n.d., 1847

« 1046

Even though I achieve nothing else, I nevertheless hope to leave very accurate and experientially based observations concerning the conditions of existence [*Tilværelsens*]. I am convinced above all that these conditions are always essentially the same. Therefore, it is foolishness for a man, congratulating himself on his good luck, to say that his life proceeds without adversities—for this can only be possible in guilt, in the guilt of not having ventured out far enough. It is ridiculous to hear a man speak of the good peaceful times in which we now live—it perhaps never occurs to him merely to think about whether he for his part has ventured enough, whether he has not cheated existence and that all this security is cheating. This is just like the paltry preacher-talk that we ought not tempt God by risking dangers, but when suffering happens to a person, etc. Rubbish! Genuine decision never happens to a man; one has to enter into decision. All the noble persons who have risked their lives for the good—if they had sat and waited for dangers to happen to them, they never would have faced danger.

The conditions of existence always remain the same. No doubt many, many, many experienced men have lived before me, but the question is—how far out have these men of experience ventured? Goethe was a great man of experience, but he swam in shallow water.

Using my diagram, a young person should be able to see very accurately beforehand, just as on a price list: if you venture this far out, then the conditions are thus and so, this to win and this to lose; and if you venture out this far, these are the conditions, etc.

VIII^1 A 127 n.d., 1847

« 1047

When one is immersed in his own thoughts and thus on the way to forgetting actuality, it is remarkable how he is called back, as it happened to me today when I was called back by a peddler woman shouting: Cherries, fifteen cents! Here are cherries for fifteen cents! What called me back especially was not merely this shout—but that familiar voice! The memory comes from my earliest childhood; only now in the later years she has changed somewhat and has acquired a crooked mouth, which somewhat influences her pronunciation of the word "cents."

VIII¹ A 226   n.d., 1847

« 1048

"The world" is the medium in which we are. Just as we say that water has such and such characteristics and the test bears it out, so must one's own life, life-outlook, circumstances, and proportions of reputation and respect bear out what one himself says about the world. If a glob of spit floating upon the surface of the water were to describe the wretchedness of the element "water" in a well-prepared and brilliantly delivered speech and prove it by the fact that gold sinks in water, there would be no rebuttal. But if the glob of spit were to attempt in some way to prove to us that it was itself gold, then we would have to answer: You contradict yourself, for are you not floating upon the water? When someone says that the world is corrupt or mediocre and is himself highly respected in the world, he practically acknowledges that he himself is mediocre or corrupt. Herein lie earnestness and a dialectical coherence. The preachers' nonsense is not much to boast about.

VIII¹ A 234   n.d., 1847

«1049

In imagination and feelings, in thought and talk, everyone, even the most capable, is usually a good distance beyond himself or beyond what he is in act and actuality. The majority of men are like a railway car detached from the locomotive—they are far beyond themselves, and in actuality they are far behind.[560]

VIII¹ A 292   n.d., 1847

« 1050

All men desire to be or to become *contemporary* with great men, great events, etc.—but only God knows how many men really live contemporaneously with themselves.[561] To be contemporary with oneself (therefore neither in the future of fear or of expectation nor in the past) is transparency in repose, and this is possible only in the God-relationship, or it is the God-relationship.

VIII[1] A 320   *n.d.*, 1847

« 1051

To want to spectate and to spectate,[562] to be exalted by the highest, is essentially sinful and culpable lasciviousness, just as sinful as any other lasciviousness—to be uplifted as a spectator instead of coming out into the tension of true actuality, spectating upon suffering as a good thing instead of suffering, etc. This lasciviousness makes the church into a theater: for the difference between the theater and the church is the relationship to actuality. The lasciviousness of spectatorship is just as sinful as a debauchee's fear of getting children; in spectating one wants the enjoyment and bids goodbye to earnestness.

IX A 154   *n.d.*, 1848

« 1052

How can anyone really go in for praising this temporal existence* [*Tilværelse*] in which a person must *either* detestably repress (a crime worse than aborting the fetus) every endeavor in the more ideal sense and every possibility of true ideality or, just as revolting, cut it in half—in order to puff up or swell up with worldly honor and the loathsome fat of reputation; *or*, if he wills it [ideality], *eo ipso* is a martyr.

No, Christianity is still the only explanation of existence which holds water. This earthly existence is suffering; every man has his share, and therefore his dying words are: God be praised; it is done with.

This earthly existence is a time of test [*Prøvens Tid*], is the examination. All this nonsense about achieving and achieving is another priestly invention for money, a kind of earnestness which does away with God. No, neither you nor I have anything to do with playing providence or with wanting to achieve. You and I are being examined our whole life long. It follows naturally, therefore, that you must work in one way or another quite differently than they who achieve, but you are freed from all conceit.

Therefore the notion that the world is progressing is nonsense and also a view of existence which does away with God. Those busy achievers in particular believe that they, as it were, are straining themselves for the human race and carrying it forward. O, spare yourself the trouble! No, you are being examined, and this existence is ordered by God in such a way that it can be just this—the examination, self-denial's test of power. You are not the one who is going to make the world over, but it is you who by living in this world must be examined.

IX A 358 *n.d.*, 1848

« 1053

* *In margin of 1052* (IX A 358):
I do not mean the world of nature [*Naturtilværelsen*] but human society (for the birds' singing is beautiful and the sparrow is amusing and the lily is lovely and the starry host eternally unforgettable, etc.—but man, creation's prodigy and adornment, as the preachers say for money —he is the only defacement).

IX A 359 *n.d.*, 1848

« 1054

In a deeper sense no one can really learn anything from the past, however vivaciously he knows how to enter into it, because it is the past and consequently can only be comprehended by the imagination. But imagination and the medium of imagination is a medium of ideality and therefore can express greatness and glory very well, but it cannot express the wretchedness of actuality except on a very foreshortened scale. The point, however, is the suffering which the good man has to endure; right here is the lower actuality or the sensuousness of actuality, of time, and of worldliness.

Thus in a certain sense we can say providence has diligently planned actuality this way in order that it can become earnestness, an actual suffering, for every one individually. If a person could completely anticipate actuality in ideality and imagination and by means of such a movement of the imagination learn to know himself, develop, etc., equally well as in actuality, then he would really have to say that actuality is superfluous, that God, if I dare say so, has behaved strangely. But this is not the case.

No, things do not go that way. So, for example, there lives now, in 1848, a youth, an intelligent youth. He has imagination and ideality enough to be grasped by what is great, and he does this as vivaciously and attentively as is possible for the imagination, everything which greatness must suffer in the world. This image now grips his soul; he cannot escape it; he will personally be this. Good! Now providence captures him, and now it becomes an earnest matter. Drawn by the image, trusting in God, he ventures so far out that he himself now stands in the situation of actuality. Now actuality brings its power to bear. Even just one year of actual suffering is a long time, completely different from anything the imagination can present. To be the superior one but still to live in actuality with all these actual human beings who prefer to regard one as crazy—this is earnestness. In imagination (consequently in relation to the past) the concept of superiority is so highly developed that it really cannot be expressed in imagination that these actual people regard the superior one as mad. The imagination cannot reproduce this actual pressure of finiteness. Take Socrates, for example. In the imagination's understanding of him he is so infinitely superior that all his contemporaries become merely something of a joke—that is, it is extremely easy for this to happen. But in actuality it was not like this at all. Socrates suffered inwardly under it all. Ideality is the very contradiction of being in actuality; only in the medium of ideality can a man be so ideal that he is ideal at every moment—in actuality this is impossible. It follows from this that actuality has a hold on him. If it has mastery over him, then he is not great; but the hold it has on him is his suffering.

IX A 382   n.d., 1848

« 1055

In Job it says that Satan, according to his own word, came to spy on and wander through the world. This suggests that there is a kind of observing which is rooted in evil, just as spectating curiosity is always rooted in evil.

X^1 A 193   n.d., 1849

« 1056 *A Little Insert*

A "highly regarded" magnificent gentleman proclaims that the truth is ridiculed, mocked, derided, spit upon: On my honor, yes, I would even say it in the hour of my death, I am so clearly convinced of it I would repeat it on judgment day. —This is nonsense! A person of status, moving only in the "best circles," movingly proclaims that Christ went about with sinners and tax-collectors and ate with them, lived in the company of the common man on the streets and avenues: On my honor, yes, I would even say it in the hour of my death, I am so clearly convinced of it I would repeat it on judgment day. —This is nonsense! A man with a fat salary and velvet paunch or with a velvet paunch and a fat salary proclaims that Christ sent out his "disciples" saying that they should own nothing, neither purse nor staff: On my honor, yes, I would even say it in the hour of my death, I am so clearly convinced of it I would repeat it on judgment day. This is nonsense!

One of two things: *either* one's life shall express in some measure that one is ridiculed, mocked; that one lives in the company of the common man on the streets and avenues and eats with tax-collectors and sinners; that one is poor and pinched; *or* one shall hold his tongue about such things and preach about the advantages of being a highly regarded, magnificent gentleman, along with the methods used in achieving "this good," about the advantages of being a person of status along with the pleasantness of moving in the best circles, about the advantages of having a fat salary along with the benefits connected with a velvet paunch.

The essential sermon is one's own existence [*Existents*]. A person preaches with this every hour of the day and with power quite different from that of the most eloquent speaker in his most eloquent moment. To let one's existence express the opposite and then let one's mouth run with eloquent babbling about the opposite is in the deepest sense nonsense and, Christianly, this means to become liable to eternal judgment, even though in the temporal world it is the way to high positions, honor, reputation, popularity, and the like.

x^1 A 650   *n.d.*, 1849

« 1057

What confuses the whole idea of "essence" in logic is that attention is not given to the fact that one continually functions with the "concept", existence [*Existents*]. But the *concept*, existence, is an ideality, and the difficulty is precisely whether existence is absorbed in the concept. Then Spinoza may be right:[563] *essentia involvit existentiam*, namely, the concept-existence, i.e., existence in ideality. From another point of view, Kant is right in saying, "Existence brings no new predicate to a concept." Obviously Kant honestly thinks of existence as not being absorbed into the concept, empirical existence. In all the relationships of ideality it holds true that *essentia* is *existentia*, if the use of the concept *existentia* is otherwise justified here. The Leibnizian statement: If God is possible, he is necessary—is entirely correct. Nothing is added to a concept whether it has existence or not; it is a matter of complete indifference; it indeed has existence, i.e., concept-existence, ideal existence.

But existence corresponds to the individual; as Aristotle has already taught, the individual lies outside of and is not absorbed in the concept. For a particular animal, a particular plant, a particular human being, existence (to be—or not to be) is very crucial; a particular human being is certainly not concept-existence. The very way in which modern philosophy speaks of existence shows that it does not believe in the immortality of the individual; it does not believe at all; it comprehends only the eternity of "concepts."

x^2 A 328   *n.d.*, 1849-50

« 1058

It is nevertheless a curious misunderstanding, a consequence of the deification of the scholarly and the scientific—namely, this desire to apply the scientific also to the portrayal of the existential [*Existentielles*]. The existential as such is far more concrete than the "scientific," (and to introduce learned science and scholarship into a portrayal of the existential is pure nonsense); the portrayal of the existential is chiefly either realization in life or poetic presentation, *loquere ut videam*.[564]

X^2 A 414 *n.d.*, 1850

« 1059 *"Science"—the Existential*

"Actuality [*Virkeligheden*] cannot be conceptualized. Johannes Climacus[565] has already shown this correctly and very simply. To conceptualize is to dissolve actuality into *possibility*—but then it is impossible to conceptualize it, because to conceptualize it is to transform it into possibility and therefore not to hold to it as actuality. As far as actuality is concerned, conceptualization is retrogression, a step backward, not a step forward. It is not as if "actuality" were void of concepts, not at all; no, the concept which is found by conceptually dissolving it into possibility is also in actuality, but there is still something more—that it is actuality. To go from possibility to actuality is a step forward (except in relation to evil); to go from actuality to possibility is a step backward.

But in the modern period the baleful confusion is that "actuality" has been included in logic, and then in distraction it is forgotten that "actuality" in logic is, however, only a "thought actuality," i.e., is possibility.

Art, science, poetry, etc., deal only with possibility, that is, possibility not in the sense of an idle hypothesis but possibility in the sense of ideal actuality.

But is not the historical actuality? Certainly. But what history? Six thousand years of the world's history is certainly actuality, but a traversed actuality; it is and can exist [*være til*] for me only as thought actuality, i.e., as possibility. Whether or not the dead have actually realized [*realiseret*] existentially [*existentielt*] the tasks which were before them in actuality has now been decided, has been concluded; there is no more existential actuality for them except in what has been traversed, which for me, again, exists only as ideal actuality, as thought actuality, as possibility.

But men are almost crazed by this pantheistic scientism. A professor thinks: Don't mind me; the few years I live, the little I am able to do—is this something to waste the slightest moment on—no, "science,

science." But this is irreligiousness, a lack of religious discipline, a lack of soberness; it is an intoxication, dreamy intoxication.

That "science" is lower than the existential [*Existentielle*] is seen very simply in the God-man. Imagine yourself as a contemporary: here "science and scholarship" is an impossibility, because the God-man is himself the existential. But when the pace is diminished, a couple centuries later, then the religiousness has become less, and then a "learned approach" steps forth. And 1,800 years later the relationship is completely turned around; then "science and scholarship" is higher than the existential.

Imagine yourself as a contemporary of Socrates. There is no science and scholarship here; this is just what he wants to eliminate; he is a gadfly, himself the existential. But then he dies; in Plato the existential is diminished, then comes "science and scholarship." Is Plato greater than Socrates? Yes, perhaps when assistant professors judge, but then they must be consistent and judge that a professor in theology is greater than Christ.

No, precisely when "science and scholarship" has become unconditionally the highest, precisely then religiousness is as good as completely gone. These are the two poles, and with respect to the ethical-religious one can accurately cast the horoscope of a generation by finding out what it judges of "science and scholarship" in the realm of the religious. "Minerva's owl flies only when it is dark," and "science and scholarship" always follows after. What Johannes Climacus[566] says is true: to transform Christianity into "science and scholarship" is the greatest possible error, and when it has succeeded completely (O, how the age will rejoice) —then Christianity is also completely abolished.

But what the Judge says in *Either/Or*[567] is also true, that the more subtle and distinguished the drink to which one succumbs, the more difficult the cure. And now to succumb to "science and scholarship." Merciful God, what a world revolution there must be to pull men out of this intoxication. When to be intoxicated is the mark of being sober, not only in one's own eyes but in the eyes of all—but what am I saying, sober, to be more than sober, sober as a god who in blessed coolness rests in the complete equilibrium of having this self-esteem and of being respected as such by all—what hope is there, then, of salvation? Anyone who speaks of this kind of drunkenness will be regarded scientifically and scholarly, by the whole world, as a contemptible drunkard.

x^2 A 439   *n.d.*, 1850

« 1060 *Socrates—Christianity*

This Socratic thesis is of utmost importance for Christianity: Virtue cannot be taught; that is, it is not a doctrine, it is a being-able, an exercising, an existing [*Existeren*], an existential [*existentiel*] transformation, and therefore it is so slow to learn, not at all as simple and easy as the rote-learning of one more language or one more system. No, in respect to virtue there is always particular emphasis on *the internal*, the inward, "the single individual."

Here I come again to my thesis—Christianity is not a doctrine but an existence-communication [*Existents-Meddelelse*].

It is of crucial importance to define the concept "teacher" in relation to Christianity. All this unholy mob of "preachers and professors" is what really, *bona fide*, has confused "the faith."

x^2 A 606   *n.d.*, 1850

« 1061 *The Judgment upon Christendom*

If it were possible to maintain that Christianity no longer has to struggle, that we cannot persecute each other any more because we are all Christians, etc., but can take life straight, not inversely—if this were the case, the proof would be that Christ would not be put to death if he were to come again.

And yet it is customary in Christendom to say that it would be like this.

If Christianity were a doctrine, it would be possible. But this would not be the case with Plato, if he were to come a second time and he had been put to death the first time.

But Christianity is not doctrine; it is an existence [*Existents*], an existing [*Existeren*]. Christianity is not the doctrine about denying oneself, about this being the right thing to do for three reasons. Christianity is to deny oneself. And if Christ this moment were to express absolute self-denial, death would be certain.

x^3 A 150   *n.d.*, 1850

« 1062 *An Apostle in Our Time*

If I were to imagine such a one in our time, he would refrain completely from preaching, in order, if possible, to draw attention to what it means to exist [*at existere*], to preach by existentially [*existentielt*] expressing self-denial, the imitation of Christ, etc. How could he cope verbally with those artists in eloquence who preach now—and completely cover up what it means to exist [*at existere*].

A man is castrated to make him a singer who can reach the high notes which no ordinary man can reach; so also these orators, Christianly understood, are castrati, deprived of their essential masculinity, which is the existential [*det Existentielle*]—but they can reach notes higher and more ravishing than any true Christian can.

x^3 A 725   *n.d.*, 1851

« 1063 *The Existential—the Art of Speaking—Eloquence*

The more a person himself strives in daily existing [*Existeren*], the less inclined he is to deliver speeches. Take Socrates. Such a person understands only too well that those glorious orators and masters of eloquence lead men not into but away from the existential [*Existentielle*], which always merely assigns these little tasks in the daily routine but does not have the spectacular situations and fascinating experiences. Such a person will therefore say: Good Lord, what is to come of an hour's declamation once a week or once a year? No, such a one therefore becomes an ironist, a teaser. And what does this mean? It means that he continually places the little things of life together with the highest, evokes awareness that although in one sense the issue hinges upon the highest, it also has to do with the most commonplace—in short, he does not hold the tasks esthetically at a distance.

On the other hand, the less a person himself exists [*existerer*] the greater is the urge toward the effusions of eloquence.

We are thinking especially now of the situation in Christendom.

x^4 A 5   *n.d.*, 1851

« 1064 *The Existential Springs*

are slack. Where previously there were springs there is now nonsense (reasons, consideration, deliberations, looking to "the others," etc.). Therefore all motion is simulated motion, motion on the spot, as if a cow were trying to fly. This is highly irregular preparation for action, something like getting ready for a foot race by putting on three overcoats, two furs, overshoes, etc.

x^4 A 62   *n.d.*, 1851

« 1065 *The Existential—an Observation*

The question is whether one day of fasting is not a far more earnest exercise than hearing or reading a sermon one hour every day for fourteen days—without changing one's way of life.

x^4 A 207   *n.d.*, 1851

« 1066 *The Meaning of Existence (Tilværelsens)*

All this about the history of Christianity, etc. is, to repeat, stuff and nonsense, and also trickery, for the purpose of dethroning Christianity as absolute power.

The meaning of this existence is: to be examined, to be examined for eternity.

God has so ordered this existence that it is impossible in this world truly to relate oneself to truth without having to suffer—and eternity judges everyone as to whether he has related himself in suffering to the truth.

Man's interest, on the other hand, is in getting hold of the truth—without having to suffer. Man, every man, has some sense of truth, but to suffer for it he in truth will not, and he will not understand that this suffering intrinsically belongs to truth.

Man's interest, then, is in getting hold of the truth without having to suffer, which is really impossible.

Existence and its examination are like this. If I were a pagan and were to talk in Greek fashion, I might say that God has organized everything this way to amuse himself. He amuses himself the way a man can by putting meat in a mousetrap and watching the mouse's skill in getting the meat without being trapped—in the same way God amuses himself over the leaping and swinging and twisting, etc., of all these millions of people as they try to get hold of the truth without having to suffer. All those millions—ah, yes, for the divine has majestic proportions, uses centuries to let mistakes make merry.

To repeat, existence is ordered in such a way that truly to relate oneself to truth is impossible without suffering. If there happens to be a single individual who, somewhat more honestly, wants to venture out into the truth—although he also would rather have the truth without suffering for it—then providence takes pity on him and helps him—really to suffer. Naturally he cries "Woe!" and "Alas!"—but it is still kindness on the part of providence, if it is certain that a person can relate himself to the truth only by really suffering and that eternity judges whether one has really suffered for the truth and rejects all Sophists.

XI^1 A 353   *n.d.*, 1854

« 1067 *To Relate Oneself to the Concepts*

Plato teaches that only the ideas have true being [*Væren*].

Thus one can also, and more truly, say that only the human existing [*Existeren*] which relates itself to the concepts by primitively taking possession of them, by examining, by modifying, by producing new, only this existing [*Existeren*] interests existence [*Tilværelse*]. Any other human existing [*Existeren*] is merely mimicker-existence [*Exemplar-Existents*], a rummaging in the finite world, which vanishes without a trace and has never interested existence [*Tilværelsen*]. And this holds true just as much for a philistine-bourgeois's existing [*Existeren*] as, for example, for a European war, if it is not placed in relationship to concepts, in which case authentic existing is still due only to the individual through whom it occurs.

Although that which relates itself to the concepts thereby interests existence [*Tilværelsen*], such an existing [*Existeren*] naturally becomes a battle with demons and powers which otherwise would not appear to be there at all. To be a Christian was originally understood to be like this, but now it has become something entirely different, and, of course, being a Christian has gained the ease, comfortableness, and indolence reserved for all triviality, and then this triviality is regarded as an advance, without any suspicion that precisely [the absence of] the spiritual trials and the battles of the demonic against something and the opposition of all existence [*Tilværelsens*] is an indirect admission—because existence is too old and too shrewd to be inconvenienced for nothing.

XI^2 A 63   *n.d.,* 1854

EXPERIENCE

« 1068

What really counts in life is that at some time one has seen something, felt something, which is so great, so matchless, that everything else is nothing by comparison, that even if he forgot everything he would never forget this, so that he could say with Benvenuto Cellini, when after sitting a long time in a dark dungeon he got to see the sun: *die Gewalt der Strahlen nöthigte mich, wie gewöhnlich die Augen zu schliessen, aber ich erholte mich bald, öffnete die Augen wieder, sah unverwandt nach ihr und sagte: O meine Sonne, nach der ich so lange mich gesehnt habe, ich will nun nichts weiter sehen, wenn auch deine Strahlen mich blind machen sollten, und so blieb ich mit festem Blick stehen.*[568]

(Goethe's *Werke*, 8°; Stuttgart and Tübingen: 1830; XXXIV, pp. 365-66.)

II A 58   n.d., 1837

« 1069 *What It Means To Desire Experience on the Gospel Story of Nicodemus*[569]

Prayer

..... and when you favor us with one of the better hours, we pray that it may not be one of the many fleeting moods which merely unsettle our minds in various ways, but that every such hour may in itself contain a promise that it will not be the only one of its kind, lest distress so overwhelm us that we are not able to collect ourselves at the time of our visitation, or lest joy so transport us that the moment of blessing fades away unnoticed and unused. We know very well that it is not granted to us frail human beings to have the divine constantly dwelling within us; yet we also know this is what we strive for and that you will not leave us without witness, that your grace is a spring which never goes dry because we drink of it but wells up all the more and bounds all the higher the deeper we dig. We are unable to determine the time or the place, but teach us to prepare ourselves inwardly so that in the opportune moment we may not be incompetent and unworthy to receive, may not be cold and unfruitful.

To have experience—yes, it is a great idea to have experienced much; to possess an inexhaustible mental treasure which can never be taken away from us is indeed a high aim. It is this desire which animates the youth when his heart swells with vague longings and he wishes nothing to escape his glance, wishes to try everything, to attempt all things— often linked to the vain wish that he might legitimately be able to say: Yes, this, too, I have experienced. And he wishes to have gone through not only the happy experiences but also the sad, in order later to remember that the cup of sorrow had also been offered to him, that he tasted its bitterness and yet held himself erect.

But the error in this is wanting to have experienced everything even before he has really begun to live.

And now the older person—we presuppose that he has experienced all this; and even though in ungodly hankering one frequently imagines that what the particular person has experienced is nothing compared with what he himself is going to experience, and even though he proudly thinks of himself as old and far richer in experience, yet he does have a certain respect for that which the older person possesses, because, after all, it has been experienced. How sad it would be to imagine an old person who throughout his whole life had been merely contemporary with his own life, who knew his own life as he knew every other external event, knew the hour and the minute, but the inward appropriation of it——. Thus we see that neither the restless craving to be out in the world nor mere living in the world is enough to constitute experience. In a certain sense such persons also have experience, but since there is not developed within them the power which surmounts the whole and surveys it, they never become *wise through experience*. For this an act of the will is needed, *which wills to have experience, which in the time of sorrow wills to remember the joy it has experienced and in the hour of joy does not forget the sorrow which threatens.*

Christian Experience

..... and this hour of devotion will now soon be over. Perhaps it will have meaning for you so that you will often remember it, or it may vanish without a trace, so that you seek in vain to recall it for a short while—this we do not know. Who knows the workings of the spirit which moves like wind[570] without our knowing whither or whence. But this we do know, that if your presence here in the Lord's house, your devotion in his temple, is not, as it were, the richest unfurling and flowering of quiet private devotion, which daily strengthens you for your work, sanctifies your joy, ennobles your sorrow . . . . .

III C 13   n.d., 1840-41

« 1070

They say that experience makes a man wise.⁵⁷¹ This is very unreasonable talk. If there were nothing higher than experience, experience would drive a man crazy.

IV A 46   n.d., 1843

« 1071

One of the seven sages has remarked how curious it was that at the race track the experts competed but the inexperienced were the judges.⁵⁷²

IV A 59   n.d., 1843

« 1072

What do I learn from experience?

Nothing—or a merely statistical knowledge. As soon as I frame a law from experience, I insert something more into it than there is in the experience. Experience's naked activity would become a tabular activity just like that which results from meteorological observations. In part it enumerates particulars; in part it gives a figure for the average. But this statistical average proves absolutely nothing; it is only a figure I pull out of the past, and then——period.

IV C 75   n.d., 1842-43

« 1073

Every human being can experience the same thing, and the difference between men lies not so much in the different things which they experience as in the modes in which they experience. No person has ever lived who has not had occasion to experience that he was a sinner; has this therefore been experienced by everyone, or has it always been most deeply experienced by the most defiled? But a past sin is not therefore annihilated and cannot be entirely annihilated in time.—

V B 213: 2   n.d., 1844

« 1074

The sad things about us human beings is really that in almost everything in our lives hindsight is best; that is, after we have done something, often badly, then we know how we should have done it.

X^1 A 238   n.d., 1849

« 1075 *The Amazing Contradiction in Our Time*

If any age or time ever put a premium on "experience" and made a great to-do over it, ours is the one. Everything is supposed to be empirical, empirical science, etc.

Only with regard to Christianity is there an unwillingness to have experience. Without willing to risk becoming involved in it, without willing to venture out in such a way that one reaches life decisions where the Christian situations come into existence [*blive til*], we want to make a judgment about it.

What has actually happened is that to become a Christian has gone out completely. Just as it was once said that war had fallen into disuse and had been replaced by diplomatic exchanges on paper, so pathos, pathos-filled acting and venturing, has been replaced by reasoning on the basis of *pro* and *con*, but the reasoner, of course, remains essentially unchanged, yes, ridiculously enough, it is almost the same whether he adopts Christianity or not.

The observation that our age, which generally is so eager for experience, makes a specific exception of Christianity, I have read in an English book,[573] but it was not used in such a way that one perceives that the author himself was quite aware of the point.

x^5 A 76 *n.d.*, 1853

THE EXTRAORDINARY, THE EXCEPTION

« 1076

In every age all those practical people[574] seem to be so dependable (judges and town-clerks, retailers, *et al.*). But those practical people are frauds. Those practical people sneak away, retire into the grave—and then, then there is no one who knows that they ever were around. If, then, the exceptional person [*den Udmærkede*] had accommodated to them, he would merely have made a fool of himself, because now, now when all these practical people have retired, he now remains.

VII^1 A 173   *n.d.*, 1846

« 1077

It is elevating and upbuilding to consider how feeble the age is, how in fact it really works against itself. It persecutes and hounds the exceptional person [*den Udmærkede*], but the more it does this, the more certainly the exception becomes immortal. To be persecuted is already something noteworthy, and a completely insignificant person could become immortal merely by having been shabbily persecuted by his contemporaries. Therefore it would be an equally ironical and touching reply if a persecuted exception were to say to his contemporaries: Thank you; with the aid of these insults my name will live a generation longer than it otherwise would; if you will be so kind as to kill me, my name will be remembered forever.

VII^1 A 174   *n.d.*, 1846

« 1078

"He who does not hate his father and mother for my sake . . . . . and sacrifice everything is not worthy of me."[575] Yes, says the preacher, but these words are not spoken to everyone, are not relevant to everyone. Why, then, are they addressed to all? Why is this not noted explicitly? How irresponsible of Christ carelessly to let these words fall this way since they are not meant for everyone! To whom, then, are they spoken? The clergy think that they are for the extraordinary individuals. Fine! But how, then, does a person become the extraordinary [*Overordentlige*]? If he is such a one by virtue of natural qualifications, therefore a genius, then he does this by himself and there consequently is no need to preach to him about this. To whom, then, should it be preached at all? To all. And it should be spoken to all in order to leave it up to each one individually whether he will or not. But the preachers' prating is unbelievable gibberish. They stack up a few extraordinary individuals—always dead ones, of course, for safety's sake—and make them into geniuses, to boot (out of this world completely)—and the rest of us are not to be concerned about such words; we are to do the very opposite—Amen!

I wonder if being an extraordinary person means to be a genius? Not at all. This is why God is said to train up his chosen ones. It takes place quite simply—something like this. At first the extraordinary has a little understanding of how to constrain himself, but gradually God comes to his assistance—helping him in his effort to forsake everything for God's sake. It is a very simple story. It must be said, too, that it is nobody's fault but his own if in this respect he has not been willing to let God help him, for God is willing to help every person in this way.

VIII^1 A 202   n.d., 1847

« 1079

There lived in a market town a small group of dancers; only one of them could leap two feet in the air; the others only a half-foot. Yet there was one among the others who could leap a half-foot plus two inches. He was greatly admired and praised. The one who could leap two feet high was ridiculed, regarded as demented and eccentric. The moral: so is it with the extraordinary in this life, especially in a market town. Within the category, "the ordinary" (which includes so many people that a great multitude can have direct profit out of their admiring, since it is a mild way of admiring oneself, inasmuch as the ones who are admired do not stand particularly high above the ordinary people), there are many grades; the upper level get A-plus plus and all the treasures of earthly life. If this is exceeded, the concept changes, because the extraordinary begins. The extraordinary comes to be looked upon as an eccentric, as ridiculous, and is laughed at, mocked, and spit upon (precisely because it is so high that no one at all has the profit of admiring himself by admiring it). No one knows anything about it other than it is some infamous something which in every way should be given over to derision. A few people may have a dim notion that this is nevertheless something extraordinary, and therefore they prefer that not even history gets to know the true situation.

The extraordinary is this: oneself humbled before God by the thought of his overwhelming grace and love, thanking him again and again—and then when one turns around to men, finding that he is ridiculed and mocked for this very reason (because of that for which he gives thanks), so that in a sense one thanks God for being mocked and ridiculed.

The extraordinary, to take an example from the most sublime, is the Virgin Mary. Never satisfying her heart's need to thank God for the mercy he has shown her, never, never herself satisfied with her thanksgiving but always regarding herself as an ingrate in comparison with God's goodness—and then being shunned as the extraordinary by the other girls, regarded as a woman of easy virtue, suspected by her husband. For many a girl this would perhaps have been enough, and only one of these things enough to drive her mad or to suicide—but it is madness to an even greater degree that Mary can never sufficiently thank God.

IX A 12 *n.d.*, 1848

« 1080

The sad thing for the extraordinary is that at the moment it looks as if the extraordinary were the only one who does not accomplish anything; even a country schoolteacher, every family man, etc., accomplishes much more than the extraordinary, does something or someone some good; whereas the extraordinary exists [*er til*] only for the idea.

The extraordinary really exists in order to record the new price and to screw up the price—this is something which in a certain sense does not interest anybody at all. The others, all who live in the established order, in what is customary, operate by doing business at the usual price.

X^1 A 608 *n.d.*, 1849

« 1081

Stick to what is customary, be like the others, why conceitedly fool yourself into thinking you are different from or more than others, etc.

This is all very well, and in a certain sense I entirely approve of such talk. However, there certainly have been extraordinary individuals—how did they happen? Yes, it is really a cruel operation. Usually it probably has happened like this. From an early age and in the most unhappy way they painfully felt their difference from others. They heard the cruel words: Why won't you be like the others—which is something like what was said to Sarah in the Book of Tobit, "Why don't you get married as the others?" (Cf. *Fear and Trembling*.[576]) Consequently they are prevented from becoming like others by sufferings and anguish—and at long last, maybe, this difference became more clearly enunciated as the exceptional difference.

x² A 180   n.d., 1849

« 1082

It is, nevertheless, very exhausting to have this discernment, to understand and be aware that one has been granted something extraordinary, and then understand that the very moment it is to be involved in actuality there is a hairbreadth line which determines whether it is to express the extraordinary in a straightforward manner and become admired or express it inversely and become repudiated by the age.

The higher one is, the more obvious these contrasts—which do not appear at all in connection with ordinary undertakings which lie within the realm of probability.

And then to keep on working in the same way for the same thing, while alternately discerning the possibility of the opposite result. In this lies precisely the discipline which turns the mind away from results and toward God in obedience to him.

x² A 220   n.d., 1849

« 1083

In margin of 1082 (x² A 220):

It is something else again when the immediate person who is aware of his own extraordinariness boldly ventures, fully convinced that only one result is possible: to win. And then the opposite happens, that is, he is ultimately victorious, but spiritually, which means to get the worst of it. This is something else entirely; for he was not dialectical, did not understand in advance that the extraordinary is dialectical, that there is a little question to pose—whether the extraordinary is perhaps so extraordinary that its adequate expression is to get the worst of it, to be regarded as madness, etc.

x² A 221   n.d., 1849

« 1084 *Most Men—the Heterogeneous*

Most men are really only sample copies [*Exemplarer*], duplicates of what has been put into the world. Of them it may be said: They derive benefit out of living, but the world has no benefit out of their having lived.

As for the other class (the heterogeneous)—it is generally true that they have no benefit out of living (humanly speaking, one may be tempted to speak this way upon seeing how anguished and filled with suffering their lives are, usually consoled only by the thought of death), but the world has benefit out of their having lived, for they are the ones who introduce what is new.

x³ A 27   *n.d.,* 1850

« 1085 *The Extraordinary, Ethically, and the Fraud of the Clerical Way*

Ethically the extraordinary is related as a matter of course to every individual (the ethical is precisely the universally human)—that he can be this, yes, that he really ought to be this. Here there is no esthetic distinction of ability or inability, rooted in conditions which are not in everyone's power.

With regard to being a Christian, consider ethically the extraordinary, which is to become a witness for truth, martyr, and the like.

What happens in preaching? Instead of expressing that every individual has to make a reckoning with God as to why he has not become a witness for truth and consequently confess that the fault lies in him, in his weakness, in his earthliness, etc., at the same time confessing that it is an indulgence granted to him that he nevertheless is a Christian—instead of this the clergyman turns the relationship around and turns the ethically extraordinary into the esthetically extraordinary, the extraordinary by distinction, and says: So high I have never dared hope—that I should become such an extraordinary. Aha! Instead of getting a minus for not becoming what in the strictest sense could be required of him, he even gets a plus for humility and modesty.

If this is not making a fool of God, then I do not know what it is to make a fool of God.

x³ A 464   *n.d.,* 1850

« 1086 *The Exception*

The universal (Mynster *et al.*) does not want to recognize that the exception [*Exceptionelle*] (the most superior as the abnormal) exists [*er til*]. Or—insofar as it is past—they explain it now by using the results, so that it nevertheless becomes something other than it was. Or, because such an exception has altered our very concepts, they do not make use of the present in order to find the exception, which, however, it was in its time.

They dare not admit the exception lest everything be disarranged. Nor do they know my method for controlling this by the existential.

But, in relationship to the exception, this is the advance—and an advance toward the ideal is always a step backward—that whereas in old times there were such men of God, now we must be satisfied with a poet, who says it is a possibility, who holds possibility open, but then again he is the strictest controller and critic of everyone who claims to be such a one.

X^4 A 32   n.d., 1851

« 1087 *The Extraordinary Is—the Sacrificed*

In the domain of the religious and ethical-religious it holds true that these two terms are inseparable, for the extraordinary is related inversely.

Attention must be paid to this above all, and then one will have occasion for a glimpse into the knavery and hypocrisy of the preaching in current Christianity. O, we men, every human being, human nature, are in fact born hypocrites, and so crafty!

This is the range: the sphere of the religious—the extraordinary. This is the true extraordinary, and as everywhere in this domain the positive is recognized by the contrasting negative, to be the extraordinary is—to be sacrificed, to become sacrificed.

But we human beings interpret the extraordinary esthetically as the superlative of the immediate—therefore to be the extraordinary becomes the highest enjoyment. Aha!

And now the clergyman preaches—these 1,000 and 1,000 who are salaried in order to confuse Christianity (it is just as upside-down as for a state to hit upon the notion of maintaining 1,000 public functionaries who are paid for defending the circle by proving that it is square)—he preaches: "To be something as exalted as a witness of the truth, an apostle, the Virgin Mary, etc.—I am far too modest and humble to ask for anything like that." You scoundrel! What you are doing is slipping in a false concept of the extraordinary. By sparing ourselves, by loving flesh and blood we assure ourselves a pleasant life in this world—and then, assisted by the priests and parsons, we aspire to the hypocritical appearance that it is—out of humility and modesty!—that we do not ask to be the extraordinary.

No, no, if there is going to be a mere smidge of meaning in the Christian proclamation, the extraordinary must be considered quite differently. If it is so that these extraordinary ones are the condition for our having permission as a matter of course to take life easier (if this is possible)—well, these extraordinary ones, these sacrificed ones at least ought to be laid as a weight upon our consciences. Furthermore, we ought not be permitted to sneak away from the extraordinary ones by making their lot out to be enviable and then sneakily attributing humility and modesty to ourselves because we do not ask for such things. No, no, if it is actually true that the sufferings of the sacrificed can permit us to take the life easier—well, then, in any case their sacrifice should be entered as our debt.

If anything is going to be said about the extraordinary, it ought to be like this: I confess before God and his holy angels that if the angel had come to me and announced to me such—glad!—tidings, I would have begged, implored that I might be free. Or if Christ had called to me and said, "You shall be my chosen instrument, I shall—glad tidings!—show you what you shall come to suffer for my name's sake"—then I would have implored that I might be free, etc.

O, you anguished sacrificed ones—you are not even thanked—no, no—for our being able to sneak out of "imitation" [*Efterfølgelsen*], and then we mendaciously turn the relationship around and your situation becomes enviable.

Detestable! But for us human beings everything, everything, hinges on getting rid of whatever reminds us, even most remotely, of "imitation." If, then, I am to thank you for all your sufferings, the affair could easily turn against me thus: But you, why do you not suffer? Why are you shirking? You see, this is what we are afraid of. So we insure ourselves—for if the extraordinary's situation were really enviable, then I escape "imitation" to the very degree that I turn modesty and humility into money, honor, esteem, and all worldly enjoyment, in which I have my life.

Here the clergy plainly have responsibility. For the mass of men are not so hardened that if this were to be laid upon their hearts they would not give it a hearing. But the preachers are afraid to let even a little truth shine forth.

It is a question, moreover, by what right they as a matter of course preach that some have suffered—so that the rest of us may enjoy life. This is pure Mynsterism, this dubious egotism. The question is whether this whole interpretation does not reduce Christianity to mere history, a merely historical teaching which at one time had to be suffered for—instead of Christianity's being examined by the eternal. Why did the earlier ones suffer? Because they renounced everything. But has Christianity abolished this requirement, or can it be an indulgence for me that others have renounced everything? But everywhere one comes across this falsification which makes Christianity into a historical teaching, a kind of learning—instead of its being the eternal's demand and promise to these first ones as to us and to every age, so that Christianity has nothing at all to do with this whole historical nonsense, but—as it says in the N.T., begins over again with every generation.

x^4 A 518 *n.d.*, 1852

« 1088 *Modesty. The Extraordinary*

In *The Laws* Plato says (cited according to Rötscher, *Aristophanes und seine Zeit*; Berlin: 1827; pp. 85-6) that modesty is what binds men in obedience to the laws (αἰδώς).

Therein lies the human; to be the single individual, the exception, is audacity.

In immediacy this power of modesty which binds individuals in obedience to the universal is essentially an animal qualification; they are not self-reflected in such a way that they could endure being different from the others; to be different from the others would be the most fearful agony.*

In times of reflection it is frequently only fear of men which intimidates the individuals into being like the others; then abstractions like the public, which are actually "the others," become the tyrant.

Yet there remains the ethical truth that a person ought to have the modesty not to be different from the universal, however much it must be maintained that this can easily become sophistry if one is not careful what he understands by the universal, that it is not automatically what "the others" express at a particular, perhaps degenerate, time.

Consider now the extraordinary. Part of his suffering is that he cannot avoid being confused with outright audacity which places itself above the universal. This cannot be avoided, for the extraordinary is vindicated by what he has to bring; but this is present implicitly and is actually to be seen only when he is dead. x^4 A 590   *n.d.*, 1852

« 1089

*In margin of 1088 (x^4 A 590):

Just as modesty forbids stripping oneself naked, so it is modesty which keeps one from forsaking privacy to be as the others and to be stripped as the single individual. —It is therefore a suffering to become the extraordinary, although it is still true that he must suffer if he is truly the extraordinary; the suffering is that the others must regard it as a lack of modesty, and that he himself in the moment of spiritual trial [*Anfægtelsens*] must also regard it this way. x^4 A 591   *n.d.*, 1852

« 1090 *Renunciation (Imitation)*

To want to be exempted from renunciation (consequently to want to enjoy life) is secular-mindedness.

But to want to carry out renunciation, but then to be esteemed as the extraordinary—this is also secular-mindedness.

On the whole, and I cannot stress this enough, the extraordinary has nothing to do with the ethical. Ethically there is nothing extraordinary, for the highest is simply the requirement; it is unjust and usurious to want to have the profit of the esteem of the extraordinary by doing what is required. At the same time, the contemporaries may desire just that, for then they get rid of such a person, then his life constitutes no requirement upon them. —The "extraordinary" is not connected with ethical fulfillment of what is commanded but is connected with the singular relationship to God.

If the medieval ascetic had not been so secular-minded as to let himself be deceived into being honored as the extraordinary, if he had said, "Stuff and nonsense! All I express is simply a striving oriented to what is required. I am not the extraordinary, but you are, you who on your own responsibility exempt yourselves from the requirement."— then he would have been persecuted. The world never agrees that renunciation is supposed to be what is required. The highest was probably achieved in the Middle Ages: men honored renunciation, the requirement, as the extraordinary—and then exempted themselves. But just this was the great error in two directions (with regard both to the honoring and to the exempting) and was the abolition of Christianity.

X^4 A 652 n.d., 1852

« 1091 *The Extraordinary*

To prevent the extraordinary from being conceited and proud, the truly extraordinary is always dialectical so that seen from one side to be an extraordinary is a suffering, and human villainy contributes repellently to make such a one the extraordinary.

No one is born as the true extraordinary; he becomes that.

It happens something like this. Little by little he may become aware that something extraordinary has been entrusted to him—yet he has this together with such suffering that for a long time he is aware only (almost) of the suffering, and the extraordinary does not tempt [*frister*] him.

Then comes the time when he takes over his task. And here it is required that he love men to a high degree and be well-intentioned toward them.

But what happens? He collides with a combination of human misunderstanding and human infamy.

Thus he is thrust back away from men; it is not he who haughtily scorns men, no, he loves them; no, it is men who partly out of misunderstanding, partly out of plain nastiness, push him away from themselves.

They cannot devitalize him, for, indeed, he has been designed for the extraordinary; consequently this treatment merely potentiates him—so that he becomes the extraordinary. The dialectical middle factor is always this suffering, the advance payment, etc.

XI¹ A 409 n.d., 1854

« 1092 *The Extraordinary*

That the extraordinary must suffer in this world is nevertheless entirely in order; yes, it is not difficult to see that in a certain sense it is even ridiculous. The contradiction (the root of the ridiculousness) is that a person has to be the extraordinary while *qua* man, etc. he externally and physically is and looks just like the others. The contradiction consists of the fact that within this likeness there must be such an enormous difference.

When the extraordinary is dead, people make use of illusions, imagine that he looked quite different from others, that the extraordinariness could be seen, could be recognized physically—all of which is nonsense.

And because this is the way it is, because the true extraordinary in a certain sense is the abandoned one, the ridiculous one, it therefore happens that whatever is a bit more than the ordinary without being the truly extraordinary (which of course rejects such means) avails itself of a certain physically recognizable difference from the ordinary. This is helped along by sparkling uniforms, robes, or clerical costumes, stars, etc. —for when the common man sees this, he thinks, yes, it goes without saying that such a man is somebody extraordinary; he does not look like the others.

XI¹ A 434 n.d., 1854

« 1093 *The Genuine Extraordinaries of the First Class*

They do not feel so happy in this world that they would want to settle down in it. No, they are travellers, on a mission, hurrying as fast as possible away again, home.

When they notice that it is drawing toward the end, when they have just about completed their mission, having produced the most intensive possible effect in the shortest possible time, they touch a little spring which only they know about—then their lives have a crashing effect and in this manner they are blasted out of this world.

Here everything is heterogeneity from first to last; to make a crashing departure from this world is as heterogeneous as possible to a smooth, placid life and a quiet death.

XI² A 247 n.d., 1854

Bibliography
Collation of Entries
Notes

Bibliography

KIERKEGAARD'S WORKS IN ENGLISH

Editions referred to in the notes.
Listed according to the original order of publication or the time of writing.

The Concept of Irony, tr. Lee Capel. New York: Harper and Row, 1966.
Either/Or, I, tr. David F. Swenson and Lillian Marvin Swenson, II, tr. Walter Lowrie, 2 ed. the Rev. Howard A. Johnson. New York: Doubleday, 1959.
Johannes Climacus, or De Omnibus Dubitandum Est, tr. T. H. Croxall. London: Adam and Charles Black, 1958.
Edifying Discourses, I-IV, tr. David F. Swenson and Lillian Marvin Swenson. Minneapolis: Augsburg Publishing House, 1943-46.
Fear and Trembling (with *The Sickness unto Death*), tr. Walter Lowrie. New York: Doubleday, 1954.
Repetition, tr. Walter Lowrie. Princeton: Princeton University Press, 1941.
Philosophical Fragments, tr. David Swenson, 2 ed. rev. Howard Hong. Princeton: Princeton University Press, 1962.
The Concept of Anxiety [Dread], tr. Walter Lowrie, 2 ed. Princeton: Princeton University Press, 1957.
Thoughts on Crucial Situations in Human Life, tr. David F. Swenson and Lillian Marvin Swenson. Minneapolis: Augsburg Publishing House, 1941.
Stages on Life's Way, tr. Walter Lowrie. Princeton: Princeton University Press, 1940.
Concluding Unscientific Postscript, tr. David F. Swenson and Walter Lowrie. Princeton: Princeton University Press, 1944.
The Present Age and "Two Treatises" by H. H., tr. Walter Lowrie. London and New York: Oxford University Press, 1940.
On Authority and Revelation, The Book on Adler, tr. Walter Lowrie. Princeton: Princeton University Press, 1955.
Purity of Heart, tr. Douglas Steere, 2 ed. New York: Harper, 1948.
The Gospel of Suffering and *The Lilies of the Field*, tr. David F. Swenson and Lillian Marvin Swenson. Minneapolis: Augsburg Publishing House, 1948.
Works of Love, tr. Howard and Edna Hong. New York: Harper and Row, 1962.
Christian Discourses, including *The Lilies of the Field and the Birds of the*

Air and *Three Discourses at the Communion on Fridays*, tr. Walter Lowrie. London and New York: Oxford University Press, 1940.
The Crisis [and a Crisis] in the Life of an Actress, tr. Stephen Crites. New York: Harper and Row, 1966.
The Point of View, including *Two Notes about "the Individual"* and *On My Work as an Author*, tr. Walter Lowrie. London and New York: Oxford University Press, 1939.
The Sickness unto Death (with *Fear and Trembling*), tr. Walter Lowrie. New York: Doubleday, 1954.
Training in Christianity, tr. Walter Lowrie. London and New York: Oxford University Press, 1941.
For Self-Examination, tr. Edna and Howard Hong. Minneapolis: Augsburg Publishing House, 1940.
Judge for Yourselves, including *For Self-Examination, Two Discourses at the Communion on Fridays*, and *The Unchangeableness of God* (tr. David Swenson), tr. Walter Lowrie. Princeton: Princeton University Press, 1944.
Attack upon Christendom, tr. Walter Lowrie. Princeton: Princeton University Press, 1946.

GENERAL WORKS ON KIERKEGAARD

BIBLIOGRAPHIES

Henriksen, Aage. *Methods and Results of Kierkegaard Studies in Scandinavia*. Copenhagen: Munksgaard, 1951.
Himmelstrup, Jens. *Søren Kierkegaard International Bibliografi*. Copenhagen: Arnold Busck, 1962.
Thulstrup, Niels. "Theological and Philosophical Kierkegaardian Studies in Scandinavia 1945-53." *Theology Today*, XII, 3, October 1955.
Woodbridge, Hensley Charles. "Søren Kierkegaard: A Bibliography of his Works in English Translation," *American Book Collector*, XII (1961), iv, pp. 17-20. "A Bibliography of Dissertations concerning Kierkegaard Written in the U.S., Canada, and Great Britain," ibid., pp. 21-22.

BOOKS AND ARTICLES

Aiken, H. D. *Age of Ideology*. New York: American Library, 1956.
Allen, W. Gore. *The Renaissance in the North*. London: Sheed and Ward, 1946.
Anderson, Einar Wulfsbuerg. *The Influence of Kierkegaard's Philosophy on the Works of Henrik Ibsen*. M.A. thesis, University of Minnesota, 1926.
Angell, John W. *The Theological Methodology of Søren Kierkegaard*. Ph.D. thesis, Southern Baptist Theological Seminary, 1949.

Anglican Theological Review (Special number on Kierkegaard). Sewanee, Tennessee: University Press, 1956.
Attwater, Donald. *Modern Christian Revolutionaries.* New York: Devin-Adair, 1947.
Auden, W. H. "A Preface to Kierkegaard." *New Republic,* 1944.
Bain, John A. *Søren Kierkegaard.* London: SCM, 1935.
Barckett, Richard M. "Kierkegaard: A Christian Protest." *America,* 1955.
Beach, Waldo and Niebuhr, Richard. *Christian Ethics.* New York: Ronald, 1955.
Bierstedt, R. "An Unripe Philosopher." *Saturday Review of Literature,* 1947.
Bjarnason, Loftur L. *Categories of Søren Kierkegaard's Thought in the Life and Writings of A. Strindberg.* Ph.D. thesis, Stanford University, 1951.
Blackham, H. J. *Six Existentialist Thinkers.* New York: Harper, 1959.
———. *Søren Kierkegaard (1813-1855).* London: Routledge and Kegan Paul, 1952.
Boas, G. *Dominant Themes of Modern Philosophy.* New York: Ronald Press, 1957.
Brandes, Georg. *Main Currents in Nineteenth Century Literature.* London: William Heinemann, 1901, reprint 1906; New York: Boni and Liveright, 1923.
Brandt, Frithiof. *Søren Kierkegaard,* tr. Ann R. Born. Copenhagen: Danish Information Office, 1963.
Bretall, R. "Kierkegaard. A Critical Survey." *Examiner,* 1939.
Brock, Werner. *An Introduction to Contemporary German Philosophy.* Cambridge: Cambridge University Press, 1935.
Butler, C. "Impressions of Kierkegaard." *Downside Review,* 1937.
Calhoun, Robert L. "Kierkegaard's Writings." *Yale Review,* 1945.
Cant, Reginald. "Søren Kierkegaard." *Church Quarterly Review,* 1938-39.
Carnell, Edward J. *The Burden of Søren Kierkegaard.* Grand Rapids, Michigan: Eerdmans, 1965.
Channing-Pearce, M. *The Terrible Crystal.* London: Kegan Paul, 1940.
———. "Kierkegaard's Message to our Age." *Journal of the Philosophical Society of Great Britain,* 1945.
———. *Søren Kierkegaard.* London: Clarke, 1948. New York: Devin-Adair, 1947.
Clive, G. "The Sickness Unto Death: A Study of Nihilism." *Harvard Theological Review,* 1958.
Coats, J. B. "Kierkegaard." *Fortnightly,* 1950.
Collins, James. "The Fashionableness of Kierkegaard." *Thought,* 1947.
———. "The Mind of Kierkegaard." *Modern Schoolman,* 1948-49.
———. "Three Kierkegaardian Problems." *New Scholasticism,* 1948.
———. *The Existentialists.* Chicago: Regnery, 1952.
———. *The Mind of Kierkegaard.* Chicago: Regnery, 1953.
———. "The Relevance of Kierkegaard." *Commonweal,* 1955.

Croxall, T. H. "The Importance of Kierkegaard." *Danish Foreign Office Journal*, 1948.
———. "Kierkegaard as Seen by an Englishman." *Danish Foreign Office Journal*, 1955.
———. *Kierkegaard Commentary*. New York: Harper, 1956.
———. *Kierkegaard Studies*. New York: Roy, 1956.
Diem, Hermann. *An Introduction to Kierkegaard*. Richmond, Virginia: John Knox, 1966.
Drucker, Peter F. "The Unfashionable Kierkegaard." *Sewanee Review*, 1949.
Dupré, Louis K. "Kierkegaard, the Melancholy Dane." *America*, 1955.
———. *Kierkegaard as Theologian*. New York: Sheed and Ward, 1963.
Evans, Oliver. "The Rise of Existentialism." *South Atlantic Quarterly*, 1948.
Fausett, Hugh I'Anson. *Poets and Pundits*. New Haven: Yale University Press, 1947.
Ferrie, W. S. "Kierkegaard: Hamlet or Jeremiah?" *Evangelical Quarterly*, 1936.
Fleissner, E. M. "Legacy of Kierkegaard." *New Republic*, 1955-56.
Flottorp, Haakon, *Kierkegaard and Norway*. Ph.D. thesis, Colorado University, 1955.
Fowler, Albert. "Water from his own Well: Kierkegaard." *University of Kansas Review*, 1955.
Friedmann, Rudolph. "Kierkegaard." *Horizon*, 1943.
———. *Kierkegaard*. London: Nevill, 1949.
Friedman, Maurice. *The Worlds of Existentialism*. New York: Random House, 1964.
Fulford, Francis W. *Søren Aabye Kierkegaard*. Cambridge: Wallis, 1913.
Gates, John Alexander. *The Life and Thought of Kierkegaard for Everyman*. Philadelphia: Westminster, 1960.
Geismar, Edward. "Søren Kierkegaard." *American Scandinavian Review*, 1929.
———. *Lectures on the Religious Thought of Søren Kierkegaard*. Minneapolis: Augsburg, 1937.
Golding, Henry J. "Kierkegaard: a Neglected Thinker." *The Standard*, 1926.
Gregory, T. S. "Kierkegaard." *Listener*, 1946.
———. "Kierkegaard." *Current Religious Thought*, 1950.
Grene, Marjorie. *Introduction to Existentialism*. Chicago: University of Chicago Press, 1959. (First published as *Dreadful Freedom*. University of Chicago Press, 1948.)
Griffith, Gwilym O. *Kierkegaard*. London: Lutterworth, 1943.
Guterman, N. "Kierkegaard and His Faith." *Partisan Review*, 1943.
Haecker, Theodor. *Søren Kierkegaard*. London, New York, and Toronto: Oxford University Press, 1937.
Halevi, Jacob. *A Critique of Martin Buber's Interpretation of Søren Kierkegaard*. Ph.D. thesis, Hebrew-Union College, 1960.

Heinecken, Martin. *The Moment before God.* Philadelphia: Muhlenberg, 1956.
Heinemann, F. H. *Existentialism and the Modern Predicament.* New York: Harpers, 1953.
Hems, John M. "Abraham and Bond." *Philosophy,* 1964, 41-55.
Hohlenberg, Johannes. *Søren Kierkegaard,* tr. T. H. Croxall. New York: Pantheon, 1954.
Holmer, Paul LeRoy. "A Comparative Study of the Philosophies of Søren Kierkegaard and Friedrich Nietzsche." University of Minnesota M.A. thesis, 1941.
———. "Kierkegaard, A Religious Author." *American Scandinavian Review,* 1945.
———. "On Understanding Kierkegaard." *Orbis litterarum,* 1955.
Hong, Howard. "Kierkegaard as a Christian Philosopher." *Scottish Journal of Theology,* 1941.
Hubben, William. *Four Prophets of Our Destiny.* New York: Macmillan, 1960.
Jansen, F.J. Billestoo. "The Universality of Kierkegaard." *American Scandinavian Review,* 1963.
Jaspers, Karl. "The Importance of Nietzsche, Marx and Kierkegaard in the History of Philosophy, *Hibbert Journal,* 1950-51.
Johannesson, E. O. "Isah Dinesen, Søren Kierkegaard and the Present Age." *Books Abroad,* 1962.
Johnson, Howard, and Mils Thulstrup, ed. *A Kierkegaard Critique.* New York: Harper, 1962.
Jolivet, Regis. *Introduction to Kierkegaard.* London: Muller, 1950.
Kaufmann, W. *From Shakespeare to Existentialism.* Boston: Beacon Press, 1959.
Kerr, Hugh T. "A Kierkegaard Centenary," *Theology Today,* 1955.
Kierkegaardiana Vols. I-VI Copenhagen: Munksgaard, 1955-66.
Killinger, John. *Hemingway and the Dead Gods; A Study of Existentialism.* New York: Citadel, 1965.
Klemke, E. D. "Some Misinterpretation of Kierkegaard," *Hibbert Journal,* 1959.
Kraushaar, O. F. "Kierkegaard in English." *Journal of Philosophy,* 1942.
Krieger, Murray. "Tragedy and the Tragic Vision." *The Tragic Vision.* New York: Holt, 1960.
Kuhn, Helmut. *Encounter with Nothingness.* Hinsdale, Ill.: Regnery, 1949.
Kurtz, Paul. "Kierkegaard, Existentialism, and the Contemporary Scene," *Antioch Review,* 1965.
Leendertz, W. "Søren Kierkegaard," *Mennonite Quarterly Review,* 1949.
Link, M. M. "Kierkegaard's Way to America." American University, Ph.D. thesis, 1951.
"Kierkegaard in France." *Times Literary Supplement,* 1935.

Löwith, Karl. "On the Historical Understanding of Kierkegaard." *Review of Religion*, 1943.
Lowrie, Walter. *Kierkegaard*. London, New York, and Toronto: Oxford University Press, 1938.
———. "Kierkegaard." *Church Review*, 1941.
———. "Qualified Retraction and an Unqualified Apology." *Theology Today*, 1959.
———. *A Short Life of Kierkegaard*. Princeton: Princeton University Press, 1942.
———. "Translators and Interpreters of Søren Kierkegaard." *Theology Today*, 1955-56.
Lucas, Ernest. "Søren Kierkegaard." *London Quarterly Review*, 1932.
McCleary, Richard C. *Existential Thinking in America 1918-1941*. Ph.D. thesis, Yale, 1961.
McEachran, F. "The Significance of Søren Kierkegaard." *Hibbert Journal*, 1945-46.
McInerny, Ralph Matthew. *A Thomistic Evaluation of the Philosophy of Søren Kierkegaard*. M.A. thesis, University of Minnesota, 1952.
McKeon, Richard. "The Philosophy of Kierkegaard." *New York Times Book Review*, 1945.
Mackintosh, H. R. "A Great Danish Thinker." *Expository Times*, 1902.
Magel, Charles R. *An Analysis of Kierkegaard's Philosophic Categories*. Ph.D. thesis, University of Minnesota, 1960.
Malantschuk, Gregor. *Kierkegaard's Way to the Truth*. Minneapolis: Augsburg, 1963.
Mantripp, J. D. "Søren Kierkegaard." *London Quarterly Review*, 1939.
Martin, Harold Victor. *Kierkegaard, the Melancholy Dane*. New York: Philosophical Library, 1950; London: Epworth (Philosophers' Library), 1950.
———. *The Wings of Faith*. New York: Philosophical Library, 1951.
Masur, G. *Prophets of Yesterday*. New York: Macmillan, 1961.
Merlan, Philip. "Toward the Understanding of Kierkegaard." *Review of Religion*, 1943.
Michalson, Carl. *The Witness of Kierkegaard*. New York: Association Press, 1960.
Michalson, Gordon Elliott. *Baron Friederich von Hugel and Søren Kierkegaard*. Ph.D. thesis, Drew University, 1947.
Miller, Samuel H. "Kierkegaard: Then and Now." *Andover Bulletin*, 1955.
Oke, C. Clare. "Kierkegaard as Major Prophet." *Expository Times*, 1950-51.
O'Mara, J. "Kierkegaard Revealed." *Studies*. Dublin: 1949.
Otani, Masaru. "Introduction to Kierkegaard." *Meddelelser fra S. K. Selskabet*. Copenhagen: 1955.
———. "The Past and Present State of Kierkegaard Studies in Japan." *Orbis Litterarum*, XVIII, 1963.
Patka, F., ed. *Existentialist Thinkers and Thought*. New York: Philosophical Library, 1962.

Pelikan, Jaroslav. *From Luther to Kierkegaard*. St. Louis: Concordia, 1950.
Pope, R. Martin. "An Impression of Kierkegaard." *London Quarterly Review*, 1941.
Ratcliffe, S. K. "Kierkegaard." *Listener*, 1946.
Read, Herbert. "Kierkegaard." *A Coat of Many Colors*. London: Routledge, 1945.
Reinhold, H. A. "S. K., Great Christian of the 19th Century." *Commonweal*, 1942.
Riding, Laura. "Søren Kierkegaard." *Times Literary Supplement*, 1937.
Riviere, William T. "Introducing Kierkegaard." *Christian Century*, 1939.
———. "Interpretation of Kierkegaard." *Christian Century*, 1939.
Roberts, David. "Kierkegaard's Writings." *Review of Religion*, 1943.
———. *Existentialism and Religious Belief*. New York: Oxford, 1957.
Robertson, F. G. "Søren Kierkegaard." *Modern Language Review*, 1914.
Robinson, F. G. "Søren Kierkegaard." *Essays and Addresses on Literature*. London: Routledge, 1935.
Rohde, Peter P. "Søren Kierkegaard and Our Time." *Arena*, 1949.
———. *Søren Kierkegaard*. Copenhagen: Ministry of Foreign Affairs, Press Department, 1955.
———. *Søren Kierkegaard*. New York: Humanities Press, 1963.
Rougemont, D. de. *Dramatic Personages*. New York: Holt, Rinehart, and Winston, 1964.
———. *Love Declared* including "Dialectic of the Myths" and "Two Danish Princes: Kierkegaard and Hamlet." New York: Pantheon, 1963.
Ruggiero, Guido de. *Existentialism*. New York: Social Science Publishers, 1948.
"S. K.: Prophet with Honor." *Christian Century*, 1963.
Safier, Fred J. *The Philosophy of Søren Kierkegaard*. Ph.D. thesis, Harvard, 1934.
Schuelke, Gertrude Luise. *Kierkegaard and Rilke: a Study in Relationships*. Ph.D. thesis, Stanford University, 1950.
Sechi, Vanina. "Perspectives in Contemporary Kierkegaard Research." *Meddelelser fra S. K. Selskabet*. Copenhagen: 1953.
Soper, David Wesley. "Kierkegaard, the Danish Jeremiah." *Religion in Life*, 1939-40.
Spinka, M. "Søren Kierkegaard and the Existential Theology." *Christian Thought from Erasmus to Berdyaev*. Englewood Cliffs, New Jersey: Prentice-Hall, 1962.
Steere, Douglas V. "Discovering Kierkegaard." *Christendom*, 1939.
Stewart, H. L. "Kierkegaard as Major Prophet." *Expository Times*, 1950-51.
Stewart, R. W. "A Neglected Prophet." *Expository Times*, 1927.
———. "Søren Kierkegaard as Major Prophet of the XIXth Century." *Expository Times*, 1949-50.
Swenson, David F. *Something about Kierkegaard*. Minneapolis: Augsburg, 1949.

———. *The Faith of a Scholar*. Philadelphia: Westminster, 1949.
Thomas, G. F. *Religious Philosophies of the West*. New York: Scribner, 1965.
Thomte, R. *Kierkegaard's Philosophy of Religion*. Princeton: Princeton University Press, 1948.
Tillich, Paul. "Kierkegaard in English." *American Scandinavian Review*, 1942.
Tyler, Parker. *Every Artist His Own Scandal*. New York: Horizon Press, 1964.
Unamuno, y Jugo M. de. *Perplexities and Paradoxes*. New York: Philosophical Library, 1945.
Untermeyer, Louis. *Makers of the Modern World*. New York: Simon & Schuster, 1955.
Updike, J. "Kierkegaard." *New Yorker*, 1966.
Webber, R. H. "Kierkegaard and the Elaboration of Unamuno's 'Niebla.'" *Hispanic Review*, 1964.
Wieman, Henry Nelson. "Interpretation of Kierkegaard." *Christian Century*, 1939.
Wild, John. *The Challenge of Existentialism*. Bloomington: Indiana University Press, 1959.
———. *Human Freedom and Social Order*. Durham, North Carolina: Duke University Press, 1959.
Willey, Basil. "Kierkegaard: the Melancholy Dane." *Cambridge Review*, 1951.
Wilson, Colin. *Religion and the Rebel*. Boston: Houghton and Mifflin, 1957.
Wyschogrod, Michael. *Kierkegaard and Heidegger*. New York: Humanities Press, 1954.
Yanitelli, Victor. "Søren Kierkegaard." in "Bibliographical Introduction to Existentialism." *The Modern Schoolman*, 1949.
Zuidema, S. U. *Kierkegaard*. Nutley, New Jersey: Presbyterian and Reformed Publishing Co., 1960.

Collation Of Entries in this Volume With Kierkegaard's *Papirer*

Numbers in the left-hand columns are the standard international references to the *Papirer*. Numbers in parentheses are the serially ordered references in the present edition.

Volume I A		Volume I A		Volume I A		Volume II A	
4	(410)	113	(751)	245	(128)	97	(279)
6	(411)	114	(24)	254	(854)	100	(832)
8	(117)	124	(849)	290	(217)	125	(1014)
27	(412)	126	(25)	301	(218)	127	(219)
28	(273)	129	(123)	316	(252)	128	(220)
33	(118)	135	(16)	324	(699)	130	(221)
38	(242)	137	(17)	325	(277)	131	(222)
40	(413)	138	(245)	327	(617)	133	(280)
46	(414)	141	(850)	334	(28)	150	(857)
50	(689)	146	(770)	Volume I C		151	(858)
53	(274)	149	(26)	40	(227)	162	(30)
54	(202)	150	(795)	80	(831)	165	(859)
55	(203)	152	(851)	Volume II A		173	(860)
56	(578)	172	(419)	4	(782)	174	(861)
57	(579)	174	(420)	5	(783)	180	(133)
58	(580)	175	(124)	6	(784)	184	(427)
74	(22)	181	(737)	12	(265)	191	(92)
84	(848)	197	(790)	13	(855)	197	(282)
86	(119)	198	(125)	15	(129)	213	(712)
89	(415)	199	(27)	18	(91)	217	(428)
90	(120)	206	(13)	30	(422)	234	(429)
95	(416)	210	(275)	39	(856)	235	(1020)
96	(417)	212	(126)	41	(266)	245	(430)
97	(418)	215	(421)	46	(131)	249	(431)
101	(29)	221	(852)	55	(769)	250	(432)
102	(23)	222	(853)	58	(1068)	251	(433)
105	(121)	232	(276)	82	(423)	252	(434)
106	(122)	234	(127)	83	(424)	258	(286)
108	(581)	236	(371)	93	(278)	261	(287)

COLLATION

Volume II A		Volume II A		Volume II A		Volume III A	
265	(243)	473	(297)	675	(281)	124	(835)
269	(582)	479	(205)	708	(1)	125	(884)
276	(288)	484	(739)	709	(766)	135	(885)
277	(435)	485	(740)	711	(1024)	154	(886)
283	(244)	489	(93)	713	(285)	184	(887)
284	(289)	496	(2)	715	(135)	185	(888)
287	(204)	499	(447)	725	(1025)	191	(230)
293	(436)	501	(873)	743	(33)	195	(741)
294	(437)	502	(874)	750	(583)	196	(682)
295	(290)	513	(875)	751	(753)	202	(889)
303	(865)	514	(876)	759	(864)	214	(883)
305	(194)	522	(586)	765	(291)	218	(801)
306	(866)	530	(877)	767	(292)	219	(802)
307	(438)	536	(878)	791	(797)	230	(890)
315	(585)	539	(139)	792	(584)	231	(785)
316	(293)	547	(448)	795	(171)	233	(94)
317	(439)	553	(798)	Volume II C		234	(95)
322	(867)	556	(1021)	34	(36)	235	(96)
329	(440)	569	(298)	37	(193)	238	(742)
333	(441)	570	(834)	47	(772)	241	(743)
338	(442)	571	(140)	Volume III A		Volume III B	
351	(833)	577	(449)	3	(37)	45:1	(806)
352	(136)	578	(879)	4	(773)	45:5	(807)
360	(443)	579	(450)	7	(754)	179:27	(756)
362	(34)	581	(228)	10	(799)	181:9	(713)
365	(444)	583	(130)	12	(800)	Volume III C	
367	(195)	593	(862)	23	(880)	6	(299)
369	(294)	594	(283)	13	(18)	13	(1069)
376	(445)	595	(284)	25	(38)	15	(587)
383	(35)	606	(425)	26	(1026)	20	(300)
388	(295)	610	(1022)	28	(881)	30	(257)
393	(620)	612	(1023)	41	(39)	Volume IV A	
409	(738)	620	(618)	62	(1027)	5	(702)
412	(137)	624	(619)	63	(882)	6	(3)
419	(296)	628	(426)	87	(229)	27	(451)
425	(138)	632	(796)	92	(755)	33	(301)
430	(868)	636	(132)	94	(803)	38	(198)
443	(446)	646	(31)	95	(804)	46	(1070)
447	(869)	654	(752)	96	(805)	57	(703)
449	(870)	661	(765)	110	(141)	59	(1071)
450	(871)	664	(134)	111	(142)	60	(267)
463	(621)	671	(863)	112	(700)	72	(774)
465	(872)	674	(32)	123	(701)	73	(897)

COLLATION

Volume IV A		Volume IV C		Volume V A		Volume VI A	
82	(898)	33	(41)	69	(706)	117	(152)
92	(899)	47	(258)	70	(768)	118	(153)
94	(732)	48	(259)	72	(912)	122	(923)
98	(900)	50	(42)	78	(6)	136	(1036)
100	(901)	72	(894)	97	(149)	137	(924)
108	(5)	75	(1072)	Volume V B		139	(1037)
112	(902)	76	(43)	14:72-73	(50)	140	(1038)
130	(145)	80	(260)	15:1	(262)	147	(630)
131	(903)	86	(895)	18	(690)	149	(631)
134	(904)	87	(261)	53:15	(51)	Volume VI B	
143	(206)	88	(196)	53:23	(97)	10	(625)
148	(1029)	90	(240)	55:4	(52)	11	(626)
149	(905)	91	(241)	55:10	(98)	27:2	(456)
150	(775)	92	(1028)	148:17	(150)	38	(632)
155	(906)	96	(896)	148:38	(913)	40:45	(633)
161	(146)	100	(197)	196	(53)	49	(56)
164	(1030)	104	(143)	198	(54)	54:3	(925)
165	(744)	105	(808)	207:3	(914)	54:10	(1039)
172	(910)	106	(809)	213:2	(1073)	54:21	(199)
173	(148)	109	(144)	Volume VI A		60:2	(634)
179	(911)	Volume V A		7	(915)	98:46	(926)
187	(253)	2	(268)	9	(254)	129	(635)
188	(1031)	5	(604)	14	(105)	Volume VII[1] A	
192	(704)	6	(1032)	17	(627)	12	(154)
213	(907)	10	(452)	19	(628)	13	(155)
222	(147)	14	(45)	25	(811)	15	(927)
Volume IV B		16	(46)	27	(916)	28	(928)
2:16	(734)	18	(622)	34	(917)	29	(929)
5:13	(776)	19	(623)	35	(918)	30	(930)
13:18-19	(891)	20	(47)	39	(172)	33	(1040)
13:21	(777)	23	(453)	43	(151)	35	(931)
13:23	(735)	25	(48)	51	(757)	48	(1041)
67	(908)	26	(454)	60	(758)	51	(156)
170	(909)	28	(49)	65	(1034)	59	(812)
173	(44)	30	(1033)	70	(919)	73	(932)
Volume IV C		33	(745)	72	(920)	79	(302)
14	(736)	35	(810)	92	(921)	80	(1042)
16	(892)	36	(714)	96	(269)	84	(759)
17	(893)	41	(767)	101	(1035)	86	(57)
20	(112)	47	(624)	102	(55)	89	(933)
21	(113)	56	(715)	109	(455)	91	(636)
27	(114)	63	(716)	113	(922)	93	(157)
32	(40)	68	(705)	115	(629)	123	(637)

COLLATION

Volume VII[1] A		Volume VIII[1] A		Volume VIII[1] A		Volume VIII[1] A	
134	(1009)	74	(839)	316	(950)	526	(249)
138	(934)	83	(304)	317	(179)	528	(473)
140	(1043)	87	(719)	319	(951)	530	(814)
144	(457)	88	(161)	320	(1050)	543	(841)
145	(717)	102	(460)	325	(468)	547	(373)
146	(935)	122	(162)	330	(306)	554	(646)
159	(158)	127	(1046)	343	(307)	564	(647)
161	(566)	128	(606)	344	(308)	565	(318)
162	(567)	129	(461)	345	(309)	583	(319)
165	(231)	130	(462)	346	(310)	601	(65)
171	(58)	143	(940)	354	(608)	621	(163)
172	(936)	144	(941)	357	(469)	622	(4)
173	(1076)	145	(305)	359	(952)	629	(374)
174	(1077)	155	(792)	362	(643)	632	(66)
178	(232)	157	(463)	363	(100)	665	(1014)
179	(937)	168	(246)	365	(470)	671	(958)
180	(1010)	189	(942)	368	(233)	673	(67)
206	(59)	202	(1078)	371	(311)	Volume VIII[2] B	
211	(605)	214	(464)	374	(312)	13	(234)
216	(1044)	215	(465)	377	(313)	30:4	(943)
217	(1045)	221	(840)	378	(314)	31:20	(1012)
232	(718)	223	(946)	391	(315)	32:22	(1113)
238	(60)	225	(182)	392	(372)	34:7	(944)
239	(458)	226	(1047)	398	(953)	58:14	(945)
242	(159)	234	(1048)	405	(247)	79	(648)
243	(459)	236	(947)	406	(720)	81	(649)
245	(1008)	238	(466)	410	(954)	82	(650)
248	(99)	241	(61)	413	(955)	83	(651)
251	(938)	243	(639)	416	(183)	84	(652)
Volume VIII[1] A		244	(62)	423	(609)	85	(653)
6		256	(640)	425	(248)	86	(654)
7	(778)	257	(786)	435	(471)	87	(655)
10	(836)	258	(787)	436	(184)	88	(656)
20	(207)	267	(467)	448	(644)	89	(657)
28	(746)	268	(63)	454	(64)	154:3	(747)
50	(208)	270	(813)	466	(645)	159:4	(748)
53	(160)	291	(948)	469	(316)	168:5	(68)
56	(837)	292	(1049)	470	(568)	168:6	(749)
59	(771)	293	(641)	492	(760)	168:8	(750)
60	(683)	294	(642)	493	(472)	171:15	(375)
62	(939)	307	(607)	494	(956)	Volume IX A	
72	(303)	312	(949)	509	(957)	2	(474)
73	(838)	314	(1011)	519	(317)	5	(475)

COLLATION

Volume IX A		Volume IX A		Volume X¹ A		Volume X¹ A	
6	(476)	301	(378)	135	(236)	432	(169)
12	(1079)	308	(379)	136	(667)	438	(501)
13	(477)	314	(961)	178	(495)	443	(502)
14	(478)	329	(489)	185	(668)	447	(340)
16	(320)	340	(1016)	188	(186)	457	(976)
20	(479)	346	(962)	190	(496)	460	(383)
21	(610)	350	(490)	193	(1055)	467	(503)
28	(480)	358	(1052)	198	(167)	471	(504)
32	(255)	359	(1053)	201	(329)	472	(505)
44	(1015)	360	(491)	204	(330)	473	(506)
51	(481)	368	(325)	208	(969)	480	(672)
56	(611)	372	(963)	212	(590)	502	(817)
57	(321)	382	(1054)	216	(669)	503	(341)
59	(322)	387	(235)	217	(497)	523	(818)
60	(376)	392	(964)	219	(762)	537	(592)
76	(69)	394	(492)	232	(331)	547	(507)
79	(658)	395	(270)	233	(721)	552	(593)
80	(70)	405	(380)	235	(670)	558	(508)
95	(691)	414	(493)	238	(1074)	566	(673)
103	(323)	418	(965)	243	(332)	579	(594)
104	(959)	419	(966)	245	(333)	580	(977)
105	(482)	439	(665)	248	(816)	587	(342)
110	(164)	440	(326)	249	(382)	608	(1080)
111	(960)	442	(209)	271	(591)	610	(978)
114	(761)	443	(967)	279	(334)	624	(343)
127	(659)	447	(165)	285	(335)	647	(788)
147	(483)	460	(569)	301	(498)	649	(509)
153	(692)	461	(494)	321	(970)	650	(1056)
154	(1051)	464	(968)	327	(971)	658	(707)
198	(660)	472	(570)	345	(671)	672	(384)
199	(377)	475	(223)	346	(168)	Volume X² A	
207	(484)	483	(224)	352	(336)	12	(674)
232	(661)	Volume X¹ A		353	(101)	16	(385)
233	(662)	3	(166)	354	(337)	19	(675)
240	(663)	5	(185)	355	(338)	22	(102)
249	(324)	7	(381)	360	(972)	23	(979)
257	(664)	38	(589)	364	(339)	27	(386)
264	(588)	48	(842)	393	(973)	37	(510)
284	(485)	49	(327)	399	(499)	38	(344)
289	(815)	51	(684)	412	(974)	57	(612)
292	(486)	122	(666)	426	(843)	58	(387)
297	(487)	127	(328)	427	(500)	73	(345)
300	(488)	132	(693)	430	(975)	78	(71)

494   COLLATION

Volume X² A	Volume X² A	Volume X³ A	Volume X³ A
79 (72)	386 (779)	172 (520)	765 (576)
85 (346)	392 (820)	173 (521)	Volume X⁴ A
86 (347)	396 (188)	186 (77)	5 (1063)
97 (271)	397 (613)	187 (174)	11 (238)
119 (187)	406 (73)	192 (395)	15 (708)
132 (763)	407 (74)	209 (522)	22 (599)
135 (388)	408 (75)	248 (990)	24 (686)
136 (348)	414 (1058)	250 (723)	28 (528)
137 (819)	419 (986)	257 (353)	32 (1086)
139 (389)	420 (514)	282 (396)	34 (687)
141 (511)	421 (515)	285 (523)	49 (577)
142 (980)	422 (352)	340 (724)	50 (357)
146 (676)	434 (722)	342 (14)	60 (726)
170 (349)	439 (1059)	344 (685)	62 (1064)
178 (981)	453 (390)	348 (213)	71 (15)
180 (1081)	455 (789)	354 (354)	76 (250)
187 (512)	460 (516)	362 (524)	78 (529)
194 (237)	462 (391)	420 (397)	115 (530)
201 (982)	466 (678)	427 (355)	147 (399)
208 (983)	491 (76)	463 (226)	149 (531)
220 (1082)	514 (392)	464 (1085)	150 (175)
221 (1083)	546 (987)	501 (78)	176 (995)
224 (984)	555 (210)	505 (398)	184 (996)
253 (694)	556 (211)	521 (597)	200 (400)
258 (781)	561 (264)	540 (189)	207 (1065)
264 (173)	592 (8)	624 (679)	212 (532)
270 (985)	593 (393)	625 (680)	222 (822)
271 (764)	603 (517)	648 (681)	234 (780)
283 (571)	606 (1060)	649 (525)	246 (600)
284 (513)	617 (844)	653 (695)	288 (104)
305 (572)	Volume X³ A	655 (356)	320 (997)
311 (350)	27 (1084)	697 (598)	362 (998)
319 (351)	54 (596)	710 (725)	387 (108)
320 (272)	60 (212)	714 (991)	388 (109)
324 (263)	66 (988)	715 (992)	418 (110)
328 (1057)	96 (106)	725 (1062)	433 (214)
348 (1017)	97 (107)	729 (793)	437 (215)
354 (7)	100 (518)	733 (526)	439 (573)
358 (225)	104 (989)	734 (993)	452 (533)
367 (677)	134 (519)	737 (994)	457 (79)
377 (201)	137 (394)	738 (527)	470 (534)
380 (170)	150 (1061)	755 (574)	473 (251)
384 (103)	151 (821)	760 (575)	506 (358)

COLLATION 495

Volume X⁴ A		Volume X⁵ A		Volume XI¹		Volume XI² A	
507	(359)	110	(403)	280	(365)	15	(367)
514	(360)	120	(20)	284	(200)	25	(368)
516	(535)	131	(362)	293	(553)	47	(559)
518	(1087)	144	(543)	307	(19)	48	(828)
537	(176)	145	(544)	308	(405)	49	(560)
549	(999)			309	(406)	63	(1067)
550	(791)	Volume X⁵ B		324	(554)	80	(614)
563	(1000)	245	(595)	326	(845)	95	(369)
571	(1001)			332	(555)	102	(561)
580	(823)	Volume X⁶ B		333	(556)	110	(562)
581	(536)	78	(9)	347	(216)	113	(1006)
590	(1088)	79	(10)	349	(557)	122	(1018)
591	(1089)	80	(11)	353	(1066)	139	(89)
594	(601)	81	(12)			140	(90)
596	(709)	233	(825)	Volume XI¹ A		164	(370)
616	(537)			358	(83)	199	(729)
624	(538)	Volume XI¹		362	(698)	200	(730)
633	(824)	13	(363)	385	(84)	221	(563)
638	(80)	28	(711)	386	(85)	229	(603)
644	(190)	38	(696)	394	(826)	247	(1093)
648	(539)	39	(545)	407	(86)	260	(688)
652	(1090)	45	(364)	408	(87)	263	(615)
658	(540)	59	(697)	409	(1091)	280	(829)
659	(361)	70	(546)	410	(794)	302	(21)
669	(1002)	91	(547)	434	(1092)	315	(564)
Volume X⁵ A		123	(548)	436	(191)	328	(181)
22	(239)	124	(549)	444	(558)	330	(256)
31	(115)	173	(111)	451	(1004)	331	(830)
32	(116)	222	(550)	479	(727)	341	(616)
36	(541)	225	(81)	483	(366)	349	(409)
42	(401)	236	(82)	503	(407)	375	(565)
76	(1075)	237	(180)	528	(1005)	381	(1007)
94	(177)	245	(404)	529	(408)	404	(192)
98	(542)	252	(1003)	546	(602)	422	(731)
99	(178)	264	(551)	565	(728)	Volume XI³ B	
106	(710)	265	(552)	570	(827)	124	(846)
107	(402)	278	(733)	592	(88)	125:8	(847)

Notes, Commentary, and Topical Bibliography

The summary presentation of basic concepts is by G. M. Malantschuk and the notes and bibliography are by the editors.

The following abbreviations have been used throughout the notes:

    S.V. *Samlede Vaerker* by Søren Kierkegaard, I-XIV (Copenhagen: Gyldendal, 1901-1906).

    Pap. *Papirer* by Søren Kierkegaard, edited by P. A. Heiberg, V. Kuhr, and E. Torsting, I-XI³ (20 vols.) (Copenhagen: Gyldendal, 1909-48). References to the *Papirer* will usually be in the form I A 1, etc.

Titles of studies pertinent to a particular theme are given under the appropriate heading. The editions of Kierkegaard's works referred to in the notes are listed in the Bibliography.

ABSTRACT, ABSTRACTION

The abstract is drawn (by thought) from concrete things and indicates the common characteristics of things. By the process of abstraction, which as a definite, conscious approach had its beginning in Greece (*Concluding Unscientific Postscript*, p. 295), the concepts of things are created which form the basis of all thinking. But thought must always return to concrete things if it is not, as with Hegel, to become "pure thought," which loses the actuality of sense and is changed to something imaginative. Climacus (Kierkegaard) in these words emphasizes the justification of abstraction in relation to solid actuality and also the dubiousness of "pure thought": "Just as existence has combined thinking and existing in such a way that an existing being is a thinking being, so also are there two media: the medium of abstraction and the medium of actuality. But pure thought is yet a third medium, quite recently invented" (ibid., p. 278. Ed. tr.).

ABSURD

The absurd is the central category in Kierkegaard's thought and is used as the designation for the logical contradiction which arises when an attempt is made to join two qualitative opposites in an existential unity. Thus when man, who is structured according to both time and eternity, must join these two opposites in his existence, not abstractly but thoroughly concretely, there is, viewed from the angle of logical thought, a contradiction. In its absolute form this contradiction is contained only in the declaration of the incarnation of God. All other forms of the absurd are only lower analogies in relation to the absurd on the highest level (*sensu eminentiori*). Kierkegaard employs the category of the absurd to delineate accurately the boundary between knowledge and faith. All knowledge has the aim of a contradiction-free objectivity, but faith continually has the absurd as its object. For a consideration of the realm of the absurd, which pertains particularly to Christianity, there is required clear, logical thought, of which Kierkegaard says: "The absurd is ... most developed thought." Kierkegaard also uses a related expression, the paradoxical. The absurd is a stricter term for contradiction. See PARADOX.

Glicksburg, C. I. 'The Kierkegaardian Paradox of the Absurd," in *The Tragic Vision in Twentieth-Century Literature*. Carbondale, Ill.: Southern Illinois Press, 1963. See also general works on Kierkegaard.

1. See *Concluding Unscientific Postscript*, pp. 503-504.
2. See VI A 17:19.
3. Belief, confidence, faith.
4. Opinion, conjecture.
5. *Fear and Trembling*, pp. 110-11.
6. *Postscript*, pp. 231-32.
7. *Postscript*, pp. 493 ff.
8. *Postscript*, pp. 540 ff.

ACTION

Action always stands in relation to a resolution consciously thought through. Without this clarity of resolution, it would have to be said of our actions that things "happen to us rather than that we act" (III C 14). Action presupposes self-knowledge so that we can be sure that our actions depend on conscientious reflections and are not in "the service of unclarified cravings" (*Edifying Discourses*, IV, p. 23).

THE ANCIENTS, THE CLASSICAL

Under the influence of ideas from Hegel's *Esthetics*, Kierkegaard is considerably occupied in his early journals with antiquity in contrast to the romantic. For him antiquity always means the limited, the harmonious; whereas the romantic "flows beyond all limits" (I A 130). The later contrast finite-infinite corresponds to classical-romantic. At times in subsequent writings Kierkegaard substitutes for the antique and classical a term he often employed: Greekness or the Greek quality [*Græciteten*]; and for him Greece is first and foremost the land of the classical.

Wild, John. "Kierkegaard and Classic Philosophy." *Philosophical Review*, 1940.

9. *Timaeus*, 22b "O Solon, Solon, you Greeks are always youths; an old man is no Greek."

ANSELM

Anselm of Canterbury (1033-1109) is known especially for his ontological proof of God and for his work *Cur Deus Homo?* Kierkegaard notes numerous observations regarding Anselm's position on ethical questions, particularly while he was reading Friedrich Böhringer, *Die Kirche Christi und ihre Zeugen oder die Kirchengeschichte in Biographien* (Zürich: 1842-49). The same reading gave Kierkegaard occasion to pinpoint the circumstance that Anselm prayed God to help him with the proof and thanked him when it was completed. Kierkegaard concludes: "Anselm prays in all inwardness that he might succeed in proving God's existence. He thinks he has succeeded, and he flings himself down in adoration to thank God. Amazing. He does not notice that this prayer and this expression of thanksgiving are infinitely more proof of God's existence than—the proof" (X^5 A 120). See also X^4 A 210.

10. Friedrich Böhringer, *Die Kirche Christi und ihre Zeugen oder die Kirchengeschichte in Biographien*, I-VII (Zürich: 1842-49).

ANTHROPOLOGY, PHILOSOPHY OF MAN

Inasmuch as Kierkegaard concentrates first and foremost upon man, it is not surprising that anthropology takes the most prominent position in his writings. But for Kierkegaard anthropology does not signify knowledge of external data about man but a penetrating understanding of man's inner life. He had gained this understanding through immersion in his own inner being, which he called "an inland journey within his own consciousness" (S.V., V, p. 48; see also V B 47:13 and XI^2 A 171) and by thorough observation of his fellow men. Therefore in his anthropology he gives a new and well-tested view of man. As the basis for his anthropology he uses the idea of man as a synthesis of two contrasting qualities. See SYNTHESIS, QUALITY.

Allport, Gordon. *Becoming*. New Haven: Yale University Press, 1955.

Brown, Gladstone L. "A Christian Criticism of the Philosophy of Karl Marx." Drew University thesis, 1958.

Buber, Martin. *Between Man and Man*. Boston: Beacon Press, 1955.

Copp, John D. *The Concept of Soul in Kierkegaard and Freud*. Boston University Ph.D. thesis, 1953.

Madden, M. C. *The Contribution of Søren Kierkegaard to a Christian Psychology*. Southern Baptist Theological Seminary Ph.D. thesis, 1940.

Price, George H. *The Narrow Pass*, a study of Kierkegaard's concept of man. New York: McGraw-Hill, 1963.

11. Johann Caspar Lavater, *Physiognomische Fragmente, zur Beförderung der Menschenkenntnis und Menschenliebe*, I-IV (Leipzig and Winterthur: 1775), I, pp. 5 ff.

12. Presumably from H. H. Clausen's lectures on dogmatics during the winter semester of 1839-40 and the summer semester of 1840.

13. See *The Concept of Dread*, pp. 32-34.

14. See II C 55.

15. See *Philosophical Fragments*, p. 47.

16. See *Repetition*, p. 57; *Philosophical Fragments*, pp. 46, 49.

17. See *Edifying Discourses*, I, p. 51; *Postscript*, p. 51.

18. Wilhelm Gottlieb Tennemann, *Geschichte der Philosophie*, I-XI (Leipzig: 1798-1819).

19. *Timaeus*, 42a ff., 90e ff.; see *Stages on Life's Way*, p. 67.

20. Ludwig Feuerbach, *Das Wesen des Christenthums* (Leipzig: 1843).

21. See *Stages*, p. 83.

22. See *Edifying Discourses*, IV, pp. 22 ff.

23. See *Fragments*, pp. 119 ff.

24. See *Fragments*, pp. 55 ff.

25. Because all have sinned.

26. Luke 7:28.

27. See *Postscript*, p. 210.

28. See Cicero, *De natura deorum*, II, 140.

29. See Plato, *Cratylus*, 399c.

30. *Homo* is related to *humus*, "of the earth," or even the ground itself. On the other hand, the Greek "man" connotes something of the spiritual nature of man.

31. See *Joyful Notes in the Strife of Suffering*, in *Christian Discourses*, p. 108; *The Sickness unto Death*, p. 153.

32. H. V. Kaalund, *Fabler for Børn* (Copenhagen: 1844).

33. Carl Daub, *Philosophische und theologische Vorlesungen* (Berlin: 1838-44), I (*Vorlesungen über die philosophische Anthropologie*) "For whom everything is a life-question, only life is of consequence and right is of no consequence."

34. See *Two Discourses at the Communion on Fridays* in *Judge for Yourselves*, p. 5; *The Point of View*, pp. 109-10; and *Works of Love*, pp. 72, 128 ff., 141 ff., and 177 ff.

35. See *The Sickness unto Death*, pp. 145-50.

36. Plutarch, *Moralia*, "Concerning the Inscription Ει on the Temple at Delphi," ch. 13.

37. Alphonse de Lamartine, *Den franske Revolutions Historie i 1848* (serially in *Berlingske Tidende*, Copenhagen: 1849).

38. Scribe, *Den første Kærlighed*, tr. by J. L. Heiberg (Copenhagen: 1832).

39. *Postscript*, p. 86.

40. Matthew 7:24, Luke 6:47, John 8:31 ff.

41. *Die christliche Lehre von der Sünde*, I-II (Breslau: 1849).

42. *Either/Or*, II, pp. 217 ff.

43. John 2:1-11.

44. John 19:5.

45. See J. V. Neergaard, *Morderne Ole P. Kolleruds, Ole Hansens, Peter Christian Knudsens og flere andre Forbryderes Criminalsag* (Copenhagen: 1838), p. 19.

46. See Plato, *Phædo*, 606. The Jowett translation does not use the figure of angles but, instead, that of two bodies with one head.

ANXIETY (Angst), Dread

Anxiety is an expression of the individual's relationship to possibility within the finite. It is the mark of freedom on the lower level of human existence, inasmuch as the individual is drawn to possibility by anxiety and simultaneously is repelled from it; thus anxiety is compounded. As an expression of freedom, anxiety is related to guilt. Since in the first stage of human existence guilt is not only individual but includes the guilt of the race also, Kierkegaard uses the concept of anxiety to throw light on the question of original sin. In his difficult book *The Concept of Anxiety* (*Dread* in present English translation) he gives a coherent presentation of the forms anxiety may take as an expression of original sin. Only by a personal assumption of the consequences of original sin and through faith in the eternal (in "faith's anticipation"; see ibid., p. 141) can the individual conquer anxiety. See FAITH, DESPAIR.

Croxall, T. H. *Kierkegaard Studies*. London: Lutterworth Press, 1948.
Hamilton, Kenneth. "Man: Anxious or Guilty?" *Christian Scholar*, 1963.
May, Rollo. *The Meaning of Anxiety*. New York: Ronald Press, 1950.
———, et al. *Existence*. New York: Basic Books, 1959.
Roberts, D. E. "The Concept of Dread." *Review of Religion*, 1947.
Steiner, Henry, and Gelser, Jean. *Anxiety*. New York: Dell, 1962.
Thielecke, Helmut. "Nihilism and Anxiety." *Theology Today*, XII, 3, October, 1955. Also editorial.
Tweedie, Donald Ferguson. "The Significance of Dread in the Thought of Heidegger and Kierkegaard." Boston University Ph.D. thesis, 1954.
Ussher, Arland. *Journey through Dread*. New York: Devin-Adair, 1955.

47. J. C. Hamann, *Schriften* I–VIII (Berlin: 1821-43).
48. See I Corinthians 6:3; Hebrews 1:13-14.
49. *The Sickness unto Death*, p. 159.

APOSTLE

For Kierkegaard the apostle is the best example of what it means to be a disciple of Christ, but at the same time the apostle differs from other believers in that he has been chosen for his work in a special way and thereby has "divine authority" ("Of the Difference between a Genius and an Apostle," together with *The Present Age*, p. 144).

50. Matthew 17:20.
51. See A. Schopenhauer, *Die Welt als Wille und Vorstellung* I-II (Leipzig: 1844), II, 2, 27. "A serpent does not become a dragon unless it shall have consumed a serpent."

ARISTOTLE

Kierkegaard ranks Aristotle (384–322 B.C.) very high among the philosophers. He extols Aristotle for thorough, fundamental thinking and in his philosophic work frequently appeals to him. For example, Aristotle's statement in *Physics* that "the transition from possibility to actuality is a change" (IV C 47) plays a very important role in Kierkegaard's thought. Kierkegaard also uses ideas from Aristotle's *Poetics* and *Politics* in his discussion of esthetics and ethics.

Durkan, John. "Kierkegaard and Aristotle: A Parallel." *Dublin Review*, 1943.

52. See *Nicomachean Ethics*, 1111 b, 6 ff. "Voluntary action"; "choice."
53. Ibid., 1113 b, 14 ff.
54. Ibid., 1145 b, 26 ff.
55. Ibid., X, 9, especially 1179 b, 32 ff.
56. *Magna Moralia*, I, 1, 1181 a, 25 ff.
57. *Nicomachean Ethics*, 1178 a, 9 ff.
58. Ibid., 1111 b, 20 ff.
59. Ibid., 1143 b, 11 ff.
60. Ibid., 1154 b, 24 ff.
61. Ibid., 1163 b, 8 ff.

ART, ARTISTS, ARTISTRY, THE ARTISTIC

Art in the narrower sense is symbolized for Kierkegaard by poetry, and in his comprehensive view of the various spheres of existence art is in the lowest sphere. In line with his stronger emphasis later upon the significance of action for existence, he turns against the artist who wants to paint Christ (*Training in Christianity*, pp. 247-49) instead of obeying him. Art as a poet's creating and forming activity is of great concern to Kierkegaard. He lays considerable weight on the artistic treatment of material and particularly on the way it is to be communicated. He develops his original theory of the art of communication. He is also attentive to the ethical and religious problems related to a poet's life. Throughout his entire authorship, Kierkegaard wrestles with the question of the extent to which poetic activity is justifiable from an ethical and religious point of view.

Croxall, T. H. *Kierkegaard Commentary*. New York: Harper, 1956.

———. "Kierkegaard on Music." *Proceedings of the Royal Musical Association*. 1946-47.

———. *Kierkegaard Studies*. London: Lutterworth Press, 1948.

Fallico, Arthur. *Art and Existentialism*. New York: Prentice-Hall, 1962.

Glicksberg, C. I. "Aesthetics of Nihilism." *University of Kansas City Review*, 1960.

Henriksen, Aage. "Kierkegaard's Reviews of Literature." *Orbis litterarum*, Copenhagen, 1955.

Stanford, Derek. "The Aesthetics of Søren Kierkegaard." *Twentieth Century*, 1952.

62. François Huber, *Nouvelles observations sur les abeilles* (1792). Huber was blind from the age of fifteen. This work appeared when he was forty-two years old.

63. See H. Gerdes, *Das Christusbild Sören Kierkegaards* (Dusseldorf: 1960).

64. A one-act drama by Scribe, translated by J. L. Heiberg (Copenhagen: 1832).

65. C. Molbech, *Forelæsninger over den nyere danske Poesie* (Copenhagen: 1832).

66. Prototype.

67. Self-seeking.

68. Johann Ernst Hartmann (1726-93), composer of the music to Ewald's *Fiskerne*. His son, J. P. E. Hartmann, was born in 1805.

69. See I C 125, pp. 307 ff.

70. See I C 105.

71. See Grimm Brothers, *Irische Elfenmärchen* (Leipzig: 1826).

72. See *Postscript*, p. 99. Behrendt (?-1821), businessman and broker, was a Copenhagen character about whom many stories were told. See No. 625.

73. See *Either/Or*, I, p. 32.

74. See *The Concept of Dread*, p. 9.

75. Flavius Philostratus, des Aeltern, *Werke* (Stuttgart: 1821-32).

76. *Poetics*, 1448b 3-28.

77. Hebrews 4:15; see II A 366.

78. *Either/Or*, I, p. 43.

79. We only hear . . . ; we know nothing.

80. *Dionysius Longin vom Erhabenen*, Greek and German, by C. H. Heineken (Dresden: 1737).

81. See *Stages*, p. 329.

82. Ibid., pp. 411 ff.

83. A consequence prevails from *to be able* to *to be*; a consequence prevails from *to be* to *to be able*.

84. See VI A 40.

85. A drama by Alexander Dumas, translated by C. Borgaard (Copenhagen: 1838).

86. L. Holberg, *Erasmus Montanus*, Act. II, sc. 3.

87. A five-act play by Bulwer, translated by N. V. Dorph, performed in July, 1844, and later.

88. See Horace, *Ars Poetica* 11.351 ff.; "in which many things are brilliant."

89. See E. Hirsch, *Kierkegaard-Studien* (Gutersloh: 1933), pp. 444 f.

90. Centenary of the Royal Theater, December, 1848, and January, 1849.

ASCETICISM

In very early utterances by Kierkegaard there is a discernible attraction toward the ascetic. But asceticism is not understood as an outward arrangement but as a claim upon the inner man not to make himself completely dependent upon the world. Kierkegaard gives expression to this by his emphasis upon "the infinite movement of resignation" (*Fear and Trembling*, pp. 46 ff.; *Concluding Unscientific Postscript*, pp. 358 ff.), whereby the individual seeks to free himself from the absolute power of finite ends in order to serve the truth. This focus does not require that one withdraw from the world, for "the person who is to remain standing in the world to witness to the truth will bring appropriate asceticism to his life" (X^3 A 588). Later there is more and more emphasis upon Christ as prototype, because, according to Kierkegaard, this aspect of Christianity has been forgotten, and asceticism in its outward visible form stands out more clearly and comes to the fore during the Church battle. See IMITATION.

91. See II A 786, II A 239.

92. See *Postscript*, pp. 482 ff., 486 ff.

93. Dr. Theol. Balthasar Münter (1794-1867), senior pastor of Holmens Kirke and teacher at the Pastoral Seminary.

94. *Über die Religion. Reden an die Gebildeten unter ihren Verächtern* (Berlin: 1843), p. 75.

95. Which had to be proved.

96. See S.V., VIII, p. 9. This Roman emperor reportedly on occasion ate only ostrich for a whole day.

AUGUSTINE

In numerous ways Kierkegaard was inspired by Augustine's ideas. Presumably the most important of Kierkegaard's discoveries therein was that Augustine, in opposition to Pelagius, held that from the Christian point of view man must go through "three stages" (I A 101), an idea which no doubt was influential for Kierkegaard himself during his development of the doctrine of the stages. Yet Kierkegaard later at times felt prompted to criticize Augustine's conception of faith, which he considered to have been developed (under Greek influence) intellectually and not existentially (XI^1 A 257).

Manasse, E. M. "Conversion and Liberation: A Comparison of Augustine and Kierkegaard." *Review of Religion*, 1943.

97. God is such a master in things large that He is not less so in things small.

98. See L. Holberg, *Erasmus Montanus*, Act I, sc. 4.

99. Books VI, VII, and X.

100. An innermost sanctuary, something secret.

AUTHORITY

According to Kierkegaard, one who has received a command to proclaim Christian truth has authority. Such a proclaimer stands by himself responsible before God and has no need of being involved in discussion with the listeners. The proclaimer is either one who has been called in a special way by God or an ordained pastor. However, as Kierkegaard made his way in presenting the requirement of consistency between proclamation and existence, he became convinced that ordination itself is not enough. Only the person whose life conforms to what he proclaims has genuine authority to proclaim.

Croxall, T. H., *Kierkegaard Commentary.* New York: Harper, 1956.

———. "Kierkegaard on Authority." *Hibbert Journal*, 1949-50.

101. See *The Present Age* and *Two Minor Ethico-Religious Treatises*, pp. 146 ff.

102. See Diogenes Laertius, *Lives and Opinions of Eminent Philosophers*, 40 ff.; *For Self-Examination*, pp. 1 ff.

103. See *On Authority and Revelation (The Book on Adler)*, passim.

104. "Has a Man the Right To Let Himself Be Put To Death for the Truth," "On the Difference between a Genius and an Apostle," included in *The Present Age*.

105. See *Critique of Practical Reason* and *The Metaphysics of Morals*.

106. Matthew 21:12.

BEING

In Kierkegaard's conception all the objects of thought and existence can be considered according to two points of view: essence and being. Kierkegaard's thought is first and foremost in the category of being, because it refers to existence. In his polemic against Hegel's purely abstract understanding of being, Kierkegaard develops in considerable detail, particularly in *Concluding Unscientific Postscript*, his own view of being and the ontological problem. He views being from both an abstract and a concrete angle. Abstract being is designated by the copula "is" [*er*], and contains no gradations. Concrete being, which exists [*er til*] as a particular being, has gradations. From his abstract point of view Climacus can say, "A fly, when it is, has as much being as God" (*Philosophical Fragments*, p. 51 n.) Only through more specific qualification (explication) in concreto will the absolute difference appear. The gradations of being in human existence follow the levels and structure of the stages. See POSSIBILITY, NECESSITY.

107. Being.

108. The different.

109. The Danish reads: *"Tilværelsen gaaer ud af det Savn."* The editors of the *Papirer* have a footnote suggesting that *det Savn* should read *das Sein*.

110. See J. L. Heiberg, "Ledetraad ved Forelæsningerne over Philosophiens Philosophie eller den speculative Logik" at the Royal Military College (ms., 1831-32), pp. 90 ff.

111. F. C. Sibbern gave lectures on "The Philosophy of Christianity" during the winter semester, 1838-39.

112. See Sibbern in *Maanedskrift for Literatur*, XIX (1838), pp. 356 ff.; *Philosophical Fragments*, p. 22 and "Interlude."

113. See *Johannes Climacus or, De Omnibus Dubitandum Est*, pp. 151-52.

114. One, odd, even.
115. See *Postscript*, p. 100.
116. Exodus 3:14.

BERNARD OF CLAIRVAUX

While reading works depicting the life of Bernard of Clairvaux, Kierkegaard recorded a number of observations in his journals in which some of Bernard's expressions are quoted and note is taken of the zeal with which he won men to Christianity (X^2 A 377). From the point of view that one should not speak to the masses to excite them but should address individuals as Socrates did, Kierkegaard is critical of Bernard's sermon to those taking part in crusades (X^5 A 133).

117. Helfferich, *Die christliche Mystik*, pt. I, p. 264.
118. Persuader to death. Epithet of Hegesias of Cyrene, head of the Cyrenaic school and advocate of suicide.

BIBLE

In the early journal entries there is a critique of the Bible reading in which commentaries and exegetical works have a dominant place. Kierkegaard's idea is that this creates hindrances to personal appropriation of the content of the Bible, which should be read as a "letter from the beloved" (X^2 A 555). Kierkegaard goes so far in his criticism of the wrong use of the Bible ("No one reads the Bible humanly any more") (IX A 442) that he finds it conceivable that reading of the Bible be prohibited in order to draw attention to the loss that would be entailed, because the Bible alone can give the answer to man's central questions. But Kierkegaard had to learn from personal experience what conflicts a man can get into when he tries to appropriate in his own existence the truth of the Bible. See CHURCH.

Dunstan, J. Leslie. "The Bible in *Either/Or*." *Interpretation*, 1952.
Minear, Paul S., and Morimoto, Paul S. *Kierkegaard and the Bible*. Princeton: Princeton Pamphlets, 9, 1953.
Perry, E. "Was Kierkegaard a Biblical Existentialist?" *Journal of Religion*, 1956.

119. See *Fragments*, p. 80.
120. *The Gospel of Suffering*, pp. 97 ff.
121. To preach Christianity properly is in a sense to preach *against* Christianity because of the possibility of offense.
122. See *For Self-Examination*, pp. 25 ff.
123. See *Stages*, p. 246.

BOURGEOIS MENTALITY, PHILISTINISM

Kierkegaard always used strong words against philistinism and bourgeois mentality, such expressions as absence of spirit and mediocrity. The basis of his charge is that the philistine, the bourgeois-minded, can never become enthusiastic for anything higher or risk anything for it but is content to live his life within a limited and spiritually narrow perspective.

Gilson, Etienne. *Being and Some Philosophers*. Toronto: Pontifical Institute of Mediaeval Studies, 1952.

124. See the characterization of Peregrinus Tysz in Hoffman's story *Meister Floh*.

125. See K. Hase, *Kirkehistorie* (Copenhagen: 1837), p. 88.

126. He who has never been drunk is not a real man. *The Concept of Dread*, p. 93.

127. See Matthew 22:39.

CALL, CALLING, VOCATION

Call and calling, according to Kierkegaard, can come to a man in two forms. (1) Men are called by God to turn to him; the way is the way of repentance. (2) Every man is called to carry out his particular task which is prepared for the particular person, for "at every man's birth there comes into being an eternal vocation [Bestemmelse] for him, expressly for him" (*Purity of Heart*, p. 140). The most important thing for a person in this respect is to win clarity about himself and this his task and to be faithful to it. There is a special form of calling when a man is called by God "through a revelation," by which he gets "a divine authority" (VIII^2 B 13) to announce a command given to him.

128. Purpose, design.

129. See *The Sickness unto Death*, p. 233; *Purity of Heart*, pp. 197 ff.

130. See *Bogen om Adler*, VII^2 B 235 (English title, *On Authority and Revelation*).

131. See *Postscript*, p. 297.

132. See X^2 A 125.

CATEGORY

According to philosophic usage the term *category* refers to a major concept, and this is true in Kierkegaard's thought. But there is not presented in Kierkegaard's thought, as in Aristotle's or Kant's, a definite number of categories. Furthermore, in contrast to theirs, his main concepts are first and foremost existential concepts. When Kierkegaard asks: "Shall the category be derived from thought or from being?" (IV C 91), his reply is that categories are to be derived from being or, which is the same, that "categories are abbreviations of existence" (VII^1 A 249), because thought abbreviates (foreshortens) and conflates the circumstances of existence in certain major concepts (categories). See *Postscript*, p. 101.

Magel, Charles R. "An Analysis of Kierkegaard's Philosophic Categories." University of Minnesota Ph.D. thesis, 1960.

CATHOLICISM

Instructed in the realm of religion and Christianity by the false steps of the preceding periods, Kierkegaard sought to take a new path (I A 54-55) and according to his conception give a true depiction of what Christianity is. In his writings he pursues this task honestly and with inflexible consistency without being bound in his attempt by confessional considerations. Therefore he recognizes the positive religious elements wherever he finds them, and thus also in Catholicism. His thoughts about resignation, dying to the world, the apostle, and the ordination of the clergy, for example, point in a Catholic direction. At the same time he firmly maintains as inalienable the Protestant doctrine of faith and the exclusion of all meritoriousness on the human side. In his later years, when he particularly emphasizes the significance of imitation for the Christian life, the tendency toward Catholicism becomes more marked in the writings. But when he finally made an attack against the Church this involved not only "especially Protestantism and more especially in Denmark" (*Attack on Christendom*, p. 145) but the whole "concept: Christendom" (ibid., p. 34). See MIDDLE AGES MONASTICISM.

Roos, H. *Søren Kierkegaard and Catholicism*, tr. Richard M. Brackett. Westminster, Md.: Newman Press, 1954.

133. Romans 3:19 ff.

134. See Schleiermacher, *Das Verhältnis des ev. Glaubens zum Gesetz*, II, 2, pp. 637 ff.

CAUSE

During his stay in Gilleleje (1835) Kierkegaard declared that he wanted to find *"the idea for which I can live and die"* and "What is truth but to live for an idea?" (I A 75, pp. 53, 55). He found this idea in his service to the cause of Christianity. Furthermore, Kierkegaard considered that it is the case for every man that the highest is to sacrifice oneself for a cause. He pointed out, however, that to serve "God's cause" is arduous both for God and for man. It is arduous for God to be involved with a human being, "a weak, foolish, carnal heart"; for man, on the other hand, to serve God's cause means "to be examined" (X^4 A 473) by God, which is not easy at all.

CERTAINTY

A person can achieve certainty only when through his relation to the eternal he finds "that Archimedean point *from which he can lift the whole world*" (I A 68, p. 42). But the path to this firm point goes through the leap of faith, and as long as one is in the uncertainty of existence, this firm point can be adhered to only in continuous "fear and trembling" (IX A 32).

135. See *Den rette uforandrede Augsburgske Troesbekjendelse med sammes, af Ph. Melanchthon forfattede, Apologie*, tr. into Danish by Dr. A. G. Rudelbach (Copenhagen: 1825), pp. 126 ff.

136. See *Postscript*, pp. 23 ff.
137. See Plato, *Apology*, 40c ff.

CHANGE, COMING INTO EXISTENCE

There are various kinds of change, as Kierkegaard observes in a note (IV C 47) endorsing Aristotle's doctrine of change. One of these is the change of coming into existence, which denotes the transition from possibility to actuality and which pertains to existence and to the coming into existence of particular concrete things. (See *Philosophical Fragments*, "Interlude.") Kierkegaard concentrates on this kind of change. Everything which exists [*er til*] has become what it is by coming into existence, and the process of appropriation, which plays the most decisive role in Kierkegaard's thought, comes within this kind of change. In his works Kierkegaard gives numerous examples of how this process of appropriation takes place very concretely in the ethical and religious spheres.

138. *Becoming no existing*. See K. Werder, *Logik, als Commentar und Ergänzung zu Hegels Wissenschaft der Logik*, I (Berlin: 1841) pp. 109 ff.

139. *Origination* and *decay*. See Hegel, *Wissenschaft der Logik*, pt. I, sec. 1, pp. 78 ff., 108 ff. (*Werke*, III; Berlin: 1833.)

140. Not *becoming* but *what has become*, i.e., *existence*.
141. *Something* and *something else*.
142. *In itself*.
143. *Being something else*.
144. *Is at the end*.
145. *What has been*.
146. *Motion, change*. Tenneman, *Geschichte der Philosophie*, (Leipzig: 1798-1819). See *Fragments*, pp. 90 ff.; *Postscript*, p. 306.
147. *Increase, decrease*.
148. *Change of quality*.
149. *Change of place*.
150. *The Concept of Anxiety* [*Dread*], pp. 302 ff.
151. See *Fragments*, pp. 95 ff.
152. Ibid.
153. See *Postscript*, pp. 99 ff.
154. See A. Neander, *Denkwürdigkeiten aus der Geschichte des Christenthums und des christlichen Lebens* I-III (Berlin: 1823-26), I, pp. 254 ff.

CHILDHOOD, CHILDREN

In connection with his illumination of the various steps in the development of the individual, Kierkegaard considers the period of childhood in some detail. Through his own experience in childhood he knew how important this portion of life is for a person's later development. In one of his early journal entries (II A 12), occasioned by his reading of Poul M. Møller's essay "On Telling Stories to Children," Kierkegaard offers his ideas on how one should present to children material suitable to their age. Kierkegaard was a keen observer of children, and the results are discernible in many places in his works. He also uses the child as illustrative of the God-relationhip pointing out that a person, through acknowledgment of his own helplessness and inadequacy in relation to God, becomes "more and more a child" (X^2 A 320) on a higher level.

155. See Poul M. Møller, "Om at fortaelle Børn Eventyr," in *Efterladte Skrifter* I-III (Copenhagen: 1839-43), III, pp. 322 ff.

156. Presumably *Prædikener*, by J. P. Mynster (Copenhagen: 1810), I, pp. 60 ff.

157. Comedy by J. L. Heiberg, in *Skuespil* I-VII (Copenhagen: 1833-41), VI, pp. 8 ff.

158. "There is a boy here who has five barley-loaves."

159. "To answer children is truly an *examen rigorosum*; it is also a masterwork to engage children and teach them through questioning, because ignorance still remains the great sophist who has crowned as many idiots as great minds."

160. "The little grandchildren on the lap of their grandmother, who is telling stories, a counterpart to the little grandchildren at the knee of their grandfather, who is telling stories."

161. See *Training in Christianity*, pp. 174 ff.

162. I Corinthians 13:11 ff.

163. See X^2 A 72.

CHRIST

The Christian-oriented influence in Kierkegaard's childhood influenced his view of Christ and decisively penetrated his entire life. In singling out the central element in this influence he says: "I owe everything, from the very beginning, to my father. When he, melancholy as he was, saw me melancholy, his request to me was: "Be sure that you really love Jesus Christ" (IX A 68). His upbringing by his father had the effect that Christ came to be in the center of his existence. The suffering Christ especially became impressed on Kierkegaard's mind (IX A 288 and 399), and this explains why Kierkegaard in his journals and in his published works frequently dwells upon the suffering of Christ and presents the imitation of Christ as an essential aspect of Christianity. Kierkegaard desired "only one thing, to suffer in some measure" as Christ suffered in this world (*Training in Christianity*, p. 178). The treatment which Christ received was for Kierkegaard proof that the good will always suffer in this world.

Croxall, T. H. "Facets of Kierkegaard's Christology." *Theology Today*, 1951-52.

———. *Kierkegaard Commentary*. New York: Harper, 1956.

———. *Kierkegaard Studies*. London: Lutterworth Press, 1948.

Heinecken, Martin J. *The Moment before God.* Philadelphia: Muhlenberg, 1956.

Sponheim, Paul R. "The Christological Formulations of Schleiermacher and Kierkegaard." University of Chicago Ph.D. thesis, 1961.

Thomas, J. H. "Christology of Søren Kierkegaard and Karl Barth." *Hibbert Journal*, 1955.

Wolf, Herbert C. *Kierkegaard and Bultmann.* Minneapolis: Augsburg, 1964.

———. "Kierkegaard and the Quest of the Historical Jesus." *The Lutheran Quarterly*, 1964.

164. Five of Kierkegaard's brothers and sisters had died between 1819 and 1834. The two older sisters died at the ages of thirty-three and thirty-four. Kierkegaard's father thought that none of his children would live beyond the thirty-fourth year.

165. Genesis 1:25 and 1:31.
166. John 19:30.
167. C. Daub, "Die Form der christlichen Dogmen- und Kirchen-Historie," in *Zeitschrift für spekulative Theologie*, ed. B. Bauer, II, 1, pp. 88 ff.
168. Luke 2:49.
169. John 9:4.
170. John 19:30.
171. Mark 1:13.
172. Matthew 27:46.
173. See *Training in Christianity*, p. 196.
174. John 13:27.
175. See *Discourses at the Communion on Fridays* in *Christian Discourses*, pp. 368-69.
176. Matthew 14:13 ff.; Mark 6:32 ff.
177. Acts 17:28.
178. Possibly a reference to Fichte's *Anweisung zum seligen Leben*. This is Kierkegaard's first expression of protest againt the domestication of the incarnation. See E. Hirsch, *Kierkegaard Studien*, II, 550.
179. Luke 2:36.
180. Luke 2:35.
181. Luke 2:37.
182. John 16:7.
183. John 19:30.
184. Luke 23:34.
185. Genesis 22.
186. See Luke 23:43.
187. Acts 7:55.
188. See *Philosophical Fragments*, pp. 31 ff.

189. John 10:11.
190. By *it* is meant the *upbuilding*.
191. Mark 14:44-45.
192. See *Training in Christianity*, pp. 151 ff.
193. Acts 7:56.
194. Matthew 18:20.
195. John 21:15 ff.
196. Matthew 11:28. See *Training in Christianity*, pp. 10 ff.
197. Matthew 27:46.
198. Matthew 27:19.
199. See *Works of Love*, p. 113.
200. Matthew 27:46.
201. Luke 2:13 ff.
202. *Vollständiges Betrachtungs- und Gebetbuch vom heiligen Alphons von Ligiuori*, tr. M. A. Hughes (Aachen: 1840).

> Sweet Jesus, in order to die,
> You go, out of love for me,
> To gain life,
> Let me die, Lord, with you.
> . . .
> Sweet Jesus, already you have died
> Out of love for me:
> Have gained life for me,
> Ah, let me die with you.

203. Matthew 27:60.
204. M. Luther, *En christelig Postille*, tr. J. Thisted (Copenhagen: 1828), I, p. 255.
205. Ibid., p. 252. See John 19:38 ff.
206. See Luke 4:21.
207. John 2:4.
208. Matthew 16:23.
209. Matthew 8:24.
210. Matthew 27:57 ff.
211. John 11:50; 18, 14.
212. Matthew 27:63 ff.
213. John 19:19 ff.
214. Matthew 27:40 ff.
215. Matthew 26:53.
216. John 14:6.
217. Luke 23:43.
218. Luke 23:15 ff.
219. Matthew 27:46.
220. Luke 12:49-53.

221. Mark 10:38.
222. Matthew 19:14.

CHRISTENDOM

Christendom is a historical concept and includes the historical stages in the attempt of peoples to appropriate the truth of Christianity. Since Christianity makes the highest demands on man, there is the possibility of various adaptations and distortions. In the process of historical development, first one and then another aspect of Christianity has been emphasized. After he had studied the experiences and false steps of centuries with regard to Christianity, Kierkegaard saw his task to be that of presenting Christianity in its original form by going to its point of departure: encounter with the person (historical) of Christ. Kierkegaard upbraids Luther because he "did not go back far enough, did not make one contemporary enough with Christ" (IX A 95). Concerning his task he says, "It is a matter neither more nor less than a revision of Christianity; it is a matter of getting rid of 1,800 years as if they had never been. I believe fully and firmly that I shall succeed; the whole thing is as clear as day to me" (IX A 72).

Bonifazi, Conrad. *Christendom Attacked*. London: Rockliff, 1953.

Fitzpatrick, Mallary, Jr., "Kierkegaard and the Church." *Journal of Religion*, 1947.

Gates, John Alexander. *Christendom Revisited: a Kierkegaardian View of the Church Today*. Philadelphia: Westminster Press, 1963.

Geismar, Eduard. *Lectures on the Religious Thought of Søren Kierkegaard*, introduction by David Swenson. Minneapolis: Augsburg, 1937.

Graham, D. Aelred. "Introducing Christianity into Christendom." *Clergy Review*, 1944.

Martin, H. V. "Kierkegaard's Attack upon Christendom." *Congregational Quarterly*, 1946.

Minear, Paul S. "The Church: Militant or Triumphant?" *Andover Newton Bulletin*, 1955.

Stewart, R. W. "Is Church like a Theatre?" *Expository Times*, 1950-51.

223. See *The Gospel of Suffering*, pp. 139 ff.
224. See *Attack upon Christendom*, pp. 29 ff. and passim.
225. See *Training in Christianity*, pp. 109 ff.
226. Matthew 21:33 ff.
227. See Tacitus XV, 44; *Training in Christianity*, p. 119; a hatred toward all of Christianity (in the fashion of a hatred of the human race).
228. Acts 3:6.
229. A. G. Rudelbach, *Den evangeliske Kirkeforfatnings Oprindelse og Princip* (Copenhagen: 1849).
230. Apparently a mistake in writing; the phrase most likely should read "the Sophists, who claimed to be wise."
231. John 18:2.

232. Friedrich Böhringer, *Die Kirche Christi und ihre Zeugen oder die Kirchengeschichte in Biographien*, I-VII (Zurich: 1842-49).

233. See P. L. Benzon, *Criminalhistorier uddragne af Danske Justits-Acter* (Copenhagen: 1827), pp. 58 ff.

CHRISTIANITY

Kierkegaard endeavored to stipulate the absolute difference between Christianity and all other religions, and he found this difference in Christ's words, "I am the truth" (II A 184). Other religions profess to have the truth, but in Christianity a single human being *is* the truth. Here thought encounters an absolute contradiction: a single human being affirms of himself that he is the truth, that is, he is God. This affirmation contains an absolute paradox whereby Christianity is on a level qualitatively different from that of other religions. But Christianity is also a teaching, i.e., the ethical and religious claims upon man. These can be compared with the ethics of other religions and life-views, and the difference is only quantitative. Here one can only say that Christianity has the highest ethical norms. Therefore Kierkegaard draws a sharp distinction between Christ's teachings and Christ as the object of faith: Christ himself is "infinitely more important than his teaching" (*Training in Christianity*, p. 123). Striving is possible in relation to Christ's teachings; one can be related to Christ as redeemer only by faith. The first relationship is the presupposition for the shaping of existence; the second is the communication of a wholly new existence.

Barckett, Richard M. "Søren Kierkegaard: 'Back to Christianity!'" *Downside Review*, 1955.

Cole, J. P. "Kierkegaard's Doctrine of the Atonement." *Religion in Life*, 1964.

Croxall, T. H. *Kierkegaard Studies*. London: Lutterworth Press, 1948.

Diamond, M. L. "Kierkegaard and Apologetics." *Journal of Religion*, 1964.

Dupré, Louis K. *Kierkegaard as Theologian: the Dialectic of Christian Existence*. New York: Sheed and Ward, 1963.

Forgey, Wallace. "A Pastor looks at Kierkegaard." *Andover Newton Bulletin*, 1955.

Geismar, Edward. *Lectures on the Religious Thought of Søren Kierkegaard*, introduction by David Swenson. Minneapolis: Augsburg, 1937.

Heinecken, Martin J. *The Moment Before God*. Philadelphia: Muhlenberg, 1956.

Kroner, Richard. "Existentialism and Christianity." *Encounter*, 1956.

Mackintosh, H. R. "The Theology of Kierkegaard." *Congregational Quarterly*, 1929.

Michalson, Carl. *Christianity and the Existentialists*. New York: Scribner, 1956.

Stewart, R. W. "Existential Christianity." *Expository Times*, 1950-51.

Thomte, Reidar. *Kierkegaard's Philosophy of Religion*. Princeton: Princeton University Press, 1948.

234. Schleiermacher, *Der christliche Glaube* (Berlin: 1830), I, p. 52.
235. See, for example, Acts 6:1; 11:1 ff.; 15:1 ff.
236. Ephesians 1:7. Forgiveness of sins.
237. See *Postscript*, p. 208.
238. See Hayo Gerdes, *Kierkegaard, Tagebücher* (Dusseldorf: 1962), I, p. 363, n. 101, for his interpretation of this entry in the *Papirer*.
239. Josty, a cafe in Fredriksberg, which adjoins Copenhagen.
240. Baader, *Vorlesungen über speculative Dogmatik* (Stuttgart and Tubingen: 1828), p. 80.
241. Matthew 11:12.
242. Philippians 2:12.
243. John 14:6.
244. Kierkegaard had in his library *Justinus Martyrs Apologier eller Forsvarskriften for Christendommen*, tr. C. H. Muus (Copenhagen: 1836).
245. See *S.V.*, V, p. 37.
246. *Augsburg Confession*, XX.
247. Isaiah 57:15.
248. For it is the power of God.
249. Psalms 139:8-10.
250. John 2:1 ff.
251. See II Corinthians 7:10.
252. See *Christian Discourses*, pp. 101 ff.
253. Ibid., pp. 103 ff.
254. Ibid., pp. 112 ff.
255. See Luke 14:26 and Matthew 10:37, also Matthew 19:29 and Mark 10:29-30.
256. Genesis 2:24.
257. Genesis 7.
258. Genesis 30:23.
259. Genesis 30:6.
260. Genesis 30:22.
261. See *Christian Discourses*, pp. 297 ff.
262. *Werke* (Stuttgart: 1821-32).
263. See *Repetition*, p. 2.
264. See *Fragments*, pp. 119 ff.
265. See *Fragments*, p. 7.
266. See *Purity of Heart*, pp. 160-62.
267. Ibid., p. 162.
268. Ibid., pp. 161 ff.
269. John 19:5.
270. See *Works of Love*, pp. 154 ff.
271. See Luke 22:61.

272. Luke 16:1 ff.
273. See *Christian Discourses*, pp. 32 ff.
274. Ibid., p. 120.
275. See *Christian Discourses*, pp. 289 ff.
276. Matthew 25:1-13.
277. See *The Sickness unto Death*, p. 233.
278. Ibid., pp. 232 ff.
279. See Matthew 6:33; Colossians 3:2; see also *Attack upon Christendom*, pp. 208 ff.
280. John 4:32, 34; 6:27, 55.
281. Matthew 8:22.
282. Matthew 7:12.
283. Psalms 37:25.
284. Matthew 27:46.
285. Acts 22:7.
286. Matthew 28:5.
287. H. Martensen, *Den christelige Dogmatik* (Copenhagen: 1849), pp. 8 ff., 14 ff.
288. I Timothy 4:1 ff.
289. Luke 18:8.
290. Matthew 7:24; Luke 6:47; John 8:31 ff.
291. II Corinthians 4:17.
292. F. Böhringer, *Die Kirche Christi* . . . (Zürich: 1842-49).
293. Ibid.
294. Matthew 7:14.
295. First lie.
296. Luke 19:10.
297. Luke 18:15-17.
298. The blood of the martyrs is the seed of the Church.
299. See *The Concept of Irony*, p. 303.

CHRISTMAS

Kierkegaard does not have much to say for Christmas. In many passages he repeats the position that Christmas began to be celebrated only in the fourth century. Christmas is a "substitute for a pagan festival" (IX A 460). And yet he can also say with reference to Christmas, "The strongest expression for our being saved entirely by grace, that we are able to do nothing, is the fact that the Savior is a child. Here there can be no talk at all about imitation" (X^4 A 439).

300. Gustav Lisco, *Das christliche Kirchenjahr* (Berlin: 1843).
301. *Postscript*, pp. 520 ff., especially pp. 527 ff.
302. Acts 6:15.
303. See *Postscript*, p. 260.

CHRYSOSTOM

Johannes Chrysostomos (ca. 343–407) is regarded as one of the great figures in the Greek Church. While reading A. Neander, *Der heilige Chrysostomos* (Berlin: 1821), Kierkegaard wrote an observation by Chrysostom which completely agrees with his own view of Christianity, that in contrast to paganism's predilection for the distinguished and resplendent, Christianity represents all that which does not make a good showing in men's eyes and is "foolishness to reason" (X^3 A 760).

304. A. Neander, *Der heilige Johannes Chrysostomus und die Kirche* (Berlin: 1821).
305. Matthew 26:69 ff.
306. Neander, p. 235.
307. Ibid., II, p. 274.

CHURCH

At first Kierkegaard was prompted to concern for the question of Church and congregation by the stir about this question created in Denmark by Grundtvig. Even then Kierkegaard maintained that Church and congregation are historical entities and only provide the framework of the Christian life. As a consequence, Kierkegaard's view is that the structure and organization of the Church is not an essential aspect of the Church, but that the religious practice of individuals is. Concerning this he writes: "the task is precisely that your own house should become a house of God" (X^1 A 212). According to his understanding the Church should "really represent 'becoming'" (X^1 A 552), which means that it should be renewed continually from within, and this renewal can be accomplished only by the individual members through their spiritual contribution. Therefore Kierkegaard increasingly emphasizes the significance the individual's inward deepening has for the Church and rejects all attempts to renew the life of the Church by change in its external structure.

Helm, Adelbert J. *Søren Kierkegaard and the Church.* Vanderbilt University, M.A. thesis, 1953.

308. See *Postscript*, pp. 25 ff. There is here an allusion to the Grundtvigians and their emphasis upon the creed as secure against critique.
309. (K.) The Church.
310. See, in contrast, *Attack upon Christendom*, pp. 194-95.
311. See Schleiermacher, *Glaubenslehre*, 23,1.
312. See *Christian Discourses*, pp. 283 ff.
313. See *The Point of View*, pp. 153 ff.
314. Par excellence.
315. J. C. Hamann, *Schriften*, I-VIII (Berlin: 1821). "A divided child is of no use to a true mother."

COLLISION, CONFLICT, ADVERSITY

For Kierkegaard, who in his anthropology defines man as a synthesis of two contrasting qualities, collisions and contradictions in existence must play an essential role. Only through inward strife and "adversity" can a man develop spiritually and gain "one more new string" in his lyre (VIII^1 A 128). It can be said that all of Kierkegaard's works contain an explication of how a man grows spiritually through conflicts and opposition.

316. Matthew 10:34; Luke 12:21.
317. Transition to another (conceptual) sphere.

COMMUNICATION

Socrates' method of presenting his thought indirectly under the cloak of irony was for Kierkegaard the first occasion for becoming occupied with the question of the extent to which the life of the individual contains specific relations and experiences which cannot be declared directly to others (I A 327). In his own life there were such things which he could not communicate directly. In working into these questions Kierkegaard was led to the discovery of a wide-ranging correspondence between indirect communication and ethical-religious truths. He discovered that these, too, can be communicated only indirectly since they contain elements of the eternal which cannot be expressed by direct verbal statement. The receiver can get hold of these eternal elements only in existence, when he re-creates them in self-activity. In order that this may occur, the receiver must be situated before a choice between two contrasting claims. On the basis of this insight Kierkegaard developed his original art of communication, the essential features of which he later wrote down (VIII^2 B 79-89). Christ's life provides the highest example of indirect speech, because here two qualitatively contrasting elements are really united. Christ communicates to men in an indirect way by posing a choice. With reference to the unique position of Christ in relation to indirect communication Kierkegaard says, "Only the God-man is in every respect indirect communication from first to last" (X^3 A 413).

Kierkegaard's entire pseudonymous authorship is indirect communication, because the intention is to incite the reader to choice. On the other hand, his upbuilding or edifying discourses are "direct communication" (IX A 222). But the contrast between them and the pseudonymous works again constitutes an indirect communication. In addition, when Kierkegaard characterizes the edifying discourses as "witness" (IX A 222) and at the same time says of "witnessing" that it "strikes the truest mean between direct and indirect communication" (X^1 A 235), the edifying discourses taken by themselves fall partially under the rubric of indirect communication.

In his edifying works Kierkegaard is attentive to more than the art of communication. Here the ethical responsibility of the writer plays the primary role. Therefore, we find additions stating that he "has no authority to *preach"* (*Edifying Discourses*, I, p. 5 and in many other places) since he was not an ordained pastor. (See AUTHORITY.) The same ethical responsibility prompted him to declare his own existential position in relation to the augmented requirements (demand) which his later works contain. In his survey of the authorship in 1849 he characterized his own position in the following words: "The edifying is mine, not the esthetic, neither [the pseudonymous works] for edification nor, even less, those for awakening" (X^1 A 593). The expression "for edification and awakening" is used in *The Sickness unto Death* and "for awakening and inward deepening" in *Training in Christianity*.

Anderson, Raymond E. *Kierkegaard's Theory of Communication*. University of Minnesota Ph.D. thesis, 1959.

———. "Kierkegaard's Theory of Communication," *Speech Monographs* (1963).

Broudy, H. S. "Kierkegaard and Indirect Communication." *Journal of Philosophy*, 1961.

Cumming, Robert. "Existence and Communication." *International Journal of Ethics*, 1954-55.

Dargan, Edwin Charles. *A History of Preaching*, II. New York: Hodder and Stoughton, 1912.

Holmer, Paul L. "Kierkegaard and Kinds of Discourse," in *Meddelelser fra S. K. Selskabet*. Copenhagen: 1953.

———. "Kierkegaard and Religious Propositions." *Journal of Religion*, 1955.

———. "Kierkegaard and the Sermon." *Journal of Religion*, 1957.

Lee, R. F. "Emerson through Kierkegaard: Toward a Definition of Emerson's Theory of Communication." *Journal of English Literary History*, 1957.

Malantschuk, Gregor. *Kierkegaard's Way to the Truth*. Minneapolis: Augsburg, 1963.

318. See K. Daub, "Die Form der christliche Dogmen- und Kirchenhistorie," in Bruno Bauer, *Zeitschrift für spekulative Theologie*, I-II (1836-37). See E. Hirsch, *Kierkegaard-Studien*, II, pp. 539 ff.

319. Matthew 6:26.

320. Mark 16:14 ff. text for May 16, 1844.

321. See *The Concept of Dread*, p. 96; *Stages on Life's Way*, p. 312.

322. In *Love of Fame*, II, 208, rather than in *Night Thoughts*.

323. Letter to Jacobi, Jan. 22, 1785 (F. H. Jacobi, *Werke*, IV, p. 34). See *Stages*, pp. 100, 122.

324. *Nicomachean Ethics*, XII, 8, 1178b, 8 ff.; *Metaphysics*, XII, 7, 1072b, 14 ff.

325. Grundtvig in Preface to *Christelige Praedikener eller Søndags-Bog* (Copenhagen: 1827), I.

326. See L. Holberg, *Peder Paars* (Copenhagen: 1823), Bk. I, Song 1.

327. *Rhetoric*, I, 1, 1355a; 2, 1357a.

328. See *Postscript*, pp. 229 ff., 241 ff.

329. See *Postscript*, pp. 361-62.
330. See *Postscript*, pp. 67 ff.
331. Ibid., p. 100; A. Trendlenburg, *Logische Untersuchungen* (Berlin: 1840).
332. *Plutarchs Moralische Abhandlungen*, tr. J. F. S. Kaltwasser (Frankfurt/M: 1786), III, pp. 452 ff.
333. See *Postscript*, p. 236.
334. Ibid., p. 223.
335. Ibid., pp. 223-24; Carl L. Michelet, *Geschichte der letzten Systeme der Philosophie in Deutschland von Kant bis Hegel* (Berlin: 1837), I, pp. 301 ff.
336. Michelet, pp. 339 ff.
337. See *Postscript*, p. 390.
338. Ibid., p. 431.
339. Ibid., p. 391n.
340. I Corinthians 9:23; 10:6.
341. Preacher at Holmens Kirke, January 19, 1845.
342. See *The Point of View*, pp. 44 ff.
343. See *Works of Love*, p. 11 (Preface).
344. See *Christian Discourses*, pp. 259 ff.
345. See *Works of Love*, pp. 9 ff. (Preface).
346. See Matthew 6:34.
347. See II Corinthians 7:9.
348. See *Postscript*, pp. 67 ff.
349. This paragraph was added later by Kierkegaard.
350. See *The Concept of Anxiety* [*Dread*], p. 95.
351. See *Training in Christianity*, pp. 132 ff.
352. See *Postscript*, p. 68; *Training in Christianity*, pp. 122 ff.; *The Point of View*, pp. 151 ff.
353. See *Fragments*, pp. 13 ff.; *Works of Love*, p. 257; *The Concept of Irony*, pp. 214-15.
354. See *Fragments*, pp. 23 ff.
355. See *The Point of View*, pp. 39 ff., 148 ff.
356. See *Works of Love*, p. 337.
357. See *Fragments*, p. 25; *Works of Love*, p. 258; "Has a Man the Right to Let Himself Be Put to Death for the Truth," in *The Present Age*, p. 122.
358. See *The Point of View*, p. 151.
359. See *Fragments*, p. 47.
360. See *Works of Love*, p. 256.
361. See *Fragments*, p. 11.
362. Potentially, to the best of one's power.
363. *For Self-Examination*, p. 14.
364. See *Works of Love*, p. 188.

365. *The Concept of Irony*, 173.
366. See Matthew 6:22 ff.
367. See *Works of Love*, pp. 195-96.
368. *Fear and Trembling*, p. 130.
369. See "The Lilies of the Field and the Birds of the Air," in *Christian Discourses*, pp. 322 ff.; Matthew 6:33.
370. I John 5:10.
371. See IX A 234.
372. *Training in Christianity*, pp. 133-34; see *For Self-Examination*, pp. 63 ff.
373. I Corinthians 2:2.
374. See *Briefe eines Deutschen an die Herren Chateaubriand* . . . (Leipzig: 1828), pp. 21 ff.
375. See *Edifying Discourses*, II, p. 12; *The Concept of Anxiety* [*Dread*], pp. 103-104; *Concluding Unscientific Postscript*, pp. 395-96.

CONSCIENCE

For Kierkegaard conscience [*Samvittighed*] means, as the word itself implies, a person's knowledge of his actions and the motives for them. But since different people in judging their actions employ different criteria, depending on their level of spiritual development, there will also be different levels in the development of conscience before it reaches its highest level. Of this Kierkegaard says: "there is no accomplishment (neither in the physical, like dancing, singing, etc., nor in the mental, such as thinking and the like) which requires such an extensive and rigorous schooling as is required before one can genuinely be said to have a conscience" (X^1 A 51). The three levels in the development of conscience are ranged in accord with the three stages of existential possibility. In paganism the external environment provides the norms of human action. Therefore, in paganism there is essentially no question of conscience. Socrates, however, inaugurates something new by finding a spiritual principle within himself. Only the ethical as man's inner reality and the eternal in man constitute conscience. Then conscience expresses man's "knowledge shared [*Samviden*] with God" (*Concluding Unscientific Postscript*, p. 138. Ed. tr.). Christianity raises the relationship of conscience to a higher power by placing the individual before a choice concerning salvation or perdition. Kierkegaard expresses this situation by speaking, as Luther does, of "the anguished conscience." Kierkegaard says, "Remove the anguished conscience, and you may as well lock the churches and convert them to dance halls" (VII^1 A 192). Therefore only Christianity, by placing men face to face with the earnestness of the eternal, brings conscience to its highest development.

376. See *Works of Love*, pp. 136 ff., especially p. 137.
377. See *Grundlinien der Philosophie des Rechts* (Berlin: 1833), VIII, pp. 184 ff.

CONTEMPORANEITY

Kierkegaard regarded the concept of contemporaneity as one of the most central of all, and he called it "the central thought of my life" (*Attack on Christendom*, p. 242). He understood his highest task to be that of pointing men to contemporaneity with Christ as the revealed truth. Contemporaneity has two main aspects. Of first importance is contemporaneity with Christ in the "autopsy of faith" (faith's own view) (*Philosophical Fragments*, p. 87), which is reached by the leap of faith. For this contemporaneity a detached historical knowledge of and insight into Christ's historical appearance are not essential, since here it is a matter of Christ as the absurd reality, which is just as difficult to believe in all ages. In this contemporaneity a person is related to Christ as Savior. Particularly in his later years Kierkegaard emphasized contemporaneity with the historical Christ, whereby the individual enters "the situation of contemporaneity" (IX A 95) with Christ, whereupon he must consider honestly how he would be related to Christ upon encountering him in his earthly existence. This latter kind of contemporaneity stresses particularly the aspect of imitation and Christ as the prototype.

Lønning, Per. *The Situation of Contemporaneity*. New York: Humanities Press, 1963.

Wolf, Herbert C. "Kierkegaard and the Quest of the Historical Jesus." *The Lutheran Quarterly*, 1964.

378. See *Fragments*, Ch. IV-V.
379. See *Fragments*, Ch. V.

CONTRADICTION

Kierkegaard regards the view which interprets life from the viewpoint of two contrasting principles ("dualism," IV A 192) as superior to that which looks on life from the viewpoint of unity (monism). From this position Kierkegaard, contrary to Hegel, emphasizes the priority of the principle of contradiction in life, because "As long as I live, I live in contradiction, for life is contradiction" (V A 68). Hegel, however, maintains that his philosophy had abrogated the principle of contradiction, whereby the principle of identity assumes the primary position. Kierkegaard concedes that the principle of identity may be considered the highest principle for abstract thought, where there are no qualitative incongruities, but never in concrete life, where such incongruities are found.

380. See *Either/Or*, I, p. 20.
381. Ibid., p. 21.
382. Reference to *Die Ethik des Aristoteles*, tr. C. Garve (Breslau: 1801) II, pp. 430 ff.
383. See Tennemann, *Geschichte der Philosophie*, I, p. 105.
384. Nothing of the things that are is the one.
385. See Hegel, *Vorlesungen über die Geschichte der Philosophie* (Berlin: 1833), I, pp. 32 and 37.

386. See *Postscript*, pp. 270 ff.
387. An end from which . . . an end toward whom.

CORRECTIVE

Kierkegaard considers that man's adaptation of the high truths of Christianity according to his wants and the resulting distortion of these truths continually require correctives. He regarded himself as such a corrective (X^4 A 15, A 596). He finally extended this task of being a corrective to embrace not only a limited period of Christendom but the entire history of Christendom.

Guthrie, George P. *Kierkegaard's Corrective of Liberal Theology*. University of Chicago B.D. thesis, 1954.

DEATH

Thought of death was not a merely theoretical question for Kierkegaard, inasmuch as he was continually reminded of it by his fragile constitution. This persistent reminder of death resulted in his living with the idea that he literally had never had "more than half a year, and hardly that" (X^1 A 234) to live. The thought of death taught him to use time in the right way and to put his trust only in eternity. At the same time he discovered that Christianity teaches men to see death from the point of view of eternity and to fear judgment more than death. This helps men to conquer anxiety concerning death, for only when they know something worse than death can death be conquered. Kierkegaard writes of this with reference to himself: "I do not fear death; just like the Roman soldiers I have learned that there are worse things" (IX A 492). (See note 164.)

388. Genesis 4:10.
389. See *Postscript*, pp. 210 ff.; *Works of Love*, pp. 317 ff.
390. *Works of Love*, pp. 317 ff.
391. See *The Sickness unto Death*, pp. 150 ff.
392. Christian Scriver, *Seelen-Schatz* (Leipzig: 1715), p. 980.
393. Diogenes Laertius, *The Lives and Opinions of Eminent Philosophers*, X, 125.

DEMONIC

In *The Concept of Anxiety*, Kierkegaard's pseudonym defines the demonic as anxiety about the good [*Angst for det Gode*] and enumerates the various forms of the demonic. The demonic person avoids communication with the good and is closed up in his own narrow and limited world. As a category the demonic is found only within Christianity, because only Christianity can inform man in a concrete way what the good is. According to Kierkegaard's understanding, modern man by departing from Christianity is moving more definitely in the direction of the demonic, because in spite of his repudiation of Christianity he cannot escape knowledge of it.

394. August Bournonville, *Faust*, presented in 1842, with Bournonville in the role of Mephistopheles. See *Fear and Trembling*, pp. 51 ff.

395. See *The Concept of Dread*, pp. 105 ff.; in particular with reference to this entry, pp. 115 ff.

396. Carl Winsløv, who acted in Oehlenschläger's *Karl den Store* in 1830 and in *De Uadskillelige* in 1834.

DESCARTES

Kierkegaard speaks of René Descrates (1596–1650) with respect. He concentrates especially upon Descartes's *Discourse on Method* (IV C 14). He seeks to show that Descartes's phase, *de omnibus dubitandum est*, which he (K.) used as the title of his philosophic observations on the essence of doubt (IV B 1; *Johannes Climacus, or De Omnibus Dubitandum Est*), was misunderstood by his contemporaries, since Descartes, in spite of all his doubt, held that "a divine revelation should be believed" (IV C 14). Nevertheless Kierkegaard criticizes Descartes because he "had made thought absolute, not freedom (IV C 11). In Kierkegaard's view freedom and being rank higher than thought.

397. Professor Martensen.

398. See Hegel, *Vorlesungen über die Geschichte der Philosophie*, III, p. 335, with reference to Spinoza.

399. See *Fear and Trembling*, pp. 22 ff.

400. On the entire theme of Descartes and doubting see *Johannes Climacus, or De Omnibus Dubitandum Est, Pap.* IV B 1. For English translation, see Bibliography.

401. Something contrary to natural light.

DESPAIR

Despair [*Fortvivlelse*] is a deeper expression for anxiety and presupposes that a person has gained consciousness of the eternal within him, which is not yet the case in the sphere of anxiety. Despair signifies the misrelationship between the eternal in a man and his concrete existence. The proper relationship is that the eternal as the primary principle penetrates temporal existence. There are two main forms of the misrelationship of which despair is the expression: *either* that a man concentrates only on the temporal *or* that the eternal is only used intellectually as knowledge which gains no significance for existence.

Clive, G. "Sickness unto Death in the Underworld: A Study of Nihilism." *Harvard Theological Review*, 1958.

Croxall, T. H. *Kierkegaard Studies*. New York: Roy, 1956.

Martin, H. V. *Kierkegaard*. London: Epworth, 1950.

402. Of Kierkegaard's published works, see especially *The Sickness unto Death*, which concentrates on the possible forms of despair.

403. See *Either/Or*, II, p. 192.

404. See "Diapsalmata," *Either/Or*, I, for the esthetic analogy. See also Graham Greene, *The Burnt-Out Case*.

405. *The Ethical Principles in Job.*
406. Wherever aridity encompasses a solitary man, there is a lowering of the spirit, a weakening of the mind, a neglect of religious practice, a hatred of professing [one's faith], a praise of secular things.
407. Melancholy, moroseness. See *Either/Or*, II, pp. 192 ff.
408. The seven chief vices.
409. See *Stages*, pp. 191 ff.; V A 33.
410. See *Edifying Discourses*, III, pp. 90 ff.; I John 2:17.
411. *Die deutsche Theologie, mit Forrede von Dr. M. Luther und Johann Arnd*, ed. F. C. Krüger (Lemgo: 1822).
412. See *Stages*, pp. 191 ff. See II A 485.
413. See *Either/Or*, I, p. 21.
414. See J. C. Hamann, *Schriften* I-VII (Berlin: 1821), II, pp. 61 ff.; also a letter from Hamann to Jacobi, April 25, 1786, in Jacobi, *Werke* (Leipzig: 1819), IV, p. 211.
415. Joel 2:13.
416. The "immediate" man. See *The Sickness unto Death*, especially pp. 184 ff.
417. See *The Sickness unto Death*, pp. 146-50.
418. Ibid., p. 147.

DIALECTIC, DIALECTICAL

By dialectic Kierkegaard understands the elucidation (exposition) of the existential situation with the aid of thought. Dialectic encompasses all the existential concepts with which Kierkegaard works and which he seeks to place in relation to each other through his dialectical method. The principal task of the dialectic, according to Kierkegaard's view, is a consistent thinking through of the central Christian concepts. He wanted to cast Christianity completely and wholly into reflection (IX A 226). Only a clear dialectical insight into Christianity's existential form can prevent the individual from confusing it with other existential forms. In this way dialectic is placed completely in the service of existence.

Aubry, Edwin Ewart. "Kierkegaard, Father of Dialectical Theology," in *Present Theological Tendencies*. New York and London: Harper, 1936.

Croxall, T. H. *Kierkegaard Commentary*. New York: Harper, 1956.

Hamilton, Lester I. *The Existential Dialectic in the Writings of Søren Aabye Kierkegaard*. University of Kentucky. M.A. thesis, 1951.

Harper, Ralph. *Existentialism. A Theory of Man*. Cambridge: Harvard University Press, 1948.

Malantschuk, Gregor. *Kierkegaard's Way to the Truth*. Minneapolis: Augsburg, 1963.

Swenson, David F. "The 'Existential Dialectic' of Kierkegaard," in *Journal of Philosophy*, 1938-39.

419. See Book of Esther, 3:1 ff.

420. See J. L. Heiberg, *Recensenten og Dyret* (Copenhagen: 1827), pp. 38 and 40.
421. Plato. *Apology*, 41a-c.
422. See II Corinthians 10:5. Height.
423. See *Either/Or*, I, pp. 37 ff.
424. See *Fragments*, title-page.
425. IV C 12, 13, 87-96, 105.
426. J. L. A. Kolderup-Rosenvinge, Professor of Law, University of Copenhagen.

DISCONTINUITY, CONTINUITY

These concepts are used by Kierkegaard particularly for the elucidation of the difference between qualitative opposites. Thus continuity corresponds to the eternal; the disconnected elements of temporality fall under the rubric of discontinuity (*Concluding Unscientific Postscript*, p. 277). As qualifications of the eternal, the good and freedom are continuous; whereas the evil can achieve only apparent continuity (*The Concept of Anxiety* [*Dread*], p. 116).

427. J. C. Hamann, Schriften, I-VIII (Berlin: 1821), p. 63.
428. Preestablished harmony.
429. See Trendelenburg, I, pp. 24 ff.; also P. M. Stilling, *Den moderne Atheisme eller den saakaldte Neo-hegelianismes Consequenser af den hegelske Philosophie* (Copenhagen: 1844), pp. 31 ff.

DON JUAN

For Kierkegaard Don Juan represents protest against the ethical claim of Christianity. Therefore the Dan Juan character is possible only within Christianity. In *Either/Or* it says that Don Juan's essence is "sensuous-erotic genius" (I, p. 63).

Grimsley, Ronald. "The Don Juan Theme in Molière and Kierkegaard." *Comparative Literature*, 1954.

DON QUIXOTE

Cervantes' *Don Quixote* gave Kierkegaard the idea for "a comic novel: 'A Literary Don Quixote,' " in which he intended to depict the hopelessness of wanting to "keep up" with everything that is written and what a mistaken notion it is to believe that to read as many books as possible is the main thing in life (I A 146). With regard to the *Don Quixote*, Kierkegaard criticizes Cervantes for not being poetically consistent in letting Don Quixote become a sensible person at the end.

430. Published by the Society for the Right Use of Freedom of the Press, I (1835-36).

DOUBT

Kierkegaard frequently polemicizes against the interpretation of doubt common in philosophy—namely, that one must begin with doubt in order to achieve truth. According to Kierkegaard this method of beginning to philosophize is "as appropriate as having a soldier slouch in order to get him to stand erect" (IV A 150). In addition he strongly emphasizes that doubt in philosophy cannot be overcome intellectually, therefore not on the basis of knowledge; only the ethical resolution to give up doubting can halt it. Kierkegaard quite often expresses the view that it is unethical to awaken doubt in a person, however justifiable the doubt seems to be, if one does not point simultaneously to the means for conquering the doubt.

431. *Vorlesungen über Glauben und Wissen* (Berlin: 1837).

432. R. Descartes, *Principles of Philosophy*, Part I, 3.

433. See *Fragments*, pp. 102 ff.

434. Diogenes Laertius, IX, 107; see *Fragments*, p. 103. Suspension of judgment, hesitation.

435. See R. Møller, *Veiledning* (Copenhagen: 1824, 2 ed.), p. x. Møller was bishop of the diocese of Lolland-Falster and father of Poul Martin Møller, Kierkegaard's favorite professor.

436. See *Works of Love*, p. 121.

DREAMS

Kierkegaard points out that as long as men had a simpler mode of life, both physically and intellectually, they believed "that God divulged his will in dreams" (X^2 A 258). Examples of this can be found in the Bible. This belief has been lost through a changed way of living and "life in the large cities." Then intellectuality gains dominance over "the unconscious life," in which men originally had confidence but now regard with distrust. As a consequence, dreams are interpreted negatively as something inferior and demonic.

EDUCATION, UPBRINGING

The interest Kierkegaard had for the mental-spiritual possibilities and growth of men led him into the practical aspects of the question of upbringing. In an early entry he sets forth the view that in instruction there ought to be an awareness of the historical and physical development of mankind, that the individual must appropriate this before he can find his own task (II A 5). A higher kind of education or upbringing begins only when a person lets himself be educated by God. He says of this kind of upbringing, which was of such great importance in his own life: "but what would you think if a person were to say: God in heaven in my teacher, and I count it an honor to be his disciple, that he educated me" (III A 231). He says of educational methods in his time, which did not reflect an understanding of the responsibility involved in education: Perhaps in no area or development does the confusion of our age appear more ludicrous than in the educational system" (VIII^1 A 258). Kierkegaard also had misgivings about the new views in education for which Grundtvig was spokesman, and he speaks ironically of the time when this kind of education comes to prevail: "When the time comes, I trust I shall be dead, although I could wish that Grundtvig might still be living then" (VIII¹ A 258). And yet he agrees with Grundtvig's observation that it is wrong to question the child, for "it is the child who should be permitted to question" (X¹ A 647).

Ford, Richard S. *A Comparative Study of the Experiental Approach to Religious Education and Some Aspects of Existentialism*. University of Southern California Ph.D. thesis, 1957.

437. See II A 12.
438. See *The Sickness unto Death*, p. 164.
439. See *Edifying Discourses*, I, p. 13.
440. Principal of the Borgerdydskole, Copenhagen, where Kierkegaard had studied. See *Efterretninger* by C. Bartholin and J. Stilling (Copenhagen: 1844).

ENTHUSIASM

According to Kierkegaard's conception a genuine and persevering enthusiasm is possible only in relation to that which is of enduring value. In the period of "leveling" which began in Kierkegaard's time and which he treats at some length in his published works (see *A Literary Review*, part of which is in English translation under the title *The Present Age*, especially pp. 27 ff.), the presupposition for persevering enthusiasm is lacking, since everything is measured by the standard of finitude. But finite and temporary things are not worthy of true enthusiasm. In many places Kierkegaard speaks of his own enthusiasm which characterized his service to the cause of Christianity and which stayed by him all his life. Among other things he calls it an "intellectual enthusiasm" and says that it placed the claim upon him of "enduring everything for the idea" (X⁴ A 560).

441. Archimedes no doubt was in mind. See S.V. VIII, p. 62.

ENVY

The opposite of envy is admiration (*The Sickness unto Death*, p. 217). In admiration the other person's good points are acknowledged positively; in envy this is expressed negatively. Kierkegaard adduces many examples of the origin and effect of envy. An extraordinary achievement will most likely be treated by contemporaries with either admiration or envy. Kierkegaard's great achievements in writing aroused more envy than admiration, and he touches on this not infrequently in his journals. He noted the consequences of this envy particularly during the controversy with *The Corsair*.

Stark, Werner, *Social Theory and Christian Thought*. London: Routledge and Kegan Paul, 1959.

442. See *The Present Age*, pp. 22 ff.

ESTHETICISM, THE ESTHETIC

The problem of the esthetic occupied Kierkegaard very much and in many forms. At the outset he was most attentive to the esthetic mode of existence, which he knew by experience during his youth when he himself practiced for a time an esthetic view of life. Then he achieved clarity concerning the implications of this philosophy of life. He discerned the inadequacy of the esthetic in that it binds a person to momentary satisfaction and "enjoyment" and therefore can never satisfy man's deepest needs.

The esthetic stance toward life is employed or is found on the lower level in Kierkegaard's shaping of the doctrine of the stages, in which the multifarious existential aspects of the esthetic are clearly delineated.

An important side of the esthetic is artistic creativity, of which Kierkegaard was particularly aware, because to a degree he regarded himself as a poet. The great question for him was how the artistic could be used in a higher service, for example, in upbuilding or edifying literature. Kierkegaard was aware of the danger that the poetic may remain within the confines of the esthetic and not point to anything higher, instead of being penetrated by ethical-religious earnestness, which not only evokes enthusiasm but can also lead to existential action.

Comstock, W. R. "Aspects of Æsthetic Existence: Kierkegaard and Santayana." *International Philosophical Quarterly*, June, 1966.

Glicksberg, C. I. "Æsthetics of Nihilism." University of Kansas City *Review*, 1960.

Johnson, David. *Søren Kierkegaard's View of Æsthetic Existence*. Columbia University M.A. thesis, 1947.

Malantschuk, Gregor. *Kierkegaard's Way to the Truth*. Minneapolis: Augsburg, 1963.

443. See *Either/Or*, I, p. 19.
444. Ibid., p. 23.
445. Ibid., pp. 132 ff.; *Stages*, pp. 38, 42, 88-89.
446. *Repetition*, p. 11.
447. See *Either/Or*, I, p. 20.
448. See *Either/Or*, I, p. 300; II, pp. 6-7.
449. *Aristoteles Dichtkunst*, tr. M. C. Curtius (Hannover: 1753).
450. Leipzig: 1816.
451. See *Purity of Heart*, pp. 27-28.
452. *Fenelon's Werke religiösen Inhalts* (Hamburg: 1823), III, pp. 322 ff.
453. Transformation into another kind.
454. See *Berlingske Tidende*, No. 20 (January 24) and No. 24 (January 29), 1850.
455. "Hjemløs," in *Nord og Syd* (April, 1853 ff.).
456. *Tillæg til den evangelisk-christelige Psalmebog* (Copenhagen: 1845), p. 38.

ETERNITY, THE ETERNAL

According to Kierkegaard the eternal may be regarded from various points of view. It is a contrast to time, which essentially is an "infinite succession" of moments which disappear; eternity, however, can be defined as a "present" which always "is" (*The Concept of Anxiety* [*Dread*], pp. 77-78). Time can never become eternal, however long it persists, because time and eternity lie on two absolutely different levels. Together with the temporal the eternal forms the synthesis of two opposite qualities, and man as an intended being is this synthesis. Kierkegaard presents the following gradations within the eternal. First there is an "abstract eternity" or the "eternity of abstraction" (*Concluding Unscientific Postscript*, pp. 277-78), which means that "the ideas" and highest concepts of abstraction have a validity which always "is." On a qualitatively higher level there is the conviction (thought) of a transcendent personal activity, God, who must now be regarded as the permanent unchangeable being (point) beneath all the changes and shifts of time. This level can be characterized as "a continuous state of fulfillment (II A 570). The highest level in the appearance of the eternal is its revelation in time, which Kierkegaard, using an expression from Paul, calls "the fullness of time" (Galatians 4:4). Then God is revealed in a single human being and the eternal appears as concrete actuality.

457. II Peter 3:8.
458. See *Either/Or*, I, p. 292.
459. See *Works of Love*, pp. 124 ff.; pp. 134 ff.
460. Ibid., pp. 123-24, 188-89.
461. Luke 16:19 ff.
462. *En christelig Postille*, tr. J. Thisted (Copenhagen: 1828), I, p. 389.

THE ETHICAL, THE ETHICAL CONSCIOUSNESS

Kierkegaard distinguishes three main forms of the ethical. First, the ethical which has its goal and criterion within the finite. This view is found in its pure form in the "Greek ethic"; nevertheless, this cannot be considered ethics in the proper sense, because it does not have a consciousness of eternally obligatory norms, which to Kierkegaard is characteristic of the genuinely ethical. The most appropriate expression for this view of ethics is custom or group morality. Genuine ethics appears in two forms, which Kierkegaard's pseudonym Vigilius Haufniensis calls the first and the second ethics (*The Concept of Anxiety* [*Dread*], pp. 18-19). In the *first* ethics there is the consciousness of eternal norms of action, and this encompasses the temporal realm. This kind of ethics is capable of many manifestations, of which the two most important are (1) Socratic ethics, which by acknowledgement of the eternally valid norms broke through the moral structure of ancient Greece, and (2) the ethics of "the law" in Judaism, commandments received from an eternal transcendent power. The *second* ethics is characterized by having the Christian teaching of sin and grace as its presupposition. Then a person has insight into how far he can attain by his efforts within the first ethics.

Within each of the "three" above-mentioned main forms of ethical outlook there must be distinguished three different modes of action which are determined or yielded by a person's relation to another person, to himself, and to God. These modes constitute the social, personal, and religious aspects of ethics (*Either/Or*, II, pp. 266 ff.). These aspects receive different emphasis in each of the main forms of ethics. Thus in the "Greek ethic" group morality or the social aspect dominates. In the "first ethics" the personal aspect is in the foreground, since a person must seek to actualize the eternal requirement through his own efforts. In the "second ethics" the redeeming grace of God is the presupposition for man's ethical decisions and action.

Bogen, James. "Kierkegaard and the 'Teleological Suspension of the Ethical.'" *Inquiry*, 1965.

Brophy, Liam. "Kierkegaard: the Hamlet in Search of Holiness." *Social Justice Review*, 1955.

Buber, M. "Suspension of Ethics," in *Moral Principles in Action*, ed. R. N. Anshen. New York: Harper, 1952.

Clive, G. *The Connection between Ethics and Religion in Kant, Kierkegaard, and Bradley*. Harvard University Ph.D. thesis, 1953.

———. "Teleological Suspension of the Ethical in Nineteenth Century Literature." *Journal of Religion*, 1954.

Croxall, T. H. *Kierkegaard Commentary*. New York: Harper, 1956.

Forrest, William. "A Problem in Values: the Faustian Motivation in Kierkegaard and Goethe." *International Journal of Ethics*, 1953.

Geismar, Eduard. *Lectures on the Religious Thought of Søren Kierkegaard*, introduction by David Swenson. Minneapolis: Augsburg, 1937.

Graham, Aelred. *Christian Thought and Action*. New York: Harcourt Brace, 1958.

Gumbiner, Joseph Henry. "Existentialism and Father Abraham." *Commentary*. 1948.

Harrelson, Walter J. "Kierkegaard and Abraham." *Andover Newton Bulletin*, 1955.

Holmer, P. L. "Kierkegaard and Ethical Theory." *International Journal of Ethics*, 1953.

Hook, S. "Two Types of Existentialist Religion and Ethics." *Partisan Review*, 1959.

MacKay, L. H. *The Nature and the End of the Ethical Life According to Kierkegaard*. Yale University Ph.D. thesis, 1954.

———. "Loss of the World in Kierkegaard's Ethics." *Review of Metaphysics*, 1962.

———. "The Analysis of the Good in Kierkegaard's *Purity of Heart*," in *Experience, Existence, and the Good*, ed. I. C. Lieb. Carbondale, Ill.: University of Southern Illinois Press, 1961.

Malantschuk, Gregor. *Kierkegaard's Way to the Truth*. Minneapolis: Augsburg, 1963.

Mourant, John A. "Ethics of Kierkegaard." *Giornale Metafisica*: 1952.

Phillips, D. Z. "Does it Pay to be Good?" *Aristotelian Society*. London: Nov. 16, 1964.

Rose, Mary. *Three Hierarchies of Value: a Study of the Philosophies of*

Value of Bergson, Whitehead, and Kierkegaard. Johns Hopkins University Ph.D. thesis, 1949.

Schmitt, R. "Kierkegaard's Ethics and Its Teleological Suspension." *Journal of Philosophy*, 1961.

Schrag, Calvin O. "Note on Kierkegaard's Teleological Suspension of the Ethical." *International Journal of Ethics*, 1959.

———. "The Structure of Moral Experience . . ." *International Journal of Ethics*, 1963.

Thompson, Hugo W. *Ethics and Religion in the Philosophy of Kierkegaard.* Yale University Ph.D. thesis, 1935.

Waring, E. *Kierkegaard and Modern Ethics.* Cambridge University M.Litt. thesis, 1955.

463. See *Either/Or*, I, p. 28.
464. Matthew 12:36.
465. Matthew 9:4.
466. See Deuteronomy 32:48; Joshua 1:1.
467. See *Postscript*, p. 490.
468. Matthew 5:37.
469. Matthew 6:3.
470. See *Fear and Trembling*, p. 56.
471. If she spins it amidst tears, sews a shirt out of it amidst tears, it will protect me better than any iron; it is impenetrable.
472. Johan Grafen Mailáth, *Magyarische Sagen*, 2 ed. (Stuttgart and Tübingen: 1837), II, p. 18 ("*Erzi die Spinnerin*").
473. W. M. L. de Wette, *Laerbog: den christelige Sædelære og sammes Historie*, tr. C. E. Scharling (Copenhagen: 1835), pp. 44, 213 ff.
474. Matthew 5:44.
475. Judges 14:14. See *Stages*, p. 27.
476. Acts 3:6.
477. See note 475.
478. See *Edifying Discourses*, III, p. 50.
479. By calculation it always sets up a god in the likeness of money, always in the midst of our conflicts it never brings back either the blessedness of peace or the joy of victory, always anxious.
480. See *Stages*, p. 165. Always investigating, always verbose, never having achieved its purpose, that they may possess, be strong, live vitally, when those things —
481. See Socrates' (Diotima's) speech in Plato's *Symposium*.
482. Lethe, the stream of oblivion; see *The Concept of Irony*, p. 48.
483. *Christosophia Der oder Weg zu Christo* (1731), pp. 387 ff.
484. See *Either/Or*, I, p. 414; II, pp. 164 ff., 184.
485. Regine Olsen's brother. This letter has not been preserved.
486. See *Either/Or*, II, pp. 268-69.
487. *Nicomachean Ethics*, II, 5, 1106b, 15 ff.

488. Ibid., III, 8, 1114b, 31 ff.
489. King, who wrote on the problem of the origin of evil (*De Origine Mali*), came to Kierkegaard's attention through Leibniz, "*Anmerkungen über das Buch von dem Ursprünge des Bösen, das kürzlich in Engelland heraus gekommen,*" *Theodicee* (Hannover: 1763) which also has an appendix on Hobbes.
490. In the text of *Papirer, ethnisk* should read, according to the context, *ethisk*.
491. See *The Concept of Anxiety* [*Dread*], pp. 15 ff.
492. See *Fear and Trembling*, pp. 91-92; *Stages*, p. 218.
493. See *Stages*, p. 27; *Either/Or*, I, pp. 288 ff.
494. See *Fear and Trembling*, p. 92.
495. Karl Rosenkranz, *Erinnerungen an Karl Daub* (Berlin: 1837), p. 24; see *Fear and Trembling*, p. 61.
496. "Every good and perfect Gift Is from above," in *Edifying Discourses*, I, pp. 35 ff.
497. See *Edifying Discourses*, II, pp. 27 ff.; Matthew 7:11.
498. Matthew 16:3.
499. See *Stages*, pp. 429-30; *Fear and Trembling*, p. 108n; *The Concept of Dread*, pp. 16 ff.
500. The reference is to *Either/Or*. Entries IV A 213-256 are marginal notes in a copy of this work.
501. Motto: "Are passions then the pagans of the soul? reason alone baptized?" Edward Young, *The Complaint: or Night-Thoughts on Life, Death, and Immortality* (1742).
502. See *Postscript*, pp. 227, 316-17, and *Either/Or*, II, pp. 136 ff. on the problem of time in the esthetic life and on the ethical view of time.
503. Act II, sc. 2.
504. See *Stages*, p. 414.
505. See *Postscript*, pp. 474-75.
506. *Grundrids til Moralphilosophiens System* (Copenhagen: 1841), p. 34.
507. J. F. Hagen, *Aegteskabet* (Copenhagen: 1841), p. 16.
508. *Fragments*, pp. 91 ff.; *Stages*, p. 430.
509. *Fragments*, pp. 89 ff.
510. See *Postscript*, pp. 291, 350.
511. Ibid., p. 128.
512. Ibid., p. 110.
513. See *Stages*, p. 430.
514. See *Works of Love*, pp. 177 ff.
515. See *Stages*, p. 433n.
516. *Opera* (Stuttgart: 1830).
517. *Ethics*, III, vi ff.; IV, Prop. VIII.
518. Ibid., V, Prop. X.

519. Luke 23:42.
520. Right and wrong are not by nature but by custom.
521. Hamburg: 1836.
522. See *Works of Love*, p. 185.
523. Plato, *Symposium*, 210 b-c. See *Works of Love*, pp. 342-43.
524. See *Works of Love*, pp. 39 ff, 58 ff.
525. Ibid., pp. 347-48.
526. Montaigne. *Michael Montaigne Gedanken und Meinungen über allerley Gegenstände*, I-VII (Berlin: 1793-99), IV, p. 273.
527. See *Christian Discourses*, p. 85; Purity of Heart, p. 66.
528. Matthew 26:69 ff.
529. Matthew 13:45 ff.
530. The Danish in the text is *praktiske*, which has the same elemental meaning as the English *practical*, in the sense of pertaining to action, practice in everyday life. It does not denote evaluation in economic terms.
531. See *Either/Or*, I, p. 23.
532. *Puf eller Verden vil bedrages*, tr. by N. C. L. Abrahams, drama performed in Copenhagen during the spring and autumn of 1849.
533. If one is permitted to speak thus.
534. Letter of November 28, 1756, in G. E. Lessing, *Sämmtliche Schriften*, I-XXXII (Berlin: 1825-28).
535. *Christian Discourses*, pp. 154 ff.
536. James 2:26.
537. *Training in Christianity*, pp. 68 ff.
538. I Peter 4:7. See Chapter I of *Judge for Yourself*.
539. Luther, *En christelige Postille*, I, p. 533.
540. Philippians 3:12.
541. *Paris's Mysterier* (Copenhagen: 1843), I-VIII.
542. *Attack upon Christendom*, p. 18. Nothing is blessed unless it is peaceful.

EQUALITY

On the question of equality [*Lighed*] and inequality among men, Kierkegaard distinguishes between inessential and essential equality. Inessential equality has to do with differences among men in inheritance, health, education, wealth, etc. These differences can never be eliminated; therefore, equality can never be established. Equality in inessentials is therefore never possible. On the other hand, men are equal in what is essential. To Kierkegaard the essential is the eternal, and in this respect all are on a level of equality, because all possess within themselves the possibility of the eternal. In the word humanity [*Menneskelighed*: man-likeness, also man-equality] is found a felicitous expression of the relation between man and the idea of equality as a task which is implied: "To realize complete equality in the medium of worldliness [*Verds-lighed*, i.e., world-likeness] i.e., to realize it in the medium the very nature of which implies differences, and to realize it in a worldly [*verds-ligt*] way, i.e., by positing the differences—such a thing is forever impossible, as is apparent from the categories. For if complete equality were to be attained, worldiness would be at an end.... It is only religion that can, with the help of eternity, carry human equality to the utmost limit—the godly, the essential, the non-worldly, the true, the only possible human equality. And therefore (be it said to its honor and glory) religion is the true humanity" ("Concerning the Dedication to 'that Individual' " in *The Point of View for My Work as an Author*, pp. 109-10).

543. See *Works of Love*, pp. 81-82.
544. Ibid., pp. 87 ff.
545. Danske, *Kirketidende*, May 7, 1848.
546. *Judge for Yourself*, Ch. I.

EXIST, EXISTENCE, EXISTENTIAL

All of Kierkegaard's thought and his whole authorship had the task of elucidating the various spheres of existence in a detailed and basic way, not only so that they would not be confused but also to show that the most important thing is for a person to become engaged in existence himself. In showing how this can be done, Kierkegaard gives us so many examples within the most varied perspectives that his entire philosophy may be called a guide and an incentive to existing. Only by venturing out into existential decisions and through existential striving can a person reach the goal of life: to become a self through relationship to God.

The Danish language has two words, *existere* (to exist as a striving person) and *være til* (to be there in time and space, *Dasein* in German); there is only one English word, *exist* (*existence*), for both Danish words. Therefore, the Danish terms follow within brackets the expression used in translation. Occasionally *existere* is used in the ordinary sense of being in space-time.

Beck, Maximillian. "Existentialism, Rationalism, and Christian Faith." *Journal of Religion*, 1946.

———. "Existentialism versus Naturalism and Idealism." *South Atlantic Quarterly*, 1948.

Bixler, Julius Seelye. "The Contribution of Existenz-Philosophie." *Harvard Theological Review*, 1940.

Blackham, H. J. *Six Existentialist Thinkers*. London: Routledge and Kegan Paul, 1952.

Broudy, Harry S. "Kierkegaard's Levels of Existence." *Philosophy and Phenomenological Research*, 1940-41.

Charlesworth, Max. "The Meaning of Existentialism." *The Thomist: A Speculative Quarterly Review*, 1953.

Collins, James. "The Meaning of Existence." *New Scholasticism*, 1948.

Croxall, T. H. *Kierkegaard Commentary*. New York: Harper, 1956.

Diem, Hermann. *Kierkegaard's Dialectic of Existence*; tr. Harold Knight. Edinburgh: Oliver and Boyd, 1959.

Emmet, Dorothy M. "Kierkegaard and the 'Existential' Philosophy." *Philosophy*. London: 1941.

Grieve, Alexander. "Søren Kierkegaard." *Expository Times*, 1907-1908.

Harper, Ralph. "Two Existential Interpretations." *Philosophy and Phenomenological Research*, 1945.

Heinecken, Martin J. *The Moment before God*. Philadelphia: Muhlenberg, 1956.

Jaspers, Karl. *Reason and Existenz*; tr. William Earl. New York: Noonday Press, 1955.

Kean, Charles Duell. *The Meaning of Existence*. London: Latimer House, 1957.

Kroner, Richard. "Existentialism and Christianity." *Encounter*, 1954.

Kuhn, Helmut. "Existentialism, Christian and anti-Christian." *Theology Today*, 1949.

Larson, W. R. Curtis. "Kierkegaard and Sartre." *Personalist*, 1954.

Lowrie, Walter. "*Existence* as understood by Kierkegaard and/or Sartre." *Sewanee Review*, 1950.

MacCallum, Henry Reid. "Kierkegaard and Levels of Existence." *University of Toronto Quarterly*, 1944.

Maritain, Jacques. "From Existential Existentialism to Academic Existentialism." *Sewanee Review*, 1948.

Martin, H. V. *Kierkegaard*. London: Epworth, 1950.

May, Rollo, et al. *Existence*. New York: Basic Books, 1958.

Michalson, Carl. "Existentialism Is a Mysticism." *Theology Today*, XII, 3, October, 1955.

Miller, Libuse Lukas. *In Search of the Self*. Philadelphia: Muhlenberg, 1962.

de Nondonca, A. "The Origin of Existentialism." *Journal of the University of Bombay*, 1952.

Perkins, Robert. *Existence and Æthetics: Some Kierkegaardian Themes*. Indiana University M.A. thesis, 1959.

Perry, E. "Was Kierkegaard a Biblical Existentialist?" *Journal of Religion*, 1956.

Rhoades, D. H. "Essential Varieties of Existentialism." *Personalist*, 1954.

Schaepman, P. M. *The Philosophy of Existence* (Kierkegaard, Nietzsche, Sartre, and Heidegger). University of London M.A. thesis, 1958.

Schrag, Oswald O. "The Main Types of Existentialism." *Religion in Life*, 1953.

———. *The Problem of Existence*. Harvard University Ph.D. thesis, 1957.

Searles, Herbert Leon. "Kierkegaard's Philosophy as a Source of Existentialism." *Personalist*, 1948.

Smith, John E. "The Revolt of Existence." *Yale Review*, 1953-54.

Smith, Vincent Edward. "Existentialism and Existence." *The Thomist*, 1949.

Stavrides, Mariam. *The Concept of Existence in Kierkegaard and Heidegger*. Columbia University Ph.D. thesis, 1952.

Stewart, R. W. "Existential Christianity." *Expository Times*, 1950-51.

Swenson, David F. "The Existential Dialectic of Søren Kierkegaard." *The International Journal of Ethics*, 1938-39.

"That Blessed Word *Existential*." *Christian Century*, 1955.

Thomas, J. Heywood. "Kierkegaard and Existentialism." *Scottish Journal of Theology*, 1953.

Tillich, Paul. "Kierkegaard as Existential Thinker." *Union Review*, 1942.

———. "Existential Philosophy." *Journal of the History of Ideas*, 1944.

Wahl, Jean-Andre. *A Short History of Existentialism*. New York: Philosophical Library, 1949.

Warner, D. H. J. *The Dialectic of Existence in Kierkegaard, with Particular Reference to Socrates*. Oxford University B.Litt. thesis, 1956.

Wild, John. "Kierkegaard and Contemporary Existentialist Philosophy." In *A Kierkegaard Critique*, ed. Howard A. Johnson and Niels Thulstrup. New York: Harper, 1962.

Williams, F. "Problem in Values: the Faustian Motivation in Kierkegaard and Goethe." *International Journal of Ethics*, 1953.

Wyschogrod, Michael. *Kierkegaard and Heidegger: the Ontology of Existence*. New York: Humanities Press, 1954. Columbia University Ph.D. thesis, 1954.

Yale French Studies, Vol. I, No. I.

Yanitelli, Victor R. "Types of Existentialism." *Thought*, 1949.

Ziegler, L. "Personal Existence: A Study of Buber and Kierkegaard." *Journal of Religion*, 1960.

547. See Revelation 2:23.

548. A family of birds including auks, puffins, and murres, whose nesting habits were obscure in Kierkegaard's day.

549. See *Either/Or*, I, pp. 320-21.

550. Luke 24:27.

551. See *Postscript*, pp. 2687 ff.

552. No great genius exists without some madness. See Seneca, *Dialog*, IX (*De tranquillitate Animi*), 17, 10; *Fear and Trembling*, p. 116. In Aristotle the expression in *sine mixtura dementiae*, as quoted by Seneca.

553. This idea impressed William James, who learned of it through H. Höffding. In *Essays in Radical Empiricism* (London: Longmans Green, 1922), p. 238, James says: "In Professor Höffding's massive little article in *The Journal of Philosophy, Psychology, and Scientific Methods* (Vol. II, 1905, pp. 85-92) he quotes a saying of Kierkegaard's to the effect that we live forwards, but we understand backwards. Understanding backwards is, it

must be confessed, a very frequent weakness of philosophers, both of the rationalistic and of the ordinary empiricist type. Radical empiricism insists upon understanding forwards, also, and refuses to substitute static concepts of the understanding for transitions in our moving life." See also William James, *Pragmatism* (London: Longmans Green, 1908), p. 223, and *A Pluralistic Universe* (London: Longmans Green, 1920), p. 244. (Letter from J. S. Bixler helpfully provided the references to James' works.) See *Repetition*, pp. 3-4.

554. See *Edifying Discourses*, III, pp. 25-26.
555. See *Fragments*, pp. 49 ff.
556. See *Postscript*, p. 281.
557. Ibid., p. 548.
558. H. Ritter, *Geschichte der Philosophie alter Zeit* (Hamburg: 1831).
559. See *Efterladte Skrifter* (Copenhagen: 1843), III, p. 241.
560. See *Christian Discourses*, p. 77.
561. Ibid.
562. See *Training*, pp. 227-28.
563. See *Fragments*, pp. 51-52.
564. Speak that I may perceive.
565. *Postscript*, pp. 288 ff.
566. Ibid., pp. 191-98.
567. *Either/Or*, II, pp. 162-64.

EXPERIENCE

There are two viewpoints for regarding experience. It can be looked upon as an external strengthening of the expectation that certain actions yield certain results. But this experience is never reliable, because one can never calculate the external results of an action. One can learn only worldly prudence (prudence about the world) from this experience, a prudence which Kierkegaard disdains. With regard to this sort of experience he says: "If there were nothing higher than experience, experience would drive a man crazy" (IV A 46). On a higher level there is the experience which looks away from petty itching for results in the external world and looks only upon "strengthening in the inner man" (*Edifying Discourses*, I, pp. 93, 98).

568. The strength of the rays forced me to close my eyes as usual, but I soon recovered, opened my eyes again, resolutely looked at it and said: "Oh, my sun, for whom I have yearned so long, I now want to see nothing else, even if your rays should blind me," and thus I remained standing with an unwavering gaze.
569. John 3:1 ff.
570. John 3:8.
571. See *Fear and Trembling*, p. 95.

572. See Diogenes Laertius, *Filosofiske Historier*, I, 103, tr. B. Riisbrigh (Copenhagen: 1811), I, p. 47; S.V. V, pp. 20 ff.

573. *Nachricht vom Leben und Character des Thomas Bateman*, tr. from English, Karl Bresler (Berlin: 1834).

THE EXTRAORDINARY, THE EXCEPTION

Through great and undeserved sufferings a man is placed outside the universal and becomes an extraordinary. In protest against suffering this man can end in desperate, demonic defiance *or* before God in relation to his suffering come to a potentiated religiousness with the capacity to discover new aspects of religious experience which can be of help to other men. Kierkegaard was such an extraordinary in a positive sense. Through his sufferings and through his "thorn in the flesh" he was matured for his tasks in the realm of the ethical-religious. How great a significance he attributed to these sufferings during his work with Christianity is apparent in this expression: "I have almost said that my genius has really been my suffering" (X^1 A 670). Because of this special existential position, he had to regard himself as a religious exception in contrast to the poetic exception, who remains within the esthetic sphere (*Repetition*, pp. 154 ff.). Yet Kierkegaard discovered that Christianity really wants to make every person a religious exception, in that it seeks to lead the individual through suffering and isolation to a deepening in the requirement and gift of Christianity. Yet there is a distinction between the extraordinary and the exception—every man can become the exception, but not every exception is an extraordinary. The extraordinary has laid upon him a special mission, in Kierkegaard's case to provide the corrective to possible distortions in the religious realm.

574. See *The Point of View*, pp. 100-103.

575. See Luke 14:26 and Matthew 10:37.

576. Pp. 111-12.